INDIAN AGENT

Number Six:
Canseco-Keck History Series
Jerry Thompson, General Editor

Peter Ellis Bean, ca. 1815–17. Photo courtesy Robert E. Davis.

INDIAN AGENT

Peter Ellis Bean in Mexican Texas

JACK JACKSON

Texas A&M University Press
College Station

First edition

The paper used in this book meets the minimum requirements
of the American National Standard for Permanence
of Paper for Printed Library Materials, z39.48-1984.
Binding materials have been chosen for durability.
∞

Library of Congress Cataloging-in-Publication Data

Jackson, Jack, 1941–
Indian agent : Peter Ellis Bean in Mexican Texas / Jack Jackson. — 1st ed.
p. cm. — (Canseco-Keck history series ; no. 6)
Includes bibliographical references and index.
ISBN 1-58544-444-8 (cloth : alk. paper)
1. Bean, Peter Ellis, 1783–1846. 2. Indian agents—Texas—Biography. 3. Indians of North America—Texas—Government relations. 4. Texas—History—To 1846. I. Title. II. Series.
E78.T4J33 2005
976.4′03′092—dc22

2005000439

To Mrs. Leona Bean Hicks, whose side of the family preserved and brought down to us the original portrait of Colonel Bean

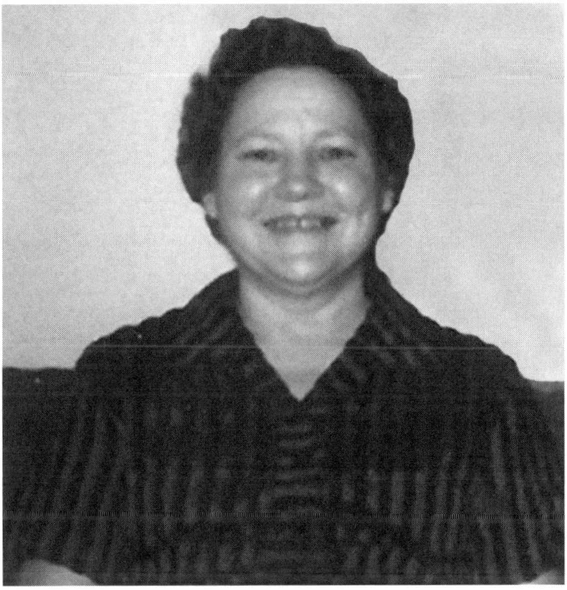

CONTENTS

ILLUSTRATIONS

Maps

ACKNOWLEDGMENTS

THIS STUDY OF the life and times of Peter Ellis Bean has been germinating in my mind for a number of years. It started in 1987 with a book called *Philip Nolan and Texas* and has continued through more recent books on the inspections of Texas carried out by Gen. Manuel de Mier y Terán in 1828 and Col. Juan Nepomuceno Almonte in 1834.[1] All three men were closely connected to Bean, and his name kept popping up in the documents gathered during the course of my research. I eventually wondered why no one had written a more extensive biography of this interesting historical figure than Bennett Lay's 1960 *The Lives of Ellis P. Bean.*[2] Scholarly fish with a voracious appetite for Texas history can only avoid this baited hook for so long.

On a research trip to Mexico City in July 2000, I was fortunate enough to gain admittance to the historical archive of the Mexican War Department. Bean's military service record of 64 *fojas* (128 pages) was examined, but no copy facilities were available. My time being limited, I was unable to do more than make hasty notes on the file. But enough to realize that here was some previously untapped information on Bean—important material by which to judge the truthfulness of his memoir and follow his later activities in Texas.

When I learned that my dear friend Caroline Castillo Crimm had been allowed to photograph some records in this archive with a digital camera—and was returning to do more work—I sent her a "wish list." Included was the entire Bean file, though I scarcely hoped that she would have the time or inclination to interrupt her own pursuits to do free work for me. But she did, even sending me computer printouts that were very clear and easy to read.[3] With this file, plus all the other letters I had already gathered, I could not justify putting off a biography of Peter Ellis Bean any longer.

Once this decision was made, the book practically wrote itself. This sometimes happens when a project has been simmering in the ol' brain for years, anxious to get out. All that remained for me to do was plug document translations into the holes of my first draft and resolve annoying questions that had arisen when things mentioned by previous Bean researchers were contradictory or did not make sense. This is the "messy," tedious part of scholarship, but it must be done if a book is to have any lasting value.

I am obliged to several people for their help in this tune-up job. Ned F. Brierley's expert translation skills allowed me to present Spanish documents to English readers more faithfully than I could have done with my severely limited grasp of the language. Galen D. Greaser, archivist of the Spanish Collection of documents at the Texas General Land Office, provided invaluable assistance in sorting out Bean's tangled land affairs in the Mexican and Republic periods. Thanks to him, this aspect of Bean's career as a real estate "speculator" and producer of the essential commodity of salt came into better focus.[4]

Jean Carefoot at the Archives Division of the Texas State Library (TSL) was also very helpful with locating Bean documents—quite a few of them—in the Nacogdoches Archives under her supervision. Unfortunately, the originals may no longer be examined, and the searcher must resort to using microfilm. Rather than go through this needle-in-a-haystack ordeal, I found the old set of Nacogdoches Archives Transcripts (eighty-nine volumes) easier to use. Jean also alerted me to the fact that the TSL has recovered a set of documents long thought lost. They are the translations of letters once in the Archives of Bexar County made in the 1850s by P. L. Buquor and X. B. Debray. Many of these originals were lost prior to the transfer of the Béxar Archives from San Antonio to the University of Texas at Austin in 1899, and most of the translations also turned up missing during the 1880s. Thus historians writing after 1900 had no knowledge of either the original documents or the Buquor/Debray Translations. Some of these "new" documents have considerable importance to Texas history, not surviving elsewhere.[5]

The Nacogdoches records compiled and transcribed by Robert B. Blake (1877–1955), from court cases and deed books, eased my research chore. Volume 52 of his "Red" typescript series is almost entirely devoted to the Bean family. Many references to Peter Ellis Bean and documents from his hand are scattered throughout other volumes, some in Spanish and others translated. Though not always trustworthy in particulars, this monumental series is a good place for researchers of east Texas to start their work.[6]

Among the historians who gave me good input on Bean were James L. Haley and Thomas Ricks Lindley. They have somewhat different ideas about what Sam Houston was doing militarily and as a spokesman for the

Cherokees in the revolutionary years. Nonetheless, their findings allowed me to place Bean in context of the times and sort out, to some extent, his relationship with Houston.[7] Linda Flores Harvey—a descendant of the "outlaw" Manuel Flores—helped with some needed east Texas materials. Dorothy Sloan told me about several Bean and Fredonian Rebellion items in a private collection not known to scholars, and J. P. Bryan generously allowed me to use various Bean-related letters he recently acquired. Joseph Musso graciously provided several photographs for this book, including one of Sam Houston that is little known, and Terry Stark did the same with a portrait of Philip Nolan he located among Minor descendants in Louisiana. Thanks also go to Dianna Everett and Carolyn Reeves Ericson for answering some questions about sources mentioned in their published works.

Unlike most earlier writers, I am not related to the Beans and have no connection, however remote, to the clan from Tennessee. Thus this book is not a "family" matter but rather an effort to learn more about Peter Ellis Bean and reach a balanced assessment of his historical significance.

An editorial remark is in order: To impart the flavor of the era—and to show that Bean was not the only "illiterate" person on the Texas frontier—letters have been left in their original form. Commas, periods, and other modern forms of essential punctuation were customarily lacking in those days, whereas a profusion of unnecessary capital letters was routinely used. Sentence breaks are indicated by triple spacing, and the use of [*sic*] has been avoided when possible.

People—even educated ones—often spelled words phonetically with little consistency. Thus Bean's own letters in English might suggest that he was a rude bumpkin, whereas translations of his letters from the Spanish give the impression that he was a college graduate. The reason is that Bean dictated most of his Spanish letters to a scribe with good knowledge of the written language. His characteristic signature and flourish seldom match the writing above. Since Bean spoke better Spanish than English (and was not accustomed to expressing himself on paper in English), "his" Spanish letters are usually in proper form and read that way. So that the reader can more fully appreciate Bean's role on the Texas frontier over a long period of time, a number of his Spanish and English letters are quoted at length rather than summarized or glossed over. From his surviving letters in English, one can only imagine the extensive editing that Henderson K. Yoakum had to perform before presenting Bean's memoir to his English readers.

INDIAN AGENT

INTRODUCTION

RARELY CAN WE FOLLOW all the major events of Texas history in the first half of the nineteenth century through the life of one man. Peter Ellis Bean was such a man. His life stretches like a fuse between 1800 and 1847 all the way from Nacogdoches to Mexico City. Once Bean's fuse was ignited, it set off charges down through the years —explosions involving every major figure in the history of both Texas and Mexico. They are all there, from Philip Nolan to Sam Houston, their powder kegs sitting alongside Bean's slow-burning fuse and triggered when the time was right. He fought with Andrew Jackson at the Battle of New Orleans and conferred with men as diverse as Jean Laffite and José Bernardo Gutiérrez de Lara. In Mexico Bean was associated with all the heroes of the revolution against Spain, men such as José María Morelos, Guadalupe Victoria, Vicente Guerrero, Nicolás Bravo, Manuel de Mier y Terán, and others. Shortly before the capture and execution of Morelos, Bean conducted Morelos's young son, Juan N. Almonte, to exile in New Orleans, where Almonte grew to manhood. They all knew Bean and respected the role he played in freeing Mexico from Spanish rule.

Likewise in Texas, there was hardly anyone who had not heard of Bean after his return to the Nacogdoches region in 1823. His role in putting down the Fredonian Rebellion in the winter of 1826–27 was a decisive one. Thereafter Bean managed Indian affairs for Mexico in east Texas until the outbreak of the revolution that took Texas out of the political realm of the Republic of Mexico—a republic that Bean had helped establish. During this decade Bean worked with men like Stephen F. Austin and his fellow empresarios to keep peace with the various Indian tribes in Texas, whether native to the region or those flocking in from the United States. These duties, of course, also brought Bean into contact with all the Mexican officials of the period, ranging from alcaldes, to political chiefs, to governors, to commandant generals, to the presidents of the nation. At one time or another they either met Bean personally or read his letters reporting the situation in Texas on a wide range of subjects.

Bean, with a colonel's commission in the Mexican army for his past services to the nation, also wanted to be an empresario himself. His aspirations were blasted, however, when it was discovered that Bean had a wife in Texas in addition to one residing in Mexico. That Bean was a bigamist is fairly certain, despite the legal niceties of the question. While in Mexico Bean claimed that he was legitimately married to a woman in Jalapa but admitted that he had a "mistress" back in Nacogdoches. While in Texas he said he was married to the woman he had brought from Tennessee (or at least lived with her and their three children in that status) and the *señorita* in Jalapa was nothing but a "mistress" whom he occasionally saw while on business trips. It seems likely that both women thought they were Bean's one and only. This aspect of Bean's behavior is rather unsavory, to modern noses especially. But even in Bean's era it was a strike against him, one that doomed his hopes of being a colonizer of the boundary reserve along the Sabine River. Although high-placed friends in the Mexican capital vouched for Bean's moral character and fitness for the job, it came to naught.

Apart from his association with the Nolan Expedition, his activities in defusing the Fredonian Rebellion, and his being a bigamist, Bean is most remembered as an Indian agent among the "savage" and semicivilized tribes of east Texas between 1826 and 1836. That aspect of his long career is our focus here. Because new documents have been brought to bear on this subject, it is hoped that some clarity will emerge on exactly what Bean was doing and why. Was Bean genuinely interested in the welfare of these Indians (the Cherokees especially), or was he only slyly manipulating them on behalf of Mexico's best interests instead of their own? Because Sam Houston, after his 1833 arrival in Texas, considered himself to be the Cherokees' main spokesman, his relationship with Bean receives much attention. Were they working together on Indian affairs or at odds with one another? This question has great significance as revolution approached, and even in the two men's dealings with the Indians after the Republic of Texas was established.

It is difficult to find a more fascinating character in the early history of Texas than Peter Ellis Bean. This study—while by no means definitive—has been undertaken to shed some new light on his long and eventful career. Although he has been regarded as a marginal and somewhat obscure "border" figure, Bean was anything but. He was on the cutting edge of events as they unfolded in the march of Anglo-Americans toward coveted Spanish possessions in the Southwest. From the time of his arrival there with the equally enigmatic mustanger Philip Nolan in 1801 until his death in Mexico in 1847, Bean witnessed it all. Republics rose and fell around him, but he survived the ordeal and lived to tell the tale. His story is the story of Texas and Mexico combined, neatly wrapped into one package.

Chapter 1

BEAN'S EARLY YEARS

Peter Ellis Bean was born in Grainger County, Tennessee, on June 8, 1783.[1] He was the eldest of eight children, and his parents were William Bean and Elizabeth Blair; they, both widowers, married in 1782. Earlier Bean writers have been silent on his mother's name, but it appears—from a recent genealogical post on the Internet, which seems to be taken from work that is well researched and documented (though not credited, as is often the case)—that she was Elizabeth Blair. Peter Ellis's siblings were William (1785), Fetna (1787), Robert (1789), Edmund (ca. 1790), Elizabeth Ann (ca. 1792), Jesse (ca. 1794), and Lydia (1796). In addition, his mother Elizabeth had at least one son from a previous marriage. This half brother later became known as Capt. William Shaw, but there may have been other children in addition to him. A Benjamin Shaw often appears in the same records as William. Peter Ellis, after his return from Mexico in 1817, visited these relatives in Tennessee.[2]

Bean's father was also married previous to his alliance with Elizabeth Blair. Around 1777 he wed Rachel Ball, and their son Ahab Bean was born January 10, 1778, on Boone's Creek in Washington (later Grainger) County. Rachel died in childbirth, as often happened to women on the frontier. Thus Peter Ellis was surrounded by brothers and sisters as he grew to manhood, and he also had numerous kinsmen in the immediate area.[3] The Beans were a well-established clan in the mountains of eastern Tennessee by the time of his birth, dating back to the foundation of Bean's Station. It stood in a gap of the Cumberland Mountains where Indian trails intersected, being branches of their Great Warpath. There, on the Holston River near a sulfur spring and a salt lick that attracted game, the Beans built their Station (or fortified enclosure) as a protection against Indian attack. It grew into an important crossroads point in what became Grainger County, Tennessee.[4]

This settlement had been founded by Bean's grandfather, Capt. William Bean (1721–82), and other members of his generation. He married Lydia Russell in 1744 and they had nine children. Among them was Peter Ellis's father William "Jr." (1745–98, also a captain), Robert, Jesse, George, John, Edmund, Jane, Sarah, and Russell Bean.[5] The death of Bean's "Uncle Russell" was reported to him in Texas by a relative in Nashville (Edmund "Been," either a brother or nephew) in January 1827, saying he had died "August last."[6] This Russell Bean, born in 1769, was probably the same who gave rise to the frontier legend with Andrew Jackson, then a judge holding court in Jonesboro, Tennessee. It is difficult to pin down this legend chronologically—and there are numerous variations of the encounter—but it seems to have occurred after the turn of the century, and Judge Jackson is always credited for his personal bravery and the way he ran his court in a "no foolishness" manner.

Russell Bean had returned from a lengthy trading venture down the Mississippi in 1801 to find his wife, Rosamond, nursing a baby by another man. Supposedly, in a "drunken frolic," he either bit or cut off the ears of this infant, was indicted for the offense, and brought before Jackson's court. Described as a "great, hulking fellow," Bean paraded into the courtroom, cursing judge, jury, and all assembled before marching out the door. Jackson ordered the sheriff to arrest Bean for disrespect. But Bean was so intimidating that the sheriff could not make the arrest and deputized the judge to do it himself. Jackson went out into the street with a pistol, pointed it at Bean, and told him to give himself up or die. A variant, which appeared in a history of Jackson published in 1834, says that they fought like cats and dogs until the judge had bested his man. The standard version says that Bean saw "murder" in Judge Jackson's eye and surrendered to him meekly. Russell Bean suffered harsh punishment for his "stupid and dreadful deed."[7]

Peter Ellis, in his memoir, says that he—in volunteering to fight at the Battle of New Orleans—"had known Jackson from my earliest recollection."[8] What he probably meant to say was that he had known *of* Jackson during his early years. Andrew Jackson's exploits against the British as a teenager entered frontier lore very early, and tales such as these were oft related to children around the fireplace on winter evenings. In any case, Peter Ellis Bean was already a prisoner with Nolan's men in Spanish Texas by the time of his Uncle Russell's encounter with Judge Jackson, if it happened in 1801.

Russell Bean's reaction to his wife's infidelity may have been something of a family characteristic. It was echoed in Texas several decades later when our Bean returned from Mexico to find his wife living with another man. Gossip—completely unsubstantiated and likely false—had

Bean cutting *her* ears off for the offense. He did, however, give her a beating and drove her out of the house to seek refuge elsewhere. It goes without saying that the Beans were not the only frontier family whose males reacted violently when faced with marital infidelity. The trait was almost universal in that day and time, especially if a child had been produced by someone else during the husband's absence on long hunts or business ventures to distant places.

Bean's childhood was spent in the wild, savage, and yet beautiful part of Grainger County that his grandfather had settled when Tennessee was still regarded as sacred country belonging to the Cherokees. Captain Bean, like his fellow frontiersman Daniel Boone, was part of the Anglo-Celtic wave rolling across the mountains into the fertile Tennessee River Valley. The captain's Station sat on what became a hub of busy county roads. Although he prospered at this location, when crowded by too many settlers the Bean clan moved on. Around 1769 Captain Bean built a cabin for his growing family near where Boone Creek emptied into the Watauga. His and Lydia's son Russell (named after her family) was born that year, said to be the first white child born in what later became Tennessee. But, of course, every family on the westward march claimed similar honors for their children.[9]

The Beans fought the French and Indians for possession of this stubborn soil, and later the British as well. The Beans, according to an eminent historian, "were always to the front when an expedition was on foot." The participation of the Beans in the American Revolution is well documented. They donned their fringed leather or calico hunting shirts and shouldered their long rifles on numerous occasions, the battle of King's Mountain being only one of them. Bean's grandfather Capt. William Bean soldiered until his death in 1782, but his sons, nephews, and cousins carried on the fight. As the migration spread west, Beans were always in the vanguard as hunters, trackers, traders/fighters with the Indians, surveyors, gunsmiths, and salt-makers. Like the Trammells and similar clans, they were "go-ahead" people accustomed to life in the wilderness and would not have it any other way.[10]

Self-sufficient and tightly interknit by marriage, the Anglo-Celtic westward movement toward Texas was greatly feared by Mexican thinkers such as General Terán. No matter what Mexico tried, these hardy folk could not be held back from crossing the Sabine and Red Rivers into Texas. Roads? They disdained roads and struck their paths through the wilderness, just as they had been doing since pushing inland from the Atlantic Seaboard.[11] Shinn, in his *Pioneers and Makers of Arkansas,* describes a frontier frolic near the White River of Arkansas, along the Southwest Trail that led to Texas: "They came with their guns and a fine old crowd it was. Colonel Miller and his boys, Colonel Peel and sons, the widow

Lafferty and sons, Major Magness and his army of boys, the Creigs, Ruddells, Trammels, Beans, Trimbles, and Kellys were all there with their guns stacked against the walls."[12] If their dogs got on the trail of a bear, Preacher Eli Lindsay, an "old neighbor from Kentucky," would dismiss services until it could be run down and killed. The women, meanwhile, gossiped, fixed food for the gathering, and tended their brood of young children. Drinking, dancing, and general hell-raising would come after lanterns went up in the trees after dark.

This, then, was the frontier milieu in which Peter Ellis Bean came to manhood in the lands wrested from the Cherokees. He had no education to speak of, but he learned his wilderness survival woodcraft early on. If he managed to pick up any Cherokee linguistic skills during his youth, it has gone unrecorded. This was still wild country, and his aunt Jane Bean was killed in 1799 by Indians when she went from the house to a spring nearby for water. Bean was sixteen at the time, and this was thirty years after his grandfather had first come to Tennessee. Indian peril was an everyday fact of life, and it is hard to imagine that a youthful Bean was not affected by it. His uncles and cousins made guns—beautiful examples of the famed Kentucky Long Rifle. Molding lead bullets and mixing ingredients into powder came naturally to young Bean. He had an inventive and tinkering streak that served him well in later years. No matter the mechanical challenge, Bean could perform.[13]

Peter Ellis beat his Bean kinsmen to Texas by several decades. It was not something he planned when striking out on his own in the spring of 1800 with a boatload of whiskey and flour, intended for sale in Natchez. He was only seventeen and his father William did not want to let him go at such a tender age, but Bean would not be denied. He craved some excitement in his life, to see new and strange places. Besides, there was an aunt who lived at Natchez who would take care of him once he reached the wild town. His father's consent or no, Bean, along with a friend, John Word, pushed his homemade flatboat into the swift waters of the Holston River.[14]

It was a foolish undertaking, as the boys soon learned. After passing the rustic town of Knoxville, they entered the broader Tennessee River. Downstream the country grew wilder. Cabins became scarce; now Indian villages dotted the riverbanks, and white people were seldom seen. Bean and Word struggled to keep their boat afloat through the Narrows and what was called the Suck, because of its hazardous swirls. Doom came to their merchandising venture at Muscle Shoals, when a rock broke their boat to pieces with the total loss of their precious cargo. (Philip Nolan had experienced a similar disaster a decade earlier. Returning from New Orleans with a boatload of fancy merchandise for his employer, Gen. James Wilkinson, Nolan's boat became frozen in near the mouth of the Ohio and later sank.) John Word had had enough and returned home, but Bean continued on with a small trunk of his clothes salvaged from the wreck.

He hitched a ride with an immigrant family bound for Natchez, only five dollars in his pocket. Amid their pigs, chickens, sheep, and farming tools, he floated past the Ohio's mouth and into the broad Mississippi. Debarking at Natchez, the teenager must have been impressed with the hustle and bustle of this river town. It had only recently been surrendered to the United States by Spain and was a polyglot of different cultures, races, and languages. Bean found his aunt, and an uncle who lived nearby sent a saddle horse so the lad could join him. A fever felled him for a month, but Bean was soon back sightseeing in town. There he learned that the renowned Philip Nolan was planning another expedition to Texas, his fourth to that Spanish province, and Bean eagerly signed up.[15]

Nolan was the beau ideal of backwoods lads like Peter Ellis Bean. He had many friends in high places, had just married a rich girl of the plantation class, and returned from his last trip to Texas with over twelve hundred spirited mustangs. These horses fetched high prices in the Mississippi settlements, and Nolan was a man on the rise. Only he knew how to pull the levers to get to Texas, obtain these animals, and get out again. Nolan was enlisting about thirty men; each was to bring back ten horses, half of which he could keep for himself. These horses, when tamed and driven to Natchez, were worth around $50 on the market, "magnificent" ones going as high as $150. The more horses, the more money. Besides a lot of money to be made, there was the excitement of seeing places that few Americans knew anything about—the "unknown land," as Nolan described it to his double-dealing patron, General Wilkinson. Bean probably understood little of the intricacies involved, but he knew enough to realize that it promised to be a real adventure.

And so it was. Bean later wrote it all down, his account being our most authoritative one extant for Nolan's final trip to the Texas plains in search of thundering herds of wild horses.[16] No other document tells us what Nolan's party saw and did as they eluded Spanish patrols to finally cross the Red River around modern Texarkana and enter Texas early in 1801. They proceeded to the Trinity and Brazos Rivers above Nacogdoches, apparently oblivious to the maelstrom of paranoia that their passing had incited among Spanish officials from the Mississippi to the Rio Grande. Their mission was said not to be catching mustangs but wresting Texas from the Spanish Empire—conquest and nothing less. For this, Nolan was working to incite the "barbaric" tribes along the northern frontier, and he was in league with revolutionary inhabitants of the province. Together they would swoop down on the Spanish settlements and deliver Texas to the hated North Americans.

Philip Nolan, ca. 1799. Photo courtesy Terry Stark.

Reaching the Brazos near the small river tributary that now bears his name, Nolan erected a combination fort and corral. It was a roofless structure intended to hold their gear while members of the party—now reduced by desertions to twenty-five—rode out on mustang-catching forays. Nolan made trips to hold councils with the Tawakonis, Taovayas, and Comanches; their chiefs also paid visits to the fort. Rather than inciting them to war, Nolan probably wanted to trade for their horses—easier than catching them himself with his greenhorn crew. But word of his general location got back to Samuel Davenport and William Barr at Nacogdoches. They were two Irishmen whose business House would suffer if Nolan were allowed to export horses and trade with the Indians.

When a Spanish force marched out of Nacogdoches to apprehend Nolan, "Guillermo" Barr rode with it.

The fate of Philip Nolan's final expedition and the disposition of his men taken as prisoners has been related elsewhere.[17] Suffice it to say that the Spaniards found him and readied their attack on the morning of March 21, 1801. After Nolan refused Miguel Francisco Músquiz's demand of surrender—delivered through interpreter William Barr—a battle ensued. Nolan was killed by a random musket shot through the head. His men, including Bean, tried to escape but were forced to surrender. Barr volunteered to take Nolan's ears and personal papers to the commandant general as proof that the invasion attempt had failed and its ringleader was dead. Then began Peter Ellis Bean's decade-long captivity as the king's prisoner—some of it rigid, some fairly relaxed. He lied about his age on the roll of prisoners, saying he was twenty-two, a native of North Carolina, and a resident of Natchez for one year. It should be noted that Bean was using the given name "Ellis" at this time, and he continued to do so until the mid-1820s. Thus Henderson Yoakum published Bean's memoir under the name of Ellis P. Bean. In Mexico he was called Pedro Elías, or simply Elías.

Chapter 2

TEN YEARS A PRISONER

EXTENSIVE TESTIMONY WAS TAKEN at Nacogdoches and San Antonio de Béxar to determine the motives for the expedition. Most of Nolan's men swore that they had only come to help their leader bring out the horses he had already arranged for delivery. For this service Nolan had agreed to pay them in horses or slaves. Several of the men, such as David Fero, had also been promised a dollar a day if the trip extended longer than three months. No one, naturally, professed any knowledge of a scheme of conquest.

This did not satisfy their inquisitors, and more relentless examinations were made of Nolan's suspected collaborators in Texas. Included were Nolan's mistress, Gertrudis de los Santos, and her husband Antonio Leal; both were helping Nolan in his smuggling and horse export business. On November 3, 1801, Nolan's men were headed south, after nearly three months at the provincial capital of Béxar. They were marched from place to place in the Interior Provinces, as no one could decide where their trial should be held. Eventually they arrived at Chihuahua, where Gen. Nemesio Salcedo y Salcedo had his headquarters—this on March 14, 1803. They were held in confinement until the king's pleasure regarding them should be known.

This took time under the snail-paced Spanish legal system. By 1804 fifteen of the prisoners had been transferred to San Carlos; Bean was among those left at Chihuahua. But their irons were removed and they were permitted to pursue their trades in the day, returning at night to sleep in the military barracks. Bean became a hatter, and in six months' time had raised his reputation so high that no one would buy a hat unless at his shop. Bean found someone to set him up in business and employed two Spanish hatmakers to work for him, "for, in fact, I was no hatter at all." He prospered but still longed for freedom. Other prisoners became reconciled to their life and thought about marrying local women and making the state of Chihuahua their home. Not Bean. He began plotting an escape attempt with other like-minded prisoners and might have succeeded except for the betrayal of one of their comrades, Jonah Waters. Bean gave him a sound thrashing at the first opportunity.

After this episode, restrictions were tightened on Bean and his fellow conspirators. They were imprisoned for a month and not allowed to leave the grounds of their respective presidios. This confinement was relaxed as time went by, and several prisoners were granted permission to take trips for their "health." In April 1807 one of General Wilkinson's officers, Zebulon Pike, was captured at a little fort he had built above Taos on an expedition supposedly to explore the upper reaches of the Red River. Professing their amazement at being on the Rio Grande, in Spanish territory, he and his men were conducted to see General Salcedo at Chihuahua. While there, under a loose form of house arrest and actually treated with considerable hospitality, Pike had the opportunity to see several of the prisoners and learn their circumstances. Upon his return to the United States, Pike sent a report on their status to the *Natchez Herald,* which the paper published on August 10, 1807. He had this to say about Bean: "Ellis Bean, of Grainger County, state of Tennesee, a hatter, formerly carried on his business in the city of Chihuahua, but being detected in an intrigue with the daughter of an officer, and refusing to marry her, was in close confinement at St. Jeronimie [San Gerónimo], a few leagues distant, in good health."[1] Bean does not mention this love affair as being connected to the escape attempt, so it must have been one of his womanizing escapades that went awry. Other prisoners had sexual partners, and one caught a venereal disease that gave him so much pain that he had to opt out of the escape plan.[2] Whether Bean got the officer's daughter pregnant will probably never be known, but that he jilted her seems fairly obvious.

Sometime after Pike's visit Bean learned that Pres. Thomas Jefferson had not done much to end their captivity. He railed against the president in his memoir because the circumstances of Nolan's expedition had been placed before him and the Spanish court as well. Jefferson had said that "he knew nothing of us, and that we should be tried according to the Spanish laws . . . But what can a poor prisoner expect, when the leading men of his country fail to see justice done him?" Bean supposed that the reason was that Jefferson "was a great friend to the prince of Peace" (Manuel de Godoy, who in effect ruled Spain because he was the lover of King Carlos IV's wife). Bean's assessment dripped with venom: "As Mr. Jefferson did not know us, and had no expectation of being benefited by us, it was less trouble to say, 'Hang them!'"[3] Some have speculated that Bean's bitterness toward the United States for abandoning them to their fate among the Spaniards led him to transfer his loyalties to an independent Mexican nation with such steadfastness.[4]

Finally, on February 23, 1807, the king ordered that one out of every five of Nolan's men be hung and the rest sentenced to hard labor for ten years. Only those who had fired at the king's men were to suffer the penalty of casting lots to decide their fate of life or death. This shrank the number to nine men, Bean one of them. Blindfolded, they knelt to throw the dice on a drumhead. Bean threw a four and a one, but Ephraim Blackburn, a Quaker, tossed a three and a one. He was hanged at the Plaza de los Urangas in Chihuahua on November 11, 1807. Peter Ellis Bean escaped death by a very narrow margin, but the odds seemed to be rolling in his favor and continued to do so throughout his life in Mexico.

Shortly thereafter came orders that Bean and three other men (David Fero, Zalmon Cooley, and William Danlin) were to be sent to Acapulco on the coast. They rode out of Chihuahua in heavy irons and headed down the central plateau of Mexico. The harsh desert landscape of yucca, mesquite, and cactus eventually yielded to a more pleasant and temperate zone of adequate rainfall with trees and fields of corn, beans, and peppers. Herds of fat cattle were frequently seen. Bean also noticed a difference in the people. "The people at every town through which we passed would flock to see us, for they had never before seen an American so far into the interior. Of those who came to see us some gave us money and others sent us provisions. They were all mixed with Indian and showed us real friendship and seemed to have humanity in their hearts. The Spaniards were hard-hearted and barbarous and seemed to have no other feeling than to make us as miserable as possible."[5]

Reaching the town of Salamanca, east of Guadalajara near Celaya, Bean described another chance to escape—one that he foolishly did not take. Given the liberty to stroll around the central plaza, which was ringed by tightly arranged houses, Bean was approached by a young and very attractive woman. She asked him if he wanted to escape. "I answered her that it was a thing impossible and I had resigned myself to my fate." She would return later, said the woman, and free him from his chains. Bean, curious at this strange offer, asked a man nearby who she was. He learned that she was María Baldonada, the wife of a very rich—but old—man, whom she had only recently married. Bean, of course, instantly realized that she not only wanted to free him but herself as well. He was to be the avenue of María's escape from a marriage that she detested and could not otherwise end.[6]

The unhappy wife later returned to the plaza and sat down beside him on a mat. She explained how the escape was to go. Once over the wall by means of a rope that a friend would extend down from a rooftop, Bean would be taken to her. He would be safe, as she owned several remotely located haciendas where he could hide. There, they could stay together until it was safe for them to escape. Bean protested that his companions would surely suffer for his getaway, but the lady told him he should best look out for himself and let God worry about the rest. When Bean mentioned that a pardon for him from the king might arrive at Mexico City any day now, and he would be free to come and go at will, María said not to count on it. A call to supper cut short further discussions between the pair.

They met again the next day, and a soldier was bribed to take a walk. María pressed for Bean to act; now was the time for him to make his dash for freedom. When the soldier returned and found Bean gone, he would desert rather than be held to account. Bean—according to Yoakum's rendition of his memoir—replied with a totally asinine excuse, given his impoverished circumstances and earlier fling in Chihuahua with an officer's daughter: "Madam, you are a married lady, and I should be a most unhappy man to receive such favors from one of your rank, and then be compelled to leave you without any hope of seeing you again. But if, by the King's order, I should get free, I could then come and spend my days in this town, where I should have the happiness of seeing you, and perhaps be sometimes in your company, if admissible."[7]

María would not be put off by Bean's if-and-when proposition of being her part-time lover. Her marriage to this rich old coot (he was fifty-five) had been arranged by her parents, and she had had to go through with it not to displease them. But she did not love her husband and refused to be bound by her marriage vows. Although Bean was a stranger in shackles, she had fallen for him at first sight. Her opinion of him, María said, was too good to suppose that he would abandon her for any other lady, no matter how fair, after she had gambled all to accompany him to his country as a matter of the heart. "Though I am mixed with Indian blood, I would trust to your honor not to cast me off."

Bean turned the charming lady's offer down, but he wrote that it was a decision he "repented" for the next three years. When the soldier returned, Bean rode back to quarters with him—but not before María had slipped him a package. It contained a tender love letter and a ring to wear so, if he obtained his freedom, he would not forget "one who is not ashamed to own that the love she has for you is more than she can bear." Bean was in a foul mood after he read this letter, no doubt realizing that in his anxiousness to avoid being "trapped" by a love-starved and rich married beauty, he had passed up the best chance so far of freeing himself. If Bean's memoir can be believed, he passed up an offer of pardon after the revolution began when marriage to some rich Spaniard's daughter was the bargaining chit. This, however, may be Editor Yoakum's high-flown prose and not Bean's down-to-earth words.

The prisoners were then conducted to Acapulco, Mexico's west coast port for the East Indies fleet that arrived once a year, bearing cargoes of spices, rugs, ceramics, gold, silver, and other rich treasures obtained from the Orient and Pacific islands under Spanish control. Guarding the port were strong fortifications, planned and built by royal engineers over many years. It was considered to be an impregnable place, its "castle" erected of stone blocks with walls twelve feet thick and containing a hundred guns of the largest caliber.[8] Shortly after their arrival, Bean was separated from his fellow prisoners and put in solitary confinement. This, he said, was because the commandant at Chihuahua had written something against him and ordered that "great care" be taken in his case. The officer's daughter that Bean had wooed and forsaken?

Here began Bean's account of his miserable circumstances at Acapulco, one of the most poignant prisoner narratives ever written.[9] He was starved and subjected to harsh treatment, his only companion a white lizard that he succeeded in taming. His interaction with other prisoners, guards, and friars usually ended in violence, which only worsened his incarceration. An escape attempt at the dock ended in failure; Bean's chains were restored and he was returned to his small cell, where he again sought companionship with his "friend Bill" the lizard. He talked a woman passing outside the prison into sending him a bladder of liquor up a rope he had woven: "I can truly say that, during the year and five months I stayed in this cell the last time, the hour I was drunk, and unconscious of everything, was the only happy time I saw."

Bean orchestrated another escape attempt by volunteering to place charges in holes that others had bored for the blasting of rocks. He assured an officer that there was nothing to it, even if none of his soldiers knew how. During the process of making matches in the gallery of a house near the rock pit, Bean bought cartridges, a brace of pistols, and a dozen knives. Money talked, and Bean still had about 150 pesos left from his hatter business at Chihuahua. He convinced some of his fellow prisoners, who outnumbered their guards, to make the try with him. They got loose, and several made their way up the coast with Bean. But the breakout attempt ended in disaster, and Bean lost his "old Spanish friend" who had joined the Nolan Expedition in Natchez years before. He may have been Luciano García, recently transferred to Acapulco, but a man of this name was later governor of Mexican Texas so the matter is questionable. Bean, without giving his name, says he died of an infected leg wound received on the getaway venture.[10]

Hauled back to Acapulco, Bean had to face the wrath of the provincial governor. Bean, with his constant escape attempts, was becoming a real administrative problem. Why, asked the governor, can you not reconcile yourself to your status and quit causing me headaches? Bean replied, "Sir, I am a prisoner, and alone; but I do not fear what you can do to me; for if you take my life, you will at once free me from tyranny." Tyranny? "What tyranny?" asked the governor. Look at your companions; they bask in the sun, soaking up its rays, and do not make trouble like you. That was because they were cowards, answered Bean, and "do not love their freedom as I do." He assured the governor that he would continue trying to regain his liberty at every opportunity. The governor shook his head in disgust and sent Bean back to prison at the castle.

There he was held more rigorously than before and chained to a large mulatto. Bean learned from another prisoner that the mulatto had been told to place Bean in total subjection; if he "took care of" the American prisoner, the governor would deduct a year off his sentence. When the mulatto yanked Bean's chain in the prison yard three days later, throwing Bean off his feet, Bean grabbed a cow skull and beat the big man senseless. After this incident Bean was separated from the mulatto and a large wheel put around his neck, so large that "I could not move with it." But he was soon relieved of this onerous punishment, reshackled, and taken back to his cell with its gentle lizard: "Here I spent my time better. All was silent, and nothing to disturb me."

The governor declared to the viceroy that he could no longer be responsible for Bean's obstreperous behavior and asked that he be sent to another fort. Plans to send Bean to Manila were interrupted by Father Miguel Hidalgo's call for a revolution to overturn Spanish rule of Mexico. This came on September 16, 1810, known as the famous *grito de Dolores.* As the revolution progressed, prisons were cleared of men willing to fight for the Royalist cause. Bean declared his willingness, and the governor released him when the castle's commandant argued that Bean's record of "venturesome" and bold escape attempts would make him a good soldier. So Bean's irons were taken off and he was given a uniform, a gun, and a sword.

This development put Bean "in a good fix for war." He was soon talking to other soldiers about what the revolution meant for them and how they ought to join it. If Hidalgo's rebellion met with success, all the Europeans who had ruled them for three hundred years would be forced to leave Mexico and then "the natives would be generals and colonels, and all the riches would fall into their hands. Those to whom I said this were well pleased; but I charged them to say nothing about it to any person that would tell; and, if they said anything to any one, not to mention my name."[11]

These seeds of dissension sown by Bean began to take root among the soldiers at Acapulco, many of them mestizos whose ethnic kinsmen were rallying to the flag of revolution. Bean's companions from Natchez told him he was crazy to talk of such things, for he would certainly be hung if the sedition was traced back to him. When the forces of insurgent leader José María Morelos approached Acapulco, Bean was among the party of Royalist soldiers sent to find and give battle to him. But Bean managed to contact Morelos through a company of patriot militia and was conducted into his presence, tied fast so it would look like he was a captured prisoner. Morelos asked Bean to join the patriot struggle, and Bean told him that "I was a republican, and that was what I had come for." Thus began Peter Ellis Bean's close association with Morelos that continued for the next five years.

Morelos had only 150 men at the time, along with twenty "old broken guns." He was also short of gunpowder, but he had a pound of saltpeter and two pounds of sulfur. Alas, none of his men knew how to mix the ingredients together with charcoal. "I told him I could do it; and got some women to grind it on the rocks they ground corn on for bread, and by night it was all ready to dry." Bean's ability to make gunpowder and refurbish cannons made him very useful to Morelos. Later in the war Bean was in charge of several complete powder mills for the insurgents, providing them with powder and ball for their military operations, along with repairing cannons and running a small arms factory.

Bean also played a significant role in the fighting at Acapulco and elsewhere throughout the revolution. He conceived a plan that enabled Morelos's small force to defeat the Spanish army sent to destroy him, whereby four hundred new recruits—"in fact, all the natives"—were gained through desertions of Royalist prisoners to the rebel side. This, along with all the cannons, arms, and ammunition taken, in one night made Morelos's force "respectable in arms and men." Subsequent actions along the Pacific coastline added to the rebel coffers and placed "our camp in a flourishing condition." More men joined the rebel banner, and the priest/general José María Morelos rapidly became acknowledged as one of Mexico's most important leaders.

Bean remained his chief confidant, and Morelos soon had him in command of cavalry troops. In one battle the governor was badly wounded, Bean's "old friend, who had kept me in chains so long." Rather than execute him, Bean sent him back to his castle to die. "After this battle," wrote Bean, "all the coast was clear of the enemy, except the strong fort at Acapulco, which I was unable to take." Shortly thereafter, Morelos received a letter that the fort would be surrendered to him by rebel sympathizers within if he appeared with his army in the darkness sixty yards from the

José María Morelos, ca. 1812. Photo courtesy Joseph Musso.

fort and waited for a lantern to be hoisted to the top of a flagstaff. At this signal, the fort's drawbridges would be let down and all doors opened. The touchholes of the fort's massive cannons were being filled with tallow to disable them.

Morelos liked the scheme and the idea of possessing the formidable fort. Bean, however, opposed the plan because—if treachery motivated it—the fort's guns could destroy the insurgent force in a matter of minutes. Morelos wanted to see it through but allowed Bean's men to approach the fort and say that all was in readiness—that Morelos had his army assembled at the designated spot. He did not, and it was a good thing because the fort's fifty cannons began blasting away with grapeshot. When daylight came, the Royalists were much disappointed to see that the ground was shredded to pieces instead of being littered with insurgent corpses. Bean asked Morelos the next day what he thought of the plan now, and Morelos admitted that "God had protected us." Yes, God and Peter Ellis Bean's lack of faith in Royalist promises—a suspicious attitude gained through years of suffering. The priest Morelos had not suffered like Bean and still placed faith in Spanish honor. In this bloody revolution, honor was a scarce commodity.[12]

As the revolution entered its phase after the capture and execution of Father Hidalgo and his generals in Chihuahua, Bean was all over the map. But Gen. Félix Calleja, made viceroy for his defeat of Hidalgo's army at Guadalajara, was marshaling a large force to snuff out the rebel pretensions of independence from Spain. Besieged at Cuautla (below the capital) by Calleja, Morelos managed to escape but with little except his son Almonte and the shirt on his back. Rebel successes were on the wane. At a battle near Orizaba, the Royalists "gave us such a complete flogging" that the insurgents were able to save their guns and ammunition only with difficulty. A retreat was made to Oaxaca, and this rich city fell to Morelos in a brief battle. Much Royalist property was confiscated, easing the impoverished condition of Morelos's force. It was here that Bean established his powder mill in an attempt to replenish the rebels' exhausted supply of munitions—an operation that Bean said was carried on successfully for about a year.[13]

At the end of 1812 Morelos marched with three thousand men to Chilpancingo and onward to Acapulco for another try at capturing the fort. Bean signed the letter demanding the fort's surrender, to which the commanding officer replied that if he would come over to His Majesty's side, Bean would be rewarded with a colonel's commission and ten thousand pesos. Bean described General Morelos's reaction when he showed him the letter: "He laughed when he read it, and said, 'Why don't you go?' I said, 'If you thought I would go, you would not say that.' He then said, 'You are right.'"[14] There was an ease between the two men that allowed them to joke about matters of serious import. Morelos had learned to trust and rely upon this foreigner in ways that few others could have won his confidence.

His health poor, Morelos left for Tehepán and put Bean in charge of "the business" at Acapulco. At a post near an island in the harbor, Bean readied his small armada of rough and badly made craft for an attack on the island. It was keeping the fort supplied with provisions, making it impossible to starve out the Royalists. In a fight with one of their schooners, Bean took some prisoners. They confirmed that the garrison was near starvation and, through them, Bean offered to negotiate terms for surrender. He refused to let the garrison march away with their arms to join Royalist forces elsewhere. No, they had to leave their weapons behind and all the king's property as well. There is likely some exaggeration here, as Bean did not have the rank to be conducting negotiations of such significance.[15]

At this point of Bean's narrative, Editor Yoakum notes that four leaves (eight pages) are missing from the manuscript. This is an unfortunate loss, because some stirring events were then taking place. Suffice it to say here that the fortress of Acapulco capitulated late in August 1813, and Morelos was now master of the southern sea. Bean's presence at the climax is doubtful, as he signed a document at Oaxaca on August 3, in which his rank was given as a major and his title as commandant of engineers. After the surrender of Acapulco, Morelos hastened back to Chilpancingo where the new Congress was meeting. Two months later Mexican independence from Spain was declared. As Bean's biographer Bennett Lay says, "Paradoxically, the siege and capture of Acapulco marked the beginning of patriot misfortunes."[16]

This was true because the seven-month siege had tied up Morelos's main army and given the Royalists time to reorganize their forces and move against him. By the time Bean's tale resumes, the insurgent cause was in serious difficulties and it was taken for granted that the king's men would triumph. Bean records another tryst with a beautiful *señorita,* this one the daughter of a rich Royalist sympathizer who—knowing of his daughter's love for Bean—urged him to appear at the altar with her. "We have now in the house for you a king's pardon, and the promise that you shall have the same command in the king's army that you now have. So, fulfil the promise to my daughter, marry her, make her happy, and yourself also. You well know of the defeat of Morelos, and that all the troops you commanded are lost; that the king's troops are daily increasing, and the patriots falling off. So, for your own happiness and mine, I hope you will, at your leisure, take all these things into consideration."[17] Bean, however, left this "young angel Miss Wakina" (Joaquina) in the lurch, even after she said that she would leave with him to share his company in an unmarried state. He gave her another one of his patriotic speeches about how he would never cease his revolutionary activities until he saw Mexico flourishing in the "enjoyment of liberty, and the despot fly from our coasts." Too much of a gentleman to allow Joaquina to be torn from her family in such uncertain times, Bean kissed her and left the room. Once again he had avoided matrimony, though he had to put spurs to his horse outside when a friar tried to keep him from riding away from the wedding assembly.

This incident, judging from its sequential placement in the narrative, must have occurred after the smashing defeat that Morelos suffered at his hometown of Valladolid near the end of 1813. This unexpected reverse stunned Morelos and left one of his generals, Nicolás Bravo, crying like a baby. When Morelos decided not to continue his retreat southward to Puruarán but make a stand against pursuing Royalist troops, he was again defeated on January 5, 1814, and his fleeing army slaughtered. Bean was in Oaxaca in March, when a Royalist army under Col. Melchor Alvarez arrived to liberate the city from the insurgents. The well-to-do citizens had fared badly under their rule and were prepared to welcome the Royalists with open arms. Thus, it appears that Bean's refusal of marriage to Joaquina came at Oaxaca, just before he fled the city and Colonel Alvarez's troops.[18]

Bean mentions Gen. Ignacio Rayón needing his help at Tentaclan del Camino (Yanhuitlán?), but Bean's mules were so worn out that he could not ride to his aid with the two hundred men at his disposal. Rayón had already gone into the mountains when Bean got there. A Royalist force was approaching, but Bean told Rayón he could lick them if sent reinforcements. No help arrived, except about forty men from Teotla, and Bean was obliged to give battle on his own. "There we gave the enemy's cavalry such a beating, that they retreated, and reported to their infantry (who never reached the battle-ground) that my force was two thousand men!" General Rayón, hearing of Bean's success, "came to my assistance when I did not need him." Although Rayón asked Bean to join his command, he remained a loyal partisan of Morelos. Bean did not think too highly of this rival *caudillo* and wrote that if he joined him, "I knew that I would always be left to fight [alone] if any danger offered."[19]

Soon after this action a letter arrived from General Morelos, "relating all his misfortunes, and requesting me, if I could pass to the United States, to do so as soon as possible; and see if I could make any arrangements to bring on a campaign against the province of Texas, and, if I could, to make some provision for a supply of arms."[20] Bean had two thousand pesos when he left Oaxaca. He raised more money from rich people at Tehuacán, who knew him and his devotion to the cause of Morelos, and set off on his journey to the coast with twelve thousand pesos in his saddlebags. Reaching the port town of Nautla, up the coast from Veracruz, Bean had some hair-raising scrapes with boats coming in and out of the port. He witnessed a fight between a British brig and the schooner *Tigre,* commanded by one of Jean Laffite's pirate captains, Dominique You.

While the *Tigre* vanquished its foe, in celebrating their victory the crew got so drunk that they crashed on a reef. Bean, in the small schooner he had recently captured (calling it "the first vessel the *Mexican* nation ever owned"), went to the rescue of the stranded crew and brought them back to Nautla. They refurbished Bean's little schooner and set sail for the pirate stronghold of La Barataria, a bay and swampy network of bayous around the island of Grand Terre on the coast below New Orleans. The voyage was made in ten days. Bean, however, did not linger long to enjoy the famous hospitality of Laffite—then indisposed by eviction orders from U.S. authorities. He reached New Orleans in the first week of September 1814.

Bean set about his business of enlisting aid for the Mexican struggle for independence. He spoke with the governor of the Territory of New Orleans, William C. C. Claiborne, whom Bean styled as "my old aquaintance" from Tennessee. Then he went up the Mississippi River to Natchez and on to Natchitoches, where he conferred with José Bernardo Gutiérrez de Lara and José Alvarez de Toledo about the possibility of another invasion of Spanish Texas. He found a large number of "poor fugitive Mexicans" at that place, "but they had become dispirited, and had no desire to make a second attempt."[21] Bean did not have the funds to back a campaign anyway, so he returned to New Orleans. There he found Gen. Andrew Jackson preparing to defend the city against a British invasion. He enlisted in the company of Capt. Maunsel White and was stationed on Bayou St. Johns.

When General Jackson visited the levee and asked him if he "understood artillery," Bean replied that he did. There was some truth in this, considering his experience in resurrecting beat-up old guns for Morelos in Mexico. Now Bean found himself working a 24-pounder, which he manned until the British troops were cut down like wheat and began their flight back to Lake Borgne. Around the time of the Battle of New Orleans, Bean sat for the portrait in military uniform that has come down to us. Family tradition has it as a gift of Laffite. With Jackson's permission, Bean withdrew from the army for his return to Mexico. Bean obtained a small schooner, bought as much arms and ammunition as his funds would permit, and set sail down the Mississippi. He eluded a British blockade of the river's mouth at Balize by taking the Southwest Pass. Another small Spanish prize was captured on the way to Nautla, with some needed foodstuffs.[22]

After delivering his cargo, Bean hastened to Morelos at the hacienda of Puruarán and described their meeting as follows: "Morelos asked me what good news I brought from the United States. I related to him how I got there, and what I had done. I told him the United States was our friend and well-wisher; but since it was at war with Great Britain at the time, it might not be able to do much for us. It was then agreed to send an ambassador to the United States, and that I should return with him. 25,000 pesos was all the money that could be raised for the purpose."[23] Toledo had written Bean from New Orleans on July 24, saying that the United States would recognize Mexican independence as soon as an ambassador arrived; he urged that arrangements be carried out quickly. Morelos wished to accompany Bean to the coast but could not because of his duties as president of the struggling republic. His desire was no doubt motivated by the fact that Morelos had entrusted his young son, Juan Nepomuceno Almonte, to Bean's care during the voyage. The lad was being sent to New Orleans for "schooling." The fortunes of war having turned against him, Morelos may have suspected that he would never see his son again in this world.[24]

After some delays and a difficult voyage, Bean, Almonte, and the Mexican emissaries reached New Orleans on November 1, 1815. Leaving his charges at their destination, Bean caught a boat back to Mexico —only to learn that during his absence Morelos had been captured and executed! "I found the country was in a desperate situation; that a great number of the former patriots had gone over to the royalists, and obtained pardons."[25] Bean made efforts to locate the few remaining holdouts, Gen. Manuel de Mier y Terán and Gen. Guadalupe Victoria among them. On his trip to reach Victoria's camp below Veracruz, Bean said he took with him "a young lady of fine family, who had lost all they had in the revolution. I married her at a small town on my way, intending to ship her with me to the United States."

So, after dodging matrimonial bliss with pretty, dark-eyed Mexican lasses for years, Bean finally found one that he could not pass up. To protect her identity, perhaps, Bean did not give her name in his memoir. Editor Yoakum, probably with information from Bean's son Isaac, said her name was Anna Gorthas. She was "related to General Morelos" and resided at her hacienda "Branderrillas."[26] For a century other writers continued to call Bean's Mexican wife by this name. In reality, she was Magdalena Falfán de los Godos. "Anna" may have been one of her several given names, as Mexican women usually had two or three. "Gorthas" might have been Isaac Bean's phonetic rendering of Godos, as he visited Jalapa shortly after his father's death and met this widow. It is likely (as we shall see) that Yoakum obtained Bean's manuscript narrative from Isaac, and he may have learned the name of Bean's Mexican wife and his date of death from Isaac as well.[27]

It seems clear that Bean—with the death of Morelos—had already decided to quit the struggle and return home by the time he wed beautiful young Magdalena. He denied it, of course, and said he continued to try and rouse his dispirited comrades to carry on the revolution. General Victoria had only four men with him when he appeared at the hacienda where Bean was staying. He had recently been defeated by the Royalists and was entirely destitute, "not having a single dollar." Bean offered to share what he had with him and urged Victoria to have another go at it: "He said it was not worth while; that the people had got out of heart, and it would be better to go to some secret place" and await a change. This convinced Bean that he would be better off heading for the United States.[28]

His every move, however, was being followed by the king's spies. When troops closed in on him, he had to leave Magdalena behind and make his escape afoot. This is Bean's story anyway, saying he abandoned her because he knew that the Spaniards would not kill a woman just because her husband was trying to avoid capture. He went to a rebel post nearby and another garrison twenty-five miles away, returning to the hacienda with some men and pulque laborers to recover his mules, horses, and dried beef. But he arrived too late, as the Royalists had withdrawn with their plunder—and presumably his bride as well. "They got all my property and money," wrote Bean, "except two hundred doubloons, which my wife saved by going for water, and burying it in the sand." Bean, his "hopes lost," may have used this money to work his way up the coast and catch a boat back to New Orleans.[29] But the certifications of his military service later obtained from old comrades in Mexico City give a different story, one that Bean did not tell in his memoir.

At this point Bean's narrative ends, and we must piece his moves together from other sources.[30] Because this story will be developed in due course, here it is only necessary to say that he revisited the Mexican exiles at Natchitoches. They were talking a lot but doing little. The invasion projects under discussion—such as that of Francisco Xavier Mina, Louis Aury, and Henry Perry—were disorganized and promised little success. Gutiérrez still hoped to mount another overland expedition against Texas, but his prospects were increasingly dim. To pass the time Bean wrote his memoir, while events were still fresh in his mind. He eventually gave up on the exile brotherhood and decided to visit his relatives in Tennessee. Bean may have reached the old home place in time to see his mother, who died around 1818. While on this visit he met and married Candace Midkiff, the daughter of a well-to-do farmer named Isaac Midkiff who lived in the community of Sparta in White County.[31]

Several years later, they picked up stakes and settled in southwestern Arkansas near the Louisiana border. A son was born to Peter Ellis and Candace in 1821 (Isaac), but Old Man Midkiff died shortly thereafter. Learning that Mexico had won its independence, Bean resolved to move his family to Texas. This occurred around January 1823, and another daughter (Louiza Jane) was born to the couple in August. They—or perhaps Bean by himself, prior to bringing his family from Arkansas—lived somewhere in the boundary reserve for a short time. He was in Nacogdoches and signed a mortgage as a justice of the peace on July 17, 1822, indicating not only residency but an official capacity. Once his family joined him, they settled about twenty-eight miles west of town at Mound Prairie just above the Neches River. It was on the Old San Antonio Road, the main artery that linked Texas to Louisiana and Mexico. Governor Trespalacios, whose term was in 1822–23, said that Bean wanted to come earlier but would not as long as Mexico was under the imperial rule of Iturbide. They possibly had some communication on the subject, and Almonte was the governor's aide.[32]

A few documents exist in the Nacogdoches Archives that shed light on what Bean was doing after his return to Texas. The details are often sketchy, but these items suggest that Bean was actively involved in the affairs of the community. The years 1822–23 are mostly a blank, perhaps because Bean was living around Ayish Bayou (modern San Augustine) or closer to the Sabine—the affairs of which were not as carefully recorded in the Nacogdoches municipal archives. Later statements speak of Bean's association with "bad men" while residing in this district, prior to moving his family to the Neches. But once Bean settled on the Neches River, we begin to find his name mentioned in public documents—and in an official capacity.

For example, Anthony R. Clarke wrote Empresario Stephen F. Austin on February 3, 1824, about elections that had just taken place in Nacogdoches: "An order has been received here from Salcauder [Political Chief Saucedo] at St Antonio for Election to be held for alcaldes, the Election was held Bean was elected for the Naches [District] Juan Seguan [Seguín] and myself for Nacogdoches and John J. [A?] Williams for the Iiesh [Ayish] Bayou."[33] On June 12 Clarke wrote Austin again, urging him not to leave his settlement as it would be "ruinous to the Colony." Then he explained the remarks he had made in his last letter to Austin about the "character" of Capt. James Gaines.

> I reflected on my self after I sent it for fear you might think I was endeavouring to traduce the Man . . . but I still think it my duty to prevent him from deceiving others as he has me, on his return from St Antonio he spoke very ill against the Political Chief and [town] counsel stating that he was fifteen days disputing with them in supporting the American settlers in this District, but gave no correct information respecting the intentions of Government about this district, Since that time a Spaniard has passed through here from St Antonio . . . [and] he informed me that Gains while at St Antonio spoke very bad of all the Americans in this settlement. I since lern that he gave Col Bean the same account but spoke more fully to him as he speaks Spanish well.[34]

Clarke went on to say that the people of Nacogdoches were quite ignorant of the government's late regulations respecting their district because "the papers that have come on have been translated by Col Bean but so badly that we can make but little sence of it." This letter provides some idea of an important figure in east Texas history, James Gaines, as well as tells us that Bean's rank as a colonel in the Mexican army was recognized by his east Texas neighbors even before being confirmed on his 1825 trip to Mexico City. Bean's difficulty with rendering Spanish documents into understandable English is also suggested.[35]

Bean at this time was still signing his name as Ellis P. and sometimes as Ellis H., an anomaly that has puzzled more than one student of his career. The testimony that was sworn before him and Alcalde Juan Seguín (different than the Juan Seguín of San Antonio who later participated in the Texas Revolution) in the summer of 1824 is an example. Magistrate Bean signed the documents as Ellis H. Bean, as he did other documents of the period. The June proceedings were against Aden Bunch, whom Bean ordered Sheriff John Foster to take into custody on June 14. The reason? Nicholas Trammell swore under oath that Bunch had murdered a man named Young three days earlier. "Tramel" gave more testimony on June 17, and it told how he had witnessed Bunch ride into Young's camp. Then he heard a "lick" and saw Bunch take off in a hurry. Pursuing him on horseback, Trammell spotted Bunch and a Negro driving a jack and two horses toward the "Angholeen" (Angelina River). This testimony, one suspects, kept the culprit Aden Bunch in jail for a while. The "lick" was a gunshot that had put poor Young in his grave, Bunch and the Negro making off with his animals.[36]

Nick Trammell, it should be said, had blazed a Trace between the Great Bend of the Red River to Nacogdoches around 1814, a road that still bears his name. It was an extension of the Southwest Trail that ran from Missouri through Arkansas to jumping-off points for pilgrims bound for Texas. The towns of Washington and Fulton later served this purpose, and Trammell's Trace was already the recognized route when Stephen F. Austin was trying to sell town lots at Fulton in 1819. Nick used his Trace to smuggle horses out of Spanish Texas, along with whatever else of value that he could secure. He moved his family to Texas in 1818, settling on the Red River around Pecan Point or Jonesboro. When he heard that an independent Mexico was giving people a league of land in the interior, away from the contested boundary, he moved to Nacogdoches in 1823—cutting another trail from these settlements that joined his Trace near what became Old Unionville below the Sulphur Fork of the Red. Thus Nick Trammell made the decision to come to Texas at the same time that Bean brought his family from Arkansas.[37]

The Trammells and the Beans were part of the same migration westward from Tennessee. Nick's father Nicholas had been killed by Indians in 1784 in defense of Nashboro (later Nashville), then a fort similar to

Bean's Station. Like the Beans, the Trammells were heavily into the manufacture of salt from licks found in the wilderness. Nick, born in 1780, was only three years older than Peter Ellis Bean, and they were both of the adventuresome breed.[38] It is very likely that they had many tales to swap when they found themselves living in the same neck of the woods around Nacogdoches. Since Bean's place of residence on Smackover Creek in southwestern Arkansas was not far from the main stem of Trammell's Trace, it is even possible that Bean reached Nacogdoches by this route. That Bean seems to have lived in the boundary reserve at first suggests, however, that he worked his way south to Natchitoches and entered Texas by the usual road across the Sabine. James Gaines maintained a ferry at this crossing and did so for years thereafter.

Nick Trammell got into many scrapes in Mexican Texas. His eviction from a league of land that he and his son Nathaniel had bought from Empresario Haden Edwards on the Trinity crossing of the Old San Antonio Road was one of the incidents that kicked off the Fredonian Rebellion in late 1826.[39] Meanwhile, Nick was involved in various disputes over slaves and horses of uncertain ownership that seemed to always wind up in his possession. The Trammells—like the Beans—appreciated fine horseflesh and loved to race. A dispute over the prize of one such race involving Nick's fourteen-year-old son Phillip came before Alcalde Bean on August 7, 1824. Young Phillip beat his opponent Holmes's horse twice, whereupon he was conceded the prize of a gilt sow "whare he could found her, for Shee was his Property." This sow was later found hidden at the Widow Bunch's, but Elison York said it belonged to him. He would only give Phillip half, but "Tramel Said if he did not git all of the hog he would not have aney of it." Someone was trying to pull a fast one on Nick Trammell's son, and racing wagers did not go uncollected on the frontier in those days. If you played, you paid.[40]

Alcalde Bean, of course, was involved with other cases of justice besides those dealing with Nicholas Trammell and his sons. These have been cited merely to show how the migration westward of Anglo-Celtic clans resulted in new contact once they reached east Texas in the early 1820s. They were still stacking their long rifles against cabin walls around Nacogdoches and having their frontier frolics. The only difference was that they were now living in Mexican Texas, where an entirely new set of rules governed their conduct. Nick Trammell was a stranger to these rules, and often ran afoul of them, but Peter Ellis Bean—with his knowledge of Spanish and his many years of experience in Mexico—could manipulate the system to advantage. Trammell could not and was constantly in trouble.

Indicating that horse thieves were active in Bean's neighborhood is the complaint that he filed with Patricio de Torres on September 6, 1824.

Several Spaniards had asked for Bean's assistance in "aperhanding ten or twelve horse thives that is thare a Steeling horses." Bean—again signing himself as Ellis H.—wanted Torres to send a posse of eight or nine men in pursuit. When they left Nacogdoches, Torres was to direct them to stop by his house: "[Anthony?] Woolf must come on to command the Partes I will let him [k]now when he comes to this Plase how he must Proseed."

On March 5, 1825, an election for a new alcalde was held in the Neches District at " Mr. Bean's." James Bradshaw received the most votes, and he was certified as the winner by Ellis H. Bean on the same day. One at first assumes that this election took place at the residence of Peter Ellis Bean, but his name does not appear on the list of electors. Instead, William Bean is shown as casting a vote.[41] Who was this William Bean and what was he doing at a house on the Neches River in 1825? Although the documentation later calls William a nephew of Peter Ellis, he may have been the colonel's slightly younger brother, born in 1785. This is hard to say with authority, as the name "William" was present in every generation of Beans going back to the Scotsman William Bean who first came to America and planted roots for the family tree, dying in Northumberland, Virginia, in 1697.[42] When applying for land in Texas, our William called himself a "hatter," perhaps a sly reference to the profession Peter Ellis had engaged in while a prisoner in Mexico. The Beans were not hatters; they usually supported themselves as gunsmiths, traders, tavern-keepers, or salt-makers—especially the last.

The fact that this William was related to Colonel Bean and living in the neighborhood of the Neches poses some interesting questions. Had the colonel moved his family west of Nacogdoches because William was already living there and had built a residence called "Bean's" house by the time of the March 1825 election? Or did this "nephew" William accompany Peter Ellis and his family to Texas two years earlier, deciding that he would locate himself near the Neches crossing of the Old San Antonio Road while his "uncle" tarried near the Sabine with his family? The possibility that William Bean was in Texas *before* Peter Ellis cannot altogether be discounted. His letters to Peter Ellis on Smackover Creek, Arkansas, describing the rich opportunities around Nacogdoches may have prompted Bean to pull up stakes and join him in Texas. Such letters are not extant but, whatever the case, the two Beans became united after their arrival.[43]

Colonel Bean, it seems, did not seek reelection for alcalde of the Neches District because he had decided it was time for him to go to Mexico and solicit recognition for his services during the struggle for independence. As Bean was preparing for this trip, his name sometimes surfaces in the public records. So does that of Nick Trammell. He had bought a

Negro in August 1824 from a suspicious character named Jackson, lately arrived from Alexandria, Louisiana. As it turned out, Jackson had stolen two horses from Esquire Stokes of that vicinity, and the Negro he sold "Nicolas Trammal near Nacogdoches" was "Stated to be a free man." John Sprowl, the alcalde of Ayish Bayou, had bought one of these stolen horses from Jackson. He passed the word along to Austin, lest this smooth-talking Jackson fellow show up in his colony and try to sell the other horse and Negro to some unsuspecting buyers like himself and Trammell.[44]

Trammell's problems continued into 1825. There was a suit against him in March over an escaped slave belonging to Mrs. François Villon, which had been freed by Trammell and taken to his house on the Angelina River. Leonard Dubois represented Mrs. Villon, and Patricio de Torres officiated in the case as judge. Trammell lost, and was ordered to pay costs of the suit. He could not (or would not), so some of his property was auctioned on March 16. Nick's black horse brought fifteen dollars, the high bidder being Joseph Durst. His "rifle Gun"—probably of the Kentucky variety and a prized possession—went to Attorney Leonard Dubois for nine dollars. This auction must have annoyed Trammell considerably, as no frontiersman could do without a good horse and gun. Although he won the case, Dubois did not have the nerve to recover Mrs. Villon's slave Gabriel from Trammell's place on the Angelina and was soon soliciting help from Austin's colony to make the seizure.[45]

Colonel Bean and Samuel Norris were appointed court interpreters for a case in May 1825, a month after Bean had written his petition to the Mexican government and received the alcalde's blessing for his trip, as discussed in chapter 3. The case involved the killing of Leonard Dubois's brother Charles by Capt. James Dill, an old and respected settler of the region. During this trial Dill was judged not guilty, being "perfectly justified in taking life of sd. Dubois." The political chief at Béxar reversed this ruling, since trials by jury were illegal in Texas. Rather than face arrest, militia captain Dill fled to Louisiana. Leonard Dubois tried to have him extradited for the murder of his brother–without success, just as he fared with the recovery of the Negro Gabriel from Nick Trammell.[46] Such was the chaotic state of affairs at Nacogdoches when Bean departed for Mexico. They would get worse when Haden Edwards was named empresario of the region in April 1825 and arrived later in the year to begin placing eight hundred "Catholic" families from the United States in possession of lands held by the old settlers—some for generations, but under dubious or lost titles from Spain.

Chapter 3

BACK TO MEXICO

In Mexico, meanwhile, events had been transpiring that would ease Bean's goal of securing favor for his past services to the nation. The empire of Emperor Agustín de Iturbide had collapsed, and he had been forced into exile. A republican form of government was adopted, along with a national colonization law in August and a constitution in October 1824. The federal government instituted liberal provisions for the granting of land, although these decisions were left up to the individual states.[1] Congress in May had passed an act joining Coahuila and Texas into a single state, designating Saltillo as the capital. In the summer Iturbide foolishly tried to return from banishment, landing in disguise on the coast of Tamaulipas. There he was captured and summarily executed at Padilla. None other than Bean's compadre in exile, José Bernardo Gutiérrez de Lara, enforced the national Congress's law on what would happen to the former liberator if he dared to violate the terms of his banishment. Gutiérrez had been elected the first governor of his home state of Nuevo Santander (now Tamaulipas) in July 1824 and took his duties seriously.[2]

This was not all. Bean's old friend of the revolution's dark and dismal days, Guadalupe Victoria, was now president of Mexico. Another former compatriot, Nicolás Bravo, was the republic's vice president. Early in 1825 the legislature of Coahuila y Texas passed a colonization law for the granting of lands to empresarios. Colonists who came as individuals, independent of empresarios, also had a right to claim lands on their own account. If they had rendered past services to the nation, of course, their petitions would receive special attention. Bean was only one of many veterans claiming this right.

The provisions of this March 24, 1825, state colonization law were exceedingly generous, even to foreigners. All they had to do to receive a league or *sitio* of land (4,428 acres) was appear before the local alcalde and take an oath to support the federal and state constitutions, giving their faith as Roman Catholic. The cost of such a grant was modest and deferred for a number of years. The applicants had to "cultivate" or "occupy" their land within six years, but—in practice—this provision was broadly construed. Seldom did it work against titleholders, William Bean being a notable exception. Grantees could bequeath but were not allowed to sell their land until it was improved, an obligation passed on to their heirs. Nor could one hold a title after leaving the Mexican republic, a provision to ensure permanent occupation.[3] Thus, the time was definitely right for Peter Ellis Bean's trip to the Mexican capital. All the pieces were in place, both on the federal and state levels. Owing to the fact that his former comrades now ran the federation, Bean must have anticipated little opposition to any of the things he would be soliciting. Mexico was free at last of Spanish tyrants!

Having made a decision to go to Mexico by the spring of 1825, Bean prepared a petition to the government, stating his case. He took it to Luis Prosela, who was serving as the alcalde ad interim of Nacogdoches after the death of his father Pedro Prosela. Luis, on April 6, gave Bean a character certificate to attach to his petition for the journey southward. It is evident from Prosela's remarks that Bean's petition asked for the land on which he resided. Bean had lived there "for the time that he cites," and Bean had served as duly constituted alcalde for the district of Neches for one year without a rival for the position. Other than that, not much was said about Bean's character, but at least he had a document proving that he was a resident of east Texas and had held a position of responsibility in the community. To get the land that Bean solicited, it was also necessary for him to appear before Alcalde Prosela and take an oath of loyalty in due form.[4]

Bean's petition to the government, dated April 5, specifies exactly what he wanted and tells us that he had been living at his "ranch" on the Neches since the beginning of 1823. This means that if he lived at Ayish Bayou or some other place in the Sabine District prior to moving his family west to the Neches, Bean must have arrived in Texas *earlier* than January 1823 (the date given by his wife in her first deposition). Also, a notation in her family Bible says that Bean returned to Texas in 1820, and there is the mortgage he signed at Nacogdoches in mid-1822 that proves —if the date is correct—his presence in Texas by that year.[5] Perhaps he left Candace and the baby boy Isaac back on Smackover Creek in Arkansas until he could check out the situation in the boundary reserve. If this is the case, what he saw must have convinced him that the Neches River west of Nacogdoches would be a better place for a man with a wife and child to live. It should be noted that Bean called himself a *man of family* in Texas, which later came back to haunt him.

Señor First Alcalde and Civil Chief of the Province of Texas

Pedro Elías Bean, [a native] son of Tenecí, of the Roman Catholic Apostolic Christian religion, of the age of forty years, before Your Lordship I appear, and I make known: That for twenty-four years I have lived on the Gulf of Mexico; and of these I have worked seven years in the defense of the Mexican Republic, with the title of colonel, in company with Generals Don Guadalupe Vi[c]toria, Don Nicolás Brabo, and Señor Morelos; they are persons who know me well and likewise they know the services that I have done in favor of our beloved independence and most holy liberty without having been remiss in what was ordered me, still less in having any tarnish against my honor.

These services should be acknowledged as useful to me; and [because of] finding myself so burdened with family, from Your Lordship I request and pray in the name of our Mexican federation that you do me the favor of giving me two *sitios* of land for me and my heirs; one adjoining [the] Nechas which is where I have placed my ranch for two years and three months; and it has cost me a lot of work in building houses and opening farm plots; and I exist with the hope of being able to live and maintain my family on this stated site; and the other, if Your Lordship's generosity concedes it to me, my request is that it may be where there is found vacant land.

Therefore I pray Your Lordship that you concede me all the expressed [land] . . . this is my legal request and allow from me this writing on the present common paper, because there is no sealed [paper] which corresponds [to the occasion]. I swear it not to be from malice, and in that [form] which is necessary, &c.

God and Liberty, Nechas, April 5, 1825. Pedro Ellias Bean.[6]

That Bean needed money to make the trip, and that he intended to seek more land than just for his family on the Neches, is indicated by the later testimony of Robert Collier when Bean's marriage status and public conduct were being investigated. Collier was a resident of the Sabine District and a prosperous farmer who benefited from slave labor. He was also thought to be involved in the smuggling of slaves from Louisiana, one of the worst border offenders in this respect. Collier said that Bean had come to his house and asked for one hundred dollars to finance his trip to Mexico, for which favor Bean would make sure that Collier received title to his land. All Collier had to do was state how many acres he had under cultivation and give him a document on the size of his family; Bean would attend to the paperwork in Mexico City.[7] Because Collier lived in the twenty-league border zone, an area in which settlement was proscribed, he may have advanced money to Bean in hopes that his influence would result in legal title to Collier's land. If Bean approached other settlers in this manner, it went unrecorded.

Bean most likely commenced his trip down the Old La Bahía Road, turning west at the junction of the Béxar–San Felipe Road. This would have taken him through parts of Austin's colony and the one that Green DeWitt was in the process of securing just below it on the Guadalupe River. If Bean passed through San Felipe, he missed meeting the empresario—according to a letter that Bean wrote Austin in 1826. Somewhere along the way Bean formed a hard impression of DeWitt, as we learn from a letter that Political Chief José Antonio Saucedo wrote Gov. Rafael González from San Antonio on June 26.

> Most Excellent Sir, I pass to the hands of Your Excellency the attached petition of the foreigner, Peter Ellis Bean, residing in the District of Nacogdoches, and at present en route towards Mexico, favored with certification from the Alcalde ad interim of that place, which is also attached; by which he solicits to establish himself with his family on the point stated that is included in the territory assigned to one of the empresarios [Haden Edwards] who are attempting to colonize this Department; concerning which matter I hope that Your Excellency will be pleased to communicate to me the decision.
>
> This individual has informed me that the empresario Green DeWitt is a criminal by having misapplied funds that he was handling for his Nation, a fugitive from the territory of Islas Negras [Black Islands, meaning Missouri]; that on his way towards Mexico he formed a list of some inhabitants who actually are trying to establish themselves under our Government, himself falsely writing on it the names and signatures of many foreigners that have neither seen the said empresario, nor have notice of his contract. All of which I believe it my duty to bring to the knowledge of Your Excellency for your determination of what is deemed proper. Bean has offered to inform Your Excellency on this point when he returns from Mexico [City] and touches at that Capital [Saltillo].[8]

Bean's motives for denouncing DeWitt's moral character are hard to determine. DeWitt, after three years of frustration, had received a contract in April 1825 to bring in four hundred families. He was still in Saltillo at the time of Bean's charge, but his agents—such as Surveyor General James Kerr—were already active in selecting a site for the town of

Gonzales, named after the governor.[9] Word of Bean's accusation was reported back to Stephen F. Austin from Saltillo on July 16 by Baron de Bastrop, Texas' lone representative in the state legislature. Bastrop said he would do what he could for DeWitt, as Austin had asked him, but Bean's claim that DeWitt had absconded with public funds in Missouri was a serious one. He told Austin to verify these charges. If true, he should advise DeWitt to sell his contract to "Mayland" (Benjamin R. Milam), DeWitt's partner in this matter, and seek colonization status instead in California or Tabasco. Bastrop reminded Austin that "you and I have many enemies," and it would not do to make more by pressing DeWitt's cause if he were guilty.[10]

The upshot is that, through the intercession of Bastrop in Saltillo and Austin in San Felipe, DeWitt was quickly cleared of Bean's charges.[11] But the fact that Bean had leveled such criminal charges could not have endeared him to these men and may have influenced their behavior toward him when his own empresarial aspirations became tainted by similar charges against his moral fitness for the position a year later.

After leaving San Antonio Bean did not travel the usual route to Mexico City. Instead, he passed through San Carlos (in the state of Tamaulipas) and visited a comrade in the struggle for independence, José Bernardo Gutiérrez de Lara. As noted, upon his return from exile in Louisiana, Gutiérrez was made governor of the state of Tamaulipas; shortly thereafter he was given military authority over the region. According to Yoakum, Bean kept a small notebook or diary of his trip to Mexico and the entry for June 28, 1825, read: "I found Don Bernardo Gutierres, with about four hundred troops, in command of the place. He was my old friend, and I was very glad to see him, as my horses and mules were giving out, and my money also; but, to my misfortune, I found him very poor, and unable to help himself."[12]

This notebook, which Yoakum had in his possession, has now disappeared—along with the original manuscript copy of Bean's memoir that Yoakum edited and brought to publication in 1855. The loss of the diary is especially unfortunate, as it would have allowed us to follow Bean's activities and movements in Mexico, all the way back to Texas, throughout 1825–26. From the few entries quoted by Yoakum—and knowing Bean's flair with words in his memoir—we have lost a truly important document to Texas history. It would have told us of Bean's reunion with comrades who, when last seen, were in despair that Mexico would ever be free of Spain. But the struggle had ended in success, and now the losers were the winners in a new constitutional republic. Their meetings with Bean must have been joyous ones, old memories pouring forth in buckets. Alas, without Bean's diary we cannot know the nature of either these personal conversations or Bean's impressions of a Mexico where freedom now reigned supreme.[13]

As Bean did not make his appearance in the Mexican capital until October 1825, he probably traveled down the coast of Tamaulipas from San Carlos and visited his wife, Magdalena Falfán de los Godos, near Jalapa. They had not seen each other since Bean's dash to escape Royalist troops a decade earlier, when she remained behind. This lady, said to be of fine family and related to General Morelos—a niece according to one early account and repeated in later ones—had managed to recover her estate several miles west of Jalapa after independence was attained. As noted, she was not mentioned by name in Bean's memoir, but Editor Yoakum gave it as "Señorita Anna Gorthas." Bean's professed plan was to send his wife to her uncle in Jalapa before putting her on a vessel to the United States. Shortly before this he suggested an overland escape route to General Victoria that involved "keeping in the mountains along the coast" until they reached exile in the United States, assuring Victoria that he knew the way and they could do it even if it "took two years." Victoria declined, saying he could not undergo such an ordeal. But Bean and his new bride were betrayed by turncoat patriots, and Bean was taken as a prisoner to Veracruz, thereafter escaping to New Orleans by boat. He probably used the same coastal route discussed with General Victoria to return to Doña Magdalena in 1825.[14]

His travel diary having been lost, we do not know how long Bean lingered at the Hacienda de las Banderillas or if, in fact, he sought out his wife prior to going to the capital. Yoakum said that he reached the Valley of Mexico by October 18, an interval of almost four months since his encounter with Gutiérrez in San Carlos, Tamaulipas.[15] Apart from his desire to see Magdalena at Jalapa, Bean may have visited his former comrade to obtain a certification of his services to Mexico in New Orleans and the Neutral Ground. Upon his return to the United States in 1816, Bean had spent over a year among Gutiérrez and his fellow exiles along the Red River near Natchitoches as they plotted another invasion of Texas. Despairing that a successful campaign could be launched, and so bored that he devoted energy to writing his memoir, Bean left in 1817 to visit his family in Tennessee.

Gutiérrez now occupied a position of high authority, even if he was penniless as usual. His word on Bean's service during the struggle for freedom would certainly carry more weight than Alcalde Prosela's, so Bean searched him out. This effort did not pay off for Bean. Gutiérrez could not help him with cash, and if he wrote a certification of Bean's services it did not make its way into Bean's military service record in Mexico City.[16]

There is a very interesting document that is dated October 20, 1825, only two days after Bean's arrival in the capital. The only known copy is in French and, as translated, its title reads "Memorial Addressed to the Mexican Republic." It is a historical review of affairs in Texas from the Louisiana Purchase to the admittance of Anglo-American empresarios. As a second part—and appended at least a year later—the unknown author, calling himself a Citizen of the United States, wrote a "Plan of an American Government for the Province of Coahuila and Texas." The handwritten copy on deposit at the Center for American History, University of Texas at Austin, has attached a partial copy of a September 5, 1826, letter (in English) from James Gaines to Political Chief Saucedo. A Bean letter to Saucedo is mentioned but is not in the file.[17]

It is difficult to say who wrote this Memorial. Gen. James Wilkinson—who was then in Mexico City awaiting word on his petition to be an empresario in Texas and who died there in December 1825—is a possibility. He was known for writing long-winded tracts about borderlands affairs as far back as when he was a secret agent for Spain while in command of U.S. military forces along the Mississippi. He addressed a similar tract on the colonization of Texas to the Mexican government when petitioning to be an empresario. But Wilkinson was in failing health, and the focus on the empresarial status of the territory between the Sabine River and Nacogdoches suggests that someone very close to the scene penned the Plan if not the Memorial itself.[18]

Was it Peter Ellis Bean? Certainly not, as may be judged by the author's remarks on his qualifications quoted below. But this American "Citizen" either had detailed information on what Bean planned to do before he left Texas or he learned about these plans after Bean reached the Mexican capital.

> What! To trust the care of populating a land [like Texas] to men of the character of the Austins, the Eduards, the Thorns, the Wevells [Wavells], the Beans, &c.! Bean, now colonel in the service of Mexico, [is] without talents, without education, and scarcely knowing how to write his name, although born and raised in a country where the most abject dock-hand off the street knows how to write his language! —
>
> Bean is not Catholic! It doesn't matter, he is not for that any less a colonel of the armies of Mexico, and furthermore also is an *impresario.* And why?
>
> Because serving under Parish Priest Morelo[s] he was a comrade of the current President of the Republic [Guadalupe Victoria]. Is it necessary to entrust him with important positions and posts which

> demand a recognized responsibility to recompense him? When one is forced to employ Beans and Gutierrezes — what should one not expect? It seems to me that if the Republic had wished to show itself grateful it would have been able to pay these men in cash, and certainly they would have preferred a double salary to all the civic rewards and even to the most beautiful title without wages.

Several remarks in the Memorial and Plan also touch on Bean's ambitions as an empresario of the boundary reserve lands: "General Wevell is obtaining still another [colonization contract] above that of Frost Thorn; finally, quite recently, Colonel Bean is put in possession of all the land that the govt. had at first believed prudent to allocate to him, that is to say, all the land comprised between Nacogdoches and the Sabine, as far [south] as the sea." And again, at the beginning of the Plan: "American Citizens. The government of Mexico is coming to the resort of putting at the disposal, not of the govt. of the United States, but of citizens of the United States, the major part of the beautiful province of Texas, in conceding, most recently, to our fellow citizen Colonel Bean, all the land allocated to him, that is to say, all this beautiful expanse of land comprehended between the Sabine and Nacogdoches as far as the Gulf of Mexico."[19] These remarks indicate that the date of October 20, 1825, is too early for this entire document, as Bean did not get his concession until the next year and did not start assembling his certifications of merit until November 1825. The fall of 1826 is a more realistic date for the Plan portion.

The Memorial is earlier and more lengthy than the undated Plan tagged on at the end. It consists of a detailed history of the struggle for Mexican independence as it occurred in Texas and the Neutral Ground. General Wilkinson was perhaps qualified to write of these events, and his name is mentioned several times as making the arrangement with the Spaniards that established this zone in 1806. Bean's trips back to the area between 1814 and 1817 gave him better firsthand knowledge of the revolutionary movements taking place in the Neutral Ground. General Morelos had commissioned Bean to coordinate these activities, including another invasion of Texas if possible. Much attention is given to the 1812–13 campaign of Gutiérrez, its failure, and his fate once he returned to Natchitoches. But Bean was *not* the author of the Memorial or the Plan. He would not have submitted such a self-deprecatory document as this to the Mexican government in October 1825. Far from advancing his goals, it would have damaged them greatly.

Could James Gaines have possibly written the Memorial? He also had been engaged in the revolutionary contest and followed its course toward independence. Born in 1776 in Culpepper County, Virginia, James Gaines was descended from the prominent Pendleton family. He was a double first cousin to Gen. Edmund Pendleton Gaines, of whom we shall hear a great deal more during the Texas Revolution. James had some education and worked as a surveyor, commissioned by Pres. Thomas Jefferson to survey lands along the Natchez Trace in 1803–1804. By 1812 he was operating a ferry on the Sabine and took part in the raising of troops for the Gutiérrez-Magee Expedition. He, by some accounts, was disgusted by the execution of Governor Salcedo and other Spanish prisoners and quit this invasion force before Gen. Joaquín de Arredondo marched north to crush the rebels in a battle below San Antonio in 1813. However, in an account that Gaines gave Lamar in 1835, as well as in another account, published a decade later, on December 4, 1845, in the San Augustine *Red-Lander,* Gaines leads us to believe that he was a participant in the Battle of Medina and escaped the slaughter.

By 1819 he returned to Texas and bought the long-established ferry on the Camino Real crossing of the Sabine. This facility he operated for over twenty years with his sons and other employees. In a letter written to the governor of Texas on September 20, 1820, Gaines and "Ramón Querk" reported the movements of Gen. James Long's army of eight hundred men and spoke of their plans. Gaines called Col. Ignacio Pérez "a true friend" and said that Pérez had given him permission to remain at his settlement on the lower crossing of the Sabine. On June 5, 1821, Gaines asked the governor for possession of the tract he occupied, along with permission as "agent" to introduce 250 families from Louisiana, then living in Arkansas, to the Nacogdoches region. They were good farmers, he claimed, and would fight the hostile Indians to protect their holdings. The governor, however, believed that Gaines wished to bring people down from Pecan Point and did not consider them desirable citizens. A tall, red-haired man, Gaines was alcalde of the Sabine District in 1824, at the same time that Bean served from the Neches District. In other words, James Gaines was a shaker and mover on the local scene with enough experience and education to have written the October 1825 Memorial.[20]

But there are problems with him as well (his knowledge of the French language, for instance, is questionable), and certain passages argue strongly against Gaines as the author. Alcalde Samuel Norris is described very critically, and he was Gaines's brother-in-law! Norris was called "the most stupid and the most ignorant being that it is possible to find." Again, the American "Citizen" said that "we should consider [him] as a true fool, a man who is not capable of aiding us at all, in any way, but who nevertheless would be able to sink us; our relations with him should be nil, our measures [for establishing an American government] should be unknown to him."[21]

The author thought even less of James Gaines, saying that "he is sold to the [Mexican] government, he is a spy against us; he is a vile being. . . . Let plenty of care be taken about him." A recent incident involving Gaines was mentioned to show how low his standing was among the local people. It was pegged to Gaines's September 1826 letter to the political chief, which denounced the Anglo inhabitants of his district in harsh terms.[22] Bean was given a copy of this letter by the governor and forwarded it to Nacogdoches, so the citizens of Ayish Bayou would know that Gaines was not their friend.

> But one might say to me, "These men are good republicans" — all right, but is Bean a Mexican republican? I deny it, and here is the proof.
>
> James Gaines, of whom I have spoken above, seeing the [takeover] movement of the Americans and knowing what they are capable of, wrote to D. José Antonio Saucedo, political chief of Sn. Antonio de Vejar, to inform him what was going on in the American establishments (I am sending you, adjoined, a copy of Gaines's letter, beside which you will find another one from the famous Bean[;] I have been obliged, in preserving the sense, to correct each and every word of this nearly unintelligible letter).
>
> What has resulted from Gaines's news items? It is that the governor of Saltillo, Victor Blanco, to whom this letter was sent by Saucedo, did not have any qualms about communicating it to Bean, who sent a copy of it to Joe Durst in Nacogdoches, recommending to him specially to communicate it to all his friends (Bean's) at Aysh Bayou.
>
> Gaines has taken refuge in the woods: they are hunting him like a beast at bay, and if he has the misfortune of falling into the hands of his compatriots, no doubt the impropriety of Victor Blanco will have for Gaines the same result [as happened] to the unfortunate [Simón de] Herrera [because of] the culpable indiscretion of Governor Clayborne.

So we are left without certain knowledge of who wrote this Memorial, but its comments on Peter Ellis Bean indicate that the author was no great admirer of his, if not something of an enemy. In fact, the writer thought that practically every prominent Anglo in Texas would be a hindrance to forming an American government in Coahuila y Texas, its empresarios included.[23]

Once Bean reached Mexico City, many leading figures of the new republic were on hand and willing to supply him with the testimony that he needed to receive recognition for his past services. They included a powerful member of the revolutionary 1813 Congress at Chilpancingo, Antonio de Sesma; a former governor of Texas, José Félix Trespalacios; the envoy that Bean had escorted to New Orleans (along with the son of General Morelos, Juan Almonte) in mid-1815, Joseph Manuel Herrera; the current vice president, Gen. Nicolás Bravo; war heroes Gen. Manuel de Mier y Terán and Gen. Vicente Guerrero; and the president of Mexico himself, Gen. Guadalupe Victoria. Did Bean prompt them or give these men a written account of his various services to refresh their memories? Or did he just ask them to list what they recalled of his contribution and then go with what he got? This is impossible to tell, but there are similarities in each document and Bean was not above "pulling strings" to accomplish his purpose.

These six certifications were made in the month of November 1825 and assembled into a customary service record form dated December 1, 1826, after Bean was already back in Texas. Through this documentation by the principal participants in Mexico's ten-year battle for independence, we may gauge the truth of what Bean wrote in his memoir. We may also determine that Bean was not lying when he "bragged" to settlers in east Texas about his role as a colonel in the Mexican army during the revolutionary years. Bean may have exaggerated a bit and spiced up the telling, but these certifications substantiate most of his claims and establish that he was well known to them all.[24]

Bean's service record, perhaps because it was prepared after he had left the Mexican capital, does not give his age or place of origin but states that he was married. Indeed, his marriage to a Mexican woman was a point in his favor, considering that he was a foreigner whose claims might have been otherwise overlooked. The fact that Bean had been so closely associated with the martyred hero of the revolution, José María Morelos, was another strong point in his favor. Bean's career as a "patriotic soldier" (he claimed) had started on November 1, 1810, a month and a half after Father Miguel Hidalgo issued his revolutionary *grito.* Bean was a captain of cavalry by December 20 and eight days later promoted to lieutenant colonel. He received the rank of full colonel of cavalry on May 2, 1815.[25]

Bean said that he separated from the army "without license" on April 12, 1817; this gives us a possible date for Bean's decision to quit hanging around the enclave of exiles in western Louisiana and visit his relatives in eastern Tennessee. His service—for which Bean had gone unpaid—amounted to six years, five months, and eighteen days. When augmented "by reason of [being on] campaign," this term of service was doubled. Further, Bean was reinstated in the Mexican army with the rank of lieutenant colonel of cavalry, with the brevet rank of colonel, on February 28, 1826.[26] This, of course, was one of the main reasons he had made the trip—along with receiving recompense due him. There is no indication that Bean ever got his back pay from the Mexican government. He was still pursuing the matter near the end of his life, after he had returned to his wife in Jalapa.

The certifications attached to Bean's service record and given in appendix A will suffice to indicate the reliability of his memoir, though told in much drier, matter-of-fact fashion than Bean's narrative. Because this information has not been presented elsewhere, and sheds new light on Bean's revolutionary years, the certifications are quoted in their entirety. For example, we learn that Bean was captured in a cave after parting from his wife and was carried to Veracruz. The Royalists planned to ship him to Spain as a prisoner, but Bean was able to escape on a boat to the United States. Bean did not mention anything about this capture/escape in his memoir, leading us to believe that he made his way to freedom overland along the coast. This new development certainly explains why Bean had to leave his bride behind. He was lucky to get away from the "Plaza of Veracruz" himself, and it would be interesting to know the manner in which he succeeded in this escape. Señor Sesma attributed it to "Holy Providence." Bean, no doubt, could have given us a more swashbuckling explanation.[27]

With these certifications in hand, Bean addressed a letter to Pres. Guadalupe Victoria on November 24, 1825. He noted that since 1810 he had devoted himself to serving the Mexican nation "in the terrible struggle that it has sustained for the cause of the independence that it now enjoys, serving principally under the orders of the Most Excellent Sr. Gen. Don José María Morelos y Pavón." Past misfortunes had delayed Bean from appearing immediately after "the cry of Yguala" to claim his rightful recompense. Bean wrote that when he finally decided to return to Mexico from the United States,

> I found out on the way that an Empire had been installed, a form of government that always has disgusted my republican principles, and for which reason I refused to come to increase the number of slaves of the Monarch [Iturbide] who had grasped the scepter, scandalously trampling the sacred rights of these peoples, and making useless their previous sacrifices and efforts to be free. . . . I have the satisfaction of appealing at this time to the presence of Your Excellency, less as to the first magistrate of the Mexican Nation than as to an eyewitness and . . . let it be permitted me to say it, with a certain noble pride, as to a companion in arms who served under the orders and the voice of the same leader whom I obeyed and loved as the most firm support of our hopes and [the] illustrious adornment of the Mexican Nation and liberty.[28]

Guadalupe Victoria, ca. 1825. Photo courtesy Joseph Musso.

Even if Bean's military service was attested to by the most respected men in Mexican politics, his record did not escape a close examination. A board of commissioners, or *junta,* reviewed the documents received in January 1826, both as to the length of time served and at what rank. The War Department, on January 27, wrote the following letter on Bean's behalf:

> The Citizen Pedro Elías Bean demonstrates the services that he has performed for the Motherland since the year [1]810 when the shout of liberty was pronounced, suffering in the attainment of such a just cause the greatest afflictions, persecutions, and arrests, until he went to the United States. [He states] that for this reason he did not present himself at a suitable time in request of the compensation that the Government lavishly bestowed, but now that he finds himself in this Kingdom, he prays that he be conceded the remuneration of which he considers himself a creditor [owed]. He includes six certifications from accredited leaders with which he justifies his disposition and good services toward the Motherland.

The response came on February 28: Bean "should be conceded the post of Lieutenant Colonel of Cavalry, with the rank of Colonel."[29]

Bean had asked on February 4 that his grade of colonel of cavalry *vivo* be confirmed, as opposed to having this rank as a brevet, "in accordance with what I was in the revolution."[30] But the board did not agree. Despite the documents he had presented, "endorsed by various known and accredited Leaders with which he proves that in the 1st period of the revolution he performed the best services," they felt that the rank of lieutenant colonel was sufficient reward to Bean. They admitted, however, that he "merited the greatest considerations from the Government, and that he never acted in a way that might have harmed him in the present evaluation." Unless it was the president's "superior pleasure," Bean's colonel rank would remain brevetted.[31]

The president tried to move Bean's petition along by writing Manuel Gómez Pedraza, secretary of war and marine, on February 18. He wanted Bean to have a colonel's commission and be paid accordingly. The National Treasury was to issue instructions to this end, all down the line. And the commandant general of the northeastern states "shall give the suitable order so that he may be recognized and put in possession of this employment . . . and [so] that his subordinates should obey the orders of service that he may give them in writing and verbally." Pedraza's notation read: "The President confers rank of Colonel of Cavalry of the Army on the Citizen Lieutenant Colonel Pedro Elías Bean."[32]

This review process lasted over six months and was not finalized until the end of the year, meaning that Bean was unable to carry a copy of his service record back to Texas. His failure to produce a service record upon demand hindered Bean with frontier officials from the commandant general on down. But with the president's personal stamp of approval, Bean could rest assured that these challenges to his authority would eventually be overcome. He probably knew that the secretary of war and marine on

February 23 had assigned him to the 13th Regiment of Cavalry as a brevet colonel and effective lieutenant colonel.[33]

Word of Bean's success at the capital filtered back to Baron de Bastrop at Saltillo from his correspondent in Mexico City, Manuel Ceballos, who was a senator from Coahuila y Texas in the national Congress. On February 15 Ceballos wrote that their friend General Wavell had been awarded a colonization contract, and so had "Coronel Mr. Elías." The only difference was that Bean was promising to introduce "honorable Mexicans" in two-thirds of his colony. This had evidently tipped the scales in Bean's favor, as the majority of his settlers would be Anglo-Americans. Wavell had contracted to introduce Europeans, thereby avoiding Mexico's concern over admitting more citizens of the United States. Bastrop replied that he had no news of the colonel's solicitation but thought that including Mexicans in the project was a good idea, as it would help "naturalize" the foreigners. Thus we learn that Bean had the government's approval for his colonization scheme several months before he actually submitted a petition for it in May.[34]

Bean felt confident enough of the confirmation process on his colonel's commission to ask for a month's leave on March 3, along with travel money to go to Jalapa. He stated that his long absence in the United States had separated him from his "family," and he wished to be reunited with them—meaning Doña Magdalena, as the couple had no children that we know of. This request was granted (at half pay), so Bean commenced the 250-mile journey from Mexico City on the national road to Veracruz. A notation on Bean's request indicates that, upon his return, he was to join General Terán's "reconnaissance of the limits of the federation."[35] This inspection, however, was delayed for two years—at which time Bean resided at Nacogdoches and did serve Terán in accomplishing his goals.

He did not overstay his leave, as an entry in his notebook (as cited by Yoakum) mentioned that Dr. John Dunn Hunter had arrived at the capital on March 19. Bean, however, may have made this entry later, after his return from Jalapa sometime in April.[36] Hunter had been sent to Mexico by Richard Fields, a leader of the Cherokees, to press for recognition of their land claims in east Texas. Chief Fields, along with Chief Bowl (Duwali), had been unsuccessful on an earlier trip to Mexico City in 1822–23. Hunter was also unsuccessful, as U.S. minister Joel Poinsett advised his government at the end of April, saying that Hunter "has lately been here" and Mexico had "refused to give them a large tract of land, where they might remain united in a body." One writer, without citing his authority, says that Bean tried to assist Hunter in this endeavor.[37] Hunter had to leave the Mexican capital without a land title for the Cherokees, or the other tribes he claimed to represent, but his and Bean's paths would soon cross again in Texas—with fatal results for Indian advocate Hunter.

Now that Bean had rank in the Mexican army, he pushed the next part of his agenda: status as a colonizer in Texas. Although Haden Edwards had been awarded an empresarial contract for the lands around Nacogdoches in April 1825, much land still remained. It included the twenty-league border reserve east of Edwards's contract, and this was the core area that Bean solicited in his petition of May 3, 1826, to Secretary of Foreign Relations Sebastián Camacho.

> [I], Citizen Pedro Elias Bean, am established and married to Doña Magdalena Falfán de los Godos, a native of Jalapa. In the best form I state to Your Excellency the following: In view of having fixed my residence in the Province of Texas, in the place called Nechas; and in consideration of the services I have performed for the Fatherland, as seen by the certifications I have submitted to justify my merits; and through my desire to increase [our] settlements for the common good, I have arranged for those empty places to be cultivated and occupied by honorable and industrious families up to the number of 300, introducing them to the environs of Nacogdoches [on a tract of land bounded] to the east by the Sabine River, to the west by the Trinity River, to the north by the Sulphur Fork [of the Red River], and to the south by the sea [Gulf of Mexico].
>
> It is desirable that these isolated and unpopulated lands be occupied by people of benefit to the Mexican Republic, and I commit myself to expel and remove all fugitives [from justice] who may have emigrated there, perhaps without knowledge of the authorities, and to take care of others of good order [qualities] in the establishment to which I aspire; [I will also] lead to pacification eight or nine nations of Indians that I can count on to fight against the Comanches, who at this time have risen up; and with these advantages [of mine] undoubtedly there will be saved, perhaps, expenses for the Nation which are very indispensable for it [to make otherwise].
>
> Therefore, I request Your Excellency, if it pleases you, that approval be conceded to me, with the end of obtaining favor with the State of Coahuila y Texas to realize an enterprise so beneficial to the Republic, so that from that distance [the state capital] there may be extended to me the necessary faculties I need for [attaining] this object.[38]

It might be noted that there is no mention here of two-thirds of Bean's colonists being honorable Mexicans, as Ceballos had intimated to Bastrop in February. Bean also revealed the name of his Mexican wife at Jalapa. This meant that when Gov. Victor Blanco saw his petition—and compared it to Bean's solicitation for two leagues of land on the Neches, where he lived "burdened with family"—trouble was bound to follow.

Bean was asking for land that could only be granted by the federal government, although state authorities had to be consulted in terms of his being put in possession. Further, in asking that his grant extend west to the Trinity River instead of ending about fifty-two miles from the Sabine, Bean was clearly intruding on the Edwards grant. How could Bean have been ignorant of this, when even the two leagues of land that he personally solicited for his family was in territory awarded to Edwards? Timing may have been a factor, because Edwards did not receive confirmation of his contract until shortly before Bean left Nacogdoches for Mexico. But Edwards had been trying to receive this grant in Mexico City since 1822, and word of his progress had surely made its way back to east Texas since Bean's arrival there in January 1823.[39] Alcalde Prosela's certification to Bean in April 1825 suggests as much, and so does the letter that Political Chief Saucedo wrote the governor after Bean showed up in San Antonio, accusing DeWitt of crimes.

Since Bean's departure, however, Haden Edwards had generated much dissatisfaction among the old settlers, whose rights he seemed determined to sweep aside. By the time Bean filed his petition for lands that overlapped those of Edwards around Nacogdoches, going west to the Trinity, Edwards was in the process of losing his empresarial contract. Even so, it is hard to say if word of Edwards's difficulties reached Bean in Mexico City by May 1826 or if it had any bearing on his decision to request lands far west of the twenty-league boundary reserve—lands that fell into the Edwards colony. About the only settlement of any size in the boundary reserve at this time was Ayish Bayou, although squatters (some of them fugitives from justice in Louisiana) were scattered west of the Sabine on small plots of land. They were a rough-edged law-breaking group, yet these were the people that Bean hoped to rule as a colonizer.[40]

Although Bean had been rewarded for his past services to a greater extent than most foreigners who fought in the Mexican Revolution, he was not above asking for more. In a letter written on June 7, he quibbled about how he had not received the proper seniority he merited and requested that his military service record be finished and made available to him. Among other things, he claimed that one of his commissions was as a "Commander of Engineers" of the cavalry branch of service.[41]

Bean wrote the Nacogdoches alcalde from Mexico City on June 28, 1826, with news of his return home and some advice for colonists who were obtaining land from Empresario Haden Edwards by purchase.

Sr. Constitutional Alcalde of Nacadoches

My Dear Sir: Since I do not know who the alcalde is this year, I write thus. I will leave this capital in 10 or twelve days for that one of Nacadoches and take with me 100 men to establish [*cantonar*] in Nacadoches and its vicinity in order to prevent trade with the Comanches and the other incidents that might arise in that place. And I hope you will provide some housing to lodge these troops. I am writing you well in advance so you will have time to arrange lodging.

On this day we have learned that Sr. Edwards wants to throw the citizens off their lands. This gentleman has no right whatsoever to lands except those west of the Trinity, and you can alert the people not to purchase from the aforesaid gentleman, because he has no right nor can he issue titles to those lands. Thus those who purchase from this individual will lose their money if he has no means of returning it to them. I am notifying you of this for your intelligence and so as to avoid lawsuits.

I am your affectionate servant Who Kisses Your Hand.

Ellis H. Bean[42]

This letter perhaps explains why Bean sought to colonize from the Sabine to the Trinity: he believed that Edwards's grant was for lands *west* of the Trinity. If this was the case, Bean's information was bad because Edwards had authority to colonize all the way east to the twenty-league boundary reserve—a point midway between Nacogdoches and Ayish Bayou usually regarded as the Attoyac. The boundaries specified in Edwards's April 1825 contract with the governor of Coahuila y Texas were as follows: beginning in the angle of the coastal and boundary reserves; up the latter line to fifteen leagues (thirty-seven miles) above Nacogdoches; west to the Navasota River; downstream to the San Antonio Road and eastward on this road to the San Jacinto River; thence downstream to the ten-league coastal reserve line. In other words, Edwards was the legal empresario for much of the same lands that Bean had asked for in his May 1826 petition. But these details were worked out in Saltillo, and Bean was not privy to the final arrangement. At least he knew that Edwards had no power to issue titles and was trying to "throw the citizens off their lands."[43]

Through other communications, possibly those of Ceballos to Bastrop earlier in the year, word of Bean's success in Mexico City made its way back to Texas. This is demonstrated by a letter that Haden Edwards's brother Benjamin wrote Stephen F. Austin from Nacogdoches on July 21: "It is reported and believed that Been has a grant to the Nuteral lands; and yet the Alcalda [Samuel Norris] is letting out lands to his favourites, suffering them to take the improvements of others, while some rely upon obtaining their titles through Been or his commisioner, and all [are] doubtful of the security of their lands eventually."[44] The empresario's brother also mentioned a man who would figure prominently into the trouble on the horizon for their colony. As we have seen from Anthony Clarke's earlier letter to Austin, and the unknown French "American Citizen" writer of the Memorial/Plan, more than one inhabitant of the region held a low opinion of James Gaines.

> What so much adds to this confusion, is the abuse of justice and the continual outrage upon the rights and liberties of the Americans by the civil authority of this place, aided and supported by the celebrated *James Gaines,* and his followers, who seem determined to put down every man who will not bow in adoration to him, and who has independence to be a freeman . . . Having been active with others in organizing two regulating companies, the object of which was no doubt laudable *at first* and has done good, he now makes use of this auxiliary aid to oppress and bear down every man, who is obnoxious to him, or who does not approve of his policy of throwing the whole country into commotion, which he has done, for no other purpose than for his groveling political views and self-aggrandisement.[45]

In July, several weeks before Bean left Mexico City, he also wrote a letter to Stephen F. Austin with some thoughts on how to get around the Mexican government's prohibition of slavery. Bean at this point expected to be named an empresario, so perhaps he felt it was time to share some good advice with the most successful colonizer in Texas.

> Dier Sir,
>
> I have not the honor of Being aquented with [you] But I think it my Duty to enform you as a friend that I Recivd a letter from Saltilla yesterday that states that the law will undoubtedly pass that all the Negros of the Provens of Texas and Quaguila will [be] set free in this case I spoke to the Presedent as he is an old frind of mine he states me the same But there is a way your Settlers can Stop it all But the sooner the Better that is to Gow in Presens of and Alcalde stating that this nigro cost you so much and when he Pays it by labor Don [then?] you have no charge against him he Discounts so much a month as any other hirid Persons a small sum so that he will be the same to you as Before and it will be no more notised this you will comunicate to the citizens on the Ais bayo so that they can take the same Measurs with thers it is ennabatebel [inevitable?] necesario as quick as Posibel—

> I have nothin in this worth your atension Please enform the widow long [Mrs. James Long] that it is imposibel that this government will alow hir any Penchen as hir husband was not [k]nown as a General on this Plase nor had no comision from this Gverment—
>
> Ellis H Bean[46]

A law that permitted slavery under the guise of indentured servitude was passed by the state legislature in 1828, prompting Eugene C. Barker to remark that Bean was "an illiterate but intelligent correspondent" of Austin's, and that Bean's suggestion had led to the solution of the "problem."[47] In other words, ignorant does not mean stupid. Peter Ellis Bean may have had little formal education, but he was a shrewd man. His education came in the school of hard knocks, and he learned his lessons well.

If we can only wonder about Bean's knowledge of the status of the Edwards colony in May 1826, no such doubt exists about the state of affairs that Bean found when he reached the state capital of Coahuila y Texas in September and talked to Gov. Victor Blanco. The governor had annulled Edwards's contract on August 23, 1826, so Bean must have considered the prospects for *his* petition fairly good. He gave Governor Blanco a copy on September 14, with a letter that added a few twists. The Supreme Government, he said, had approved his colonization petition and referred it to the state government. These lands being solicited would be settled by "sons of the country," Germans, and North Americans numbering three or four hundred families. Bean emphasized that he and his colonists would subject themselves to the laws of the nation, also to the particular laws of the state and the governor's conditions for awarding a contract to him.[48]

The governor wrote the secretary of foreign relations four days later concerning Bean's petition as an empresario in Texas. Because of its variances (added number of families, Germans, etc.), he considered Bean's letter to him a second petition. Still, Blanco said his government was of the opinion that Bean's project should be admitted, as long as he respected the property of private individuals and companies who already had just titles to their holdings within the limits "that may be designated" to him. This decision had been reached in fulfillment of the president's resolution.[49]

From this letter it seems that Gov. Victor Blanco was willing to respect Pres. Guadalupe Victoria's wishes in making Peter Ellis Bean an empresario in the sensitive boundary zone. If so, this is surprising in light of the governor's activities a few months earlier, as we shall see.

On September 23 James E. B. Austin wrote his brother Stephen that he had just arrived in Saltillo after a "fatigueing journey" and consulted with Baron de Bastrop about the slavery question then before the legislature. The baron thought that a further introduction of slaves was impossible but planned to present a bill that would allow Austin's three hundred families to hold their slaves already in Texas. The empresario's younger brother closed with "E Bean is here he has the comission of Col. and permission to settle the reserve on the Sabine and Edwards Col[on]y as far as the Nachez [Neches]."[50] Bean no doubt was spreading word to this effect, fully expecting that his contract would sail through confirmation procedures on the state level.

Chapter 4

QUESTIONABLE MARRIAGE STATUS

BEAN REMAINED IN SALTILLO until October 17, at which time he headed to San Antonio and arrived there at the end of November. It is unknown if, during this month's stay in the state capital, he discovered that the governor had initiated an inquiry the past July 10 into his personal conduct. On that date Blanco wrote Political Chief Saucedo at San Antonio, charging him

> to notify the Alcalde of Nacogdoches and Citizen Stephen Austin to examine beforehand some witnesses in their jurisdiction who have the best reputation of honest men, and who have known the aforementioned Pedro Elias Bean, on the following points:
>
> 1st, Let them say, as to his public conduct, all that they may know, or that may be evident to them concerning this individual.
>
> 2nd, If the aforesaid Elias Bean is married, what is the name of his wife, of what place she is a native, and where she was married [to him]. If she has children, how many, and what are their names.
>
> 3rd, What is the public reputation which Elias Bean has among the inhabitants of that district.[1]

This letter launched an investigation of Bean's private and public life that was to plague him for years. Who tipped off Governor Blanco and aroused his interest in Bean's marriage status at Nacogdoches? Was it Bastrop (the most likely suspect), or someone in Mexico City? Bean made no secret of his Mexican wife while in Mexico, using this marriage to advance his projects at the capital. It is doubtful that he was foolish enough to mention to these officials that he also had a wife in Texas, even in macho bull sessions under the warm glow of free-flowing alcohol. Yet it is obvious that Blanco's letter, with all its concern about Bean's wife and children, hinted at the question of bigamy. Austin was not even married, but it did not disqualify him as an empresario or cause his private conduct to come into play. Nor was this type of scrutiny usually leveled against other aspirants.

Someone had raised the issue of morality and advised Blanco to pursue it before Bean's colonization contract was approved. Was this a payback for Bean's year-old accusations against Green DeWitt for misappropriating public funds, the coin being even more serious morality charges? Men in Mexico sometimes dipped their fingers into the proverbial cookie jar, but few of them were married to two women at the same time. No good Catholic could tolerate such behavior, even if he was married and kept a mistress in a *casa chica* across town. From this point on, Bean's marriage status became intertwined with the fate of his proposed colony in the border zone. The two considerations run side by side, and it is impossible to separate them. Thrown into the blender were his activities as an Indian agent. While he was being praised for keeping the peace with the Indians, he was also being denounced as a bigamist—often by the same officials.

Austin was the first to take testimony. On August 3, 1826—about the time Bean was heading north from Mexico City to Saltillo—Austin called on Martin Allen, "a respectable and honorable inhabitant of this Jurisdiction," to tell the truth about what he knew of Bean. Under oath Allen stated that he had

> lived a number of years in the Same Section of Country in the Arkansas Territory with Said Bean and was intimately acquainted with him and his family for Six years and was frequently at his house both in Arkansas and on the river Neches in the district of Nacogdoches where he now lives— The Said Bean had a wife when this deponent first saw him in Arkansas, does not know where he was married but believes in the State of Tennessee— The common and universal belief of every one was that the said Bean was legally married to his wife according to the laws of the country where he lived— his Father in law was by the name of Metcalf and was well known to this deponent. He had the character of a respectable and honorable man and was a Justice of the Peace in Arkansas territory, and [deponent] does not believe from the character and standing of said Metcalf that he would have permitted the Said Bean to live with his daughter unless they were legally married.
>
> This deponent thinks Bean to be an honest man he is very fond of boasting and telling large stories about his exploits in the Mexican revolution and said he was a Colonel in the regular army of Mexico.
>
> This deponent cannot positively state how many children Said Bean has at this time but believes he has *three* [emphasis added].[2]

Austin let the taking of depositions lapse at San Felipe until August 24, when aspiring empresario Sterling C. Robertson was in town. Robertson, calling himself a sergeant major and a native of Tennessee, declared that

> about five or six years ago [1820 or 1821], as best he can remember, he traveled in company with Ellis Bean from the town of Memphis on the Mississippi to the town of Columbia in Tennessee, and the said Bean told him that he was going to the community where he married his wife. With reference to business he also said that he had been in the Mexican Revolutionary Army and that he had a wife in Mexico, but said that he could not return to her because the Army to which he was attached had been defeated. Also he said that at that time he was living in Arkansas Territory near the Red River of Natchitoches, where the woman whom he married in Tennessee was living, and that he was planning to go to Texas to make an investigation about the lands which they promised him for his services, as soon as he returned from his trip. This deponent understood that the said Bean married his American wife in Franklin County, Tennessee.[3]

This testimony was strong evidence that Bean had two wives, one in Texas and another in Mexico. According to what Robertson said, Bean freely admitted to strangers that he had married a woman in Tennessee and was presently living with her, although circumstances kept him from returning to his first wife in Mexico. Could Bean have said the same to old war buddies in Mexico City, the men who were now running the country? Allen's deposition ruled out the possibility that Bean's Tennessee marriage was a common-law arrangement, a point that later became critical to Mexican authorities. Judge Austin sent this testimony to the political chief on August 28, calling both deponents very respectable, honest, and well-known men. He apologized for not pursuing the matter further: "Since Bean's family lives on the Nechez River, fifty leagues from here, I have not been able to find here many men who have knowledge of him; for this reason, I have not taken more depositions on the matter."[4] Austin need not have bothered; the two statements he forwarded were already damaging enough to Bean.

Alcalde Samuel Norris did not start his testimony-taking process at Nacogdoches until early September, but it was also damaging. Called were his brother Nathaniel Norris, an ensign in the civil militia, and their brother-in-law James Gaines, who—as seen—commanded a vigilante group that made life miserable for the new colonists introduced by Haden Edwards. Nathaniel said that he had known Bean for two years, after he had been selected an alcalde by voters, and Bean was always trying to oppose the interests of the old residents of the town. In one instance it was necessary to devote a whole day in closed meeting to overcome Bean's objections "since he wished that the authority which ruled in this town should go to one of the opponents of these residents." Another episode was mentioned to indicate that Bean's "words were very sweet but his deeds very bad." From this it seems that the old-settler faction at Nacogdoches viewed Bean as in the enemy camp, allied with the interests of Empresario Haden Edwards.[5]

James Gaines claimed knowledge of Bean for about three years, and said that Bean had an American wife and a son and a daughter. "They went away to settle by the Neches River," suggesting that Bean had earlier lived in Gaines's neighborhood along the Sabine, where Gaines operated a ferry. Gaines accused Bean of associating with "very bad people, the same who have been driven to the other side of the Sabine." These people were eagerly awaiting Bean's return, in order to again enter Mexican territory, proclaiming that "now they have an empresario of their own!"[6]

James Gaines, it should be noted, had come into possession of certificates for 466 leagues of land from José Bernardo Gutiérrez de Lara, with whom he had served in the 1813 campaign. Gutiérrez, of course, had no legitimate right to confer land on this scale, as his government never got off the ground. Gaines, like other fighters in the Mexican Revolution who had acquired land for their services, became upset when empresarios such as Austin would not recognize these scripts. In November 1824 Gaines lectured Austin about how, in the coming year, "the first will be Last and the Last first, the Great Small and the Small Great." Steps were being taken, he said, to secure from Congress the rightful compensation that was due Gutiérrez's veterans. This actually happened in 1825, when claims were pressed at the capital for foreigners who had fought with Gutiérrez. That Gaines considered Bean's empresarial aspirations in the boundary reserve a threat to his own control of the area requires no great leap of the imagination.[7]

Gaines's 1826 testimony was but a shorter version of the undated deposition given by the alcalde at Ayish Bayou, John Sprowl. He certified that

> Ellis Been, during his temporary residence in this District, uniformly associated with men of the worst character, and particularly with those who have been driven out of the country, by the companies of Militia, mentioned in the Petition to which this is annexed, and lived with them on a footing of the most familiar friendship. I also certify that since the rumour has circulated through the country that Colonel Been has obtained authority from [the] Government to colonize this Section of the Province, the most infamous characters in it have exhibited an indecent exultation and triumph over the peaceable and honorable citizens, who have hitherto been able, by persevering exer-

> tions, to keep them under some restraint and subordination. They have boasted that "Now they have an Empresario! now they are fixed," as if they had now no longer any obstacle to surmount in the commission of the worst of crimes.[8]

James Gaines was one of those characters who would say different things to different people, depending on how it served his interests at the moment. His reign of terror over those who opposed his vigilante activities against the Edwards faction and other "bad people" in the Sabine District has been noted. A decade later Haden Edwards accused Gaines and his supporters of using some pretty outrageous tactics to "clean up" the region. "On [Edwards's arrival with his family in August 1825] he found the organization of two corps or volunta[r]y assosiciations of men controld or commanded by James Gains under the style and name of *Regulators.* They had been in the habit of taking the law into their own hands. Under the pretext of punishi[n]g crime, they would often shoot men at their own houses under slight suspicions of guilt and many of the lives of our best men were then sacrifised— It was urged against these arbitrary *Regulators* that they were nothing more than freebooters, that they plundered those they killed or imprisoned—"[9] This being the case, it is small wonder that Peter Ellis Bean did not wish to live in the environs of the Sabine when he brought his family to Texas in 1823. The imperious way that Nick Trammell and family were evicted from his ferry on the Trinity crossing of the Old San Antonio Road is evidence that Alcalde Norris and his civil militia (Gaines backing him up when necessary) employed rough and high-handed measures as well.

It may also be argued that Alcalde John Sprowl was unfit to speak on the question of Bean's character, and certainly he was from the Mexican point of view. When the Edwards brothers' Fredonian Rebellion broke loose at the end of the year, Sprowl was a member of the "Committee of Independence" that ratified the document declaring Texas independent of Mexico on December 21.[10] If Bean was such a detestable fellow with bad habits and friends, then why was he so instrumental in putting down this rebellion against Mexican rule—a rebellion that Sprowl had become a turncoat to embrace?

As noted, Robert Collier on August 22 gave a deposition to Elbert Hines, acting alcalde of the Sabine District, that Bean had come to his house and asked for one hundred dollars to help defray his travel expenses to Mexico the year before.[11] This statement is ambiguous; it could mean either that Bean was gouging local people for money or that Bean represented their hope for recognition of land titles in the boundary reserve, a region that no other agent of the government had been authorized to colonize. Bean, once in Mexico, applied for a colonization contract that—

when approved—would give him the power to place men like Collier in legal possession of the land they cultivated.

On the same day that Collier gave his statement, another district alcalde was taking testimony about Bean that was far less ambiguous. In fact, it was the most spectacular piece of evidence gathered in the Nacogdoches region, because it came from Bean's wife, Candace Midkiff (often spelled "Metcalf"). Alcalde Demetrius Hayes of the Neches District reported the following to Alcalde Samuel Norris at Nacogdoches on September 5, 1826.

> This day [August 22] there has presented herself in person before me the Alcalde of the Neches District [Hayes], Candes Masquef and she says the following: I was married to Elias H. Bean in the State of Tennessee, District of Juaite [White], and I [was] married by McDaniel who was authorized by the marriage law of said State, and further I say that I have two children by the aforesaid Bean. Their names are as follows: Asigues F. [Isaac T.] Bean, born in the Arkansas Territory in the United States of America in the year of '21 on March 5th; Lenallin [Louisa Jane] was born in the Province of Texas the year of 1823 . . . [on] August 15th [and] They [the family] returned to the province of Texas in the month of January [1823].[12]

Alcalde Norris forwarded his depositions to Political Chief Saucedo on September 5. Saucedo combined the Nacogdoches testimony with that taken at San Felipe by Austin and sent the file to Governor Blanco on October 1 with something of a disclaimer: "I lack knowledge of this individual [Bean] and the judicial proceedings obtained do not furnish sufficient data on which to base my report, which by [your] aforesaid order is asked of me in this matter. Therefore I transmit them without this requisite."[13]

These proceedings reached Governor Blanco only several days after Bean, on October 17, had departed Saltillo for Texas. Even if the governor was not aware of the results of the investigation he had ordered the previous July, he knew—when this foreigner appeared before him in September, speaking grandly of his triumph in the Mexican capital and how he had received the president's blessing for his colonization project—that there was something fishy about this newly minted colonel of the Mexican army. Blanco wrote Saucedo on October 20, acknowledging receipt of the file on Bean and ordering that a spy be designated to follow his moves, a person "throughly reliant and honest." Bean had just left for San Antonio, "en route to the frontier with the rank of Brevet Colonel in the National Army of the Republic." Nonetheless, the governor wanted him watched closely. The spy was to snoop around "privately" and report back more definitely on the following aspects of Bean's marital arrangement: "His conduct towards his wife Candes Midkiff, who lives in Neches with two children of the aforesaid Colonel; if he recognizes her as his legitimate wife and the same with his offspring; if he lives with her as a husband; whether he supports her and her family; whether that lady acknowledges him to be her lawful husband; and if she is married according to common law or for life."[14] Blanco was obviously not satisfied with the dirt on Bean uncovered the past summer and wanted Saucedo to nail down the bigamy question once and for all. As we shall see, the political chief at San Antonio was more than willing to perform this task, though the situation in east Texas was about to erupt in armed confrontation that would dominate everyone's attention.

Bean did not have at hand all the documents he needed to convince Governor Blanco of why he was going to Texas, or with what authority, but enough paperwork crossed Blanco's desk to assure him that Bean was not just full of hot air. For example, on October 14 the principal *comisario* at Saltillo certified that Bean had been included in the state budget for salaried officers of the "Commandancy General of These States." Only Gen. Anastasio Bustamante could issue orders to this effect, upon notification by the secretary of war and marine that Bean was entitled. The *comisario* noted that he had furnished Colonel Bean the sum of one hundred pesos, four reales, for "his march to Texas." This advance would be deducted from Bean's pay for the month of November, with another third "by reason of two payments that he received in advance in the month of July last in Mexico City."[15] Later documents show that Bean's annual salary as a lieutenant colonel, brevetted colonel, in the Mexican army was eighteen hundred pesos, boosted somewhat by campaign "gratifications." But the majority of Bean items in the Béxar Archives reveal that payment of his salary and especially reimbursement for gifts he made to the Indians were often snarled in red tape. It could take years for him to pry loose money from the government and usually did.

Part of the problem was that the *comisario particular* at San Antonio was Erasmo Seguín, who was a real stickler for bureaucratic paperwork. Unless claims were properly documented and submitted in official language, Seguín would not pay them. Bean sometimes tried to dodge these formalities, as if his word were sufficient proof that an expenditure had been made and payment was due him. Seguín could not claim ignorance of Bean's duties, for the commissariat general of San Luis Potosí wrote him on October 23 that Bustamante had sent the following order to him on October 13. "The Citizen Colonel of the Army, Peter Ellis Bean, Lieutenant Colonel of Cavalry, goes, by order of the Supreme Government, to be situated in Nacogdoches; and it being necessary that in said point he may receive the payment that corresponds to his office, I thank Your

Lordship to give your order so that, through the particular commissariat of Béxar, there may be paid to him at the proper time, monthly, that which is included in the budget for the provision of those companies."[16] Despite this, Seguín was soon questioning amounts that were due Bean on his march to Texas and particularly pay for his services in defusing the Fredonian Rebellion. Besides the records available in the Béxar Archives, some of these snarls went up the bureaucratic chain to Mexico City and wound up in Bean's military service record at the War Department.

Nor could Governor Blanco at Saltillo claim that Bean was a fake, proper documents or no. Four days after he acknowledged receipt of the incriminating file on Bean from the political chief, he again wrote Saucedo. This time it was to pass along a letter the commandant general had written him on October 21. It spelled out something on Bean's commission in Texas. He was to go to Nacogdoches and see if the friendly Indian nations on the frontier were disposed to make war on the Wacos in union with the Cherokees, as the latter had proposed earlier in the year. Bean was also commissioned to inform the Supreme Government on the political situation in this part of the republic, relying on the civil militia if necessary.[17] While Bean's commission was later stated more fully, the governor of Coahuila y Texas certainly knew that he had been entrusted with delicate duties on the northeastern frontier by authorities on the federal level. This must have given him pause, considering the new round of secret investigations about Bean's private life that he had ordered only four days earlier.

Chapter 5

THE FREDONIAN REBELLION

COLONEL BEAN REACHED San Antonio near the end of November, just as open rebellion against the Mexican authorities at Nacogdoches was coming to a head. Empresario Haden Edwards received notification that his colonization contract with the Mexican government had been annulled by a letter from Governor Blanco dated August 23, 1826. Three reasons were given:

> 1st, Edwards had insulted the dignity and usurped the authority of the State by publishing an edict in Nacogdoches on October 25, 1825, in which he falsely styled himself as military commander of the region and required old possessors of lands to present their titles or else they would be evicted and their lands sold to the highest bidder.
>
> 2nd, He had despoiled several of the inhabitants of that frontier of their lands, so that he might give them to others.
>
> 3rd, He had sold part of the lands in his colony, appropriating the proceeds, "believing himself to be absolute Lord and Master of those lands."[1]

Edwards thought that this decision might be reversed, but Blanco upheld it in a letter of October 20: "I have decreed the annulment of his contract and his expulsion from the territory," he told the political chief. The only way that Edwards could appeal the governor's decision was by mail, *after* he had removed himself from Mexican territory.[2] The empresario later claimed that there was "some doubt" the governor had written a letter expelling him and his brother from Texas. He also maintained that the first news of his contract's cancellation did not reach him until late in 1826, upon his return from Louisiana. Edwards claimed that this letter left him "thunderstruck" and unable to divine "the cause of this high handed measure."[3]

This cancellation of his contract led Haden Edwards and his brother Benjamin to consider drastic measures in order to salvage years of effort and fifty thousand dollars spent in securing their empresarial rights. Benjamin often attended to the affairs of the colony while Haden was in the United States, trying to recruit settlers. They were opposed by the old settlers and by those in control of the local government. This faction was led by Alcalde Samuel Norris. He was backed by his brother Nathaniel, brother-in-law James Gaines, and the newly elected captain of the local civil militia, José Antonio Sepúlveda. The latter individual had been warning the political chief for almost a year that Edwards and the other foreigners at Nacogdoches were planning a revolution and that he wished to make the old residents his "slaves." Once Haden Edwards lost his contract, these warnings about revolution proved true.[4]

Apart from Edwards's domineering attitude toward the people that he found occupying his grant with prior claims to ownership of desirable tracts of land, some dating back several generations, two incidents seem to have led to armed conflict in his jurisdiction. Ironically, both of them originated with abuses of the constituted alcalde, Samuel Norris. First came the eviction of Nicholas Trammell from the crossing of the Trinity River on October 20 by Captain Sepúlveda and ten of his militiamen, acting on Norris's orders. Trammell's son, Nathaniel, had purchased a league of land at the crossing from Edwards, but one Ignacio Zertuche swore that he had an earlier claim and that he, a native Mexican, should be favored with title instead of the foreigner Trammell. This case became a political football and doomed any chance that Edwards might have had in retaining his empresarial contract. Both the political chief and the governor became involved with the implications of the dispute, which was still festering when Bean returned to Texas the next month. In the meantime, Nick Trammell had been forced to flee with his family to Pecan Point, back up the Trace that bore his name.[5]

The other incident involved John Bassett, a young gentleman who had just arrived in Texas but was warmly received among the new American population. He was recruited by a trader named Horatio Seymour to sell some goods among the Indians, expecting to operate under his employer's license. When Alcalde Norris learned of this, he demanded that Bassett buy a new twenty-five-dollar license from him and have his goods examined before going among the Indians. Bassett refused and was supported by the Anglo colonists, who insisted that this license was actually a tax from which they were exempt under the national colonization law. Bassett left for Natchitoches to pick up his trade goods and proceeded directly to the Cherokee village. There Chief Richard Fields told him that the alcalde had commanded them to fine Bassett twenty-five dollars. This Fields refused to do, and the trade goods were received.

When Bassett returned to Nacogdoches, accompanied by John Dunn Hunter, he went by the alcalde's office to pick up some papers deposited there earlier. Scarcely had he left when he was arrested by ten or twelve armed "ruffians" sent after him by Alcalde Norris. Bassett was then taken to the Sabine by a guard of men who either had orders to kill him or threatened him with death if he returned to Texas. Undeterred by these threats, Bassett went to Ayish Bayou where his employer resided.[6]

After he told the local people how he had fared at the hands of Alcalde Samuel Norris, they decided to oust the ignorant and corrupt old-settler faction that ruled political affairs at Nacogdoches. Among the forty men that rode to arrest these councilmen and their henchmen was Martin Parmer, newly arrived in Texas but already known as the "Ring-Tailed Panther" from his military exploits back in Missouri.[7] They reached Nacogdoches on November 22 and soon had the Norris faction in detention—except James Gaines, who "made his escape out of his own house through a window in his shirt tail." Like Bean, Gaines was adept at making fast getaways.

Parmer secured the Old Stone Fort, confiscated weapons from residents, and took charge of the town's archives, which he combed for proof of the charges he planned to bring against Norris and his cohorts. He then instituted a court of inquiry to determine the guilt or innocence of the prisoners, including Haden Edwards, although his arrest was mostly for appearance's sake. As one might expect, this kangaroo court returned guilty verdicts against the officials most detested by the Ayish Bayou people. A reward of one hundred dollars was issued for James Gaines, whether taken "dead or alive."[8]

Parmer's court left a reluctant Joseph Durst in charge of the archives as interim alcalde. They warned Norris and Sepúlveda that they would come back on December 15 to make sure these men did not try to reassume their old functions. Then they rode to their homes in Ayish Bayou, confident that they had straightened out things in Nacogdoches and that the civil government would henceforth pay more attention to their interests. They proclaimed that their loyalty was to the Mexican nation and that their actions were strictly motivated by a desire for good government. Thus, they were not rabid revolutionists but solid citizens.

Both Norris and Sepúlveda bombarded Political Chief Saucedo with accounts of how the predicted revolution against Mexican authority was now a reality—this at the time that Bean made his appearance in San Antonio with a commission to report on these problems to the Supreme Government. On November 12, shortly before Bean's arrival, Saucedo notified Governor Blanco that he had received his order to select someone to watch Bean's movements and report on his marriage status. "In its fulfillment, I shall effectively take care of its punctual and prompt observance on the occasion that I myself have to go in person to the Town of Nacogdoches close to the place where his wife Candes Metcalf has established herself." Saucedo promised to give the governor a complete account of his findings after a proper investigation had been made of the points raised.[9]

A list of documents received at Béxar by the political chief for the month of November 1826 indicates that four official notifications concerning Bean heralded his arrival.[10] Suggesting that either the governor, the commandant general, or the political chief had not fully apprised the military commandant of Texas of Bean's commission is a letter of November 28 that this official, Lt. Col. Mateo Ahumada, wrote Bean. He asked Bean what were his instructions in coming to Texas, perhaps to learn how and if his own authority was compromised.[11] It seems that Bean, on his every move, was preceded by news that either left a bad impression of him or complicated his life somehow. Was this just Bean's bad karma, or did it represent an institutionalized frontier bias by Mexicans against foreigners from North America? From this vantage point it is difficult to say, but Bean encountered problems in Texas unlike those with his revolutionary brethren in Mexico.

The situation in east Texas continued to deteriorate rapidly, this due to the Indians of the region and their possible involvement with the disillusioned Haden and Benjamin Edwards. The Cherokees were also disillusioned. After John Dunn Hunter returned from the Mexican capital with news that the government would not honor its previous promises of a large communal grant of land, war drums began to beat in the Piney Woods. Chief Richard Fields was especially enraged about what he regarded as a betrayal of his people by Mexican officials. He and Hunter decided to cast their fate with Empresario Edwards, who was promising them all of Texas north of the San Antonio Road if they would help him establish his Fredonian Republic.[12] Someone who attended a committee meeting, at which Chief Fields spoke, passed along his speech to Bean, who then forwarded it to Austin in his own inimitable version of English.

> In my old Days I travilid 2000 Miles to the City of Mexico to Beg some lands to setel a Poor orfan tribe of Red Peopel that looked up to me for Protasian I was Promisid lands for them after staying one year in Mexico and spending all I had I then came to my Peopel and waited two years and then sent Mr. hunter again after selling my stock to Provide him money for his expenses when he got there he staited his mision to [the] government they said that they New nothing of this Richard fields and treated him with contampt— I am a Red man and a man of [h]onor and cant be emposid on this way we will lift up our tomahauks and fight for land with all

> those friendly tribes that wishis land also if I am Beaton I then will Resign to fait and if not I will hold lands By the forse of my Red Warriors—[13]

This speech was not given until—true to his promise—Martin Parmer rode back to Nacogdoches on December 16 and again took over the Old Stone Fort. This time he was accompanied by Benjamin Edwards, and they bore a flag of two red and white stripes with the legend "Independence, Liberty and Justice." Five days later Benjamin Edwards and Herman Mayo drew up a treaty of alliance with the Cherokees and other Indian nations represented by Richard Fields and John Dunn Hunter, said to compose twenty-three tribal groups. This treaty was ratified the same day by eight Anglos, including both Edwards brothers and Martin Parmer as "president" of the Committee of Independence, and by five Indian chiefs who composed the Committee of Red People. It was probably at these proceedings that Chief Fields made the speech that got back to Bean in late December.[14]

Edwards, in a letter to Aylett "Strap" Buckner of Austin's colony written the day after Christmas 1826, crowed that "the flag of *liberty* now waves in majestic triumph on the heights of Nacogdoches, and despotism stands appalled at the sight." The Indian tribes represented by Hunter and Fields—both signers of the treaty—"are now our decided friends, and by compact as well as interest are bound to aid us in effecting the *Independence* of this country." More such letters were dispatched by the rebellious faction in an attempt to entice Anglo settlers in Austin's and DeWitt's colonies to join the red-and-white standard of independence from Mexico.[15] But alliances between white men and red savages—as the "civilized" tribes were generally regarded—were never certain things. This aspect no doubt worked against the Edwards brothers as they tried to rally recruits to their banner of revolution.

Bean left San Antonio and traveled to Goliad (then known as La Bahía) during the first week of December. The commandant at that post was told of Bean's coming by Ahumada, who wrote him on November 30 that—by the commandant general's order—he was to give Bean any assistance he required in fulfillment of his commission from the government.[16] Bean needed assistance because he had not ridden to Texas at the head of one hundred troopers as expected. In fact, Commandant General Bustamante assigned only two men to serve under Bean, but these orders did not arrive in a timely fashion.[17] On December 6 Colonel Bean wrote Political Chief Saucedo that he had seen an official communication directed to the alcalde of Guadalupe Victoria dated five days earlier, "saying that Nacogdoches and the Judges of that place are very rebellious and not doing as the Señor Don Stephen Austin has advised them." Bean was going "to march swiftly" to San Felipe de Austin where the empresario would no doubt inform him of the latest information. It might be necessary to take the militia of Austin's colony and march with it if events required: "According to the news I may receive from Austin, I shall give you immediate notice, in case you may find it convenient to pass to me news directed to you from Nacogdoches, for my guidance and the ends that correspond to the good of the Nation."[18]

Bean was being very diplomatic in this letter, possibly because he had sensed that Saucedo and Ahumada at San Antonio were hostile to his reasons for returning to Texas. It is not likely that he learned of the ongoing bigamy investigation against him, certainly not from the political chief himself. But the military chief's query as to his specific orders was enough to make Bean realize that his actions—with the Indians and the Anglo rebels—were subject to intense scrutiny. Yoakum, quoting an entry in Bean's "memorandum book" of the same day, says that Bean made a wager on the situation in east Texas: "If the justices of Nacogdoches are imprisoned, or hindered in their functions, then I pay twenty-five dollars; if not, then Señor Y—— gives me one jack and three bottles of wine." Various writers have said that this bet suggests that Bean was not taking the trouble at Nacogdoches very seriously. At this point it probably looked more like local squabbling of a petty nature to Bean, the sort of thing he knew happened on a daily basis.[19]

Upon reaching San Felipe around the middle of the month, Bean heard that the trouble was indeed serious and likely to get worse if the Indians became involved. Austin had been busy writing letters to people who were arraying themselves against Mexican authority, in the certain belief that any uprising would damage his own prospects as an Anglo empresario. On December 14 he wrote several residents of Ayish Bayou, saying he had heard "with the deepest regret and astonishment of the late proceedings against the Authorities at Nacogdoches; it appears as tho the people in your quarter have run mad or worse—they are distroying themselves, building up the credit of their enemies with the Govt. and jeopardising the prospects of hundreds of innocent families who wish to live in peace and quietness in the country." He told John A. Williams and Burrell P. Thompson—the former switched sides and supported Mexico; the latter remained a Fredonian and a signatory of the independence document a week later—that "Col Bean is going on [to Nacogdoches], he is an officer in the mexican army. *Advice with him* and put aside all your ill timed and I must say injudicious and obstinate republican nicity, and allay all your passions and excitements and take prudence for your guide and above all throw away your arms."[20]

Did Bean, while he was in San Felipe, hear about Austin's testimony-taking process in August? Did he have any hint that his marriage was the subject of considerable interest to Mexican authorities in both San Antonio and Saltillo? The documentation does not reveal an answer to this question, and Austin—though fully aware that Bean was said to have two wives—was probably too circumspect to open the subject with Bean. On December 16, however, Austin wrote Saucedo that he had received notice of his obligation to inform Postmaster Patricio de Torres at Nacogdoches that he was to verify Bean's conduct. Bean himself was leaving that day and would be accompanied by Captain Sepúlveda and some men who had arrived several days earlier. Strangely enough, it was Bean who was asked to deliver Austin's notification to Torres, whereby the postmaster learned that he was to spy on Bean! Austin either had no other certain way of getting the message through, or considered Bean honorable enough not to open and read his letter to Torres.[21]

Colonel Bean and Captain Sepúlveda left San Felipe on December 16 with about thirty-five men, intending to sniff out the situation at Nacogdoches rather than provoke a confrontation. They retired without incident to some unspecified point, perhaps along either the customary crossing of the Neches or Trinity Rivers, where Bean wrote Austin on December 23.

> I have just got news from Nacodoches and thare is about 100 Americons and three Injin chiefs Richards is one of them and also Dr. Hunter is with them they have formed a comity and is about to Declar war and if all the Ingins Joine them this will be a serious affair field has said that he will furnish 400 warriors for his Part he sais that the Spanard has Desived him in his land But I have Rote to him and I hope that when he Recives my leter that I shall Brake him off also I have Rote to a man in the Aish Bayo and I hope that I shall Suckseed in Deviding them I have to lay out and not be seen for to hear from my letters and if I Dont Suckseed I shall cross [back to?] the trinity the[y] are for marching as soon as posibel to take your Coloney you will comunicate this as quick as Posibel and if it is in your Power you ought to send as meney men as you can and stop [at?] this crossing of the Trinity. this is all that I can state at present. God & Liberty. Pedro Ellis Bean[22]

The "man in the Aish Bayo" that Bean had written was probably Elisha Roberts, because his reply (given below) mentions Bean's letter of December 22. Also, we have Bean's letter of that date, addressed to "Mr. Elisha Roberds, Esq." from the Neches, and—as he stated to Austin a day later—this letter certainly was meant to divide the opposition.

Dier Sir with much surprise I have heard of this Disturbans that is Rening [reigning?] in your setelment and Nacagdoches, is it Posibel that good men and men of understanding will be led astray By men that has nothing to loose[?] no I cant Belive that you will expose your Selvs and Property [to certain ruin.] I hope that you will take my advise and try to Put a stop to all this fuss as quick as Posibel if you all are quit [quiet] you all will git your land also the [institution of] Slavery is admitid to Continu and what more do you Wish[?] thare is now a Comisenor Coming on to fix all the land Besness and it will be of a grate Benifit to you to hold your land and emprovements,

But my Diar Sir if you all Prosist in foley you may consider your Selvs Runed for all will fall threw I hope that you will Strive to Put all of this Bisness Down if you can for the Maxican Goverment is friendly to wards you all, you all Stand high and is it Posibel that you will Brake threw the Bounds of Reason and Do your Selves so much engery[?] it is onley four years now till the Constitution can be changed and then I will inshur you that thare will be liberty of Consians [i.e., freedom of religion] that will suit you all.

Sir I hope to hear from you as soon as Posibel and hear allso that you have Put a stop to all this Confusion. Brake it up if it is in your Power this is from your friend and Welwisher to you all. You will Keep this a secret to your self.

Yors — Peter Ellis Bean

P. D. I have heard that Capt. hins [Elbert Hines?] has had nothing to Do with this fus you can Join him and Put a stop to all Bean[23]

Further supporting the conclusion that Bean had not yet withdrawn to the Trinity to await the arrival of reinforcements is the letter that he wrote Austin on December 28 from "Netches."

Dier Sir thare is one Express goan to your Colony [from the Fredonians] to make it Rais in arms and in this Date thare will starte an other I hope you will keep a good lookout for those Villions counts on you and your men But i now have more k[n]owledge of things then to be led astray to save [those] men from their crimes they find them selvs lost and will swim against stream as long as they can I have devided them so that I now have 70 me[n] coming from Irish Bayu to attack 30 that is in nacodoches and my leters from [to] field [as] yet I have had no answer But I am wating howerly for the answer if I Suckseed in Braking him of[f] I then put out the fier instantly and thare is litel Doubt with me in my mind But that I shall suckseed You will look out for they are trying to sedus your Coloney your most sincere frind. Peter Ellis Bean[24]

It is obvious that Bean had also been attending to personal affairs at his place on the Neches while awaiting word from Chief Richard Fields. On December 28, the same day as his letter to Austin, his wife Candace appeared before the alcalde of the Neches District, Michael Whatley, and gave another deposition that suggests some strong prompting from Bean, to say the least.

> **question the first** Did you ever Swear befor Demtris Hays Alcalda for the District of Natches . . . that you was lawfully married to Peter Ellis Bean[?] . . . She answereth no that She never Did.
> **question the 2nd** Did not the above named Demetries Hays State to you that if you had not answered his questions that Samuel Norris the Chief Comma[n]dent at Nochogdoches Would send Malitia and have you taken a prisoner and confined in the Stone house at Nacodoches[?] . . . She answereth he did State as named in the Within questions—
> **question thc third** Did you State on examination Before the above named Hays that you was lawfully married to Peter Ellis Bean[?] . . . answereth . . . that She Did State before the Sd. Hays on examination that She was lawfully married to Peter Ellis Bean.
> **question the fourth** Why did you answer in the way you Did to the third question[?] She anwereth . . . the cause Why She answered the third question as She Did was to save the property of Peter Ellis Bean in her hands as She Supposed he never would return
> **question the fifth** Was you ever Lawfully married to Peter Ellis Bean[?] to this question She answered She never Was[25]

Handy Wane and Daniel McLean witnessed this declaration, and it soon came into Bean's hands—if he had not actually framed the questions and been on the scene when the deposition was taken from her.

Here is the situation that Bean found at his homestead near the Neches. Candace Midkiff Bean was a woman in her mid-twenties with two small children. Bean had left her to fend for herself in the wilderness and been absent a year and a half. It is doubtful that he tried to communicate with her from Mexico, involved as he was with grand schemes and spending time with his Mexican wife at Jalapa. But Bean did write the Nacogdoches alcalde in June, saying he was about to leave for Texas, and the news was probably passed on to his wife. Word supposedly reached Candace in the early fall of 1826 that Bean had been killed in Mexico. Believing herself to be a widow, she accepted the advances of that "Ring-Tailed Panther," Martin Parmer.[26]

According to an account that Parmer's son Thomas gave Moses Austin Bryan in 1874, the family started for Texas in the spring of 1825 intending to settle in Austin's colony. Misfortune struck them just east of the Neches River at "Bradshaw's Prairie" where Parmer's wife died in August and Indians ran off their horses. Parmer and his motherless children were stuck in the neighborhood of Bean's house, this shortly after Bean had departed for Mexico. Like Bean, he was much older than Candace, and neither had spouses around. How soon they began their affair is unknown, but it may have started as a matter of convenience. Eligible Anglo women were scarce on the frontier, and no doubt Candace had other suitors besides Parmer. But Parmer was a charismatic, commanding figure and won her hand. They were married sometime around Christmas Day 1826, though they had probably been sleeping together on the Neches much earlier. It is uncertain when and how they tied the knot, as available marriage records at Nacogdoches do not start early enough to contain an entry for them. Most frontier couples took vows before a district official, promising to sanctify it when a priest was available. This was the custom in Mexican Texas where priests did not usually circulate among the backwoods Anglo settlements, if at all.

Shortly after the newlyweds' supposed marriage, word reached the Bean homestead that Peter Ellis Bean was very much alive and on his way home from San Felipe, where the informant had seen and spoken with him. This may have been how Bean learned of his wife's "infidelity." Parmer wisely returned to Nacogdoches to avoid an unpleasant meeting with the husband.[27] Candace was still somewhere in the Neches District, as indicated by her deposition before the local alcalde on December 28. Bean surely stopped at his house in search of her. If he did not find Candace there, he probably learned her whereabouts from the men who were occupying his house. At this point in time it seems they were rebels. If so, they did not question Bean's right to appear at his own home. There is also the possibility that Bean talked them into switching sides, as he soon did with some of the Indians.

According to three men later sent to negotiate with the Fredonians, they found an outpost of insurgents stationed at Bean's house. They "had taken possession of the Boat, all of Beans property and declared it confiscated. On our arrival at said post [early in January 1827], the soldiers informed us that the country was revolutionized from that [Neches] to the Sabine River." This is curious because Bean, in a letter given below, stated that the seventy volunteers he used to rout the rebels at Nacogdoches were quartered "at my own house on the Neches" when he had arrived. Also, a letter written to "Col." Benjamin Edwards by H. Haile, "Lieut. Comd. at Naches," indicates that Bean's house was occupied by a small group of rebels as late as January 23. Loyalist prisoners from the neighborhood were still being sent to Nacogdoches, with cases formed against their conduct. Either there was a quick evacuation by men of the fractious element and an equally quick reoccupation of the premises by men loyal to Mexico, or Bean did not want to name names and make enemies after the rebellion fizzled out.[28]

What Bean found going on at his place may account for the remark in his letter to Austin of December 28 about not being "led astray to save men from their crimes." Martin Parmer, one of the leading rebels, was assuredly on Bean's list as a man who should suffer for the crimes of seducing and shacking up with, or marrying, his wife. The "crimes" of lesser figures, some of them his friends and neighbors, Colonel Bean could pardon.

Nicholas Trammell was another man who thought that Parmer was guilty of crimes and should be punished for them. About the time Nick was being evicted from the Trinity crossing in October 1826, Parmer had shot and killed his half brother Morton "Mote" Askins at the house of Daniel Clark on the Angelina. Although Alcalde Samuel Norris ordered Parmer's arrest, he was not brought to justice. Once Trammell had made his way back to Arkansas, he was obliged to take in and rear the orphans of his slain kinsman, with whom he was very close. Thus Parmer's motives are rather suspect when he rode into Nacogdoches with his fellow Ayishians the next month to clean out the corrupt civil officials. Norris, who had ordered his arrest, was one of them. In Parmer's kangaroo court, Norris was judged deserving of death but spared because he was so ignorant and under the control of his violent vigilante brother-in-law, James Gaines. Norris, however, was barred from ever holding public office again. Stripped of its political rhetoric, this amounts to a very convenient way for an accused murderer to clear the court docket of charges against him.[29]

Bean sent Candace's deposition to Austin on December 31 from the Trinity River, with a long letter on the fast-developing situation at Nacogdoches, which is quoted fully below.

> With this I send you a proven certificate Declerid Before esq. Grisham it is in english you will Do me the favour to translate this and send it on this is a favour that I Ever shall esteem that woman was maried to Pamer But when she hear of my coming on shee left him and has given him a bill of sail on all my stock of catel and hogs Mr. hais [Hayes] that was the magistrit that staited

> she swore shee was maried to [me] and took the Bill of Sail for my Property Run of[f] when he heard of my Coming and [fled] Past Sabine. I am sir with Dew Respect your Sencer frind Peter Ellis Bean[30]

From this letter, and its personal information, several things are evident. Bean wanted Austin to have a statement from his wife that proved they were not legally married, and he asked Austin to translate it into Spanish and "send it on" to higher authorities. This indicates that Bean was aware of the bigamy charges against him. Also evident is that Bean had stopped by his house to learn what had happened to his wife and his property as well; the sentence "shee left him" indicates that Parmer and Candace had parted ways and neither of them was at his place. But someone was there to tell Bean how former Alcalde Hayes had come into possession of his livestock before heading for Louisiana. Bean clearly had some friends in the neighborhood, regardless of which side they were taking in the rebellion.

Apart from attending to his personal affairs, Bean was actively sowing discord among both the Anglo rebels and the Indians whom Richard Fields and John Dunn Hunter were trying to rally to the Fredonian cause. Bean's letter of December 22—addressed to Elisha Roberts, a leading citizen of Ayish Bayou—has already been given. He wrote Chief Fields on December 26. According to the entry in his notebook quoted by Yoakum, Bean sent it to the Cherokee chief by "an express," meaning a fast rider. Two days later Bean sent another express to Ayish Bayou and a spy to Nacogdoches.[31] In his letter to Austin of December 31, he copied one received from Roberts.

> I Recived your frendly letter under the Date of the 22nd of the Present month you tell me you are surprised to hear of the Disturbans in the Neighourhood and Nacodoches it apears at Preasnt imposibel to say which side to take to save our families and Property it appears at Prasant the onley corse to pursue is to lie still and take no Pert on no side the People of this [district] Intendid to try to Put Down the Rebellion untill they was eformid that the Ingins had Joynid them they then came home and is Pasing thier familey and Property over the Sabean as fast as posibel as they are not abel to contend with the Combind Ingins But the Peopel is very much Devidid thare is not more than 30 americans of the Rebel Perty But the Ingins is of a grait number Shawneys Dillaways Socks and quicapus and Cheris all those [that] have Movid in this quarter so it is almost emposibel to do any thing Elisha Roberds[32]

Bean, apart from trying to disengage Chief Fields and Hunter from the Fredonians, also had agents active among the tribes they claimed to represent. These efforts were paying off. The Cherokee leaders had returned to their villages for ratification of the treaty of alliance signed at Nacogdoches on December 21, but they encountered opposition. Some of the tribes were away on hunting expeditions, and the Kickapoos—who despised all white people—were unwilling to join the alliance with the Fredonians. There was a division even among the Cherokees, one that Bean exploited in the coming weeks. As he told Austin in his December 31 letter, to put out the fire of rebellion, the Indians had to be detached from Haden Edwards and his insurgent force.

> I also wrote to Richard fields and Dr. Hunter fields Did not Rite me But sent me word that I was to[o] late if he had of saw me one month sooner Perhap we might of come upon tirms that is all the satisfaction he gave me.
>
> But if Mr Sauceda will come as quick as posibel on Perhaps we can make a compremise with the Ingins for they are all that is to be feard they ame at marching to Sn Antonio if some thing is not quickly done, also from your coloney they have Recived letters that states you cant Raise 30 men they will all Join them as I have found out those letters is from esqr. Commins and aman By the Name of Buckner . . .
>
> So my Dier sir the onley way to stop this is to come [send] forward Señor Sauceda and give them lands or the Countrey will [be] entirely lost if we can Brake of[f] the Ingins the thing is setled you will hurry Sausada and let him [k]now what I Right you.[33]

Bean's concern with the prompt arrival of a military force under Political Chief Saucedo and Colonel Ahumada—not to mention the subject of land titles for the Indians—was well merited. They had been delayed in San Antonio until December 13, not reaching San Felipe until January 3, 1827. Rains, bad weather, and flooded conditions caused them to rest and regroup in Austin's town for three weeks, during which time they wrote a ream of letters to their superiors about needed reinforcements. They also wrote the principal conspirators in the revolution, urging them not to oppose Mexican rule and even offering amnesty to those who laid down their arms. Not until January 22 would Saucedo's troops march for the Trinity, where Austin was to join them with militiamen from his colony.[34]

Meanwhile, Colonel Bean had been busy. During the first week of January, he wrote letters to Haden Edwards and Richard Fields. He told

Edwards, "with whom he had not the honor of being acquainted," that the political chief had granted amnesty to all persons who had taken up arms and assailed the Mexican political authorities. Austin had cooperated in securing this pardon. Bean urged Edwards to desist from further hostile movements. It was not too late, he said, and past errors could be forgotten. A rupture with the Mexican nation, "to whom I have the honor to belong, must prove fatal to you." Bean wisely warned the former empresario that prudence should suggest to him that what could be obtained as a favor from the government ought not to be demanded by force. In closing, Bean asked Edwards to communicate his future intentions.[35]

To Fields, he said that it had never been the government's intention to do an injustice to him. Bean understood that Fields, on his trip to Mexico City in 1822–23, had been told to return to Coahuila y Texas and apply for the lands that best suited him. If Fields had not sought possession of those lands in legal form, he could hardly blame the government. Further, if Fields had subsequently engaged the services of persons to represent his interests in the Mexican capital (meaning Hunter), "and did not succeed as you expected," it was because his agents lacked the proper credentials and consequently the government doubted whether they were really sent by him. Bean, who was in Mexico City pushing his own land project at the time Hunter was doing the same for the Cherokees, knew whereof he spoke. The fact that they both returned to Texas at the end of 1826 makes one wonder if the two men spent time traveling together. Even if they did not, Bean was surely aware that Hunter's efforts in Mexico City had gone unrewarded.

This was a very delicate business, Bean assured Fields. Any premature rupture with Mexico "would bring serious evils upon us." The troops of the Republic of Mexico stationed in the Department of Texas "and which I have the honor to command," were adverse to the shedding of their fellow citizens' blood—especially the blood of the Cherokees or any of their allied tribes. He asked Fields to meet him at the upper crossing of the Trinity River for a conference between himself, Saucedo, and Austin. "I dare say that you would not be displeased with the results." Bean reemphasized that the Mexican government had not the "remotest idea of declaring war against the Cherokees or other tribes with which they were allied." He closed by saying that he had written "with my usual frankness," confident that Fields as a man of honor would inform him of his sentiments. In all likelihood, Bean met Chief Richard Fields before his trip to Mexico in mid-1825. Otherwise, Fields would not have known anything about Bean's plainspoken "frankness."[36]

On January 4 Bean sent a fast express to Austin from the "Natches." Again he urged the troops to come forward and reported that the Fredonian forces were divided, the Indians as well.

> I came Back to this Place as I found out that those Rascals is Braking of[f] from Nacodoches at this time thar is a guard of 12 men onley in the stone house I wish you to hurry on the troop as fast as Posibel for now is our time Before the Ingins geather But by a leter that I Recived this Day from samuel Noris I find the Ingins is also Devidid and it apears that they wont be hear bary shortly but the troop must hurry all that they can at Mr. Comins at the trinity River — thare is two caggs of Powder and two Pigs of lead you will see that they are taken and Brought on By the troops as that articul will Be wantid hear you will let the Commander [k]now the contents of my leter your friend and Ser[van]t. Pedro Ellis Bean[37]

Historian Henry S. Foote has questioned why Bean, with this information on the scanty force at Nacogdoches, did not immediately ride with the men available to him and capture the Old Stone Fort, either killing those who resisted or putting them to flight. The answer lies with the Indians, and the possibility that they would reinforce the few white men who still occupied Nacogdoches. Bean had not yet broken off the leadership of the Cherokees or met with the other tribes. Until this was accomplished, he was reluctant to force an engagement that might lead to a hasty and shrill tocsin involving the Indians under Fields and Hunter.[38]

Samuel Norris did not have Bean's caution. Shortly after his letter to Bean, Norris rode into town "with a drum beating and the National Standard of the Mexican Republic unfurled." With him were about seventy local Mexicans and ten or twelve Americans of the old-settler stripe. Their purpose was to arrest the Edwards brothers and reestablish Mexican authority, the authority they had earlier lost to Parmer and his rebels. Parmer commanded only about fifteen men, plus a few Cherokees under Hunter. Nonetheless, he charged the attacking loyalists and within ten minutes had routed them. Although this was to be the Fredonians' last victory, it showed that a five-to-one advantage did not necessarily mean that the rebels could be defeated. Far from being a shirker or a coward, as Foote implied, Bean was smart enough to await developments with the Indians that he knew were essential to "putting out the fire" of rebellion.[39]

These developments came on January 25, when Bean had a meeting with chiefs of the Cherokee, Shawnee, Delaware, and Kickapoo tribes. He induced them to stay loyal to Mexico, no doubt with the argument that their long-sought lands would be given to them by a grateful nation. Bean reported that he persuaded them that they had been deceived by Fields, and the chiefs agreed to kill him and arrest Hunter.[40] Later events show that Bowl and Big Mush (Gatunwali) were the main leaders in this Cherokee decision. There does not seem to be evidence that Bean paid them money to eliminate Fields and Hunter, although Bean later filed a claim on "debts" he had incurred (118 pesos) in putting down the "fractious ones" at Nacogdoches prior to Ahumada's arrival.[41] This could have been money Bean spent for council gifts, as was the custom. Bowl and Big Mush probably attended to this business themselves, because of the compromising position that the actions of Fields and Hunter had placed the Cherokees in. They, by joining the Fredonians prior to any tribal council called on the subject, had virtually doomed hopes that the Mexican government would put the Cherokees in possession of land in Texas. Now, Bean had restored their hope.[42]

After this arrangement was made, Bean moved quickly. He had seventy American volunteers, including thirty-five men of Austin's militia who had joined him on the Trinity by January 26. He rode at the head of this force to the Neches and on to Nacogdoches, where he found that the rebels had already made a "hurried escape." This occurred on the evening of January 28, when the last rebels left in town abandoned their fortification and fled to the Sabine. Bean pursued them hotly, stopping in the Ayish Bayou settlement only long enough to detain three suspicious characters and put them in the custody of John A. Williams, who already had six other men under arrest.[43] Thus the Fredonian Rebellion collapsed, due in no small part to the activities of Col. Peter Ellis Bean. Not only had he performed the duties of a soldier, but he had made an important beginning to his commission as an agent among the Indian tribes of east Texas.

Chapter 6

AFTERMATH OF REBELLION

BEAN, FROM YEARS OF hard experience, was aware that gaining military distinction was different from receiving recognition for it. Consequently, he wrote a number of letters to people all along the pecking order to make sure they knew how his contribution had turned the tide. One of these letters to Commandant General Bustamante was even published in a Mexico City newspaper under Bean's name, spreading the word that the rebellion fomented by ungrateful foreigners had been put down and Texas was still attached to the Mexican nation.[1] Bean initiated this "public relations" campaign with a letter of February 7 to military commandant Ahumada.[2] This was a day before Colonel Ahumada was able to march uncontested into Nacogdoches with part of the 12th Permanent Battalion, colors flying and martial music blasting as if it were a victory parade. Political Chief Saucedo was in the entourage and soon set about restoring order.

Both Bean and Ahumada wrote the commandant general on February 9, providing a summary of events that had preserved the integrity of Mexican territory. Ahumada admitted that Bean had played a considerable role, pursuing the rebels all the way to the Sabine. Bean's letter recounted how he had placed four Indian tribes in "complete peace and tranquility," separating them from the men who had stirred them up. "At the same time I arranged that the life of the leader Fields would be taken, and I still have hope that they will bring me Hunter, who is fleeing with the rebels." This done, he was then free to ride at the head of "the 70 volunteers who were quartered at my own house on the Neches."[3]

Upon reaching Nacogdoches, they found the town abandoned by the enemy, owing to their realization that Bean had subverted the tribes upon which they had "counted [as allies] and placed all their hopes." Bean's volunteers chased the rebels to the border of the United States. Once there, he had asked permission of the commandant at Fort Jesup to continue in pursuit of those who had escaped. Bean even enclosed a copy of the officer's reply, giving his name as "Isac Mane, Colonel of the 7th Regiment." Colonel Many professed ignorance of any revolutionists crossing the Sabine to enter U.S. territory but said he would send someone to investigate the allegation. If verified, "I shall immediately impede these vile, unauthorized plans." This was diplomatic doublespeak. Before and after the Fredonian Rebellion, former and/or present U.S. citizens regularly passed within sight of Fort Jesup, either bearing arms for the trouble in Texas or fleeing from it.

Then Bean shifted to the subject of a war against the Comanches, using the services of the tribes that he had formed an agreement with. "In my conversation with the Indians, I touched on the point of their making war on the Comanches, and they offered me their services, as that was what they desired. In another council that I shall have with them, I will deal with all the particulars and inform Your Excellency of the results. We now have peace and tranquility in this country, which I have achieved with my activities to the benefit of the Fatherland."[4] Modesty was not one of Peter Ellis Bean's notable characteristics. And now, with the bigamy controversy swirling around him, he could not afford the luxury of being modest even had he been so inclined.

But others also spoke favorably of Bean's role in bringing down the insurrectionists. John A. Williams described the colonel's decisive sweep through Ayish Bayou: men were arrested and their property seized. One of them was Adolphus Sterne, who had been on a trip to Louisiana to obtain arms and supplies for the rebels.[5] Unfortunately, Haden and Benjamin Edwards had made their escape to the United States, but neither Richard Fields nor John Dunn Hunter was so lucky. Fields was killed by his fellow tribesmen (some said Choctaws) near the Sabine and Hunter by his supposed Indian friends—all to demonstrate their loyalty to Mexico.[6]

Why did Bean not demand the life of Hunter from the Cherokees, along with that of Fields? For one thing, Hunter was a white man and a literary figure of note, even if he looked and acted like an Indian. It would have been against the racial/cultural standards of the era for Bean to engineer the killing of a man of this class by Indians. The Cherokees, under tribal law, routinely imposed the death penalty on their own, but —to them—killing a white man was another matter entirely. Only if they regarded Hunter as having betrayed their trust would a council agree to rub him out. It is also possible that Bean and Hunter had become friends in Mexico City, and Bean sympathized with this white-man-turned-Indian who was devoting his life to the advancement of Indian land claims in Mexican Texas. One writer has said that Bean tried to assist Hunter in achieving this goal, but the available documentation gives us no satisfactory answer.[7] In any case, the celebrated "Dr." John Dunn Hunter would trouble Mexico no more.

His friend Herman Mayo—a newspaper editor then living at Nacogdoches and coauthor of the Declaration of Fredonian Independence—wrote, in 1827, a touching account of Hunter's assassination. He claimed that Hunter had met his end on a creek near an Anadarko village while trying to return to Nacogdoches and valiantly fight on without help of the Indians who had spurned his alliance. In Mayo's words, it was a tragic fate for a man who deserved better. Herman Mayo no doubt considered Col. Peter Ellis Bean responsible for the untimely death of his heroic John Dunn Hunter.[8] So have later historians—whether they be supporters of the Indian position or those sympathetic to the goals of the larger Fredonian Rebellion itself.

Rather than going to the Sabine, Martin Parmer headed west with his son Isom, intending to hide out with friends in Gonzales until the excitement died down. This he did, but word came that he had best get out of Texas; it was too risky for his friends to protect him. Taking Isom and a guide, Parmer made his way east off the beaten path. William P. Zuber, who later married into the Parmer clan, tells one of those "great-if-it's-true" yarns about the Ring-Tailed Panther's escape.[9] Colonel Bean, Parmer learned when reaching the Neches crossing, was tearing up the roads with fifty soldiers to capture him. When Parmer asked the ferryman (who did not recognize his passengers) if Bean had a warrant for the arrest of this man, the ferryman replied: "No, he needs no warrant. Parmer is an outlaw and any man who finds him has a right to arrest him without a warrant." Parmer, it should be noted, was one of those four Fredonian rebels who had been excluded from the general amnesty because of the gravity of their activities.[10]

Parmer then asked the unsuspecting ferryman if he wished Bean success. When he replied "I do," Parmer said, "Perhaps you would like to arrest Parmer yourself?" Again came a yes answer, and the ferryman avowed that if he could find the wanted man, "I would *show* him that I could." This was more impudence than Parmer could stand. He revealed his identity to the aghast fellow, cocked and aimed his rifle to send him on an eternal boat ride down the river Styx. Isom grabbed the gun and tried to wrestle it out of his father's hands, assisted by the guide. Had not the ferryman poled his boat back across the Neches and fled into the brush during this scuffle, Martin Parmer would have had the blood of another man besides Nick Trammell's half brother on his hands. Parmer eventually made his way to the Louisiana frontier and stayed there until Mexican rule—and the prospect of his being brought to justice as a murderer under its authority—was finished.[11]

Even while Bean was being praised in the excitement of victory, the political chief was busily complying with his orders to determine Bean's marital status. On February 12 he wrote the governor as follows: "Through my own efforts I have found out that Colonel D. Pedro Elias Bean, established on the Neches River, was married according to the laws of the United States to a woman of that country; and because of [his] having mistreated her in his actions, she abandoned him and went to the other side of the Sabine River, carrying with her a child and leaving the other of the two which they had to the Colonel."[12] Moreover, Felipe Músquiz had told him that Bean was legally married to a woman in Jalapa. Saucedo promised to forward more information as it came forth. By March 19 he was able to do so, and two documents were sent. One was a copy—certified by Samuel Norris, now reestablished as the Nacogdoches alcalde—of Candace's deposition that she had never been lawfully married to Bean. She placed her "X" on the document before Norris on February 26.[13]

The other deposition was executed by the administrator of mails, Patricio de Torres, on February 15. Because of his reference to a "confidential" letter of the past November, it is certain that Torres was the spy that Saucedo had designated to collect impartial evidence on Bean and watch his movements.

> Since I came to this place I have known Señor Don Pedro Elías Bean as a married man, having a wife and two small children; the said señor recognized and gave the necessary means of maintenance and needed articles of apparel to his wife and two children until the day of his departure for Mexico, placing his interests and house under the administration of his wife. I have received a letter from the aforesaid Colonel Bean in which there was enclosed one for his wife, entreating me to have it handed to her, which I did.
>
> His wife having news, by word of mouth, that the señor Elías Bean was married in the land abroad, or rather not having any news of her husband over so long an absence, she married Col. Parma [Parmer]; and as soon as certain news was known of señor Elías Bean, she separated from said Parma. Coming to his house, Col. Don Pedro Elías Bean mistreated his wife with sticks and blows and chased her out of his house. Dispossessed of all her goods and furnishings, she passed through this village and told her troubles to trustworthy persons, saying to them that she was the legitimate wife of the aforesaid [Bean] and that she viewed him as [her] legitimate husband, and that her documents [to prove it] existed in [North] America.[14]

Thus, Saucedo was sending contradictory evidence on Bean to the governor. Candace's own words stated that she was not legally married to Bean and had only said so earlier because Alcalde Norris threatened to put her in jail. Her reason for giving false testimony was simply to secure ownership of Bean's property in case he never returned. The fact that the Neches alcalde, Demetrius Hayes, had wound up with Bean's cattle and hogs, before absconding with them, certainly suggests that Candace's first deposition was coerced. Then a well-respected citizen who seemingly had no personal grudge against Bean, Postmaster Patricio de Torres, had made it clear that the colonel's homecoming was not a happy one. Bean had vented his anger against her in what we now call spousal abuse and driven the poor woman out of their house with little more than the clothes on her back. She probably took her infant daughter with her and left the five-year-old boy with the colonel. And this from a man who had been wrapped in the fond embrace of another woman—also his wife—in Mexico every chance he got! But the couple later reconciled long enough for another child to be conceived.

Bean, perhaps in an attempt to salvage something of his property, sold to Mary Ronald all his stock of hogs, marked or unmarked "that runs with them on the Said warters whare Said Bean Livid." Hayes may have missed some of Bean's razorbacks rooting around in the Neches River bottom, but the price of this sale went unrecorded as did Mary's success in her porker roundup.[15]

Hardly had the dust settled when Bean took the opportunity on February 25 to respond to Commandant Ahumada's query as to his commission. He said that, by the Supreme Government's orders, he was in Nacogdoches to fulfill the following commission: to pacify the Indian towns of that frontier; to learn what force could be counted on from the civilized tribes in a war with the Comanches and other barbaric nations that had broken the peace with the Mexican nation; to see what plans could be made to cut off commerce from the north (i.e., from traders based in the United States) with the Comanches, and how this might be best effected; to inform himself where the friendly tribes could be placed *with benefit to Mexico's interests;* to investigate which tribes should be admitted to settle in the republic; and to determine "what class of sacrifice" Mexico should make to gain the friendship of those Indian nations who had emigrated from the United States.[16] The phrase about benefiting Mexico's interests has been emphasized because it governed all of Bean's conduct with these tribes in the coming years.

Several days later Bean shed more light on his business in Texas by producing a copy of Pres. Guadalupe Victoria's eleven-point memo on what Bean was to accomplish on the frontier. It embraced many functions, and maintaining good relations with the Indians was only part of his job. General Terán, in light of his anticipated boundary survey, probably helped formulate the items of concern. This memo is summarized as follows:

1. To learn the "origin of possession" of both nations (Mexico and the United States?) and their projects toward the present settlements, north to south;
2. To investigate the defense of Mexico's "external line" by means of cantonments, as well as the placement of towns to mutually aid each other in a manner suitable to military measures, pacifying the Indians, and obtaining other advantages;
3. (To learn?) points of foreign colonization;
4. To cut off commerce of Indians in the northern states and the means to effectuate it;
5. To determine if it was suitable to raise fighting companies of domesticated Indians on behalf of Mexico, with an explanation of their utility and what could be achieved by such means;
6. To investigate which are the preferred points for (colonization by?) nationals;
7. To examine which places should be sustained, or reserved, for the Indians; which ones to admit; and to make a plan of defense that would count on their services;
8. To estimate what force was necessary, between the friendly Indians and the colonists, to pacify the barbaric tribes;
9. To recommend what class of authority Mexico needed between the two nations (on the frontier?);
10. To say what measures should be taken to make our commerce flourish in that land (of northeastern Texas?);
11. To inform the government what sacrifice the Nation should make to win over the Indians of these countries.[17]

There has been some confusion as to whether Bean left Mexico with the commission of Indian agent to the east Texas tribes, or whether he received this position as a reward for his services in the rebellion. While Bean's success with the Cherokees no doubt contributed to solidifying and extending the term of his work among the tribes of Texas, there is little question that his discussions in the Mexican capital had convinced the president and his advisers that Bean was capable of handling Indian affairs on the frontier in Mexico's best interest. He reiterated his ability to unite the immigrant tribes into an effective force against the Comanches in his petition for empresarial rights in the boundary reserve. Likewise, his North American heritage would make him the logical person to deal with the problem of squatters who were flooding across the border. Bean was not a "man without a country," but rather a man with two countries. His service during the Mexican Revolution had satisfied the top officials in the government that Bean could be trusted with duties in Texas that other North Americans might have performed with less devotion to their adopted nation.

On February 27, 1827, Bean petitioned Political Chief Saucedo for a grant of land on the margins of the Neches to the north. He wished to cultivate this league of land as a "settler." Compared to Bean's request to be an empresario, this petition for the land he already occupied breezed through. Governor Blanco ordered that he be given a league of land on April 6, even though Alcalde José María Mora did not appoint a surveyor (James Gaines) until August 6, 1828. Gaines finished the survey a week later.[18] Bean's original grant of a square league can still be seen on General Land Office maps of Cherokee County. The Old San Antonio Road crossed the Neches just below Bean's land and ran diagonally through his grant to what later became Alto, thence onward to Nacogdoches.[19] Was this grant a reward for Bean's services in the just-concluded rebellion? Quite possibly, even though he had asked the state government in 1825 to obtain this particular tract of land for his *family,* before going to Mexico City and deciding to expand his efforts to a much larger colonization project. Perhaps Governor Blanco thought Bean would be satisfied with a mere 4,428 acres and drop his empresarial ambitions. If so, he did not know Peter Ellis Bean.

On the same day, February 27, 1827, the colonel's "nephew" William Bean also petitioned the political chief for a *sitio* of land on the Neches to the northeast. It was likewise approved by the governor and surveyed by James Gaines in 1828. His field notes and plat map of the survey show that the grant was on the creek called Arroyo de las Salinas (Salt Creek), or, as later styled, Las Salinillas (Little Salines, or Little Salt Creek). Because the two grants to the two Beans were applied for, conceded, and surveyed at the same time, there has been much confusion on which grants were where—something of a puzzle.[20] The puzzle is worth our attention because William and/or Peter Ellis wanted to locate this league on the famed Neches Saline. It was in what is now southwestern Smith County, just above the Cherokee County line, and this saline figured significantly into the later disputes between Chief Bowl's tribe and the Republic of Texas, as we shall see.[21]

To complicate things, William sold the rights to his league of land to Peter Ellis on November 17, 1827. Had he decided to leave Texas, or did he think his "uncle"—being an officer in the Mexican army—would have better luck in getting approval for the tract? The latter explanation is unlikely, as Governor Blanco had already approved William's petition on April 6, the same day as Peter Ellis's. Little else is heard of William Bean, so perhaps he had concluded that things did not suit him in such an unstable place as Texas. If he was the colonel's brother, William M. Bean

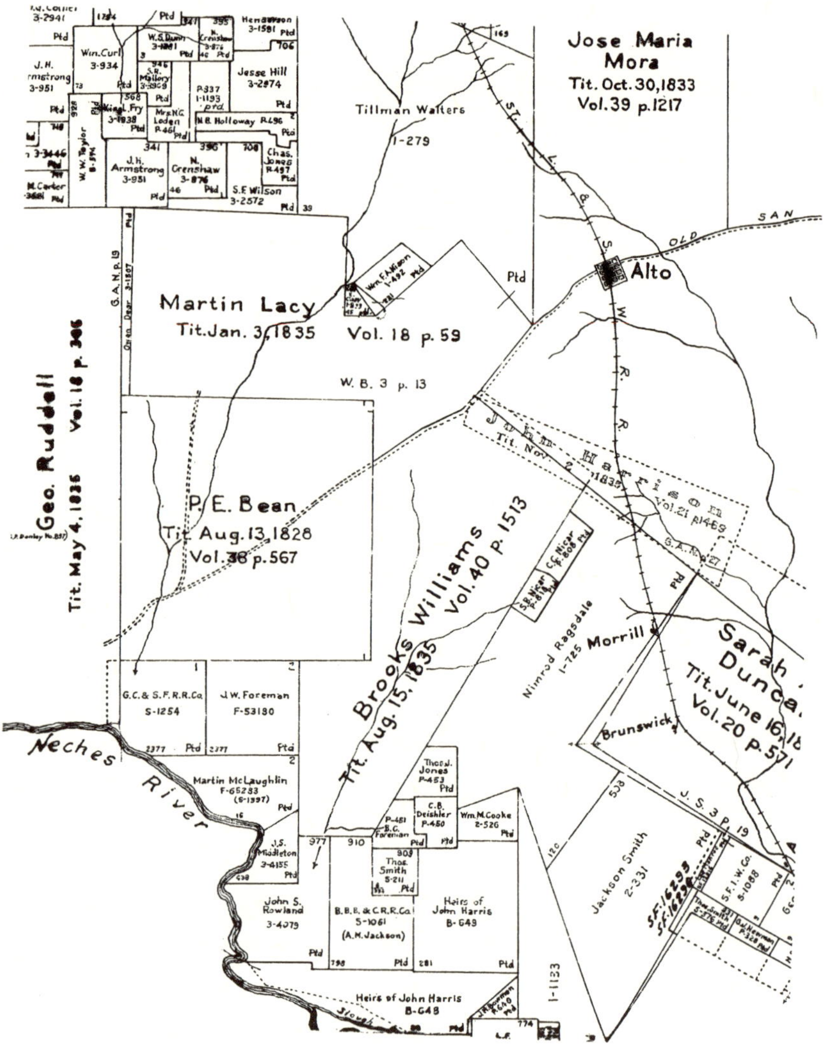

Bean's original league of land in Cherokee County.
Courtesy Texas General Land Office.

born in 1785, he died in Scott County, Illinois, in 1867. The signature on his original land petition contains no middle initial to help resolve this question.[22]

Be that as it may, when title was conferred to this Saline League on September 24, 1828, it was in the name of Peter Elías Bean. Signing the deed of title were Alcalde José María Mora and James Gaines, along with witnesses Luis Prosela and José Pineda. No matter whether William Bean had stayed or gone, Peter Ellis Bean was now the legal owner of the saline—or so he thought.

Finally, on February 27 Bean asked that he be paid the field compensation due him according to his rank. Although Ahumada forwarded Bean's request to the commandant general, saying that in his judgment the petition was "just," it resulted in a debate about whether or not officers on campaign against the Indians were entitled to these "gratifications" in addition to their regular pay. They were rather like a modern per diem travel allowance, amounting to twelve reales (1.5 pesos) for each day spent in the field. It would be quite some time before Bean learned the decision, or actually received anything that he claimed was owed him on the march to Texas.[23]

As proof that Bean had worked miracles among the Indians, Chiefs Bowl and Big Mush with seven other Cherokees visited Nacogdoches on February 28, 1827, and presented themselves to Saucedo. They declared that they wished to live in peace and harmony with the Mexicans, announcing that they had killed Chief Richard Fields and John Dunn Hunter. They brought with them Hunter's pistol, some papers, and the Fredonian flag that Fields had displayed in his house.

Colonel Ahumada forwarded the revolutionary papers and flag to Commandant General Bustamante on March 11, assuring him that both chiefs had pledged obedience and loyalty to Mexico but also noting that the Cherokees were anxiously awaiting formal title to the lands they occupied. He called Mohs [Mush] and Buls [Bowl] civil and war chiefs, respectively, and said that they had "agreed to and given orders" to kill Fields and Hunter. Ahumada was in favor of conceding the Cherokees their desired land "in order that the reward may be granted them which they have earned by the valuable services they have rendered, and in view of the fact that they have offered to arrest and deliver the Edwards [brothers] and other leaders of that faction in case they should cross to this side of the Sabine and visit their village."[24]

Bustamante's reply, from La Bahía, was about as close to an approval for Cherokee land claims as the tribe would ever get.

> With your note of the 11th of March last, I received the documents and revolutionary flag mentioned. It is with pleasure that I learn of the complete restoration of public tranquility in that district, and that the honor of our Government and the Mexican flag is still unsullied. The death of the treacherous demagogues, Fields and Hunter, is certainly a very fortunate circumstance for the happiness of the tribes who had been enticed by them into rebellion, as well as for the security and peace of the territory which they claimed to rule.
>
> I have especially recommended to the Supreme Government the merits of Mohls [Mush] and Buls [Bowl], who commanded a breach of the pledge with said visionaries and offered to arrest for you the

> Edwardses and as many of the rebels as recrossed the Sabine to stir up the tribes. I have also recommended the application of these Chiefs for land, for the regular settlement of their tribe, and doubt not but that it will be done by the Supreme Government. I hope you will induce them to settle where they may live happily and contribute to the permanent and profitable pacification of the Comanches, assisted by our [military] forces and fellow citizens of Béxar.[25]

Bustamante suggested that the most fertile territory, and the one best suited for the attainment of both objectives, was the valley of the San Sabá. But if the Cherokees should insist that lands be granted them on the northeastern frontier, where they presently lived, "let it be where it best serves the interests of the Mexican Republic, consulting as far as possible the welfare of the Cherokees, to whose present Chiefs you will offer the assurances of my particular esteem." He asked to be informed with regard to their selection of lands, so he could present their claim to the president in due form.

In addition to this letter of commendation for the Cherokee leaders that had remained loyal to Mexico, Bustamante wrote a letter to Ahumada thanking him for his forced march to Nacogdoches in difficult conditions "without forgetting our worthy fellow-citizens Bean, Austin, Williams, and other persons who contributed largely to the success of that important undertaking."[26] On April 7 Bustamante wrote Austin a personal thanks, mentioning Colonel Bean as the other individual whose services in putting down the rebellion he was going to bring to the attention of the Supreme Government.[27]

Austin, seemingly, had avoided his worst nightmare: that the Indians would unite to pillage his colony, and that Mexico would consider his settlers no more loyal than the rebellious Anglos at Nacogdoches. Bean's place on the frontier had also been made more secure. He could only hope that his performance would lead to approval of his colonization scheme. Haden Edwards was now out of the way, so there should be no problem with extending his border-zone domain westward to the Neches, if not the Trinity.

The situation at Nacogdoches was so stabilized that Saucedo left for San Antonio on April 6, arriving there on May 4. Colonel Ahumada reached San Antonio a few days earlier, having stopped at La Bahía to consult with Commandant General Bustamante about Indian problems.[28] Ahumada, it seems, was still concerned with the role that Bean was going to be exercising in Indian affairs and how it would conflict with his own authority. In a letter to Bustamante on April 16 he conceived the idea of forming a *junta* to deal with the Indians, composed of himself, Austin, Lt. Col. Francisco Ruiz, and Benjamin Milam. Bean was not on his list.[29] Colonel Ruiz had been left at Nacogdoches in command of the 12th Permanent Battalion, along with Captains Cosío and Roxo. It amounted to 129 men and nine officers, enough to foil any intentions that the Fredonians had of making more trouble. Colonel Bean, of course, was there too in case the Indian alliance unraveled. The old settlers started drifting back, regardless of which side they had taken in the rebellion, and life returned to normal in the Piney Woods.

Chapter 7

A MULTITUDE OF INDIANS

GENERAL ANASTASIO BUSTAMANTE had left his headquarters in Monterrey and traveled to Texas to be on hand in suppressing the Fredonian Rebellion should it flare out of control. By the time he reached La Bahía early in 1827, however, the revolt was on its last legs. This collapse left Bustamante in a position to devote time to his real interest, which was regulating the Indian affairs of Texas—whether it be through war or peace negotiations with the diverse tribes that now inhabited the expanses of the state. This was not a new realm for Bustamante, as he had signed treaties of peace with the Lipan Apache and the Comanche nations under the empire of Emperor Agustín de Iturbide, prior to the formation of a republic.[1]

To understand the situation that Bustamante faced—as well as that of the men who would have to deal with this Indian situation on a face-to-face basis, such as Peter Ellis Bean—a brief review is necessary.[2]

During the eighteenth century, tribes now considered "native" to Texas had retarded the province's growth and restricted settlement to small enclaves around San Antonio de Béxar, La Bahía del Espíritu Santo (Goliad), and Nacogdoches, the latter of which was not established until 1779 and the former two around 1720. In this period most of the trouble came from Karankawan groups on the coast and Apaches in the interior, the Lipans in particular. The Caddoan groups in east Texas, including those around later Nacogdoches, were mostly peaceful agriculturists although they resisted the missionization process and kept to their villages. On the coast around Galveston Bay were the Orcoquiza, with the Bidai—possibly a related group—inland from them. Neither tribe was regarded as capable of much mischief. In south Texas the Indians were largely Coahuiltecan subgroups, who were not considered a serious threat to the Spaniards and who formed the majority of mission converts. Epidemic disease kept their numbers low and required the missionaries to constantly seek new neophytes.

This situation changed when the Comanches entered Texas from the north around 1720 and began to exert pressure on the Apaches, forcing them southward out of the prime buffalo habitat on the plains. Soon after San Antonio was founded in 1718, the Apaches began to menace the settlement. By 1730 they were stealing the presidio's horse herd from outlying pastures on the lower Cibolo; sometimes their raids were in the town itself. Although a treaty was made with them at midcentury, the Apaches continued to be a threat to ranchers in the region. They were still decimating mission herds of cattle on the coastal plains at the close of the century.

Meanwhile, Wichita groups were making their way across the Red River into north-central Texas. They included the tribes later known as Wacos, Tawakonis, and Taovayas—all of which were still considered a menace to Anglo colonization in the nineteenth century. It appears that the Tonkawas were not native to the central Texas region but had fled north from Coahuila and Nuevo León in the colonial period and congregated at a place on the Brazos River called "Ranchería Grande." By the time we are considering, they were regarded as a contemptible and indolent small tribe that stayed near the Anglo settlements to escape the wrath of their many enemies. Also in this mix were the Quichas/Kichais, later called "Keechis," Ionis, Anadarkos, and several splinter groups of the Southern Caddos near Nacogdoches. The Taovayas, who mostly remained in their fortified villages on the Red River, later were known as the Towash. The spelling of names for these various groups was usually irregular in Spanish- and Mexican-period documents and remained so once Anglos began referring to them in English.

As the nineteenth century commenced, a whole different set of Indians began to make their way into Texas from the United States, although much of the territory they came from was still owned by Spain. The first arrivals were from the Southeast, tribes such as the Choctaws, Chickasaws, Creeks (often called Muskogees), Alabamas, Coushattas, and Biloxis. Other small groups such as the Seminoles eventually made their way to Texas. But the immigrant tribes that Indian agent Bean usually had to deal with had come from the Northeast, mostly because of pressure from westward-expanding Americans such as his own people. These tribes, starting about 1820, included the Shawnees, Kickapoos, Delawares, and especially the border Cherokees. As seen, all had figured into the Fredonian Rebellion with the dire prospect that Chief Richard Fields and John Dunn Hunter could unite them on behalf of the Fredonians. These various tribes had established themselves north of Nacogdoches, mostly between the Trinity and Sabine Rivers but all the way up to the Red River. They were generally referred to as "the Cherokees and their allied nations" because of the influence that various Cherokee spokesmen had on them at councils called through the years.

By contrast, the Southeastern tribes preferred to remain in the woodlands between the Trinity and the Sabine, south of Nacogdoches. They had no particular spokesman in a united sense, although the Coushattas were often considered the most important tribe for reaching a consensus of opinion. Usually Mexican officials, and later Texan officials, had to deal with these tribes individually. They were mostly a pacific people, devoting themselves to farming, stock raising, and hunting. Peter Ellis Bean, though stationed at Nacogdoches, was often called upon to assist them in various ways. His main duties, however, involved the Cherokees and "allied tribes" in terms of their usefulness to campaigns against the feared Comanches. Since the Comanche range lay westward, north of San Antonio in the plains and hill country, their depredations did not usually affect the east Texas settlements, or even Austin's colony along the Brazos. In this region the feared tribes were the Wacos and Tawakonis. Thus they became the key players and major concern, lest they ally themselves with the Comanches—as they had the previous century in terms of both warfare and trade. Their combined strength would have enabled them to desolate the Anglo settlements, which were already creeping up the Brazos and Trinity watersheds to threaten the Indian way of life. They occupied lands too fertile for cotton planters to resist.

How numerous were these tribes? The figures, as we shall see, vary for who was giving the estimate and their motive for doing so. High figures usually come from Austin and other empresarios who wanted to call the government's attention to the problem these Indians represented in terms of their colonization efforts to "tame the wilderness" and make it a safe place for the settlers they had contracted to introduce. Little regard for any prior rights of occupation these Indians might have enjoyed was in evidence when the "census" figures were forwarded to officials in Mexico. Most estimates were accompanied by alarming statements on how savage these tribes were and how their influx had to be contained, lest civilization be lost for generations to come. Bean himself, once he got situated in the 1830s, constantly warned the government about the dangers of unrestricted Indian immigration to Texas from the United States. Stephen F. Austin, however, remained the most vocal opponent of the Indians with an intensity bordering on nothing less than paranoia against the "Cultural Other" that they represented.[3]

In 1826, some months before the Fredonian trouble erupted, Chief Richard Fields had asked permission for the Cherokees to make a campaign against the enemy nations of Comanches, Wacos, Tawakonis, and

"Tahuallas" (Taovayas). When Chief Bowl first brought his band of Cherokees to Texas in the winter of 1819–20, they had tried to establish their village on the Three Forks of the Trinity, near the present site of Dallas. The stronger prairie tribes had forced them out, and the Cherokees were obliged to settle about fifty miles north of Nacogdoches. In the next five years, Bowl's core group of sixty warriors and their families was augmented by more Cherokee immigrants, plus the other tribes that had come across the Red River. With their help, Chief Fields wanted to exact some revenge and believed the time was right. Although Political Chief Saucedo in October had ordered Alcalde Norris to give Fields permission for this campaign, the Fredonian Rebellion intervened.[4]

This project, however, remained on the front burner because it was one dear to Bustamante's heart. When he reached La Bahía and was informed that the Fredonian business had been terminated, he wrote a letter to Col. Mateo Ahumada on April 7, 1827, ordering a well-coordinated campaign. Because the Comanches were the most numerous, warlike tribe committing depredations in the settlements of Texas, "it is thus necessary to fight them in their own villages with an energy equivalent to the perfidy and cruelty of their outrages." Ahumada, after consulting those individuals best acquainted with their mode of warfare and the territory inhabited by these Indians, was to submit a plan of campaign. A statement of troops and provisions deemed necessary was needed, along with how these troops should be divided; the direction they should follow; and finally, the number of armed men that could be relied on from Austin's colony and settlers of Nacogdoches.

> Colonel Bean says he can rely on twenty friendly tribes. The Lipans, under their Chiefs Castro and El Cojo, have offered me their services for a campaign against the Comanches, and even against the Tahuacanos and Wacos if these latter refuse to make peace. It would be advisable, under the circumstances, to send a strong division to the Tahuacano village, thence to march against the Comanches, it being immaterial whether that division is received by them as friends or enemies. But I think it best that their fields and villages should in no case be destroyed, because this would reduce them at once to wandering tribes. These have always been more hostile and more prone to break their treaties, for the reason that they have no home and consequently nothing to lose.[5]

The commandant general considered it a good idea to wait until the friendly tribes, and even the Tawakonis, had worked their fields. In the meantime, reinforcements of cavalry that were already underway would have arrived. He wanted Ahumada's plan of campaign as soon as possible, so that it could be communicated to the government for approval of funding.

Bustamante's call for a campaign against the Comanches, using the services of the Wacos and Tawakonis if possible, became a guideline for activities throughout the rest of the year. Ahumada, Austin, and Ruiz had already written letters in February to the Waco and Tawakoni chiefs, inviting them to come in and make a treaty of peace. As noted, on April 16 Ahumada proposed that a *junta* be formed of himself, Austin, Ruiz, and Milam to deal with Indian affairs—an arrangement that would have excluded Bean, even though Bustamante mentioned him as being able to deliver the assistance of twenty friendly tribes. Ahumada's list, we must suppose, included only those men who had some expertise or direct contact with the Comanches.[6]

Lieutenant Colonel Ruiz was the man who best fit this description. During the struggle for independence he was first a Royalist, then supported the rebel side. After the Battle of Medina he fled to Bayou Pierre, Louisiana. For the next eight years Ruiz spent part of his time in Comanche camps or in those of their allies on the plains. After independence was achieved, he was pardoned and commissioned as agent for these tribes. It seems they trusted him as much as any white man. He accompanied a Comanche delegation to Mexico City in 1822, where a peace treaty was made with them on December 13. Bustamante signed for Emperor Iturbide's Mexico on the Comanche treaty, as well as the peace accord reached with the Lipan Apaches at the capital on August 17. In the years following, Ruiz was the recognized Mexican authority for dealing with the Comanches. Ruiz also had good standing among tribes like the Shawnees and their kinsmen from North America.[7]

Benjamin Rush Milam had a little experience with the Comanches, having visited their camps on the Colorado River in 1818 as a trader. Like Bean, he had been involved (to a lesser degree) in the Mexican Revolution and received a colonel's commission from the new government. Mexico gave him a colonization contract fronting the Colorado River in 1825, and he also served as Gen. Arthur G. Wavell's agent for the contract that had been awarded this Englishman in the boundary zone. Wavell's tract was west of the Great Bend of the Red River, bounded to the south by the Sulphur Fork of the Red. It included the raw settlements of Jonesboro and Pecan Point, neither of which was subjected to Comanche raids. On the contrary, trade routes to the Comanche villages ran west from these places.[8]

Milam had just made a report to Ahumada on the district, saying that he found it mostly occupied by Indian families from the north: 300 Shawnee, 110 Kickapoo, 75 "Dilues" (Delaware), 80 Cherokee, and 150 Quapaw—a total of 755 families. At 5 persons per family, Milam estimated that

3,775 Indians were in Wavell's territory, as opposed to the 200 American families clustered around Pecan Point and Jonesboro.[9] Milam and Bean were friends, and they probably helped each other attend to business in the Mexican capital in 1825–26. In fact, Milam's report is of the same date and in the same handwriting as Bean's eleven-point instructions from Pres. Guadalupe Victoria. The government may have intended for them to fulfill these instructions jointly. Or, more likely, Bean may have had Milam make the copy because his handwriting and grammar were better than Bean's, which they assuredly were.

Ironically, Austin—who had less actual dealings with the Comanches than any of the other *junta* members did—was the one who submitted the most elaborate plan for the campaign. He even drew a map of the northern portion of Texas so that his ideas on total warfare against the Comanches and their Plains allies would be more clear. It showed rivers, Indian villages, and routes to be taken by various attack divisions. His campaign plan and map were dated at San Antonio on August 28, 1827.[10] As we shall see, by this time peace talks were well underway and a treaty signed with the Comanches and the two tribes Austin was most concerned about, the Wacos and Tawakonis.

Ruiz, at Nacogdoches, informed Ahumada of the latest developments on April 14. He and Bean were leaving that day for the Keechi village with the object of inviting the Wacos and Tawakonis to make peace. Capt. Mariano Cosío would remain in charge of the troops in town. While the emissaries were in the Keechi village on April 24 and 25, they spoke with two Tawakonis who said that both their people and the Wacos were in favor of peace. This visit would bear fruit in June. On June 2 Ruiz wrote Austin that the chiefs of the Wacos and Tawakonis had appeared in Nacogdoches, with a number of warriors and women, offering to make "a true peace with our government, and that they will never again go on the warpath anywhere, especially in that colony of yours, along the Colorado, etc." The Comanches were also in the mood to do the same, and Ruiz planned to accompany the entire party to San Antonio so that a treaty with all three tribes could be signed with Commandant General Bustamante.[11]

In this letter to Austin, and the correspondence that follows, one can detect something of a rivalry between Ruiz and Bean. Perhaps it was only resentment for the new man on the scene, a brash *norteamericano* who seemed to want all the credit for himself when it came to Indian affairs. Ruiz told Austin he had to go with back with the chiefs because "it has been impossible for me to make them march with Colonel Peter Ellis Bean, who will also perform the same [peacemaking] operation, although he does not have any influence [among them] or greater knowledge." Ruiz expressed the same sentiments to Ahumada the following day, when

Bean was among the gathering of witnesses to the peace proceedings held in the lodging of the military commandant. Ruiz said that the chiefs had demanded that he ride back with them for their meetings with the Comanches because "of the knowledge, esteem, and influence that no one else has in said Nations." They, said Ruiz, opposed his suggestion that Bean accomplish the mission alone because "neither these [tribes] nor the Comanches had knowledge" of Bean.[12] This was probably true, but there is a tinge of condescension in the way Ruiz phrased his remarks about the new Indian agent.

If Ruiz saw the letter that Bean wrote Austin on June 3, no doubt his resentment of Bean intensified.

> Dear Sir I am happy to inform you that yesterday I have maid Pease with the Waco Nesion and tawacanys also the chiefs of Both nasions is now in this Plase you can now treat them as friends and can let your uper setelment [k]now it tommorow I shall start with them to meet the Comanches and gow with them to Sn Antonio to Settel all in this thare is nothing [else] worth your notis to Right you all is quiot
> Peter E. Bean[13]

Bean, in effect, was taking sole credit for the peace made at Nacogdoches and sounding as if he were going to do the same when all the chiefs were paraded into San Antonio. Two weeks later, Commandant General Bustamante wrote Austin that all three tribes had approached *him,* through *his* envoys, to make treaties of peace. He invited Austin to come to Béxar and contribute to the peace process or form a war plan against them if peace failed. Austin then submitted his map and plan for war on a grand scale. In any case, everybody on the scene wanted to take the credit for making peace with the Indians in 1827.[14]

Bustamante was a busy man when it came to making treaties—and war—with Texas Indians. The Karankawas were defeated in a joint action involving the militiamen of three empresarios (Green DeWitt, Martín de León, and Stephen F. Austin), plus troops from La Bahía and other soldiers under Bustamante's command. On May 27 Bustamante signed a treaty with the Karankawas at La Bahía. They were represented by Father Miguel Muro, to whom they had fled for protection, and Chief Antoñito made his mark on the document. It fixed the Indians' eastern range at the Lavaca River—out of Austin's colony. Antoñito promised to bring all the Karankawas and Cocos into a peaceful condition or abandon them to their fate in warfare with the colonists. This treaty, like so many others made with the Karankawas dating back into the colonial period, would not endure.[15]

Watercolor on ivory of Bean, ca. 1815–17. Photo courtesy Robert E. Davis.

The duration of Bean's stay among the Wacos and Tawakonis is uncertain, but the evidence suggests it was well into July. How strange this trip to their Brazos River villages must have been for Bean. He had visited this region with Philip Nolan twenty-six years earlier when he was still wet behind the ears, a lad not out of his teens. They had chased mustangs and traded with these same Indians, the Comanches as well. Then it had all ended on the crisp morning of March 21, 1801, when a Spanish force from Nacogdoches surrounded their mustang pen "fort," killed Nolan, and hauled Bean and his companions off to prison. What memories must have stirred within Bean as he rode through these fertile plains. With such experiences behind him, no wonder that Bean considered himself as good a man as any to negotiate with these tribes.[16] Still, he was not shy about taking credit for whatever gains he made—or helped make—with the Indians.

Prior to this June trip, Bean was mentioned in an incident involving the Cherokees. Ruiz wrote Ahumada on May 14 that he had been visited by Chiefs Big Mush and Bowl with thirty-six warriors of the Cherokee tribe. They were upset because they had heard from John Williams (probably John "Cherokee" Williams rather than the John A. Williams of Ayish Bayou) that the government of Mexico had sent a letter to the "Arkansas," perhaps a letter meant to be published in some Arkansas newspaper. This letter stated that all the Indians who had immigrated into the Department of Texas would be compelled to leave, and that the arrival of Mexican troops was expected to carry out this expulsion. This news had made the Cherokees uneasy.

Williams added that Bean had torn up this letter so it would not reach Arkansas, which made them suspect that the news was true. They were at a loss to understand why the Mexican government would take such a measure against them, and had come to learn if the bad news was true or false. Happily, Williams was in town so Ruiz called him in to explain the situation. Williams said that the Indians had misunderstood him, that the letter had been given to Ben Milam to deliver at Pecan Point or Arkansas, as told to him by Bean. Then the chiefs began talking to Williams in their own language, which he spoke. After this they declared that Williams had been lying about the whole thing, and they would not again listen to any news that did not come directly from the government. They mistrusted these North Americans who were continually deceiving them, but were satisfied that the news of their expulsion was false. The Cherokees, they said, would continue to live in peace with their adopted country, to love and trust the Mexican government. Ruiz's account implies that Bean was one such *norteamericano* whose word the Cherokees could not trust.[17]

The chiefs returned the following day to discuss another matter. They had killed Richard Fields as a traitor and rebel, but his widow and seven young children were left unable to support themselves. Fields had a few cattle, which the family was subsisting on, but he also had left some business debts. The Cherokees feared that holders of these notes might deprive Fields's widow and orphans of their scanty inheritance and leave them destitute. Therefore, they asked that the Mexican government act as a father to these children—who should not be made to suffer for the sins of their father—and exonerate them of his debts. Ruiz could not give them a decision but said that he would hold off any debt collectors until the government ruled on the matter. Finally, Ruiz told Ahumada that the chiefs wanted a "Mexican officer" to visit their village, and he had promised to do so that week as it "will enable me to observe more closely their conduct."[18] Ruiz was clearly undercutting Bean's authority as a representative to the immigrant tribes of east Texas and assuming it himself. How much of this he told Bean about is unknown.

Speaking of authority, Ahumada had written another letter to Commandant General Bustamante on April 16, while they were both huddled at La Bahía discussing Indian policy. Because of how Ahumada's orders to the military commandant at Nacogdoches (Ruiz) might conflict with what Bean was doing, especially with the "barbarous" Indian tribes of the region, he asked Bustamante to specify exactly what Bean's commission involved and the authority that had been conferred on him. Bustamante wrote a marginal note on this request and forwarded it to the War Department.[19] As he already knew the general thrust of Bean's commission, Bustamante probably did so to placate Ahumada, the peevish military commandant of Texas. But Bustamante was also fuzzy about the details, as indicated by his cover letter of April 19.

> I enclose for Your Excellency a written communication in which the Commander of this Department asks what is the commission with which the Citizen Colonel Pedro Elías Bean finds himself on the frontier, so that, with Your Excellency deigning to ask the Most Excellent Sr. President, there may be extended a formal instruction of all the objects of the said commission [to Bean].
>
> Although His Excellency, before my coming to these States, indicated to me verbally that the said leader went charged with obtaining all the possible advantage from the peaceful Indians of the frontier in order to make war on those [tribes] who are harassing us, and to achieve afterward a lasting peace, I do not remember well all that [the President] told me; and desirous of certainty, I would like there to be sent me said instruction in order to satisfy, as much as possible, all the beneficent aims that in this particular [matter] may be proposed by the Supreme Government.[20]

In mid-May a search was made in the war ministry for a copy of Bean's instructions. It was not found, which meant that President Victoria had to be quizzed about the extent of what he had commissioned Bean to do. He probably did not remember either, which would account for his catch-all reply.

On June 19 Bustamante conveyed to Ahumada the letter of the secretary of war and marine, dated a month earlier. It said that the president had been advised of the question concerning Lieutenant Colonel Bean's commission, and "His Excellency orders me to say that this *jefe* [Bean] can be very useful for whatever the commandant general may order, by virtue of the knowledge that he has of the frontier and Indian relations, as [proved by] the incident with the Cherokees, and consequently Your Excellency may occupy him in what is deemed convenient."[21] This was a polite way of saying "President Guadalupe Victoria recognizes Bean's worth, and you had better make good use of him!"

But there was still no word on Bean's empresario status. Any hope that he had of his boundary-zone grant being extended west to the Trinity was dashed when the government gave much of the former Edwards colony around Nacogdoches to David G. Burnet in December 1826. At the same time a German merchant in Mexico City, Joseph Vehlein, received a contract to settle the southern portion of Edwards's grant from Nacogdoches to the coastal reserve.[22] Edwards's son-in-law Frost Thorn had managed to survive the Fredonian Rebellion with the right to colonize the strip of land above Burnet's new grant, northward to the boundary reserve. Wavell's grant extended to the Red River above Thorn's. This flurry of colonization contracts meant that most of the land the Cherokees and their allied tribes were petitioning the government for had now been awarded to empresarios with very little sympathy for their prior claims. Bean's task in maintaining friendly relations with these tribes had suddenly become more difficult.

Moreover, the governorship at Saltillo was in transition. Blanco was gone, and José Ignacio de Arizpe now occupied his place. Arizpe, on April 20, acknowledged receipt of the documents "relative to the marriage of Colonel Don Pedro Elías Bean" that Saucedo had forwarded the past February.[23] This file would go on to Mexico City and be added to Bean's growing bigamy folder. Apart from a letter that another governor wrote in May, evidently in an interim capacity, nothing more was heard on the subject during 1827.

Instead, the War Department focused on the question of pay that was due Bean—231 pesos and odd change—for the months of October, November, and December 1826. It is amazing how much paperwork was generated by this trifling amount of money. Bean, in San Antonio during the summer, applied again for the sum. It represented gratifications from the time he left Saltillo on October 17 until January 20 of the current year, corresponding to ninety-five days at twelve reales each plus thirteen "daily rations." General Bustamante approved the application, saying it was certain that Bean had left Saltillo on the given date for "pacification of the barbarous Indians" and he had performed "good services." Bustamante added, "Also I believe it my [duty] to call the justified attention of Your Excellency, not only toward the good services of [Bean], but with respect to the increased costs that are caused in traveling through these deserts, by reason of the scarcity of foodstuffs and commodities." This amounted to an extra plug for honoring Bean's claim, since a soldier on field duty had to be paid according to military regulations. Bustamante's own expenses in Texas likely prompted this remark.[24]

The lack of a military service record for Bean also became an issue in 1827, no doubt because army men on all sides were challenging his rank, commission, and authority. Bean's service record may also have been needed to expedite payment to him, but one suspects that it was part of the standard procedure for delaying payment to soldiers as long as possible (if baser motives were not involved). He had anticipated problems of this nature before leaving the Mexican capital. On June 7, 1826, Bean complained that although he had received the military rank he asked for, the rightful patent of antiquity had not been conceded to him—in other words, dating back to when he first joined the struggle for independence in November 1810. He asked the secretary of war that the actual commencement of his service be recognized, but the military *junta* had not finished its review. Until then, his formal service record was unavailable to anyone—including the ministry of war.[25]

But the process was moving along. On August 11, 1826, the board ruled that Bean's seniority should be recognized for a total of twelve years, eleven months, and eight days. Of this he served three months and ten days as a "Patriot"; sixteen days as a captain; and twelve years, eleven months, and eight days as an effective lieutenant colonel—of which three years and eleven months were at the rank of brevet colonel. Bean could not receive credit for his time served outside the Mexican republic "because it was [taken] without leave from the Government although it *was* necessitated by the bad condition of the revolution in the whole country. He is a patriot by any standard and worthy of the considerations of Your Excellency because of the utility with which he always has sacrificed himself for our liberty." At the end of 1827 this service was upgraded to thirteen years, eight months, and nine days.[26]

In his request for this record, in a letter written at Béxar, Bean said that "since the last year of '26, the originals of the justificatory documents of my services were turned over by me to the Sr. Brigadier Don Vicente Filisola, who as Commander-General of the State of Mexico passed them on to the head of the Divisional Staff, so that there would be made out for him the corresponding record." But not having this documentation yet, Bean asked that it be completed and remitted "to give fulfillment to the superior order in which it is required of him." Bustamante forwarded this petition to the War Department on August 16, 1827, the same day Bean wrote it. In a marginal note he called Bean's petition "very just."[27]

The reason Bean was in San Antonio the summer of 1827, as suggested by the above discussion, had to do with his mission to the Wichita-related tribes. He and Ruiz found it necessary to pass beyond their villages on the Brazos and negotiate with the tribes living on the upper Trinity as well. The Wichitas told them that it had been "some time" since their young men raided south, and they had decided it was better to end the trouble. In July Ruiz and Bean rode into San Antonio at the head of a large delegation of Wichitas, Caddos, and Southern Comanches. A treaty that has been described as a "cease-fire agreement" was signed with these Indians on July 28. The names of Bustamante, Saucedo, Ahumada, and Ruiz, but not that of Bean, are on this document. He was still not part of the "inner circle."[28]

The Comanche signatories were Chiefs Yncoroy, Quelluna, and Quellucare, who said that their principal chieftains were off fighting the Osages. Thus they could only agree to a suspension of hostilities with the Mexicans until their leaders returned to negotiate a more lasting peace arrangement. In the interim the Comanches promised not to "hurt or insult" Mexicans (which included Anglo citizens of Mexican Texas), and the Mexicans would not visit their villages without a passport. This provision was probably in reference to a defeat that had been inflicted on the Comanches at the river Agua Fria by troops under Capt. Nicasio Sánchez earlier in July, or it could have been designed to keep unauthorized traders from going to their villages. Two months later another ceremony at Comanche Peak (in modern Hood County) brought pledges to end warfare with other Comanche leaders, at least those most accessible to the white men who sought them out. It appeared that progress was being made with the hostile Comanches, and that a warlike combination between them and the Wichitas had been thwarted. But Austin was not so sure, writing his war plan for Bustamante in San Antonio at the end of August.[29]

The empresario had been scheming to launch hostile strikes against the Waco and Tawakoni villages a year earlier. News of this sort of activity usually reached the Indians, so it is amazing that Ruiz and Bean were able to get them to trust peace overtures. Austin, as early as May 1826, put his militia on alert and devised a plan of war to exterminate these tribes. Without consulting Ahumada, he proposed an alliance to the Cherokees, Shawnees, and Delawares. His militia would strike the Waco and Tawakoni villages on the Brazos, while his immigrant Indian allies, on the appointed day, would storm the Tawakoni town at the head of the Navasota.

Austin wanted the campaign to continue until the Taovaya village on the Red River was destroyed. He said that, by engaging in this action, the immigrant tribes would prove their loyalty to Mexico, and perhaps it might give them more hope to be rewarded with legal possession of the land they were occupying—a somewhat cynical reason for trying to enlist the Cherokees to do fighting for his colonists. Ahumada vetoed the alliance, lest the peaceful Indians come to believe that the whites were dependent on them.[30] Austin was still pursuing plans for this campaign at the end of July 1827, even after Bustamante had signed a peace treaty with them at Béxar.

Coincidentally (perhaps), at this very time Austin, Ben Milam, and David Burnet wrote Bustamante a long letter on the dangers that the immigrant tribes posed to the peace and tranquillity of Texas. All three were empresarios, Burnet having received his contract to colonize part of the Edwards grant during the past December. Milam was then mostly involved as an agent for Wavell's grant on the Red River. On March 30, 1827, Milam wrote Austin from Natchitoches, complaining about the news that the Shawnees had the governor's approval to settle around Pecan Point with "all the privaleges of other citizens in cais they cultivait the soil." Milam was not happy with this prospect—or his own as Wavell's agent in luring more settlers to the region. "If this be the cais we may bid adue to our antisapated pleasure for society never will improve under those circumstances. . . . I leave this [town] in the morning for pecoun pint [Pecan Point]. A little Tristy [gloomy] in consiquens of the inducements Extended to the Indians by the Government. I feare they will be a little troublesom to the setelments but I will distroy Every thing like discord as fair as is in my power and hope for a chainge a spedy chainge for the better."[31]

The lengthy petition to Bustamante that Milam cosigned with Austin and Burnet on July 2 was obviously directed toward effecting such a change for the better. It began with a description of U.S. policy toward Indians that had originated with Pres. James Monroe in 1823, whereby all tribes then occupying organized U.S. territory were to be moved west of the Mississippi River. Considering the fertility of Texas, and the lack of Mexican military forces on the frontier, it was only a matter of time until these "barbarians" crossed into Mexican territory: "And we conceive it to be perfectly competent and reasonable for Mexico to protest against the settlement of these Savage Tribes in her immediate vicinity, inasmuch as it must subject that part of her territory bordering on such settlements to an absolute dereliction or render it fit only for the habitation of other Nations of Savages."

Indeed, some of these Indians had already taken up residence "beneath the brighter skies of Texas" and declared their determination not to relinquish their "forcible, uninvited and unauthorized possessions." They were listed by the number of families in each tribe: Shawnee, 550; Kickapoo, 500; Delaware, 250; Cherokee, 80; Quapaw, 150. Supposing 5 souls to each family gave 7,650 Indians, with probably 1,530 of them warriors. If these well-armed Indians were allowed to obtain a permanent foothold in the country, their barbaric kinsmen would follow them just as "the Goth and Vandals swarmed into Italy." But that was not the worst: "Another and very imminent danger connected with this emigration is found in the great probability that these strangers will form at least a temporary alliance with our ancient enemies the Comanches, the Whacoes and the Tawackanies, and combine with those treacherous people to devastate the exposed frontiers of the Republic." Such a combination, they argued, would be "replete with mischief and might require the utmost energies of the nation to suppress it."

If steps were not quickly taken "to arrest the progress of a fearful and growing evil," then all of Texas down to the Rio Grande would fall victim to "the *tomahawk and scalping knife* of a ruthless and savage foe." The three empresarios urged Bustamante to make no "promises of concessions of Lands, either temporary or perpetual, and of offering any other rewards or emoluments, whether it be by military appointments or civic honors, to any of the Chiefs or head warriors of these barbarous Tribes."[32] By this invective we can see that neither Burnet nor Milam wanted Indians on his colonization grant, nor Austin on his projected upper colony. They opposed *any* land for Indians, especially as a reward for their services in the recent Fredonian Rebellion. Even news of Bustamante's plans to give recognition to Chiefs Bowl and Big Mush aggravated them. One wonders how Col. Peter Ellis Bean, as Indian agent to the tribes of east Texas, could have shared much common ground with men so narrow (if not racist) in their thinking about Indians. His job was not an enviable one.

On August 4, only a few days after the signing of the treaty at Béxar, Bean received some articles that indicated his role in the Fredonian Rebellion had been recognized by his old comrade, Pres. Guadalupe Victoria. On that day he signed a receipt for *comisario* Erasmo Seguín, stating that two small boxes had been delivered to him. They contained a pair of golden epaulets, a golden saber tassel, a crimson uniform coat made of wool, a sword belt with guards of gold and an ironwork buckle, and some white cashmere pantaloons with a decorative galloon (sash). Besides this was a "fine sword with yellow engraving, all sent by the Most Excellent Sir President of the Federation." A hat for Bean had become separated from the shipment. Once Colonel Bean donned this impressive uniform, he must have been the envy of his military detractors in Texas. How could they continue to question his authority when Bean had been decked out in full military regalia by the president himself?[33]

After Bean received this uniform, Commandant General Bustamante (as noted) began to assist him with paperwork to the War Department concerning Bean's service record and back pay. Paymaster Erasmo Seguín was involved in this process, writing letters of August 30 and October 31 on the subject. On August 30 Seguín noted that Bean had been paid since January 20 of the current year but not for the three earlier months. As it turned out, the problem occurred because Bustamante had failed to enclose his certification of this service in his communication to Seguín, or the superior order that was required before payment could be made.[34]

Bustamante tried to explain the situation on November 8. He produced a letter that the ministry of war had written to the minister of the treasury earlier in the year, which he had sent to Seguín from La Bahía (or thought he had) on the previous April 3. It discussed the question of whether the commissary general at San Luis Potosí should pay field compensation to troops serving on the frontiers of the East. "The President has resolved that the troops of the Army who may find themselves on the frontiers enjoy the field compensations while the war with the barbarous Indians lasts." Thus Bean, Ruiz, and other officials involved on campaign were due this compensation or "gratification." On December 27 Bustamante forwarded these "lost" records to the War Department so payment could be authorized and Seguín alerted to the fact.[35]

Likewise, the business about Bean's service record was not settled until 1828, when Francisco García Conde and Vicente Filisola finally got around to certifying on January 1 the information about Bean that had been assembled two years earlier. Their distillation or abstract of Bean's military career shows that this information had been confirmed by review, and it was now a formal part of his service record. Bean was credited with going to the United States in an attempt to form "advantageous ideas of our emancipation" and enlist North American aid "for our glorious Independence." On a second trip to New Orleans he accompanied Plenipotentiary Herrera, who was entrusted with formal negotiations on behalf of the revolutionary government, but a few months after Bean's return to Veracruz "he had the misfortune of being surprised by the enemy troops. The sufferings of this leader to uphold the present system are notorious, according to the credentials that demonstrate his extreme patriotism and valor."[36] It appears that a copy of this service record was sent to the commandant general during January, removing all doubts about Bean's past military distinctions and the salary that he was to currently receive.

Bustamante also got involved in Bean's bigamy case, seemingly in a supportive role. On February 2, 1828, Secretary of War and Marine Manuel Gómez Pedraza advised Secretary of Foreign Relations Juan de Dios Cañedo that he had received and was transmitting Bean's bigamy file that Bustamante had sent to his ministry the past August 14.[37] Because Cañedo's ministry had Bean's empresario petition under review—and the power to grant or refuse his colonization request—from this point on the bigamy question became a factor in whether or not the government should bestow this privileged status on Bean. Throughout 1828 documents bounced back and forth between both ministries. The two questions became inextricably meshed as these officials tried to reach a decision on Bean's moral character and determine if he was qualified to represent Mexico as a colonizer in the boundary reserve with the United States.

Cañedo wrote the governor of Coahuila y Texas on April 22 about Bean's request to bring three to four hundred families to the border reserve, and his "other" request to extend his territory to the neighborhood of Nacogdoches. Since these lands were not in dispute with those claimed under authority of the state of Tamaulipas, the president had acceded to Bean's request.[38] José María Viesca, who had come to the governorship in September 1827 and would occupy this position until October 1830, replied to the secretary of foreign relations on May 5. He used strong language. Bean had bigamy charges filed against him that the War Department had known about since May 28 the previous year. Until this matter was resolved, Viesca thought that Bean's colonization plans should be suspended. He asked to know how the matter was decided "because it does not seem to me that this government should enter into a colonization contract with *a man of criminal reputation* [emphasis added]."[39]

To make sure that Cañedo realized the import of the matter, he enclosed a copy of his "predecessor's" May 28, 1827, letter to the secretary of war and marine. Oddly, it was signed by Viesca, not Blanco or Arizpe.

> It having come to the notice of the Govt. that the Sr. Brevet Col. of the Mexican Army Pedro Elías Bian was married to two women at the same time, that the one was existing on the Nechas River of the Department of Texas, and the other in Jalapa of the State of Veracruz, it ordered in July of 1826 to verify if it was true that he was married on the frontier of this State; since there was no doubt of it being so in that of Veracruz—because of a declaration of the same [Bean] in a representation that he directed to the Supreme Government about colonization of lands in this State—and that I remit for the information of this Government. And with there proving true the existence of the two marriages according to the evidences that are in the expediente, I have the honor of directing it to Your Excellency [in the] original so that you may be pleased to determine what is most convenient.[40]

In the margin was a note saying that the governor of Coahuila y Texas had sent the original documents of a file formed against Colonel Bean who was "married to two women at the same time." Upon receipt of the governor's latest letter, Cañedo forwarded a copy to Pedraza in the War Department.[41] Governor Viesca was clearly no friend of Bean's, even if he had to defy the wishes of the president of Mexico to bring Bean down.

Yoakum's portrait of Bean, 1855.

Pedraza responded to Cañedo on June 2, saying that the commandant general had been aware for a year now that there was a charge of bigamy against Colonel Bean. Bustamante had not reported his findings on the case, and consequently the governor's "doubts" could not be satisfied. Pedraza admitted that the governor was correct in not wishing to enter into a colonization contract with Bean at this point, even though it amounted to depriving Bean of his private rights as a citizen of the nation.[42]

We will again pick up the thread of Bean's colonization/bigamy investigation as it approached resolution later in the year, but at this point it is proper to examine the governor's motive for denouncing Bean in such harsh terms. Viesca called Bean a criminal and brought a new moralistic dimension to the two-wives debate. He considered the evidence gathered in Texas conclusive about Bean being legally married to Candace Midkiff, even though most of this evidence was hearsay and she herself gave contradictory testimony. Was this woman really his wife, wedded in legal fashion, or were they just living together without the recognition of church or state? Either way, Viesca seemed absolutely positive that Bean was a sinner, and thus he had no business being an empresario. This attitude suggests that Governor Viesca was either a moral crusader or a man completely out of touch with how the "institution of marriage" worked on the Anglo-American frontier.

Possibly contributing to Viesca's hostile attitude about Bean's empresarial contract was the fact that it had the blessing of President Victoria and Minister Cañedo. The federal government was telling him to grant this fellow Bean a colonization contract without even knowing that land in the same region had already been awarded by the state. Cañedo, of all people, should be keeping track of these grants, as it was his responsibility to do so. Thus, the governor may have been taking out on Bean a bit of his frustration about colonization decisions made in two different places, with the right hand not knowing what the left hand was doing. The two-wives issue could have been the straw that broke the camel's back with Governor Viesca. Another (more likely) possibility will be examined shortly.

After the big Indian peacemaking ceremony at San Antonio, Bean returned to Nacogdoches. No doubt he donned his new uniform and made a grand entrance. As noted, Alcalde José María Mora had received orders from the new political chief, Ramón Músquiz, to put Bean in possession of the league of land he had requested.[43] On March 1, 1828, Bean wrote General Bustamante from Nacogdoches about the alarming migration of the Kickapoos (two hundred) and Muskogees (six hundred). Both were "bad nations," and their arrival had put the frontier in danger. Bean called them "an enemy very fatal and numerous."[44] This letter, it seems, marked the beginning of Bean's concern over uncontrolled Indian emigration from the United States. It was a theme Bean returned to many times in the coming years. Was Bean influenced by the ideas of Milam, Burnet, and Austin concerning the threat represented by immigration of foreign tribes? It is hard to see how he could have escaped the peer pressure of these influential men, who were telling Bustamante the same thing. And they were not the only ones.

Raids into Texas by hostile Anglo freebooters also bothered Bean—quite a change from his own behavior with Philip Nolan in earlier times.

On March 4 Bean wrote Gov. George Izard of Arkansas Territory that a man named Dayton was engaged a little above Cantonment Gibson in raising a force of men to start, "as soon as grass rises," on a plundering and murdering expedition in Texas. It is uncertain if Bean went to Pecan Point to get this information or if it was relayed to him.[45] Suggesting the latter is a communication Bean sent to Austin the next day on the same subject, in which the bearer's name (John "Cherokee" Williams?) is mentioned. Bean's informant was a friend "that Dont wish his name statid." This friend called himself a "Cityson of this Government" and considered it his duty to pass on his news because Bean was "the nearest [Mexican] ofiser to this Plase." He said that a band of armed men had recently ridden by Pecan Point

> that call them selves advans guard of a large army of Republicans, But if I should name them I should call them a Band of Robers thare is onley fifteen strong at Present and they git no Recruts hear in this Cuntrey but they say they have two or three hundrid troops hourly Expected my informasion is from the noted Doctor Dayton who seems to head the Party he told me that he intendid to fall on St Antonio first if he should git men enough but if he should fail he intended to take Dilions [De León's] fort firs and was varry sertin that Dewits Coloney and Austins would Join him he also states that the Peopel on Ish bayo and those near Nacogdoches are to keep up a constant alarm in order to Draw the troops to that Plase, he says thare is fifty men on the way to meet him at the mouth of the Poorwashitau.[46]

Bean's informant then proceeded to name people involved in the plot. Among them were Baley Anderson, a young man named Blunt, Captain Firth, Mr. "Prater" (probably Stephen Prather, who "would use all his influans with the Ingins"), and a Mr. Litten. The latter was to meet the others on the Colorado with a company of men: "he say that they are to Join under the name of a traping Expadision as to other Particulars you can inquire of Mr Williams who will give you this letter." In passing the letter to Austin, Bean mentioned a Captain Hall of his colony, who was also supposed to link up with the expedition, bringing his company of men. He urged Austin to take watchful measures and let him know how things worked out.

Dr. Lewis B. Dayton did make an appearance in Austin's colony and was tarred, feathered, and run out of town for his trouble. Considering all the specifics given in this letter from Pecan Point, it is understandable why Bean's informant did not want his name revealed. The raid being hatched by people on the Red River—had it come to fruition—was nothing less than a full-fledged invasion with sacking and looting of Mexican towns as its objective.

The citizens of Pecan Point did not know whether they were in Miller County, Arkansas, or responsible to officials in Texas. Bean, because of his friendship with Milam, became drawn into the territorial dispute. His responsibilities as Indian agent also gave him an interest in the affairs of Jonesboro and Pecan Point, for the Shawnees had the oldest and most valid claim to the lands fronting on the Red River. They had begun negotiations with the first Mexican governor of independent Mexico, José Félix Trespalacios. Similar to later understandings with immigrant tribes, it allowed them peaceful possession of these lands while the matter was being decided. This agreement was upheld by Trespalacios's successor, Gov. Rafael González. In 1824 he granted each Shawnee family that came to Texas a square mile of land on the south bank of the Red River.[47]

Typical of the outrage that such open-ended and vague "titles" generated among the Anglo settlers of the area is the letter directed to Governor Izard by J. G. W. Pierson, who styled himself major commandant of the 9th Militia at Pecan Point, Miller County. Pierson considered it his "indispensible duty" to give the governor notice of the dangerous situation faced by the white settlers of the district. These dangers he attributed to the Mexican authorities who had given the Shawnees written permission to settle there. Pierson stated that the tribe was about to come in considerable numbers, building their huts next to the cornfields of the whites, driving their horses and cattle into the settlement, cutting down pecan trees for timber, "pillaging" houses and corncribs, killing hogs, and so forth. "All which, when we mention to them, they say the soil belongs to them; they have their right from the Govr of St Antonio and if we are not pleased with their conduct we may remove—This settlement is at present weak, a number of families have abandoned their homes & fields, and more contemplate going in case the Indians are not removed from among us, which if not done shortly it is my candid opinion the total abandonment of the settlement will be the inevitable concequence."[48] Pierson wanted the Arkansas governor to remove the Shawnees by force, saying that the troops at Cantonment Towson would cooperate with his militia. Alas, there were no more than forty regulars at the fort and "that number is daily diminishing by discharge." This letter is marked with an endorsement on the back: "Miller Co April 1828 Shawnee Inds—Major Pearson—Mexn Col. Bean." Evidently a copy was carried to Bean at Nacogdoches by John "Cherokee" Williams, who also brought the letter from an unnamed informant at Pecan Point (Ben Milam?) that Bean forwarded to Austin. Bean almost provoked an international incident by going to Pecan Point two years later with a small troop of Mexican soldiers.

Early in May Bean also received notice that he had been cleared for payment of the money due him for the months of October, November, and December 1826, since it was owed to all troops of the army serving on the frontier. This payment, however, would only come to him "on the first remission of cash that was available." Such was also the case with Bean's expenditures for the Indians, as shown by the account that had been remitted by Commandant General Bustamante. It had taken over two years, but Bean's claim was honored—at least on paper. Getting the cash was another matter entirely.[49]

Of Bean's private life at this time, it is difficult to say much. It appears that his wife Candace returned to him and they lived under the same roof. She gave birth to their third and final child, Ellis M. Bean, on May 8, 1828, which suggests they were together in the latter part of 1827 if not earlier. William P. Zuber—a notorious tale-spinner responsible for Travis drawing a line in the sand at the Alamo, Rose going over the wall, and other historical embellishments—gave an account of Bean's married life to a grandson of Martin Parmer's that rings true, despite the fact that Zuber himself was married to one of Parmer's granddaughters. He wrote in 1902: "Early in 1828 my father, then on a visit to Texas, visited Bean on business and stayed with him during a night, but did not rest well. Bean and his wife quarreled during the entire night. Bean continually cursed Parmer, and reproached his wife for her unfortunate transaction with him; while the poor woman could only plead innocence of wrong intention on the plea of her belief that her husband was dead, declare her inexpressible grief at the event and implore his pardon."[50]

From the timing of Ellis's birth, Candace would have been in the advanced stages of pregnancy "early in 1828." Samuel Belt, a man who operated a trading post near the later Fort Terán, where Bean was commandant, told Mirabeau Lamar that Bean had cut off his wife's ears in one of his rages. Descendants of the couple vigorously denied that such a thing had ever occurred.[51] Nonetheless, Peter Ellis and Candace had more than the usual set of problems that married couples have to deal with. In September César Lafitte gave Bean a power of attorney over his house and *solar* (lot) in town.[52] Bean may have lived there on his frequent visits to town—separately from Candace, their two children, and newborn son. But the fact that the child was named Ellis suggests that there was no doubt in Bean's mind that he was the father. This would not have been the case if Candace were living separately from him with the possibility/opportunity of sleeping with other men.

Chapter 8

TERÁN VISITS TEXAS

THE THING THAT OCCUPIED most of Bean's time in 1828 was the arrival of Gen. Manuel de Mier y Terán and his Boundary Commission. Terán and his team members were charged with making observations of the line of limits between Mexico and the United States, reporting on Anglo-American penetration of the frontier zone, and gathering information on the situation with Indian tribes in Texas—especially those tribes who had emigrated from the United States and settled in the northeastern portion of the state. Terán was also to observe the flora and fauna of Texas and make a report that would guide Mexico in developing its potential. His commission was all embracing, and Peter Ellis Bean would figure largely into Terán's activities once he reached Nacogdoches on June 3.

For the next seven and a half months Nacogdoches would be Terán's base of operations. During this time he was almost daily regaled by Indian visitors—all seeking title to the lands they occupied—and Bean assisted his old revolutionary war comrade in these discussions. Though they were men of drastically different background and education, Bean and Terán had talents that enabled them to work well together. Through the course of their time in each other's company, it is apparent that Terán came to rely heavily on Bean's knowledge of the frontier and thought highly of him. If Terán was aware of the bigamy charges circulating against Bean in the ministries of Mexico City, there is no mention of it, nor did it seem to affect his opinion that Bean was suited to be an empresario in the boundary reserve.[1]

Terán, in coming to Texas, brought with him a lithographed map of the state bearing the date 1826. It was drawn by Florencio Galli and printed by Claudio Linati, two Italians who had immigrated to Mexico and are credited with introducing lithography into the country. This map (the only copy known) shows empresario grants made in Texas, including the now-annulled colony of Haden Edwards. To the east of Edwards, the boundary zone fronting on the Sabine is shown as "otorgado al [given to] Sr. Bean." His grant also extends westward above the tract of Frost Thorn. Moreover, two roads from the Red River go down to a point called BEAN, which is lettered more prominently than the town of Nacogdoches slightly to the east. Although this map was derived from the general type that Austin had circulated in the Mexican capital on his first trip, it is possible that Bean provided additional information for it during his 1825–26 visit.

Why else would his house on the Neches be given such significance on this map? Austin's prototype maps show no such location, only the little "cerritos" (Indian mounds) at the river crossing. In any case, Bean's empresarial aspirations are shown as an accomplished fact on the map that General Terán carried to guide his movements on his inspection of Texas. It is generally recognized as the first printed map to depict Texas as a separate geographical/political entity.[2]

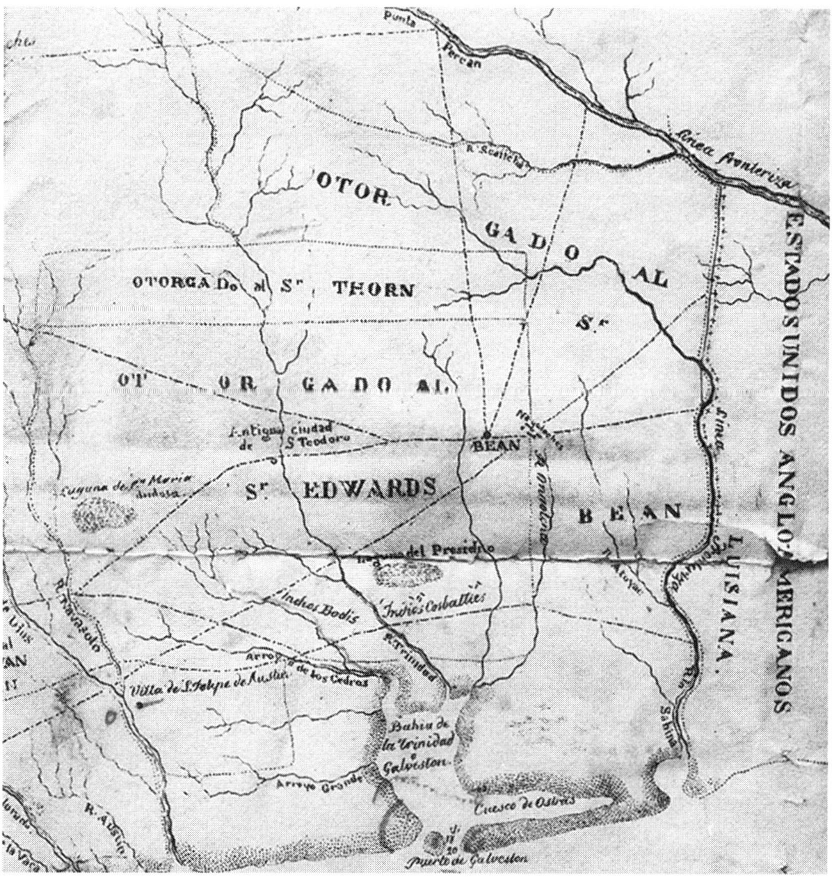

Right portion of the 1826 Galli map, showing Bean's house and his boundary reserve grant. Author's collection.

On June 9, 1828, Terán reported to the minister of foreign relations, Cañedo, that he had been visited by the war and political chiefs of the Cherokees (Bowl and Big Mush). They showed him a letter from the minister of war that stated, among other things, that they would receive the land they desired as soon as a commissioner arrived to mark the boundaries between Mexico and the United States. This letter was probably sent in the summer of 1827, when Bowl—despite the protest of Burnet, Milam, and Austin—received the commission of colonel, a Mexican army uniform, sword, and other recognition of his loyalty to Mexico during the Fredonian Rebellion. Terán told the chiefs that his instructions did not permit him to grant them specific lands, but "so as not to make them doubt that promise [by the government]," he would request instructions to that end. He advised the minister, "If we admit them [the Cherokees], I think they can remain at the same place [they presently occupy], which is consigned to Colonel Bean's colony. Up to now [this arrangement] has not been effected, but he is agreeable to accomodating them."[3]

Later in the month Terán wrote the governor of Coahuila y Texas about the problem of Anglo squatters in the boundary reserve and how their introduction needed to be regulated by recognizing them and awarding them titles to the land they occupied: "The colony founded by [Peter Ellis] Bean could well receive them, and this individual—who is so experienced in Mexican affairs—through his personal influence is in an [ideal] position to familiarize them with Mexican law, about which they currently know or care little."[4] Governor Viesca, it will be recalled, at this very time was denouncing Bean to the federal government as a criminal and a man with two wives, a man unfit to be an empresario. Yet here was a Mexican general of the highest standing, telling him that Bean was just the opposite—a man who could bring order to the region and deserved to have his colonization contract finalized.

Bean's petition for colonization rights was fatally damaged when, in April 1828, an agent of Lorenzo de Zavala applied for a contract to bring five hundred families to the same region. Zavala was governor of the state of Mexico, a prominent figure in Mexican politics, and a personal friend of Governor Viesca. Zavala sought the grant entirely for speculative purposes and had no intention of introducing settlers to it. Like many other Mexicans who involved themselves in the land game in Texas, whether through seeking empresarial rights or securing purchases of free-floating eleven-league grants, Zavala hoped to make a short-term profit. No matter his intent, Zavala enjoyed a decided advantage over the "foreigner" Bean, and his agent actively pressed for confirmation during 1828. It seems likely that Governor Viesca's moral crusade against Bean was motivated, to some extent, by his friendship with Zavala.[5]

Be that as it may, Viesca strongly recommended that Zavala's petition be sanctioned by the federal government while remaining opposed to Bean's. This did not escape the notice of the ministries in Mexico City. Cañedo asked him why, in recognizing the application of Zavala, he did not mention that the question should hinge on the resolution of Bean's application? Bean, after all, had previously been conceded the lands that Zavala wanted. On June 11 the governor answered rather testily that the recommendation he had made, at the "insistence" of Señor Zavala, was with the idea that the concession earlier made in Bean's favor "would be revoked because he had a case pending against him," that is, the bigamy case that Viesca had made such a high-profile issue.[6] This sounds like a fixed job, worked out in smoky back rooms. Viesca suggested that Bean, because of his services to Mexico, should instead be remunerated with a "private dominion of land to the maximum extent that the law permits." As the governor well knew, that would have amounted to a purchase of eleven leagues—nowhere near the size of the reserved boundary territory that Bean wanted to colonize.

It is doubtful that Governor Viesca conveyed this news to General Terán while he was in Texas, preferring to fight his battle for Zavala on the bureaucratic level at Mexico City. Bean, for sure, would not have known what was afoot—unless he caught wind of it through the military grapevine. For example, Capt. Mariano Cosío at Nacogdoches gathered some information on Bean's conduct late that summer for Commandant General Bustamante, and it is unlikely that Bean failed to hear about the inquiry. Col. José de las Piedras conveyed the orders for Cosío to handle Bean's bigamy case, and he no doubt told General Terán about it.[7] None of this seems to have prejudiced Terán against Bean. On July 5 he wrote Cañedo a letter about the small tribes around Nacogdoches and how the introduction of "wild tribes" from the United States had made it difficult for the "old tribes" to survive. Terán thought that if these tribes were entrusted to an agent, an inventive man like Colonel Bean, and if they were given farm implements and instruction, they might be able to prosper like the Cherokees.[8]

While this debate on Bean's moral character was taking place, he was organizing the immigrant tribes for a council to let them know that the Mexican government had not forgotten about them. The council took place on July 2, and Bean reported the results to Terán on July 11. His remarks were quoted in the diary of José María Sánchez as if a first-person account, but neither Sánchez nor Terán attended the meeting north of Nacogdoches. Bean went as the inspector general's representative and recorded some of the speeches made, including his own address to the gathered tribes. His report would have been longer, except that "my pencil had run out on me."[9]

Bean said that some three hundred Indians attended this meeting at the Cherokee village. Represented were the following tribes: Cherokee, Shawnee, Kickapoo, Delaware, Alabama, Coushatta, Navadacho, and Hainai. In his speech he reminded them that when he had returned from Mexico, he "found the black flag of war" flying in their towns. But after his council with their chiefs, who were present today, they "opened their eyes, and saw that a few evil minds were going to involve them in a war without [the chiefs] knowing why." They had smoked the pipe in friendship, and "since that day, there have been no more clouds or darkness."

In a reference to Dayton and his troublemakers from above the Red River, Bean said that these evil men—outcasts in their own land—had told the Indians that Americans were going to make war on the Mexicans. It was a lie, and if these men returned to their villages, they should be arrested and carried to Nacogdoches. They only came to create disturbances and steal Indian horses (as some of them apparently had).

Bean told the assembled Indians that Terán, whom they had already met, was here "to give you lands so that you might build towns, plant corn, and raise cattle so that your women and children will not be hungry." The president of Mexico was also very contented with them, as they knew from the paper he had written them. Bean assured the Indians that this was the "total truth" and that he never spoke with a forked tongue.

Terán, when he read Bean's report, must have caught his breath. True, he recommended to the government that these tribes be granted land, but he knew that he, personally, was not empowered to do so. Did Bean have instructions from Terán to make such a promise, in order to keep them attached to Mexico's interests? He must have, or it was unwise of him to have included this statement in his report to the inspector general. Perhaps both men were hoping that this commitment would nudge officials in Mexico City to give these Indians the lands that they merited for their service in the Fredonian Rebellion. Otherwise, Bean and Terán were playing a game as cynical as Austin's: say anything to keep the Indians happy.

The Indians were reminded that, twelve moons ago, he had smoked the pipe of friendship with the Wacos and Tawakonis on behalf of the chiefs now present. But these two tribes had proved false to their word and were again stealing horses. Bean told his listeners that if they wished to make war on the Wacos and Tawakonis they were free to do so, taking their horses and mules for their own. Bean closed his address with a remark that suggests he thought he was still in the running for a colonization grant: "I am thinking of a good place—which I will soon make available—for you to build your villages. I remain the father of the Red men, who are the friends of the Mexicans."[10]

The question arises of how Bean was able to communicate with these Indians in the councils he held with them through the years. There is no evidence that Bean spoke Cherokee or any other Indian language, despite frequent reports of his "talks" with various tribes. It seems that Bean was obliged to use the services of an interpreter who had knowledge of these tongues. Otherwise, it is doubtful that Bean—either through use of sign language or a smattering of lingo he may have possessed—would have been able to convey complex ideas of Indian policy to them. It seems likely that Bean retained frontiersmen like John "Cherokee" Williams and Stephen Prather to do his talking for him. Williams was frequently in the villages of various tribes. Prather was a trader with the immigrant Indians and much respected by them. These men and others like them, whose names are lesser known, could speak their languages, or enough to be understood. As might be expected, misunderstandings sometimes occurred.[11]

At this time Terán wrote several reports on the Indians of Texas. Although his informant in San Antonio about the plains tribes was Francisco Ruiz, Bean was probably responsible for most of Terán's information about the immigrant tribes in the eastern woodlands. These two reports, dated June 9 and July 7, 1828, are titled "Noticia de las tribas de salvages conocidos que habitan en el Departamento de Tejas" and "Adicion a la noticia."[12] The number given for each tribe was in families, not individuals. Here are Terán's "census statistics" for the Indians of Texas in 1828, comprising thirty-four tribes of anywhere from 3,852 to 4,372 families. The two figures were given because so little reliable information was available about the plains tribes. Applying the standard estimate of 5 individuals per family gives 20,960 to 23,560 Indians in the state. No attempt has been made here to "translate" Terán's original spelling of the tribal names, but most are recognizable: Lipans del sur 150; Lipanes llaneros 80–100; Comanches 1,200–1,500; Chariticas 250; Caihuas 140; Huecos 160; Tahuacanos 80–100; Tancahuas 80; Tarancahueses & Cujanos 100; Vidaises & Ocoysaus 40; Cutchates 50; Alabamo 35; Navadachos 15; Kichaes 37; Tejas & Ainais 23; Nadacos 29; Beloeses 20; Tamayacas & Huichites 58; Cheroquees 80; Savanas 300; Delawares 150; Kicapoo 110; Cuapas 150; Deluas 75; Chactas 10; Aix 160; Pacanabo 200; Tahuayaces 200; Yguanes 40; and Cados 300. Colonel Bean and other Texans would complain constantly about how the numbers of these tribes were swelling in the years to come as word of the fertility of Texas prompted their kinsmen to join them. These figures should be compared with those given by Jean-Louis Berlandier (a member of Terán's Boundary Commission) in his 1830 report on the Indians of Texas.[13]

When Terán's health improved enough for him to make several excursions late in the year, Bean either assisted him in securing the services of an expert guide (Pierre Roubleau) or went with Terán himself. The trip in October–November enabled Terán to make astronomical observations in the boundary reserve, and he crossed the Sabine to visit the environs of later Shreveport. On a second trip in December, below Nacogdoches down the Neches and Trinity Rivers, Terán learned much about the Southeastern tribes that had settled this forested region. Altogether, Bean was occupied most of the second half of 1828 performing good service for General Terán, who would shortly become Mexico's most important figure in the affairs of Texas.[14]

No doubt Bean tried to use his influence with Terán to further his empresarial dreams, but—apart from the several letters already mentioned—it does not appear that Terán actively made demands on Bean's behalf. Terán was more preoccupied with the prospect that Mexico would lose Texas due to the uncontrolled influx of North Americans. Bean represented only a small cog in this giant wheel. Still, Bean's prospects were yet alive, as indicated by a letter that Elisha Roberts wrote Stephen Austin on July 18. He said that he had received Austin's letters in which it was stated that the twenty-league border reserve had been granted to three Mexican gentlemen to colonize, "which is good Knews to me and the settlers in this country." Roberts asked Austin to do what he could with the empresario who had power to complete title to his lands and advise him what course to pursue. In a postscript he added, "Col. Bean says he is appointed to Colonize the 20 border Leages; please inform me if he is one of the gentlemen Aluded to in your letters."[15] No record of Austin's reply to Roberts has been found. It would be interesting to know his thoughts on Bean's chances as a colonizer of the border leagues at this time, as well as his opinion of the man's abilities.

While General Terán was stuck in Nacogdoches, ill and suffering from the summer heat, Bean attended to routine matters. On July 22 Alcalde Mora wrote the political chief that Amos Edwards, a brother of the ex-empresario, had appeared with his family and slaves, seeking admission as a settler. He was of advanced age and had presented five certificates favorable to his character. Bean examined the documents and assured Mora that they were good testimonials. He recognized the signatures on two of them, Jackson and Carroll—both "generals of troops in the United States of the North." Mora sought the political chief's advice in the matter, no doubt because of the Edwards family's role in the recent rebellion.[16] Bean was probably consulted on many questions involving the entry of people coming to Texas from beyond the Sabine. Later he also helped rebels such as Burrell Thompson gain reinstatement as citizens, though it is doubtful he would have done the same for that "Ring-Tailed Panther," Martin Parmer.

Haden Edwards's son-in-law Frost Thorn had been allowed to keep his colonization contract above Nacogdoches after the Fredonian Rebellion, but he was having a hard time fulfilling his obligation to introduce settlers to lands fronting on the northern boundary reserve. In a letter to Austin of July 22, he added his name to the list of empresarios who had Indian squatters on their lands: "My Colony is at this time totally ocupied by the Indians. The Cherokees and Shaunesse are Agriculturists, and do not live in villages but in a compact settlement. They raise much corn. and I have myself this season purchased from the Cherokees alone, not less than 1000 Dollars worth of Corn and pease."[17] But unlike Austin, Milam, and Burnet, Thorn thought that "it would improve there condition to Colonize them." Perhaps Thorn hoped to fulfill his empresarial contract by awarding land to the Cherokee and Shawnee families already tilling the soil of his colony. He promised to write Austin "frankly" on this subject in a short time. If he did, Austin probably convinced him that giving land titles to Indians was a terrible idea. Whatever the case, Thorn failed to introduce enough settlers to his colony, which was then awarded to Gen. Vicente Filisola in October 1831.[18]

Now that it was certain to Bean that he had a place on the frontier, and would remain at Nacogdoches as an Indian agent, he petitioned the governor for four *varas* of land that adjoined the lot on which he had built his town house—either on the Lafitte lot or another that Bean had acquired. This property was granted to him, "without damage to a third party."[19] In October 1828, however, the ayuntamiento protested that this lot where Bean wanted to build a *chimenea* (literally a chimney, but also a hearth or fireplace) belonged to the corporation of the town and thus could not be conceded to Bean. It was described as ground previously given to the troops guarding Nacogdoches because they "truly needed it" to expand their quarters. Bean may have planned to erect some sort of furnace at the site, which the townspeople objected to because of its heat, smoke, and noxious fumes.[20]

So extensive were Bean's later dealings in town lots and outlying tracts of land that they will receive but brief mention in later chapters. As noted, James Gaines completed the survey of Bean's league of land on the margins of the Neches on August 13, 1828, and he was put in possession. This ranch, with portions devoted to agriculture, became only one of Bean's many holdings around Nacogdoches.[21] On some of them, such as lands that contained salines, he was obliged to engage in bitter disputes with other people to obtain them—often with the *ayuntamiento* (town council) itself.

As an example of how Bean tried to stretch the rules of the land-grant game is the case that he initiated in December 1828 on "behalf" of a relative, William Bean. The exact identity of this William has already been examined, with questions about him still unanswered. As noted, possession had been granted to Peter Ellis—not William—on September 24, by virtue of William's conveyance of title. According to Colonel Bean's petition of December 21 to Political Chief Ramón Músquiz, his nephew "Guillermo" had been awarded a *sitio* of land in April 1827 along the Neches River to the northeast on the Arroyo de las Salinas. This, as discussed, was in modern Smith County.

Peter Ellis commenced to make improvements on what he called lands "situated on Salinillas Creek." When this petition went to Saltillo, Governor Viesca ruled that such a sale was in violation of Article 27 of the state colonization law of March 24, 1825. William Bean had not taken possession of this grant, nor had he cultivated it for the specified period. Nor did William Bean's signature "WBean" on the transfer document look anything like the signature on his petition, fully written out. That Bean had forged this signature was implied but not stated in so many words. In any case, the contract of sale between William and his uncle Pedro Ellis Bean was a nullity, as it infringed on the cited article of the state law pertaining to land grants. This decision did not come until February 18, 1829, so Bean assumed his title from William was good and kept arguing fine points of law about salines.[22]

Viesca's adverse ruling in this case, however, was insignificant compared to the decision then climaxing on Bean's boundary-reserve colonization scheme. He may have been telling people around Nacogdoches that he had been "appointed" empresario over this reserve, but his plans were not faring well in Mexico City. On August 2, 1828, Secretary of Relations Cañedo told Secretary of War Pedraza that it was very necessary to resolve the bigamy case against Bean, as the president had ordered. On the same day Cañedo wrote Governor Viesca that the president wanted to know whether or not Bean knew about his order of the previous April 22, which had approved Bean's colonization project. Also, what was the status of the governor's suggested alternative—giving Bean some land elsewhere?[23]

Governor Viesca replied on August 18, saying, "In no way has this government made known to Bean the Superior Order of last April 22, by which there was approved the colonel's project, nor have I been able to determine that there has come to his notice in any other way the said resolution, whereby he could have started his enterprise and considered himself as the possessor of those lands." It was well known that if any empresario began operations—especially in exempt lands—prior to receiving superior approval, he was doing so at his own risk. "Thus if Colonel Bean has admitted some families and awarded lands to them, in confidence that his enterprise would be approved, his acts—in the government's judgment—are null." Viesca said that this was in fulfillment of the president's order in a letter written on August 2.[24] The governor of Coahuila y Texas was clearly keeping Bean in the dark, and making no apologies for it.

Thus the matter stood when Zavala's agent began pressing for a decision on his empresario contract. Cañedo wrote the governor on September 27 that "because the [bigamy] case pending against Bean was not sufficient reason for revoking the agreement by which his empresario application was approved, the government could not make this revocation without more solid foundation."[25] In other words, there was still a question of whether or not Bean was a bigamist, because the documents in the file were inconclusive. Even if Bean did not have friends in the state capital, it seems that powerful officials in Mexico City were still looking out for his interests.

Commandant General Bustamante was also on Bean's side, and by November he got around to forwarding the results of his inquiry on Bean's marital status to the War Department. Pedraza, on November 22, sent this file to Cañedo in foreign relations because "the governor of Coahuila was interested in the result of this matter."[26] Interested indeed.

Cañedo turned the file over to Luis Gonzaga Cuevas (later to head the ministry himself), and Cuevas wrote a lengthy opinion on November 25. He said that the governor of Coahuila y Texas had started this proceeding against the conduct of Bean, his marriage status, and his reputation among the citizens at Nacogdoches. Reviewing the first batch of depositions, Cuevas thought they amounted to nothing more than Bean having some "bad" friends, being considered an "enemy" of certain citizens, and a man whose words, it was said, were "sweet but his actions very bad." Others certified that Bean lived with Candace Midkiff as if married to her, and she claimed that they were legitimately married in Tennessee. But this same lady later confessed that the marriage was not legal, and she had only said it was to secure Bean's property for herself. Captain Cosío's subsequent investigation, taken from the "most honorable" citizens of the community, likewise revealed contradictory results. Some told him that she claimed to be married to Bean while others did not know if it was legitimately, although admitting that she had lived with him as such.

The governor had passed this *expediente* to the War Department without knowledge of Cosío's investigation, which came later. Viesca considered Bean guilty of the crime of bigamy, for it was certain that Bean—by his own admission, when he had petitioned for an empresarial contract—had a wife in Jalapa, Doña Magdalena Falfán de los Godos. But it was Commandant General Bustamante's judgment that Candace Midkiff must be considered a "mere concubine" and not as a wife, this by virtue of her statement that she and Bean had never been married. Thus Bean was not a bigamist. He ought to be reunited with his legal wife in Jalapa, thought Bustamante, but the fact that he had not been able to do so should not jeopardize his colonization contract, nor should it detract from Bean's many services to the nation.

Cuevas rendered his opinion on the basis of two things. First, because of what was in the evidence thus far submitted, no sure verdict could be formed on Bean's crime of bigamy. Second, supposing that the verdict might affect Bean's colonization project, this case should go back to the War Department for final resolution—the idea being that nothing could be agreed on it in Bean's favor as long as his bigamy case was pending and therefore his rights as a citizen remained suspended. Cañedo referred the matter back to Pedraza three days later, requesting of him a resolution.[27]

Meanwhile, as 1828 came to an end, other people were also seeking closure. Zavala's lawyer, Lic. Rafael Delgado, was one of them. On December 27 in an "imperious manner" he asked that his client's colonization request be decided.[28] Not mentioned, however, was the fact that Zavala already had agents active, trying to sell his grant of land in the United States. Their activities, of course, could not amount to much until Zavala had the government's contract in hand. Bean wrote the governor on January 6, 1829, complaining that so far he had received no response at all to his "memorial" of the past July 22 about lands that the Supreme Government had recommended he should receive in 1826. "I don't desire an advantage," said Bean, but the decision should be governed by the laws of colonization, and the inhabitants of the region ought to be "tranquilized" by receiving possession of their lands from a duly constituted authority.[29] He wanted to be that authority and was tired of being jerked around.

A change of leadership in the federal government at this time also negatively impacted Bean's chances of vindication. A contest developed between Pedraza, who was the president-elect, and Gen. Vicente Guerrero, who thought he had been cheated out of the presidency in the recent election. After a military uprising, Guerrero was seated by Congress as president in January 1829, and Pedraza went into exile. Esteban de Moctezuma took his place as secretary of war and marine, while José María Bocanegra replaced Cañedo as secretary of foreign relations. Zavala became head of the treasury on April 18, while still occupying the governorship of the state of Mexico. General Bustamante was confirmed as the duly elected vice president, but he remained on the northeastern frontier or wherever he was needed. Felipe de la Garza became commandant general in his stead. This is not to say that these new men were hostile to Bean's situation, only that most of them were unfamiliar with the ins and outs of his colonization petition over the past three years. Lorenzo de Zavala, of course, was the exception.[30]

In January the new heads of these ministries again passed Bean's file back and forth, each claiming it was the other's duty to rule on his colonization project. In view of how Zavala's agent had "agitated" the question before the Supreme Government, Bocanegra decided to take the matter in hand. On February 10, 1829, he sent his decision to Governor

Viesca at Saltillo. Because of Zavala's many sterling qualities, his colonization petition should receive favor instead of Bean's. The president had only awarded the boundary reserve earlier to Bean because he lacked a material understanding of the laws involved. Lorenzo de Zavala was to be notified that he had received preference to Bean for these lands. But His Excellency the president had also disposed—because of Bean's past services, and the love he had always shown for Mexico—that it was "recommended to Your Excellency [Viesca] that he [Bean] should be attended to in the grant of some other lands that he might aspire to, whenever the difficulties that up to now he has had, because of his private affairs, are resolved."[31]

It is uncertain if outgoing president Guadalupe Victoria or incoming president Vicente Guerrero had been "disposed" to order this resolution in Zavala's favor. Both men were comrades of Bean in the revolutionary struggle, and both had certified to his service late in 1825 when Bean was seeking reinstatement in the Mexican army with the rank of colonel. (President Victoria's term officially ended March 31, 1829.) Gov. José María Viesca was certainly pleased by Bocanegra's decision, as it represented victory for his personal friend Zavala. Moreover, it validated his own suggestion for how Bean's empresarial contract should be handled: revoke it and give Bean a smaller amount of land elsewhere.

Gen. Vicente Filisola, who had considerable hindsight when he wrote a history of the "War in Texas" near midcentury, said that Bocanegra's "true reason" for granting the border reserve to Zavala was that he was a Mexican and Bean was a foreigner. It was not thought wise to place lands that bordered the United States in the hands of a native of that country, for fear that Bean would allow entry of "all classes" of North American colonists "under the umbrella of the enterprise belonging to Mexicans."[32] Bean probably would have, but so did other empresarios on the frontier—including Lorenzo de Zavala. Modern Mexican historian Eduardo Enrique Ríos pronounces that when the government awarded this contract to Zavala, Bean was "unjustly" deprived of his land concession.[33] So it would seem to most historians, especially considering that Zavala did not concern himself with introducing the kind of settlers that Mexico wanted in this region and less than two years later sold his contract to speculator interests in New York City.

Governor Viesca wasted no time informing Bean of the result. First, on February 23, he wrote Secretary of Foreign Relations Bocanegra that Zavala would get his contract remitted to him, pursuant to the president's approval. He also promised that Bean would be conceded land in the vacant places he might designate. On February 27 he passed on to Bean the Superior Government's decision that Zavala was to be the colonizer of the boundary reserve, and not him. The governor did not gloat, adding

ELLIS P. BEAN.

Thrall's portrait of Bean, 1879.

that this had been done with the "concept" that Bean would be awarded the maximum limit of land in the empty spaces of Texas, that is, eleven leagues.[34]

How Bean took this bad news can only be imagined. Not only had he lost out on his colonization project, but the granting of compensatory lands to him outside the boundary reserve seemed contingent on the outcome of his bigamy status—his "difficulties" of a private nature, as Bocanegra had so politely phrased it. If Bean had any clue to Governor Viesca's role in these deliberations, he must not have considered his chances very good for obtaining land at the state level. For the time being, he would have to acquire more land by purchase rather than on the basis of his past service to Mexico. Bean, by virtue of being a Mexican citizen, was entitled to buy eleven leagues of land *without* this ruling or any of the grief he had suffered from aspiring to be an empresario. He had been defeated, no question about it. Bean was down, but he was not out—as we shall see.

The military situation in Texas had also undergone changes in the past year. Mateo Ahumada had been replaced as commandant of the department by Antonio Elozúa, who kept his headquarters at San Antonio de Béxar. In Nacogdoches Col. José de las Piedras was at the helm, as he had been while General Terán was in town. It was Piedras who kept Terán informed of developments on the frontier after Terán left for Tamaulipas at the beginning of 1829. Colonel Piedras seems not to have thought very highly of Bean, and Bean's regard for the haughty Piedras was probably reciprocated. Piedras devoted his time to making money by cornering the market on goods from New Orleans, which did nothing to endear him to the local merchants of Nacogdoches. Bean was left to his land affairs and Indians, certainly the latter more than when Francisco Ruiz was commandant at the post. Still, the Indians had to deal with Piedras when matters of substance were discussed, matters that had to go to higher authorities.

On occasion Colonel Piedras was consulted on more private relations between the Indians and the Mexicans. An example of this came a year earlier, on January 8, 1828, when Chief Bowl visited Nacogdoches and informed Piedras that he desired to tighten the bonds of friendship and offer his people an example of how they might demonstrate their gratitude and goodwill to the republic they had offered to protect. To cement this relationship and perpetuate it into the future, Bowl wished to place two of his young sons in the government's care. He wanted them educated and instructed in public affairs, in some location away from the distractions of the Cherokees or any other tribe of Indians. In effect, Bowl was asking that his sons be raised as Mexicans. While this prospect must have been flattering to certain Mexicans, who wished to amalgamate these foreign Indians into the Mexican social system, Bowl probably made the offer so he would have sons more adept at furthering the tribe's interests. Obtaining legal possession of their lands, of course, ranked high on the Cherokees' list of priorities.[35]

Bean went to New Orleans at the end of 1828 and was still there at the beginning of 1829. Before he left, he had pushed his claim to the league of land that contained the valuable "little salines," this by virtue of purchase from William Bean. Colonel Bean, at the same time, was trying to get possession of another tract closer to Nacogdoches. He had petitioned for this league as a "settler" on October 30, 1827, probably because his original request in April 1825 was for two *sitios.* Bean was placed in possession of the first league (the one east of the Neches on the Old San Antonio Road) earlier in 1828, but now he wanted another. Gov. Rafael Ecay Músquiz conceded title on October 11, 1828, just ten days after he took over the governorship from Viesca on an interim basis. It eventually got surveyed on the opposite (west) bank of the Neches, a mile below the San Antonio Road in present Houston County. Although not specified, it may also have contained salt deposits or mineral springs that Bean prized so highly.[36]

It must have seemed to the Nacogdoches community leaders that Colonel Bean wanted every desirable tract of land for miles around. He had already been given possession of the valuable Neches Saline, plus a league on the main road, and here he was, asking for—and getting—more. The ayuntamiento on January 19 wrote the political chief, soliciting that he remit Bean's original document of possession (the one with the phony-looking signature). In the meantime, they asked that Bean's right to the "little salines" be canceled and he be made to understand—upon his return—that he had to locate his grant elsewhere.[37]

It seems that the citizens of Nacogdoches were accustomed to using these salines to gather salt themselves, and they did not want Bean to have possession of the land on which they were located. Why these protests had not started earlier is hard to say. The residents must have been thrilled when they learned that Governor Viesca had annulled Bean's title on February 18. It took time for word to reach Nacogdoches, but this news traveled fast.

Bean was back in Nacogdoches by March 10, 1829, for that was when he responded to the ayuntamiento's demand of the same day. This document shows that Bean either had some detailed knowledge of Mexican law, or an attorney who did. He began by saying that there were seven salines in the neighborhood similar to the one he was asking for. In fact, they were not salines as defined by the law that reserved such salt deposits for the federation, such as those near the towns of Reynosa and Refugio (Matamoros, referring to the old Sal del Rey). In question here was water gathered from depressions in the ground; when boiled down in iron pots, the water rendered salt similar to that obtained from seawater. If such places belonged to the federation, Bean said he would have taken them as provided in Article 35 of the law governing salines. "But since they are not those covered [in the law], I have begun operations for the making of salt, which before was brought from the United States to this village at a very high price."

More articles were cited from the federation's "Guide of the Treasury" relating to salines and the use that could be made of them. It was his understanding, said Bean, that the Constitution rewarded resourceful men and encouraged with advantages those who devised plans to benefit the republic. He hoped his industry for the common good would merit the government's approval. The gentlemen of the ayuntamiento were not ignorant and should not claim that these "little salines" belonged to everyone, when they were in an entirely different category.[38] Bean was still arguing with the political chief a year later on the difference between *salinillas* and *saltierra* ("salty earth").

It might be noted that the Nacogdoches alcalde at the time of this controversy was José Ignacio Ibarvo. He wrote the political chief in September, saying that he had "repeatedly made claim to title for the land that was granted to William Bean, and by him transferred to his uncle, the Citizen Don Peter Ellis Bean, on November 17, 1827." Although this transaction had been annulled, Colonel Bean still remained in possession of the land. Ibarvo prayed that this matter would be resolved—in his favor, of course.[39] Thus did politics intermingle with personal interests on the frontier. Bean became heavily involved in the production of salt around Nacogdoches, but it was an uphill struggle.

For example, there is documentation in the Nacogdoches Archives to show that one W. S. Thomas was actively bringing out wagonloads of salt from the "Naiches Salt Works" in the summer of 1829. In June Thomas agreed to deliver one hundred bushels to Leonard "Duboy" (Dubois) as ordered by merchant Frost Thorn. There were wheel problems on the wagons, and Thomas had to delay delivery because his help ran off.[40] Bean is not mentioned in these documents, but in 1833 he leased the saline to Stephen Prather, noting that Thomas had formerly been in charge of the works.

After his return from New Orleans in March 1829, Bean wrote Austin to clarify the alarm that Colonel Piedras had spread concerning the Spanish expedition that was supposed to be forming in Havana for an invasion of Mexico. "The Reason that Col. Pedras Rote this ofisial Was that a Mexican Rote By me and Before he [Piedras] ast me aney thing about it he Startid an Extreordenero Express [to you] as he Done onse Before When he Said that the Royalists was in tranity Bay But you will See that all is Nothing." Bean thought that the rumor of a Spanish "Expodision" was false, but in this he was mistaken. Later in the year an invasion was made at Tampico, which General Terán played an important role in defeating.[41]

Several months later Elozúa, the military *jefe* at Béxar, informed Piedras that the Supreme Government had ordered that Bean's bigamy case "be perfected and concluded." Consequently, he was naming as prosecutor the battalion captain José Ortega, who was under Piedras's command; Lt. Gavino Aranjo was to assist Ortega as secretary in the proceedings.[42] Such orders would scarcely have come to Piedras at Nacogdoches without a complete file on Bean's two wives and all the dirt connected to the case. No matter how commanders changed, this yoke was still on Bean's neck and soldiers continued to circulate coarse jokes behind his back. Something to the effect of "Why hasn't Colonel Bean returned to his wife in Jalapa?" "Oh, he's having too much fun with the young wife he has here!" "Yuk, yuk."

The Indians high on the frontier near the Red River were also troublesome at this time, as evidenced by a letter that General Bustamante wrote Colonel Elozúa on March 23 from Soto la Marina, Tamaulipas. Bustamante, who was more concerned with Texas than the man who replaced him as commandant general, Felipe de la Garza, wanted Elozúa to coordinate a decisive strike at the Tahuayases (Taovaya) village and completely annihilate it. This "perverse Tribe" had been invited to make peace several times, but they had not wanted to be reduced to a peaceful state and were attacking frontier establishments "more and more every day." Now it was indispensable that they be wiped out, making use of the friendly tribes along the frontier to accomplish it.

Elozúa was to coordinate his activities with Colonel Bean and Lieutenant Colonel Austin, so that the civil militia of the latter colony would march at their own expense toward the Tahuayase village and combine with Elozúa's force from San Antonio. But since the Wacos and Tawakonis, together with the Comanches, had honored their peace treaties up to now, said Bustamante, when their villages were approached they should be notified that the troops had no hostile intentions toward them. In fact, they could join the campaign if they wished and help destroy the Tahuayases. The precise arrangements for the campaign were to be worked out with Bean and Austin. Lieutenant Colonel Ruiz was to give his advice "because of the information [about the Indians] which these Leaders possess."[43]

Political Chief Ramón Músquiz avowed to Austin on May 28 that he knew nothing of the proposed campaign and thought that he and the state government were due explanations. The recent deaths near San Marcos of two Mexicans at the hands of the Wacos and Tawakonis "who have brazenly been engaging in hostilities since the month of January" suggested to Músquiz that the project against the Taovayas ought to be changed. Because the two openly hostile tribes were closer to the Anglo settlements, he said it might be necessary to call on the militias for any strike made against these Indians. Músquiz promised to operate in conjunction with Austin in the matter, "knowing that I can count on your important cooperation."[44]

As these discussions progressed, the focus of the campaign shifted entirely to the Wacos and Tawakonis instead of the Taovayas. They were declared to be in greater need of extermination, the Wacos first and after them the Tawakonis. Austin no doubt contributed to this reevaluation of what tribes were the worst enemies of his colony, for he had always wanted to be rid of these Indians. But Bean, in his 1828 talk with the friendly immigrant tribes, had also urged them to take vengeance against the Wacos and Tawakonis for proving false to their pledges of peace. By mid-1829 the decision had been made to strike their villages, and the San Felipe ayuntamiento was asked to have 150 mounted militiamen ready. On June 23 Austin signed an order raising several of those companies, but —as usual—his company captains protested the lack of "suitable" horses for their men. Perhaps having to undertake the march at their own expense dampened the militia's enthusiasm for the campaign.[45]

Militia captain Martin Allen (the same who had testified at San Felipe about Bean's marriage status) wrote Austin on July 5 that the town of Harrisburg had just been visited by a "large number" of Indians of diverse tribes. They included "Caddoes Anadarkoes Ieshes Inies Beedies Coshaties Delawares and Kickapooes," all of whom were friendly and showed every intention of remaining so. But the Kickapoos, after purchasing all the powder in town, "put off amediately." Allen, in speaking to the Indians who remained, informed Austin that they were very inquisitive about whether or not the whites "were going against the WayCoes."

> I kept them as much in the dark as posable in order to Learn from them how the Different tribes Stood affected to wardes our inimyes —they seemed to All be against the waycoes except a part of the Caddoes who told me that the waycoes and them ware Friends which I believe to be the Case—
>
> I have Learnt a few days Since from a very Smart intilagent Co shatty who Stayed at my ho[u]se All night Directly from the Villiege —he informed me that a jenril Expedition was to be fitted out against the waycoes, of All the different Tribes between the Brazors and Red river nameley the Coshatties Alabammoes Baluckshes Chocktoas Cherokees Kickapooes Caddoes and all the other Small tribes in ther vicinity he says they are to devide them Selves in different bands and all march at one time by different routs So that the enimy Can have no Chance of ascaping—he says they intend to kill all men wimmen and Children—he says they are to March in two moons [September].[46]

Allen thought that the Indian who gave him this information had not heard anything about the planned expedition from white people. In closing he offered his opinion about the need for secrecy: "I think it would be good policy when there is an expedition on foot against the Waycoes or aney of them tribes to keepe it as much from the Knowledge of other indians as posable—there being so much Communication from one tribe to another."

Martin Allen's letter seems to have ignored the possible influence of one white man over these immigrant Indians, that of Peter Ellis Bean. But if Bean was organizing a coordinated campaign by all the Indians between the Red and Brazos Rivers, he would have to do it without the army's help. Colonel Elozúa notified Austin at the end of July that the commandant general had ordered the campaign against the "Tahuasis" (Taovayas) suspended, news that no doubt also went to Bean. A week earlier Francisco Ruiz told Austin that the fall campaign against the Indians was a good idea, but there were obstacles—in his opinion—that would cause it not to happen, "one of many being the metallic cry of *money money money.*" Hard cash had "completely disappeared," and nobody could get credit anymore. Even with this situation, he thought that the Tawakonis "will continue to keep the peace." Then Ruiz offered his thoughts on the immigrant tribes.

> As for the emigration of the barbarians from the North, I have said a great deal and to the government itself, or, to be more specific, to the Commandant General of these States [Bustamante]. On repeated occasions I have expressed my opinion to him, which is: namely, that, if not very soon, then some day so many tribes are going to be harmful to us, and all the more so if they, as may be expected, band together with those already in this Department. . . . I believe that all too late our Government will recognize this evil, and perhaps when it is already too late, when it could have been cut off if action had been taken at the proper time.[47]

It is a shame that we do not have similar personal letters from Indian Agent Bean, revealing his thoughts about the continual influx of tribes from the United States. Instead, his letters are mostly "official" protests about the lack of diligence of U.S. authorities in stemming the tide of these Indians into Mexican territory. Lacking are Bean's opinions on whether they were savages incapable of being assimilated into white society—be it Anglo or Mexican. It seems he mostly kept such thoughts to himself, a wise decision considering how quickly this type of information became generally known and might be used against him in his relations with these tribes.

Austin's sentiments about Indians in general, and especially the tribes flocking into Mexican territory from the United States, are made clear from the notes attached to his latest manuscript map of Texas that Austin sent to President Guerrero at this time. Austin listed the various tribes that had been immigrating to Texas for the past two years, saying "it is to be fundamentally feared that the majority of the millions of savages" that the policy of the U.S. government was forcing west would cross from "the dry and sterile plains of Arkansas" into a more fertile and inviting Texas: "The idea that they can be contained [within their western reserves] is an illusion, or [that they can be] made useful citizens, in the case of their incursion within Mexican territory, nor is it to be hoped that they will remain quiet in their new homes; and if they enter Texas in their present state, the country will be lost to civilization for centuries and its inhabitants given up to the [scalping] knife."[48] These strong anti-Indian ideas echo those given to General Bustamante by Burnet, Milam, and Austin two years earlier. The legends on Austin's map reinforce his thesis that eastern Texas was about to be overrun with hordes of savage tribes from the United States. Col. Peter Ellis Bean, like Ruiz and these other men, was also alarmed at the dimensions of this migration.

Bean, however, kept working among the friendly tribes for a strike against the Wacos, seemingly in conjunction with militiamen from the Nacogdoches region. On August 25 he conveyed orders to the alcalde of Ayish Bayou, Benjamin Lindsey, that elections be held for officers in all militia companies of the district. These companies were to be composed of sixty men, according to a proclamation received from the governor of the state. Bean wanted Lindsey to send him a list of the men in these various companies with the officers elected, so that commissions could be brought to them. James Gaines was to do the same in his district, as well as the new alcalde in Tenaja. "I hope that the Setlers of this country will turn out & fulfill this [service] . . . of greate advantage to them & the government."[49]

Alcalde Lindsey did not take kindly to being told what to do by Bean, suggesting that the colonel's authority was challenged by his fellow Anglos as well as by Mexicans. He wrote his counterpart at Nacogdoches: "I have never had any knowledge of Col. Beans having been invested with the faculties of Chief of department; if he possesses such power I presume you are oficially notified of the fact." If Ibarvo had "Such oficial onformation" in his archive, Lindsey asked for a copy "& if Col. Bean Possesses any such power I am at all times ready to Comply with his Order on the Subject but untill I receive some oficial information of the fact I shall only put the Militia in readiness according to your request."[50]

How this matter was resolved is unknown. Bean's instructions from President Victoria did tell him to use militias on the frontier, but this was a prerogative zealously held by ayuntamientos of each district and presided over by the political chief. Empresarios like Austin and Green DeWitt also figured into the equation, actually issuing orders that ranging companies be raised to protect their colonies. DeWitt's settlers were particularly subjected to Indian raids in 1829, often directed at Tonkawas in their midst. DeWitt suggested that the two empresarios support a "Company of Rangers, or the public troops [meaning the local militia]" to patrol the limits of their territory and spread the word if large raiding parties were sighted. Smaller ones these rangers could deal with themselves, as they sometimes did.[51]

Even without the local militia units of the Nacogdoches region, Bean could still rely on War Chief Bowl and his Indian allies. They had their own reasons for wanting to make war on the Wichita tribes on the upper Trinity and Brazos Rivers, extending north to the Red. According to historian John Henry Brown, this fall campaign against the Wacos was indeed carried out in 1829—at least by the Cherokees. Brown obtained the details from his old friend, Capt. Thomas Barron, who said that a band of fifty-two Cherokee warriors from the Red River, near the southwestern corner of Arkansas, had attacked the main Waco village and killed "a large number" of their foes.[52] Bean's role in this particular raid—if any—is unknown. From Allen's report to Austin, it sounds like Bean hoped for a much larger strike involving all the east Texas tribes. Perhaps he and Chief Bowl had to settle for something less in 1829.

Meanwhile, Bean sold two portions of his league astride the Old San Antonio Road along the creek called "cerrito de Nechas." In September he sold a fourth of it to Levi Bostick for 500 pesos; Bostick sold the land to James Bradshaw the next month. In November Bradshaw increased his holdings by buying from Bean a tract ("una parte de un sitio de tierra en el Serrito de Nechas") bounded on the north by Bostick's purchase, the price being 550 pesos. This means that Bean only had half (or less) of his original league on Mound Prairie by the end of 1829, and it soon became known as "Bradshaw's Prairie." But Candace remained at Bean's house on the Neches, and several thousand acres were more than enough for her to plant a garden. It is uncertain how many slaves Bean owned at this time to help Candace with chores. He bought a twenty-five-year-old female named "Qusdet" from Bostick in September for 500 pesos.[53] Several slaves were mentioned in his will made in 1843, more than a decade after he and Candace had split the blanket. In lawsuits that followed, Bean was said to have owned twelve or fifteen slaves; most were a family unit that he had seemingly acquired in 1830 if not before.

The prize of the lot was a field hand named Dory, although it is uncertain when and how Bean came to own him. When Robert Collier was murdered in September 1826, an inventory of his estate was formed by Alcalde Elbert Hines of the Sabine District. Item six read: "Dory a field hand aged about 21, property of Nath[aniel] Collier."[54] The same month that Bean bought the female slave Qusdet, he was ordered to appear before Alcalde Ibarvo concerning the declaration of Nathaniel's sister Susana Collier. She said that Dory belonged to her brother as a gift from their grandfather and had not been part of their father Robert's property. It appears that Bean had either bought, or was trying to establish control over, Dory—seemingly because he was Nathaniel's guardian.[55] After Bean left Texas, a number of lawsuits were filed, charging that he had unlawfully deprived Nathaniel Collier of Dory's labor since the year 1830.

Perhaps Bean parted with some of his league on Mound Prairie in 1829 because of his plans to relocate east of Nacogdoches. In July Bean bought a tract of land on the left bank of La Nana Creek from Juan José Mata Medina, at a cost of forty pesos. In September he paid Vital Flores four hundred pesos for a league of land that extended on both sides of Carrizo Creek, or "Bayou" as it was sometimes called. In the sales document Flores referred to the purchase as "mi rancho en el Carrizo" two leagues from town and said it embraced "all my land." During the fall and winter, Bean built a sawmill and house just west of the creek. According to Robert B. Blake, it was on the Old Camino Real and later called the Upper Melrose Road. Once this sawmill was in operation, Bean opened a lumber yard in town and sold all sorts of building supplies. Despite local lore about the residence, which stood until the 1950s, Bean does not seem to have brought Candace and the children to this house. It may have been his "bachelor" quarters, intended to distance himself from a marriage that was not working out. One suspects that Bean's trips to Mound Prairie became less frequent after he had a dwelling of his own, right next to his bustling sawmill. Bean himself later admitted as much.[56]

Throughout the summer Colonel Piedras and Political Chief Músquiz exchanged letters on the alarming situation all along the border with the United States. A possible invasion worried them, as U.S. troops were said to be massing on the boundary line. Indians continued to stream into east Texas from the United States in what amounted to an invasion itself. Bean's influence with the Indians was mentioned favorably in this correspondence. Erasmo Seguín wrote similar letters from Béxar on border problems, begging the government's attention lest Texas be lost to the Mexican Federation.[57]

Following his victory over the Spaniards at Tampico in September 1829, during which Felipe de la Garza was eased aside by Gen. Antonio López de Santa Anna (technically in command of the operation), General Terán functioned as the actual commandant general of the Eastern Interior States. As this jurisdiction embraced the states of Tamaulipas, Nuevo León, and Coahuila y Texas, these pleas for military reinforcements in Texas soon crossed his desk. Terán's 1828 inspection had already convinced him that the Mexican hold on Texas was in dire peril from peaceful but unrestricted Anglo immigration into the eastern section of Texas. The prospect of U.S. troops marching across the Sabine to fan the spark of revolution that the Anglo colonists might ignite themselves was more than General Terán could abide. By the end of the year he was forming plans for a display of military strength in Texas to head off any revolutionary sentiments that might be brewing. These plans he pursued into 1830, although Bustamante's revolution in the interior of Mexico prevented any troops being sent to Texas in 1829.

As suggested, the federal government was undergoing another rapid transition. President Guerrero's cabinet had been under attack by opposition forces on both political and military levels. It consisted of Lorenzo de Zavala as minister of treasury and head of the cabinet, the same who had received confirmation of his Texas colonization contract in February 1829; José María Bocanegra as minister of internal and foreign affairs, the same who had awarded Zavala his contract in preference to Bean; José M. Herrera, who headed justice and ecclesiastical matters; and Francisco Moctezuma, minister of war and navy. The opposition coalition struck not so much at Guerrero as at his cabinet. Zavala was practically forced to resign; Bocanegra was shifted to the treasury department, and Agustín Viesca—brother of the governor of Coahuila y Texas who had discredited Bean—took Bocanegra's place.

The opposition, now led by General Bustamante, would not accept this reshuffling of a cabinet that they deemed too liberal if not corrupt and ineffectual. Vice President Bustamante, under the pretense of restoring constitutional order, proclaimed the Plan of Jalapa in December 1829. According to Article 4 of this Plan, a complete change in the officials of the government was demanded. Various states rallied to the Plan, and after a short contest Bustamante's troops were victorious. When Guerrero abandoned the struggle, his partisans—including General Santa Anna—fell into line. Bustamante became chief of state on January 1, 1830, and true to his promise he named a more conservative cabinet. Lucas Alamán was made minister of internal and foreign affairs, while José Antonio Facio was given the war portfolio. Bustamante had offered the job to Terán, but he declined in favor of his friend Facio. Terán was busy enough with his duties as commandant general, which were confirmed. Thus Col. Peter Ellis Bean had several friends in high position at the beginning of 1830.[58]

His standing at Nacogdoches and San Augustine, however, was still in ill repute. One individual who did not think too highly of Bean was Thomas F. McKinney, a prosperous young merchant of the "upper class" who resented Bean's influence on local affairs. On September 9, 1829, McKinney wrote Austin a letter that—after denouncing Colonel Piedras as a Spanish sympathizer in vicious fashion—tore into Bean: "The Ayish Byou settlers are perfectly disposed to sustain the present institutions [of government] it is true that they have been much decieved as respects their land titles by pompous stories which Bean has told them relative to his controling powers as empresario and Comisioner of the reserve Lands having been thus disappointed repeatedly they have perhaps been unmindful some of them that these were impositions of an individual and not of the Govt and expressed themselves in that [angry] way." McKinney admitted that it was a breach of confidence to be telling Austin these things, as he had received his information from a friend of Bean's "and [he] expressly requested [me] to Keep it a secret but in order to give you an idia of his excessive stupidity and vanity I must inform you that he has obtained permission to visit Mexico and the object of his visit is to have texas stricken of[f] into a teritorial Govt and get himself the appointment of Governor he also says that his plan is supported by G[enera]l Terran this I can not believe however I know the Genl esteemed him as a good but ignorant man."

To McKinney's way of thinking, such an appointment would justly subject the government to censure and keep the local people in disorder. He enclosed a copy of one of Bean's letters to the alcalde of Ayish Bayou (probably Bean's letter on militia organization) so that Austin could have "a distant idia of his presumption and the imposition which he practices upon these people which in my opinion has a great tendency to keep up confusion among them for he never says when any enquiries are made of him that he does not know [the answer] he in some way or other always gives positive relations of all things."[59]

McKinney, as slanted against Bean as his statements are, reinforces Bean's own "All's Quiet on the Eastern Frontier" letters to people on a variety of subjects ranging from Indian problems to outright revolution. Bean seemed to want to put a positive spin on life, and this attitude of his was no doubt expressed to settlers in the boundary reserve. Little is known about the supposed project between Bean and Terán to make Texas a territory separate from Coahuila, an arrangement that Bean—with Terán's support—would administer as "Governor." Even if remotely true, this prospect would have made Austin a bitter enemy of Bean, as it did with others who advocated a territorial status for Texas in opposition to Austin's desires for separate statehood. McKinney went on to say that the only thing that could remedy the situation was the appointment of "an inteligent and virtuous man" with authority over the region, and the arrival of a commissioner "to give them titles to lands an oficer of the Govt to whom they could apply with confidence for necessary instructions who knew his duty and fulfilled his obligacions." In McKinney's mind, Peter Ellis Bean was definitely not that man.

The gossipy McKinney was far from finished spreading malicious information about Bean to Austin. Next he talked about Bean's abilities as an Indian agent: "The indians too have been much disapointed by Bean who to gratify his own vanity tells them many things which they find him uncapable of fulfilling and the Genl song among them is that Bean lie heap . . . the Shawnees have talked of going for some time to see a big man at St Antonio who they say is a good man no lie and a good friend to the indians [Francisco] Ruis."[60]

This "lie heap" label has unfairly become affixed to Peter Ellis Bean in terms of his relations with the Indians. McKinney seems not to have realized that it was beyond the power of either Bean or Ruiz to place Indians in possession of the lands they occupied. Not even General Terán had such authority, so they had to keep stringing the Indians along until a decision was made in Mexico City by the president and his minister of relations. If Bean was making promises to the Indians that he could not keep, which he probably was, it was scarcely his fault when the government did not deliver. Bean was in a virtual no-win situation, and it is not surprising that the Indians thought he "lie heap." Modern historians should discard such catchy labels and probe for the underlying reasons that brought them into use.

McKinney closed by begging that Austin keep secret his breach of the confidence of Bean's friend who had told him about "Beans pretencions to the *Gubernatorial* Seat of the anticipated Territory of Texas." He said he would like to know if Austin thought "there could be any possibility of the Govt being duped by him [Bean] in such a manner and if Genl Terran would possibly promote such schemes." But once started, McKinney couldn't shut up on the subject of Colonel Bean's shortcomings. He rambled on about how Bean had written an address to the people of Ayish Bayou, informing them of his visit to Mexico, tendering his services on their behalf, and thanking them for their former attentions to him. Bean, said McKinney, also made verbal requests of them to draw up a petition for him to represent them in Mexico, "though his scheme does not seem to take he is anxious in my opinion to get in his possession some document which will induce the Govt [to believe] that he has Standing among us which no Doubt [will] fail."[61]

Little can be said about this letter except to show how mean-spirited were the enemies with whom Bean had to contend. Interestingly, McKinney was already suggesting at this early date that Texas should establish and support "a respectable Govt independant of that of Mexico," although it would be "perfect madness" to express such an idea until the American position was stronger. He was feeling out Austin on this subject. Austin, whose motto was "Fidelity to Mexico" in these years, did not encourage such ideas.

In the latter part of 1829 Bean made a trip to San Antonio. His purpose was to press for payment of his salary and gratifications owed him by *comisario* Seguín, pursue the question of title to the league of land he had bought from his "nephew" William, and attend to other business matters. Bean wrote the political chief a heated protest regarding the saline dispute on August 18, after the ayuntamiento had presented to him the null-

and-void verdict. Músquiz had reinforced the edict in a letter of August 5, saying that the authorities were "insulted" by the devious way Bean had gained his possession. Bean protested that he had already paid surveying and filing fees on the tract and spent more than three hundred dollars making improvements on the saline. He told Músquiz that he was coming to Béxar, where he as William Bean's attorney would "answer in person all charges, and exhibit proofs to confuse false reports" that had been circulated against his rightful title.[62]

Bean was there at the end of October and did not return to Nacogdoches until the end of the year. He had no success with Political Chief Músquiz. On November 29 (after Bean had left Béxar) Músquiz ruled that the colonel's purchase from William Bean was illegal, just as Governor Viesca had considered it in February, and that the saline was to be declared vacant.[63] It appears that old settlers Raymond Norris and Raymond "Querqui" (Quirk) also were trying to gain possession of the Neches Saline, and that their petition was more favored by the ayuntamiento. Regardless, the saline was now up for grabs. If Bean was going to win out, he had to try something different; the purchase from his "nephew" did not work.

Just as McKinney told Austin, Bean had received in July permission to go to Jalapa but was unable to make the trip. He remained in Texas and was authorized to carry payment for the troops at Nacogdoches in November; by mid-December he reported the delivery. On December 22, he wrote Commandant Elozúa the following letter.

> I have arrived here without news, finding all peaceful, although there was displeasure with the [president's] order freeing the Negroes; but [the citizens] are quiet and awaiting the arrival of the Señor Commissioner for giving the settlers of these frontiers possession of their lands; then they will be completely satisfied and will have landed property to defend, for which reason they are bound to be good patriots. If something happens in this respect, I shall give Your Lordship prompt notice.
>
> It is said here that the United States are trying to purchase this frontier to the Rio Grande, but there is nothing certain up to this time. On this date I am going to write the Most Excellent Señor President of the Republic of Mexico, urging that he not agree to this sale, because it would be the loss of the best part of the Mexican Government's territory. On the 14th some of the soldiers I brought, and others, left for Béxar. God and Liberty.[64]

Does this sound like the letter of an ignorant man, unfit to manage political affairs on the northern frontier? Perhaps not as McKinney and Austin would have desired, but Bean shows a grasp of what President Guerrero's September 15 decree, abolishing the institution of slavery in Mexico, meant to the plantation/slave owners in Texas. It threw them into near apoplexy, until they learned that Political Chief Músquiz was not going to publish or enforce the emancipation proclamation without first appealing that Texas be exempted. Gov. José María Viesca forwarded the appeal to Mexico City, with a strong endorsement, while his brother Agustín was still minister of relations. Through him President Guerrero issued a decree in December, stating that Texas would be exempt from the law abolishing slavery in Mexican territory. Guerrero sent Commandant General Terán a confidential letter at the same time, telling him to inform the Texans that they could keep their slaves but no new ones were to be introduced.[65]

Where did Bean get news that the United States was trying to purchase Texas? Probably from Anthony Butler, who was passing through Texas at this time with instructions from Pres. Andrew Jackson for that very thing.[66] These became Butler's own instructions when he reached Mexico City to find that Joel Poinsett had been recalled and he was to take his place as U.S. chargé d'affaires to Mexico. Bean, in other words, was privy to some inside information. When it became known in Mexico that Butler had arrived with instructions to buy Texas, national outrage was provoked.[67] McKinney, of course, would have regarded Bean's intention to write President Guerrero and urge him not to accept this offer, as another example of Bean's "vanity." Perhaps so, but presidents of nations need to hear sound advice from their loyal citizens, men like Bean who had fought in the struggle for Mexican independence. If this is vanity, more patriots should be guilty of it.

Chapter 9

COLONIZATION SHUTS DOWN

PRES. VICENTE GUERRERO had more serious problems to worry about in December 1829 than any U.S. purchase scheme afoot. He was already en route to retirement at his hacienda when Bean planned to write him, and Bustamante was on his way to Mexico City to take control of the government. Foreign Minister Alamán, however, was the brains behind the conservative movement that this military overthrow represented; it was said that he regarded the tough old Indian fighter Bustamante as a "simpleton." But Alamán could not regard the well-educated Terán in this light, and he soon started listening to the alarming reports about Texas that General Terán was forwarding to the capital. Bustamante, of course, knew firsthand about the problems besetting Texas, and he also respected Colonel Bean's role as a peacemaker among the Indians. Simpleminded or otherwise, Bustamante could be relied on to back Terán's proposals for saving Texas.[1]

With order restored, Alamán in February presented to a closed session of Congress some of Terán's ideas about the steps that needed to be taken to preserve Texas for the Mexican federation. This resulted in the notorious law of April 6, 1830, that decreed even stiffer measures than Terán had pushed for. All colonization contracts were suspended (except those of Austin, DeWitt, and De León) and further emigration from the United States was prohibited. No more slaves were to be brought to Texas, even by settlers headed to the colonies of the three men who were ruled to be in substantial fulfillment of their contracts.[2] Terán was given permission to establish the forts he considered necessary in Texas, and he was soon named as commissioner of colonization—in addition to the military power he already wielded as commandant general of the Eastern Interior States and the political clout he exercised as the nation's boundary commissioner on the northern frontier. For the next two and a half years, Gen. Manuel de Mier y Terán was "the Boss" (as Austin called him) where Texas was concerned.[3]

Even before this hated law was passed, Terán was writing Minister Alamán about colonization problems in Texas. On March 15 he suggested to Alamán that Anglo and Indian families who had illegally come to east Texas should be gathered into the land between the Sabine and Neches Rivers, from their origins down to the Neches and Angelina junction. He impressed upon Alamán the seriousness of having so many illegal settlers scattered about the frontier, and urged that the federal government do something to regulate the situation. Terán sketched a crude map of the region where this proposal was to be effected, calling it "a simple version of my itinerary."[4]

Col. Peter Ellis Bean, of course, had been Terán's companion and guide through this country in 1828. Was this the "Territory" over which Bean hoped to be governor? Did he and Terán reach an understanding, as they traveled the boundary reserve together, on how the squatters—both Anglo and Indian—could be awarded land in this district under a territorial arrangement? The lands for which the immigrant tribes, as well as Bean's fellow Anglos, were petitioning the government were between the Sabine and the Neches. Bean, as "Governor" over these lands, could satisfy both groups. And if the region was given territorial status, he would only be responsible to federal officials—not fouled up with the state governor of Coahuila y Texas, his bitter enemy. Documentation to support this theory has not yet been located, but it may turn up. The possibility also exists that Bean's planned trip to Jalapa in the summer of 1829 was actually to confer with General Terán and iron out the details, on the way down to see his wife.

While it is true that Burnet, Zavala, and Vehlein held colonization contracts in this region, the politicians at Mexico City who had made the decision and signed the paperwork were now out of power. None of the three empresarios had introduced settlers. Moreover, by March 15, 1830, Terán knew that such contracts would be canceled by the initiative that Alamán had introduced to Congress in February; it became law only three weeks later. Thus the reserved lands on the boundary would revert to the federal government, along with other lands not awarded to colonists when the empresarios' contracts expired. With Minister Alamán's power, and the certain backing of President Bustamante, these lands could be set aside from Coahuila y Texas and made a "Territory." It was Austin's worst fear; he wanted Texas to be made into a state separate from Coahuila, not have the eastern swath designated as under territorial (i.e., federal) rule. McKinney's September 1829 letter about Bean's grandiose scheme, and General Terán's possible interest in furthering it, must have alarmed Austin considerably.[5]

Meanwhile, Bean took advantage of the governor's promise a year earlier to concede him the "maximum" amount of land in the empty portions of the state. On February 27, 1830, he wrote Viesca requesting that eleven leagues be granted "in places most convenient to my interests, whether all together or separate, provided they are entirely vacant." Bean offered to settle and cultivate these lands as the law stipulated, agreeing also to pay for them in installments until the full sum was covered. Viesca passed this application on to the commissioner general of lands, Juan Antonio Padilla, for review. Padilla, on April 25, attested to Colonel Bean's past services and good qualities, pronouncing, "I judge him meriting this solicitation." Still, it was not until January 1831 that Viesca "granted in sale" the land that Bean had asked for—eight leagues instead of the eleven. No reason was given for the governor's decision to sell Bean less than the "maximum" to which he was entitled, and which Viesca had promised to award Bean during the contest with Zavala. Was it because of the two leagues already granted to Bean as a settler, plus the annulled league he had purchased from William Bean? If so, Governor Viesca had been keeping a sharp eye on Colonel Bean's land affairs in distant Texas.[6]

General Terán was soon swamped with problems that resulted from the April 6, 1830, law, colonization affairs being no small portion of them. There were also the problems associated with erecting forts in Texas and garrisoning them with soldiers to safeguard Mexico's territorial integrity on the frontier. Of these, Fort Tenoxtitlán was the first to go into operation. It was located on the Brazos River a short distance above the Old San Antonio Road, and Col. Francisco Ruiz was made its commandant. Later in the year, forts were built at the mouth of the Trinity River (Fort Anáhuac, under command of Col. Juan Davis Bradburn) and on the lower Lavaca River (Fort Lavaca, where Rafael Chovell was commissioner). During 1831 others were added: Fort Lipantitlán on the lower Nueces under Col. Enrique Villarreal, and Fort Terán on the middle Neches, where Col. Peter Ellis Bean was in command. Another small fort was built at Velasco, near the mouth of the Brazos.[7]

But during 1830 Bean was mostly engaged in relations with the Indians. In April his decision not to give gifts to the Tawakoni leader Cacarahue was approved.[8] The *Texas Gazette* of San Felipe carried one of Bean's reports of May 29 that the Cherokees, Shawnees, and Kickapoos had gone to war with the Wacos and Tawakonis. So far one battle had been fought, with thirty losses to the defenders and only five to the attackers. This war of total extermination between the tribes of "northern Indians, lately removed to Texas" would be extended to the Comanches. The article reported that the Comanches had been driven from their hunting grounds at the heads of the Brazos and Colorado Rivers by a tribe of Indians "heretofore unknown to them." They had supposedly

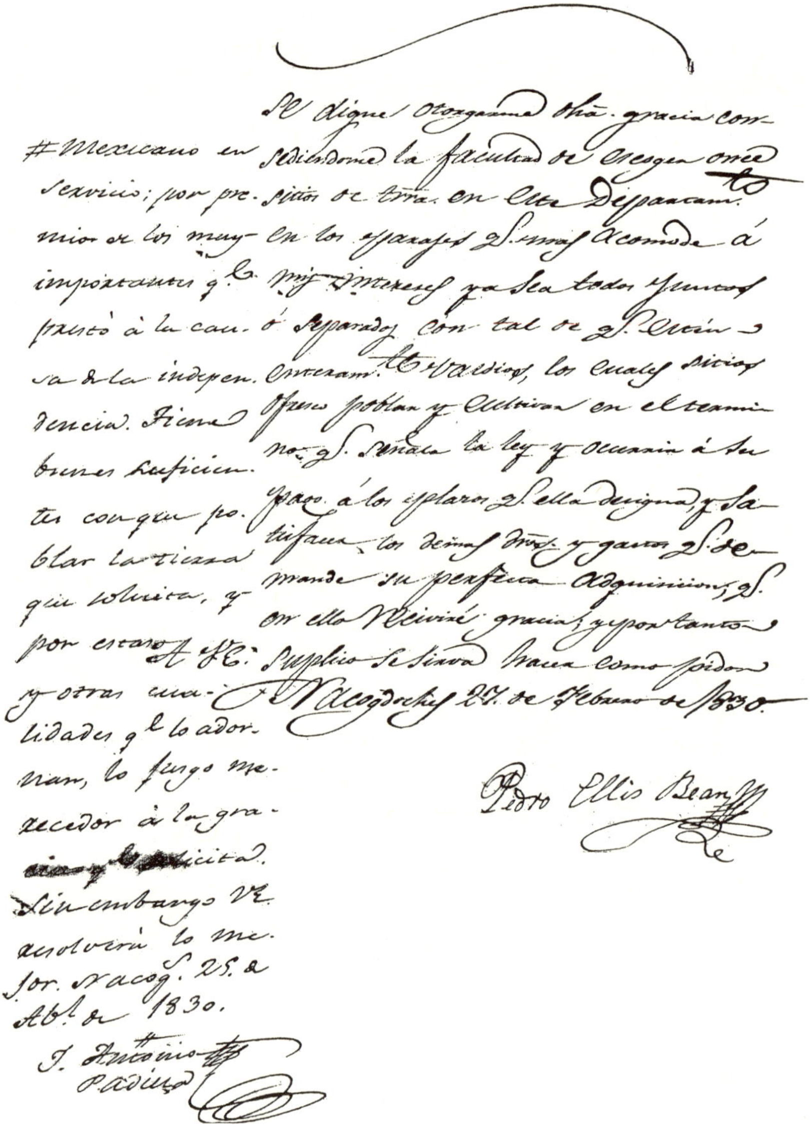

Bean's signature page of 1830 petition for eleven leagues of land. Courtesy State Archives of Coahuila.

sought refuge in the southwestern part of Texas, on the Nueces and Rio Grande.[9] This was wishful thinking.

Bean wrote Colonel Elozúa an account of the battle on June 22. He said that eight tribes of Indians on the frontier had declared war against the Tawakonis, Wacos, and Taovayas. The Cherokees had made their campaign, hitting the Tawakoni village. They killed thirty-six, "although some of them were women," and there were twenty-eight wounded, many of whom had since died, and they burned the village. The Cherokee war party numbered sixty men, of whom they lost six. Not a single one of the Tawakonis would have survived, except for an underground fort in which they took shelter: "The Charaquíes were killed while setting fire to the fort, but it did not burn because it was underground; and at present they are planning a strong campaign with the different tribes that they have gathered together, and without doubt the Malefactors of the Plains were left well punished; the Frontier is tranquil, and the roads are open."[10]

Elozúa forwarded Bean's good news to Commandant General Terán on July 6, with his opinion that "such occurrences cannot help but redound to the benefit of this Department." Since these three tribes were the only Indians who continued to be hostile, they were now left in a position where they could no longer "continue to do us harm." The new establishment of the Alamo Company at the Upper Crossing of the Brazos River would ensure that.[11] On the same day Elozúa thanked Bean for his efforts in bringing this Cherokee campaign together (though not in so many words) and also gave Colonel Ruiz notice of the victory.[12] Ruiz received Bean's report "with the greatest satisfaction" and did not doubt that —"if it turns out as Señor Bean indicates"—Texas would benefit.

But Ruiz, in his reply to Elozúa, pursued the implications of what this victory and the forthcoming campaign of the immigrant tribes against the Wacos, Tawakonis, and Taovayas meant: "Although it may not achieve their total extermination, it will at least make them abandon their lands or villages and go away from our settlements." Now was the time to press them to the "last extreme," delaying their peace overtures and not admitting them to any towns where they might obtain gunpowder or munitions. Thus they would be thrown back on trade with Americans to the north or the Indians called "Aquases," the latter of whom could not satisfy their needs. There was also the possibility that they would join up with the large Comanche nation "with which they are in great harmony," particularly the "Tauaces" to whom they would flee if persecuted. Ruiz believed that "gentle and prudent means" should be taken so the Comanches would not admit these tribes to their villages, making them understand that they (the Comanches) were at peace with Mexico and did not appreciate being subjected to their problems.[13]

Colonel Bean was also queried on the subject of traders who might be supplying arms and ammunition to the three Wichita tribes. He told Elozúa that no traders had left from Nacogdoches to carry on this commerce. The "Anadacos" and French traders who came in secretly from Bayou Pierre were the guilty parties. They wanted to involve the Comanches in stealing horses so they could buy them cheap. They were using the Wichita tribes as middlemen, and it was through their lies that the Comanches were led to believe the people of Nacogdoches wanted to destroy them. As for the Cherokees and their allies, they should be permitted to "avenge themselves against those bad tribes." They would not harm the Comanches, but the Comanches must not unite with the Wacos and Tawakonis to make war on Bean's Indian friends. He blamed the Anadarkos for spreading these lies, all to protect their monopoly on the stolen horse market in Louisiana.[14]

Terán, when advised of these developments, wrote Bean. He told Bean that he was ordering Colonel Piedras to "furnish you a cash fund" so that the Cherokees could be supplied with shot and powder for their campaign as they had requested. The "savages" were to function freely in carrying out their operations, but Bean, by "every means within your reach," was to prevent them from forming an alliance with the Kickapoos, Shawnees, and other tribes mentioned, "since it will never be beneficial for our small establishments to have so many Indians joined together." The day would come when they got the idea of attacking some detachment, especially the Cherokees, who knew how to carry on tactical warfare and were "less stupid" than the other tribes.[15] By this we can see that General Terán was asking Bean to do almost the impossible—keep the Cherokees battling the Wichita tribal groups but without the help of their immigrant allies.

July 1830 was a busy month for Bean. On July 7 U.S. Indian Agent Jehiel Brooks wrote him from Louisiana, asking that Bean convince the Cherokees not to attack the Caddos. Evidently Bean succeeded, and the Caddos were "spared the wrath of the more powerful intruder."[16] Bean also received orders from Terán that month to take a troop of soldiers and go to Pecan Point, where he was to see how things stood. Colonel Elozúa was advised by Colonel Piedras on July 19 that Colonel Bean, Alférez Jesús de la Garza, and ten cavalrymen had left Nacogdoches pursuant to Terán's orders.[17] Garza, his men all sick because of the "bad climate at those points," returned to Nacogdoches on September 14. Bean had taken the road to Natchitoches to see if there was anything to fear from the Caddo tribe or if it was planning to reunite in Mexican territory. Alférez Garza told Piedras that the settlers at Pecan Point who wanted to be subjects of the Mexican nation were being "badly mistreated" and yearned for a boundary survey that would resolve the question of which nation they belonged to.[18]

Bean reached Nacogdoches several days later. In his subsequent reports to Terán he made it clear that U.S. officials in Arkansas Territory were trying to carve out a chunk of Mexican territory as their own fiefdom. Already they exercised control over the citizens on the south bank of the Red River. This, of course, was Miller County, which had been organized as part of Arkansas Territory. On September 27 Colonel Piedras wrote General Terán of the situation that Bean had found on the Red

River. The governor had ordered Milam to cease his colonization operations in the region, and the lack of a recognized dividing line had "paralyzed" any development that might occur. Good families who wished to establish themselves in the Wavell-Milam colony were dissuaded because no one knew who "owned" the territory.[19]

Bean wrote Terán directly on November 22, saying that some of the settlers at Pecan Point had been introduced by Milam while others had come on their own—thinking that these lands belonged to the United States—but none had arrived at the invitation of Señor Wavell, "as this gentleman never was known [in Texas]." Milam was acting as his agent, with the approval of both the federal and state governments. According to Bean, there were "about three hundred families who are settled on the banks of the Red River on the southwestern side belonging to the Mexican Govt., and more who are emigrating, [all] desirous of the protection of this Government." He promised by the next mail to send a map, "although badly made," so that Terán could be better informed about the country at risk.

Bean also passed along information that the president of the United States had bought or exchanged lands of the Choctaw and Chickasaw Indians. They had three years to move west, taking the lands that faced Pecan Point to the east of the Red River. He reminded Terán that only the shallow river divided the Indians from Mexican territory. For the exchange of lands, the president had given to each warrior a carbine, a blanket, and twenty thousand pesos per year, which were to be divided between the two tribes at twenty thousand pesos each year for the term of twenty years. "These Indians are very peaceful; they never have made war on the whites, but their number is large, and some day they may cause us to regret [their relocation]; calculating the number of children and adults, they come to 28,625 souls."

When Terán transmitted Bean's letter to the secretary of foreign relations on December 30, it was with his own thoughts about the danger represented to Mexico's interests by the North Americans. In the colonies of Texas, families from the North were introducing themselves without anyone's knowledge or permission, taking possession of the land, and then an empresario, "no more than because he has taken the trouble of requesting that he be called one, enters into schemes with the intruders, from which he alone draws benefit. In sum, Most Excellent Sir, there has been conceded to some private persons the right to sell a beautiful country that is property of a whole Nation." Foreigners were being attracted to a place where they did not belong, and Terán wanted them thrown out. He suggested that, because these settlers were in violation of the law of last April 6, the government should suspend all such enterprises, "even those that already had the approval of Superior Authority," because neither the empresarios nor the government of the state of Coahuila y Texas understood the issues involved.[20] Based upon Bean's visit and reports, Terán became engaged in a diplomatic contest with José María Tornel —Mexico's own representative in Washington—over whether this was Mexican or United States soil. Terán correctly maintained that it belonged to Mexico, even if inhabited by North Americans and immigrant Indians from the rival nation.

After Bean returned to Nacogdoches from this assignment, Colonel Piedras wrote Commandant Elozúa on September 28 about recent horse thefts that had occurred near the Neches on the main road—in other words, where Colonel Bean's family lived. Tawakonis, possibly with some Keechis, had stolen horses belonging to the Shawnees. The latter tribe and the Cherokees were avowed enemies of the thieves, and this incident had provoked their wrath. Piedras believed that now was the perfect time to organize a major strike against the Tawakonis and Wacos, whose frequent outrages made the roads unsafe and kept any kind of progress from happening: "Taking advantage of the favorable attitude of the aforementioned [Shawnee and Cherokee] tribes, I have ordered Colonel Don Peter Ellis Bean to go to that city [Béxar] for the purpose of proposing to Your Lordship an expedition of three or four parties that together can operate against the aforesaid Tahuacanos and pursue them in all directions until they are exterminated."[21] His ideas for the campaign much resemble those earlier advanced by Austin, but Bean had probably adopted similar search-and-destroy tactics in his own war councils with the friendly tribes. Bean, said Piedras, was going with a Cherokee chief to discuss plans for the campaign with Elozúa at Béxar.

Elozúa notified Commandant General Terán on October 22 that Bean had arrived a few days earlier. As soon as Bean reached town, the two of them consulted the "experts who have lived among the Huecos and Tahucanos, and who are informed of their customs and their territories." These conferences brought forth the information that it was customary for these Indians to abandon their villages in the winter months and withdraw to creeks and forests where they engaged in hunting. No one knew where they might be found at present, except it was possible that—after their defeat on the Brazos and San Gabriel Rivers by Nicasio Sánchez's force in September—they had mixed in with the Comanches. Consequently, Elozúa told Terán that "it appears that the season or the opportune moment for our expedition to go out has not arrived yet." Better information was needed on the whereabouts of these two tribes, their strength, and so forth. Colonel Piedras was advised by mail the next day that the campaign had been postponed, but the letter did not reach him until Bean brought it on his return to Nacogdoches.[22]

Once this matter was behind him, Bean gave Elozúa some alarming news about Pres. Andrew Jackson's Indian Removal Policy. He may have seen this article from a Washington newspaper on his trip to Natchitoches and brought it home with him. It revealed that Congress had placed at the president's disposal five hundred thousand pesos (dollars) for the purpose of buying Indian lands and moving the tribes inhabiting them west of the Mississippi. Bean broke down the totals from seven states and territories, noting that 109,412 Indians were involved: "And there is no doubt that, when these [tribes] cross the Mississippi River, many of them are bound to come and infiltrate through our frontiers, and this is a threat which we should take measures to avoid and keep them from coming in."[23] Elozúa forwarded this letter to Terán the same day, no doubt increasing the commandant general's own fears that these removed tribes would penetrate the porous boundaries of Texas and complicate further an already unstable situation with the immigrant Indians living in the department.

Then Bean tackled a more personal subject, one that had been eating away at him for almost four years. "Some time ago [he wrote Elozúa on October 22] I heard, from bad reports, that you all have been wanting to file some kind of charge against my honor and my conduct, saying that I had married two different women. I have waited with much patience, and now I am asking that, if I am delinquent, I be declared as such, and therefore I beg that said charges be presented to me so that, in view thereof, I can vindicate my honor, as I very well can."[24]

Nothing disconcerted the Spanish military system so much as having to deal with a demand that dirty laundry of this sort be washed in public, out in the open instead of remaining behind closed doors. Elozúa wrote Bean that his case was in the possession of Capt. José Ortega at Nacogdoches, to whom had fallen the responsibility of documenting the charges against him in the form stipulated by the Supreme Government. He was being told to bring it to a speedy conclusion, and Elozúa assured Bean he had "no doubt that the reputation of Your Lordship will be vindicated in the manner which it justly deserves." Captain Ortega was promptly notified of Bean's request, "which he, with so much justice, is demanding."[25] Although this sort of flattering language was customary in delicate situations, the pressure was now on Ortega to wind up his investigation. Colonel Bean wanted to either be cleared or proclaimed a bigamist. The verdict might cause him to be drummed out of the Mexican military service, but Bean insisted that a decision be reached.

Ortega wrote Elozúa on November 22, 1830, saying that Bean's case was suspended, "awaiting the reply from the Judge of the District in which they assert he married—to whom I resorted, seeking a certificate of said marriage—in order to be certain [that Bean was actually married].” Since no other party had appeared with conclusive evidence, it was “impossible without this document to prove in judgment the bigamy [charge] of which he is harrassed.” Ortega had, with the previous day’s date, again repeated his request for Bean’s marriage certificate, availing himself of the High Judge of Natchitoches, “and if, in the ordinary course of things, I do not receive his reply, I shall give Your Lordship an account of the condition in which it [Bean’s case] is found.”[26]

This seems to be the end of the matter, as no documentation has been located to indicate if Captain Ortega ever received a copy of the certificate uniting Peter Ellis Bean and Candace Midkiff in matrimony, holy or otherwise. Nor have any proceedings been found in which Colonel Bean vindicated his honor, as he avowed he very well could. A recent Bean genealogical post on the Internet claims that they were married in 1818 in the community of Sparta, White County, Tennessee, Candace having been born in Nashville on December 12, 1802. Thus she was only sixteen when tying the knot with a man almost twenty years her elder—a man much experienced in worldly ways.[27] (The birth entry in her family Bible, however, gives the year as 1800, making her a more respectable eighteen when she married Bean.)[28] Considering that Candace was joined in Texas around 1831 by her brother Isaac, it is odd that she did not ask him to bring proof of her marriage to Bean.[29] Perhaps it only amounted to an entry in the Midkiff family Bible, not the sort of thing Ortega would have needed to close the case to the government’s satisfaction. It appears that the investigation died a slow death.

Because the vital records of White County, Tennessee, are so fragmentary for the decades of the 1810s–1820s, we may never find the conclusive evidence that Captain Ortega was seeking in 1830. Marriages before local justices in small settlements are particularly lacking, creating problems for modern genealogists who try to trace the roots of their family in this region.[30] In short, it remains unknown if Peter Ellis Bean and Candace Midkiff really did become “officially” married by a man named McDaniel in 1818. Nonetheless, they lived together as a family in Texas and were generally recognized as man and wife by the people of Nacogdoches. In demanding that he be allowed to defend his “honor,” Bean may have intended to argue technicalities—such as he did with the distinction between little salines and salty earth.

The colonel left San Antonio shortly after writing these letters. He passed through Fort Tenoxtitlán, delivering funds to Colonel Ruiz and his Alamo Company troopers. This was acknowledged by Ruiz on November 12.[31] Near the Trinity River, Bean came across a group of families probably bound for Robertson’s colony. Because they were North Ameri-

Painting of Bean by his great-grandson, Haskell Bean. Photo courtesy Carolyn Reeves Ericson.

cans without passports, Piedras had detained them when they passed through the town of Nacogdoches—this in fulfillment of the provisions of the law of April 6, 1830. But these men had slipped away with their families, in total disregard of his orders for them to remain at the Rancho del Carrizo, and were doubtless headed for Austin's colony. Austin was advised not to admit them as settlers, considering their furtive entry and subsequent exhibition of blatant disrespect for Piedras's authority.[32]

Colonel Piedras, upon Bean's arrival, learned of the "just motive which exists for the suspension of the expedition against the Tahuacanos." He wrote Elozúa that he would "wait, as you suggest, for a more opportune occasion to undertake it." Commandant General Terán also received Elozúa's news with regret. He ordered that the campaign be pursued at a more favorable time, "with Your Lordship limiting yourself, for the present, to whatever is appropriate for the safety of the new establishment at Tenoxtitlan."[33]

Terán also passed on to Secretary of Foreign Relations Alamán Bean's information about how the North Americans had established a district and part of another in Mexican territory and how the governor of Arkansas Territory was opposing Ben Milam's activities in this region.[34] Terán wrote Milam as well, suspending his operations because the settlers he was introducing were from the United States instead of Europe. Thus Milam's efforts as agent for the Wavell grant violated the provisions of the April 6, 1830, law. Terán even ordered Piedras to impede Milam's land commissioner (José Antonio Navarro) and surveyor (José María Carvajal) so no titles could be issued to the lands around Jonesboro and Pecan Point. These decisions irked Terán, as he knew this was Mexican territory and should be colonized under Mexican authority. His desire to stop the unauthorized entry of North Americans, however, was greater than his consideration for the settlers already in place—especially when officials of the United States were behind this takeover. Thus the settlers of the region were left in limbo.[35]

Meanwhile, a larger problem for Terán was taking place in the United States. Lorenzo de Zavala, David Burnet, and Joseph Vehlein on October 16, 1830, sold their land concessions to a speculative organization called the Galveston Bay & Texas Land Company, based in New York City. Their contracts covered an area lying west of the Sabine to the San Jacinto River, and bordered at the top by a line running twenty leagues north of Nacogdoches. It was an immense area comprising almost four million acres. The combined grants were soon being portrayed as one entity on Texas maps, all in an effort to sell land script to other speculators or directly to people interested in becoming settlers.[36] Even documents in the Mexican archives linked the three empresarios together, such as the file pertaining to Zavala's concession in the old Secretariat of Fomento (Development).[37]

Although these men had sold their empresarial contracts abroad, they did not entirely disassociate themselves from the colonization process. And even though none of them had introduced colonists by the time their contracts expired, all three—through the company's agents in Mexico City like John T. Mason—managed to get their contracts extended. Those of Burnet and Vehlein were renewed for three years in 1832, and Zavala's was renewed for four years in 1834. Agents eventually appeared on the scene in Texas, and grants were made in the names of the three empresarios—as if they had not relinquished control of the territory. This arrangement was opposed by Terán for two reasons: the sale violated the intent of the national colonization law, and the law of April 6, 1830, prohibited the introduction of settlers from the United States. To Terán, who was the commissioner of colonization for Texas, it was nothing but a big real estate scam whose object was to deliver this rich part of the state to foreign control.[38]

On February 2, 1831, Terán was obliged to write a sarcastic letter to José María Tornel, Mexico's representative in Washington, because Tornel had agreed with Secretary of State Martin Van Buren that Milam's colonization project and Bean's "surveying" work on the Red River would be suspended until a boundary survey took place between Mexico and the United States.

> Colonel Bean, carrying out my orders, went to Pecan Point to make an examination necessary to the Mexican service, the reconnoitering of the situation of the savage tribes, and preventing the entrance of [foreign] adventurers. In the execution of this commission, nothing occurred that should have called the attention of the Governor of Arkansas Territory [to it], or that ought to give rise to a political question, unless the mere presence of a detachment of twelve men, at points incontestably on the Mexican frontier, be assumed as a sufficient motive. The Colonel reported on his return that the commissioner, Maylan [Milam], had been notified by Governor Pope of Arkansas to suspend the formation of his colonization establishment; I had already notified him to the same effect, but for different reasons.[39]

Terán went on to say that there was a settlement of North Americans forming in the district, "which will possess itself of the country unless the Mexican government intervenes." If Governor Pope was so keen to stop Milam's activities on behalf of Mexico, then he should devote equal energy to stopping his own citizens from setting up shop in territory disputed by the two nations. Terán assured Tornel "with the greatest certainty" that Pecan Point was in Mexican territory. Tornel, by suspending these discussions "as Your Excellency has done," had laid aside Mexico's rights. This was a serious charge, perhaps why Tornel published a defense when he was called home.

Meanwhile, Peter Ellis Bean devoted himself to land affairs. In mid-February Alcalde Manuel de los Santos Coy wrote the political chief about the little salines in dispute with Bean. Santos felt confident that Bean's claim was no good and asked about the price that people should have to pay for taking a barrel of salt from the works. Bean wrote the alcalde on February 23, pointedly reminding him of the governor's decree of October 11 last. A month earlier Alcalde Santos had questioned Colonel Piedras about Bean's instructions for the Indians to turn over to him any Negroes found in the countryside, so he was on Bean's back for different reasons as 1831 began.[40]

Bean wrote again on the first of March, this time to the political chief, about the league of land with "little salines" that he had previously asked for, obtained through purchase from William Bean. Ignoring the adverse verdict already handed down, he rehashed his arguments on how these salines, "vulgarly called salty earth," were not salt deposits as recognized by law. Bean described again the process whereby salt was derived from such places by boiling down water taken there in kettles. He recited the articles of the laws governing such things, begging that his solicitation be recognized. At the end of the month Músquiz replied that he could not place Bean in possession of this *sitio* of land on the margins of the Neches because of the protests the Nacogdoches alcalde had made on behalf of the citizens of his community. The decision had to be reached by the governor, to whom all documents were being forwarded.[41]

At this time the governor of Coahuila y Texas was José María Letona, who had just replaced Viesca. The change of authorities at Saltillo, however, did not help Bean. On April 28 Letona ruled that the saline, "which at various times the Colonel Don Peter Ellis Bean has attempted to have granted him as private property," was to be "enjoyed indiscriminately by all the citizens of the State until the Supreme Government shall decide otherwise." Colonel Bean "may select a vacant place more suitable, in order that he be given possession of the territory that this government has granted to him."[42] Reference was to the leagues of land that the government of Coahuila y Texas was about to sell to Bean because he was a citizen of Mexico with past services to the nation and had lost out to Zavala on a larger bid for lands. At least the question had to be ultimately decided by the federal government—rather like Indian petitions for their lands—so Bean still had cause for optimism.

Músquiz forwarded this good news to the Nacogdoches ayuntamiento on May 12, saying that "all citizens can enjoy the benefits of said salines" until a higher ruling came from Mexico City; in the meantime, Colonel Bean could choose some other vacant place if he desired.[43] But Bean wanted this location, and he continued to push for it until he eventually won. It is likely that he kept his salt works in operation, allowing the local citizens limited access. Bean was not one to invest money in something and then let it lie idle.

It appears that one of Viesca's last acts before turning over the governorship to Letona was to grant Bean sale of the eleven leagues he had petitioned for a year earlier as a Mexican citizen. Even though only eight leagues were conceded, Bean always claimed that the sum was eleven leagues.[44] This is difficult to sort out because Bean—like many other Anglos in Texas—was buying eleven-league grants that had been conceded in other people's names, people with Spanish surnames who were citizens of Mexico. Bean acquired control of one such grant in 1831 from

Lt. Gavino Aranjo, the soldier who was designated to act as secretary when Captain Ortega was investigating Bean's marital status for Commandant Elozúa in 1829. At least one other Mexican soldier at Nacogdoches also acquired part of an eleven-league grant and transferred it to Bean. He was Alférez Jesús de la Garza, who led the small troop of soldiers to Pecan Point under Bean's command. They were probably put up to it by Bean—who then completed the surveys in choice spots and obtained title to the tracts, acting as their "attorney." When the land was sold, the money went into Bean's pockets. In all such cases, it is hard to say what soldiers like Aranjo and Garza or Mexican inhabitants of the town received when assigning their rights to "go-ahead" men like Bean. Usually the only document filed in the Nacogdoches clerk's office was a power of attorney.[45]

Not much has been known about Bean's religion or attitude toward education. Evidence that he was a Catholic and desired that his children have some formal schooling comes on March 10, 1831, when Bean—as a member of the *junta* or "Board of Piety" formed on the subject—signed a circular to the "Settlers of the Frontier." His name was second on the announcement, right after that of Colonel Piedras. It called for the erection of a church and a school in Nacogdoches, praising the benefits of both to the community.[46]

Bean continued to acquire town lots. At the end of November 1830 he paid Father Ignacio Galindo 160 pesos for "all the piece of land" that the priest owned in town. A month later José Pineda sold Bean a town lot for a mere 10 pesos; Bean sold it six years later for $500—quite a profit. On May 15, 1831, he bought a large lot (166 by 480 *varas*) on the hill just west of town from Doña María Catarina Amador, wife of the postmaster, Patricio de Torres. This cost him 100 pesos, but it had quite a view of Nacogdoches from what is now known as Irion Hill. At the time it was called "la Loma," and State Highway 21 descends from this elevation to cross the railroad tracks into town. A few days earlier Bean bought one hundred acres from Juan Lazarin, paying a peso (a dollar) an acre. The tract was a league and a half west of town on the Arroyo de los Ailitos at the place known as Moral, and one suspects it was farmland.[47] Although Bean was tending the orchard of his land business at this time, it did not come to fruition until some years later. Let us return to the Cherokees and General Terán's efforts on their behalf.

It has been the opinion of at least one historian that Terán "would not help them" obtain titles to their land.[48] This is a mistaken view of Terán's motives and an unfair accusation against him. Terán, during his 1828 inspection of Texas, was favorably impressed with the work ethic, prosperity, and cultural achievements of the Cherokees—the fact that they could write using their own alphabet especially. Yes, they drank too much, but critical observations like this were mostly confined to his diary. In a letter to the secretary of foreign relations dated June 9, 1828, Terán spoke highly of the Cherokees and recommended that they receive lands in Texas. He did the same with the Shawnees, begging that the matter be brought to the president's attention.[49] But Terán did not have the authority to place these tribes in possession of their lands, and he acknowledged that "in order to establish them in the place I have mentioned, we [also] need the permission of the state government." This was the fly in the ointment, because state officials were usually more inclined to please the Anglo empresarios who had control over these lands than press for the rights of Indians who occupied them.

Once Terán realized that he could not induce a sufficient number of Mexican settlers to migrate and occupy the frontier zone as a balance to North American dominance, he opted to place the friendly Indian tribes in legal possession of their lands. As commissioner of colonization for Texas he now had this authority, even if it meant browbeating state and local officials into compliance. The letter that Terán wrote Governor Letona on August 15, 1831, should put to rest any accusations that he was derelict or responsible somehow for the failure of the Cherokees to obtain titles to their Texas land.

> In compliance with the promises made by the Supreme Government to the Cherokee Indians, and with a view to the preservation of peace with the rude Tribes, I caused them to determine upon some fixed spot for their Settlement; and [they?] having selected it on the headwaters of the Trinity and the banks of the Sabine, I pray Your Excellency may be pleased, in order that possession be given to them with the corresponding Titles, with the understanding that it will be expedient, that the commissioner appointed for this purpose should act in conjunction with Colonel José de las Piedras, commanding the military force on the frontier of Nacogdoches.[50]

Governor Letona conveyed this order to Political Chief Músquiz so that he might take the necessary measures. The Cherokees could petition the government for these lands through an attorney, after the issuance of a decree similar to the one made for the Alabamas and Coushattas on July 19.[51]

Then commenced the red tape that choked Terán's superior orders to death. Músquiz told the governor that he would issue the necessary orders for the Nacogdoches alcalde to notify this tribe that they must select an attorney empowered to represent them in negotiations with the state government for the grant of land they required. But the Cherokees, just like the Alabama-Coushattas, would find it difficult to defray the expenses of an attorney. Even if they could afford this expense of hiring someone to go to the capital—doubtful because "they are uncivilized and poor"—there were the fees associated with a land commissioner or surveyor, not to mention the cost of stamped paper for issuing proper titles. Músquiz predicted it would all come to nothing, unless Commandant General Terán admitted the tribes as colonists in his new military settlements and the federal government picked up the bill.[52]

Governor Letona, however, overrode the political chief's attempt to bog down Terán's mandate—though it took him six months to do so. On March 22, 1832, he wrote Músquiz that Colonel José de las Piedras had been commissioned to put "each of the families, composing the Tribe of Cherokee Indians, in possession of the lands which, with consent of this Government and that of the Nation, they are possessing in this department." Piedras was to be furnished with the stamped paper needed for issuing titles, but on his own responsibility.[53]

Piedras accepted his commission on May 7, requesting more precise instructions on how he was to go about adjudicating the claims that each Cherokee family might submit to him. The governor sent these additional instructions on August 9—too late for Piedras to do anything for the Cherokees. As we shall see, by that time Colonel Piedras had been expelled from Nacogdoches by a force of Texans in the name of federalism. Ernest William Winkler, whose well-documented study on the Cherokees dates back a century but is still one of the best, states the result in these words: "This event terminated the measures that had been taken to put the Cherokees in possession of their lands; despite the fact that General Terán, heartily seconded by Governor Letona, had been very anxious thus to ensure the friendship of these Indians."[54] By awarding them their lands!

The question might be asked why General Terán named Colonel Piedras as commissioner for the Cherokee land concession instead of Colonel Bean. Bean, after all, was the government's agent for the Cherokees and their immigrant allies. He was also Terán's major informant on developments concerning these tribes. Bean wrote Terán two reports on Indian affairs a month prior to Terán's decision to place the Cherokees in possession of their lands (letters in the Mexican military archive that are not presently available to researchers), and he may have recommended this action to his friend, the commandant general. The answer, perhaps, lies in the fact that Piedras was the chief military authority at Nacogdoches—a man whose legal activities on behalf of the Mexican nation would carry more weight and respect with the local people than Bean's. Land titles issued by Piedras might also silence the objections bound to be raised by the empresarios, or their agents, who claimed authority over the lands being apportioned within the limits of their contracts. Added to this was the fact that Terán had already selected Bean for another important job: commandant of the fort being built on the Neches, where the colonel would be occupied for the coming year.

Chapter 10

BRIEF INTERLUDE AT FORT TERÁN

On September 25, 1831, Piedras wrote Commandant Elozúa that Bean had left the day before with twenty dragoons and ten foot soldiers to set up a post on the Neches. It would be called Fuerte de Terán in honor of the man who had suggested and implemented the fortification of Texas against U.S. designs.[1] The site chosen was on the west bank of the Neches above its confluence with the Angelina, about forty-five miles south of Nacogdoches, and it was intended to facilitate communication with Fort Anáhuac on Trinity Bay.

Fort Terán was astride a much-used crossing of the Neches, a pivotal location from which roads radiated upward to Nacogdoches and Ayish Bayou (called San Augustine after 1833), southward to the Indian villages on the Trinity and below to Liberty and Anáhuac, and—most important—eastward to the Anglo settlement of Bevil and beyond to Louisiana. Since Terán's objective was to cut off unauthorized entry to Texas by North Americans, Bean's fort was ideally situated to accomplish this goal. The spot is still in a very remote area, and although some debate continues on which side of the river Fort Terán stood, the evidence is fairly clear that it was on the west bank in present Tyler County, not on the opposite bank in Angelina County.[2]

The number of men stationed at Fort Terán under Bean fluctuated according to circumstances at Nacogdoches. Samuel Belt, who soon opened a store or trading post nearby and maintained a ferry across the Neches, gave the garrison as fifty strong with "Martinez" as Bean's second-in-command. Lt. Gavino Aranjo is also mentioned as a soldier at the post, and this was possibly when Bean talked him into selling his eleven-league grant. Aranjo had received the grant from the governor of Coahuila y Texas on March 17, 1831, and Bean obtained power of attorney over it from the lieutenant on October 27—a month after they had marched out of Nacogdoches to establish Fort Terán. Close to five leagues from the

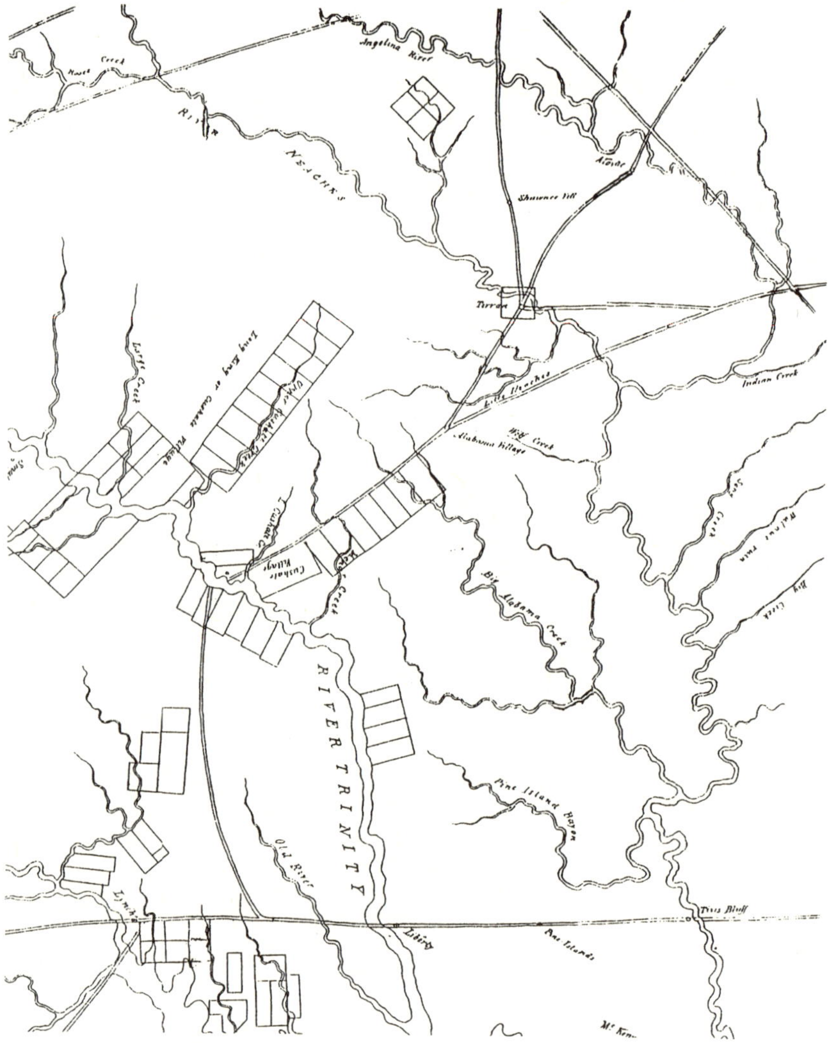

Map of surveys, ca. 1834, showing Fort "Terran" on the River "Neaches" and roads. Courtesy Galen Greaser.

Aranjo grant were later located in the general vicinity of the fort—but to the west, on the boundary of modern Polk County. This was by title issued on March 17, 1834.[3]

Land acquisitions were much on Bean's mind at this time, as hinted at by one of his visitors, George W. Smyth: "Early in 1832 I went to Fort Teran, situated on the Neches in what is now Tyler County. Here Col Peter Ellis Bean was stationed with a few Mexican soldiers. I remained a few weeks under the hospitable roof of the col. and was invited to Nacogdoches to do some surveying."[4] For Bean, one suspects.

Fort Terán quickly grew into something of a small settlement with eight or ten houses around it. Bean himself was in charge of its construction, no doubt with lumber from his own sawmill—the same that Piedras bought from Bean, on credit, when building a new and larger *cuartel* for his troops at Nacogdoches. (The citizens charged that Piedras diverted these materials to build a private residence for himself, known as the Red House.) In April 1832 Piedras noted that he was still in search of a bricklayer to complete work at Fort Terán. Traces of such work at the actual site are hard to find, indicating that it was not a fortified place built of brick or stone but rather an observation point constructed mostly of perishable wood.[5]

Bean did not expect to have to repel an armed invasion from the United States so much as monitor the influx of unauthorized settlers from across the Sabine. With growing unease he observed the escalating tensions between these people and the Mexican government. What would his position be if open conflict resulted, he a soldier in the National Army of Mexico yet with sympathies to many of the new Anglos coming in? Men such as George W. Smyth, who had useful talents? As always, Bean's situation was unenviable.

There is not much documentation available on what Colonel Bean was doing at Fort Terán, except for news that Colonel Piedras occasionally forwarded to Elozúa at Béxar. Judging from the documents extant in the Béxar Archives, this news was not very exciting. Mostly it deals with routine matters such as the search for a bricklayer or stonemason that Bean needed at the fort. In October 1831, a month after Bean left Nacogdoches to establish Fort Terán, came notice of the two "unassigned officers" who were paid their allowances and annual salaries by the commissariat at Béxar. Bean's salary as a lieutenant colonel of cavalry amounted to 1,808 pesos, and as a "campaign gratification during the same time," he was due another 889 pesos. The salary of Francisco Ruiz, the captain of cavalry, ranking lieutenant colonel at Tenoxtitlán, was 1,130 pesos, but he also had 615 pesos of gratifications owed him.[6]

Since gifts to friendly Indian delegations or visitors were sometimes classified under the category of "gratifications," it is likely that both men continued their peacekeeping activities on the frontier. Ruiz, on the Brazos, was mostly having to deal with problems involving the Wichita tribes and the immigrant Indians of northeastern Texas who wanted to make war on them. Bean's Indian relations, on the other hand, were with the Southeastern tribes from the United States—the same Indians whose entry he had opposed as harmful to the best interests of Mexico. It is suspected (without much supporting evidence) that Bean was able to perform his diplomatic duties in a satisfactory manner with the Alabama-Coushattas, Creeks, Choctaws, and Biloxis who inhabited the southeastern forests of Texas. Later incidents involving Bean and these tribes indicate as much.

Did Peter Ellis Bean, a man who liked to keep on the move, regard his new command as "banishment" from the life to which he was accustomed? This is hard to say, considering the dearth of information available to us. It appears that he relaxed a bit and concentrated on personal affairs of a business nature. One writer suggests that he may have profited a bit from the smuggling trade that regularly crossed the Sabine. If so, Bean was smart enough to cover his tracks, and any "payoffs" that merchants like Belt made to him were small enough not to arouse the cupidity of Piedras.[7] Colonel Piedras, during his five-year tenure as commandant at Nacogdoches, had already earned the hostility of the local Anglo merchants because of his virtual control over the sale of goods that were introduced from Louisiana. Mexican politics aside, this opposition was a large factor in Piedras's downfall later in 1832, after which Colonel Bean took his place.

Bean had land matters to attend to, now that his purchase of eight leagues of vacant land was approved. He had to decide where he wanted to locate these leagues, get them surveyed, and file the paperwork. Then there was his sawmill and the league that contained the "little salines." Even though local people could extract salt there, the federal government had yet to rule on Bean's private possession of the tract. Somebody had to keep these operations going during Bean's absence. Across the Neches north of Fort Terán was a salt lick used by Indians from time immemorial to extract salt. Bean, not one to miss an opportunity, leased this salt lick—although from whom is uncertain.[8] Then, as usual, he hired people to extract salt from the "mine" on some kind of a profit-sharing arrangement. His involvement was mostly limited to looking in from time to time to see how things were going. If they were not going well, Bean had the mechanical expertise to increase production.

Meanwhile, by mid-1831 the always tenuous peace with the Southern Comanches broke down. Their raids—usually attributed to parties of "young men," acting without the approval of the band's chief—hit outlying ranches around Béxar, Goliad, and even south to the Rio Grande settlements. Alarmed by these developments, Commandant General Terán rode north at the end of August to a "Campo sobre el Río de las Nueces," possibly the site where Fort Lipantitlán was under construction. At this camp Terán wrote letters to Commandant Elozúa at Béxar amplifying his August 23 orders that an active campaign be carried out against the Comanche camps. At all costs Elozúa was to secure a "just vindication for the repeated hostilities of said Comanches," and this campaign was to continue until "beyond doubt" the aggressors had been punished.[9]

Issuing orders was easier than obtaining results, but Mexican forces did have some battlefield successes against raiders. They were helped by the Shawnees, who inflicted a defeat on warriors from Chief Yncoroy's *ranchería,* killing an estimated twenty in their first blast. This attack was precipitated because the Shawnee chief's wife was "insulted grossly" while visiting Béxar by a Comanche "who endeavored to abduct her by force to his camp." She managed to escape and returned to the Shawnee encampment with news of the route the Comanches would take when they headed home. John Linney (called Linia), second chief of the Shawnee tribe, waited until the Comanches left town with their gifts/loot and then wiped them out at Bandera Pass.[10] But the leaders of other Comanche bands still tried to maintain the peace and bring the offenders into line. Thus the situation remained unstable, and travelers could never be certain if Comanches encountered on the road had hostile or peaceful intentions.

Colonel Bean, tending to his little fort on the Neches, was not involved in these difficulties. Nor does it seem that he was called upon to enlist the immigrant tribes in General Terán's campaign against the Comanches. At this time another foreigner, named James "Santiago" Bowie, took Bean's place as Elozúa's point man with the fierce tribes on the frontier above Béxar. The several expeditions that Bowie led in late 1831 and early 1832, however, were more interested in finding silver deposits around the abandoned fort of San Sabá than finding Indians and bringing them to peace. Nonetheless, Bowie's two expeditions had Elozúa's sanction, and the results were reported to him and Political Chief Músquiz.

Bowie's report of his first expedition to "that section of the country, formerly occupied by Mexican citizens and now in the hands of several hostile Indian Tribes" is dated December 10, 1831. He had left Béxar on November 2 with his brother Rezin, eight men, and a "boy" named Charles. Despite the warning of a Comanche encountered on the trail north that 124 Tawakoni, Waco, and Caddo warriors were looking for Bowie's men and intended to slaughter them, Bowie kept heading for the silver mines. His party was intercepted before it could reach the Spanish ruins. This gave rise to the famous San Saba Fight that ensured Bowie's reputation as a leader of men who could be counted on against insurmountable odds. No one at Béxar—including his bride of seven months, Ursula de Veramendi—expected to see Bowie's party come limping into town on the night of December 6.[11]

Disappointed with the results of his first expedition, Bowie launched another on January 23, 1832. This time he left Gonzales with twenty-six men, and his avowed purpose was to fight the "Tahuacanos and other hostile Nations." This was nonsense, of course, but it gave his treasure hunting and land scouting a legitimacy with Commandant Elozúa and Political Chief Músquiz—the latter of whom Bowie gave his report

James Bowie, ca. 1831. Author's collection.

dated April 23. After heading to the Pedernales, Llano, and San Sabá on the headwaters of the Colorado River, Bowie went east to the Brazos. But in all of this "long and tedious route we met with sign of only six Indians that could be relied upon as being Tahuacanos." Thus Bowie headed back to Béxar, "having in the meantime expended two months and a half in a fruitless search." He told Músquiz that the hostile tribes had seemingly abandoned their former country and removed elsewhere.

Sounding much like Peter Ellis Bean, Bowie explained why. He observed that the "great number" of northern Indians that frequented and inhabited Nacogdoches and its vicinity were at war with the Tawakonis, Wacos, and other nations of Indians hostile to the peace of the country. "These northern Indians [from the United States], being well-equipped and possessing good rifles and every warlike accessory, have always been successful against their enemies." Their frequent harassing of the Tawakonis and Wacos was one of the principal causes for the withdrawal of these hostile tribes to their now distant locations, this to escape the disasters recently inflicted on them.

"Further," wrote Bowie, "it is now my opinion that little or nothing is to be anticipated or feared from hostilities with those Indians known to be at this time at war with the citizens of the country. [I believe that] the depredations that are committed daily under the name of Tahuacanos, Wacos, etc., are done by other tribes considered as friendly." In this report Bowie praised the future prospects of the country he had passed through, not only because of the fur-bearing animals found on its rivers but because of its lands that were "not excelled in this or any other part of the country" for agricultural purposes. Revealing the actual reason for his expedition, Bowie promised to give Músquiz samples of "different specimens of mineral that I was able to collect"—all in hopes that his discoveries would prove "advantageous and beneficial to that section of the country."[12]

It is not certain when James Bowie first met Peter Ellis Bean. Bowie, born in 1796, was thirteen years younger than Bean. They may have crossed paths at Nacogdoches in 1828, on Bowie's first visit to Texas, which supposedly took him by Bean's sawmill outside of town. However, it is fairly certain that Bean did not build this sawmill on the Carrizo until the winter of 1829–30. In Nacogdoches (or possibly San Augustine) Bowie visited his relatives by marriage Stephen Prather, a man well known to Bean from his actions in putting down the Fredonian Rebellion at Ayish Bayou, and Prather's nephew Thomas F. McKinney, the vain young merchant given to accusing other people of vanity—Bean among them. Even if Bowie did not meet Bean at Nacogdoches in 1828, his frequent trips between Louisiana and Texas thereafter would have provided the opportunity.[13] Regardless of Bowie's limited knowledge of Texas Indians, he and Bean shared a big interest in common—acquiring tracts of Texas land for speculative purposes, the larger the better. Bean could not hold a candle to Bowie in this regard. Bowie's speculations in Louisiana were on a large scale, so brazen that they gave him something of a bad reputation. It was not long before Bowie gained a similar reputation in Coahuila y Texas.

Chapter 11

THE REIGN OF PIEDRAS ENDS

THIS BRINGS US TO the "disturbances" at Anáhuac and Nacogdoches in the summer of 1832. When General Santa Anna proclaimed his Plan de Veracruz against the Bustamante government at the beginning of the year, many states adhered to the Plan and the revolt spread northward. General Terán, sick and discouraged at this latest internal discord and convinced that it would result in the loss of Texas, killed himself in July. A month earlier at Fort Anáhuac the actions of Terán's chosen commander, Juan Davis Bradburn, caused a group of disgruntled settlers to march on the town and demand that Bradburn release the Texans he had placed under arrest. They were lawyers Patrick Jack and William B. Travis. A prisoner exchange agreement was signed on June 10, and the insurgents retreated to Turtle Bayou to await the release. There, on June 13, they adopted resolutions in support of Santa Anna's call for a return to the Constitution of 1824 and the end of Bustamante's military regime. Thus their personal opposition to Bradburn's "tyranny" escalated into warfare in support of federalist goals.[1]

During this lull in hostilities, Bradburn scrambled for reinforcements from Béxar and Nacogdoches. He had only 160 men at Anáhuac, with another 60 at Velasco under Col. Domingo de Ugartechea. When Piedras received word of the situation, he ordered Ruiz at Tenoxtitlán to march part of his command to the aid of Bradburn; Ruiz was unable to comply, owing to a shortage of horses and supplies. Bean, at Fort Terán, had forwarded news of the disturbances to Piedras. On June 19 Piedras wrote Commandant Elozúa that he was leaving Nacogdoches with two companies of the 12th Battalion, some cavalrymen, and nineteen men of the civil militia who had responded to his call. Bean had been instructed to assemble the Shawnees, Alabamas, and Coushattas; they, with the cavalrymen at Bean's post, would augment his force. Capt. Francisco Medina was left in charge of Nacogdoches.[2]

Once Piedras reached Fort Terán, he learned that the rebels had endorsed Santa Anna's Plan of Veracruz. He, a loyal centralist officer, was about to be thrust into a civil war—against the well-armed and numerous Anglo-Texans of Austin's colony. Bean, from his long relationship with Bustamante, was in a similar predicament. Should he battle the insurgents at Anáhuac in support of Bustamante's regime—which General Terán also served—or cast his fate with Santa Anna? These thoughts were no doubt on Bean's mind as he rode toward Bradburn's fort near the mouth of the Trinity River. Piedras's little army consisted of about 100 men and 9 Coushatta scouts. The rebels were said to have 160 men, with more arriving to assist them all the time.[3]

Our most detailed account of Bean's activities during the rescue operation is one gathered around 1837 by Mirabeau Lamar from two informants named "Fields" and "Belt."[4] The latter was no doubt Samuel Belt, who owned a store near Fort Terán and who likely was responsible for Lamar's garbled account of Bean's wife and how Bean had cut off her ears. The former was probably Joseph Fields, who owned a tract of land on the left bank of the Trinity near Aaron Cherry's place. Their plantations were about seventy miles below Fort Terán and about thirty miles north of Liberty. Since most of the action described takes place at or around Fields's house, he must have been Lamar's principal informant. Whether it was Fields or Belt who called Bean an "infamous scoundrel" and an "infernal brute," relative to his conduct toward his wife Candace Midkiff, is unclear. What is clear is that one or both of these men (and perhaps Lamar, who wrote the account) did not think too highly of Bean's valor on the march to reinforce Bradburn.[5]

A rumor was circulated of American spies in the neighborhood of Fields's house. Piedras became alarmed and concluded that the entire American force was close upon him. Bean was dispatched to scour the swamp with a small party, among which there was an Indian. Bean's advance was interrupted by a tremendous rain shower, lasting a few minutes. As soon as it was over, Bean discovered fresh horse tracks within a few steps of him. "To be so near a foe of whom he was in search & yet not see him, being himself all the time observed & narrowly watched, had rather a tendency in conjunction with the shower to cool the ardor of the *vali[a]nt* Colonel," wrote Lamar.

The Indian proposed to follow the fresh tracks and overtake the American spies, but Bean "feeling uneasy in his situation, immediatly left the swamp & returned to camp." His report satisfied Piedras that the American forces were between him and Bradburn, and that he could not advance without encountering them or retreat without being pursued. "In this dilemna[,] dreading persuit [and] not caring to persue [his march to Anáhuac,] he sent some of his officers with a flag of truce to the ame[ri]-

ca[n]s inviting them to a conference, with a view to an amicable adjustment of the difficulties." Afterward when it was ascertained that only two or three American spies were in the swamp at the time Bean left it, the Indian reproached Bean openly before his face of cowardice, and Piedras had him under arrest. "This created hostilities between them, so that when Pedraz was afterwards beseiged at Nacogdoches, Bean refused to assist him."[6]

Whether or not Colonel Piedras put Colonel Bean "under arrest" or just gave him a stern rebuke for reporting information that supposedly caused him to open negotiations with the insurrectionists—instead of riding into Anáhuac with guns blazing—there is little doubt that it caused hard feelings. Piedras was not exactly anxious for a confrontation, as demonstrated by the terms of the agreement he signed with the rebels before even talking to Bradburn. All their demands were met, including the removal of Bradburn as commander of the fort. Piedras remained at Anáhuac only long enough to satisfy himself that the settlers were calm and headed back to Nacogdoches on July 8. He feared, rightly so, that the revolt would spread to Nacogdoches and San Augustine. Before leaving he assured the downcast Bradburn that the centralist regime would soon recover from its recent setbacks, and the opportunity would arise to make the rebellious colonists "obey the laws and reduce them to the blindest obedience." Bradburn fled to Louisiana skirting the Opelousas Road, convinced that assassins were right behind him.[7]

Upon his return to Nacogdoches, Colonel Piedras found much to alarm him. Men were gathering in secret meetings and rebellion seemed to be in the air; the successes against Bradburn were infectious. On July 24 he wrote Commandant Elozúa of his misgivings.

> With much circumspection it has been said to me that Colonel Peter Ellis Bean has offered his services to the Americans to declare himself for Santa Anna and to attack this garrison. On the 21st instant said Colonel presented himself to me, having come from [Fort] Terán where he was commandant without any order from me; and realizing it, he told me that he came in person to inform me of that [a revolt in the name of Santa Anna] was the general opinion, and to be able to discuss the means that he ought to take [if such an event transpired].

That night Piedras was told that Bean had been present at a meeting in the house of (Elisha?) Roberts "and swore he would place himself at the head of the revolutionists." This meeting, however, was indecisive about an uprising, and Bean was not able to gain a consensus or form a plan. Thus he was obliged to operate with precaution. Piedras continued:

> Last night Colonel Bean disappeared, as said by his orderly, who did not expect him [to return] that night. With this event my doubts [about Bean's loyalty] are vanished, and I expect that in the morning the force of Americans must come. The civil authority, who has been advised of all that has occurred, is far from taking any measures; rather, it has remained in apathy, permitting meetings to be held in the streets and stores, where plans are formed. The civil militia has not gathered itself together [to support me], neither do I think there is any hope to be expected from them. Thus, I am reduced only to my military force, without provisions or any other kind of assistance. I expect momentarily to be attacked, and I shall resist until I lose my life.[8]

According to Mary Austin Holley's 1836 history, Piedras tried to rally the Cherokees and Shawnees to support him against the rebels. He admitted as much in a report of the situation written on July 12, saying that the citizens of Ayish Bayou had abstained from their "revolutionary movements" upon learning that the Indians were assembling at his orders. That Piedras planned to utilize the Indians against the settlers was greatly resented and led the people of Ayish Bayou to draft resolutions opposing such a measure. They did not want to see the Indians involved "in our affairs in any manner whatsoever" and stated that "the people of the country cannot put their trust in a government whose officers are capable of settling domestic difficulties with the tomahawk and scalping knife."[9] Apart from Piedras's stranglehold on the region's economy, another factor thus came into play for his opponents as armed conflict neared: his radical role in Indian affairs.

Responding to this complaint, the Nacogdoches ayuntamiento on July 28 drew up a list of grievances against Colonel Piedras. They charged him with calling upon and "employing" the Indians "to assist in his premeditated acts of violence, thereby endangering the lives and property of ourselves and fellow citizens, exposing us to the dreadful outrages to be expected from his savage auxiliaries." In effect, when ayuntamiento members Encarnación Chirino, Juan Mora, Antonio Menchaca, Charles S. Taylor, and Augustus Hotchkiss asked that their neighbors at Ayish Bayou support them in rallying around "the flag of Santa Anna," Colonel Piedras was being depicted as an officer low enough to incite savage warfare against those opposed to his political views. Holley says that someone neutralized these Indians, after which the rebels were confident enough to attack Piedras's position.[10]

Was that "someone" Agent Bean? Resolutions adopted by the Texas Convention that met in October 1832 contain remarks that suggest as much and give the reason: Bean had been stripped of his authority over the Indians by a spiteful Piedras, who was now determined to align the immigrant tribes in hostile array against the colonists—all in a desperate attempt to maintain his centralist rule of the Piney Woods. Bean, of course, could not condone such an extreme measure by his commander. It led to an open rift between them and shifted Bean to the ranks of his fellow citizens. These remarks will later be quoted from another 1836 history of Texas, that by David B. Edward.[11] Suffice it to say here that in 1832 one of the complaints against the government of Coahuila y Texas was its failure to place the immigrant tribes in possession of their lands, which had left these Indians very discontented. The Convention suggested that this situation be rectified, lest it lead to trouble with the white settlers on the northeastern frontier.

Colonel Bean, it appears, had reached a decision: it would be Santa Anna instead of Bustamante as the leader of Mexico. And best of all, if the revolt was successful, Col. José de las Piedras would be shipped back to Mexico, just as Col. Juan Davis Bradburn had been obliged to flee for his life. Even if Bean had no intention of commanding the rebel forces at Nacogdoches, he was placing himself in their midst. No doubt he assured them that many soldiers of the garrison had federalist sympathies and would not fight to sustain Piedras. This was true, as events soon proved. Fields and Belt told Lamar: "Bean joined the Americ[a]ns and went to St Augustine to gather forces; he was taken sick [there] and was not at the fight."[12] Bean himself, in a letter written the next year, claimed that he was sick at the end of July, so illness may have indeed kept him from fighting. Conveniently, it also gave him the excuse that he had not borne arms against Mexico, just in case the federalist revolt was put down and President Bustamante remained in power.

Whether or not Bean so skillfully manipulated the military/political situation in east Texas, it worked out to his advantage. Three hundred colonists converged on Nacogdoches from the surrounding districts by the end of July and gave Piedras an ultimatum to surrender. He refused, and the Texans elected James Bullock as their commander. They marched to the town plaza on August 2 and were attacked by Piedras's cavalry. After a brief but bloody battle, Piedras decided to evacuate Nacogdoches when night fell. Bullock did not pursue and seemingly lost control over his men; no one knew what to do after they discovered that Piedras and his troops were gone, leaving only their wounded behind.[13]

At this point James Bowie arrived, sent by Austin to calm the settlers and keep them from causing more trouble. Bowie rose to the occasion, but not as Austin had intended. He mustered twenty volunteers and put them on the trail of Piedras's three hundred or more soldiers. Circling around the Mexican column, Bowie had his men hidden at the Angelina crossing by the time Piedras reached it. Shots rang out and three Mexican saddles were emptied, but Bowie withdrew his men from the tree-shrouded river crossing without revealing how small his force was. The next day he boldly demanded that Piedras surrender. This Piedras refused to do, but his officers persuaded him. Capt. Francisco Medina, one of Bean's friends, drew his pistol and put it to Piedras's head to force the issue. Piedras handed his sword to Medina—his command with it—telling Medina to do whatever he damn well pleased.[14]

Captain Medina accepted Bowie's terms, the soldiers were disarmed, and the whole troop marched back to Nacogdoches. Once again James Bowie had triumphed against overwhelming odds, and his reputation was enhanced accordingly. He was designated by the town's civil leaders to escort Piedras and his *soldados* to San Felipe, from whence Colonel Piedras was put on a boat that eventually took him to Matamoros. Bowie continued on with the column to Béxar, receiving thanks from Captain Medina for his kindness and consideration during the march. Bowie, not one to miss a trick, somehow got a power of attorney over Medina's ten-league grant on March 14, 1833, seven months after the captain had headed his troops to Matamoros from Béxar.[15]

Gen. Vicente Filisola, in his 1849 history of Texas, explained why it had been so easy for the colonists to rid themselves of Piedras. He noted that there was a division of opinion among the inhabitants of Nacogdoches, then the only town where a respectable Mexican force remained. Some supported the resort to arms while others opposed it. But the businessmen, "who were the most influential, were in favor of it, and, in addition, they were against Colonel Piedras personally for business reasons, for this chief had imprudently established a monopoly on almost all the items that sold best and brought in the most money, since he had things shipped in from New Orleans on his own account, and he took the profit away from many merchants, so they wanted to throw him out of there, hoping that he would be succeeded in command by Colonel Peter [Ellis] Bean, a North American who had been living in the said town for many years."[16]

When Col. Juan Almonte reached Nacogdoches two years later, he received a slightly different story—no doubt from Bean himself.

> Former Colonel José de las Piedras, who commanded this post and whose devious conduct was in every way in keeping with the policies of the previous [Bustamante] administration, so exasperated these inhabitants with his abuses that in the year 1832, they were forced to revolt against him in order to adhere to the plan of salvation of His Excellency the General [and] President [Santa Anna] proclaimed in Veracruz on January 2 of that same year. They were headed by Colonel Sr. Don Pedro Elias Bean, a longtime patriot who at that

time was under the command of the aforesaid Piedras, who persecuted him [Bean] for his political opinions. When he asked Piedras whether he would embrace the Plan of Veracruz or prepare to fight against it, the former opted for the second extreme, from which resulted a battle in which he was defeated.[17]

From this account it sounds like Bean, in his talk with Piedras on July 21, had posed the question of whether the commandant would "embrace" the Plan of Veracruz or resist it. Piedras's negative answer was probably why Bean had "disappeared" on July 23, to put himself beyond the reach of his centralist superior while consolidating the rebellious movement with inhabitants of the town and surrounding districts. Most of them knew of Bean's leadership in the Edwards affair and respected his role as a diplomat among the Indians. They would have appreciated his delicate situation as a commissioned officer in the Mexican army and understood why Bean had to stay in the background when it came to a fight —this assuming that it was a prearranged understanding and not sickness that actually kept him out of the battle. Either way, Bean helped organize the revolt and lent legitimacy to it because he wore a Mexican uniform. Like his fellow citizens he had no use for Piedras, and the recent episode on the march to Anáhuac still galled him. Knowing Bean, he probably said that if he received their backing as commandant at Nacogdoches, the merchants would prosper and the region as well.

If Piedras was expecting help from the Indians, Bean's advice likely kept them quiet or delayed them long enough not to be a factor in the outcome. It should be remembered that, shortly before this revolt, Piedras had been named as the commissioner to put the Cherokees in possession of their solicited lands. Thus, if Piedras was driven out of Texas, the Cherokees' best chance yet of receiving title to their lands went with him. This may account for reports that Chief Bowl was on his way with sixty warriors in support of Piedras but failed to reach town before the surrender took place.[18]

Austin wrote the political chief an account of the Nacogdoches uprising, claiming that Piedras had "threatened to gather up the Indians against the inhabitants, thus kindling a war of extermination." In his mind, this justified the citizens' actions against the commandant and his garrison—many of whom had since embraced Santa Anna's cause. Frost Thorn wrote Austin on August 28: "The Indians doubtless were employed as auxeliaries and it required much explanation to counteract his [Piedras's] influence over the cherikees, but I am inclined to believe that these feelings at this time are entirely changed, and that we have but little to fear from them." In this instance Piedras's "influence" was no doubt based on the understanding that he was empowered by the government of Coahuila y Texas to finally grant the Cherokees their long-expected lands. Thorn told Austin that he and John Durst planned to visit Chief Bowl the next day, just to make sure that there was no misunderstanding of what it all meant.[19]

However it transpired, Bean came out of the revolt smelling like a rose. He remained at Nacogdoches as Mexico's Indian agent and general troubleshooter—still on the payroll, more or less, as interim commander. The downside was that Bean had no soldiers to command and no way of enforcing whatever measures he thought necessary to the security of the frontier. Now he had to be a diplomat not only with the red men but his white and brown neighbors as well. As Almonte stated Bean's position in 1834, "only to his good offices and the prestige which he enjoys among these people is due the preservation of order in this part of our territory, where for nearly two years not a single [Mexican] soldier has been seen."[20]

Bean was carrying a heavy load, and it is not surprising that for the next several years he devoted himself mostly to his land interests. As interim military commander at Nacogdoches without any men to back him up, how could he have done otherwise? His letters for the remainder of 1832 are mostly about what to do with the arms and supplies left behind by the 12th Permanent Battalion. On November 24 he inquired about the status of the church edifice that had been evacuated by Piedras's troops, formerly used by them as a barracks. At the beginning of February 1833 he asked the acting alcalde if the funds of the 12th Battalion could be transferred to some place where they might be more secure.[21] Bean—as Mexico's only military representative in east Texas—was now responsible for the safeguarding of all vestiges of the ousted centralist regime.

Chapter 12

LAND AFFAIRS FOREMOST

THE ADVENT OF 1833 brought another major shakedown of the federal government. Throughout 1832—since Santa Anna's Plan of Veracruz—support for the Bustamante regime had been weakening. Members of his cabinet offered to resign in language that, if accepted, would have meant that Bustamante also had to step down. He rejected these offers and tried to rally the support of the military establishment. Acting executive Bustamante must have experienced déjà vu during the year, as these were the same sorts of unacceptable cabinet shuffles that had brought him to power. A compromise was worked out in December whereby Manuel Gómez Pedraza, the president-elect whom Guerrero had overthrown, was allowed to take office until a new president could be elected. On January 3, 1833, Pedraza and General Santa Anna entered Mexico City riding in the same carriage.

Everyone knew, of course, who would hold the reins of the new government. In March the state legislatures elected Santa Anna as president of Mexico and Valentín Gómez Farías as vice president. Santa Anna, pleading that he was "too ill to take office," retired to his estate of Manga de Clavo so he might be at a safe distance to watch how the promised reforms worked out. On April 1 Farías, a steadfast liberal, became chief of state in the absence of the duly elected president. Lucas Alamán, José María Bocanegra, and other former cabinet members were soon being persecuted for their activities during the Bustamante centralist regime.[1]

A letter that Santa Anna wrote on January 18, before his transition to power was complete, shows that he was not fooled by recent events in Texas. He was satisfied that the Anglo colonists had a "strong inclination to declare their independence of the republic," and was well aware that they had cloaked their attacks on Mexican authority as support for his Plan. This was almost a personal insult. Santa Anna thought it "absolutely necessary" that General Filisola march into Texas, as planned, with good officers and "the largest force possible." The pretensions of the foreign colonists he considered "insolent," and they had to be shown that they could not conduct illegal meetings and draw up proscribed memorials. As far as Santa Anna was concerned, "all their grievances and complaints tend to that [separatist] object," even if they "have been wronged on several occasions." He wanted Filisola's army "to see that justice is done to the colonists, and that they are treated with the proper considerations." Santa Anna's idea of "justice" and "proper considerations" for traitors to the Mexican nation can be imagined.[2]

This letter came to the attention of Vice-Governor Juan Martín de Veramendi in mid-February, and he forwarded it to Political Chief Músquiz with stern instructions to tell the colonists that their political "excesses" would lead them to "utter ruin." Veramendi correctly foresaw that more such consultations would be held, saying that their object was to separate Texas from Coahuila if not to accomplish full secession from the Mexican republic. He warned Músquiz against allowing these things to occur, and predicted that a constitution for self-rule would be next on the colonists' agenda. Thus we learn that Santa Anna believed, as early as January 1833, that a military response was necessary to force the Anglo-Texans into showing more proper respect for Mexican institutions. We also learn that Veramendi had a clear idea of what was going on among his son-in-law James Bowie's circle of Anglo friends at the time. This rather amazing letter has received little notice from historians. Among other things, it has a bearing on Austin's chilly reception in the capital later that summer and on the reason Col. Juan N. Almonte was sent on an inspection of Texas at the beginning of 1834.[3]

Back in Texas, 1833 also saw the arrival of Sam Houston, who splashed across the Red River from Indian Territory in December 1832. He came armed with a commission from the U.S. War Department to persuade the Comanches and other wild tribes of the plains into traveling to Fort Gibson for peace talks. Houston also had schemes of his own, which involved the semicivilized tribes that the Jackson administration was pushing west of the Mississippi. Upon reaching Nacogdoches, Houston—considering his Indian-diplomat cover story—was probably introduced to Colonel Bean by Adolphus Sterne, another Tennesseean and prosperous merchant who was the recently installed alcalde.[4] That politics were also discussed is strongly suggested by the letter that Bean wrote Houston on February 4: "As it apears that it is the wish of the Citizons of this Cuntry that you Should be a member of the Comitty for to form this estern Part into a Stait that has formerly Bin governed by Cuahuela I feel myself willing to Suport you as far as my Millitary orders will admit."[5]

Houston, after returning to Nacogdoches from a trip to San Felipe and Béxar with James Bowie, may also have suggested that Bean write Secretary of War Lewis Cass a letter about uncontrolled U.S. Indian immigration into Mexican Texas. Houston, or someone else with better grammar and spelling skills than Bean, may have even drafted the letter that Bean signed and dated February 24, 1833, before mailing it to Cass. Assuming that he did lend his compositional skills, Houston's motives for "helping" Bean are unclear, as with much of Houston's literary output during the period of his exile among the Western Cherokees of Indian Territory. But the letter reflects the concern about this influx of foreign Indians that Bean had already expressed to the Mexican government, and the rational thrust of it is clearly Bean's. His central thesis was that Article 33 of the treaty recently signed by the two governments made the United States responsible for preventing its Indians from crossing into Texas. This was not being done, and Bean cited several episodes involving representatives of the Choctaw, Seminole, and Creek tribes who had crossed the frontier line and declared their intention to immigrate with all their people in the near future.

> I trust that the enlightened policy, as well as the character for morality of the President of the U.S. of the North, will suggest to him the propriety of preventing any attempts on the part of the Creek Indians to trespass on the territory of Mexico and more particularly that of this Province.
>
> You will feel at once the peculiarity of my situation, and acknowledge that it is my imperious duty to inform immediately my Government of these facts, in order to cover my responsibility. I am &c.
> Pedro Elias Bean[6]

Bean was true to his word, and copies of his letter were forwarded to officials in Mexico City and also to the Mexican consul in New Orleans. Col. Peter Ellis Bean was going on the record in regard to a problem that Pres. Andrew Jackson had largely caused by his policy of Indian Removal. Bean's position on how the treaty had made it the responsibility of the United States to keep these Indians out of Mexican territory was a position soon aggressively advanced on the diplomatic level of international politics. Colonel Bean may not have been the first to articulate this spin on the treaty, but he did it with a flair from the ground level. With his own eyes he could see the pattern of immigration, though officials in distant places might deny that it was happening. These Indians were native to the United States; to Bean, they should be settled in lands reserved for them by the U.S. government in Indian Territory—above the Red River, and not below it in Mexican territory. Attention was being called to Bean's protest by an article in the *Natchitoches Herald* as late as June 3, 1835.

Eleven days before Bean dated this letter to Secretary of War Lewis

Cass, Sam Houston wrote President Jackson (from Natchitoches) his first report of what he had witnessed in Texas. His Indian commission was barely mentioned, no doubt because it was incidental to the real reason Jackson had sent him to Texas. Houston said that nineteen-twentieths of the people wanted the United States to acquire Texas, and they were determined to form a state government separate from Coahuila. It was his opinion that the Convention being called for April 1 (in which Houston served as a delegate from Nacogdoches despite his brief residence) would declare all of the country north of the Rio Grande as "Texas proper" and form a state constitution. As noted, Bean told Houston that he would back him as a member of this separatist "Comitty," and it is likely that he did. Houston assured President Jackson that Mexico was too weak to maintain its grip on Texas, and that Texas must inevitably transfer its allegiance to another power.[7]

Although Sam Houston played a prominent role in the April 1833 Convention, helping to draft the constitution and giving some impassioned speeches, it appears that he did not take up the standard for the Cherokees. Perhaps he had yet to gain standing among Bowl's tribesmen and learn how their claims to Texas lands were still a matter of dispute. So Houston said in speeches after the Cherokees had been driven from the republic. Whatever the reason, he did not push for even the recognition of Indian land rights that the 1832 Convention had deemed essential to the security of the frontier. The memorial that supported the proceedings of the new Convention was written by Empresario David G. Burnet. Not surprisingly, it contains nothing on how the immigrant tribes needed to be given possession of their lands. Burnet's focus was on how the influx of foreign Indians needed to be stopped.[8]

As 1833 commenced, Bean signed an agreement with merchant Frost Thorn that caused his land dealings to accelerate. On January 24 Bean granted Thorn his power of attorney to represent and sell for him twenty-three leagues of land. They were listed as eleven leagues obtained from Gavino Aranjo, four leagues from Jesús de la Garza, and "five & three" leagues that had been conceded to Bean by the Supreme Government. These were the eight leagues that Governor Viesca had sold Bean in 1831, but why the figure was broken into two parcels is unknown.[9] A report from the state government dated a year earlier shows that eight hundred leagues of land had been sold to various Mexican citizens.[10] Bean's name and his eight leagues are among those listed. Massive sales of eleven-league grants continued into 1833, and they were snapped up by men like Bowie, Thorn, and Houston. But locating the tracts, getting them surveyed, and filing proper titles took time—all necessary steps before money from sales could start flowing in.

In the meantime Bean had to raise money in other ways. One involved a lease agreement that he signed with Stephen Prather on March 19, whereby Prather was to take over operations of the saline that Bean claimed title to and whose ownership was still tied up in Mexico City. Prather was an old-school frontiersman who had gathered friendly Indians in an action against the Fredonian rebels at Ayish Bayou in 1827, throwing the rebels into disarray and making many sympathizers have a change of heart. Besides Bean, he was most often credited by observers as having played a key role in defusing the rebellion.[11] Now Bean wanted him to replace a man named W. S. Thomas in harvesting salt from the Neches Saline. As noted, Thomas was having trouble making deliveries from the "Naiches Salt Works" as early as 1829.

> Articul of agreement maid and contracted this 19th day of March [1833] in the town of Nacogdoches—Between Peter E. Bean and Stephen Prether Both of the same town Wharas [t]he said P. E. Bean is posessed and the proper owner of a surtain Salt lick on the warters of the Natches it being the same formerly ocupied [and worked] by W. S. Thomas he the said Bean hearby on his part leases or rents unto him the said Prether the Salt Lick above mentioned for and during the tirm of five years counting from this Date he the sd. Bean Doth hear by warent and defend the posasion of said Lick for the tirm above mensioned unto him the sa. S. Prether and to no other person, he the sd. Bean further binds him self that no purson shall establis to make salt for sail at said lick, But aney won may for his privit use won or two bushels make. But in all other cases the sole wright and peasabel posasion shall be visited in sd. Stephen Prether for the tirm above mensioned Definding him the sd. Prether in the same, alowing at the same time the privilege of the use of wood, wreter [water] and stone &c. for the use of said Lick.
>
> He the said Prether binds himself on his part for use of sd Salt Lick to pay to him the sd. P. E. Bean three barrels of Salt the first year and one hundred bushels of Salt anualey for the succedding four years and at the expirasion of the tirm of five years above mensioned to give up to sd. P. E. Bean posasion of the premisis above mensioned. But he the sd. Prether Reserving to himself the Right of Removing his Kittels and working tools leving all other Improvements to the Benefit of said P. E. Bean.[12]

This contract was signed by both men and witnessed by Frost Thorn and "H." Edwards. He was Haden Harrison Edwards, son of the empresario Haden, who lived with his brother-in-law Thorn at Nacogdoches. H. H. Edwards would soon become active in the acquisition of land in east

Texas, some of it from Bean. He is often confused with his exiled father in these activities.

Bean's salt-making deal with Stephen Prather was cut short by the latter's death a few months later. Prather's son Freeman gave Bean a town lot as security for the salt owed by his deceased father, an obligation that Bean quickly put on record. He claimed that "counting from the date of the contract March the 19th 1833 untill the 14th June 1833 the said Prather falls in debt one hundred twelve bushels of Salt." Thus Freeman Prather had "shewed me the boundary lines of a sertain lot belongin to his desast father and said that I must keep posasion of the same untill I was Paid or he would make me a Right as soon as it was past [passed] to him."[13]

As a further example of how Bean teamed up with Frost Thorn is the September 20, 1833, purchase that they jointly made of a league and fifty acres of land five miles south of town west of La Nana Creek. Thorn and Bean, said the deed, already owned a mill at the mouth of the creek, on the road to the house of "Pierre Robleau." He was Bean's friend who had guided Terán through the east Texas backwoods on his 1828 inspection. The sale was made by José Morin, and the price paid was only 150 pesos. This suggests that Bean and Thorn had already obtained the place from Roubleau or another grantee, because a league of land usually brought ten times that much in the 1830s. Morin either needed money badly or was already in debt to the purchasers. In any case, Bean built or renovated a second sawmill, this time in partnership with one of the leading men of the community. Altogether, the saw- and gristmill on La Nana Creek was a valuable piece of property that generated considerable income for its owners through the years.[14]

One of those frequent cases involving slaves of questionable ownership occurred at Bean's other mill in the spring of 1833. These slaves had belonged to John Berry, recently deceased. Berry's widow Milly learned, after his death, that some of them had been shifted from the Nacogdoches jurisdiction to that of Ayish Bayou. A number of the slaves had been left with Benjamin Lindsey, who later certified that Berry's widow had the "unlawful" plan of driving them to Louisiana before the estate was probated. She hired Elisha Clapp and Isaac Lee to scour the countryside for her husband's slaves. Samuel Stiddum got into the act, claiming that he was the appointed guardian and tutor of Berry's minor children. He appealed to the Nacogdoches alcalde to help him recover any of Berry's slaves that might still be in the jurisdiction. Two of them, a woman named Daina and a young man named "Salamon," were said to be in Bean's possession.[15]

A party of armed men converged on Bean's house by his mill in the dead of night, led by the Nacogdoches *procurador.* They took away Daina but Solomon fled to the woods, stopping the operation of Bean's mill. It appears that the posse caught him and that both slaves were hauled off, under the pretext that Bean had stolen them from Berry's estate. Bean lodged two strong protests with Alcalde Ignacio Ibarvo, saying that both Negroes were his property, by virtue of a bill of sale from Berry a year ago—which was on record in the municipal archives. Bean wanted to know why the alcalde had authorized this sort of outrageous search and seizure without even first asking him to present the Negroes in court so his ownership could be proved. He said he would have done so if cited. "Destructions like this are not permitted by our laws, nor by the Constitution of our State." Far from being stolen, they were his property "because they cost me my money." Bean wanted the two slaves back and damages paid to him as well.[16]

According to the *List of Titles* issued by the Nacogdoches authorities, by September 26, 1833, Bean had received title to five and three-fourths leagues on Galveston Bay near the mouth of the Trinity River. Actually, it covered the peninsula that juts out between Trinity Bay and East Bay, well below the Trinity's mouth. Smith Point is now near the tip of the peninsula. The survey was made by José María Carvajal on September 25, and his plat map is quite accurate. The grant lies in present Chambers County—later disallowed by the Republic of Texas because it was in the coastal reserve. Commissioner Vicente Aldrete noted that Bean had already paid the government 750 pesos for the eight leagues purchased.[17]

By the end of the year Bean (no doubt with Thorn's assistance) had title to another two and one-fourth leagues, which adds up to the eight leagues he bought from the state of Coahuila y Texas. Nonetheless, all of Surveyor Carvajal's paperwork is dated December 14, 1834. Of the latter sum, one league had been located on the Red River ten miles below the mouth of the Kiamichi. Bean used the quarter league for land on La Nana Creek, north of town. Carvajal completed all these surveys, and the paperwork for them is in the same box at the General Land Office.[18]

The final league of this two-and-one-fourth-league survey was in modern Smith County, near the headwaters of the Neches on its east bank. It was on Saline Creek, the same leased to Prather in March 1833 and the tract later referred to as "Bean's Saline." Documents on file at the General Land Office prove that this was the same league that Peter Ellis had tried to locate on the Neches as an attorney for William Bean. What Carvajal "surveyed" in 1834 and the plat map he drew are virtually identical to the field notes and plat made by James Gaines in 1828. Thus is explained how José María Carvajal could cover so much ground in such a short time. In the case of Bean's Neches Saline, Carvajal may not have even gone to the tract. He probably sat at a desk and did the paperwork for Bean, as his field notes are a word-for-word copy of Gaines's. His plat map is also very similar, though not as detailed as the one drawn by Gaines six years earlier. Whatever his other failings, James Gaines was a very competent surveyor.[19]

So this is how Bean worked the system: after the ayuntamiento's protests botched his attempt to use William's purchased league for securing this saline, and after political chiefs and governors ruled the sale invalid, Bean took another approach. He quit trying to argue the distinction between salines and salty earth, dropping William's concession that had been declared null and void. Instead, he decided to use one of the eight leagues purchased from the government to secure title to the same location where Freeman Prather had his salt kettles bubbling away. It worked, meaning that Colonel Bean's name is linked to one of the most important salt deposits in the history of the Republic of Texas. For when Chief Bowl decided to resist the taking of this saline by Texan troops during the Lamar administration, it resulted in the expulsion of the Cherokees from lands that they had claimed as their own. Because of his influence with the Indians, however, Bean managed to extract salt from this rich deposit. Few other white men were allowed to do so—unless under Bowl's and the colonel's auspices.[20]

In 1834 more such locations were staked out by Bean as "attorney" for the Aranjo and Garza grants. Frost Thorn became heavily involved in selling not only Bean's grants but many of those he had obtained for himself through similar purchases from Mexican grantees. These activities led to Thorn's status as the first "millionaire" of Texas, although a number of other men at Nacogdoches were competing with him for the honor.[21]

Meanwhile, life continued as usual in 1833. Starting in the summer, Bean brought suit to seize the property of Col. José de las Piedras at Nacogdoches in lieu of the debts that Piedras owed him. This was for the lumber that Piedras had bought on credit from Bean's sawmill to bolster the strength of his garrison's buildings. It was not easy to get payment on federal military projects that had been abandoned, especially when the seizure involved an officer's private property, and Bean was denied permission by the commandant general in September: "Since what Bean demands of Colonel Piedras is actionable before civil authority because he [Piedras] is deprived of his [military] employment, this Commandancy General has nothing to do with it. Let the interested party have recourse in the civil courts in accordance with the laws."[22]

This decision came to Bean at the end of October, and he relayed it to Alcalde Ibarvo on December 5, along with his intention to pursue it until obtaining satisfaction.[23] On another matter, John Durst, a wealthy man of property at Nacogdoches who was also the administrator of rents, was called upon to explain his failure to pay Bean 180 pesos as ordered. He claimed, on November 4, it was because there were insufficient funds in his cash box; obligations to Thorn and Santos had taken all the money presently available. Also in November Bean told the alcalde that he wanted the curate to have use of the church, which had been taken for quarters by the 12th Battalion.[24]

That summer also marked many transactions between Bean and William Goyens, a free black of the community who was a blacksmith, freighter, innkeeper, and trader with the Indians. Goyens may have been part Indian himself, as he was sometimes used as an interpreter among the immigrant tribes. Later he was sent as an agent to the Comanches or other plains tribes. He was also living with a woman said to be white, Mary Pate Sibley, and they married either in 1834 or 1835. Bean, it is suspected, had used Goyens's services in his dealings with the Indians perhaps as far back as 1827.[25]

In August Goyens borrowed $160 from Bean, promising to pay him "in good Second Rate Cows and Calves at ten dollars [each] on or before the first Day of May next," this being the going value. Also in August Goyens agreed to pay Bean $500 worth of lumber "at the old Selling Prise and Despach the Same as the Bills may Come in." Below this contract Bean signed receipts for money paid, including one stud horse valued at $150; these payments continued into 1835. In another August transaction, Goyens agreed to deliver to Bean a "good well finished Wagon that Shall be abel to Carry thirty Hundred [pounds?]." This was due Bean upon demand in December for value received. Since the value went unstated, it was added in a note below: "this wagon is to be worth 250 dollars." Another note was for sixty pounds of iron that Goyens needed. More such business dealings likely occurred between the two men than those of record.[26]

Military matters received slight attention. On June 17 Bean wrote Commandant Elozúa about a corporal of the Alamo Company named Eligio Alvarado. This soldier had been regarded as a deserter since the previous July, and Elozúa wanted him reunited with his company. Bean defended the soldier, saying that he had presented himself on August 1, 1832, and "since that day I found myself seriously ill," Bean told Alvarado to retire to the ranches of the jurisdiction. This, of course, was while the coup against Piedras was forming. Bean likely sent Corporal Alvarado away so he would not have to participate in the battle on the centralist side. Then, on October 25, Alvarado came into town and "since this date this individual has remained under my orders, discharging some affairs of the service," despite there being no money to pay him. Bean would send Alvarado on to Béxar if Elozúa desired, but "he has absolutely no horse on which to ride."[27] Thus Colonel Bean was not only clearing this man of desertion charges but reminding the military commandant of his sparse resources at Nacogdoches.

On July 10 he relayed to the alcalde an order received from the commandant general pertaining to former secretary of war Facio and minister of foreign relations Alamán. Both men were physically described, and they were to be arrested if they tried to leave Mexico through the northeastern states.[28] In mid-July Bean passed on the news brought from Matamoros by Augustus Hotchkiss, probably a cousin of the Archibald Hotchkiss who arrived the following year to figure prominently in the affairs of Nacogdoches—its land affairs especially. Hotchkiss said that a month earlier Colonel Piedras, at the head of his 12th Permanent Battalion in Matamoros, had pronounced against the federal system. The commandant general of the Eastern Interior States, Gen. Vicente Filisola, was placed under arrest; another revolution was in the making. Since Elozúa had just ordered Bean to recognize Filisola as their legitimate military superior, Bean wondered how this new attempt to reestablish centralist power ought to be viewed. "I give knowledge to Your Lordship that on this frontier, I observe at present that the general opinion of this public, in its greater part, is not inclined to cooperate in sustaining the [reactionary] voice that has been raised; and more so when, as a consequence, it is known at first glance that such pronouncement wants to establish a Government that hereafter will place us in the unhappy condition of slavery, and deliver us all into the hands of the Spaniards."[29] Bean said that the people of Nacogdoches opposed the action of Colonel Piedras, all being "bound to die" in sustaining the federal system. He wanted to know what Elozúa thought about it all, so he could work in conformity with his orders. Still, Bean made it quite clear that under Santa Anna the republic had been placed "in quiet and peaceful tranquility," a state of affairs that Piedras and other centralist diehards wished to disrupt.[30]

Governor Letona died of yellow fever in late 1832 and was replaced by the vice-governor, Juan Martín de Veramendi. He was a liberal native of San Antonio de Béxar, generally considered as friendly to the interests of the Anglo-Texans. Despite being James Bowie's father-in-law, he was not in favor of the separate statehood scheme that Bowie's Anglo associates had hatched at San Felipe in their April Convention. This we know from the prophetic remarks Veramendi made while transmitting Santa Anna's letter to Political Chief Músquiz at San Antonio earlier in the year. Some months later a Cherokee delegation went to Béxar to meet with the new interim political chief, Miguel Arciniega, and pursue the matter of their land title. On July 20, 1833, Arciniega wrote a letter to the secretary of state of Coahuila y Texas, telling him to expect visitors. Enclosed were the original applications, in English (together with a translation into Spanish), of the Cherokee Indians, in which they requested to be put in possession of the land they had designated in accordance with the previous offer made them by Governor Letona. "To attend to the particulars [enumerated in their petition] a commission of three, selected from the six representatives present, will proceed to the [state] capital in order to treat in person upon an affair in which the honor of the government is already compromised. The commissioner José de las Piedras, to whom this matter was entrusted, was not able to discharge it because of his departure from Nacogdoches, whither he has not returned up to this time."[31]

Nor was Piedras likely to return anytime soon, for troops loyal to Santa Anna had put down the centralist uprising with a minimum of bloodshed. The Cherokee petition was well written and a reasonable request, considering the promises that had been made to them by Mexican officials in the past. But the Cherokees were asking for a lot of prime real estate, more than anyone—including Peter Ellis Bean—wanted to see them control. Their claim also did not mention the fact that the land they had decided on was inhabited by other immigrant tribes, supposedly their friends and allies.

> The subscribers state that the tract they have selected under the promise of the government is located in the vicinity of Nacogdoches, and it is bounded as follows: Boundary begins where the Bexar road crosses the Trinity river, and follows said road in the direction of Nacogdoches to the Angelina river; thence it proceeds up the right bank of said Angelina river to where José Dust [Joseph Durst] now lives; thence it continues with a course to the northeast till it touches the Sabine river; thence up the right bank of said Sabine river to its headwaters, thence west till it touches the Trinity river; and finally from thence down the left bank of said Trinity river to the point of beginning.[32]

After the government had promised to award the Cherokees this tract, they settled on the land and cultivated it in the hope of securing complete ownership. But some years had passed since the government made them this promise, so they requested that a commissioner be sent to put them in possession. They recommended Don Manuel de los Santos Coy, a resident of Nacogdoches, as qualified to issue their land titles.

The chiefs then complained that various Americans had selected for their own use some of the best places in this tract of land and told the Cherokees it was done with the government's authorization. The Indians wanted their title issued immediately and asked that it be held by them communally instead of individually. Further, they wanted the Americans removed from the land that the Indians had occupied in good faith after receiving the government's promises. They did not want any of these American claims—doubtless of the eleven-league variety—located on lands belonging to the Cherokee tribe. Then a bit of statistical information was given, perhaps as an explanation of why so much land was being asked for.

> The subscribers further state that it is now four years since they sent to the government the census of the population of their tribe, and that since that time there has been an increase in the number of individuals of the tribe amounting to 190 or 200 persons. This increase is due to our boys growing into men and to the immigration of our fathers and brothers, who have come to live with us. We desire that these persons be entitled to the same privileges as those who came earlier. The tribe at present numbers about 150 families, comprising about 200 men, the total number of persons being about 800. The property of this tribe consists of about 3000 head of cattle, about the same number of hogs, and of 500 or 600 horses. The subscribers inform you that said tribe lives chiefly by tilling the soil and by raising cattle. They believe that the land designated will be sufficient for their farms and ranches.[33]

One would hope so, considering the huge region being solicited for a mere eight hundred people! The petition was signed by "Colonel Boles, John Boles [his son], Richard Jestice [Justice], Piggion, Andrew M. Vann, and Eli Harlin [Harlan]." Chief Bowl and the latter two individuals were the ones chosen to carry the petition to the state capital, then at Monclova. Political Chief Arciniega commented on each of the points raised in the petition, with an overall favorable endorsement—except for considering the amount of land they wanted as excessive. These Indians were almost civilized, he said, and their establishment would bring advantages to Texas—provided that they learned Spanish and adopted Mexican customs and laws, so far as possible. With Mexican settlers placed among them, they would be naturalized and slowly integrated into the Mexican nation.[34]

Bowl and the other two Cherokee representatives set out for Monclova in August, a hot month for travel. They met with Governor Veramendi shortly before his death in a cholera epidemic that was then raging across Mexico. On August 21 he gave them another one of those documents typical of the *mañana* treatment Cherokee leaders had received from government officials since they first pressed claim to Texas lands. Veramendi noted that the lands they solicited were in the colonization grants awarded to David Burnet and Gen. Vicente Filisola. It was not possible for him to approve the Cherokee petition until the contracts of these two empresarios expired. To this the chiefs replied that their rights to the land predated those of the empresarios; because the Cherokee claim was older, it was better and should be recognized.

Veramendi countered that they had no documentary proof of what had been conceded to them in Mexico City during their 1823 visit other than the president's word and a map that he had delivered to them, on which was marked the territory they were now asking for. His ruling specified that "said tribe shall not be disturbed for any reason whatever, until the Supreme General Government may decide whether in truth it granted to said tribe the concession to which reference has been made at the aforementioned time." Or, he continued, until the termination of the extension of time that Congress had granted to David G. Burnet. In either case the chief of the Cherokees would be notified, so that he might hire an attorney to represent him in the state capital for the purpose of concluding a "suitable" contract for the tribe.[35] Thus the Cherokee land claim languished for the next two years, until a successful revolution by the Anglo colonists took authority for such matters out of Mexican hands.

Bean's role—if any—in this latest round of Cherokee land negotiations is not a matter of record. As seen, in the month of August he was doing business with William Goyens at Nacogdoches and trying to seize property of Colonel Piedras for debts owed him. But word spread of the Cherokees' small victory at the capital—in terms of their right to occupy the claimed lands without molestation until a higher decision was reached—and officials in Texas began scurrying to learn exactly what the deceased governor Veramendi had promised them. This occasioned another bout of brainstorming by people familiar with the situation and whose opinion might guide its resolution.[36] One such person was Col. Peter Ellis Bean, and he had read Veramendi's letter that the Cherokees brought home from Monclova. No one else knew its contents except the Nacogdoches alcalde, who had examined the document but failed to make a copy for his archives.

Bean gave Commandant Elozúa his ideas about how the Cherokee land matter should be handled on October 7, 1833. He admitted that the vice-governor of the state, in his letter to the Cherokee chief, did not want the tribe "inconvenienced from the place where they find themselves living while the S[upreme] General Government resolves [the question]." Further, Veramendi recognized that the Cherokees had more right to the land they occupied than Empresario Burnet "because of the Cherokees being earlier rooted in it," although the Indians had no document that vouched for this. All they had was the word that the government gave the chief conceding them permission to live in it.

Bean's warning was phrased as follows:

> That in consequence of the preference which the said tribe believes itself [to have] obtained the said lands, they already are beginning to form ideas; and they only hope that the expressed lands will be given them in due form so as to make enough families come from their own nation to plant them on the said land. For this reason, it has seemed to me suitable to tell Your Lordship that, if these Indians come to put themselves in possession of a land that is only found distant from here [no] more than five leagues at most, there remains no doubt that with the coming of those who must already be trying to do so, these lands will be filled with a class of barbarous people. [Once they are here] it will become more and more difficult to make them go back, and I believe that they will do irremediable harm to all those who inhabit this frontier.

This said, Bean proposed a solution to the problem. If the government wished to award land to the Cherokees, he suggested "that these places may be in [their] possession on the lands that are nearest to the nations with whom we are frequently at war. Because in this case, and with such a provision, there will be avoided in the future the hostilities that our enemies the Comanches, Tahuacanos, &c., have been accustomed to carry out; and the Cherokees will be attended to in what they have tried to obtain from the Supreme Govt.—land on which to live."[37]

If ever there was a defining moment for Bean, vis-à-vis the Cherokees, this letter might be it. He was their agent and was supposed to look out for their interests, insofar as compatible with the best interests of Mexico. He visited their villages on numerous occasions and knew their customs and way of life as well as any white man. Yet here he was, expressing the opinion that it would not do to have these "barbarians" so close to the settlement of Nacogdoches. If the government wanted to honor its promises of land for these Indians, it should be farther away—out west where the Cherokees would be obliged to constantly battle the Wacos, Tawakonis, Comanches, and others. Bean had seemingly fallen into line with the land merchants in Nacogdoches, who coveted the rich territory between the Trinity and Sabine Rivers north of town for themselves. If the Cherokees had been hostile to the whites, what Bean recommended to Elozúa might be more excusable. But no, they were peaceable Indians who only fought against plains tribes that Mexico called its enemies. And Peter Ellis Bean wanted to keep them at it.

Did self-interest also figure into Bean's recommendation that the Cherokees be uprooted from the lands they had occupied above Nacogdoches for over a decade? This is a possibility, because the lower boundary the Cherokees were asking for cut through Bean's league of land astride the Old San Antonio Road, the first tract that he had received from the government. He may have still owned a section of this grant below the road, even if James Bradshaw owned the upper portion. Bean also had plans to locate the four leagues that he had obtained from Jesús de la Garza on the east side of the Neches, about ten miles above the road. Moreover, it would jeopardize Bean's plans for locating one of his own leagues on the Neches Saline (southwestern corner of modern Smith County). These lands were squarely within the tract that the Cherokees were soliciting from the government, and Bean had knowledge of the boundaries in October 1833 if not before. Through him, and Alcalde Adolphus Sterne, word would have spread like wildfire to other land traffickers at Nacogdoches.

Bean avoided part of the problem by changing his mind and locating the Garza tract elsewhere. On April 5, 1834, he received title to four leagues—by virtue of the power of attorney he had received from Alférez Garza in April 1832 and then transferred to Frost Thorn. The tract was nestled between the Neches and Angelina Rivers where Cherokee, Houston, and Angelina Counties join. Bodans Bayou runs through the survey—well below anything the Cherokees were asking for or had a right to claim.[38]

But Bean persisted with owning the Neches Saline in Smith County. Carvajal surveyed it, based on Gaines's earlier work, at the end of 1834 as part of Bean's other two and a quarter leagues from Coahuila y Texas, and title was confirmed to him on December 14, 1835. As we shall see, this was around the time that Sam Houston was preparing to sign a treaty with the Cherokees on behalf of the rebel government, a treaty that would guarantee *them* possession of this region. Bean had already sold the Saline League by then, so he could afford the luxury of being disinterested in whether or not Houston's treaty would be ratified and put into effect.[39] More likely, from early on he had an understanding with the Cherokees to work the saline himself and give them part of the profits. This is suggested by the 1833 contract with Prather and later events at the site, connected with his neighbor Martin Lacy.

As a result of the April Convention, Stephen F. Austin had traveled to Mexico City in the summer of 1833, bearing a petition for separate statehood from Coahuila and a proposed constitution for the new state of Texas. Although the Convention was controlled by independence-minded people like William Wharton (as president) and Sam Houston, Austin agreed to present their proceedings to the federal government. It appears he felt that the time had come to press for separate statehood. Had Austin known about Santa Anna's letter of the preceding January—warning the government against exactly the sort of "revolutionary" documents he was bearing—it is doubtful that Austin would have been

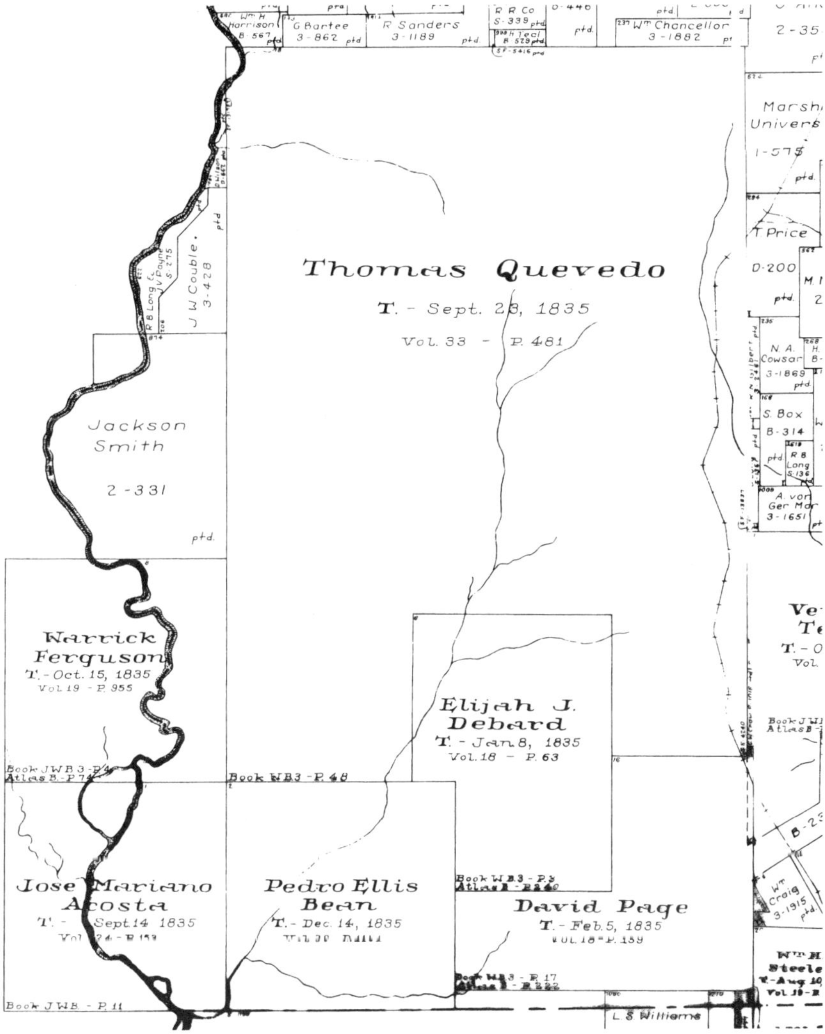

Bean's "Saline League" in Smith County. Courtesy Texas General Land Office.

foolish enough to venture into the lion's den. His decision was no doubt prompted by the actions that other men were taking to give Texas a territorial status, some of them agents for the Zavala, Burnet, and Vehlein concessions now called the Galveston Bay & Texas Land Company. John T. Mason was one of their representatives, and Austin regarded him as a foe. U.S. Chargé d'Affaires Anthony Butler was another devious opponent, who was scheming with James Prentiss and other speculators to buy Texas from corrupt politicians in Mexico.[40]

Austin met with frustration in the Mexican capital and found that his "enemies" had the ear of Vice President Farías and other top officials. He made remarks about how the just demands of Texas could not be put off indefinitely and how military force by Mexico was not an option. Farías interpreted these remarks as threats, and they hurt Austin's case. In his exasperation, Austin wrote to the ayuntamiento at Béxar on October 2, advising them to organize a government separate from Coahuila and tell other municipal councils to do the same. This letter, when brought to the attention of higher authorities, resulted in Austin's arrest on charges of treason. He remained in jail throughout 1834, and his colonists were adrift without their leader. They feared to take any action, lest it endanger the life of Austin or contribute to a verdict of guilty.[41]

Chapter 13

ALMONTE'S 1834 INSPECTION

COINCIDING WITH AUSTIN'S ARREST—and partially motivated by it—Vice President Farías authorized Col. Juan N. Almonte to go to Texas and gauge the rebellious sentiment of the foreign colonists. Almonte was the illegitimate son of Peter Ellis Bean's revolutionary war mentor, Gen. José María Morelos, and an Indian woman. Bean had conducted thirteen-year-old Almonte to New Orleans shortly before the capture and execution of Morelos by Royalist forces. There Almonte had remained until independence was achieved. Once Bean quit the struggle and returned to Louisiana after the death of Morelos, he probably spent time with the lad and looked after his interests as much as possible. And now the son, grown into a thirty-year-old colonel in the Mexican army, was coming to Texas. Apart from their personal relationship, Bean's military duties in east Texas made him Almonte's chief informant about public affairs in that section of the Mexican republic.[1]

Almonte did not reach Nacogdoches until April 26, having been assured while in Natchitoches by Bean that his reception would be a friendly one. Just before Almonte's arrival, Bean had petitioned Land Commissioner Vicente Aldrete to put him in possession of the eleven leagues he held on behalf of Gavino Aranjo. As already noted, the surveys were completed on April 4, 1834, by José María Carvajal in two tracts. One of them was described as below the San Antonio Road on the waters of the Neches and Angelina.[2] This tract was five leagues of Aranjo's eleven located west of the defunct Fort Terán, and we know from a later sale (arranged by Frost Thorn in 1835) that Bean located the other six leagues on the Red River near Pecan Point.[3] According to this document, Bean received his title on May 18, and less than a week later he and Thorn sold a portion of it to J. K. (John Kirby) and A. (Augustus) C. Allen for five hundred dollars.[4] They were brothers from New York and big-time speculators in the Nacogdoches region, later founders of the city of Houston.[5]

Being on the main road to Texas from Arkansas and points east, lands in the Pecan Point district had a hot sales potential to incoming immigrants. It will be recalled that Bean had located one of his own eight leagues on the Red River in 1833, placing it ten miles below the mouth of the Kiamichi. In 1834 Bean also had the Garza four leagues surveyed for him—not ten miles above the main Camino Real, east of the Neches as planned—but well out of any conflict with Cherokee claims; title was conferred on April 5.[6]

These extensive land operations of Bean's were put on hold (for a short time, at least) once Almonte got to town. In his first communication from Nacogdoches, Almonte mentioned the ten or twelve men whom the inhabitants themselves termed "land speculators." These men Almonte considered in association with Austin. Like him, they hoped to make Texas into a separate state "in order to deal at will in the lands of this most fertile country and create their patrimony from it."[7] While Bean was operating on a much smaller scale than these speculators, he was friends with most of them (Frost Thorn and Adolphus Sterne in particular) and selling his grants to several of the largest land merchants. Thus Bean was treading on thin ice when he told Almonte about the dimensions of the land game around Nacogdoches. Like Terán, Almonte believed that speculation of this sort by foreigners undermined the territorial integrity of Mexico.

Monitoring the situation with the immigrant tribes in east Texas was also one of Almonte's responsibilities. He was given two sets of private instructions, and in what appears to be an earlier draft these Indians were a topic of concern. All "nomadic" tribes were to be informed that Mexico would award them lands and they would be integrated into the Mexican federation, as long as they settled at permanent sites. They were even allowed to choose their own authorities for governing themselves and, when their numbers allowed, could create territories under self-rule with the federal government's protection. If Almonte thought it indispensable that "some concessions or favors" be made to their chiefs, "giving them the most flattering expectations for this purpose," he was to immediately notify the government "for its corresponding approval."[8]

While Indians are not mentioned in Almonte's other set of private instructions (its focus being on the Anglo colonists), once he got to Texas he set about complying with the set that specified Mexico's policy toward the immigrant tribes. The important point here is that Almonte did not have the power to put these Indians into possession of the lands they desired. He could only "flatter" their expectations and recommend to the federal government which tribes deserved approval of the lands being solicited. This Almonte did repeatedly throughout the year. Tribes like the Cherokees believed that Almonte, as "land commissioner," had the authority to award titles. But in this they were mistaken and ultimately disappointed.

Colonel Bean arranged a council among the friendly tribes so Almonte could meet with them face-to-face. No doubt Almonte's Indian heritage, stamped plainly on his facial features, did something to persuade the assembled leaders that this man might at last fulfill the government's long-delayed promises to them. General Terán, after all, was a white man who held his nose and avoided touching or hugging Indians unless hard pressed; his seemingly good intentions had come to nothing.[9] But here among them was a man of bronze, and they carefully listened to his reassuring words.

Bean reported the results of the council to Political Chief Músquiz on June 16. He said that Almonte, "First Commissioner for the Supreme Government of the Federation for the Direction of Colonization in Texas," had been in Nacogdoches more than a month and a half. He "told me as soon as he arrived that he wished to have an interview with the Indian tribes living in this Department." Bean set a date with the tribal leaders and on the first of June he went with Almonte to one of their villages where more than five hundred Indians of the following nations had gathered: Cherokee, Shawnee, Kickapoo, Creek, Delaware, Choctaw, and Nacogdoche. "We were received with the greatest hospitality, and Sr. Almonte explained to them his purpose in coming, which in essence boiled down to offering them the paternal protection of His Excellency the President of the United States of Mexico and to give them lands as long as they settled in one place and built villages. They showed great joy and promised to obey the orders of the Supreme Government and devote themselves to farm work, with the sole [condition] that their internal government be left to them."[10] The chiefs insisted that their lands must be marked out through rivers, lakes, or hills, which were the only boundaries they understood. Bean and Almonte stayed two days among the Indians, then returned to Nacogdoches.

After this council Almonte began sending reports to the secretary of foreign relations, Francisco Lombardo, urging that the land claims of the Cherokees in particular be recognized. He met with their civil chief, Big Mush, noting that War Chief Bowl could not attend the council because he was seriously ill. His efforts had kept the Cherokees out of the Fredonian Rebellion. Bowl had been made a colonel, given a few gifts, and promised land for his people in 1827, said Almonte, "but these have never been granted to them, even though they are perfectly disposed to obey the commands of His Excellency the President."[11] The other tribes, though not as organized politically as the Cherokees, desired lands where they could settle in peace and devote themselves to hunting, growing corn, and raising cattle.

Almonte reported the following population figures for the various tribes: Nacogdoche, 300; Delaware, 300; Shawnee, 400; Cherokee, 500; Choctaw, 500; Creek, 600; Kickapoo, 800—for a total of 3,400 souls. Of these, there were more than 800 warriors who "could be of enormous service to the government because of their loyalty [to Mexico]."[12] In his November 1834 Secret Report to the Mexican government, Almonte included statistics for all the tribes in Texas: an estimated 15,300 Indians, of whom 10,800 were considered hostile and 4,500 friendly. The Comanches alone numbered 10,000, and Almonte believed that they must be subjugated before Coahuila y Texas could ever prosper.[13] Austin reported larger Indian figures to the government.

Recognizing the importance of interim commandant Bean at Nacogdoches, Almonte said, "Colonel Bean is the one who manages affairs between one tribe and another, and they regularly come to him to settle their disputes. Given this aspect, Col. Bean would be difficult to replace here."[14] Bean continued to supply Almonte with political, military, and Indian information after the inspection was over. On December 10, 1834, Almonte forwarded a message from the Shawnee, Cherokee, Kickapoo, and Creek tribes, dated August 25, asking the president for their lands. This petition was received from Bean. Almonte translated the document for Santa Anna's benefit and stressed the urgency of acceding to their request.[15]

Once Almonte left Nacogdoches for San Felipe sometime after the end of June, Bean's life returned to normal. No doubt encouraged by Almonte, Bean wrote Gen. Pedro Lemus on June 30 about how lack of pay had put him in a difficult position.

> I, the citizen Lieutenant Colonel of Permanent Cavalry with the rank of Colonel, Pedro Elías Bean, before Your Excellency respectfully say: That from the year 1827, in which I was assigned to this frontier, to the end of July of 1831, I was satisfied in my wages as is on record in the adjoined stop-payment order by the subordinate commissariat of Béjar.
>
> And that in attention to the notorious scarcities of the public treasury from that date until the present one, I have remained without any salary and exposed to the greatest miseries. It is now impossible for me to subsist in this sad and desperate situation, and much more with exercising a public position on a frontier frequented by foreigners.
>
> And this consideration, as much as that of my own subsistence, obliges me to raise the present request to the high justification of Your Excellency so that in your view you may be pleased to order that I be paid my due salaries, in the federal treasurer's office or

> where you may consider convenient; determining at the same time where I should collect my wages hereafter, because here there are no troops nor does the subordinate commissariat of Béjar have any funds available.[16]

Lemus, to his credit, endorsed this petition on September 25, saying that Bean was "very deserving" of his salaries because it was "certain that he has remained at Nacogdoches in the service of the Republic . . . charged exclusively with keeping tranquil the tribes of barbarous Indians which live on the frontier." If Bean had not "justified his existence" on a monthly basis to the commissariat at Béxar, it was because of the great distance at which he found himself and lack of a regular mail service between the two points.[17]

On July 4 Bean wrote Lemus again, this time regarding the 269 pesos' worth of gifts he had provided for the Indians during Almonte's visit. Attached to the cover letter were receipts for his expenditures: "There daily occur these little expenses, which custom has made indispensable for maintaining the peace among the friendly Indians; and as I have found myself for more than three years without any salaries and suffering the greatest privations, I shall see myself in need of abandoning this frontier if there are not facilitated for me some resources with which to subsist and pay the aforesaid expenses."[18] He begged Lemus "in deference to justice" to recommend payment of his expenses as soon as possible "so that I will be able to continue attending to the requests of the said Indians."

Both of these requests reached the War Department by the end of the year, and Bean's threat to "abandon" the frontier worked magic. The word came down on January 26, 1835, to let his claims be paid and charged against "extraordinary expenses of war." Almonte, then at the capital, vouched for Bean's claims and called attention to the two stop-payment orders. They were seemingly still in effect and had kept Bean from being paid anything since their date of issue, that is, shortly before he had taken command of Fort Terán. The exact reason for these "pink slips" remains unknown, but having to serve Mexico three years without pay must have tested Bean's faith.[19]

To maintain himself while the government dragged its heels reimbursing him for his services as Indian agent and military commandant, Bean fell back on his landholdings. In October he sold Morgan "Enyer" (Cryer?) 1,280 acres of land on the Red River for two hundred pesos, it being part of Aranjo's eleven-league grant that Bean had acquired.[20] More significantly, on October 16 Bean sold his "Saline League" to Archibald Hotchkiss for two thousand pesos. It was noted that Bean had possession by virtue of it being one of the eight leagues that the government of Coahuila y Texas had awarded him on February 29, 1831. This Saline

League, therefore, was the one in Smith County, not the league lying along the west bank of the Neches in Houston County that Bean had applied for as a "settler." Although Bean warranted the title, he must have known—as Hotchkiss should have—that it was in territory claimed by the Cherokees.[21]

There may have been some difficulties with Hotchkiss over the matter, because Bean was soon protesting a survey run for him on Cherokee lands and reporting that Hotchkiss was endeavoring to introduce a horde of warlike Creek Indians to Texas at considerable personal profit to himself. Hotchkiss was an agent for the Zavala, Burnet, and Vehlein grants—not a man to have as an enemy. It appears that Bean became one, along with Sam Houston. In the spring of 1835 Houston sued both Hotchkiss and his fellow land agent George Anthony Nixon for a considerable amount of money they owed his client, whose name was John C. Leplicher, a clerk whom Hotchkiss had accused of embezzling company funds and fired. Hotchkiss being absent in New Orleans, his agent and attorney Arthur Henrie was ordered to answer the charges. This was at the same time that Houston, as a single man, applied to Burnet's commissioner (Nixon) and attorney (Henrie) for a grant of land. He was awarded a third of a league (about 1,480 acres) in May 1835, but had to settle for less because Austin had already granted him a full league (4,428 acres) in his colony when Houston applied for it as a married man.[22]

Bean's wife Candace Midkiff applied for a league of land of her own in December 1834. She called herself a widow with three children who, "attracted by the generous provisions of the Colonization laws of this State," had come with her family to settle as a colonist therein. Her petition was addressed to the commissioner for Empresario Burnet's colony, the aforementioned "Jorge Antonio" Nixon. Alcalde Vital Flores certified that she was a lady "of very good morality, customs, and industriousness, a lover of the Constitution and laws of the place, and a Christian." Without waste of time, Nixon put her in possession of a league next to the one conceded to her brother Isaac. The survey was between the Trinity and the Neches, below the San Antonio Road in present Leon County. The margins of a Bean and Thorn adjoining tract were mentioned in the survey notes, but there is no reference to Colonel Bean's relationship to the "Widow" Midkiff.[23]

Was she finally striking out on her own? So it would appear, either with or without the help of her notable husband. On the 1835 census of Nacogdoches "from West to Angelina River," Candace again called herself a widow, aged thirty-two. Four children were in her household, but one may have been the nephew Samuel M. Bean who had been taken in by the colonel, possibly the son of William Bean. Candace's twenty-three-year-old brother Isaac Midkiff is living next to her on the 1835 census. He, a farmer, has an eighteen-year-old wife, Latha Jones, and one child. Nearby is a single man, Isaac Hicks, aged twenty-three and also a farmer.[24] He would marry the older "widow" Candace two years later. Candace, of course, was not a widow in the traditional sense of the word; Bean was still alive and kicking. Did this marriage make *her* a bigamist? Rules governing marriage on the Texas frontier were strange, and quite a bit looser than we are now accustomed to.

Chapter 14

STORM CLOUDS GATHER

IF THE YEAR 1835 had its dark moments as revolution approached, it also had bright spots for Peter Ellis Bean. For example, he was notified on March 12 by the new commandant of Coahuila y Texas at Béxar, Col. Domingo de Ugartechea, that he had finally been named as the "Comandante Principal of all the Departments of these Frontiers." It was a welcome development to a man who had been serving Mexico for three years on an interim basis with no help to speak of. This promotion Bean received "with the greatest satisfaction, congratulating myself, and manifesting to Your Lordship my good disposition and positive desires of receiving your orders for giving them due compliance." Bean asked what disposition he was to make of the things in his custody left behind by Piedras's 12th Permanent Battalion—muskets, ammunition, war chests, and other military articles.[1]

Also on April 7, Bean wrote Ugartechea about his order of February 9, relative to being reimbursed for the 269 pesos he had expended for maintaining peace with the Indians. A superior order had come from the commandant general (Martín Perfecto de Cos) that Bean be paid this sum, but he had no way of getting the money except to beg, "as in fact I do beg," Colonel Ugartechea for it. Taking the groveling position so characteristic of Mexican supplicants in this era, Bean implored Ugartechea to order that 269 pesos be taken in his name from the paymaster's chest under his control "since on this frontier there is no branch of funds from whence to take them." Even with his promotion, Bean had difficulty wresting funds from the Mexican military, nor does it seem that any troops were sent to Nacogdoches to serve under him. Finally, on June 4, Bean received a letter saying that Commandant General Cos wanted him paid the 269 pesos for Indian gifts.[2]

In the spring of 1835 there was a minor Indian scare at Nacogdoches, as Justo Liendo and Lorenzo Boden were charged with inciting the Cherokees to rise up against the whites. Testimony was taken in mid-February, and one of those questioned was the *coyote* (half-breed) Benjamin Hawkins. Sam Houston was his lawyer, strange considering the charges that Houston brought against Hawkins in September.[3] Though it amounted to nothing, twenty influential citizens asked at the end of the month that—because of the Indian danger—they be given arms "deposited in the hands of Sr. Colonel Bean."[4] Later in the year, more such requests were made for guns in Bean's custody.

On April 24 Bean gave testimony in the case of *William Goyens v. Isaac Lee.* They rode to Lee's house to get cows and calves that Goyens owed Bean, amounting to a debt of twenty-five dollars at five dollars per animal. Lee, it seems, was pasturing the cows and possibly sharing in their increase with Goyens. According to Bean, Lee "said that Gowen had Bin Shufling and he would not Pay more than one Cow and Calf." The blacksmith said he would sue him and did. Goyens won, and thus Bean recovered the debt for cows and calves owed him.[5]

Judging from the numerous land transactions that occurred in the early part of 1835, Bean was not short of money. On April 11 Frost Thorn, in New Orleans, made a very lucrative sale to two gentlemen from Mississippi, Nathaniel Ware and Thomas Perez. For $15,000 Thorn sold them an undivided portion of ten leagues (specified as 22,140 acres) that he controlled on the south side of the Red River, embracing part of the Pecan Point district, all duly surveyed and recorded at Nacogdoches. Four of these leagues were granted in the name of Francisco "Remerez" on May 4, 1831, being part of a five-league grant, which Thorn had located by Ramírez's power of attorney given on August 12 of that year.

The other six leagues in the sale were part of Gavino Aranjo's eleven-league grant. Title was given by Commissioner Vicente Aldrete on May 18, 1834, to Peter Ellis Bean, acting under Aranjo's power of attorney —which Thorn was now acting under, as Bean had transferred the right to him on January 24, 1833. (The other five leagues of Aranjo's grant had been located on the Neches west of Fort Terán by Bean.) It is unknown how much Bean received from this sale, but $15,000 was a lot of money in 1835. It is not likely that Bean gave Thorn power over his tracts of land without either money in hand or a stake in the eventual sale of these lands to well-heeled buyers from the United States such as Ware and Perez.[6]

More such land sales were made directly by Bean in the coming months, leading some observers to suspect that he was trying to unload his real estate in the event that revolution upset his Mexican titles. A curious twist came on April 15, when Archibald Hotchkiss sold a half interest in Bean's "La Salina" league to Frost Thorn for a mere ten dollars. This was probably an inside deal to involve Thorn in promoting its eventual sale at considerable profit to both of them. That Bean remained as an interested party somehow in money made off of such a sale is suggested by a document filed with the county clerk on July 8, 1837. Hotchkiss and Thorn verified the ten-dollar sale before the revolution, saying that half of the purchase money "paid *or to be paid* [emphasis added]" to Bean would be defrayed by Thorn. The pair retained possession of "Bean's Saline," leasing it to one Thomas Gardner for six years in 1842. Gardner terminated this arrangement by selling his salt-making equipment to Thorn and Hotchkiss in 1845; a lawsuit resulted.[7]

A document dated April 14, 1835 (one day before the Hotchkiss-Thorn transaction), also indicates that Bean had a problem of some sort with Hotchkiss over the saline or lands around it. On that date the political chief of Nacogdoches (Henry Rueg) wrote the alcalde about how Surveyor "Henere" (Arthur Henrie) had surveyed three *sitios* of land for "Archibaldo" Hotchkiss within the claimed lands of the Cherokee Indians. It was done contrary to the government's positive orders and "against the remonstrances of Colonel Bean." Sheriff James Carter was ordered to examine the surveyor and witnesses to the case. If these proceedings satisfied the charge that Hotchkiss was intruding on Cherokee lands, the surveyor would have to pay a fifty-dollar fine to the benefit of public funds.[8] Similar cases involving unauthorized surveyor activities in Cherokee lands came during the year. As we shall see below, Commandant Bean and Political Chief Rueg also brought more serious charges against Hotchkiss in the month of April.

Nor were these the only land transactions that put money in Bean's hands in mid-1835. On May 5, he sold to Thorn his quarter league north of town on La Nana Creek for 100 pesos. It was noted as part of Bean's eight leagues from Coahuila y Texas, title from Aldrete.[9] The next day Bean sold the Allen brothers a fourth of his six leagues on the Red River from the Aranjo grant for only 150 pesos, adding to what they had bought the year before.[10] Was this sale made by Bean without knowledge of Thorn's sale in New Orleans of the entire tract on April 11? If so, it is small wonder that the land business of the era was accompanied by much litigation. Compared to Thorn's nab of $15,000, Bean's $150 was pocket change. At the end of May he also sold his own league on the Red River (one of the eight he received from Coahuila y Texas) to Haden H. Edwards for 500 pesos. It was Bean's tract on the Kiamichi but noted as ten miles *above* its mouth into the Red.[11] Most of the land concessions in this region were later ruled invalid by the Republic of Texas because they fell within the twenty-league boundary reserve with the United States and involved eleven-league grants. For the time being, however, sellers like Bean and Thorn prospered. Also, when it came time to defend these titles, the buyers were often stuck with the job.

Bean also divested himself of property within Nacogdoches at this time. On May 26 he sold a town lot on the central plaza to Haden H. Edwards and his brother-in-law Frost Thorn for an astounding 800 pesos. Bean had acquired it in 1828 from Juan Amelon and Juliano Alexander, and its location must have made it valuable to the purchasers. In mid-May María Catarina Amador sold the lot on "la Loma" that had formerly belonged to Colonel Bean. It was the Irion Hill property with a scenic view of the town.[12]

To return to Bean's activities as Indian agent and military commandant at Nacogdoches, at the end of 1834 and early in 1835 he sent Colonel Almonte several reports that caused alarm in Mexico City. One letter in December dealt with the results of a reconnaissance that Gen. Henry Leavenworth had made into Indian Territory in the summer of 1834, hoping to treat with or otherwise pacify the Comanches and allied plains tribes along the northern boundary between Mexico and the United States. Almonte, while at Nacogdoches, had been asked to accompany this expedition but wisely declined. The clipping that Bean sent Almonte convinced him that the U.S. government was engaged in a military buildup along the Red River frontier and was trying to make allies of the wild tribes that were hostile to Mexico—suspicions he had voiced when first learning of Leavenworth's plans. This was indeed occurring, and treaties were being signed while Bean wrote.[13]

Bean also informed Almonte about the increasing tide of Indian immigration: four thousand Quapaws had either come or were on their way to Texas. This subject he wrote about again on January 12, telling Almonte that "Each day more of the tribes of the United States of the North emigrate to this frontier, and you know the measures I have employed to contain this problem. But up to now I have achieved nothing."[14] Bean maintained that, according to Article 33 of the treaty of commerce and navigation between the two republics, "the United States of the North are obligated to keep their Indians within their borders and not allow them to cross into our Republic." He named the immigrating tribes as the Creeks, Choctaws, and Quapaws, urging Almonte to bring this threat to the attention of the president in time for his information to be useful.

Bean's complaint became the subject of an official protest to U.S. Chargé d'Affaires Anthony Butler, who expended prodigious energy in February to rebut it.[15] From Mexico City Bean's complaint traveled to Washington, where Secretary of State John Forsyth responded to it and a related complaint by the political chief of Nacogdoches (Henry Rueg) in October. He said that the War Department had no information about any Creek Indians moving from Alabama to Mexican Texas, and President Jackson had always "discountenanced" projects of this kind. "From this it would appear that the political chief of Nacogdoches has been misinformed. But should it be otherwise, it may be doubtful whether under the 33rd. article of the treaty the intervention of the United States could be claimed or afforded unless the Indians manifested some hostile intent. If Indians going from the U.S. or elsewhere should migrate to the Mexican territories with peaceable intentions, it will be for the Mexican Government alone to decide upon their admission or exclusion."[16] This was the same argument that Butler had used earlier in the year, just the latest in a continuing controversy over the intent of Article 33. The United States clung tenaciously to its interpretation and Mexico likewise. As we shall see, Bean was not finished with protests of this nature.

In his letter to Almonte near the end of 1834, Bean also advised him that agents had arrived from the New York company that had "bought or assumed responsibility for the settlement of the vast Zavala, Vehlein, and Burnett land grants." These agents were likely Archibald Hotchkiss and George Nixon, or their representatives such as Arthur Henrie. Almonte reported, "They wish to hold the settlers' land like sultans, which in the view of that commandant [Bean] can cause an upheaval."[17] From this it appears that Bean had some problems with Hotchkiss, at least, and they probably came shortly after Bean's sale of the Neches Saline League to him.

Proof, of sorts, came on April 12 when Political Chief Rueg wrote the secretary of state of Coahuila y Texas about the doings of land agent Hotchkiss. He was in New Orleans negotiating a contract to introduce the Creek Indians to Texas, along with a *coyote* of the Creek tribe named Hawkins. This exodus was directed toward Filisola's empresarial grant. The sum of 20,000 pesos had changed hands, with another $60,000 due after rights to the land had been secured from Filisola's representative. Rueg had his information from Colonel Bean, who had gotten it from another *coyote* of the tribe. If Hotchkiss was allowed to pursue such a project in opposition to laws of the Supreme Government, said Rueg, it would be "very prejudicial" to the interests of the country and result in "innumerable evils" for the inhabitants of the frontier.[18] It is likely that Rueg's letter about Hotchkiss and the Creeks became part of the diplomatic protest that Bean launched in January 1835 by writing Almonte. More protests were made in September.

While he was in Texas, Colonel Almonte had stressed the need for a campaign against the Comanches, even begging Gen. Pedro Lemus to come to Nacogdoches and personally get it underway. When Almonte reached Monclova, he penned a detailed plan on how this campaign should be organized and carried out. It involved enlisting the friendly tribes from the United States who were inhabiting east Texas, white colonists of the ranger type, and other civilian volunteers who were accustomed to warfare with the savage tribes. Almonte attached this plan to the Secret Report he wrote for the Supreme Government in November 1834, after his return to Mexico City. Almonte had also written the new governor of Coahuila y Texas, Juan José Elguezábal, about these problems and how the citizens would perish unless given relief from constant raids by the warlike Comanches. Otherwise, he assured the governor that the beleaguered citizens might seek protection from a rival power, that is, the United States.[19]

Almonte's call for a war to the finish with the Comanches was an influential one, and it soon gained the approval of President Santa Anna and Commandant General Cos. On March 26, 1835, Ugartechea forwarded to Bean Cos's orders for him to hold talks with the Shawnees, Cherokees, and allied tribes. For their help these warriors were to be provided powder and shot for their weapons. They could also retain as spoils of war any animals captured from the Comanches that were unmarked; those with brands had to be returned to their rightful owners. Copies of Cos's orders went to the ayuntamientos of various towns, urging them to contribute to the campaign however they could—be it with cash donations, horses, or fighting men.[20]

On May 18 Bean responded by saying it was his opinion that the chiefs of the friendly tribes would not take part in the campaign unless they could keep *all* horses and mules captured, both branded and unbranded. The civilized tribes were no dummies. They knew that the majority of the stock taken would wear brands, because the Comanches had stolen them from Anglo or Hispanic settlers who had marked their animals. Wild horses *sin fierros* (without brands) would not be sufficient to reward their efforts. Colonel Ugartechea acknowledged receipt of Bean's letter on June 4, and said he was sending it to Commandant General Cos.[21]

It is interesting to note that the state government about this time published a decree aimed at awarding the Cherokees and their immigrant brethren their long-desired land. Gov. Agustín Viesca on May 12, 1835, circulated the following law:

> [Article 1.] In order to secure the peace and tranquility of the State, the Government is authorized to select, out of the Vacant Lands of Texas, that land which may appear most appropriate for the location of the peaceable and civilized Indians which may have been introduced into Texas.
>
> Article 2. It shall establish with them a line of defense along the frontier to secure the State against the incursions of the barbarous tribes.[22]

Bean, of course, had recommended this policy in 1833. It was part of the barrier approach he had pursued with the friendly tribes against the Comanches since 1826, first elucidated in his petition to be an empresario. Early on, it was simply a matter of whipping up the Cherokees to fight the plains tribes; now land was the inducement—but land out on the western frontier, away from the settlements and close to their "barbarous" enemies. It must be wondered if this legislation was passed just in case the friendly tribes should refuse to participate in the Comanche campaign for spoils of war alone. Everybody recognized that their help was essential, and Peter Ellis Bean was the man who could swing it. Now he had another carrot to dangle when meeting with the leadership of the "peaceable and civilized" tribes.

These tribes needed help as well. Throughout the summer of 1835, but starting in February, Chief Bowl complained that five or six families of Anglo squatters were occupying land in the limits that had been promised to them. One man named Cook and "the widow of ——" had established themselves within Cherokee pasture lands, doing much damage by killing their cattle and deer. Bowl wanted these squatters evicted by the sheriff, and orders came from Béxar to do so. But the problem continued. Surveyor Jeremiah Strode even "dared to have surveyed lands within the boundaries of the Cherokee Indians so as to include the house of one of their chiefs called Big Mush," this in direct contravention of orders that the Indians were to have peaceful possession of their land until the Supreme Government decided otherwise. Strode was fined fifty pesos and cost of the suit when it was learned that he had acted contrary to the instructions of his commissioner.[23] Likely story.

In April Bean also alerted Ugartechea to a party of traders from the United States who had established a "commercial house" on the banks of the Red River at the old village of the "Tahuayaces" (Taovayas) within Mexican territory. Thus the tribes at war with Mexico were able to secure weapons and ammunition, through their exchange of stolen horses with these men. In order to "stop this evil" and get these traders to withdraw from the frontier, Bean suggested another protest that their actions violated the terms of the treaty of peace and commerce between the two nations.[24]

Colonel Ugartechea forwarded Bean's report to Cos. General Cos, then at Matamoros raising troops for the occupation of Texas, replied in June. He agreed that the operations of foreign traders were "extremely harmful to the security of the frontier." Ugartechea should urge the political chiefs of various departments to arrest them, since the friendly Indians were "showing a repugnance to doing so." Colonel Bean's knowledge might be "useful in the matter," so Ugartechea was to work in combination with him. Bean's warning made its way to the Mexican War Department, where it was passed along to the secretary of foreign affairs in mid-June.[25] The presence of these traders received more attention in the following months.

On May 12 Cos told Bean, through the medium of Ugartechea, that the Coushattas were to be left in quiet possession of the lands they occupied. As always, this was contingent on the Supreme Government's disposition, but the tribe had petitioned the government for title to their lands and it was necessary to keep them quiet. American squatters and holders of land certificates were intruding on what had been recognized as Alabama-Coushatta territory, similar to the problem that Chief Bowl was having with land "owned" by his tribe. Once Cos reached Texas in September, he issued further orders on the policy to be pursued with the Coushattas.[26]

At this time the federalist government of Coahuila y Texas was under attack, partly due to four-hundred–league sales that had been authorized to raise militia forces to combat hostile Indians. A number of prominent Texans, including John Durst from Nacogdoches, immediately gobbled up these lands. When Governor Viesca opposed the federal government's annulment of these sales, General Cos disbanded the legislature. Most of the speculators beat a hasty retreat to Texas and some kept going past the Sabine, their land certificates clutched tightly in hand. Viesca and a small party of his supporters, including Ben Milam, James Grant, and Jim Bowie, were arrested as they sought to evade centralist troops loyal to Santa Anna's regime. It was a very confusing situation, and few people knew which side to take.[27]

Bean wrote Ugartechea on June 15 about how this latest turmoil in the state government was affecting people at Nacogdoches. "Around here there are some of the speculators in the 400 leagues of land, which have been sold by this State, and they have tried to cause some uprisings; but they have been unable to do so up to this date, nor have they accomplished anything, because these inhabitants want to support the Sovereign Government and not become involved in supporting [land] speculations of the State. I am alert, and I am going to have to use my political influence to oppose it as much as possible because I do not have any troops."[28]

In another letter written the same day, Bean acknowledged receipt of Ugartechea's letter of June 4 informing him that Cos had been notified that the peaceful tribes would only make war on the Comanches if allowed to "keep for themselves anything that they may take away from the Indians of the plains." Bean had good news. He had met with the chiefs of four different tribes on June 12 and 13; they were "all in the best humor, and, according to the information which they give me, 500 men from these tribes can go out [on the Comanche campaign], not counting some Mexicans and colonists who will go."[29] Thus it seems as if Bean had the friendly tribes poised and ready to undertake the campaign that Almonte had considered so necessary if Mexican colonists were ever to be induced to come to Texas. Until the Comanches were punished in campaigns such as this, and the frontier made safe, Almonte thought it impossible to balance the Anglo-dominant demographics in Texas with more Mexican settlers.[30]

The Comanche campaign, however, was put on hold due to the ugly political situation then developing in Texas. Many of the speculators who had managed to reach sanctuary talked loudly of how Santa Anna planned to purge Texas of foreigners. They would all be driven from their lands and swept back across the Sabine by his "mongrel" soldiers. When James Bowie managed to escape from Matamoros and reach Texas at the end of June, he reported the danger to Political Chief James B. Miller at San Felipe. Bowie said that he left Matamoros on June 12. All the boats in the port were being seized for the purpose of transporting troops to the coast of Texas. Commandant General Cos had prohibited all foreigners from being in the city under any circumstances. Bowie fled and managed to arrive safely at the Lavaca dwelling of Sylvanus Hatch. He told Miller that three thousand men had marched to Saltillo destined to Texas: "I will be with you in a few days by way of Brazoria. I am detained here today because of the bad health of my companion *de voyage* Mr. Despalliers who is sick with fever."[31]

A month later Bowie showed up in Nacogdoches, making trouble for Colonel Bean. But the tumult throughout Texas, caused by reports such as Bowie's, led to an increasingly difficult position for Bean. He, after all, was a Mexican soldier obliged to stay in communication with Mexican military authorities in Béxar and elsewhere. How could he say that things were calm at Nacogdoches and the citizens loyal to the Supreme Government when increasingly fewer of them were? When he told the truth in letters to Ugartechea, or named names, he would be considered an enemy of his fellow Anglo-Texans if such letters were intercepted by them. Bean was aware this was happening, as he explained on July 28.

> I have for some time passed answered no official communication from Your Lordship, for the reason that I have received information that my correspondence has been intercepted on the Brazos; the fact of having received no answer [from you] to my letters confirms that information. I have, therefore, thought it to be more advisable to remain silent, under the actual delicate circumstances. However, I avail myself of this occasion to assure you that a majority of the inhabitants of this frontier have refused to take part in the revolution and have agreed to remain quiet, notwithstanding the inducements

tendered them by some citizens of Bexar, and those of San Felipe, who have committed atrocities at Anahuac.

In the vicinity of the Colorado, they have killed an express rider; but the authorities, those who are not [already] compromised against the Supreme Government, are determined that the guilty not be brought to account.[32]

The "atrocities" at Anáhuac of which Bean spoke involved the taking of the Mexican customs house by hothead William Barret Travis and a crowd of volunteers on June 29, whereupon Capt. Antonio Tenorio, the customs collector, and a small detachment of soldiers were forced to leave. Travis thought he had struck a blow for freedom and was much surprised when his return to San Felipe was greeted by harsh criticism of his actions. But in the eyes of Mexico, armed revolution was already underway in Texas, and William Barret Travis was Public Enemy Number One.[33]

James Bowie, when he appeared in Texas, was a marked man as well. Not only had he participated in the 1834 Monclova three-hundred–league sale to John T. Mason, a wheeling-and-dealing agent for the Galveston Bay & Texas Land Company, but he had attempted to rouse militiamen to defend Governor Viesca against General Cos and his centralist troops. Bowie also had his detractors in Texas. Old settlers like James Kerr thought that Bowie and the other speculators were crying "wolf wolf, condemnation, destruction, war, to arms, to arms!" in hopes of protecting their massive illegal land purchases, even if they had to foment rebellion to do it. A chastised Travis cautioned Bowie that the time was not right for armed revolt and they had best lie low for a while.[34]

Bowie got to Nacogdoches early in July. Political Chief Rueg, for some reason, decided to urge the citizens to form a civil militia. By July 13 about one hundred men had gathered in the public square and named Bowie as their "colonel," either in response to Rueg's call or on their own hook. Near the end of the month a portion of them marched to the local storehouse where Bean kept his small armory of weapons that had belonged to Piedras's 12th Permanent Battalion. Bean reported the result to Rueg on July 30.

Yesterday there came to my house Señor Buy, and James Grante and others, and the first requested from me some guns of those that are under my charge and that belong to the Federal Government; and as it is not within my power to dispose of said arms without a general order, or [an order] from the Municipal Council of this Villa, it did not seem to me suitable to turn over the said arms.

> Señor Buy said that he would take them by force, which he effectuated, and went to the magazine and took out some guns, but I do not know the number; and he has taken them with the pretext, according to what they say, that they want to fight with some Indians. By virtue of which I communicate it to Your Lordship, making you aware that I am not responsible for the said [confiscated] arms.[35]

On the same day Bean wrote Ugartechea about the incident, declaring that he would take measures to quell any move by the revolutionists. Rueg, however, cautioned Bean in a letter dated July 31 against pursuing an inflammatory course with Bowie and his men: "In answer to your communication of yesterday, I have to say that I regret deeply the rashness of James Bowie who, at the head of a small band of men, took forcible possession of some muskets, the property of the Nation, that were deposited in the armory in your charge." Rueg expressed the "mortification with which I view the deplorable state of our affairs," but the excitement that prevailed among the citizens led him to consider as dangerous any measures taken in this instance. Because Rueg had no force at his disposal and the militia had not yet been organized, he thought that "we should act with great caution, in order to remove even the pretense for an outbreak [of violence]."[36]

Bean transmitted Rueg's letter to Ugartechea on August 11 with observations of his own on the way things had worked out. "Notwithstanding the offense committed by Santiago Bowi and the reckless men who came to the frontier for the purpose of disturbing public order, they could not succeed in carrying out their intentions. We hear nothing further of those turbulent men, and I am convinced that they have given up any hope of gathering the fruit of their former movements. They are not countenanced by the people of this frontier, who continue living in peace and show themselves obedient to the Supreme Government and to the authorities of this Department."[37]

By the time Bean wrote this letter, James Bowie had indeed disappeared, but not without creating quite a row. Shortly after arming his men with Brown Bess "Mexican" muskets, Bowie learned that a packet of letters to the Mexican consul at New Orleans was being held at a house in San Augustine, awaiting a rider to deliver them to the Sabine. Bowie paid a visit, demanded the letters, and returned to Nacogdoches, where he read them at a public gathering on the main plaza. The news—about how the rebels in Texas like Travis would be arrested for treason and how an army was being raised to set things right—aroused indignation and made Bowie something of a local hero.[38] But Political Chief Rueg recognized Bowie as a troublemaker and soon devised a way to get him out of town. Colonel Bean provided the means.

On July 3 Bean had received a letter from a friend of his in the United States who had promised in March to send him a report on traders who were operating on the frontier and receiving stolen horses from the Comanches. This report dealt not only with the situation of Holland Coffee's traders, but with the regiment of U.S. troops under a Major "Mazen" who had marched west to visit the Comanches, Taovayas, and other tribes in that direction. Their goal was to induce these tribes to await the arrival of a battalion of infantry with U.S. Commissioners Stokes, Arbuckle, and Armstrong, who were superintendents of Indian affairs. These gentlemen, said Bean's informant, had the objective of making a general peace with the plains tribes. Bean relayed this information to Ugartechea with his own feelings. If the commerce that these traders were carrying on so frequently was not cut off from the Comanches, wrote Bean, "we shall never in the future be able to have a perfect and lasting peace on this frontier, and the other points in the State, as long as they are encouraging the said tribes to continue committing their thefts, so that they will have something with which to carry on their trade, by buying from them the horses which they steal."[39]

Bean asked that this information be forwarded to Commandant General Cos because it was "one of the principal objects that should be attended to." Well might Bean describe it, because on August 24 the Stokes Commission met with chiefs of the Comanche, Wichita, Cherokee, Creek, Choctaw, Osage, Seneca, and Quapaw tribes at Camp Holmes on the Canadian River and signed a treaty that promised peace between the removed and plains Indians. Only the Kiowas refused to sign, mainly because of their anger at the Osages for an attack in which many of the Kiowa women and children had been killed and mutilated a year earlier. This was a more substantial pact than the one Col. Henry Dodge had negotiated with the plains tribes at the end of 1834. White traders always established posts in the wake of such agreements, and the Red River villages of the Wichitas offered ideal locations.[40]

When Henry Rueg learned that these traders were enabling the Comanches and their plains allies to carry on warfare against the settlements, he asked John Forbes to direct the sheriff to evict these traders from their post. The expedition, said Rueg, should be placed under the command of Colonel Bowie—perhaps the first time that the famed knife-fighter was given this rank in Texas. Bowie, full of himself and perhaps a little drunk, demanded that Sam Houston give him his horse. Houston refused, and Bowie replied, "I am going to take him." After he left to saddle Houston's horse for the outing, Houston asked Bowie's friend Caiaphas Ham if he thought it was right to let Bowie have his mount. Ham advised him that, under the circumstances, it might be a good idea. Flustered by Bowie's demand, Houston snarled, "Damn him, let him take the horse." Thus did

Rueg and Bean rid themselves of a man who seemed intent on bringing their town to armed insurrection.[41]

Just as Bean reported on August 11, James Bowie's expedition to oust Holland Coffee from his trading post on the Red River above the Cross Timbers did not amount to much. Bowie rode north through Cherokee country, stopping at Bowl's village to pick up a few scouts for the trip ahead. Bean may have given Bowie a letter to Bowl, asking this favor for Bowie and telling Bowl to also help with the Shawnees and other tribes beyond. An informant on the Neches told Bowie that many warriors of the Comanche, Tawakoni, Waco, and Taovaya tribes were at Coffee's trading post, and he was encouraging them to kill Mexicans and bring their livestock to him in exchange for trade goods they needed. Coffee might have as many as two hundred Tawakonis and twenty-five renegade whites protecting him at his trading establishment. After sending news of this intimidating development back to Rueg at Nacogdoches, and asking for reinforcements, Bowie was heard from no more. Perhaps, in Bowie's mind, the excursion was mainly to scout promising sites for locating surveys on Mason's three-hundred–league purchase, for which Bowie was the appointed commissioner.[42]

Evidence that Bean's position at Nacogdoches was becoming increasingly uncomfortable is found in a letter he wrote Ugartechea on August 18. Bean did not name names this time, but his report would have been very incriminating to him had it fallen into the hands of the people he was writing about: "I have informed Your Lordship, by last mail, of the state of affairs in the locality, up to this time. I must now tell you what has occurred since. Three days ago, some men who endeavor to spread armed rebellion agreed to hold a popular meeting in this town. The generality of the inhabitants, however, refused to attend it." No further steps had been taken since, said Bean, besides announcing that they would meet another day, not yet stated. From what he could learn, it seemed that they were trying to form an alliance with the Indians of this frontier. "But I do not believe they can succeed, because the Indians are not disposed to be hostile to Mexicans." Word was that the plotters hoped to receive money from New Orleans for the support of the revolution.

Bean could not say much about all their movements, as they were kept secret. He had learned that, as soon as they could succeed in holding another meeting, they intended to pass a resolution to the effect that all those who refused to assist their revolutionary plan must forfeit their property, to the benefit of this faction. Bean was convinced that "a great many persons" were opposed to such an extreme measure, and it would be difficult to put into practice. However, the troublemakers altered their views and plans every day, according to the rumors continually kept afloat. "Such is the state of affairs in this section of country. It may prove fatal to the generality of the inhabitants, and more particularly to the native Mexicans. It would, therefore, be advisable for the Supreme Government not to delay in sending troops to this frontier, but they should come in large numbers to impose respect. Otherwise, the stationing of a small party of soldiers here would induce the disaffected to persevere in their mischievous designs, and to call to their assistance reckless men of the neighboring country. These are not few."[43] Bean closed by begging Ugartechea to give him a one month's leave of absence so he could come to Béxar and discuss other business of importance "that cannot be trusted in writing, inasmuch as I am convinced that my correspondence is opened at San Felipe." To transmit letters such as this, Bean must have relied on private individuals who were traveling to Béxar instead of consigning them to the usual mail couriers. These riders were now routinely stopped as they passed through the settlements and being relieved of Spanish correspondence in their mail pouches. The Nacogdoches Archives contain many such items, personal letters marked "Unimportant."

The meeting to which Bean referred did indeed take place on Saturday, August 15 at Mr. Veal's Tavern. James Bradshaw was chairman, and those who took part in forming resolutions were William Logan, Solomon Peck, John Forbes, Richard Sparks, Thomas Rusk, and Sam Houston. In this meeting four men (Bradshaw, Houston, Rusk, and Sparks) were appointed "to council and treat with the different Indian tribes within the limits of Texas, according to the promises made to them by the Mexican Government, and whatever else they may deem proper, to do the Indians justice, and preserve peace with them." There was much rhetoric about the rights of free men in these proceedings, but here began the concern of the east Texas revolutionists with forming an alliance with the Indians of the neighborhood in case war should break out. Bean was also right about other resolutions, including the loss of citizenship and property for those who "desert the country" in case of a conflict. Houston made a motion that a convention be called at San Felipe "at as early a day as possible."[44]

These proceedings did not go over very well at Nacogdoches, nor did the plan to call a follow-up meeting. When Mosely Baker visited town in October to spread alarm about the coming Mexican invasion, Houston advised him to keep quiet. The War Party was not yet popular in east Texas (just as Bean reported), and the ayuntamiento had even forbidden the election of delegates to a convention.[45] No, the time was not right for anything that might be construed as a call for revolution against Mexico, and certainly not for outright independence. Thus when the Consultation did meet in November, revolutionists like Houston went along with separate statehood for Texas within the Mexican federation, and restoration of the Constitution of 1824 that Santa Anna had replaced with a dictatorship. Bolder action did not come until the March 1836 Convention.

As these events were about to unfold, Bean's life at Nacogdoches pursued its usual course. In July he received a letter from Capt. Francisco Medina in Mexico City, responding to an inquiry that Bean had written him earlier on May 31. It was about property that Medina still owned and Bean wanted to buy. Medina judged his town lot and house to be worth 1,300 pesos. The house alone should be valued at 800 pesos because it was solidly built of wood. His *solar,* thought Medina, ought to bring 500 pesos—more than enough to satisfy Señor Frost Thorn for what Bean had paid him on the captain's behalf. Medina could not discuss the sale of his ten *sitios* because Edward Gritten was acting as his representative and 2,200 pesos had already changed hands. In closing, Medina mentioned that Señor Austin was leaving in the morning for his colony. Despite all the impositions and calumnies that Austin had suffered in Mexico City, Captain Medina considered him a "good friend."[46]

At the end of August Alcalde Radford Berry ordered Sheriff Henry Teal to bring before him two men named Weeks and Hogan "to answer charges that will be preferred against them by Peter E. Bean." The nature of Bean's charges are unknown, but Teal performed his duty promptly.[47] Bean, throughout 1835, attested to the good character of a number of Anglos (and Mexicans) who were seeking admission as settlers. On September 9 he vouched for Burrell Thompson, one of the Fredonian rebels. Bean said that when he went to Ayish Bayou with Colonel Piedras, serving as his interpreter, Burrell had presented himself and wanted to take the oath of allegiance to Mexico as provided for in the general amnesty. But Piedras had refused and told Thompson he could not remain in Texas as a colonist. Bean testified that since 1827 Burrell Thompson had resided in the United States, and the certification was a means for his readmission as a citizen.[48]

Bean was involved in several lawsuits in the latter part of 1835. At the end of October Alcalde Berry ordered the sheriff to summon Mariano Mora and Miguel Cortines to answer charges brought by Bean, the nature of which is uncertain. This file has the notation "None Suited" with a cost of $6.50.[49] Thomas J. Rusk later called Cortines/Cortinez "one of the few [local] Mexicans whose energies have been used in our cause."[50] Perhaps so, but a man of the same name was also later mentioned as a companion of Manuel Flores in attempts to stir up the Caddos and other tribes on the upper Red River to slaughter the citizens of Nacogdoches. This could be a case similar to that of other Tejanos at Nacogdoches such as Juan Seguín and Antonio Menchaca, whose activities are often confused with men of the same name at Béxar. Either that or there were two men named Miguel Cortinez in east Texas

On November 13 Bean sued Josiah Thomas over a farm he had rented him for a year. The defendant was ordered to give Bean security for the arrangement within fifteen days. Thomas was Bean's neighbor west of the Neches, and his house was one of Almonte's stopping places as he traveled from Nacogdoches to San Felipe on his 1834 inspection.[51]

As ethnic tensions increased at Nacogdoches, it is interesting that Bean was requested by Alcalde Berry to release weapons from the armory—the same that Bowie had earlier raided—to the 1st Company of the Civil Militia at Nacogdoches. This company was mostly Mexicans headed by Capt. Vicente Córdova, an old settler much involved in the difficulties yet to come. Twenty-two of these militiamen were without guns, and it seems that Political Chief Rueg thought they should have them to protect their interests against the "reckless" men who were fomenting revolution against Mexican rule throughout Texas. But Bean told the alcalde, "All the guns that I have have no locks," except for "them in your ofis." Berry ordered the weapons released.[52] A few days later Rusk, as captain of the "Volunteer Company of Nacogdoches," also asked Berry for public arms for his men.[53] Everybody in town wanted weapons from Bean's storehouse in case hostilities broke out.

The question arises of Bean's actual relationship to the Anglos of Nacogdoches who were plotting revolution at this time—men such as James Bowie and Sam Houston. This is especially so with Bowie, whom he denounced to Colonel Ugartechea for confiscating arms belonging to the nation. No doubt Bean resented his authority over these muskets being trampled upon by Bowie, but one wonders if his outrage was genuine and not merely Bean's way of absolving himself should he be called to account for missing weapons in his charge. This suspicion is grounded (to some extent) on the oft-repeated story that, after Bean's death in Jalapa, his son Isaac visited his Mexican widow and brought back to Texas Bean's gold-tipped walking stick, which bore the inscription "Presented to Colonel Ellis P. Bean by James Bowie." Bowie's death at the Alamo in March 1836 suggests that he had given Bean this token of esteem prior to the rifle-taking incident in July 1835, and that the two men were friends. Bowie's use of "Ellis P. Bean" also suggests that the gift dated back to the mid-1820s, after which time Bean started calling himself Peter Ellis or Pedro Elías.[54]

In the case of Sam Houston, who resided in Nacogdoches, the evidence is more definite. Houston, like Bean, was also engaged in acquiring eleven-league grants, or portions thereof, from Mexican recipients and trying to sell them for windfall profits. As a lawyer, Houston had an edge over Bean in this regard. There was also their Indian connection, and Bean held the position of authority over Houston in such matters. As Mexico's agent to the friendly tribes, Bean enjoyed influence with these Indians that Houston only wished he could have—with Houston's adopted Cherokee brethren in particular. If Houston resented Colonel Bean's influence over these tribes, he nonetheless worked with him in opposition to men like Archibald Hotchkiss and his scheme with the Creek Nation.

On September 11 Bean addressed a letter to Pres. Andrew Jackson that very closely resembles one that Houston and his circle of friends wrote Jackson on the same day. Bean reminded the president that he had written his secretary of war, Lewis Cass, in February 1833 about the problem of Indian "incursions" into Texas from the United States. If any steps had been taken to halt this exodus, Bean said he was not aware of them. Benjamin Hawkins and another individual (Hotchkiss) now had a plan to introduce twenty-four thousand Creek Indians to Texas and were pushing ahead with it, despite Bean's opposition.

> Previous to the departure of Hawkins and his friend to meet the chief at New Orleans, he applied to me, as superintendent of the Indians in Texas, and informed me that a grand speculation could be made out of the Creeks in the old nation by permitting them to move to lands in this country; that a large sum of money could be obtained from them. I promptly assured him that no such thing could take place—nor be permitted by me, as it was contrary to the laws of the republic, and the existing treaties with the United States. Disregarding my instructions, he persisted in violating the solemn laws of both countries. Your excellency will at once perceive that the avarice and cupidity of [these] individuals, is to make a barter of human life, without [unless] your excellency will most strictly enforce the stipulations of the treaty, and prevent the emigration and incursions of those Indians to any part of Texas.[55]

Bean did not remind Pres. Andrew Jackson that he had been placed in command—by the then General Jackson—of a big gun on the levee on January 8, 1815, or that these guns did much to win the Battle of New Orleans and ensure Jackson's bid for the presidency. If Bean was as vain as Thomas F. McKinney considered him to be, he might well have jogged the president's memory on this past association. Bean did not, stating his case in a forthright manner and alluding to a sense of duty that Jackson could understand.

The letter that John Forbes as chairman cosigned with Samuel Houston, Henry Raguet, David A. Hoffman, Solomon R. Peck, William G. Logan, and George Pollitt on the same day, also addressed to President Jackson, gave additional details on the plot to bring Creeks to Texas. Archibald Hotchkiss, "an empresario," was named as the driving force behind the scheme, along with Hawkins, called a "quarteroon Creek Indian." The land they planned to buy for the Creeks was in the grant conceded to "general Felasolo [Filisola]" by the Mexican government. Going to New Orleans to meet with the Creek chiefs, Hotchkiss and Hawkins had already received twenty thousand dollars. They then proceeded to New York to close the deal with Filisola's agent (perhaps James Treat), but "they failed in the purchase." Undeterred, Hawkins and Hotchkiss returned to Texas, and the former soon left again for the United States "with the avowed and manifest intention of introducing into Texas not less than five thousand Creeks," others to follow later. The writers went on to flatter Jackson's military prowess against these Indians while he was in command of "the chivalry" of Tennessee and Georgia (at Horseshoe Bend) and ended by imploring him to enforce Article 33 of the treaty and keep these warlike Creek Indians out of Texas.[56]

Just as with Bean's 1833 letter to Secretary of War Lewis Cass, it is likely that Sam Houston had a hand in composing this appeal directly to the president by Bean. It is odd that Houston should adopt such a position against the Creeks; he knew Benjamin Hawkins from previous business deals back in Tennessee, before Houston resigned as governor and went into exile among the Western Cherokees. Hawkins was privy to Houston's plan to call a council of various tribes on either the Brazos or Trinity River in mid-1834. Moreover, during 1834 Almonte had learned (from Surveyor José María Carvajal at Nacogdoches) that Houston was scheming to introduce vast numbers of Creek Indians to Texas himself. Almonte and other Mexican officials warned the government to put a stop to Houston's project—the same sort of thing that Houston was now asking his mentor President Jackson to derail with Hotchkiss and Hawkins.[57]

Houston's motive for doing so is open to question. Was Houston jealous that Hotchkiss and Hawkins had been paid a considerable amount of money for something he had been unable to do? And mad because Hotchkiss might yet complete the deal with Filisola's agent and receive more money—money that Houston had earlier set his heart on receiving for himself? This is difficult to say, but once Hotchkiss learned that he had been denounced to the president of the United States in a letter published in New Orleans newspapers and the prominent *Niles Register* of Baltimore, he was much incensed at Houston. Bean had wisely kept Hotchkiss's name out of his letter—which was also published in the media—mentioning only the less powerful Hawkins, an Indian with an in-

Sam Houston, ca. 1840. Photo courtesy Joseph Musso and John R. Gangel.

fusion of African blood. At least we can see that Bean and Houston, along with other influential men at Nacogdoches, were working to a common purpose involving Indians from the United States as revolution neared.[58]

Several weeks later, however, Houston and his young friend Thomas Jefferson Rusk struck out on their own with the Cherokees. Houston, along with Nathaniel Robbins, had certified as to Rusk's good character when he moved to Texas in February 1835. Rusk was rather awed to be in the company of the ex-governor of Tennessee and Andrew Jackson's protégé.[59] But William Goyens—not Bean—was their contact person in talks they hoped to hold with the Cherokees and Shawnees on the Brazos River now that war was looming with Mexico. The letter that they wrote to "Our Friend Big Mush, Col. Bowles, and the other Red men" on September 24 gushed with Cooperish white-on-red sentiment, as indicated by the following excerpt: "[W]hen you have heard our talks and they are interpreted to you [then] you can Know what we have said and Know that we will not talk with forked Tongues but that we speak with on[e] tongue only and walk in a straight path as long as the Trees bring forth leaves and so long as the rain shall fall on the Earth[,] so long shall our words remain true . . . White men shall not trouble you by making [survey] marks on the trees of your lands. If they should attempt to do so . . . they will be punished as the [white] people wish at all times to meet our Red Brothers in peace and hold them by the hand forever."[60] If they attended the council on the Brazos, all their expenses would be paid and they would be treated as "friends and Brothers." Because "Mr. Goings" was a man who did not lie to either white or red men, he would make the arrangements and attend the talks.[61] Despite Bean's recent cooperation on the matter of Hotchkiss and the Creeks, he was not in on this affair. So began Houston's efforts to wean the Cherokees of Colonel Bean's influence.

General Cos was now in Texas, and the Anglo settlements were preparing to resist his military occupation of the country. Stephen F. Austin had been released from the "house arrest" that had kept him in Mexico City since the beginning of 1835 and also made his way home. A changed man by his ordeal in Mexico, Austin was now adding his voice to armed resistance against Santa Anna's centralist regime. We know that some of Colonel Bean's warnings about the unstable situation at Nacogdoches were getting through to headquarters because, on September 8, Ugartechea forwarded to Cos three of his communications received in the "last mail." According to Ugartechea's assessment of what Bean said, the east Texas situation was grim: "These communications will give you an exact idea of the slim hope to be entertained in preserving public peace for any length of time within that Department, and that of San Felipe, unless energetic and prompt measures are taken to restrain the revolutionists."[62] From Goliad on October 3, Cos acknowledged receipt of Bean's correspondence through Ugartechea and told him to grant Bean a leave of absence to Béxar. This would enable Cos, when he reached the town, to inform himself "with greater precision concerning the condition of affairs" at Nacogdoches that Bean had mentioned. Sensitive matters that Bean dared not trust to words on paper.[63]

Colonel Bean did not have time to make this trip, because open warfare had already broken out between the Anglo rebels and Mexican soldiers. On October 2 shots first rang out at Gonzales, where a detachment of soldiers had gone to demand a cannon that DeWitt's colonists used for protection against Indians. Only a few days after Cos departed Goliad, more rebels captured the old presidio from Mexican troops stationed there. Ben Milam, recently escaped from prison in Mexico, was among the assaulting force. Hard choices had come for Bean at Nacogdoches. He had to decide which way to go; riding the fence was no longer a viable option.

Chapter 15

THE TEXAS REVOLUTION

HISTORIANS HAVE NOT been able to supply much definite information about Bean's role during the revolution, except to say—as did Henderson Yoakum in 1855—that "neither party appeared willing to trust him." It has also been said of Bean that, once revolution was an accomplished fact, he surrendered himself to rebel authority at Nacogdoches as a Mexican "prisoner of war" and was released on his parole of honor. Parole granted to Mexican officers at the beginning of the war was a very lax arrangement, usually meaning that the parolee had to remain in town and report periodically to whoever had granted him parole. Yoakum gave the following account of Bean's situation: "Of these several classes [of Texan Tories], many arrests were made, and their persons secured until the danger was over. It is not unlikely that some were thus confined who ought not to have been. Among those arrested was Colonel Ellis P. Bean. He had been appointed a member of the committee of vigilance of Nacogdoches, but, as it appears, took no part in their affairs. At the beginning of the war, in the fall of 1835, he had applied to Colonel John Forbes to place him in arrest, the better to enable him to draw his pay in the Mexican army; but Colonel Forbes declined to do so, unless for some offense."[1] Forbes, as noted, was one of Houston's cosigners of the September protest to President Jackson.

John H. Reagan, who first met Bean in the summer of 1839, remembered the circumstances a little differently: "The year the war of the Revolution broke out he went to General Thomas J. Rusk and received his parole as a Mexican prisoner." Reagan thought that Bean's willingness to accept parole from an officer of the rebel forces indicated that he was "not in sympathy with the Texas Revolution." On the other hand, Reagan admitted that Bean's long residence in Texas during and after the revolution, "in amity with the people . . . would tend to a different conclusion."[2]

So there is conflicting information about whether Bean "surrendered" himself to Forbes or Rusk, and what kind of detention he was placed under. Yoakum's claim that Bean was a member of the Committee of Safety and Vigilance at Nacogdoches is also questionable, as none of the many documents issued by this committee—which formed in July 1835 and dedicated itself to the rebel cause until victory came at San Jacinto in April 1836—bear Bean's name or even mention him.[3] In this and the next chapter a reevaluation of the evidence relating to Bean's conduct during the Texas Revolution is offered.

Considering Bean's long record as a survivor of the tempestuous waves that had crashed around him during his fifty-two years of life, it is likely that he tried to ride out this storm with his accustomed savoir faire. If continuing to correspond with Mexican military men made him a traitor to Texas, then he assuredly was. Bean's sense of duty to his adopted country, despite all the hassles it had put him through, was seriously taken. He had prospered in Texas, and—like many other so-called Tories who had prospered under the liberal land policies of Mexico—was beholden to it. At the same time Bean was a man of republican principles who was not too keen on military dictatorships. He wanted stability, however, the type that would guarantee ownership of the property he had managed to obtain. If he knew, for instance through Sam Houston, that an independent Texas might annul land grants in the coastal and border reserves, that alone would have given Bean pause. Why support a revolution that would sweep away his landholdings?

As evidence that Bean—from the start—favored the Texas cause and was willing to participate actively is a letter that George Anthony Nixon wrote to Stephen F. Austin on October 10. Even though Nixon was a well-to-do man and an agent for the vast Galveston Bay & Texas Land Company, his spelling is almost as bad as Bean's. Nixon said that he had received Austin's letter about the victory at Gonzales and a printed handbill, which "semes to unite all." A meeting had taken place at his house three days previously and twenty-one hundred dollars was pledged to purchase guns; Captain English had gone to buy them, carrying Austin's messages to San Augustine, where another subscription meeting was to be held: "I have had a Part of the hand Bill translated and will have it Read to the Maxacans; yesterday I had a taulk with with [*sic*] Col. Bean and he has promised me to try and Rase the Maxacans and go on with them [to join you]. I have promised the Maxacans 500 Dollar in Cash and all my influance will be yoused to Git them—to unite and Joine the [insurgent] arme and at Present from what tauk I have had I am in Good hopes."[4]

Troops were on the way to assist Austin, said Nixon, including "a Bout 120 Good maxacans that will Joine the Cause." But, due to the impositions made on them by overbearing Anglos, Bean's influence with Córdova and the native Mexicans of Nacogdoches was diminished. They decided to take no part in the conflict and resisted efforts by the Anglo authorities to confiscate their weapons. An uneasy standoff developed between Rusk's men, plus the U.S. volunteers streaming through Nacogdoches to Béxar, and Córdova's militiamen. The latter were mainly interested in protecting their property and families from Anglo assaults as a "home guard." Although Bean or Nixon could not get them to march to the front as a unit, individual Tejanos joined the war effort and contributed to it—especially before the struggle evolved into independence from Mexico, as opposed to defending the federalist Constitution of 1824. Bean at this time donated a horse, saddle, and bridle valued at fifty dollars to the Committee of Safety and Vigilance.[5]

Near the end of October Bean scored a victory of sorts: title was finally granted him to the league of land touching the Neches on its west bank. This league had been approved by acting governor Rafael Ecay Músquiz on October 11, 1830, and granted to Bean as a "settler." Consequently, it was similar to the headrights that the Republic of Texas granted to citizens. This league was not one of the eight that Bean had purchased from the state of Coahuila y Texas, but local protests had snarled title to it. Alcalde Radford Berry responded favorably on October 12 to the petition of Bean's attorneys William Whitley and Leonard Williams that he be given possession of the tract. Bean had granted them this authority on June 17, 1833. The survey, completed eight days later by James Bradshaw, noted that Bean's league was on the right bank of the Neches about a mile below the San Antonio Road. It was a long and narrow tract in present-day Houston County, similar to the one owned by Williams adjoining on the west. Ironically, Bean may have been out of the picture by the time his title was perfected. His "attorneys" sold the league to someone else in 1836.[6]

Until the Consultation could convene on November 1, a "Permanent Council" ran the affairs of Texas in revolt. Its "president," or chairman, was Richardson R. Royall, although he acted as if Stephen F. Austin were in control. On October 18 Royall advised Austin that three ranger companies had been authorized to protect the exposed northern frontier from Indian attack. Also appointed as commissioners to deal with the chiefs of various tribes—mainly the Cherokee and Shawnee—were three men: Jacob Garrett, Joseph L. Hood, and Pierre ("Peter") Menard. They were given the "Power to council with them and give Pledges of the Public faith to Respect their rights to land with assurances that the convention will conform." The principal chiefs had been invited to San Felipe but had not yet appeared, so it was thought best to seek them out and satisfy their doubts about how they would fare under the insurgent government. Royall said that John Durst had recently visited the Cherokees, who wished to be neutral in the conflict, but Durst believed that "If we were Vanquished they would turn against us."[7] This possibility greatly worried everyone involved in the revolution.

The commissioners' instructions, formed the same day, authorized them to "repair immediately to the villages of said Indians, with full power to hold a consultation with them, for the purpose of ascertaining their grievances, and for giving them full assurances that their case [the adjustment of their land claims] will be properly attended to, as soon as the consultation meets." The committee admitted that "unwarranted encroachments" had been made upon lands occupied by the Indians, and it was now necessary to assure them that their "rights and privileges as citizens of Texas" would be recognized.[8] Circulars were printed of these proceedings, which the commissioners were to distribute among the Indians.

A very detailed report of the situation with the immigrant tribes was given to the Council by Mosely Baker and Frank Johnson on October 23. They had just returned from a several-week visit to Nacogdoches, attempting to rouse the citizens with news of General Cos's arrival. They spoke of "much division" in east Texas and said that great excitement prevailed on the "supposition that the northern Indians were unfriendly." Investigation of the matter, however, had disproved such rumors, and "no doubt now exists of their friendly intentions." About a month earlier Bowl and the other chiefs had visited Béxar, where Colonel Ugartechea had endeavored to enlist them to his side. After this visit a general council of twelve tribes was called at the main Cherokee village, "at which no white man was permitted to be present." All of their abuses at the hands of the Americans were discussed with some recrimination, but the council decided "to remain friendly with the Americans, and to appeal to the convention for protection and redress." Baker attended a subsequent meeting with the chiefs in Nacogdoches and was convinced of their good disposition: "Secure them in their possessions, treat them in a frank, manly, independent manner, and you [will] secure their friendship, and hereafter, if necessary, their [military] co-operation." Bowl, Big Mush, and three other chiefs were on their way as delegates to the Consultation, with full powers to speak for all the northern Indians.[9]

Local affairs remained quiet when the long-awaited Consultation met at San Felipe on November 1. Neither Peter Ellis Bean nor Henry Rueg were delegates, but Sam Houston played a leading role. Henry Smith was elected governor. He, with advice from a General Council, would manage affairs of a Texas still attached to the Mexican federation but engaged in a battle to restore the Constitution of 1824—which Santa Anna had managed to scuttle during the past two years. On October 27, one of the interim Permanent Council's last acts had been to close land offices until the end of the war. This bold action was sustained by the Consultation in November, lest speculators rush to file titles while soldiers were off fighting. Moreover, upon Sam Houston's motion, the "fraudulent" four-hundred–league grants made by the last state legislature were nullified.[10]

It was also decided, on November 13, 1835, to award land to the Cherokees and their "twelve associated bands" within a specified area, the boundaries of which were given and all surveys of grants therein canceled.[11] This decision was facilitated by steps taken by Houston's associates at Nacogdoches. On November 8 John Forbes wrote the "Permanent Council of Texas" about how the question of Indian land rights required immediate action. He had been requested "by a Number of respectable Setlers in the Vicinity of the Cherokees" to suggest that commissioners be appointed to "treat with the Indians for their Possessary right of the Lands they are now occupying and the putting them in possession of other Lands upon such terms as will best secure their Rights."[12] If the Indians were unwilling to leave their present lands, the commissioners should be authorized to arrange with their chiefs the boundaries and conditions needed to put them in "quiet and undisturbed possession." Those individuals in the near vicinity of the Indian settlements would receive title "floats" for vacant land elsewhere if they relinquished their lands to the Indians. Fair compensation would be given the white settlers for their improvements on the yielded land, plus their moving expenses.

Jacob Garrett wrote Sam Houston from Nacogdoches on November 9 that negotiations with the Indians were moving ahead: "I was sent Back with two more gentlemen of Commissioners to act with the Cherichez Indians we met the Chief [and] they appeard to be well sattisfyed."[13] When interim governor Henry Smith addressed the Council on November 16, the Indian problem was Item 7 on his agenda. "Some of our red brethren of the Cherokee, Shawnee and other of their associated bands, are located of certain lands within our limits, to which it is generally understood that they have a just and equitable title. They have lately been interrupted in their title by surveys and locations within the limits which they claim, which has created among them great dissatisfaction, I therefore recommend that you second the measures of the late [1832] Convention in this matter, and never desist until the objects contemplated by that body be carried into effect."[14]

This was a solid endorsement for Indian land claims that seemed to bode well for keeping them tranquil in the fight with Mexico. A report was given to the Council on November 26 by Indian Commissioners Menard, Garrett, and Hood. They had left Nacogdoches and proceeded to "Mr. Sim's farm" where they met ten or eleven Cherokee chiefs, then on their way to San Felipe. A powwow was held with these chiefs (unnamed), and the intentions of the Council with regard to their lands were explained to them: "and on securing from us assurances that their rights should be respected, they appeared perfectly Satisfied, and assured us that they never had any idea of going to war, They also told us, that (as the convention was not then in Session) they would return home and send their young men against the wild or prairie indians, which were daily Committing depredations on the inhabitants of our frontier, and also on the indians Stealing their horses &c. We then told them that if they sent any force against the wild indians we should furnish them with powder & lead."[15]

Menard then sent an express to the Shawnees. Four days later his courier returned to Nacogdoches with two chiefs and six young warriors. Another council was held, and they "appeared perfectly contented" with what he told them. They might even join the Americans to fight the Mexicans if their tribe agreed. Menard judged that the other small tribes of the region would cause no problems as "they were very much frightened and dreaded that the americans should drive then away—having been told so, by medling persons living near or trading with them."[16]

Chief Bowl was not present at the council that took place on Sims's farm. When advised of this, Houston wrote Bowl from San Felipe on November 22 to assure him that the Cherokees were at last going to get their lands. It was only a matter of more commissioners coming to fix the lines and sign a treaty. Houston said that he expected to be one of the commissioners and would bring with him the "Great paper that was signed by all the council."[17] At this time various Texan spokesmen to the Cherokees and allied tribes made the promise that powder and lead would be given to them if they wished to fight on behalf of Texas. Commissioners like Menard (and the Council members who sent them) actually wanted the powder and lead used on Mexicans instead of "wild indians," and they should have made the distinction more clear. That they did not became evident in the treaty-signing council Houston held with Bowl's Cherokees in February 1836.

Sam Houston left the Consultation with much prestige and the rank of major general in an army yet to be raised. But Governor Smith soon became locked in bitter ways-and-means quarrels with his General Council, led by Lt. Gov. James Robinson. In January the governing process broke down entirely and anarchy prevailed. When John Forbes returned to Nacogdoches to enforce the laws of the Consultation, he was met with hostility. The old political establishment refused to surrender the archives to Judge Forbes and S. H. Everitt, the representative of the Bevil District who was supposed to handle land matters. Nor would Political Chief Rueg or ayuntamiento members like George Nixon, Radford Berry, and David Hoffman cease their duties or surrender their documents to the Consultation's men. They were joined by wealthy entrepreneurs such as

John K. Allen, Adolphus Sterne, Frost Thorn, Henry Raguet, and others —many of whom protested the shutting down of their land business and sought exemption status. In such a rebellious atmosphere, Bean's "parole" and his exact whereabouts were small matters indeed. The people of Nacogdoches had bigger concerns.[18]

Sam Houston, in his attempt to stop Frank Johnson's and James Grant's volunteers from plundering Matamoros, had little success at getting them to recognize his authority. If the expedition materialized, Smith and Houston wanted James Bowie in command. At least Houston managed to raise doubts and delay the ill-advised invasion. After sending Bowie to Béxar, Houston returned to the seat of government—shaky though it was. There, early in February, he decided that the time was right to visit the Cherokees in an effort to either bring them and their allied tribes into the war on the rebel side or, at least, to secure a guarantee that they would stay out of the conflict altogether. Orders for the undertaking had been issued by Governor Smith and Lieutenant Governor Robinson at the end of December, before the government fell apart. Houston had as his fellow commissioners John Forbes and John Cameron, the latter of whom could not attend the council. Governor Smith's instructions provided that

> —you will in all things pursue a course of justice and equity towards the Indians, and to protect all honest claims of the Whites, agreeable to such Laws compacts or treaties, as the said Indians may have heretofore made with the Mexican Republic.
>
> You will provide in said treaty with the Indians, that they shall never alienate their Lands, either separately or collectively, except to the Government of Texas— And to agree that the Said Government, will at any time hereafter purchase all their claims at a fair and reasonable valuation— You will endeavour, if possible, to secure their effective cooperation at all times when it may be necessary to call the effective force of Texas into the field and agreeing for their Services in a body for a specific time— If found expedient and consistent, you are authorised and empowered to exchange other Lands within the limits of Texas not otherwise appropriated in the room of Lands claimed by said Indians.[19]

From a letter that Houston wrote Chief Bowl on February 5, it sounds as if earlier attempts to reach an understanding with him had gone unrewarded. Houston said he had heard that Bowl was "in trouble" and had called all the tribes together for a council—probably after the talks with Ugartechea at Béxar. Despite the chief's earlier promise to come to town and talk, "I have looked for you, but you did not come!" This was a shame, said Houston, because a visit to Political Chief Rueg would have satisfied

Bowl that the "Talk was good" from the Texan government. He asked Bowl to bring some chiefs of the other tribes in for a council with Rueg. If Bowl did, Houston promised that "Your sun will shine bright upon you, and your sleep will not be troubled any more!"[20] It would appear that Houston thought that Rueg had undergone a change of heart and was now a supporter of the rebellion. While Rueg's earlier actions as political chief do not so indicate, a letter that he wrote to Rusk on November 9 describes his efforts toward "relief and reinforcement" of the Texan army at Béxar.[21] Rueg was caught in the same net of conflicting loyalties as other Nacogdoches citizens, Bean among them.

This invitation for the chiefs to come to Nacogdoches did not work out, so Houston and Forbes went to Chief Bowl's village and signed a treaty of thirteen articles with him, Big Mush, and six other Cherokee chiefs on February 23, 1836. Interpreting for the council was another Cherokee, Fox Fields, and signing as witnesses were Harry Millard, Joseph Durst, Alexander Horton, George W. Case, and Mathias A. Bingham. George W. Hockley also signed as secretary of the commission. Although none of their chiefs were present at the powwow, the Cherokees claimed to be acting on behalf of the Shawnee, Delaware, Kickapoo, Choctaw, Quapaw, Biloxi, Ioni, Alabama, Coushatta, "Caddo of the Neches, Tahocuttake, and Unataqua" tribes. All of these tribes were obligated to move into the lands assigned by the treaty. But no other tribes or bands of Indians not already living in Texas were to be admitted. (Bean's 1833 letter had expressed concern that the Cherokees would continue to increase their numbers this way if given lands above Nacogdoches.) The settlers in the neighborhood of the saline on the upper Neches were not to be molested until a council took place and the wishes of the Convention were known. Also, an effort was to be made to protect honest claims by whites in the Cherokee reserve.[22]

The key part of the treaty for the Cherokees, of course, was Article 2, wherein the limits of their reserve were specified. Though not as huge as what Mexico had promised them earlier (but failed to deliver), it was a large area. Stated simply, it lay north of the San Antonio Road, running up the Angelina to near present-day Henderson, northeast and north to the Sabine, west along its headwaters into Van Zandt County, south to the Neches and downstream to the road. The tribes were left to govern their internal affairs, so long as they were not contrary to the laws of the state of Texas, and one or more agencies could be established in their midst. At least one agent would reside in the principal Cherokee village to look after their interests and see that no injustice was done to them. Sam Houston had satisfied the land-ownership aspirations of the Cherokee chiefs, but the treaty made no mention of their joining the Texans to fight against Mexico or make war on the Comanches. It did not even promise their neutrality in the conflict.[23]

Houston and Forbes explained the two-day proceedings in a letter to Governor Smith at the end of February. The Cherokees had firmly opposed exchanging their lands for vacant land elsewhere, so the idea was dropped for fear it would defeat the treaty altogether. Even though this meant that the Indians had to be given the lands they presently occupied, Houston suggested that the "salt works" were so valuable that the government should retain them. He and Forbes also tried to enlist the chiefs "in the cause of the people of Texas" and talk them into enrolling a force "to act against our common enemy." This shocked the chiefs, and "they informed us that *the subject had not before been suggested to them* [emphasis added]." They, however, promised to hold a general council in April and let the Texans know their decision.[24] Someone, it appears, had not laid sufficient groundwork to ensure that the Cherokees and their allied tribes would join the rebels in their struggle against Mexico. Thus Houston was kept guessing about the loyalty of these tribes even as the Mexican advance pushed his army toward the Sabine.

Why was Peter Ellis Bean not one of the Texan emissaries to this important council, or at least a witness who signed the treaty document? He, after all, had been their principal agent for nine years, advising them on matters large and small. Yet there seems to be no evidence that Bean was under consideration at this time for participating in any manner in the deliberations—either by the Cherokees or by the Texans. Sam Houston was now the driving force behind the treaty and relations with the friendly tribes. Was it because Bean had served Mexico's interests in those years and Houston wanted a fresh start, untainted by Bean's earlier negotiations with these tribes while wearing a Mexican uniform? Did he, perhaps, think that Bean would disrupt the negotiations in a manner prejudicial to Texan interests, or urge the Cherokees not to fight against Mexico? Whatever Houston's reasons, Bean was snubbed and it must have pained him to be an outsider to this momentous event.

But there is another possibility: that Bean did not want to attend the council, and if asked would have refused. He knew, from his experience with how the land game worked in east Texas, that whites could not be kept out of lands designated for the Indians, and any treaty signed to that end could not be enforced. Men such as Archibald Hotchkiss, George Nixon, James Bowie, John T. Mason, John Durst, David Burnet, the Allen brothers, and a host of other speculators would find ways to defeat the treaty and introduce white settlers to these lands. Although Bean had earlier sold his Saline League to Hotchkiss, it appears that he still had an interest in it. The Cherokees were already aggravated about squatters on their lands, and the situation would get worse when big-time speculators went into action. Peter Ellis Bean may have stood aside, content to watch Sam Houston make promises to the Cherokees that Bean knew could not be kept—promises that eventually would lead to Houston's downfall as a respected spokesman among the friendly tribes. This is all speculation, but Bean was out of the treaty loop and there must have been reasons for it. Was Bean's affiliation with Mexico the only reason?

Mexican troops under General Cos had been expelled from Béxar by mid-December 1835, Bean's immediate authority Colonel Ugartechea along with the rest. Letters would no longer flow between them, perhaps to Bean's relief as he knew that these letters were often intercepted. Did Bean continue to "correspond with the enemy" as later suspected by the Texans? Evidence that he did is found in a letter that the president of Mexico and commander of its armies, Antonio López de Santa Anna, wrote to his second-in-command, Gen. Vicente Filisola, from Saltillo the day before he marched northward to Texas. In this letter Santa Anna acknowledged Filisola's report that the "military commandant of Nacogdoches [Bean]" had a "favorable disposition." Santa Anna said that, regarding this matter, he would "determine upon my arrival there whatever is best."[25]

Thus it would seem that by the end of January 1836, Bean was still managing to communicate with the invasionary force in letters that indicated he was "favorable" to Mexico's putting down the revolution. Even the hint that he might be expressing such ideas would have been sufficient to brand Bean a traitor and keep him out of negotiations with the Cherokees. The last thing that Texas needed was a war on two fronts—southwest with General Santa Anna's Mexicans and northeast with Chief Bowl's Indians. Houston's treaty and its concessions were dedicated to guaranteeing peace and quiet on the eastern frontier while Texas faced the Mexicans coming across the Rio Grande. Even so, Houston failed to gain the active participation of the Cherokees in the war with the Mexicans, as Bean had managed to do on numerous occasions in warfare against the hostile plains tribes.[26]

Once it was known that a large army under General Santa Anna had arrived in Texas and laid siege to Béxar, some of the dissension within the Texan ranks died down. It now seemed that independence was the only way to go. Support for the revolution simply could not be raised in the United States under any arrangement that kept Texas within the Mexican federation. A Convention called at Washington-on-the-Brazos on March 1 quickly adopted a Declaration of Independence from Mexico. Signers included the "Ring-Tailed Panther," Martin Parmer, who had reasserted himself as a political figure. James Gaines of the Sabine District also signed, only one of many old settlers known to Bean. Land merchants, new and old, were well represented at the Convention. In spite of their clout, the constitution invalidated three types of claims: the three hundred leagues acquired by John T. Mason in 1834, the four-hundred–league sales enacted by the legislature in 1835, and eleven-league grants that had been located in the U.S.-Mexico boundary reserve (later extended to lands in the ten-league coastal reserve by various court decisions).[27] Thus would much of Bean's landholdings evaporate during the coming years, as the Texas General Land Office refused to recognize his titles along the Red River and those near the mouth of the Trinity.

Sam Houston, as usual, played a key role at this Convention and on a daily basis, despite indulging in conviviality the night before. Oddly, the people of Nacogdoches did not send him as one of their four delegates. In a field of seventeen candidates for the four seats, Houston finished next to last! Instead, Thomas J. Rusk, Robert Potter, Charles S. Taylor, and John S. Roberts were elected on behalf of Nacogdoches. Houston was a delegate from Refugio, a district he had only visited briefly in his attempt to redirect or terminate the Matamoros expedition. Why had Houston fallen so low in the esteem of his fellow citizens at Nacogdoches? Was it because word had gotten out about the treaty he was going to sign with the Cherokees, and the treaty's sweeping concession to them of prime real estate north of town? Or was it just because of his drinking problem? Whatever the reason, Sam Houston had to enter the Convention from a back door to the south, far away from his northeastern home ground.[28]

Houston's February 23 treaty with the Cherokees, the ink on it hardly dry, was presented but not ratified by the Texas Convention during these hasty proceedings. It would not have mattered anyway, as all land offices remained closed for the duration of the war. No titles could be perfected until the offices reopened. In order to hedge their bets, Bowl's Cherokees received several Mexican emissaries into their villages during February and March.[29] Santa Anna, writing to Secretary of War José María Tornel on February 16, noted that the Cherokees "held a solemn promise from the government to give them lands." If the Indians were awarded these lands, they could be used "to good advantage" by Mexico. If not, these friendly tribes would needlessly become Mexico's enemies. It is fairly evident that these were the ideas of Colonel Almonte, who was Santa Anna's chief aide on the campaign. If Almonte wrote any letters to his old friend Bean, urging him to keep the Cherokees and their Indian allies loyal to Mexico, such letters are unknown.[30]

Committees of vigilance continued to act at Nacogdoches and elsewhere as a system of communication for threatening developments. The fall of the Alamo on March 6, with no survivors, and the massacre of Fannin's men at Goliad on February 27 intensified the need for rapid response by local committees. Would Houston's pact with the "friendly" tribes hold up, or would they fall upon the women and children fleeing toward the Sabine in what was generally known as the Runaway Scrape? On his retreat toward the Brazos, Houston was also concerned that Mexican agents—such as Bean, perhaps—would sow discord among the Cherokees in an attempt to get them to rise up and slaughter the whites. Houston, with this possibility in mind, wrote Chief Bowl on April 13: "You will get your land as promised in our Treaty, and you and all my Red brothers may rest satisfied that I will always hold you by the hand, and look at you as Brothers and treat you as such!"[31]

Chapter 16

INDIAN ALARM IN EAST TEXAS

What was Col. Peter Ellis Bean doing at the time of the Runaway Scrape? Was he talking to the Cherokees and other tribes, as one might expect of him in such uncertain times, or was he lying low and rebuffing any efforts to draw him into the tempest? His actions are only vaguely understood in this period, when many whites at Nacogdoches were convinced that they faced imminent attack by every Indian tribe on the frontier. But, as we shall see, these professed fears were somewhat meretricious and being articulated for purposes that had nothing to do with any local Indian uprising.

Chief Bowl, aware that Houston's cause was experiencing some notable reverses and aware that hostility against his people was on the rise, visited Nacogdoches. He advised the inhabitants to leave before the fighting reached town and said he would look to the safety of their property while they were gone. Was this a threat? Some Texans took it that way. On the same day that Houston wrote Bowl, the civil chief of the Cherokees, Big Mush, wrote the Nacogdoches Committee of Safety that an American named Wilson had been in his village for several days. On his way back to Nacogdoches, this man had spread lies that the Cherokees had killed some settlers and were planning to attack other white families nearby. Wilson's tale had caused many settlers to pack up and leave, and Chief Big Mush did not appreciate false rumors of this sort prejudicing the whites against his people. The Cherokees, he said, were living "all in peace and quietude."[1]

Not so with the white settlers; they were in an uproar, fleeing to the Sabine as fast as they could from whatever enemy—Mexican or Indian—that might be dogging their trail. In their mass exodus the settlers had abandoned "the corn in the crib, the meat in the smokehouse, their poultry, cattle, and furniture," as one observer described it.[2] Many things that they managed to take with them soon littered the road east, cast aside in the haste to escape. James Gaines, on his return home from San Felipe, wrote interim president David G. Burnet that he had "found our agents . . . had Blown the Very Trees up by the Roots, and that Every Settlement was at the point of Breaking up . . . Bean Durst and many others of the St. ana Corps, circulated a report that produced a perfect hurricane, which caused the whole community to leave, in the order of a Blue Streak I throwed myself in the way to stop the stompide reasoned, cursed, damned, to prove the whole false . . . all to no effect."[3] This account by the irascible ferry keeper indicates that Bean was considered by at least one of his neighbors in east Texas as an adherent of Mexican objectives on the 1836 campaign. Regardless of the truth of Gaines's assertion, Bean's Toryism was making its way into the public consciousness.

Bean was again passed over when, on March 19, Burnet commissioned Michel B. Menard to secure peace with the immigrant tribes of northeastern Texas such as the Shawnees, Delawares, and Kickapoos. Burnet said that "no other citizen is as fully qualified as yourself" to perform this service and gave Menard a draft of two thousand dollars on the merchants of Nacogdoches for Indian presents. The president cautioned him not to make any treaty promises of land to these tribes, especially those that "may compromit the interests of actual settlers." In fact, it might be best not to talk about land at all, using the excuse that Texas was too much involved in its struggle for survival to make "positive treaties." Once freedom from Mexico was attained, that would be the time to negotiate such matters, but Menard was authorized to suggest that "lands adequate to their wants will be fully granted for their exclusive use."[4] In blunt terms, thinly disguised hypocrisy was the Indian policy established by Texan leaders such as David G. Burnet and later president Mirabeau B. Lamar. But what of Sam Houston? The evidence will be reevaluated in due time.

Michel Menard was a well-connected trader of French-Canadian extraction who had followed the Shawnees to Texas around 1828. He settled with them below Pecan Point and carried on an extensive fur business with the Shawnees and other tribes of the region. As we have seen, his cousin Pierre ("Peter") Menard conducted talks with the Cherokees and Shawnees in November 1835. Through his trade in furs, and his other activities dealing in horses and lands, Michel Menard became rich; by 1834 he owned forty thousand acres of land between the mouth of the Trinity and the Red River. He had tried, as Juan Seguín's "attorney," to locate a league of land on the vacant east end of Galveston Island in 1834. Turned down because he—Seguín's consignee—was not a Mexican and because this island was in the forbidden coastal reserve, Menard bought the entire island from the Republic of Texas soon after independence. This was a very controversial purchase for Menard and his partners, such as Samuel May Williams, Thomas F. McKinney, and other men who helped them ram it through Congress.[5]

As the Runaway Scrape was in progress, people in Nacogdoches scrambled to enlist the help of U.S. troops stationed at Fort Jesup. They sent alarming reports of an Indian uprising along the frontier that involved tribes from the United States, either those presently living in Texas or east of the Sabine in U.S. territory. Mexican agents such as Manuel Flores were active among these tribes, inciting them to warfare against the whites. If proof could be obtained, then President Jackson—by virtue of Article 33 of the treaty with Mexico—could order his army to cross into Texas to keep these Indians quiet. Once there, it was hoped by the hard-pressed Texans that an incident might occur involving Mexican troops, some incident in the isolated backwoods of Texas between the Sabine and the Neches. Since Jackson claimed that the land between these streams rightfully belonged to the United States, a fight that drew American blood "on American soil" would enable him to declare war against Santa Anna's Mexico. To military thinkers the ensuing conflict virtually guaranteed the freedom of Texas and its speedy acquisition as a territory if not as a state.[6]

Land speculator John T. Mason initiated the drive for American intervention in the pitiful affairs of revolutionary Texas. This was generous of him, considering that the constitution adopted by the Convention had just wiped out all of his huge land acquisitions three days before. On March 20, from Nacogdoches, he wrote the commandant at Fort Jesup a letter that would be much embellished by others in the coming month. But Mason already had all the key features figured out.

> Dear Sir: This moment news of the most disastrous character has been received from Bexar: Travis and all his men captured and murdered. An apprehension of a serious character exists here that the Indians are assembling to fall upon this frontier, particularly those from the United States. I have taken pains to inform myself of the facts, and I have no doubt they have been prepared to move in the event of Santa Anna's success. He is determined to wage a war of extermination against Texas, and has engaged the Indians to aid him. The committee of vigilance here will address you on the subject of the threatened danger from the Indians. Is it not in your power to send a messenger to them, particularly the Caddoes, to make them keep quiet? To the extent of your authority, every principle of humanity and safety to the inhabitants of both borders requires an exertion of your powers to avert the disaster of an Indian war; and I have no doubt you will exert all your energies to that end.[7]

Upon receipt of the Nacogdoches committee's deliberations, Chairman Augustus Hotchkiss—relative of the land merchant who had hoped to profit by introducing the Creek Nation into Texas—wrote the San Augustine committee's report the following day. He said that "large bodies of northern Indians, composed of Caddoes, Shawnees, Delawares, Kickapoos, Cherokees, Creeks, and other renegade Indians from the United States of the North" were then assembling at the three forks of the Trinity (near present Dallas). Their known intentions, "clearly proven to us, are to make war upon the inhabitants of the frontier." Since this was the case, two men were being sent to Fort Jesup to discuss "the particular crises of affairs."[8]

Maj. Gen. Edmund P. Gaines, commandant of the Western Department with headquarters at Natchitoches, was soon calling for troops from the governors of Louisiana, Mississippi, and Tennessee because of the war in Texas, "which has of late assumed a sanguinary and savage aspect." General Gaines—a first cousin to James whose ferry on the Sabine was astride the main road between Natchitoches and Nacogdoches—said that the president had also instructed him to write the commanders of both armies in Texas, telling them that "should they approach our boundary, or suffer the Indians near them to commence hostilities," he would inflict as many casualties as possible on the enemy now menacing the frontier settlements. These Indians had to be taught some respect, so that in the future they would honor their treaties. But, "should the war in Texas be brought to a close without the apprehended Indian hostilities," the volunteers would receive prompt discharges.[9] By this we may judge that General Gaines was poised for action and needed little convincing that the Indian menace was real.

Nonetheless, his cause for crossing the Sabine into Mexican Texas had to be documented, so Gaines set about obtaining proof. Statements were put on record about how Manuel Flores, commissioned by the Mexican government, had recently visited the tribes on the U.S. side of the border enticing them to join Mexico "in the war of extermination now raging in Texas." Flores, accompanied by a stranger (later revealed as Miguel Cortinez), then passed up the Red River and "produced excitement among the Caddo Indians." Many of "our Indians," said Gaines, "have lately gone over to the Texas side of the line." The general wrote that he could not "sit still and suffer these movements to be so far matured as to place the white settlements on both sides of the line wholly within the power of these savages."[10] No, if there was ever a time when Article 33 of the treaty with Mexico should be employed and activated, this was it.

Depositions were taken by the committee at Nacogdoches on April 11 to add strength to what General Gaines had been able to learn from informants at Natchitoches. From John "Seurt's" house James and Ralph Chesher professed themselves ready to defend Nacogdoches with their men because "the Indians are imbodied and are preparing for hostilities." They appealed for aid since the Indians and Mexicans, conducted by the Caddos, were on this side of the Trinity. Charles Sims said he had just visited the Cherokee village thirty miles west of town and found them "with very hostile feelings, and in a state of preparation for war." They were drying beef, preparing meal, and sending off their women and children. They had murdered an American trader among them, Brooks Williams, and were only awaiting the arrival of an estimated seventeen hundred warriors from the Caddo, Keechi, Ioni, Tawakoni, Waco, and Comanche tribes to attack the American settlements. Chief Bowl had advised Sims and his brothers to "leave the country, as there was danger." William Sims, in his own deposition, seconded everything his brother had said. It was at the Sims farm that talks had been held the previous year.[11]

The last statement before Chairman Henry Raguet's committee, composed of himself, Frost Thorn, David A. Hoffman, and John S. Roberts, was made by the republic's new Indian agent, Michel Menard. He blamed the Cherokees for the coming onslaught, not the Shawnees, Delawares, and Kickapoos residing about seventy-five miles north of Nacogdoches. Menard had visited their villages at the committee's request and found them of a "friendly disposition." It was true that Chief Bowl of the Cherokees had recently met with their chiefs "to induce them to take up arms against the Americans," saying that his tribe meant to "speedily fall on the Americans." But Menard's Indians refused to join Bowl in his campaign.[12] On the same day, the committee asked Mason to proceed to Fort Jesup and deliver another plea for soldiers "in the name of helpless women and children, [in] relief from death and torture."[13]

A flurry of more such resolutions was also adopted on April 11 and the days thereafter. One called for spies to act in the "neighborhood of our enemy," lest some surprise attack be made.[14] The "enemy" in this case consisted of Mexican residents of the town then hiding out, such as Vicente Córdova, whose sentiments were more suspect than ever. Colonel Bean, although his name does not come up in any of these panic-laced documents, was probably another local resident whose movements these spies were to monitor. Especially so since Bean had wielded such influence with the Cherokees in former times and was a known friend of the native Mexicans in town. With Santa Anna's army now across the Brazos below San Felipe and General Gaona's force thought to be approaching Nacogdoches from Bastrop on the Colorado, even Sam Houston was issuing orders for the arrest of men considered sympathetic to Mexico—men well known and respected as old Texans. Houston, from his "Camp

West of Brasos," wrote acting secretary of war David Thomas on April 11: "I pray you be vigilant. I have ordered spies everywhere." Men already in custody were to be watched closely.[15]

Was Col. Peter Ellis Bean one of them? This has been the general assumption, but let us see if the evidence sustains it. Editor John Jenkins, in his multivolumed *Papers of the Texas Revolution,* contains an entry (no. 2740) that claims that Sam Houston ordered Nacogdoches committeeman and alcalde David A. Hoffman, on April 13, 1836, to arrest Bean.[16] In his notes Editor Jenkins says that Houston's original letter was "not located" and tells us to see Yoakum's *History of Texas.* Yoakum, on the pages cited, says, "It appears that in April 1836, some report had come into circulation relative to an alleged correspondence of Bean with the enemy, which induced the secretary of war to order his arrest. As the truth of the report was *very questionable* [emphasis added], he was ordered into custody, and detained only as a Mexican officer and alien of the republic. But when the enemy retreated, nothing further was heard on the subject."[17]

Editor Jenkins supplies the names of Houston as the writer and Hoffman as the addressee, giving the date, based on Yoakum's note at the bottom. Yoakum, however, does not say where he saw the arrest order. This is very poor evidence upon which to found a conclusion that Bean was actually "incarcerated" in the Old Stone Fort for a second time, the first occurring with Philip Nolan's men thirty-five years earlier. Yet this is what Bean's most notable biographer, Bennett Lay, claims—adding that it "underscored the irony of his life." Bean, he writes, was a "sojourner in both Mexico and Texas, friend of both, yet treated as an enemy by each."[18] Tear-tugging language, but perhaps not the way it happened the second time around in Nacogdoches, based on what Lay knew when his book saw publication in 1960.

Flora Lowrey, in her 1945 master's thesis at Southern Methodist University on Bean, does not go into dramatics about this arrest question. But she (citing Robert B. Blake) does say that Bean's second imprisonment in the Old Stone Fort "caused him to leave Texas forever."[19] Why, then, did it take him almost eight years to do so? Bean's trauma was not so severe that he packed his carpetbag and left immediately upon release. Lowrey's study—mentioned by Lay as one of the sources for his book—mostly repeats Yoakum's information about how Bean received his parole from John Forbes when the revolution broke out. She calls it a form of "technical arrest" that Bean was asking for and notes that Forbes refused to take him into custody. Yoakum, with the qualifying "it appears," does say that Bean was "ordered into custody" in April 1836. But he fails to mention his source for the letter that gave him good authority—as it turns out—for what he stated in 1855.

In his 1969 book *Men without Countries,* John Edward Weems observes that Bean's outstanding trait was his "slipperiness." Perhaps so, but Weems also quotes Bean's later application for a league of land under the Republic of Texas in which he declared "that I was a resident citizen of Texas at the date of the declaration of Independence, that I did not leave the country during the Spring of 1836 to avoid a participation in the struggle, that I did not refuse to participate in the war, and that I did not aid or assist the Enemy."[20]

Was Bean still being slippery, or was this a truthful account of his activities? Without more persuasive evidence to the contrary, one is inclined to take Bean at his word. Yoakum in several instances suggested that Bean embraced the rebel side at heart. But he was getting up in years, was "very poor," and did not wish to "compromit either his office [i.e., his commission as a Mexican officer] or his [North American] countrymen."[21] That Bean failed to take a militant role in the Texas Revolution—on either side—cannot be denied. Numerous other old Texians fell into the same category. It made them something like modern draft evaders, but seldom did it mark them as traitors in the eyes of their contemporaries.

Also, by the time Bean applied for this league of land (in 1839), there were many people still living who would have known if he was actually under arrest as a Mexican collaborator in April 1836. Petitions for land were rejected on grounds such as these, yet Bean's was approved. In terms of the Nacogdoches commandant's "favorable disposition" that Santa Anna mentioned at the end of January, it probably amounted to Bean saying that the Indians would not take the rebel side in the conflict and that the majority of the citizens still supported the Supreme Government. In other words, nothing of great military significance—just more of Bean's usual "everything's quiet up here" assurances. If so, Bean was justified in claiming—in the standard jargon of the day—that he did not "aid or assist the Enemy."

Houston *did* order Bean's arrest, and Editor Jenkins had good reason for stating his entry no. 2740 as he did. He, it appears, just lost his notes on where the letter came from! It was—and is—in the Andrew Jackson Houston Collection (no. 367) at the Texas State Library, and Paul D. Lack cited it properly in his *Texas Revolutionary Experience* (1992). Lack says that Bean "played a more dangerous game" than Political Chief Rueg, who delivered his archives to the alcalde and moved to "a safer vantage point" across the Sabine at Natchitoches. Bean, according to Lack, "seemed to lend support to the Texan cause in relation to area Indian affairs while in fact having secret communication with Santa Anna. Houston learned of these activities too late—his April 13 arrest orders failed to reach Nacogdoches in time to lead to the incarceration of the *slippery* [emphasis added] Bean."[22]

Apart from the credit due Lack for finding an important document that Editor Jenkins said was unlocated, there are a number of problems with his analysis of Bean's predicament. As we have seen, Colonel Bean was shut out of Indian affairs by Houston, Smith, Burnet, and other representatives of the insurgent government. That he may have helped the Texan cause by keeping the Indians quiet is possible, but it is not a matter of record. And if Bean did so, it was on a personal basis. Menard was the republic's designated man for keeping the peace with immigrant tribes above Nacogdoches, and Houston—with the help of his newfound friend Forbes—took it upon himself to deal with the Cherokees. How does Lack know that Bean managed to slip away before he could be jailed and presumably placed in irons? His source seems to be the John Sprowl "character" certificate written about Bean a decade earlier. Sprowl's remarks about Bean have no bearing on the situation in 1836.

Here, then, is the letter that Sam Houston, from "Head Quarters at Groces," wrote Alcalde David Hoffman on April 13, 1836—a letter that Henderson Yoakum must have examined in Houston's collection of papers and made notes on when he was researching his *History of Texas:*

> Army Order. Sir: You are hereby Commanded to take Col. Peter E. Bean, and detain him in San Augustine until the result of the report is known— If it is true, it proves a correspondence with the Enemy, and if false it shows a disposition to mislead the Commander in Chief, and render the Army ineffective against the Enemy— At all events Col. Bean is a colonel in the Mexican Army, and as such the rules of War, based upon the law of Nations, direct his confinement and detention— My Order is that Peter Ellis Bean be forthwith taken into Custody, and detained until further orders as a Mexican officer and Alien of the Republic— By Order of Thos. J. Rusk, Secy of War.
>
> Sam Houston, Com. in Chief[23]

Secretary of War Thomas J. Rusk seems to have issued the order for Bean's arrest after he turned over his duties to David Thomas. Rusk had joined Houston in the field on April 4, so the "report" on Bean likely came to their attention on April 13—the very day they crossed the Brazos on the steamboat *Yellow Stone* and finally got the army in motion against Mexico's arrayed forces. Thus Yoakum was correct in saying that the "secretary of war" had ordered Bean's arrest, even though Sam Houston relayed the order to Hoffman at Nacogdoches. Rusk supposedly issued the order—not Houston—on the basis of some report received that Bean was corresponding with the enemy. But even if the report *was false,* Bean had said or done something to mislead Houston and "render the Army ineffective against the Enemy." A tantalizing use of words that suggests much but conveys little.

The reality is this: Sam Houston, either because Bean might sway Chief Bowl against the Texans or nix somehow the "arrangement" he had with General Gaines on the Sabine, wanted Bean kept under wraps until Rusk's report was investigated—or, in Houston's words—"until further orders." That Houston considered Bean, a Mexican officer, as a likely suspect for treasonous activities in the Redlands goes without saying. He was ordering the arrest of Edward Gritten at the same time as a "spy of Santa Anna," this for letters to Mexican officials intercepted the previous winter. Houston was also telling Thomas to detain old settlers like John Linn of Victoria for suspicious activities.[24] But, lest anyone think that Bean's detainment was a personal matter, Houston justified his arrest under the Rules of War. A week earlier Houston wrote Henry Raguet: "Don't get scared at Nacogdoches— Remember old Hickory claims Nachez [Neches] as 'neutral Territory.'"[25]

Some Houston admirers will be dismayed to learn that he did not fully trust Chief Bowl and had placed spies among the tribe as early as November 1835. According to the sworn deposition of one of his spies, Jonathan C. Poole of Nacogdoches, Houston kept him there until after the victory at San Jacinto. Poole, in 1881, asked for 1,280 acres of land for his service. Before E. C. Stuart, county judge of Falls County, he appeared and stated that

> he was a soldier and actually rendered military service to the Texas army . . . That he entered such service on or about —— day of September 1835 and was not formally discharged but served with Capt Mike Cossley [Costley] about three months when he was detailed and ordered by Genrl Sam Houston to guard and watch the movements of the tribes of Indians commanded and controlled by the Chief Bowles, and was directed to remain near or to be with said Bowles after the killing of Brooks Williams and report to General Houston every move or indication of hostility towards Texans, which he did untill after the Battle of San Jacinto sometime after which, no danger apparent, he returned home to Nacogdoches.[26]

The Sims brothers reported the killing of Williams on April 11, 1836, but it is uncertain had much earlier his death occurred. In any case, Sam Houston was taking no chances with Chief Bowl, *before and after* he signed the treaty with him in February. Poole may have been only one of Houston's spies in the Cherokee villages. Any "indication of hostility towards Texans," of course, would have allowed Houston to press the red-button alarm he needed to get General Gaines's soldiers marching across the Sabine.

Even with conclusive evidence that Houston ordered Bean's arrest, we are thrown back on speculation as to whether this order reached Nacogdoches in time to be acted upon, or whether—if it did—Hoffman actually took Bean into custody. Bean, as Lack claims, may have quietly left town during this subversive-hunting frenzy and stayed at one of his ranches. Many other citizens of Nacogdoches, regardless of which side they took, were also leaving town for the countryside if not Louisiana. (Alcalde Hoffman was among them, fleeing Texas during the Runaway Scrape!) Bean probably did not go among the Cherokees; it would be dangerous for him to have been seen at their villages in April 1836, when hysteria against Bowl's tribe and Mexican agents in their midst was building. Or, as Yoakum says, Bean may have been taken into custody for a week or so. Of proof there is none.

Col. Peter Ellis Bean was an old, respected settler and had too many prominent friends at Nacogdoches for him to remain in "jail" very long. Certainly he was not clamped in irons and imprisoned in the Old Stone Fort, as he was by the Spaniards after the Nolan episode. Lay's summation of Bean's "bitter thoughts" during this second incarceration is too melodramatic and overwrought, considering that we do not know for sure if the man was even taken into custody. Plus the fact that Houston / Rusk ordered Hoffman to "detain" Bean in San Augustine. This village had no Old Stone Fort, and that Bean was detained in the one at Nacogdoches is doubtful.[27]

But what about Bean's opinion of Houston after he learned that Sam had ordered his arrest, as Bean must have at some point in time? Things like that were hard to keep secret in a small community. Did he regard it as a betrayal by a man he considered a friend, or did he merely shrug it off as the fortunes of war? Bean had been a Houston supporter when the Raven (also known as the "Big Drunk") first showed up at Nacogdoches from Indian Territory early in 1833, and they had been pulling together on the Creek protest to President Jackson as recently as September 1835. But then Houston began negotiating with the Cherokees without Bean's services, as if his experience with these Indians counted for nothing. This must have galled Bean's pride and sense of honor, based as much on Mexican as on Anglo-Celtic cultural traditions.

Imagine this Johnny-come-lately calling him "an Alien of the Republic!" Peter Ellis Bean, given his efforts to free Mexico from Spain while Sam Houston was still trying to grow whiskers, could not have taken kindly to being accused of passing along information that rendered Houston's army "ineffectual." That amounted to high treason, with stiff penalties involved. One suspects that the report on Bean, the truth of which Yoakum called "very questionable," was a story concocted by Houston and Rusk simply to get Bean out of the way in the short term. Sam Houston had a card up his sleeve as he was camped on the Brazos opposite Groce's Landing, and his couriers were riding back and forth to Fort Jesup on a regular basis. That Bean might get wise to what was transpiring —and pass the information on to Santa Anna—was a risk that Houston and Rusk could not afford to take. The fact that no more was heard about it after Houston's victory at San Jacinto supports this line of reasoning. Furthermore, the two men were conducting business together a few months later, even if in a very cautious manner.

In the Raguet Papers is an interesting account of the situation around Nacogdoches between April 11 and April 16 that may explain why Houston ordered Bean's arrest. On the morning of April 12, men named Love and Adams brought word that a combined force of Mexicans and Indians had spent the night of April 10 camped at the Neches Saline. Lt. James Carter was ordered to scout in the direction of the enemy and learn the truth of this report. Panic quickly took hold of the community, worsened when one Randall came galloping into town—"white as a sheet"—screaming "to arms, to arms!!" He claimed that he had been disarmed by an advance guard of the enemy. Even when Lieutenant Carter returned from the principal Cherokee village at three o'clock on April 13, saying that he had seen no enemy Mexicans anywhere, the exodus from town continued. If any of these men happened to mention Bean's name in their frantic reports, it could very well have caused General Houston to issue orders for his arrest until the truth be known.[28]

Meanwhile, the Nacogdoches committee's efforts to prove that an Indian uprising was imminent went ahead with gusto. Texas agents at Natchitoches were also busy, some of them sent by Burnet's interim government. Miguel Cortinez swore on April 12 that he found his brother Eusebio in Bowl's Cherokee village, and Eusebio held a commission from General Cos to raise the Indians against the Texans. This made Miguel angry at his brother, he professed, but Chief Bowl said that he would join Eusebio and "fight while a man of his tribe remained."[29] "General" Mason hastened on his way to Fort Jesup with the depositions taken at Nacogdoches. At the same time, Judge John A. Quitman from Natchez was advising the officers at Nacogdoches that he was proceeding with sixteen men to observe the situation and "assist in the retreat of your women and children."[30] This was when Sam Houston wrote Chief Bowl his reassuring letter about the treaty, telling him "there are not many of the enemy now in the country"—a bald-faced lie.[31]

Mason reached Fort Jesup after dark on April 13, writing General

Gaines a lengthy letter the same night. He assured Gaines that Nacogdoches was by now in the hands of the Mexicans and Indians. The inhabitants were fleeing for their lives and, if pursued, "all must be massacred, without instantaneous relief [from you]." Unless five hundred men were immediately sent, the massacre would extend to the Sabine. As its banks were flooded, hundreds of families crowded together at the muddy crossing would be sacrificed. "The road from Nacogdoches to the Sabine is one unbroken line of women and children, on foot, with nothing but their clothing on their backs. Such is the distress, and a small picture of it," claimed Mason to a man fresh from fighting treacherous Seminoles in Florida.[32]

Samuel P. Carson had also arrived at Natchitoches, even though he was delegated by President Burnet to obtain aid farther east in the United States. Carson, the republic's new secretary of state, was an old friend of Houston's from North Carolina who had barely arrived in Texas in time to sign the Declaration of Independence. Carson assured Burnet and his cabinet that General Gaines would use his amassed troops to "protect the frontier and the Neutral Ground also to keep the Indians in check and repress savage aggressions. This he is bound to do in fullfilment of treaty stipulations between the Govt of the U States and Mexico." Moreover, "Jackson will protect the neutral ground, and the beauty of it is, he claims to the Nesches as neutral ground."[33] The web to catch Santa Anna unaware was being spun in high places. The threat of savage Indians gave Jackson the diplomatic excuse to enter Texas, but Houston's bedraggled and retreating army had to serve as the lure. Santa Anna's troops must be drawn closer to the border.

After speaking with Gaines, Carson wrote Houston: "My view is that you should fall back, if necessary, to the Sabine. I am warranted in saying that volunteer troops will come on in numbers from the United States . . . You must fall back, and hold out, and let nothing goad or provoke you to a battle, unless you can, without doubt, whip them."[34]

Judge Quitman reached Nacogdoches on April 15, reporting that there was not a woman or child left in town. The panic had done its work, and all were in headlong flight; at least three hundred men with arms in their hands were seen going east, away from the battlefront. "Perhaps they condisered the contest hopeless, and did not care to throw away their lives." An exodus was also taking place at San Augustine, and Quitman admitted that reports of the enemy's "overwhelming numbers and bloody intentions were indeed alarming." He told Gen. Felix Huston, "The houses are all deserted. There are several thousands of women and children in the woods on both sides of the Sabine, without supplies or money." On the road to Nacogdoches, "We must have met, at least, 1000 women and children, and every where along the road were wagons, furniture, and provisions abandoned. Almost every house was deserted, and its contents left open to depredation."[35] Scavengers were not long in taking advantage of the situation.

But what of the Indian menace? Quitman thought that a body of Mexican cavalry had been sent a month earlier to cooperate with the Indians on the upper frontier in making a descent on the unprotected settlements below. It was said that the Cherokees had promised to support them. But the incessant rains, unprecedented floods, and sogginess of the soil had kept this "cavalry" from swinging into action on the eastern side of the Trinity. The Cherokees, learning that the northern tribes could not join them as planned and that General Gaines had resolved to keep them in check, were now professing friendship. Santa Anna's army was responsible for the flight.[36]

John T. Mason, at James Gaines's ferry on April 16, wrote that Gen. Edmund Gaines had marched the day before with six hundred troops from Fort Jesup and camped ten miles beyond. He was going on to the Sabine but would not cross and enter Texas "till circumstances justify it." In the meantime, he would construct rafts and offer protection to the women and children clustered on both sides of the river. Mason asked that any evidence of Indians "embodying, or committing outrages" should be immediately communicated to Gaines by express.[37] Despite the hardships being suffered by the Texan refugees, a pretext for Gaines crossing the Sabine was still needed. That he would then aid Houston's men was assumed by everyone.

General Gaines, eager to have such a pretext, had dispatched 1st Lt. Joseph Bonnell of the 3rd Infantry at the beginning of April to the Caddo villages on the upper Red River. On his march upriver Bonnell heard that Manuel Flores and Miguel Cortinez had earlier been among the Caddos, urging them to help destroy the white inhabitants of Texas. Flores promised them "free plunder," but the Caddos had refused his offers and sent him on his way. They expressed great joy at Bonnell's arrival, relieved that he was not coming to destroy them as rumors circulating had made them fear. Chief Cortes asked Bonnell to say to Gaines that the Caddos would only look on and take no part if they saw the Americans and Mexicans fighting.[38]

This report, of course, was not what General Gaines wanted to hear. Since some of the Caddos still lived on the United States side of the border, even though they had sold their lands to the government, their participation in the Texas disturbances would have given him clear right to invoke Article 33 of the treaty. At least he had more confirmation that Mexican agents Flores and Cortinez had tried to stir up these Indians against the whites. Cortinez may have given his earlier deposition about his brother Eusebio's activities among Bowl's Cherokees to get himself off the hook in Louisiana.

This little charade was almost over, as Sam Houston's victory at San Jacinto on April 21—and Santa Anna's capture—made it unnecessary for President Jackson and General Gaines to play their trump card. For years Peter Ellis Bean had used this card, Article 33 of the treaty, to try to keep U.S. Indians out of Mexico, only to be foiled by the State Department's narrow interpretation of the article. If Bean knew that the military buildup on the Sabine was occasioned by resort to this article, he must have considered it a supreme irony. The U.S. government had always claimed that the provision could not be invoked to stop its Indians from flooding into Mexican Texas. Yet here the Americans were, ready and willing to help Texas gain its freedom from Mexico—aided by many U.S. citizens and a few "deserters" from Gaines's army—and Article 33 was the holy writ being used. It is obvious that Indian hostilities were nothing more than a pretext for Gaines to get his men into position for a jolly good fight—with Mexicans, not Indians.[39]

News of Houston's "decisive victory" did not reach General Gaines until April 28. Until then, he continued his activities dedicated to marching across the Sabine in force. He sent warnings to Chief Bowl to toe the line with his Cherokees. He did not consider Lieutenant Bonnell's report as conclusive that the Caddos were quiet and would not fall under the influence of the Comanches and other hostile tribes. He intended to warn the commanders of both armies in Texas that he was on the border to ensure that they abided by the treaty concerning inhabitants on both sides of the line. Even if the Indians of the frontier remained pacific, Gaines suggested that a sizable force of his men marching into Texas would "produce a moral effect upon the Indians and the inhabitants "of this "panic-striken frontier." Moreover, his men would gain valuable knowledge of the country useful to future operations. What "future operations" one wonders?[40]

Secretary of War Lewis Cass on April 25 gave General Gaines the latitude he wanted—including permission for a march as far as "the old Fort Nacogdoches, which is within the limits of the United States, as claimed by the Government." The president, said Cass, did not wish to take advantage of present circumstances and thereby obtain possession of any portion of Mexican territory. Still, the neutral duties and rights of the nation justified the United States in taking all measures to "prevent a violation of their territory." In view of how agents had tried to induce the barbarous Indians to join the Mexican troops in their pillage and plunder of Texas, President Jackson had authorized Gaines "to take such position, on either side of the imaginary boundary line, as may be best for your defensive operations."[41]

General Gaines wrote Houston on April 25 about how he was dispatching several officers, bearing the American flag, to confer with him and the commander of Mexico's army. Should any hostile Indians be found on either side of the unmarked boundary line, Gaines avowed that he would not hesitate to "inflict on the Indians, as well as on those who may be found acting with, and aiding them" the punishment necessary to protect the frontier from a "savage war." This meant, of course, that if Gaines's soldiers found a squad of Santa Anna's cavalry among the Indians, a shooting war would begin between Mexico and the United States. In a postscript Gaines said that he had just "heard rumours of a Battle in Texas." If the fortunes of war should place Houston "in a situation requiring, or rendering desirable, the humane offices of a friendly neighbour, I will take great pleasure in extending to you, any act of kindness in my power, not incompatible with the laws governing the conduct of neutrals."[42] This was a tactful way of saying, "Sam Houston, ask and you shall receive."

Chapter 17

OLD SAM JACINTO'S "BIG RANCH"

Once General Gaines had certain, but "unofficial," news of Houston's victory, he sent the details to Secretary of War Cass. The movement of the volunteers called on from various states could now be suspended, as the situation was well in hand. President Santa Anna was Houston's prisoner, along with his officers and most of his troops, "the residue having been killed." As to the Indians, Gaines had been assured that "the Cherokee chief, Bowles, and others hitherto disposed to be disorderly, had determined to keep peace among the Indians."[1]

What was Bean's situation as the war scare subsided? It was on May 5 that ferry keeper James Gaines had told President Burnet about how "our agents (say Palmer and Benton)" had "Blown the Very Trees up by their Roots" on their way back from the Convention, meaning—one supposes—that they bore tales of Santa Anna's success at the Alamo and how his army was advancing to slaughter them all. This was when Gaines accused Peter Ellis Bean, John Durst, and others of the Santa Anna Corps of circulating a report that caused a "perfect hurricane," despite his valiant effort to stop the "Blue Streak" of flight to Louisiana. In this letter Gaines noted cryptically: "Genl. Gaines and Troops are near their object is to be guessed at."[2]

A letter written to Gen. Thomas Rusk by Haden H. Edwards on May 11 also provides a glimpse of Nacogdoches and what it must have been like for Bean and other suspected Tories. After making bad-health excuses for why he had not joined Rusk in the field, Edwards mentioned a recent incident by a company of volunteers from "Tenahaw" headed by Captain "Braddy": "They made use of Some very Rough measures & threatened to Burn & plunder Nacogdoches—under the plea that all the Inhabitants were Torries—& had combined with St Anna— They went so far as to threaten the Life of Col Thorn & other Individuals of this place, & I have no doubt but they would have executed their threats— If they had not found out that it would have been rather an unpopular & dangerous undertaking—"[3] Frost Thorn was not only the richest man in town but had served on the local Committee of Safety during the revolution! He, as noted, was Haden H. Edwards's brother-in-law, and they were in business together. If rowdy "patriots" were threatening Thorn's life for being a Tory, one can imagine the sort of rough treatment they thought Bean deserved. Edwards assured Rusk that his family was safe and living at San Augustine.

Empresario Sterling Robertson wrote Rusk from that place on May 27 in regard to the difficulty of raising troops for the war with Mexico that was still not over, even though four thousand soldiers under Filisola's command were then retreating to the Rio Grande. Robertson had found the inhabitants of both San Augustine and Nacogdoches "lukewarm" to the idea of signing up for a summer campaign. "I am affraid that I shall not get many if any to march to the field though it is admitted on all hands that men are necessary at this time to enable you to follow up the blow of San Jacinto." The problem, said Robertson, was that the people of this section expected General Gaines to fight their battles for them. Since the United States was claiming that its territory extended to the Neches, the people believed they would be protected by U.S. troops and were content to stay home and enjoy life.[4]

This attitude grew when Camp Nacogdoches was established in July by Col. William Whistler, on the basis of Gaines's claim of continued Indian unrest; it was a move supported by the inhabitants and the Texas government. They were all glad to have U.S. soldiers on hand, especially the merchants, stockmen, and farmers with produce to sell.[5] A young soldier who was stationed at Camp Nacogdoches with Whistler's troops wrote his family on August 14, 1836, describing the place and its people. He considered east Texas as a "land that flows with milk and honey come all of you and possess it." The inhabitants were another matter: "The dress of the americans or the sett[l]ers from the united states differ from what you are acustomed to see part of thear apparel consists of 1 or 2 braces of pistols or large knife a sword and gun a furious look and frequently use thear implements on each other the other day a frien of mind was un armed and under took to save the life of a man by nocking up the gun of a monster which caused the deamon to turn on him the inosant man was to slay him with his own knife."[6]

The soldier mentioned frequent desertions from the army and made an interesting comment about the Indians who visited town: "[W]e see Indians of different tribes every day they appear to possess a considerable degree of pride and say that [they] are glad that Jacksons men have come hear to see that all things goes on well. If general gains does not take his troops back to the united states in 10 or 15 days I expect as how he will be clean of help as thear not a night passes that thear is not several disirions [desertions] thear is mutiny in the camps which cause 10 to start on to our army [in Louisiana?] last night Gains will not cary I expect."[7] As late as November 30, 1836, there were 428 officers and men at the camp. They were not withdrawn east of the Sabine until December, despite the repeated protests of Mexico's diplomatic representative in Washington.

These U.S. troops had to remain around Nacogdoches, or at least stay east of President Jackson's claimed boundary of the Neches River, and keep an eye on the Indians. The republic was therefore obliged to raise its own volunteers to meet any Mexican attempt to reconquer Texas from the south. From documents extant in the archives division of the Texas State Library, Bean at this time was supplying various volunteer companies being raised for the summer campaign with beef, corn, hogs, fodder, tobacco, and at least one horse. While some may argue that these supplies were being provided to the Texan military forces by Bean regardless of his sympathies for the revolution, signed receipts by various company commanders indicate otherwise. He was helping the Texan cause, and later got reimbursed for his efforts.[8]

Life was indeed returning to normal. This meant that Bean had to scramble for money, as he could no longer even remotely count on his salary as a Mexican officer. His landholdings had to see him through. In February he had transferred the town lot he held as security from Freeman Prather "to Briget Najara that she may hold the lot or recover the rent Dew me." Bean sued William Skinner that month for a debt of $73.75 and won. He also served as foreman on a Nacogdoches jury in February 1836.[9]

Another sale came after the dust from the revolution had settled a bit. Haden H. Edwards and James Carter paid Bean sixteen hundred dollars on June 28 for his undivided half of the tract of land five miles south of town on La Nana Creek, the same that Thorn and Bean had bought from José Morin. This league and fifty acres included the saw- and gristmill, houses, and fields jointly owned by Bean and Thorn.[10]

A bigger sale to Sam Houston came shortly thereafter. It was to cause some serious problems between Bean and Houston in the next two years.

> Agreement made and entered into on the 24th day of August in the year of our Lord 1836 between Sam Houston of the municipality of Nacogdoches on the one part and Peter E. Bean, also of said municipality on the other part.
>
> Witnesseth the said Bean has sold unto Houston a piece or parcel of land (one league, more or less), distant about two leagues easterly from Nacogdoches known by the name of Bean's Plantation. . . .

For the sum of $5,000, which the said Houston obliges himself, his heirs and assigns, to pay within one year from the date of this instrument, and for failing to do so hereby agrees to forfeit this contract, and also $2,000 to be paid to the said Bean.

And the said Bean hereby promises, on receipt of the $5,000, before named, to make a title to said Houston of said land; and for refusal to make a title on notice of said Houston's readiness to pay the said sum, the said Bean agrees to forfeit and pay to the said Houston the sum of $2,000.

And for the fulfilment of this agreement each party binds himself, his heirs and assigns, in the penal sum beforementioned, and submit themselves, without liberty of appeal to the honorable judges and judiciary of the country, that they may compel them to comply with the terms of this agreement.

Thus Bean sold his "Plantation" estate of 4,428 acres about five miles east of town to Houston, who did not have the five-thousand-dollar purchase price but promised to pay it by August 24, 1837. It may safely be said that the tone of this contract is guarded, not to mention the penalties imposed for nonfulfillment. One wonders how Houston, if he could not raise the five thousand dollars for the land in a year's time, could manage to pay a two-thousand-dollar default penalty with nothing gained.[11]

While Houston was in Nacogdoches buying a league of land from Bean, he circulated an alarm "To the Citizens of Texas." Reports had reached him that some Cherokees "with the *notorious* Cortinus" had just returned from Matamoros. They were saying that the prairie tribes were about to attack the white settlements of Texas in combination with a Mexican force. Houston called out the militias of all surrounding districts to help sustain the U.S. troops then in town "until reinforcements can arrive from Genl Gaines." His rallying cry was "All the men of Texas must have their arms in order! To secure liberty we must be watchful."[12]

He wrote General Gaines the same day, August 29, requesting more men and explaining that the Texian army was spread too thin to arrive in time to meet this emergency. Cherokees had gone to Matamoros, and some had returned with assurances that Mexican troops were on the march through Laredo. They would arrive in eight days or less. The Indians were regarding the U.S. troops camped near Nacogdoches "with evident contempt." If these men should be cut off by an attacking force of Mexicans and Indians, Houston said that it would "blur an escutcheon more glorious than I can ever hope to see again," that is, the star-spangled banner. He promised to "omit nothing" in placing the country in a state of defense, but asked Gaines, "must we not anticipate a panick again?"

Houston assured the general, "Borne down by [superior] numbers [all] must *perish*!!!" and ended with "You can save Texas!!!"[13] What was this about? Why was Houston casting doubt on the loyalty of Bowl's Cherokees, and who gave him this report?

Several weeks later Houston, in the name of the Republic of Texas, ordered Bean's neighbor Martin Lacy to take possession of the Neches Saline, "which is under the control of the Government." It was on Bean's one-league survey that he had sold to Hotchkiss for two thousand dollars in 1834, and title was confirmed on December 14, 1835. Martin Lacy had brought his family and six slaves to Texas from Louisiana around 1830. After briefly residing near Ayish Bayou, he acquired land two miles southwest of modern Alto and built a house so imposing that it was known as "Lacy's Fort." Through Bean, he won the trust of the Indians and developed a prosperous trade with the Cherokees and other nearby tribes. Now, soon-to-be President Houston wanted Lacy (probably with Bean's help, though not stated) to engage in the production of salt, selling it as cheaply as possible. He was to pay Chief Bowl six bushels per month and trade with the Indians "in all things" except liquor and lead. Houston gave him a two-year contract, coinciding with his term of office. Lacy established a trading post at the saline, which should not be confused with his "Fort" on the Old San Antonio Road.[14]

Did Houston want more of Gaines's soldiers in Nacogdoches in case the Cherokees should oppose Lacy's taking over this valuable saline on lands given them by the treaty? Was this his reason for calling out over two hundred militiamen in the meantime, urging them to report without delay? As Houston told Gaines, he had news from one "Bascos" that an Indian delegation—including Cherokees—had visited Gen. José Urrea at Matamoros in mid-July and made promises of military cooperation with Mexican invasionary forces.[15] News like this was also coming from other sources.

For example, at the beginning of August, Indian Agent Menard sent a local Tejano (Isadore Pantallion, disguised as a Mexican military officer) to Bowl's village. He was admitted to a council then in progress, called because U.S. troops had just marched from Fort Towson slightly north of Jonesboro on the Red River to Nacogdoches directly through Cherokee territory. Bowl had called the council to determine what the Indian response should be to this "invasion." Menard's spy returned with tall tales of how Chief Bowl had sworn never to prove false to his Mexican friends and how he was raising the other tribes to assist Urrea's troops when they marched north.[16] Menard, of course, had provided similar information when it was needed to spur Gaines to action in April 1836.

It seems that Houston was willing to believe these exaggerated reports, or say that he did, partly because he knew that Bowl was unhappy. The interim Texan government had not yet delivered on Houston's treaty promises for a title to Cherokee lands. And Houston was about to order Martin Lacy to take over their saline! It might be the last straw for Bowl, and Houston wanted to make sure he had more of General Gaines's soldiers on hand in case of another Mexican-agitated "Indian uprising." When Bowl learned from Menard's spy that the U.S. troops from Fort Towson were in Nacogdoches because President Jackson claimed the boundary was at the Neches, the chief muttered that this was "just like Americans, always stealing [our land] piece by piece."[17]

Houston kept up his efforts to lure the Cherokees to the lone star banner, even if he had to work against Chief Bowl to do it. One of his schemes was to enlist warriors as "rangers" who would patrol the frontier from the Sabine westward to the Comanche crossing on the Trinity. This company of twenty-five men would receive ten dollars a month for their services and all the booty they could take from the Comanches. It was an appealing offer and meant that Bowl's pro-Mexican stance in tribal councils would be undermined by warriors willing to fight on the side of Texas against their long-standing enemies, the prairie tribes—and get paid for it.[18]

Younger men were now making their feelings known, and the old chief's influence was slipping as nothing materialized on the treaty he had signed with Houston. But the Raven was about to become president of the Republic of Texas, so maybe his promises would be kept. Bowl adopted a wait-and-see attitude, while still trying to keep his options open with Mexican generals down south. This was a reasonable approach, and Bowl had been threading such needles for many years. Could Houston trust Bowl in the summer of 1836? Probably about as much as Bowl could trust Houston.

Sam Houston became the first elected president of Texas in October 1836. After a stint at Columbia, he held the reins of government at the impressive capitol building that the Allen brothers had erected in their new town named—what else?—Houston. This transfer of the seat of government took place in April 1837. But Houston still had many interests at Nacogdoches, including Anna Raguet (the winsome daughter of prosperous Henry Raguet) and some land speculations that had been left dangling when the revolution hit. The treaty that Houston had signed with Bowl's Cherokees was still not ratified by the Senate, and he attempted to mollify them at the new capital. A delegation came to see him in May, and Houston arranged a smoking session with them, his cabinet in attendance. Another meeting was planned for the following month in east Texas, closer to their villages.[19]

Anthony Butler, the U.S. chargé d'affaires who had been ejected from Mexico at the end of 1836, did not do much to set Houston's mind at ease about Bowl's Cherokees. While at Matamoros awaiting deportation, Butler had seen a party of about one hundred Indians in town, including Cherokees and Kickapoos. They had just concluded an agreement to cooperate with Mexico in cleansing Texas of the whites. As a reward, "the Indians were to possess thereafter the whole of Texas in absolute right and full sovereignty, and were to form a cordon between the U. States and Mexico." When Butler reached Texas in the latter part of April, he talked to President Houston and passed on his Indian information. Houston was anxious to know if Chief Bowl was among the delegation to Mexico, but Butler could not say. Butler reported that Houston was loathe to believe his tale of Indian treachery and expressed doubt that Mexico was strong enough to carry the scheme into execution.[20]

Because of a July 3 letter that Houston wrote William Goyens on this trip to Nacogdoches to attend an Indian council, a few historians have assumed that Houston used the services of Bean in his relations with the Cherokees. Virtually no letters exist between Houston and Bean that touch on their relationship after the revolution or enable us to say if they remained friends or not. But the letter to "Agent" Goyens quoted below at least mentions Bean.

> Sir, I send on the same sheet, a letter to my Brother Bowl, and would be glad if you cou'd take it to him, and have it explained, and brought down with the other chiefs Let wor'd be sent to the other Tribes; as directed. If you do not go, see that the letter goes directly to him. I will be happy to see you as soon as you can return. I will only have a short time to stay in this place. If you see Colonel Bean tell him I am very anxious to see him here. Give my compliments to your family.
> Your Friend, Sam Houston
> Mr. Goyens, Let the Delawares be sent for by the Bowl.[21]

At first glance it appears that Houston is "anxious" to see Bean about the Indian matter being discussed, in which Bean's help might be needed. Perhaps so, considering Bean's awareness of the comings and goings of tribal delegations to Mexico and elsewhere. He might know the truthfulness of Butler's assertions better than Agent Goyens. But the public letters soon being published in a back-and-forth exchange between them make it fairly obvious that Houston wanted to see Bean because his note on Bean's plantation was about to fall due.[22] As soon as it did, Bean posted notice of Houston's default in the *Texas Chronicle* at Nacogdoches.

Houston published his reply of November 15, 1837, in the capital's *Telegraph and Texas Register* on November 25 and kept running it into December: "A Certain Peter E. Bean having published a notice in the Nacogdoches Chronicle that I had forfeited a contract made with him on the

25th [24th] August last [1836], now this is to notify all persons that the bargain is not void, as I notified said Bean in writing dated as early as the 15th July, 1836 [1837], that the cash would be ready on the day on which it should fall due. The tenant whom I left in possession of the premises I shall hold responsible to me for their delivery in good order."[23]

The many mistakes in this public notice suggest that lawyer Houston did not compose it while sober. Houston wrote Henry Raguet the day after penning this letter that his health had been wretched and "this is the first letter written by me since my convalescence." Private perhaps, but not public. He said that it was his intention, as soon as Congress adjourned, to visit Nacogdoches and "commence improvements at Egeri so that I will have a home, when my term expires." But this "Egeri," if it stood on Bean's plantation, was slipping away from Houston's drunken grasp.[24] He published another letter in the *Texas Chronicle* on February 28, 1838, having written it earlier than the one sent to the *Telegraph and Texas Register.*

> BEWARE — I have observed that Peter E. Bean of the County of Nacogdoches has issued a public notice, declaring that a contract which he made with me, has been forfeited by me, and is void. He is aware that this is not the truth. More than one month before the money came due I notified said Bean that the said money would await his application when it became due, unless he chose to give [more] time on the payment; and, in that event, I would give him ten per cent interest—payable every six months—subsequently to which time, he stated to a gentleman of the highest respectability and character, that he had accepted my proposition, and would not send to receive the money. He has slandered my title; the law will chastise him for it. The tenant whom I left in possession of the premises, I shall hold responsible for the rent and delivery of same.
> Sam Houston
> City of Houston, Nov. 10, 1837.[25]

These were strong words from the president of the Republic of Texas to a common citizen. In effect, he was calling Bean a liar and promising that the courts of the land would punish him for slander. It is hard to imagine that "friends" would behave in such a manner. Houston had an ax to grind with Bean, and it probably went beyond mere late payment on a note that Houston owed Bean. Was it because of Bean's influence with the Cherokees under the Mexican realm, influence that Bean still had and Houston feared losing? Or was it because Bean had lost all faith in Houston's ability to honor their contract because of his alcoholism? The record is silent.

After this letter was published, Bean must have considered his chances very slim that Houston's land commissioner would approve title to *any* of the tracts of land that he had registered under Mexican law. But he was full of fight. On May 2, 1838, Bean came back at Houston in the *Telegraph and Texas Register* by publishing the contract between them. This "Notice" was prefaced by Bean: "There has been much said about my contract with Gen. Sam Houston and myself." Therefore Bean thought it "proper" to let the public know the exact language of the contract, so they could decide who was in the right when he declared it void for nonpayment. It was certified as a true copy at Nacogdoches by John K. Allen, Robert A. Irion, and Nathaniel Amory, all close associates of the president.[26] It appears that Houston abandoned the contest. When he received a "generous settlement" (of about what he owed Bean) for his revolutionary services on February 23, 1838, he used the money to buy a tract of land at Cedar Point, overlooking Galveston Bay.[27]

Sam Houston had a lot on his mind at the end of 1837, and his drinking did not do much to help him maintain focus. Mexican agents such as Manuel Flores, Eusebio Cortinez, and Vicente Córdova were still active among the Cherokees. When Bowl left on a peacemaking trip for Houston to the plains tribes earlier in the year, the pro-Mexican element among the Cherokees listened to these local Tejanos; trouble seemed imminent. Big Mush tried to keep these men out of the Cherokee villages, without much success. William Goyens offered help by interpreting and carrying messages to the Cherokees. Bowl returned early in May, reporting some progress with the Caddos, Ionis, and Keechis. They seemed ready to talk peace and no longer wanted vengeance against the white Texans. Not so with the plains Comanches and the Wichitas living on the Red River; they carried on a thriving trade with Holland Coffee and expressed no interest in making treaties with the new rulers of Texas. Bean conveyed this information to Houston on May 6 and Goyens did the same four days later. Thus we learn that Colonel Bean still had some influence among Bowl's Cherokees, and they used him to report the latest developments in frontier Indian affairs to President Houston.[28]

Shortly thereafter Bowl received word that the Comanches wished to trade with both the Americans and the Cherokees. News of such a thing alarmed Houston, as he was still hoping the Cherokees would fight the Comanches—not trade with them. At this point he ordered Rusk to take steps to enlist the Cherokees, Shawnees, Kickapoos, Coushattas, Choctaws, and Biloxis against the Comanches. Houston tried to attend a June council on the Sabine, but his guide got lost and he missed the affair. From Nacogdoches he ordered Bowl to assemble the tribes there for another council. Houston told Bowl to be sure and bring the treaty with him, the one with ribbons and a seal, but Bowl was silent. Houston nonetheless offered the chief two thousand dollars a year if he would take the field as a brigadier general for Texas against hostile Indians, or one thousand dollars just to align himself with the republic and do nothing.[29] It was during this visit to Nacogdoches that Houston was "anxious" to see Bean—probably about the plantation bought on credit a year earlier, payment for which was about to fall due.

One William A. Force wrote a very interesting letter to his brother and sister on July 10, 1837, that reveals much about the conduct of Houston and his entourage while staying at the same Nacogdoches boardinghouse.

> Politics if you please president Sam Houston and suit are here and boarding at the same house and eating at the same table with myself together with Hon. Felix Houston [Huston] 1 minister to foreign country & attorney General and a number of our [unintelligible] you will think I am boasting on what respectable company I keep what do you think[?] I want to boast of keeping company with as miserable and drunken set of vagabond[s] as ever disgraced a community[?] no no I have not got so low as that Yet thank God here they have been for 8 or 10 days I have seen them all drunk but their negroes I have seen them drunk with Indians hugging 2 or 3 at a time hooping and yelling like them throwing their arms round one another hugg them up and cry O my Brother my brother[!] a squaw shows her head Sam Houston was the first man to catch her haul her up to the bar pour out make her drink whiskey and drink after her and he has not drawn a sober breath since he has been here nor hardly any of his suit of officers I know the people of the United States many of them think H[ouston] is all powerful in Texas but they are much mistaken for all thinking men here [are] all unanimous [and] say the government must change . . . or we must . . . sink.[30]

This, then, was the man that Peter Ellis Bean had sold his plantation to a year earlier, and Houston now wanted William Goyens to fetch Bean because he was "anxious" to see him. No wonder that Bean promptly declared their contract void after it fell due the following month! Houston's condition at Nacogdoches must have spoken eloquently that he could no longer raise the five thousand dollars to pay Bean for his land, as he had been able to do in former times. Considering that the Vital Flores land had only cost Bean four hundred pesos, he was risking a lot of profit money by ending the deal with the Hero of San Jacinto.

It must also be said that going on drunken binges like this was not abnormal behavior for Houston. Thomas Rusk, one of Houston's firmest supporters, told his wife Mary in February 1835 that "Gov. Houston lives in this place and has made over two thousand dollars in the last twelve months But he is very dissipated and in very bad health."[31] "Dissipated" in the parlance of the day meant drunk all the time—a habit that Houston had nurtured during his exile in Indian Territory. Lucky that sweet and innocent Miss Anna Raguet did not walk into that boardinghouse on the night(s) that Mr. Force described. Houston's drinking problem only got worse, not better, between 1835 and 1837 and continued in a downward spiral.

"Alien of the Republic" Bean still owned substantial tracts of land, but now he was selling them instead of buying more. The same applied to his holdings in town. Here will be summarized some of these transactions during 1836–37. In August 1836 he sold another town lot on the central plaza, four *varas* in width and eighty deep, to Solomon R. Peck for five hundred dollars. It bordered on the south with a new east-west street being laid out. Because Bean had only paid José Pineda ten pesos for the lot, this sale was very profitable—rather like the one with Sam Houston promised to be.[32] In December Bean's attorneys Williams and Whitely sold his "settler" league to one George Bondies. It had three small buildings and a forty-acre improvement, but it is uncertain if Bean received anything from this sale or if he ever lived on this property in Houston County. Leonard Williams had the long, narrow league that adjoined Bean's to the west.[33] Bean still owned land on the west side of the Neches, according to a sale that neighbor Thomas Goss made at the end of December 1836. It was the south half of Goss's headright (2,224 acres) in Burnet's grant, which "corners with Bean on the west" and was bounded by the Neches on the east. This was a different tract than the Bean-Williams-Whitely league, seemingly one that Bean had purchased from its original owner. These tangled land affairs are difficult to sort out.[34]

Land sales either by or concerning Bean continued into 1837. A big one came on March 20 when he sold Garza's four leagues to Frost Thorn and J. T. Pinkney (probably Pinckney) for ten thousand dollars. At the same time he sold Aranjo's five leagues to them for another ten thousand dollars, although it appears that the Garza sale was not completed. On July 12 Bean parted with a small tract on La Nana Creek to three gentlemen for three hundred dollars. It was on the east bank along a main road bordered at the top by lands where "Padre Mata" resided in 1829. Bean had obtained it from Juan José Mata Medina the same year, paying a mere forty pesos.[35] This tract may have adjoined Flores's former Carrizo ranch.

Most of the land in this area had been granted to Vital Flores, an alcalde at Nacogdoches, from whom Bean bought the league upon which he built his house and first sawmill. Although the deal with Sam Houston fell through, later sales indicate that Bean's plantation was about four miles east of Nacogdoches and a mile or so west of Carrizo Creek, on the south side of the road. It is uncertain how close Bean's house was to the sawmill, but he was said to be living at this house in the early 1840s, or perhaps another built on the same ground.[36] We know from the diary of Adolphus Sterne, however, that Bean also had a residence about twenty-eight miles west of Nacogdoches at this time, so it appears that he leased the tract to others once he moved west. It was not until the end of 1838 that Bean began disposing of his plantation league, a process that continued after he left Texas in 1843.

Antonio Menchaca on August 9, 1837, made a bond with Simon Weiss, claiming as his own a lot that abutted the back of Frost Thorn's store and "the building usually called the store house on same lot of land levied upon by the Sheriff against Jose de las Piedras for P. E. Bean."[37] Bean's suit against Piedras was filed in May 1837, when Piedras was called "an absconded debtor," and Bean's tally came to $696 including interest. These debts were for lumber and building supplies that Bean had given to Piedras on credit between December 1830 and December 1831, when Terán's forts were being built in east Texas. The transactions were itemized, suggesting that Bean was a careful record keeper. Since Piedras would never return to Texas and Bean had no other way of obtaining satisfaction for what he was owed, he received a writ of attachment and had Sheriff David Rusk seize Piedras's properties.[38]

Among the parcels were two houses and lots, one occupied by Thomas McIver and the other by Thomas Rusk, probably where he had his law office. They were noted as adjoining property where stood the "Large Red House." Another was a lot on North Street, 128 *varas* on the front and 80 deep. Yet another was an unoccupied lot north of Thorn's store, perhaps the one sold to Menchaca, and finally, the house and lot on the public square then being used by Dankworth and Bondies as a grocery store. Bean was given legal possession in July and sold them all in August to Thomas Rusk for over one thousand dollars. One suspects that Rusk (his brother being the sheriff) talked Bean into reviving his suit against Piedras, which had been denied under Mexican rule.

In the process, Piedras's landholdings in east Texas were cleaned out —including rural properties. One tract of two thousand acres was on the west side of Carrizo Creek near lands owned by José María Mora. Another was a league between Atascosa and Pontesuela Creeks, beginning at the mouth of the Carrizo. At the same time that he sold the town lots, Bean sold the league for $480 and the two thousand acres (to Sterne and Davis) for $350. All told, Bean managed to make a substantial profit off his lumber deal with Colonel Piedras before rebellion forced him out of Texas in 1832.[39] He was not the only one to go after Piedras. In mid-1836 Adolphus Sterne and his brother-in-law Charles S. Taylor had brought

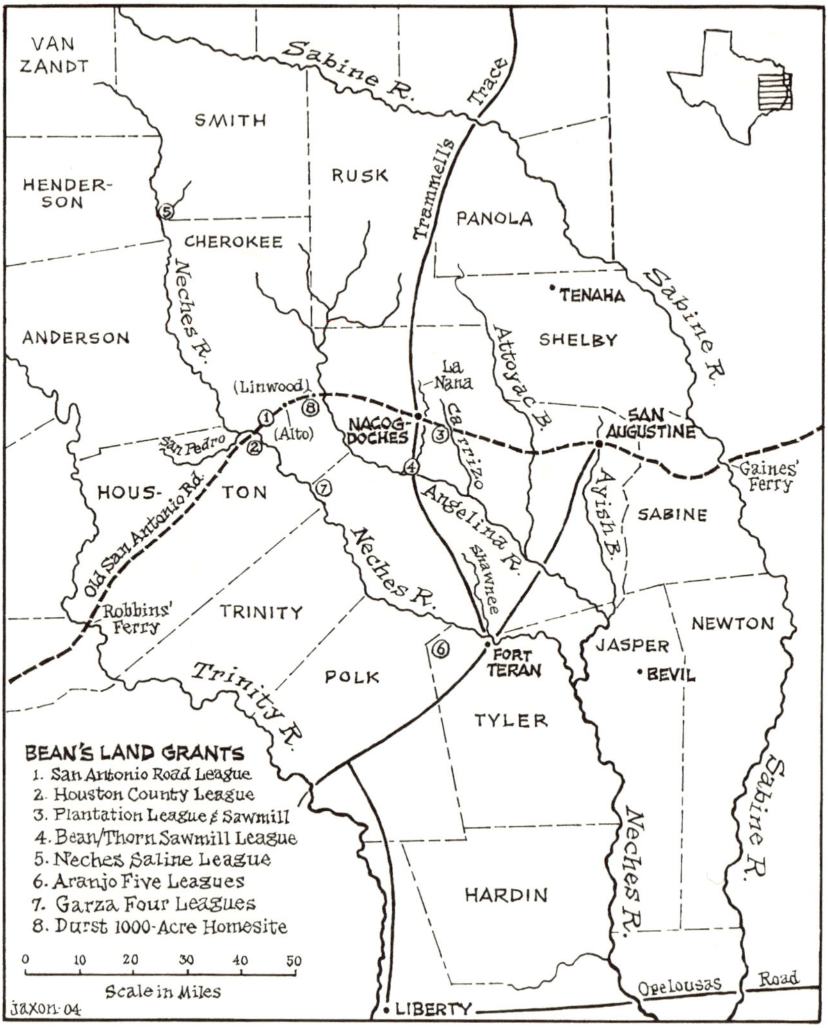

Bean's land grants in east Texas. Map by Jack Jackson.

suit against Piedras for a debt owed them of $478. They were awarded two town lots.[40]

Bean filed another suit at this time against Francisco Medina, likewise called an absconded debtor. One of his debts to Thorn from January 1831 had been paid by Bean (said to be $205, which Medina had authorized him to pay on May 14, 1835). Interest of $88 had boosted the figure, for which Bean obtained a judgment against the house and lot where James Boulter resided. This was likely the house and *solar* that Medina mentioned in his July 1835 letter to Bean as being worth 1,300 pesos, the wooden house alone valued at 800 pesos. Bean then sold it to Tom Rusk for $300, covering his expenditure on behalf of Medina and a wee bit more.[41] Francisco Medina was the captain at Nacogdoches who had marched Piedras's soldiers out of Texas in 1832 and a friend of Bean's. But business was business, and Peter Ellis Bean did not like to be left holding the short end of the stick. Thus, through legal action, Bean acquired some town property in 1837 as well as parted with it.

A much larger transaction occurred in July 1837 between John Durst and Ira R. Lewis, in which Durst received $1,207.41 and transferred to Lewis his right to a "good" league of land that Bean owed him. When Durst sold his Angelina Estate of nine leagues (roughly forty thousand acres) to Lewis in April, one thousand acres "where Bean now lives" had been withheld in return for Bean's promise to locate one of the leagues he owned as payment to Durst. He had not yet done so, though continuing to live on Durst's one thousand acres. If Bean could not convey a good title to a league of land somewhere in the Zavala-Burnet-Vehlein grants to Lewis, he must yield the one thousand acres to Lewis. But if Bean succeeded in delivering such title, then Lewis was bound (as Durst had been) to give Bean a deed to the one-thousand-acre tract where he resided.[42] How this matter was concluded is unknown, but Bean left the property to his minor son Ellis when he made his will in 1843. It was known as "Bean's Prairie Place" and had a substantial house on it called Bean's "fort."

Peter Ellis Bean had residences in various locations through the years. One, a picture of which is in Lay's book, stood outside Nacogdoches to the east on land he acquired in 1829; it has been razed and only a 1936 historical marker commemorates the site.[43] Lay, in his caption for the photograph, calls this house the "last remaining home of Candace and Peter Ellis Bean." Perhaps so, but how long they lived under its roof is questionable. Their last child, Ellis, was born in 1828, by which time their marriage was on the rocks. How long (and even whether) they lived together—much less where—has been hard to determine. Robert B. Blake remarks, "There is nothing to show that P. E. Bean and Candace ever lived together after 1826, but she remained at Mound Prairie, while Bean engaged in various activities, mostly around Nacogdoches. In 1829 [a year after the birth of Ellis M. Bean] he built a home and sawmill about four miles east of Nacogdoches on the Carrisso."[44] As noted earlier they do not appear either as a family unit or individually on a Mexican census until 1835. Bean is not on this census, but Candace is. By this time she was calling herself a widow, living alone as a single mother with her three kids and another youngster thought to be Samuel Bean, and had possession of her own league of land west of the Neches. Blake says, "That she was not then living with P. E. Bean is evident, since the officials in Nacogdoches were certainly aware of the true situation at that time."[45]

This situation changed on November 7, 1837, when "Miss Candis Medkiff" wed Mr. Isaac Hix before Justice of the Peace Charles Grayson at Nacogdoches. Hix was a single man living near Candace on the 1835 census. Although she sold her league of land to Nathaniel Robbins on July 3, 1836, the groom may have had her fat purse in mind when tying the knot. The marriage did not last long. Accused of horse theft, Hix abandoned her and fled the country. Lay suggests that Bean may have had a hand in bringing charges against Hix, if not staging the horse theft, "for he and Candace apparently lived together after her marriage to Hix."[46] This is at variance with what Blake says, but Blake's date of "after 1826" cannot be correct because of Ellis M. Bean's birth in 1828.[47] Living together or not, they cohabited long enough to produce a third child—nine years before Candace married Isaac Hix.

William P. Zuber, his facts scrambled as usual, wrote that Mrs. Bean was not respectable: "After Bean's death she married a tramp bearing the name of Hicks, who soon left her, and soon thereafter was whipped and expelled from the country for horse theft."[48] Whatever the circumstances of Isaac Hix's/Hicks's exit, Candace Midkiff was very unlucky in marriage. Oddly, she continued to use the name "Candace Hicks" and not that of Bean. Most historians have ignored this fact, including those who erected a marker in her memory. To them, she was "Candace Midkiff Bean," as simple as that.

The July 1837 Durst-Lewis transaction tells us that Colonel Bean was living on the Angelina west of Nacogdoches. His sales of property to Sam Houston and others suggest that Bean had decided to divest himself of most of his holdings east of town on Carrizo and La Nana Creeks, including his sawmills. He was now residing closer to Candace, even if she was about to marry Mr. Hix. Did Bean want to spend more time with his children? Was he beginning to feel guilty for his years of parental neglect?

This is all conjectural, but Bean's reaction to Candace's November 1837 marriage may perhaps best be judged by the fact that he filed divorce proceedings against her with the Congress of the Republic of Texas two years later. Moreover, Bean's petition clarifies—and resolves—some of the previously vague assertions about their relationship as noted above.

> To the Honorable Congress of the Republic of Texas
>
> The petition of Peter E. Bean with respect represents unto your Hon. Body that he was married to Candis Midkiff some time in the year 1817, that he had offspring by said marriage, and that he continued to live with his said wife until some time in the year 1829 at which time your petitioner ceased to live with her as his wife. And your petitioner further avers that said Candis Midkiff, as will appear from the copy of the [Marriage] Records of the County Court and its affidavit of John Morrison hereto annexed . . . has since married

one John [*sic*] Hix. Wherefore your petitioner prays your Hon. Body will grant him a divorce a vinculo matrimonia. . . .
Nacogdoches, 28 Sept. 1839 Peter E. Bean[49]

Attached to Bean's petition was a certified copy by County Clerk Daniel Lacey of the marriage license and certificate of Mr. Isaac Hix and "Miss Candis Medkiff," dated November 3 and 7, 1837, respectively, and a statement that John C. Morrison made before Justice of the Peace Adolphus Sterne on the same day. He swore that "Candis Midkiff, the within mentioned woman who was married to Isaac Hix as herein specified, was the wife of Peter E. Bean, and that the said Bean has children by said Candis Midkiff which he acknowledges to be his—and further this deponent saith not."[50]

From this petition for divorce, we may be fairly certain that Bean regarded Candace's latest marriage with disgust and wanted to be legally quits with her because of it. He was content to live separately from her for years, but when she married Hix he would tolerate the situation no longer. And, despite all of his earlier denials to Mexican authorities, Bean here admits that he *was* married to Candace—and that it occurred in 1817, not 1818 as usually thought. Bean also gives the year of 1829 for when he broke off with Candace and "ceased to live with her as his wife." This, as noted, was the year that Bean acquired property on the Carrizo east of Nacogdoches and built a house and sawmill. Bean's 1839 divorce petition thus answers some questions about the marriage that Crocket, Blake, Lowrey, Lay, and other authorities have labored to solve with circumstantial evidence. None of them were aware that Bean filed for divorce and, in the process, solved the riddle himself.[51]

Meanwhile, to go back a bit, the Texas Senate had begun its deliberations on whether or not Houston's treaty with the Cherokees should be ratified. A committee composed of Isaac W. Burton of Nacogdoches, Sterling C. Robertson of the Milam District, and Gen. Thomas J. Green of San Antonio rendered its comprehensive report on October 12, 1837. It amounted to a discussion of all the tribes in Texas, their numbers, cultural habits, and places of residence.[52] Much of it seemed tailored to refute President Houston's pacific policy with these tribes, and with the Cherokees in particular.

The committee report called the Cherokees "the most savage and ruthless of our frontier Indians"—a shocking assessment, considering how Bowl and Big Mush had preserved the peace in east Texas for years. After reviewing the so-called claims that the Cherokees held to their land under the Mexican regime, the committee judged that no such rights had been conferred. Proof of this was the fact that the Mexican government had awarded these lands to Empresario David G. Burnet in 1826. Under the false assumption that the Cherokees held a valid entitlement from Mexico, the Consultation had been led to sustain their rights in 1835. It was a mistake, meaning that the Cherokees had no just claim to these lands from the Republic of Texas. Consequently, the three commissioners proposed a resolution that Houston's February 1836 treaty with Bowl's Cherokees be rejected.[53] The Senate, by a vote taken in a secret session on December 16, 1837, nullified the treaty.[54] Treaties with other tribes were to be negotiated on an individual basis, effectively isolating the Cherokees from their traditional role under Agent Bean.

Sam Houston, of course, was devastated by the vote (or so historians have said).[55] He had placed his reputation on the line with his Red Brothers, had promised them time and again that the treaty would be honored. What could he tell Bowl, now that "his" government had rejected the agreement? There would be no title for the Cherokees—just more excuses like they had received from Bustamante, Terán, Almonte, and a host of other government people through the years. Nothing had changed, except the culture that had spawned these lying men. When Colonel Bean got the news of Houston's defeat, a twisted smile must have played at his lips. Sam Houston had wanted to hog all the glory of dealing with the Cherokees, and now they would blame him for the results. How the mighty had fallen!

Chapter 18

ALIEN CITIZEN OF THE REPUBLIC

DURING 1838 PRES. SAM HOUSTON kept up his bold stance among the Cherokees with little benefit to them or himself. Why did Houston continue to fight a losing battle when most Texans —including some of his close political supporters—thought that the Senate had acted properly in rejecting his treaty with the Cherokees? The generous assessment of his motives (one subscribed to by most historians) says that Houston really cared about the fate of the Cherokees and acted out of the highest moral principles in defending them.[1] But there is a less generous explanation: he was playing a double game with the Cherokees from the start and was willing to promise Bowl the moon if it would keep his people from taking the Mexican side during the revolution. Now that the Republic of Texas was established, free and independent of Mexico, all Houston had to do was keep the Cherokees out of any combination with Mexican agents and disenchanted Tejanos around Nacogdoches. As usual, his bargaining chip was that the treaty would be honored and enforced—by him, personally, if necessary.

And there was much Mexican activity among Bowl's Indians in 1838, enough to test Houston's diplomatic mettle. The land offices reopened with a rush by speculators, ordinary settlers, and war veterans eager to register titles to land within the boundaries claimed by the Cherokees. Bowl became more disgruntled at Houston's inability to control the situation. All the president could do was make eloquent speeches to the Texas Senate, such as one delivered in May: "The Indian lands are forbidden fruit in the midst of the garden; their blooming peach trees, their snug cabins, their well-cultivated fields, and their lowing herds excite the speculators, whose cupidity, reckless of the consequences which would ensue to the country, by goading the Indians to desperation, are willing to hazard everything that is connected to the safety, prosperity, and honor of the country."[2] Stirring words, unless the senators happened to be involved in such speculation themselves. Some were, including Houston's own friends and supporters in the Senate or back home at Nacogdoches.

After learning that the Senate had rejected the treaty, Chief Bowl went to the capital to speak with his "friend" the president and find out what course should now be taken by his tribesmen. A conference was held, after which Sam Maverick told his wife that Bowl was heard saying that Sam Houston—now that he had become the "Great Father" of the whites—was no longer a Cherokee. And this after Bowl had made Houston a "big chief" among his people and given him his daughter for a wife. Regardless of the accuracy of this gossip, Bowl was discontented with the way things had worked out under the Raven's stewardship of an independent Texas. He had a right to be.[3]

Bowl, preparing for the worst, called on his Cherokee kinsmen in Indian Territory for assistance in defending tribal land rights in Texas. If they—along with the Creeks and Seminoles—beat the Texans, Bowl said that Gen. Vicente Filisola would give them possession of the entire territory. The Western Nation, however, was being swamped with Cherokee emigrants from the East. They decided not to involve themselves in a war with another nation (Texas) until their own situation was stabilized.[4]

This meant that Bowl was thrown back on promises of help from Mexican military men at Matamoros, and these were not lacking. As part of Mexico's projected reconquest of Texas, an alliance with the civilized tribes of the eastern region was envisioned. Working in conjunction with disaffected Mexican inhabitants of Nacogdoches, various Mexican generals hoped to bring a campaign to fruition: their troops would attack from the south, marching up the coastal corridor from Matamoros, while the friendly tribes would sweep down on the Texan settlements from the north in a pincer operation. As always, the Mexican scheme involved supplying the Indians with powder, lead, and tobacco. But more important, they would receive title to their lands once Mexican authority was reestablished in Texas. This promise was replayed like a broken record in the coming years—even after the Cherokees were expelled from Texas in 1839.

From the Mexican military perspective, one might assume that Col. Peter Ellis Bean was a logical candidate to serve as a go-between for the plans being hatched at Nacogdoches—not only with Bowl's Cherokees and their allied tribes, but with the renegade Tejanos and Anglos operating among them. One writer, Dianna Everett, has suggested that Bean was "in league with" the main conspirator, Vicente Córdova, when armed confrontation broke out that summer. Her basis was an undated Bean letter supposedly taken from the pouch of a Mexican officer slain on the Red River in August, a letter that this writer has been unable to find as cited.[5] As we shall see, there is no conclusive evidence that Bean was involved with Córdova in these troubles. It amounted to suspicion by some Anglos that he still sympathized with Mexican objectives and was, at heart, loyal to Mexico instead of the Republic of Texas. Also, Bean's name is nowhere mentioned in the Mexican documentation connected with these activities, either in his military service record or in the voluminous War Department files on the planning of the 1838 "campaign." If Bean had played any role on behalf of Mexico, or even been considered as a possible agent to expedite the uprising, it is likely that his services would have received favorable mention. They do not.

Since the revolution, the native inhabitants of Nacogdoches had undergone some harsh treatment by their Anglo neighbors. In September 1836 a petition was addressed to Congress by eighty-two "american citizens" calling for disenfranchisement of the Mexican population of the town. They had repeatedly refused to aid Texas in its struggle for independence and thereby forfeited their rights as citizens. To allow them to vote was a "dangerous principle," as well as a violation of the rights of "patriotick Citizens of the republick" who had engaged in the revolutionary struggle. The local Mexicans never had, remaining "unfrenly to our Cause" and always opposed to "the Independance of our Country."[6] Tensions between the two ethnic groups remained high, and the Tejanos could only look to leaders like Córdova for protection of their lives and property. The legal system—now dominated by Anglos—offered them no recourse, and their landholdings slipped away under a variety of pretexts as well as legitimate sales.

As alarm spread through the community that the local Mexicans in their frustration were stirring up the Indians, appeals were made to Congress in the spring of 1838 for a mobilized force to combat the uprising. Unsuccessful, the citizens then demanded that Congress raise and arm an "Independent Volunteer Corps, to be styled *The Nacogdoches Guards.*" Such a force was deemed necessary to protect the safety of the town "and the lives of our women and children" from the Indians and the Tejanos who were arousing them to bloody insurrection. Meanwhile, Vicente Córdova, Antonio Menchaca, and three other old residents wrote a letter to Houston in March asking his assurance that hostilities would no longer be directed against them by Anglos of the neighborhood, so they could "retire and attend to our private affairs." Rusk did not deliver this letter to Houston in a timely manner, according to Houston's note at the bottom.[7]

In May 1838 Capt. Pedro Julián Miracle was commissioned to march from Matamoros to east Texas with Córdova and meet with the various tribes concerning the forthcoming campaign. With a force of 138 men, composed of "citizens," former soldiers of La Bahía, and twenty Cherokee and Caddo Indians all poorly supplied, Miracle was instructed to work with Flores and other sympathizers in enlisting the support of these Indians. Talks with Bowl's Cherokees and representatives of other tribes took place on July 20. Córdova, who held a military commission from General Filisola as did Miracle, wrote to Flores about the meeting the day before. Córdova asked that he appear at the council with all the men available to him as a show of strength. Córdova told Flores to bring the pipe he had in his possession so that it could be smoked with the Cherokees "and other tribes, who have promised me to unite as soon as possible for action."[8]

Miracle had his first meeting with the Indians on July 8, but rain delayed any talks until the following day. Due to bad interpreters, nothing much was understood. Another council was called in ten days. Until then, Bowl shifted the Mexican agent from house to house so as to hide him. On July 15 a hungry Miracle registered his disgust: "I am in a great passion . . . because these cursed Indians are as lazy as the devil, and I am so much enraged [at them] that I wish the devil would seize me, body and soul." That day he was taken to another Cherokee house and fed some buttermilk, cheese, and cornbread, which made him feel better. But problems arose at the meeting on July 20. A Shawnee objected to beginning attacks on the whites until the Mexican army arrived, so it was agreed that the tribes would hold themselves "in readiness at a moment's warning." By including the Tejano rebels from Nacogdoches, Miracle exaggerated by saying "we have 540 men."[9]

After this council, Miracle moved northwest to confer with more tribes. He was killed in August by a former "prisoner" named Pineda near the Red River and the Cross Timbers. His diary and papers then came to the attention of the Texan government, leaving little doubt that agents of Mexico were engaged in a conspiracy with Houston's "pet Indians" to regain Texas.[10] Again, Bean is not mentioned in Miracle's diary or in any of the letters found on his body. Nor do Miracle's dilatory proceedings with Bowl's Cherokees and other tribes of the region above Nacogdoches indicate that Bean helped with the endeavor. Had Peter Ellis Bean been involved with organizing these councils, things would have moved along at a more rapid pace. By inference, if Bean was consulted at all, his private advice to Chief Bowl was that the Indians stay clear of Mexican attempts to foment rebellion against the whites.

On August 10 Córdova and eighteen other citizens of Nacogdoches—seemingly in response to a proclamation that President Houston had just issued—took the rash step of declaring open rebellion. Bean, of course, was not foolish enough to affix his signature to such a document, but a few Anglos (including old settler Nathaniel Norris) were. In his mid-fifties, Bean was too old to go charging around the countryside in some kind of war with his neighbors, even if he had been so inclined. He was not. Besides, Bean had too much property to risk losing it in a quixotic uprising such as Córdova and his compatriots swore to pursue with the Texans who were reducing them to second-class citizenship. "The citizens of Nacogdoches, tired of suffering injustices and the usurpation of their rights, cannot but state that having gathered together with their weapons in hand, they are determined to shed their last drop of blood in order to protect their individual rights and those of the [Mexican] Nation to which they belong. They confess, as they have in the past, that they have no knowledge of the current laws by which guarantees of their lives and property are offered. They ask only that their families not be molested, in return promising their good conduct toward yours."[11] To Bean, this must have sounded something like the manifesto that had launched the Edwardses' Fredonian Rebellion. He helped put that one down, but there is no evidence that he participated in this one on either side. Bean, however, did have access to the rebel encampment shortly after Córdova issued his proclamation and later testified as to what he saw on his visit. Joseph Durst gave similar testimony on a visit made to the camp with Chief Bowl. Durst also told Rusk that a battle seemed to be looming.

Thus Houston was confronted with the problem of keeping Bowl's Cherokees out of the Córdova Rebellion while at the same time acting decisively to ensure that the dissident Mexicans (Tejanos) were punished as traitors to his "Barnyard Republic." General Rusk, who was placed in charge of the military response, had no high regard for either Indians or Mexicans. He kept urging an encounter with Córdova's men in the Cherokee villages, while Houston was plastering their chiefs with assurances that Rusk would not attack them if they expelled these troublemakers and abided by the treaty. As the trouble escalated, Houston even appointed surveyors to mark the boundaries of their treaty lands that the Senate had rejected less than a year earlier. Elias Vansickle, while surveying around the Neches Saline, was captured by Córdova's Indian allies and held until the end of the year.[12]

One must wonder if this was not a calculated move on Houston's part to keep the Cherokees out of the rebellion. He knew, better than anyone, that this survey would never be upheld. And as Rusk approached the Angelina with his troops, Houston was telling him how to avoid a surprise attack by these sneaky Indians.[13] Imagine Houston's chagrin when Chief Bowl sent word that he would talk to no other white man than Col. Peter Ellis Bean! Bowl did not want to see Charles Sims, George May, Jeff Wright, Martin Lacy, or any of Houston's other agents for the tribe; he wanted Bean to tell him the truth about what General Rusk was doing with so many armed men close to his village. Rusk reported to Houston on August 14 that Bean was "the only one through whom communication[s] have been had with Bowles for several days."[14] On August 12 Houston urged Agent May to keep telling Big Mush how the Cherokee lands would be marked before the leaves fell "or I will give them my life or my land . . . I will never tell a Red Brother any thing but the truth." In a postscript he noted, significantly perhaps, "Our force now in the field is 600 and at least 500 on the march to join them."[15]

In a letter to Bowl two days later Houston made it clear that the Cherokees faced overwhelming odds if they contemplated any kind of opposition to his wishes or failed to separate themselves from Córdova's followers.

> My Bro When I wrote to you last I hoped that trouble would have ended. It has not been so— I am told the enemy are in your village— They must not stay in your country or it will make trouble — Two thousand men on Red River are ordered under arm and the United States and cannon on the Sabine are called from under the treaty [with Mexico] and will come— In ten days we will have more than one thousand men here, and I hope to the Great Spirit that my red Brothers will not make war nor join our enemies; for if they gain a little now they must soon lose all, and ruin will come upon them and their people.
>
> Remember your words spoken to me and my words to you shall stand for I lie not to my red Brothers. Be at peace and happy. Gen. Rusk says if you are peaceful that you shall not be hurt nor your people. Remember me and my words. We have not asked you to join us to make war but to remain at peace.[16]

General Rusk, shortly thereafter and contrary to Houston's orders, marched his militia across the Angelina and entered Bowl's village. Córdova's rebels had beat a hasty retreat but were spotted about two miles from the village. Rusk gave Chief Bowl a stern warning about how blood would flow the next time he found that the Cherokees were harboring the enemies of Texas.[17]

In the aftermath of the rebellion, charges of treason were brought against thirty-one Tejano "ringleaders" at Nacogdoches. Witnesses in the trial of eight of these individuals included Adolphus Sterne, Joseph Durst, and Peter Ellis Bean. The latter two testified that they had visited the Mexican encampment in the Cherokee Nation around August 11 or 12. Bean said that the military camp had about 140 men in it; none had arms in their hands, but he saw arms "setting against the trees in the encampment" and several men had "pistols in their belts." All of the prisoners at the bar, Antonio Menchaca among them, "did not appear to have been forced there, they mingled freely and cheerfully with the others at the camp; witness left the camp in a short time."[18] Colonel Bean's testimony tells us several things. He had access to Córdova's camp as the rebellion was forming, just after their manifesto had been issued. But his being called as a witness in the post-rebellion treason trials is a good indication that he was not implicated in the uprising and—more important—was not a suspect himself.

So Sam Houston had finally come full circle with the Indians he always professed to cherish as Red Brothers. Bowl was perceptive enough to understand that Houston—despite his comforting words—would employ naked force against the Cherokees if deemed necessary. He probably guessed that Houston's surveying team was a ruse to keep Big Mush's villagers quiet and that the running of imaginary lines would guarantee nothing to his people. If Bowl learned of Houston's overtures to other tribes, such as the Shawnees, Delawares, Kickapoos, and Alabama-Coushattas at this time, he could not have understood it as anything other than an attempt by Houston to displace the Cherokees from their traditional role as mediators for these Indian allies.[19] Had not Houston recognized Bowl as the representative for these tribes in his February 1836 treaty? And styled him as a "General of all friendly tribes" as recently as January 1837? Yes, he had, but now the Cherokees were being swept aside by Houston, just as Bean had been discarded.[20]

Vicente Córdova wisely decided to withdraw from the hornet's nest he had stirred up in the vicinity of Nacogdoches and operate against more remote Anglo settlements farther north. On October 5 Córdova and a force of warriors from several tribes massacred thirty Neches Saline settlers, including eighteen members of the Killough family at their settlement inside the Cherokee claim. Other such attacks brought Rusk into the field again, and he—acting on Big Mush's tip—led his two hundred men into a battle at the Kickapoo village. Arrayed against Rusk on October 16 were Mexicans, Kickapoos, Caddos, Coushattas, and Keechis. At least one Cherokee, a warrior named Tail, was among the eleven casualties that Rusk inflicted on the Indians. When advised of this, the Cherokee leadership said that Tail was a worthless fellow who would not listen to wise advice and deserved his fate.[21]

In November Rusk confronted and disarmed Caddos living on an island nestled in a loop of the Red River near Shreveport, Louisiana, almost creating a diplomatic furor between the U.S. State Department and the Republic of Texas. Robert A. Irion, Sam Houston's secretary of state and a close friend, justified Rusk's conduct because tribal members in Texas were notorious enemies and "their perfidious actions present a continuous catalogue of depredations on the most exposed and defenseless settlements of the country." Their kinsmen still on the U.S. side of the boundary were probably supplying them with weapons and ammunition for these depredations. Hence Rusk's confiscation. Many Caddos, after selling their lands to the U.S. government in 1835, had moved to Texas without Mexican consent. Irion, writing the republic's minister in Washington on November 29, 1838, said that the president wanted measures taken to expel the entire Caddo Nation from Texas.[22]

To mollify the Cherokees, it is said, Houston then ordered Alexander Horton to complete a survey of the Cherokee lands. Houston had earlier urged Rusk to run the lines, saying if it was not done "there will be another runaway scrape and Eastern Texas will be desolated."[23] To prevent trouble such as the abduction of Elias Vansickle, Bowl gave Horton's crew an escort of twenty-five Cherokees. They stayed in the field during Rusk's campaign and finished the survey in less than a month. Horton reported that he had to constantly assure Bowl that his people would not be attacked by the whites. At the completion of the job, Bowl seemed satisfied that the Cherokee property lines had been laid out. How could he not be? At last he had from President Houston's authorized representative, Surveyor Horton, words on paper that the Mexicans had never given him. Bowl could only hope that the demarcation, now being an accomplished fact, would lead the Texas Senate to acknowledge its legitimacy on the second time around. If so, he was mistaken. The September 1838 election of Mirabeau B. Lamar as Houston's successor (he took office in December) doomed any chance the Cherokees had of remaining in Texas, much less owning any land.[24]

Houston's recent biographer James L. Haley puts a rather benevolent spin on these events, saying that Houston could not afford to have a war with Bowl's Cherokees in east Texas, and he was not "flailing in any romantic miasma about his hearty red yeomen" when writing reassuring letters to their chiefs. Haley sums up the situation Houston faced with these words: "He was still trying to convince natives to yield to white authority while also trying to guarantee native rights under that white authority, all the while trying to keep undisciplined, Indian-hating, land-hungry whites at arm's length. In sum, he tried to procure some semblance of justice for all concerned."[25] Perhaps so, but Thomas Rusk and most of the upstanding Texan citizens who rode with him would not have taken kindly to Haley's assessment of them or their motives. And the fact remains that very little "justice" was procured for the Cherokees by virtue of Houston's words and/or actions in 1838. In their view, "justice" meant a title to their lands.

In November Houston, with only a short time left as head of state, returned to the seat of government and urged the new Congress to ratify his treaty with the Cherokees. He admitted that he had run the boundary line as specified by the 1836 treaty, even though the Senate had declared it null and void. Why? Because "If ever prompt action has been necessary for the salvation of Texas, it is necessary at this time to tranquilize and conciliate the tribes yet friendly on our northern frontier." He argued that the system being pursued by speculators to locate and survey their tracts within the Cherokee claim was responsible for the "calamities" of the region.[26] As Houston biographer Marshall De Bruhl says, "His sincerity cannot be questioned, but his timing can." De Bruhl wonders why Houston did not return to the capital at the beginning of the congressional session to push his Cherokee agenda, instead of waiting until three weeks before his term of office ended. It is a legitimate question that casts doubt not only on Houston's timing but his sincerity.[27]

President Lamar, with David G. Burnet as his vice president, made his policy on the Cherokees quite clear as soon as he took office. He intended to exterminate or remove them from Texas, the sooner the better. Other tribes native to the United States also belonged in Indian Territory, and Lamar planned to mark the boundaries of the republic with a sword. Events soon played into his hands.

There is little doubt that Colonel Bean kept up his contact with the Cherokees as this storm was brewing. On May 2 he was in the "Charoque Nation" with his friend Indian Agent Martin Lacy. Together they drew up a statement by an Indian namesake of the colonel's, Little Bean, whereby he granted freedom to two of his slaves, Billa and Mima. For eleven hundred dollars paid in hand to him by Billa and Mima, Little Bean declared that from now on they were to be "ther own oners." The document was witnessed by Bean, Lacy, and Chief Bowl. In terms of his civil status under the republic, Bean was called as a juror for the April term of court at Nacogdoches. He was excused because of his absence, possibly on the trip with Lacy to the Cherokees. Bean was noted as then living at Bean's Prairie, just west of the Angelina, actively engaged with his private affairs. He also took an oath as a land commissioner for the Nacogdoches District in this year. Whether he served is uncertain.[28]

At the end of May 1839, J. S. Thorn wrote General Rusk on behalf of Chief Bowl, saying that—despite Bean being away—Bowl was willing to undergo alone "the hardship" of visiting and treating with "those wild tribes as they are very anxious to become friendly."[29] This suggests that Thomas Rusk at Nacogdoches enlisted Bean's services as a peacemaker among the frontier tribes, even if Sam Houston and Mirabeau Lamar had appointed other men to do the job. It also suggests that Colonel Bean—despite his Mexican military commission—was willing to help the Republic of Texas maintain friendly relations with the very tribes that Mexico was trying to enlist as auxiliaries in a campaign against Texas. If an incriminating letter by Bean had been taken off the body of Mexican agent Miracle the previous August, it is highly unlikely that Bean would have been trusted to work among these tribes at all. Especially not by President Lamar and Vice President Burnet, as suspicious as they were of Indians and "Mexicans" in their midst. Rusk was of like mind.

Although military command of the Eastern Interior States changed frequently at Matamoros following the Texas Revolution, one idea did not change. It was the abiding desire to enlist the aid of the friendly tribes of east Texas in the projected reconquest of the department in rebellion against Mexico, a department that had boldly declared itself an independent nation. Mexico chose not to regard Texas as such, so plans went ahead to use the Indians as auxiliaries in the continuing struggle. Gen. Valentín Canalizo renewed this conspiratorial plot in the spring of 1839. His agent Vicente Córdova had been driven from east Texas, but he was still active between the San Antonio River and the Rio Grande. It appears that he also maintained contact with Bowl's Cherokees and the chiefs of other tribes above Nacogdoches. Manuel Flores, however, was the agent chosen by General Canalizo in February to hold talks with these Indians. Córdova was to arrange the meeting and follow Flores's instructions for uniting them to Mexico's interests in the campaign.[30]

Flores began his journey north in March with an escort of thirteen Mexican militiamen and eleven Indian auxiliaries. He bore Canalizo's letters to the chiefs of the Caddo, Kickapoo, Shawnee, and other tribes, as well as to Chiefs Bowl and Big Mush of the Cherokees. Flores stupidly committed some depredations in the neighborhood of Seguin, which put a group of rangers on his trail. They tracked him to the San Gabriel River, north of present Austin, where an engagement took place on May 17. Flores's men were routed in the attack, and some thought that he was among those slain. According to a later item in the *Colorado Gazette,* however, "the person supposed to have been Flores was only the commander of a small party who had the papers and baggage of Flores in charge."[31] No matter. With the capture of these Mexican commissions and related correspondence, President Lamar had the evidence he needed to expel the Cherokees from Texas.

Was Colonel Bean implicated in this latest Mexican attempt to rouse the Indians against the Anglo settlements? Once again, the answer is no. All of the correspondence taken from Flores's party—as well as that taken the year before when Miracle was killed—was translated and published in the U.S. Senate's *Executive Document 14.* Also in this report are the letters that Texas officials wrote about the Indian problem on the frontier with the United States and how Mexico was inciting them to savage warfare. Replies from the U.S. State Department and responses from the Mexican Legation are likewise included. Yet, not a single document from this thick file talks about Bean as an instigator. There is no letter from Bean that suggests he was "in league" with Córdova, nor a letter that mentions him at all.[32]

The story of Lamar's summer campaign against the Cherokees is so well known that it need not be told again here in great detail.[33] In summary, after the captured documents came to his attention, Lamar wrote Bowl that he would not tolerate his tribesmen living as a nation within a nation. The Cherokees had to leave Texas, "peaceably if they would; forcibly if they must."[34] He placed Gen. Thomas Rusk, already well known for his militant hostility toward Indians and now no great admirer of Sam Houston, in charge of his army of expulsion. After a series of fruitless councils with Bowl, who was playing for time, Rusk entered his village to find the Cherokees already gone. Rusk's troops pursued and engaged the Indian rear guard in several skirmishes. On July 16 a decisive battle was fought with the Cherokees and their Shawnee, Delaware, and Kickapoo allies. Bowl, eighty-three years old and virtually alone on the field at the end of the battle, was murdered and his body mutilated. Big Mush and an estimated one hundred warriors were also battle casualties. The survivors split up and made their way north toward the Red River. Rusk and his men returned laden with spoils.[35]

The greatest spoil of victory, of course, was the fertile territory claimed by the Cherokees. With the Indians driven from these lands, the whites no longer had to worry about a possible dispute of title clouding their own surveys. Rusk's fellow commissioners in his councils with Chief Bowl included several men with vested interests. One was Isaac Burton, the committee chairman who had recommended that Houston's treaty be rejected by the Senate in 1837. Another was Vice President Burnet, and the Cherokee lands about to be conquered were within his empresarial grant that still appeared on Texas maps. Burnet had reminded Bowl that Texas was "ours," by right of conquest from Mexico, yet the Cherokees persisted in harboring the enemies of Texas in their villages. Rusk simply pointed out to the chiefs that the Cherokees were caught "between two fires" and would be destroyed if they did not place their marks on the proffered treaty and go.[36]

When Lamar had ordered troops to occupy the Neches Saline earlier in the year, Bowl threatened resistance. Chief Bowl had an arrangement with a Mr. Debard (probably Elijah DeBard/Debard, of whom we shall hear more) to work the saline, even before the massacre of the Killough family nearby in October 1838. Maj. Baley C. Walters withdrew his small force to await further instructions from Lamar, who was greatly aggravated that the Cherokees would presume to defend this valuable source of salt that belonged to the Republic of Texas.[37] It will be recalled that Sam Houston, as president of the infant nation, had ordered Martin Lacy to take possession of this saline in September 1836. Interestingly, Lacy was chosen by Lamar to deliver his eviction notice to Bowl before the war broke out. He was still an agent to the Cherokees, Shawnees, and other emigrant tribes from the United States, even though Lamar had specified in his commission that their "claim to territory or even occupancy, has not yet been recognized, and is now the subject of grave deliberation on the part of the Texian Government."[38]

As we have seen, Lacy was a close acquaintance of Bean's, and their leagues east of the Neches adjoined one another—Lacy's lying to the north and east while Bean's was below it, squarely on the Old San Antonio Road.[39] Their relationship was further cemented on January 11, 1841, when Bean's daughter Louisa Jane married Martin's son William Young Lacy. He remembered Bean affectionately in later years, and old-timers recalled how he had loved to talk about the "ups and downs" of his father-in-law.[40] While many men—including Archibald Hotchkiss and Frost Thorn—claimed ownership to the saline as time went by, so did the Republic of Texas. Others came and went to lease the operation (Debard among them), but it usually had to be with Chief Bowl's say-so. To him, this saline belonged to the Cherokees, as promised by Houston's treaty, and the ratification technicality did not matter. The treaty was garnished with ribbons and a seal as proof of its validity and bore the unmistakable flourish of Sam Houston. In the eyes of the Cherokees, if such a document had no meaning then nothing did.

Accompanying Martin Lacy on the ultimatum-delivery chore was a young man named John H. Reagan. He lived a long and distinguished life in Texas and is responsible for a surprisingly truthful memoir on the Cherokee War and the death of Chief Bowl. It was published in 1897, in the first volume of the *Quarterly of the Texas State Historical Association.* In response to a query on Bean's sympathies during the revolution, Reagan also wrote a letter that was published in a 1902 issue of the same journal, volume six.[41] It is of interest here because it mentions Bean's memoir, later published by Henderson K. Yoakum. Reagan said he first became acquainted with Bean in the summer of 1839—the same summer that the Cherokees were driven from Texas. Bean, at the time, was living in what was then Nacogdoches (but now Cherokee) County "near where the town of Alto stands." Reagan said he "knew him well from that time until he left Texas [in 1843] to return to the Mexican Republic. . . . Soon after I became acquainted with Colonel Bean he showed me his autobiography, and we read it together—a fair sized volume in manuscript. He requested me to edit and publish it. This I was in no condition to do. Afterwards he requested me to go to Mexico for him, and take letters to the government officials, complaining of their leaving him in prison so long, and demanding the payment to him of about twenty thousand dollars, which he said was due him from the government for his services, and also to take letters to his wife at Jalapa. This I declined to do."[42]

From this we know that Peter Ellis Bean still possessed his memoir in 1839, despite remarks that historian John Henry Brown made about Bean in an 1853 issue of *DeBow's Review,* published in New Orleans. Brown claimed that Bean, after his return to the United States from Mexico, had visited his Tennessee relatives for a short time in 1817 "where he wrote out a detailed history of his singular career, and left it with his half brothers, by whose kindness we were allowed, several years ago, to read it several times, and, from memory, have sketched the foregoing account [of Bean's life]."[43] When his *History of Texas* was published in 1892, Brown gave further information on Bean's autobiography, which he called "a collection of imperfect notes jotted down by him while temporarily sojourning on Red River, near Natchitoches, in 1817, and left among his kindred [in Tennessee?]. The author of this [present] work, in 1846, had possession for some time of this manuscript, the same from which Yoakum afterward wrote his sketch of Bean. Bean's illiteracy, as regards the English language, rendered the narrative, as prepared by him, difficult to understand. In Spanish he was far more proficient, and subsequent associations with the Americans, both in Mexico and Texas, greatly improved his knowledge of English."[44]

Henderson Yoakum not only gave an account of Philip Nolan's activities in Texas based on Bean's memoir but published the memoir itself in his 1855 *History of Texas.* Where did Yoakum obtain his copy of the manuscript? Probably through Bean's eldest son Isaac, and Bean must have left it behind when he headed to Mexico in 1843. Was this the only copy of Bean's memoir? Perhaps not. Yoakum tracked down Bean's half brother in White County, Tennessee, Capt. William Shaw, and got some documents from him. One he cited as Shaw's manuscript "Memoirs," giving it as his authority for saying that Bean reached the captain's residence in the spring of 1818. "After remaining here for some time, he formed a matrimonial alliance with the daughter of Isaac Midkiff." (But Bean, in his divorce petition, said that he married Candace in 1817.) They left together for Smackover Creek in Arkansas. For three years they settled and raised stock at this location without a neighbor for thirty miles, at which time Bean's father-in-law died. Bean, learning that Mexico had gained its independence, thus decided to move to Texas. Yoakum's information came from Captain Shaw.[45]

Yoakum says Bean's memoir was "written by himself, about the year 1816," that is, prior to his visit to his half brother's place in Tennessee. This is at odds with Brown's statement, which says that Bean wrote his memoir while among his half brother*s* in Tennessee, through whose kindness Brown was allowed to read the manuscript and commit it to memory. He declared it to be the same memoir that Yoakum had published in 1855. Were there variant copies, one left with William Shaw and another that Bean still had in his hands when Reagan met him in 1839? Besides Shaw's own "Memoir" Yoakum collected other Bean material, such as the "notebook" of Bean's 1825–26 trip to Mexico, which he quoted and cited on several occasions. In an introductory note to Bean's memoir, Editor Yoakum says, "In publishing this memoir, it is proper to state that Colonel Bean was but poorly educated, and his long residence in Mexico had caused him almost to forget his own language. Hence it has become necessary to correct his manuscript, and to rewrite it. In doing this, great care has been taken to preserve, as far as possible, his style and language."[46]

As Flora Lowrey has observed, we cannot tell how diligently Yoakum pursued his editorial mandate: "The extent to which Yoakum inserted new material or expurgated Bean's narrative is impossible now to determine."[47] If Yoakum culled any steamy sexual references from the manuscript, or placed Bean's remarks about the Mexican *señoritas* who fell at his feet in more "proper" form, he would not have been the first nineteenth-century editor to do so. (Editors continued this censorship policy into the twentieth century, the Mexican War "Confession" of Sam Chamberlain being an example.) There is a high-toned morality concerning women in the narrative that one suspects was not Bean's. He, after all, was a man soon to have two wives. But because Bean's original is lost, or has yet to surface, we may never be able to judge the extent of Yoakum's alterations.[48]

That Yoakum was loaned the original he worked from by Bean's son Isaac is strongly suggested by a letter he wrote the author a year after Yoakum's *History of Texas* saw publication. In this letter Isaac said that he was still waiting to receive the promised copy of Yoakum's book. He noted that it had received some critical acclaim and asked about the royalties he was supposed to get for letting Yoakum use his father's manuscript. It may be that Yoakum had intended to publish Bean's memoir as a booklet of its own (promising Isaac to do so), instead of using it as an appendix in his two-volume history. Isaac wanted Yoakum to return the original, as he had been approached about selling it but was unsure how much to ask. What did Yoakum think it was worth? Then Isaac confessed, "I do not want to sell it." He chided Yoakum for getting his father's name wrong on the memoir. It was P. E. Bean, not Ellis P. Bean: "I think that should be Rectified." It is unknown if Yoakum ever returned Bean's original manuscript to the family. He, however, must have returned the watercolor on ivory of Colonel Bean—the basis for his engraving—because this portrait is still in family hands.[49]

Colonel Bean's thoughts about Lamar's campaign against the Cherokees went unrecorded. His young friend John Reagan was there and begged Capt. Robert Smith not to kill old Chief Bowl, who was wounded, on the ground, and unable to resist. Smith ignored Reagan, put a pistol to Bowl's head, and blew his brains out. The Cherokee chief, Sam Houston's beloved Red Brother, was then scalped and straps of skin cut from his back to make bridle reins for the horses of some Anglo volunteer's children. It was a barbaric deed, unworthy of civilized men, but was excused because the Cherokees had supposedly killed Smith's father-in-law, Jesse Watkins. Still, it is evident from Reagan's 1897 article on the expulsion of the Cherokees (a letter written to his children in 1865) that he believed a great injustice was done to these Indians in the summer of 1839.[50]

Sam Houston felt likewise, even though he had chosen to absent himself from Texas as the plight of the Cherokees reached its climax. Did he know what was coming and—aware that he was powerless to prevent it—pick the first half of 1839 to "get out of town"? Did a well-deserved vacation, now that Houston's term of office was over, become extended because of what he was reading in Texas newspapers? Regardless of the explanation, Sam Houston distanced himself from the events transpiring with the Texas Cherokees. Upon his return to Nacogdoches, however, he scalded the residents with a speech about the unjust war—and how Bowl was a better man than his murderers—that turned many former friends against him. These included Adolphus Sterne and Henry Raguet. His relationship with Thomas Rusk (none too good because of events with the Cherokees the previous year) never fully recovered, even though they served together as Texas' first senators to the U.S. Congress after annexation.[51]

Houston continued to deepen these rifts when he went to the Texas House as a representative from San Augustine later that year. Early in December he gave an impassioned two-day speech, scorching the Lamar administration for defrauding the people of east Texas in the location of the new capital and trying to profit as a "*speculator*" in the sale of town lots. His remarks extended to the unjust war against the Cherokees, and he rose to a defense of their claims to Texas lands. Their title, Houston argued, predated Burnet's empresarial contract, and he would introduce documents to prove it. The Cherokees, instead of being "intruders," had come at the invitation of Mexican authorities as far back as Governor Trespalacios. If their title was worthless, then so were others issued under the same authority. As to the republic's conduct toward the Cherokees, Houston raged that they "had been treated with duplicity and fraud; that the government had acted towards them in bad faith, and that the Cherokees had been driven *unjustifiably,* from their country and their homes." Previous to the adjournment of Congress, Houston promised to put this issue in "the right place—*where it should stick like a blister.*"[52]

On December 22 Houston followed up with another tirade on his Cherokee Land Bill. The issue before Congress was whether to carve the

Cherokee lands into 640-acre sections and sell them to the benefit of the public treasury or allow speculators to locate scripts they already held on these lands, as many had intentions of doing. Some had pushed their surveys into these lands even before the war, which Houston said was largely responsible for Indian resistance. In making these charges, Houston resurrected the activities of Archibald Hotchkiss. He had earlier tried to bring twenty-four thousand hostile Creeks to Texas but failed in the attempt. Now he (or possibly his kinsman Augustus who resided in San Augustine and was also a land merchant) was loudly denouncing Cherokee rights because he would profit handsomely if permitted to locate his scripts on their former lands. This would happen, said Houston, if his Land Bill failed. In lawyerly fashion he built his case, interjecting emotional outbursts such as "now forsooth, they must be cheated out of their rights while others were crying out *land! land! give me more land!!!*"[53]

In 1840 Houston returned to Texas from another trip with a very respectable young bride on his arm, Margaret Lea of Alabama. None of Houston's friends expected the marriage to last, but they admired him for making the effort. In September he was returned to Congress, where he continued his assault on Lamar's Indian policy and other crackpot schemes that had left the republic near bankruptcy. In December he tried to renew his Cherokee Land Bill of the year before. The measure had passed "by almost an unanimous vote," Houston said, and was vetoed by Lamar, then made law by an override of his veto. But the question was far from settled. There was the debate on appropriations to put the law into effect, along with amendments that various members proposed to sidetrack the issue. David S. Kaufman, for example, wanted to appropriate over a million dollars "as a remuneration to settlers, and such [individuals] as hold claims in that part of the country." Houston argued valiantly against these speculator windfall schemes, giving another eloquent speech but to no avail. The House-Senate Conference Committee killed the bill.[54]

This antipathy continued in the next presidential election, when Houston called Burnet a hog thief because he had confiscated and driven off a herd of Cherokee swine once the fighting was over. Burnet branded Houston as a drunk (which he assuredly was, though Margaret was trying to redeem him) and an Indian lover to boot. Houston nonetheless trounced his opponent in the September 1841 election. He reversed Lamar's Indian extermination policy and sought to quiet the frontier by giving gifts and making treaties with various tribes.[55]

Given Houston's harsh invectives and rousing speeches on behalf of the Cherokees at the end of the Lamar-Burnet administration, one wonders why he took such an unpopular political position. Houston must have known that he was making many more enemies than friends in this process, not just with his political opponents (and supporters) but with the general populace as well—voters in the coming election. The Cherokees were driven from Texas and few white people wanted them back; nor did Texans think that the government owed them anything for what had been won by conquest. If Sam Houston was guilty of duplicity in his dealings with the Cherokees, as has been suggested elsewhere in this study, then why did he rise to their defense so eloquently and determinedly once their expulsion was an accomplished fact? And keep at it throughout his life, even when he was arguing Indian policy in the halls of the U.S. Congress as a senator from Texas?

This is admittedly puzzling, as it suggests that Houston was a genuine friend of Bowl's Cherokees without intentions of cheating them. But he was also very concerned about how his actions would look to future generations, to History. This was a trait that Sam Houston displayed on numerous occasions, such as who was responsible for the disaster at the Alamo and who was due credit for the victory at San Jacinto. In speeches on the latter subject, he alienated many former comrades—seemingly without regard for their feelings or their actual contribution. Houston was his own "spin doctor" and labored prodigiously to ensure his historical legacy.[56] This may have been the case with his speeches on the Cherokees in 1839 and 1840: Houston going "on record" to cover himself and put the blame elsewhere. Nor did it cost him as many ballots as one might suppose. He got 7,508 votes to Burnet's paltry 2,574. If nothing else, the speeches Houston made to Congress are evidence of his powerful oratorical skills. Even battling for a lost cause, no one could beat Sam Houston on his feet before an audience, hostile or otherwise.

Very little is heard from Colonel Bean in these years. Reagan says that he "lived on terms of amity with his neighbors, apparently as much as any other Texan." There is some irony to this statement, as Texans of the day were continually fussing, fighting, and killing one another in secret vendettas or open feuds—the 1839–42 Regulator-Moderator War in east Texas being an example. Two of his children were grown, and the third a large boy. Tax lists for Nacogdoches County of the period 1839–41 show that Bean was holding his own. In 1839 he had (or declared) 5,428 acres of land valued at $9,428; seven slaves valued at $2,350; eight horses valued at $225; one hundred cows valued at $975; and fifty hogs valued at $225. This (with $40 miscellaneous property) came to a total evaluation of $13,243, his taxes being $66.21. Sales of land—summarized below—and livestock reduced Bean's taxes to $43.75 in 1840. He was not a rich man but was far from being poor.[57]

At the end of 1838 Bean began the complicated process of selling his plantation four miles east of town that Sam Houston had failed to acquire. He started by reaching a settlement with Vital Flores and the widow of

Encarnación Chirino on land that he had been occupying but that belonged to the Chirino estate. Uriah Cummings was mentioned as Bean's tenant at the time.[58] This dispute settled, a series of sales commenced that lasted until 1845—all involving the "Bean tract" that he had purchased from Flores. Some of these sales stuck but others were bought back and resold for a higher price. As land-hungry settlers swarmed into the region, Bean eventually topped the sky-high price that Houston had agreed to pay in 1836.

David Muckleroy bought two tracts of 640 and 697 acres in December 1838, paying $1,100 and $1,198 for a total of $2,298. Bean sold 1,345 acres in April 1840 to William Long for $4,035. Something must have gone amiss with this sale because in November 1842 Bean and his son-in-law William Young Lacy bought the land back from Long for $3,310, except for 100 acres that he had sold to one Draper in the meantime. Less than a month later Bean and Lacy resold the 1,245 acres to John Graham for $3,500. In November 1840 Radford Berry bought 100 acres in the Flores tract, paying Bean $150. March 1841 saw Bean posting a $2,000 bond to William Arnold and David Woods involving a complicated deal with their headrights of 640 acres each. Bean, for locating their claims next to the land sold to Berry (south of the road), would get 225 acres of land once they received title. Had he known about these profitable sales of "his" plantation, Sam Houston could not have been happy.[59]

Just before the Cherokee War, on April 4, 1839, Bean appeared before the Board of Commissioners at Nacogdoches and applied for a league and labor of land as a citizen of the Republic of Texas. His oath (quoted earlier) is dated the day before. He said he was a man with family who had been in Texas prior to the revolution and was thus entitled to receive a headright. The commissioners, including Charles S. Taylor, issued him certificate no. 690. In other words, Bean's application was approved, as witnessed by Adolphus Sterne and John Roark. They were old residents who knew of Bean's Tory past and the fact that he had already received several leagues under Mexican law. But they gave him another one anyway, something they perhaps shouldn't have done. Bean had already staked out the land he wanted, because the survey notes by Isaac W. Burton are dated August 1, 1838. At the top a notation reads, "About 9½ miles N from Buffalo." This first-class headright lies in modern Kaufman County just west of the town of Kemp, later described as about seven miles from the Trinity River. King's Creek, a tributary of larger Cedar Creek, runs through the survey.[60]

Later in 1839 Bean decided it was time to collect on what the Republic of Texas owed him for provisioning various military companies in the summer of 1836. He assembled his vouchers and gave David S. Kaufman his power of attorney in September to go to Austin and receive payment of $166 due him. Kaufman had been wounded in the battle with Bowl's Cherokees a few months earlier (Kaufman County was later named for him). Bean gave him an affidavit saying that his expenses were "just, true and original, that he owes the Government nothing on his own account nor on account of any other person, that he has not retained, sold nor embezzled any arms or munitions of war or any other property belonging to said Republic." Kaufman was Speaker of the House of Representatives and one of Houston's opponents in the debate on the Cherokee Land Bill, probably too busy to handle Bean's vouchers. On November 17, 1839, Bean gave another man, K. H. Muse, his power of attorney to attend to this business at the state capital. His claims were paid as submitted.[61]

It was at this time that Bean filed his petition for divorce from Candace Midkiff, mentioned earlier. Mr. Muse presented it to the House on December 5, 1839, but it was tabled on motion of Mr. Jack. Judging from the notation on the petition ("Dec. 5th. Ordered to lie on table."), the matter was not resurrected in subsequent sessions of Congress. But Bean had made his point: Candace married Isaac Hix while lawfully married to him, and children were involved. If he was a bigamist, then so was she. Perhaps Bean did not pursue the matter lest charges be brought against her for such an offense. In any case, Candace continued to use the name Hicks instead of Bean.[62]

Peter Ellis Bean remained a respected citizen of east Texas, as evidenced by entries that Adolphus Sterne made in his diary in 1841:

> *Tuesday the 1st June* fine weather, left home for Crockett, to Col Bean's 28 miles— good fare, an old friend of 15 years standing [i.e., since 1826, when Sterne was involved with the Fredonian Rebellion and only got out of trouble because of his Masonic connections]— spent a pleasant Evening with him, talked over Auld lang sine—
>
> *Wednesday June 2d* fine weather, left Col Bean's early in the morning traveled slow to Jacob Master's, an other old friend of 13 years standing, this day is the 13th anniversary of my marriage to my dear wife—
>
> *Wednesday the 18th [of August]* warm & sultry— had a Storm in the afternoon but no rain— Town perfectly healthy, brought up my magistrate Dockett, wrote to Col Bean—
>
> *Monday the 20th [of September]* sultry weather— was very sick all night, left sick this mornings to Debards where I staid till 2 p.m.

> felt well enough to come on to Col Bean's where we staid all night—
>
> *Tuesday the 21st* very sultry weather last night left early this morning to Jno Durst to Breakfast, rained for about two Hours very hard, wind changed suddenly to the North arrived at home [Nacogdoches] at 3 p.m. found all well. . . .
>
> *Monday the 13th [of November 1843]* Cold, windy and occasionally cloudy— all day at Rusk's office interpreting [for and] examining witnesses in the case of John Smith vs watkins & others, did not sleep last night my Bile hurting me so much, opened it this morning, feel relieved, heard of the Death of Mrs Y. W. [W. Y.] Lacy, a Daughter of Col P. E. Bean—

The last entry in Sterne's diary mentioning Bean comes on January 4, 1844, after he had left Texas for a milder climate. The entry indicates that Bean's title to lands in the coastal reserve was being disputed, and his old business associate Frost Thorn was having to defend it against the Republic of Texas:

> *Sunday the 4th* wind changed last night and this morning it is clear and cold, it is getting colder every hour, and near dark it was *winter again,* answered some Interrogatories send [sent] from Liberty County in a case in which Frost Thorn and others are plaintiffs and the Republic of Texas Defendant. it is respecting some Leagues of Land the State of Coahuila & Texas made to Col P. E. Bean—[63]

This was no doubt the five and three-quarter leagues that Carvajal had surveyed on Trinity Bay as part of the eight that Bean had purchased from the state of Coahuila y Texas. It was nullified by the General Land Office of the Republic of Texas: coastal reserve lands. If his purchases of eleven-league grants from Mexican citizens like Gavino Aranjo were invalidated, it was mostly because of where Bean and Thorn had located them. They, of course, were not the only ones to suffer from the republic's land policy in this regard. Big speculators were sometimes able to win these legal battles. If not, they filed claims with the U.S. government after the Mexican War that often allowed them to recover huge settlements of their "investments" in lands that, for one reason or another, they had lost because Mexico had forbade them to colonize these lands. Since these sums were subtracted from what the United States had to pay Mexico under the terms of the Treaty of Guadalupe Hidalgo, government officials could have cared less if their citizens got the money instead of the Mexican government. Thus speculators like James Prentiss and his Galveston Bay & Texas Land Company friends grew even richer than they already were.[64]

Peter Ellis Bean was not playing in this league, but Frost Thorn was and became a millionaire. Of all the thousands of acres of land that Bean once held in Texas, most had already been sold. Just as well for him, as the Republic of Texas voided his leagues on the Red River and on Trinity Bay that had been acquired from the government of Coahuila y Texas. His Neches Saline League in Smith County and the "settler" league below the Neches in Houston County were upheld, but Bean had long since parted with them. Upheld also was his original league below Alto on the Old San Antonio Road, but—from tax rolls—it does not appear that he still owned any of it. About all that Bean emerged with out of this era was the thousand acres from Durst and his headright league and labor up near the Trinity in Kaufman County. This totaled 5,428 acres, the same figure as reported on tax rolls at the end of the decade. But money had flowed into his pockets through land deals before the bubble burst, and it had been good while it lasted.[65]

Bean, as he had for many years, still tried to fulfill his public duties as a citizen of Texas and be a good friend to his neighbors. In July 1842 he, along with James Durst and Joseph Lewis, agreed to be securities for the estate of Thomas H. Luckett. He was another old-timer who had participated in the Mexican Revolution—seeing action at the Battle of Medina in 1813 and survived to tell the tale. Luckett acted as Zavala's agent and negotiated the sale of his empresarial contract to Anthony Dey (one of the principals of the Galveston Bay & Texas Land Company). Even though this was the grant that Bean had hoped to acquire colonization rights for, it appears that he was willing to let bygones be bygones with Thomas Luckett. The extent of their relationship in Texas, prior to the death of Luckett, is unknown.[66]

Bean, Durst, and Lewis pledged fourteen thousand dollars on behalf of Thomas's widow, Matilda, so she could administer the estate.[67] But now Bean's physical condition limited his ability to get around, as he informed Judge William Hart on November 12, 1842. His friend and sometime legal representative Thomas Rusk probably wrote the letter to which Bean affixed a "cramped and tortured" signature, unlike his distinctive flourish of earlier years.

> My Dear Sir: Mrs. Luckett has called to see me and ask me to be one of her securities on her Bond given to you as administratric on the Estate of her husband. I will be one of the securities and I hereby

empower you to sign my name or, if that will not do, I will come in town on the first warm day and sign it myself. Or if you will let Genl. Rusk bring the bond to me as he goes out to Crockett Court I will sign it and let him take it in again to you. I am crippled and can't come in.

Very respectively, Your Obt. Servt. P. E. Bean Bean's Prairie[68]

In a note below, Bean authorized Rusk to sign for him as surety, and so Rusk did as Bean's "attorney" when the document was filed with Judge Hart.

Chapter 19

THOUGHTS OF MEXICO

BEAN'S HEALTH WAS NOT GOOD as the 1840s began. His bones were creaking, and arthritis in his hands made it difficult for him to hold a pen to write. All of Bean's years of imprisonment in dank Mexican dungeons were beginning to catch up with him. Besides the chilling winters, where the temperature could drop thirty degrees in a few hours, the heat and humidity of Texas summers were also bothering him worse than they used to. As his children matured, he began to think more of himself. His thoughts also turned to Doña Magdalena in Jalapa. If Bean read the articles about the Santa Fe Expedition prisoners by George Wilkins Kendall that started appearing in the *New Orleans Picayune* in 1842, it may have prompted him to quit Texas and spend his last days in Mexico. The woman Kendall described—despite being older than he judged—was without a doubt Bean's wife, and she still longed for her husband's return. Within a few miles of Jalapa, as Kendall's coach rattled down the slope from Perote into the tropical zone on its way to Veracruz, where "at every step new beauties [of nature] presented themselves," a stop was made at a hacienda.

> We entered the dwelling [wrote Kendall], the front of which was almost concealed from view by creeping vines and different species of rose and other flowering bushes. The mistress of this sylvan retreat, a stout, handsome-faced woman, some thirty years of age, instantly beset us with inquiries in relation to some American she had known formerly—a colonel she called him, but the name I do not remember. His hair, features, size and all were described with a minuteness which convinced us that his image still lingered in the memory of the fair questioner, but not one of us could give her information which seemed satisfactory. She kindly asked us to partake of refreshments; but mingled with her pressing invitations were farther inquiries

> about the colonel—thoughts of one, who evidently occupied a strong hold in her affections, never left her while there was a ray of hope that some of us might possibly know him. When we were on the road, the driver informed us that for many years this woman had been earnest in her inquiries respecting the colonel. In her artless simplicity she had asked all foreigners alike for information—one she knew so well must surely be known to others . . . Love, as a matter of course, was at the bottom—some roving American had won her affections in early life, and those affections continued as warm as ever.[1]

How could a man, with any vigor left in his loins and a throb pounding in his heart, read such words and not be stirred to action? We, of course, cannot say that Bean actually saw Kendall's serialized account, but something caused him to put his affairs in order.[2] He drew up his last will and testament, filing it with the county clerk of Nacogdoches, O. L. Holmes, on April 12, 1843.

> *In the Name of God, Amen*! I, Peter Ellis Bean of the County of Nacogdoches in the Republic of Texas, owing to the great oncertainty of this mortal life, the advancement of age and laboring under a lingering bodily disease, also being on the eve of starting to the Warm Springs in Arkansas, or elsewhere, for the preservation of life and the Great oncertainties of the Effect it may have in regards to my disease, have thought proper to make the following distribution as my last will & Testiment. I own and acknowledge three children, Isaac Thomas Bean, Louiza Jane and Ellis M. Bean, two sons & one daughter.
>
> *First*: I give & bequeath to my eldest son, Isaac T., a negro girl, Louize, also the undivided half of my headright of a League and Labour located on or near the Trinity river.
>
> *Next*: I give & Bequeath to my daughter, Louiza J. Lacy, a negro girl, Matilda, which she now holds in possession.
>
> [*Next*]: I also Give & bequeath to my son, Ellis M. Bean, the two old negroes, Dory & Vina, his wife, also the remainder of their children, three girls & one boy, Emmeline, Harriet, Sarah & Pendleton, together with the Tract of land on which my dwelling & plantation are situated containing one thousand acres and all the Stock of Cattle, Hoggs & horses, including my fine Stud Horse Bolton, also all my household & kitchen furniture. One Waggon, all my oxen & farming utencils & all things pertaining to the farm.
>
> I hereby nominate, ordain, authorize & appoint Samuel M. Bean

& Jesse E. Bean, my Executors, to this my last will & distribution, also Guardian for my minor son, Ellis M. Bean, until he become of age. Giving them, my said Executors, full power & authority in all & every thing or things necessary to carry out the full interest & meaning of this instrument.

Given under my hand & seal this the 6th Feby. 1843. P. E. Bean[3]

Several things jump out of this document, mainly the fact that Bean makes no mention at all of his "ex-wife" and the mother of his children, Candace Midkiff. Nor is she named as the inheritor of any of his property. She was still alive and living not far from Bean's one-thousand-acre plantation, but we know from his divorce petition that their husband-wife relationship had ended in 1829. He asked the Republic of Texas to grant him a divorce from her a decade later and evidently considered himself a divorced man, even if his petition was tabled. Although Bean did acknowledge Candace in the divorce proceeding as having borne his children, in his will he does not. This is a mite peculiar, further evidence that they did not live together beyond 1829 and certainly not after her husband Isaac Hix was chased out of the region. It also suggests that their parting had been an acrimonious one that predated her marriage to Hix and may have started with the Parmer affair. Despite local lore claiming that he and Candace lived in such-and-such a house, they may not have. It is not even clear if she had "custody" of the children and reared them, or if they stayed part of the time on Bean's plantations with their father. The boys probably did, as they grew older.

Another strange thing is Bean's reference to his headright on the Trinity River. Although he held a certificate for this land and it had been surveyed, Bean did not get it patented until September 20, 1844. In other words, that was the date when the Republic of Texas issued title to Bean. And who was the president who ordered that this league and labor of land be given to Bean, his heirs, and assigns, forever? Sam Houston, the same who had ordered that Bean be arrested as an "Alien of the Republic" during the revolution!

But Houston and his land commissioner, Thomas Ward, had little choice. Once a certificate was issued by commissioners of local land boards, awarding a patent for the grant was only a technicality. Bean had already left for Mexico by then, and it is unknown if Houston gritted his teeth when signing Bean's land title with his usual bold flourish.[4] Bean was so confident of his headright grant that he sold half of it on July 16, 1842, to Helena Nelson for twenty-two hundred dollars. It was noted as his certificate no. 690, "located about 8 miles from the Trinity."[5] This is why his son Isaac was only given half of the league and labor when Bean made his will the following February. A considerable amount of cash had already gone into his wallet—all before Sam Houston made the grant official on behalf of the Republic of Texas.

This will and disposition of Bean's property also had a fatal legal flaw, since a will cannot be probated and title transferred to heirs until the maker is known to be deceased. If Bean, when he rode eastward shortly after making his will, did not expect to return—or feared that circumstances of his malady might cause his death—why not simply deed this property to his children before leaving? The fact that he did not attend to this paperwork caused problems later on, especially with the estate of his minor son Ellis. This was the case because Samuel Bean proved to be a poor executor and guardian of Ellis's interests, endangering his inheritance either through incompetence or perhaps jealousy that he had received nothing himself. Witnesses who knew the family later said in a lawsuit that Samuel was reared on the same standing as Bean's two sons, and they had always assumed that the three boys were brothers.[6]

Bean's estate was further complicated by the untimely death of his daughter Louisa Jane in November 1843. Two of her children by William Young Lacy had died as infants, and now she was in the cold ground beside them. But the grieving widower could not get title to the slave Matilda away from the executors—a role that Sam Bean preempted for himself—until it was known for certain whether Peter E. Bean was alive or dead. Title to Isaac's portion of the Trinity headright league was also in limbo, and minor son Ellis was only fifteen when Bean made his will—leaving the lad the majority of his property.

Other lawsuits sprang up after Bean left Texas. One involved fourteen promissory notes that Bean had been forced to pay when Hiram Vansickle and Elijah Debard defaulted, Bean having signed the notes as surety in December 1840 to the tune of $1,327. John S. Blair held these notes, and when they fell due, Bean—to recover his money—brought suit against the pair in the spring 1842 term of court at Nacogdoches. Obtaining a writ of attachment, Bean had the sheriff seize a slave named Jim and a three-year-old sorrel mare called the Red Mariah. Also seized were two tracts of land: one a quarter league situated twenty-five miles west of town, and the other a full league in the "Cherokee Nation" two or three miles east of the Neches Saline, formerly occupied by Debard. He was probably the same man who had operated the saline in "partnership" with Chief Bowl in 1838. Debard managed to get the slave and mare back on a replevy bond in the spring of 1843, but the term ended before the matter was resolved.[7]

After Bean's mysterious departure in mid-1843, Debard and Vansickle came roaring into the fall session of court with adamant claims that they were the rightful owners of the slave Jim and the sleek mare Red Mariah. The plaintiff Bean, said Debard, "is and was at the institution of this suit an officer in the Mexican Service, and as such drew pay, and since the last continuance of said cause has become an open enemy of the Republic of Texas; that he has alienated himself from the said Republic and domiciliated himself in the Republic of Mexico, then waging and carrying on a war against this Republic and the citizens thereof; and that the said Peter E. Bean is now under the legiance of the said Government of Mexico."[8]

Yes, they had suspected that Colonel Bean was a traitor to Texas all along, and now he had proved it by hightailing it to Mexico. Mr. Debard had earlier admitted that he was indebted to Bean, but now—in an attempt to recover this mortgaged property—was using the anti-Mexican sentiment then astir among his fellows citizens in the wake of two raids made against San Antonio in 1842 and the disastrous Texian Mier Expedition at the end of the year. Once again Bean was being denounced as an enemy alien and a traitor—and all so Debard could escape an outstanding debt to a man who had helped him!

At least the people in Nacogdoches knew that Bean had returned to his Mexican wife, instead of heading to Arkansas to soak in its warm springs as stated in his will. But Bean did say "or elsewhere," probably meaning Mexico. Executor Jesse Bean knew where to go to find him early the next year, so his destination was no great secret. Did Candace and the boys know? One suspects they heard the truth very quickly, despite the later tales about how they believed Bean had been treacherously murdered by Indians and how Candace was so distraught at his fate that she went into prolonged mourning. This notion was surely put to rest by the court cases being aired in public at the time in Nacogdoches, and it is amazing that such romantic nonsense found so many willing believers in the twentieth century.

Blair soon piled on, claiming that Bean, "who now resides beyond the jurisdiction of the Courts of this Republic," had never paid some of the notes he held against him as surety. Bean had "unjustly" deprived Blair of the sum of $1,830, despite his frequent requests. With interest—plus other obligations that Bean had assumed, such as one for Martin Lacy—Blair declared that Bean owed him $3,000. His lawyers (Rusk and Henderson) demanded that Bean or his agent be required to appear in court on the first Monday of May 1844 to answer suit.[9] In the meantime, at the beginning of February, action was taken to seize Colonel Bean's property. This was done by Sheriff David Rusk in the presence of Jesse Bean and Margaret Roark.

The list was a long one. It included eight slaves and a stud horse named Bay Bolton. Then there were 150 head of cattle (branded with the letter *B*) and six stock horses. James Morgan, plaintiff Blair's lawyer in the suit, also attached two pieces of Bean's real estate: nineteen hundred acres lying about four miles east of Nacogdoches, and one thousand acres lying twenty-four miles west of town "whereon Peter E. Bean formerly Resided and adjoyning Helena Nelson and authers." The attachment was granted because Blair would "probably lose the debt" as Bean had absconded.[10] Rather like Piedras and Medina, one supposes, and we have seen how Bean cashed in on the property they left behind. But the wheel had turned and now Bean's estate—in his absence—faced some serious legal problems. This was only the beginning, as will be detailed in the following chapter.

Grappling with these legal difficulties fell to the other executor, Dr. Jesse E. Bean. He was probably Peter Ellis's younger brother, born around 1794; later testimony so indicates.[11] When he came to Texas is uncertain, but Bean must have been in contact with him awhile and known that he was capable of being a responsible executor. His "doctor" status suggests some degree of education, although the term was used loosely in nineteenth-century Texas. In the case of Samuel Bean, however, the colonel made a bad judgment of his character. Early in 1844 Jesse Bean took news of this legal trouble to Jalapa, bearing a letter from William Roark. He, with David Muckleroy, had witnessed Bean's will. Bean replied to him on April 9.

> Mr. William Roark my old friend Esqr.—
> Recived your leter by Dr. Bean and see that Sam Bean is a Raskel But one [k]nows not who to trust [He] is a Rogue and a lyar But let him goeu my fingers is yet stiff and I cant Wright good But I am a giting well fast Dr. Bean can stait to you all Remember me to your lady. If when the weather becomes cool yo[u] will see me.
> Remaining your old friend Peter E. Bean[12]

The colonel's rheumatism and arthritis were still plaguing him, even though Jesse Bean reported back that he was living "in comfort and ease." Even so, Peter Ellis was alarmed that his property was slipping away and knew that something had to be done quickly or it would all be gone. It appears that he was well enough to return to New Orleans with Jesse and transfer ownership to him of the slaves that Blair was trying to seize. On May 3, 1844, for three thousand dollars the colonel sold Jesse the same eight slaves, plus a baby boy named Bluford only four months old. The others were Dory (aged forty-five), Stephen (twenty-nine), Vina (thirty-one), Emaline (fourteen), Tilda (ten), Harriet (eight), Pendleton (six), and Sarah (three).[13] They were a family unit, and this "sale" was made to keep them together and confound Blair's attempt to take them away from

Bean's heirs. That money actually changed hands between Bean and his executor Jesse is doubtful. However this may be, in November 1844 Morgan-Blair said that they had received full satisfaction and payment of all debts owed them, and Jesse Bean could dismiss the suit by paying court costs thereof.[14]

If Bean was living at Jalapa "in comfort and ease," the last item in Bean's military service record indicates that he needed, or wanted, some help to maintain himself. On March 8, 1844, José Joaquín Herrera (who would become president of Mexico at the end of the year) replied to the secretary of war's note of March 4 that Colonel Bean had sent a petition for "something" in the way of assistance for his great loss of fortune and many sacrifices on behalf of Mexico. Writing on "Council of Government" letterhead, Herrera said that Bean's petition had come before the Council with the decision to pass it along to the Commission of War, seemingly as an endorsement.[15] This petition has not been located, nor is it known if Bean was awarded a pension.

In any case, he had only a few more years to live. According to Dr. Jesse Bean, Doña Magdalena was making them comfortable ones, and it is very doubtful that Bean reached her hacienda penniless and destitute. His many land sales in recent years argue against that. He rode a saddle richly inlaid with silver, mounted on a fine horse. When Bean strolled around Jalapa with his wife, he used the gold-tipped cane that Jim Bowie had presented to him years before. No—except for being crippled up a bit—Peter Ellis Bean at age sixty-one still cut a fine figure. His return must have been a joyful one for Magdalena Falfán de los Godos de Bean, who had never given up on him or stopped asking foreign travelers if they knew where her beloved American colonel might be. At her side again, Bean probably wondered why it had taken him so long to leave Texas in the first place.

When Peter E. Bean reached Mexico early in the year 1844, Santa Anna was still the president of Mexico but his popularity was fading. He and his secretary of war, José María Tornel, had been promising the reconquest of Texas for years. Despite their demands for millions of pesos to pursue the war, little had been accomplished in the North. Several campaigns in 1842 amounted to hit-and-run attacks with few tangible results. The United States was on the verge of annexing Texas, and Sam Houston was playing his usual coy games as the negotiations proceeded. Bean's young friend Juan N. Almonte—now a general—was Mexico's minister to the United States. He was engaged in a losing battle to prevent annexation. A treaty of annexation was signed on April 12, 1844, by Secretary of State John C. Calhoun and the republic's two representatives, but it had to be ratified and signed into law. Almonte hoped to delay the process until Congress adjourned, and the nation's attention became focused on the presidential election. He was heartened when the U.S. Senate failed to ratify the treaty that summer.[16]

James K. Polk won the election and soundly defeated the Whig candidate, Henry Clay. Polk had vigorously campaigned on a Texas platform, which Clay had opposed. Annexation seemed inevitable. But outgoing president John Tyler did not wait for Polk to exercise his electoral mandate. Tyler broke the Senate deadlock by proposing that Texas be brought into the Union on a joint resolution. As it required fewer votes than a two-thirds majority, annexation became an accomplished fact early in 1845—pending the acceptance of Texas within one year.[17] Almonte packed his bags and demanded his passport in March, returning to Mexico soon after. It is unknown if Almonte's coach stopped at Bean's hacienda outside Jalapa on his way back to the Mexican capital. Bean probably knew he was coming, because Almonte's breaking of relations with the United States was front-page news everywhere.

Houston's man Anson Jones was sworn into office as the last president of the Republic of Texas on December 9, 1844. Mexico also had a new president shortly thereafter. This was occasioned by the Revolution of Three Hours on December 6, 1844—actually a riot in which the people of Mexico City pulled down Santa Anna's statue and dragged his embalmed leg through the streets. The president accepted defeat, and Gen. José Joaquín Herrera was selected to rule the nation. He was the same officer who had reviewed Bean's pension application earlier in the year. Herrera attempted to open discussions with Texas officials on recognizing its independence, which made him very unpopular with diehards like Almonte. When President Polk sent troops under Gen. Zachary Taylor to occupy Corpus Christi in mid-1845, cries for war became more shrill in Mexico and opposition to Herrera hardened. Bean, seemingly, had waited too late for a peaceful retirement in Mexico.[18]

Hostilities broke out when General Taylor marched his army to the Rio Grande in the spring of 1846. Victories at Palo Alto and Resaca de la Palma in May brought the rapid capitulation of Matamoros, and Gen. Mariano Arista marched his bloodied troops toward Monterrey. Taylor followed at a leisurely pace, once more volunteers arrived, and captured the capital city of Nuevo León in fierce fighting early in September. Many Texans participated in the battle, but they were younger men who had arrived long after Peter Ellis Bean left his imprint.[19] His battles had begun when Texas was under Spanish rule and continued as Mexico freed itself to become an independent republic. His contribution to the independence of Texas remains fuzzy. If he helped, it was in quiet ways—even though Bean had always been a lover of liberty and a staunch opposer of tyranny. To this day people are not sure which side Bean was on during the Texas Revolution. It was Bean's misfortune to be on both sides, his long legs straddling the Rio Grande. He had a wife in Mexico and a wife in Texas. He spent most of his time with the one in Texas but returned to the one in Mexico at the end. Ever since Yoakum published his history in 1855, we have believed that the old warrior died at Jalapa on October 3, 1846—less than a month after American forces triumphed at Monterrey.[20] One hopes that it was with a smile on his face and with his "all's peace and tranquility" disposition intact.

But—as with most everything else in Bean's life—there might have been an entirely different scenario. This is the case because entries in three different Bean family Bibles—including the one kept by Candace herself—give the year of his death as 1847, not 1846.[21] By October 1847 the situation around Jalapa was anything but tranquil; it was just the opposite. Gen. Winfield Scott had bombarded Veracruz into submission in March. Then Scott defeated Santa Anna's army at Cerro Gordo in April and marched into Jalapa, which he made his headquarters before pushing on to Puebla at the end of May. Guerrilla bands were already attacking his communication and supply lines to Veracruz, and the situation worsened as his army headed for Mexico City. The main road back to the coast was unsafe for anything but heavily protected supply trains and the most well-mounted and elusive couriers. Guerrilla strikes along this lifeline intensified after the Mexican capital fell to General Scott's troops in mid-September 1847.[22]

To combat this unrelenting guerrilla menace, Col. John C. "Jack" Hays was sent to the region with a regiment of his Texans, many of them former rangers. As his adjutant John S. "Rip" Ford later recalled: "During the fall of 1847 the Mexican guerrilla bands were giving considerable trouble outside the walls of Vera Cruz." Hays's men armed themselves with a shipment of the new Walker Colts and moved inland to fight their own style of guerrilla warfare. The man who had helped design and get this formidable new six-shooter into production, Capt. Samuel H. Walker, was killed in a fierce fight at the small town of Humantla on October 9, 1847—only six days after Bean family Bibles say that Colonel Bean passed to his eternal reward. One of Hays's camps in November was "two miles beyond" Jalapa, and they returned to it various times as their operations extended into 1848.[23]

Rip Ford did not mention whether the Texan encampment was on lands belonging to the Hacienda de las Banderillas, or if the Mexican lady who owned it had recently lost her North American husband. Nor did George Wilkins Kendall, on his passage through Jalapa, record anything about revisiting the hacienda where years before an attractive *mexicana* had showered him with pleas of news concerning her long-lost *norteamericano* colonel. Had Bean—because he was an old gringo—been killed by Mexican guerrillas in their frequent raids along the main road between Veracruz and the capital? Or did he die peacefully at the hacienda outside Jalapa in these chaotic times? He was only sixty-four years old, but they had been hard years with many sufferings and privations. A man without a country? No; Peter Ellis/Pedro Elías Bean had two of them and was comfortable in both settings. This makes him a man way ahead of his time, a man whom Texans and Mexicans might envy today. Except for the two wives, of course.

Chapter 20

THE LEGAL WHIRLWIND

As SUGGESTED BY the actions of Debard, Blair, and their crew of legal representatives (including his old friend Tom Rusk), Bean was hardly out of town before litigation against him began to crowd the Nacogdoches court docket. These cases lasted for years, almost as long as he or his children held property in Texas. In the fall 1844 term of court, one James Bracken tried to gain control of Bean's slave Dory, "of great value, to wit of the value of seven hundred dollars." Bean, it appears, had earlier been the legal guardian of Nathaniel Collier, "a person *non compus mentis,*" who had perhaps thought that Dory belonged to him. He did, at least in September 1826 when Robert Collier was murdered and an inventory of his estate was prepared by Alcalde Hines. As noted, item 6 read "Dory, a field hand aged about 21, property of Nath. Collier."[1] It is unknown if Bean legally acquired this field hand from Collier's widow Harriet or the estate. But Dory, "a slave for life aged about forty years," must have been a prime specimen because Bracken—now calling himself Collier's guardian—wanted him badly. So badly that Bracken was still pursuing the case five years later, after Nathaniel Collier was deceased.[2]

On November 16, 1849, Bracken filed an "Amended Petition" as follows:

> Your petitioner would respectfully represent that on or about the first day of January, A. D. 1845, the said Peter E. Bean departed this life in Mexico; that at the time of his death he was legal and equitable owner of fifteen slaves worth about five thousand dollars which slaves he left in the County of Nacogdoches; that said Bean left at the time of his death two sons, to wit Isaac Bean and Ellis M. Bean, who were his only heirs at law, now both of mature years. That there has been no administration upon said Peter E. Bean's Estate & that he died intestate. That shortly after his death the said Isaac Bean &

> Ellis M. Bean took possession as heirs at law of said Peter E. of all his estate [and] made an equal division of the same between them and have ever since enjoyed the same and still do enjoy it to the exclusion of the petitioner. That among the negroes thus taken . . . is the slave Dora [*sic*], for the recovery of whom this suit was originally brought, which negro they have also appropriated to their own use.[3]

Isaac Bean was then residing in Walker County (formed in 1846 with Huntsville as the county seat) and Ellis Bean in Cherokee County (which had been formed out of Nacogdoches County in 1846, Rusk its county seat). Bracken wanted the brothers to deliver up the slave Dory and pay him a substantial amount of money for the "serveses and detention" he had missed while the colonel and his heirs were enjoying Dory's labor.[4]

Now that he was approaching adult status, Ellis began to reckon with his inheritance. On December 21, 1846, for the price of four hundred dollars he sold to James H. Durst the one thousand acres known as "Bean's Prairie place" with all its improvements. The exact limits were better described in John Durst's sale of his nine-league tract to Ira Lewis, from which the one thousand acres had been withheld. The deed was signed first by "Candis Hicks" (she made her mark "X"), followed by Isaac T. and Ellis M. Bean.[5] They were literate, even if their mother was not. Mrs. Sophia Peevey later told people of the region that she visited the family often. She said that "this second Mrs. Bean was a case." Besides being illiterate, "she was little and as ugly as can be." Because so many of Mrs. Peevey's other yarns about Colonel Bean and his family are factually wrong or made up, perhaps this one was as well.[6]

Strangely, on October 23, 1849, Ellis Bean again sold James H. Durst the same one thousand acres given him in Bean's will—this time for two thousand dollars. As three years before, the tract was described as four miles west of the Angelina adjoining the Old San Antonio Road on its south side "known as my father, Peter E. Bean's prairie place and the same on which he used to reside, now occupied by James Selman."[7] The Selman clan had moved to Cherokee County and were related to the Beans by marriage. Some of them, like Benjamin Selman, went on to be state legislators and men of prominence in east Texas. Benjamin's wife was Sarah "Sallie" Bean, a cousin of the colonel's.

So why had James Durst paid young Ellis five times as much as the original sale? Hard to say, unless someone had successfully argued that he had taken advantage of a lad barely eighteen years old and his illiterate, small, and ugly mother. Even more curious is the fact that James's uncle John Durst, on March 15, 1847, "for a valuable consideration" had sold him the one-thousand-acre tract "where the Young Beans now reside."[8] James Durst seems to have been assembling evidence in case evicting the Bean family became a legal matter. He brought one William A. Hagood into the fray in June 1847 by selling him "an undivided moity" in the tract for one hundred dollars.[9] Instead, Durst did the right thing and paid Ellis M. Bean a large sum of money two years later to buy the place. By this time, his mother Candace Hicks was in her grave.

Jesse Bean came before the spring 1847 term of court and said that Isaac and Ellis Bean were "setting up claim to Eleven Negroes, slaves lately in the possession of your petitioner." He named them, being the same slaves that he had purchased from Colonel Bean in 1844 "for a valuable consideration," to wit, three thousand dollars. But Bean's sons, under a plea of title from their father's will, had "decoyed" said slaves from Jesse's control and "has them now in their possession under their pretended claim, which your petitioner avers is null and void if such will was ever made." Jesse, named as an executor of Bean's will, was surely talking nonsense here and swearing falsely under oath—even if Bean's will had been misplaced at the courthouse and did not turn up until 1850. He may have been filing this petition to establish his ownership of the slave family and to keep people not of the Bean clan from getting them.[10]

William Y. Lacy—who *was* a member of the clan—brought suit against the colonel's sons in the fall 1848 term of court. The brothers, he asserted, had injured and damaged him to the extent of ten thousand dollars because they were claiming the slave Dory and his family. They were named and a value was placed on each of the slaves, adding up to sixty-two hundred dollars "lawful money." Lacy said he owned them by a finding of the court, yet the Beans had "fraudently" refused to yield possession despite his frequent requests. His petition was filed so that the brothers could not remove the slaves out of state while the suit was pending.[11] William was their brother-in-law by virtue of his brief marriage to their sister Louisa Jane. Despite the fact that he had remarried and started another family (and because he later did business with Isaac and remained close to the Beans), perhaps William's court action was prompted by what Isaac had recently done with three of these slaves. Given them away!

The colonel's eldest son Isaac married Nancy A. Boone in August 1847. She, it is said, was a niece of the frontiersman Daniel Boone, then eighteen years old. In what appears to be a prenuptial agreement—phrased as "in consideration of the marriage about to be consummated and solemnized between himself and Miss Nancy A. Boon of said county"—Isaac deeded to her the half league of land in Henderson (now Kaufman) County near the town of Buffalo that he had inherited from his father. Also conveyed were three slaves, Stephen, Matilda, and Liza.[12] (Lacy had valued them at two thousand dollars.) Despite the precaution implied, this marriage worked out; twelve children were born to the couple between 1849 and 1871. It is partly through these descendants that the

Isaac Bean, eldest son of Colonel Bean. Photo courtesy Robert E. Davis.

Bean name survives in Texas today, as will be discussed in more detail a bit later.

Ellis M. Bean came before the June 1849 term of court in Cherokee County with news that his mother "Candis Hicks" had died in 1848 (date later revealed as November 21). She had "no fixed place of residence at the time of her decease" but owned about one thousand dollars' worth of property in the county and had died intestate. Ellis, being her son "and one of her nearest of kin," thought that her estate would be wasted and

Isaac Bean's wife, Nancy Boone. Photo courtesy Robert E. Davis.

squandered unless he was named to administer it. He, along with John N. Irby and N. D. Whaley, posted surety of two thousand dollars on July 2, 1849, for pro tem rights.[13] Ellis was recently married. If he was living with his new bride in the Old Bean House or "Fort," as it was also called, Candace may have been staying there as well. Other sources, however, have her living with her brother Isaac Midkiff and family at the time of her death, so she may indeed have stayed here and there. Ellis is sometimes remembered as the family member attending to her burial, though Isaac was probably there too. Old neighbors recalled that her funeral was well attended.

So Candace Midkiff Bean Parmer Bean Hicks had finally passed to the next world. Testimony taken after the turn of the century, from people who knew and remembered her, indicates that Candace died at "Bean's Fort" on Bean's Prairie and was placed to rest about one hundred yards south of the Old San Antonio Road. One lady named Elizabeth H. Selman, who was William Roark's daughter, said that her grave had a stone wall around it and her tombstone was carved out of rock. She swore that Candace was never moved from this resting place. Others called it the Dursts' Old Linwood Cemetery near Douglass in Cherokee County. Still others said it was known as the Selman, or Roark, burial plot. Candace's family Bible was produced in this 1909 court case: it shows her born on December 12, 1800—not two years later. If correct, she was still only forty-eight years old when she died, a rather young age for a woman to have no "fixed" residence and be dependent on relatives.[14]

Legal problems soon shifted to her husband Peter Ellis Bean's estate, which was considerably larger than the one Candace had left. What brought this on is a bit of a mystery. In the March 1850 term of court, William Martin declared that the colonel had died intestate in Mexico, leaving all of his property (real and personal) in Cherokee County, "and further that no person has yet been appointed by the Probate Court . . . to administer said Estate." Neither Bean's wife nor his heirs had applied or qualified for letters of administration. Martin solicited these powers over Bean's estate and was appointed. He, as it turns out, had married the widow of executor Samuel Bean.[15] But in the July term another would-be administrator appeared. He was William A. Hicks. If he was a relative of Candace's husband Isaac "Hix," it was not stated. He was given control of Bean's estate until the next term of court upon depositing a bond of six thousand dollars "with the Will annexed."[16]

This will had been introduced into the court records by William Martin on May 13, 1850. It was a startling discovery, and not even Martin had known about it (so he claimed) when being appointed to handle Bean's estate. But since that time "he has discovered that said Bean left a last Will and testament unrevoked at the time of his death." One of the executors was dead (Samuel Bean), and the other (Jesse Bean) had refused to take it upon himself to exercise these powers. Martin was ready to do it before Hicks showed up and contested the issue. Martin's powers were revoked by the court when he and Ellis Bean failed to appear in July.[17] "Carmelette" Bean, on May 9, 1846, testified that she was the widow and heir of Samuel M. Bean, deceased. They had one son named Joe. Much later she was remembered as the daughter of an Alamo martyr named Joseph Rutherford who had been raised as an orphan by Joe Durst's wife

Delilah Dill. Since Sam Bean often claimed to be a son of the colonel's, his widow's new husband (William Martin) may have hoped to profit from administering "Sam's part" of the estate. This ploy did not work out for the Martin heirs until sixty years later.[18]

William Hicks was still the administrator of Bean's estate in March 1856, when Helena Nelson came to court. Although she had paid Colonel Bean for what was called a "title bond" to half of his headright, full title had never been received. She had passed this half league to her daughter, Helena Berryman, by deed of gift and prayed that Hicks would now execute a proper title on behalf of Bean's estate. The colonel's July 1842 sale to Nelson was put on record. William Lacy had attested in 1849 that he saw Bean sign and execute this document. It, along with later proceedings in the case, was introduced as evidence.[19]

Although William Young Lacy remarried after the untimely death of Louisa Jane Bean, he kept close ties with the Beans and remembered his first father-in-law fondly. In April 1856 Lacy acted as Isaac Bean's attorney in a rather large land sale made to David Snively of Refugio County. The sales price was thirty thousand dollars and it involved fifteen leagues of land. Eight of these leagues were in Cherokee County, three in Anderson. They were said to be the eleven-league grant of José Pineda's, possibly another one of Colonel Bean's acquisitions that he had stashed away. The other four leagues in the sale definitely were, being the grant to Jesús de la Garza that Bean had bought and located in Cherokee and Angelina Counties. How had his family managed to retain these huge tracts, neither of which was mentioned in Bean's will? There is much mystery to land dealings in the nineteenth century. Grants were seemingly sold, with money changing hands, only to reappear later and be sold again by heirs of the same party. At least we know that a decade after the death of Peter Ellis Bean, his eldest son Isaac was still landed gentry.[20]

Mary Scott, who was a Selman before her marriage, remembered in 1909 that after this sale, Isaac Bean (nicknamed "Ike") had moved his family to "West Texas." Actually it was only to Bell County, but considered "West" in the days when Comanches still ruled the western plains. She thought that a man named McBee had bought Isaac's land, which Robert Lewis then obtained.[21] All of the elderly people who gave testimony in this trial—no matter which side they were on—spoke highly of Peter Ellis Bean. Delilah Allen, aged seventy-five, said he "was a prominent man in his neighborhood, he had considerable property, and was well thought of by his neighbors and friends." Others considered him not rich or poor but "well to do" and "quite a noted man."[22] They could not believe that the plaintiffs' lawyers were trying to tell them that Peter Ellis Bean and Ellis P. Bean were two different men, because of what historians Yoakum and Thrall had written. Hell, everybody who knew *anything* knew that they were one and the same person, and that he and Candace had settled on the Neches River near later Alto when the whole country was an Indian-infested wilderness![23]

To go back a bit, the 1850 term of court was a messy one for Bean's estate. James Bracken renewed his claim to the slave Dory, as guardian for the deceased Nathaniel Collier. He claimed that Colonel Bean had deprived Collier of Dory's services ever since July 1830. At $200 per annum, Bean's heirs owed $2,142 in damages plus the Negro or his worth, $700. The jury found for plaintiff.[24] After the turn of the century, four of Bean's neighbors said that Dory always called the colonel "Ellis." He told them that "Master Ellis" had freed him, but all the commotion over who should own him suggests that Dory—like most other slaves in Texas—had to wait until Juneteenth of 1865 for his freedom.[25] Also in 1850 three men were again appointed to appraise the value of Bean's estate, no doubt because of the contest between Martin and Hicks over which of them should be appointed administrator.[26]

Finally in that year, we learn that Ellis M. Bean had inherited some of his father's bad traits with women—or at least those with Candace Midkiff. On September 23 Ellis's wife Mary Ann Bean appeared in court to say that she married him on July 1, 1848, and had remained with him to the present time.

> Your petitioner further says that since her marriage with the said Bean she has ever been a kind, affectionate, generous, and dutiful wife and that it ever was her constant care to contribute in all things to the benefit and happiness of her said husband Ellis M. Bean. But that [he], disregarding her kindness, her services & attention on him most generously bestowed, as also his duty and obligation to the said Mary Ann Bean, on or about the first day of May in the year of our Lord one thousand eighty [eighteen-hundred] and fifty at the County of Cherokee did wilfully, wickedly and violently and cruelly assault, beat and abuse said Mary Ann Bean and at divers times [since has] continue[d] to abuse and ill treat her.
>
> Your petitioner further says that the said Ellis M. Bean has even neglected to provide with necessarys the said Mary Ann Bean, leaving her upon the mercy of the world, all of which treatment [she] says is cruel and beyond forbearance.[27]

The distressed bride of only two years demanded that her husband be made to answer in court her spousal-abuse charges. Meanwhile, she had had enough and asked to be divorced from Ellis. She wanted him kept off "the premises" as might be required.[28]

It appears that Peter Ellis Bean was a wife-beater and so was his namesake son. According to a family Bible, Ellis M. Bean (called "Dick") died on April 15, 1851—seven months later at age twenty-three.[29] He had no children with his wife, and it is hoped that Mary Ann (née Rainey) found herself a more kind and loving husband as time passed. Of course, we do not know Ellis's side of the story, only hers. Some of his relatives and neighbors could not recall that he was ever married before his death. Once Isaac Bean moved his family to Bell County in the mid-1850s, the last of the colonel's descendants were gone from the Piney Woods.

Chapter 21

BEAN AND THE HISTORIANS

BEFORE BEAN'S MEMOIR saw print in the mid-1850s, historians knew little of Philip Nolan's exploits and even less of Bean's. Books published in the 1830s, such as Mary Austin Holley's *Texas* (1836) and David B. Edward's *The History of Texas: Or the Emigrant's, Farmer's & Politician's Guide* (1836), were more directed at luring American settlers to the land of milk and honey than telling its history. In the minds of these writers, the real history of Texas only dated back to the arrival of Austin's Anglo-American colonists.

At least both authors presented historical documents of interest. Among the many documents that Edward published was a petition that delegates to the October 1832 Convention at San Felipe had addressed to the Mexican Congress, naming many of the ills suffered because of the union with Coahuila and supporting separate statehood for Texas. A section of this petition (drafted by Charles S. Taylor) demonstrates uncharacteristic Anglo-Texan concern for the Cherokees and how they had become "discontented, unfriendly and hostile" because the Mexican government, that is, that of Coahuila y Texas joined, had not made good on its promises of land. This deplorable situation, said the petitioners, had to be corrected lest it lead to trouble. Is the following passage an oblique reference to Indian Agent Bean?

> The Indians' repeated request to obtain their rights, are unattended to; because an accredited agent of the government has been illegally suspended, by a military officer of the last dynasty, who, in continuance of his system of deception and conciliation, and with a view to enlist their aid [against us], declared to the Cherokees (at the time we began to evince a disposition of throwing from our necks the insupportable weight of military oppression)—"The Americans grasping for land, intend making the attempt of driving *all* my

countrymen from this State; and an extirpation of *you all* will soon follow."[1]

It seems likely that Bean is the "illegally suspended" agent and the quote comes from Piedras, "a military officer of the last dynasty" who was trying to rally the Indians to his side in 1832. As previously noted, the fact that Piedras was willing to use the Indians in his contest with the Anglo and Tejano rebels doomed him in their estimation. The prospect of anyone "settling domestic difficulties with the tomahawk and scalping knife" was more than the settlers could abide. Better to trust a man like Bean with keeping the Indians quiet, as he had in the past. Even with Piedras's ouster in August, it was generally recognized that some action was necessary on the question of Indian land rights. We may be sure that events at Anáhuac and Nacogdoches were fresh in the minds of the fifty-eight delegates who met in October. But the political chief ruled that their proceedings were illegal and did not forward the colonists' "Address" to the Mexican Congress.[2]

Despite this rebuff, another gathering was called in April 1833. As observed, Sam Houston played an important role in this Convention, chairing the committee that drew up the constitution and making rousing speeches on how Texas needed to chart a course of its own. Oddly, the "Memorial" to Congress in support of the proposed constitution has nothing about the plight of the Cherokees and their unrecognized land claims in Texas. Perhaps this is because the document bears the name of David Burnet and not Sam Houston. Why had Houston not pushed the Cherokee agenda to the extent that delegates did in 1832, shortly before his arrival on the scene? He later claimed it was because he did not understand the issues involved, but surely news of Bowl's land problems in Texas had reached him in Indian Territory where Houston had been adopted into the Cherokee tribe. Edward was convinced that the Cherokees and allied tribes were going to be gypped out of their lands above Nacogdoches, no matter how the imminent Anglo-Hispano struggle ended. Texans hated his book because he had such a low opinion of their manners, morals, and state of civilization. Houston, however, read portions to Congress in his 1839–40 defense of Cherokee land rights—confusing the author with the empresario Haden Edwards.[3]

Two important books appeared in 1841 that actually had pretensions of being histories. One was Henry Stuart Foote's *Texas and the Texans: Or Advance of the Anglo-Americans to the South-West.* But he only had a bare mention of Colonel "Beene's" role in putting down the Edwards revolt. The Englishman William Kennedy did no better in his *Texas: The Rise, Progress, and Prospects of the Republic of Texas,* which was mostly an attempt to promote colonization by his fellow English citizens. Kennedy mistakenly said that Bean, one of Nolan's prisoners, was "pardoned on account of his youth." Bean must have cursed a blue streak if he read this sentence, and grumbled to himself at a later passage in Kennedy's book: "A man named Bean (the same who had survived the wreck of Philip Nolan's expedition), arrived in Nacogdoches about this period. At first a partisan of the Fredonian cause, he speedily altered his views, and seeking Bowles, urged the Cherokee chief to abandon the insurgents, saying that if his tribe wanted land, the way to get it would be to propitiate the government by sacrificing Hunter and Field[s]. His arguments were effectual."[4]

As we shall see, this is almost a direct quote from information that Haden Edwards gave Mirabeau Lamar around 1837. Kennedy probably gained access to it through President Lamar, who supported the author's ideas on luring colonists and capital to Texas from Great Britain.[5] In truth, Bean had not "speedily altered his views" about the rebellion, and here was a foreign fellow basically accusing him of being an assassin—or bribing Chief Bowl to do the killing. This was not very favorable publicity for a community leader and man of considerable property, which Bean was in 1841.

When Henderson King Yoakum published Bean's memoir in 1855, eight years after his death, there was no chance that Texans would forget the rip-snortin' Tennesseean. Nor would they fail to remember Philip Nolan as the leader of the first armed Anglo-American "invasion" against a Texas held by Spain. No matter that Nolan, Bean, and the rest of this small party of men were after horses—in it to make some money, and not to wrest Texas from Spanish rule. But Philip Nolan had led the way, and many others followed after him. Once Texas became a free republic—independent of both Spain and Mexico—it became fashionable to say that Nolan had started the whole revolutionary movement without the help from Jefferson's government that he deserved. His death was given a romantic shroud, only one of many Anglo deaths that stirred Texans to avenge themselves against Hispanics as the struggle with Mexico continued until mid-century.[6]

Yoakum was also the first historian to publish a picture of Bean. It was an engraving taken from a watercolor on ivory that the Beans held as a family heirloom. Yoakum's engraving was a faithful likeness, except that Bean faced the opposite direction (left) and his thinning hair was bushed out a bit. Yoakum's portrait was the source for all later reproductions of Bean that made their way into the books of other historians.[7] Yoakum is also responsible for the erroneous year of Bean's death, unless it was a mundane typesetting error by his publisher, Redfield of New York City. Later historians followed Yoakum, and thus 1846 became embedded in the literature for a century—as did his wrong name for Bean's Mexican wife.

If Edward Everett Hale of Boston had read Bean's memoir in Yoakum's book, he would not have used Philip Nolan's name in his 1863 fictionalized morality play *The Man without a Country.* Had he not done so, it is unlikely that Bean would also have come to bear this designation—lumped in with Nolan and General Wilkinson, for example, in John Edward Weems's 1969 book *Men without Countries.* It is a catchy phrase with deep psychological undertones, but not an apt description of Peter Ellis Bean and his life.[8]

So how—given this built-in perception—has Bean fared with historians? How have they judged him as a man and assessed his role in the history of Texas and Mexico? As one might expect, it has been a mixed bag and not all of it favorable. Despite his role with Nolan as a "pathfinding filibuster," Bean had a lot of things going against him. First, he was a bigamist, and one of his wives was a Mexican woman. He, it was said, loved her tenderly but beat up his American wife. Second, he became a Mexicanized Texan and wore the uniform of a colonel in the Mexican army right up to the time of the revolution. This, needless to say, made his loyalty suspect as the Republic of Texas was being formed. Third, he was Mexico's agent to the Indian tribes of Texas, so the whites could never be sure what kind of mischief he might be cooking up with these "savages." And finally, Bean was a big talker who liked to "brag" about how he knew everybody important in Mexico and how he had almost single-handedly won Mexico's independence from Spain. This irritated Bean's listeners in Texas, because they liked to brag themselves. No matter how tall they spun their tales, Bean could always top them.

As to his memoir, it became customary to say that Bean had made up the whole thing. As John Henry Brown wrote in 1892, "Portions of Bean's narrative savor of the improbable, not to say the marvelous." He noted that Bean was not even mentioned in William D. Robinson's respected history of the Mexican Revolution, then added the cut, "This history in nowise, however, contradicts Bean's statements as to his having rendered important services, but does indicate that he had not won the distinction claimed."[9] A pity that Brown had no knowledge of the leaders of Mexico's revolution who attested to Bean's distinctions in his military service record.

Although Yoakum's *History of Texas* is still recognized as a classic, his volume one was very weak. This was because the writer—as he admitted himself—did not have the documents necessary to tell the story "from its first settlement in 1685," as his subtitle reads. Bibliophile John Jenkins says that Yoakum's account of early Texas is "ill-proportioned, incomplete, and generally unsatisfactory." Yoakum redeemed himself by the inclusion of Bean's memoir, which Jenkins calls "one of the most important resources on Texas history during the early part of the 19th century."[10] Why was this the case? Because in that period one could not talk about "Texas" history without reference to what was happening in Mexico. This Bean did, from firsthand experience and in an appealing style, laced with human misery and romance.

In fact, Bean's narrative is considered by modern Mexican historians as an essential document for studying and understanding their own nation's struggle for liberation. This is especially true because of Bean's close connection to the revered patriot Morelos. Rarely do Mexican sources speak of the hardships involved—and in such intimate and plainspoken language—as did the narrative by this foreigner, Pedro Elías Bean. It is not surprising that a number of Mexican scholars quote him, either from Yoakum's English edition or the Spanish translation published in 1959 (after Jean Delalande's French edition) as *Aventuras en México y Texas del Coronel E. P. Bean: Sus Memorias.* Delalande ranked Bean in the same story-telling genre as Alexandre Dumas and thought it a pity that so little was known of this "extraordinary man." Despite his many accomplishments, said Delalande, the story of Bean's life had to be pieced together from fragments scattered far and wide.[11]

Nineteenth-century Texas historians usually fell into either pro-Houston or pro-Lamar camps. Yoakum was in the former while Foote was in the latter. Depending on what these two presidents of Texas thought of Bean, their remarks or insinuations about him usually were reflected in their advocates' histories. Lamar considered it a crying shame that Mexico was able to put down the Edwards brothers' Fredonian Rebellion (although it is odd that he did not find the Red-White Alliance aspect offensive). Thus Bean's role was negatively viewed and not appreciated in the accounts that Lamar gathered from informants such as Haden Edwards. The former empresario, now that he was reestablished in Texas, gave Lamar a very self-serving account of his rebellion. Bean is mentioned in the following passage.

> Hunter went among the Indians and enlisted many to join the war— Fields was active with his own [Cherokee] Tribe— Bowls was also busy with the Indians— There seemed every prospect of uniting & combi[ni]ng the force of all the tribes in the affair— A circumstance of treachry occurred however by Bowles which brought disaster on the cause— A man of notoriously bad character by the name of Bean (the same who had been with Knowlan [Nolan] in his enterprise) arrived in the contry. He at first favored the Fredonians, but soon changed and seekings Bowles, he urged upon this chief to abandon

> the cause, telling him that if his nation wanted Land this was not the way to get it; that he would pledge his life that if he [Bowl] would kill Fields and Hunter who were the leaders among the Indians, the war would be at an end and that the Govt. would give them Lands they desired. This argum[en]t had the intended effect — Bowles became a traitor and sent one of his men in persuit of Hunter & Fields . . . The death of these chiefs ruined the prospects of the Freedonians.[12]

Yes, Chief Bowl was a "traitor," and Lamar could be glad that his expulsion of the Cherokees in 1839 had resulted in the old chief's death. And Bean—a man of "notoriously bad character"—had caused Bowl to defect and "ruined the prospects" of Haden's noble cause. Foote, in 1841, took the cue and wrote critically of Bean's failure to storm the Old Stone Fort when the Fredonians were in such disarray. Colonel "Beene," says Foote, was preparing the Indians "to take part in this terrible enterprise" (of destroying the white Fredonians) before the gallant Major Edwards even rode for the first time into Nacogdoches in "hostile array." Rubbish. Bean was working to keep the Cherokees and their allied tribes neutral—*out of* the rebellion. He never intended for Bowl to attack the whites, whether rebels or otherwise. It would appear that accepting "history" as told by actual participants has its perils.[13] When Lamar was gathering source materials in the 1830s for a history of Texas that he planned to write, why did he not talk to Colonel Bean and get his side of the story? Bean was around Nacogdoches in these years and easy to find. But Lamar wanted to produce an Anglo-Saxon imperialist view of Texas history and Bean was too Mexicanized to fit the mold.[14]

Yoakum, while "cashing in" on Bean's memoir, still took some jabs at him. Sam Houston stroked the author, allowing him to use his papers and even took him on a guided tour of the San Jacinto battlefield. It is unknown how much of Houston's ideas are reflected in Yoakum's words that "neither side appeared willing to trust" Bean as the conflict was approaching. General Houston, by ordering Bean's arrest, certainly demonstrated his feelings on the subject. Yoakum also states that Bean failed to participate in the battle against Piedras in 1832 because he did not want to risk losing his commission as an officer of Mexico.[15] Piedras, however, was convinced that Bean was leading the conspiracy against him through meetings held with the rebels. Even if he did not fight in the battle, Bean was a revolutionist in his commander's mind, and Piedras denounced him as such.[16]

The implication is that similar motives kept Bean from helping Texas in its struggle for independence—protecting his paycheck from Santa Anna's Mexico—and Yoakum states as much, though tempering his remarks by suggesting that "Bean's real feelings were in favor of the Texans." Bean in reality was paid seldom and little, but he may have had hopes of retiring on a military pension. For a man getting up in years, there is nothing unreasonable about that. As we have seen, Yoakum's statement about Bean's arrest in April 1836 came from a Houston letter to David Hoffman, as may have Houston's assurance that "when the enemy retreated, nothing further was heard on the subject."[17] Sam Houston could afford to be forgiving of Bean, since so many other good and decent Texians had taken the Sabine Chute. Few Tories suffered legal reprisals for their actions during the revolution, unless they happened to be "Mexicans" who owned desirable tracts of land.

There was also the possibility that Bean knew something about the retreat, the false alarm with the Indians, and how Houston was manipulating the situation to involve General Gaines's troops against Mexico's widely dispersed army. Things that Bean would blab about loudly if he were put on trial, things best kept quiet. So nothing came of Bean's suspect loyalties, and he was soon supplying east Texas companies of men with needed provisions. Not only that, but in mid-1836 he sold his plantation to the very man who had styled him an enemy "Alien of the Republic," the illustrious Gen. Sam Houston whose victory at San Jacinto had made Texas free of Mexican rule. Because Houston insisted on taking most of the credit for this victory in later years, he alienated many of his former comrades and friends.[18]

As with his sympathies during the revolution, Bean's motives for his behavior toward the Indians in his dealings with them are equally enigmatic. Most historians have given him credit for keeping the civilized tribes quiet, and a few have acknowledged his influence and ability when it came to organizing them against the hostile tribes. All of Bean's efforts were at a time when Mexico could field few troops to fight these battles. Nor were the empresarios able to call on their colonists in sufficient numbers for sustained campaigns. Thus the diplomatic maneuvering with the friendly tribes fell to men like Bean and Ruiz. Time and again they were able to enlist the services of Cherokees, Shawnees, and other tribes on the northern frontier. They may have promised them land, but so did Houston—and even then he could not get them to go to war against the enemies of Texas.

Much has been made of Bean's 1833 recommendation that the "barbarous" immigrant tribes, including the Cherokees, be resettled on the western frontier as a line of defense to protect the white settlements. In other words, to give up their forested lands above Nacogdoches and move to the open plains. A century ago E. W. Winkler called attention to this letter. He did not suggest that it represented a turncoat attitude on Bean's part against the Cherokees. On the contrary, he credited the ideas of Bean and the political chief for the passage of Decree No. 313 in May 1835, which allowed the "peaceable and civilized" Indians to select vacant lands and finally be placed in possession of them.[19] The object was to form a barrier against hostile incursions, no doubt about it, but this was not a new idea and it did not originate with Bean. General Bustamante in 1827 was suggesting that the Cherokees be rewarded for staying out of the Fredonian Rebellion with land in the San Saba valley—right in the middle of Comanche territory. In 1833 Bean was only advocating the same solution that most experienced thinkers did when trying to keep the hostile tribes at bay. But his words do have something of a racist tone, which has not set well with his detractors.

Among the "new historians," Bean's most outspoken critic has been Richard Drinnon. In his book *White Savage: The Case of John Dunn Hunter* (an agenda-driven work if there ever was one), Drinnon classifies Bean as a "violent, remorseless, plundering squatter" straight out of a James Fenimore Cooper novel, like Ishmael Bush in Cooper's *The Prairie.* Bean, in other words, was representative of all the leatherstocking frontiersmen who, with a long rifle cocked and balanced on their shoulder, had driven the Indians from their path as they relentlessly marched west. This is what Drinnon says about Peter Ellis Bean: "He was the embodiment of all of Bush's archetypal qualities as a superfluous man, with no productive place in the society behind him, except that he wandered even farther from home, had the imagination to become a spy and a soldier of fortune, and the audacity to become a bigamist."[20] Drinnon, as one might suspect from the subtitle of his book, castigates Bean for using the "time-worn" Anglo divide-and-conquer tactic among the tribes that Hunter and Chief Fields were trying to rally to the Fredonian flag. He blames Bean and Stephen F. Austin for the assassination of Hunter and Fields, even though other men—red men—actually "pulled the trigger."[21]

In his moral outrage over Hunter's fate, Drinnon says that Bean was as much of a racist and Indian hater as Austin, which Bean assuredly was not. Actually, Drinnon thinks that Bean was the more reprehensible of the two, for Austin merely was trying to get rich by evicting Indians from lands that he wanted white settlers to colonize for him. In other words, Austin was a good businessman, as these Indians lessened the value of his real estate. Bean, on the other hand, was an insincere backstabber, and Drinnon uses Bean's 1833 letter about where lands should be given to the Cherokees as his smoking gun. Quoting his remarks, Drinnon intones, "Too late Bean's 'barbarous people' discovered they could not trust the man of many promises." Thus all the faults of the Mexican government's policy of awarding land to Indians, or withholding same—plus the white man's devious mode of dealing with these Indians for the past two hundred years—are simplistically placed on Bean's shoulders. It is fair to say that Drinnon indulges himself in agenda overkill.[22]

In contrast, Sam Houston's relations with the Cherokees and other tribes of Indians have usually been praised and admired by historians. Few Houston biographers have suggested—much less strung together documentary confirmation—that he was as sneaky as Bean, or using the Indians as pieces on some chessboard that Houston moved here and there in a game of his own. No, Sam Houston has gotten good marks as a great champion of the Cherokees. Apart from the autobiography that Houston ushered to publication in 1855, fondly recalling his early years among Chief John Jolly's tribe on the Hiwassee, this advocacy began and took root with Marquis James's prize-winning *The Raven* in 1929. A more recent example is the 1967 book by Jack Gregory and Rennard Strickland, which focuses on Houston's 1829–33 "exile" period among the Cherokees in Indian Territory. While admitting that Houston had a drinking problem and a fondness for Indian women, the authors claim that his literary output to the *Arkansas Gazette* and his "basic attitudes" formed in these years were the springboard for Houston's position on Indian affairs in Texas throughout his life.[23]

On the surface, of course, there seems to be no contradiction; Houston's ideas about Indians read as consistent and do not dramatically change with the passage of time. But through the eyes of Peter Ellis Bean, things look a little different. We see a newcomer to Texas—jealous of, if not hostile toward—a man authorized by the Mexican government to deal with the same tribes that Houston wished to exercise influence over. As Houston rather immodestly told Mary Austin Holley in 1844, the Cherokees "had great confidence in me—I loved them—none could do so well [in keeping the border quiet in 1836] as I," this because of his youthful experiences with the tribe in Tennessee. And when revolution came (as Houston hoped it would), Bean had to be pushed aside lest he sway Bowl's Cherokees to remain loyal to Mexico. After all, Bean's *every action* as agent among these tribes had been dedicated to affirming such loyalty and enlisting them as allies to fight Mexico's enemies. He promised them lands, most assuredly, but so did Houston on behalf of an independent Texas. Houston failed to deliver on his promises even more than Bean, yet he has received recognition as the Indian's Friend. Bean's reputation as a man who "lie heap" to the Indians is undeserved when measured against Houston's greater false promises.[24]

During the 1870s several books saw print with references to Bean. In *A Texas Scrap-Book* (1875) DeWitt Clinton Baker recounted Bean's exploits in Mexico and made the following remarkable statement: "A volume containing an account of his almost fabulous adventures was written by Bean in 1817, and published soon afterward." No such book predating Yoakum's 1855 publication of Bean's memoir is mentioned by other sources. Homer Thrall, in *A Pictorial History of Texas* published in 1879, had little to say about Bean in his text. In his "Biographical Notices," however, he included almost a two-page entry on Bean. It is a rather flattering account, much of it drawn from his memoir. Thrall says that Bean and Houston were "intimate personal friends" and that Bean kept the Indians of east Texas "quiet during the exciting campaign of 1836." Thereafter he returned to the elegant lady he had married during the Mexican Revolution and "spent the evening of his days very happily at her hacienda near Jalapa."[25] A bit romanticized, but certainly better than what Bean's fellow citizens were saying about him after he left Texas for Mexico.

In 1883, four years later, "Colonel" Frank Triplett published a book called *Conquering the Wilderness.* It was an unabashed tribute to the brave "Pioneer Heroes and Heroines of America" and their push toward the setting sun; its subtitles cover an entire page in small print. Triplett devotes a whole chapter to "Ellis P. Bean and Others," styling Bean's career as "one of the most romantic imaginable." His information is mostly drawn from Bean's memoir and other Yoakum material, and he reproduces a copy of the Baker/Thrall portrait. But Triplett finally gives Bean his rightful place as a shaker and mover of the Mexican Revolution with passages such as these: "Brave as a lion in action, Bean never lost his coolness or his prudence and speedily rose to the rank of colonel, gaining each step of this promotion upon the field. When not fighting he was building powder mills, preparing the foundries necessary for casting cannon and the armories and machinery for turning out small arms and ammunition."[26] Repeating Thrall, Triplett summarizes Bean's "firm policy" for keeping the Indians quiet in Texas during the 1836 revolution, calling his services "invaluable." Bean then returned to his lovely wife, and "the hero spent his declining years at her hacienda."[27] Altogether a fairly factual treatment, even if heavily glossed with Triplett's "hurrah-for-us-guys" historical paintbrush.

Hubert H. Bancroft, in his influential histories published in the 1880s, presents Bean's accomplishments in a matter-of-fact manner. Bancroft supplemented Bean's memoir with numerous Mexican sources and pointed out how earlier historians had gotten some things wrong. But his story of Bean's return to Texas, where he settled as "a colonist, and remained there many years" is all too shallow, barely a blip on the radar screen. Likewise he repeats the standard Anglo aging-male fantasy about how Bean's beautiful Mexican wife had recovered her fabulous estate near Jalapa "and the last years of his adventuresome life were passed in peace" in the sunny tropical zone, a piña colada in one hand and the other—we can imagine where. Twentieth-century historians found this fix on Bean too charming to resist by altering the details much, with only a few noteworthy exceptions.[28]

As earlier discussed, the 1892 *History of Texas* by John Henry Brown cast doubt on the veracity of Bean's memoir and said that "when we scrutinize the very full and unquestioned recital of the military operations of the patriot General Morelos" given in Robinson's history, it was odd that "the name of Bean does not appear." Brown could not resist using Bean's memoir, but it was with his "precautionary suggestions" that a lot of it might be bull: "That an unlettered back-woods boy of twenty-two, with no means of perfecting his education from the time of his capture [with Nolan's men in 1801] to the commencement of his career as a Mexican soldier [with Morelos in 1810], should understand how to make hats, and be able to teach the Mexicans how to manufacture gunpowder, blast rocks, drill soldiers, etc., seems to be an overdraft on credulity."[29]

Brown did not read Bean's memoir closely enough to learn how he "made" hats, nor did he know enough about Bean's upbringing to understand how he acquired mechanical skills involving guns, the manufacture of powder, and so forth. Nonetheless, he thought Bean's career a remarkable one. There was enough truth in his account "to render it deeply interesting to those who would be familiar with the events that marked the overthrow of despotism in Mexico and the achievement of liberty for Mexico and Spanish America."[30] Not too bad an assessment of Bean's significance to our history.

Dudley G. Wooten's 1898 *A Comprehensive History of Texas* reprinted Yoakum's 1855 work, supposedly with new notes, but there is nothing new on Bean except to call him "a hard case." Bean's memoir was dropped from Wooten's edition.[31] In 1903 George P. Garrison, head of the history department at the University of Texas, published a book with a title that —in our present era—might raise a few eyebrows, *Texas: A Contest of Civilizations.* His readers, of course, knew which "civilizations" were being referred to and who had won the "contest." While much attention was devoted to Nolan's final expedition, Bean is but briefly mentioned: "Only one of them [the prisoners] appears in subsequent history, that one being Ellis Bean."[32] Garrison does not comment on Bean's activities in the Edwards revolt, or in any "subsequent" episode of Texas history. Did he regard Bean as on the wrong side in this epic contest between the Anglo and Hispano civilizations?

Frank W. Johnson's *A History of Texas and Texans* saw print in 1914, heavily edited by a young and on-the-rise Eugene C. Barker. There is really nothing on Bean's role in the Fredonian Rebellion, because Barker printed every Austin letter he could find on the subject. The reader is left with the impression that Austin conquered the rebels with a pen instead of a sword. They all shrank and melted away after reading the logic-based missives of Barker's hero, Empresario Stephen F. Austin. Sure they did. Barker, no doubt, would have been shocked by Drinnon's assessment that Austin's letters to the Cherokee leadership amounted to threats of genocide. By contrast, Louis J. Wortham in his 1924 five-volume *A History of Texas from Wilderness to Commonwealth* gives Bean proper credit for his "effective work in persuading some of the chiefs to have nothing to do with Edwards."[33] Then silence; Bean is invisible during and after the revolution.

Neither have more recent writers given Bean added depth, Bennett Lay's 1960 biography and John Edward Weems's 1969 triple hitter on Nolan, Wilkinson, and Bean being the only notable exceptions. T. R. Fehrenbach's widely read *Lone Star* (1968), for example, only mentions Bean twice. Once is with Nolan's expedition, where Bean is called "a recalcitrant but remarkably resourceful prisoner." Fehrenbach goes on to say, "Surviving all this, he returned to Mexico a few years later, after independence, and was made a colonel in the Republican Army. He married rich, and died in bed." His second reference to the "old filibuster" has to do with how Bean "successfully separated the restive Cherokees from the Fredonians."[34] Nor does Weems's entry on Bean in *The New Handbook of Texas* add much to our subject.[35]

So what may we say about the life of Peter Ellis Bean? That he was an ingenious "go-ahead" man typical of the frontier should be obvious from the foregoing evidence. He was also a survivor who had learned to work his way out of tight spots throughout his life in circumstances that would have daunted lesser men. He was unlettered and unschooled but still managed to leave us one of the most important narratives of his era, beginning with Philip Nolan and ending with José María Morelos. After Mexican independence Bean received recognition for his services: the rank of a colonel, appointment as Indian agent for the tribes of east Texas, and a grant of land. He would also have become an empresario, except for the scheming of petty politicians who wanted their friend to have the lucrative position instead of this "foreigner" from North America. The question of Bean's two wives played into their hands, and delayed the decision until Lorenzo de Zavala got the contract that Bean justly should have been awarded.

Even so, Bean remained in Texas and faithfully kept the peace with the many tribes that streamed across the unguarded border. At one point he was Mexico's sole military representative in the Nacogdoches region, and—as Almonte acknowledged—it was largely to his influence that things had not gone to hell with the Indians. As noted, Bean stood in the background during the Texas Revolution and played no prominent role on either side. Apart from Houston's letter ordering his arrest in April

1836 (for which Houston may have had paranoid and devious reasons for issuing), there is no evidence that Bean was working against the rebel cause. Bean inciting the Runaway Scrape? What man, woman, and child struggling through mud to reach the Sabine was not? Nor can we say that Bean was a conspirator with Mexican agents in 1838–39 to raise the disillusioned tribes in a rebellion against the white Texans. None of these accusations hold up under close scrutiny, and historians should quit making such assertions.

Bean, despite his failure to be an empresario, acquired vast lands in Texas—at one point over one hundred thousand acres. He was far from the violent, marauding vagabond that Drinnon makes him out to be, nor can he be typecast as a simple border ruffian fleeing from failures behind him on America's expanding frontier. Bean stood up for his rights and spoke his mind on all things that concerned him. He was a good citizen of both republics, as the term is generally understood; he paid taxes, testified in court, served as a guardian to minors, went people's bond, sued and was sued, gave certifications of character, witnessed deeds, and did whatever most citizens usually do. Bean was also a good businessman, involved with real estate, sawmills, salt works, agriculture, and stock raising. His homes were open to friends and passersby with a hospitality marking true Texans. If he had a macho attitude toward a wife led astray, and kept quiet about his own infidelity to her, he was not alone in the era. William Barret Travis fled to Texas for similar reasons. And Bean loved to talk and brag about his many adventures, another genuine Texan characteristic.

There is a story handed down in Bean lore that, if not true, ought to be.[36] It goes like this: After Peter Ellis Bean made his will and rode off into the sunrise, his family began to worry when he did not come back. A long search was made to find him, after which Candace began to grieve, thinking her husband had been taken by hostile Indians and killed. Several years later a traveler from Mexico came across Bean's son Isaac, either at the Bean house on his prairie or while Isaac had taken a break from plowing and was eating his lunch near the Angelina River (the stories differ on the location). The sojourner stared at Isaac and said, "Son, you sure look like Colonel Bean who I just saw down in Jalapa, Mexico, with his wife." Isaac replied, "No wonder; he's my father, and I'm mighty glad to know he's still alive!"

Isaac Bean, a single man about twenty-five years old and in the prime of life, saddled up and headed straight to Jalapa, or maybe caught a boat to Veracruz. He found the hacienda where Colonel Bean had lived with Doña Magdalena, but too late to see his father—who had died just a month before his arrival. Doña Magdalena's reaction to this son of her beloved colonel by another woman—she supposedly thinking herself to be Bean's only wife—is not part of the charming tale. In any case, she showed him Bean's grave and told him when he died. When Isaac returned home, he brought his father's favorite horse, his fancy Mexican saddle inlaid with silver, his bridle and bit, and gold-tipped walking cane inscribed "Presented to Colonel Ellis P. Bean by James Bowie." Isaac must have wondered why the legendary Bowie got his father's name wrong, just as he corrected the historian Yoakum a decade later for the same offense. Where these relics are now is anybody's guess.[37]

Colonel Bean's descendants, all of them through Isaac T. Bean and his wife Nancy A. Boone, are still scattered throughout Texas. Some years ago when I was working on a book about Philip Nolan for the recently deceased Robert E. Davis of Waco's Texian Press, he gave me photos of Peter Ellis Bean, his son Isaac, and daughter-in-law Nancy. The one of the colonel was a miniature watercolor of him painted on ivory, set in an ornate circular gold-leaf frame about the size of a saucer. Family tradition had it as a gift to Bean from the pirate Jean Laffite, which, if so, would probably date it around 1815 when Bean was in his early thirties. It is even said in the family that Laffite painted the portrait himself, using a turkey feather for a brush—quite unlikely because of its excellence. There is also the possibility that Jacob Marling was the artist, painting it several years later when Bean visited his relatives in Tennessee. In any case, the portrait went to New Mexico with a female descendant. When Colonel Bean's grandson Joe visited her, he found that she was using it to prop open her bedroom window! Thankfully, he brought the portrait back to Texas where it remains today.[38]

Joe Bean's daughter would not sell the watercolor portrait to Davis, but allowed him to make photographic copies of all three pictures. Bob Davis, a keen collector of Texana, would not tell me the lady's name, and I eventually quit pestering him about it. He probably was put on the trail by an endnote in Bennett Lay's 1960 book, which says that this "portrait of Bean, painted on ivory, is in the possession of Mrs. Leona Hicks of near Moody, Texas. Mrs. Hicks is the great-granddaughter of Ellis P. Bean."[39] She is dead now, but her niece has the portrait and is well aware of its significance to Texas history. If such a valuable relic of Peter Ellis Bean's legacy is still in the family, why not other things like his cane from Bowie, saddle, weapons, Indian artifacts, papers, and no-telling what all? Alas, only the portrait of Bean is presently known. With the exception of that of Philip Nolan, it is one of the earliest likenesses of any old "Texian" who shaped our history.

I know from my own personal experience that families keep and hand down items like this, guarding them with devotion. A treasure trove of old papers and tintypes came to my attention after I circulated a brief family history I had written to long-lost Jackson kinfolks at a 1978 reunion in Stockdale, Wilson County.[40] Just because things are not in archives or museums does not mean that they do not exist. If and when they surface, we might have to take another look at Bean and discover that we did not know him at all. This is why history is such an interesting topic; it is not dead and gone but in a slow process of birth. This book is only one contraction in the effort to understand the life of a man who has never gained the credit he was due, whether for his services to Texas or Mexico.

EPILOGUE

As with most historical figures, questions remain about Peter Ellis Bean and the people with whom he was intimately involved. Except for looking at microfilm church burial records in the city itself, I have made no attempt to search the archives around Jalapa for documentation about Bean. When his wife Doña Magdalena Falfán de los Godos died, if in fact she was related to Morelos, and if her hacienda was really called Las Banderillas all remain undetermined. Does some church record of her marriage to Bean still exist in Huatusco or another village around Veracruz? Or of Bean's date of death outside Jalapa? Did he record a last will and testament in Mexico before he died? Again, unknown.

In terms of Bean's wife in Texas, Candace Midkiff, a bit more information is available. She died near Douglass, Texas, in November 1848—outliving her husband by two years, or maybe one if we rely on her family Bible for Bean's date of death (as I think we should). According to Mattie Austin Hatcher, who wrote a postscript to Bean's memoir for publication by the Book Club of Texas in 1930, Candace pined away and died of a broken heart after Bean left Texas. Her last request was to be buried on the Old San Antonio Road along which Bean had ridden out of her life forever.[1]

In 1936 J. Frank Dobie accused Hatcher of being "bent on fixing up the prettiest romance of love and trust about the whole matter possible." He railed against the sort of mentality being demonstrated by temple guardians of the Texas Centennial, saying that historical figures like Bean had been treated "when treated at all—in a way better calculated to illustrate intellectual dishonesty on the part of the treaters than to allow the light of truth to illuminate all sides of the subject." He included Sam Houston in this category, mentioning his drunkenness in Oklahoma and how

1936 marker for Candace Bean. Photo courtesy Thomas Ricks Lindley.

he had a "squaw for a mate" before coming to Texas to reap "most bountifully of what other men had sowed."[2] Did Dobie have Bean in mind as one of those other men? No matter. Dobie was a sexist by today's standards, and even in his time was considered an iconoclast and detractor of things held sacred—merely a common man's folklorist. Still, few writers have captured the flavor of Old Texas as he did.

Candace lies buried in the Selman-Roark graveyard at Linwood, eight miles from the town of Alto in Cherokee County. People in Nacogdoches have long regarded her as a heroine. A marker was erected to the memory of "Candace Midkiff Bean" in 1936 by the Texas Centennial Commission. It calls her "one of those pioneer women who braved the Indian menace and rocked the cradle of Texas liberty." None of her other husbands are mentioned.[3]

It does not appear that their third child, Ellis M. Bean, had children. Louisa Jane Bean Lacy had two, but both died in infancy. Thus, the eldest son, Isaac T. Bean, and his wife Nancy A. Boone are responsible for all the direct descendants of Peter Ellis Bean past and future. Those that are known, anyway. A lawsuit was brought against these descendants in 1909 by people representing Samuel Bean, one of Peter Ellis's two executors and the lad he had raised as a son. This suit was over land in Houston County that the descendants still held but that Samuel's "estate" said belonged to them, on the basis of his being Bean's son and some deed that Bean had signed but was accidentally destroyed by fire. Reference has already been made to this 1909 suit, and the testimony by people who remembered the family's ins and outs (some of it quoted earlier) is quite interesting.[4]

Witnesses were able to convince the jury that Samuel Bean *was* a son of Colonel Bean's. They had heard Samuel's wife (Carmelita Rutherford) say that her deceased husband was Bean's son. Others stated flatly that Sam, Isaac, and Ellis were brothers—all three the colonel's sons. They said that Colonel Bean called Sam "son," and Sam called the colonel "father." Both Elizabeth Selman and Delilah Allen testified that Sam was one of Bean's four children. All that Bean's descendants through his son Isaac could do was argue that Samuel was not produced through the union of Peter Ellis Bean and Candace Midkiff—sidestepping the question of whether their grandfather might have sired him by another woman. The jury, however, ruled in favor of the plaintiffs. We are left with the assumption that Samuel Bean was either an illegitimate child of the colonel's or the offspring of a marriage that preceded the one to Candace Midkiff in Tennessee. Perhaps this was J. Frank Dobie's basis for making the unsubstantiated statement that Bean had a "third wife elsewhere."[5] No such marriage has been documented.

To prove that Samuel Bean was not a son by Peter Ellis and Candace Bean, but rather Bean's nephew or a more distant relative, documents were introduced into the court record. One item was Candace Midkiff's family Bible, which listed birth dates for her children by Bean and other genealogical information. As with other families, when children came of age, married, and commenced having children, they copied this information into family Bibles of their own. Thus Isaac Bean passed down not only his Bible to his children but his mother Candace's as well. Because it is not given elsewhere in published form, allow me to present this vital data below as combined from five different "Exhibits" in the court record.[6]

BIRTHS & DEATHS

Ellis P. Bean born in Tennessee June 8, 1783; died Oct. 3, 1847, at Jalapa
Candace Midkiff Bean born Dec. 12, 1800; died Nov. 21, 1848
Isaac Thomas Bean born March 5, 1821; died July 5, 1899
Louisa J. Bean born Aug. 27, 1823; died Nov. 11, 1843
Ellis M. Bean born May 8, 1828; died April 15, 1851
Nancy Alkmena [Boone] Bean born March 14, 1829; died Oct. 23, 1893
Andrew Deckard born July 24, 1866; died May 9, 1894

Andrew Deckard is shown as Andrew Deckard Bean in Ellis A. Bean's Bible. The names of his parents are not given, but he may have been the final child of Isaac and Nancy, born in 1876 instead of 1866. This is doubtful, however, because Nancy would have been forty-seven if the year of his birth was 1876, and a daughter (Cornelia) was born to them in 1866. Nancy Alkmena Bean is no doubt Isaac's wife Nancy Alkmena Boone, even though one of the exhibits has the year of her death as 1793—probably miscopied by the clerk or mistyped by Blake. Then the children of Isaac Bean and Nancy Boone are listed (the bracketed information comes from the 1909 court case and the recent "larkcom" and "Family Group Sheet" Internet posts on the Bean family).

Candace America Bean born May 16, 1849; died Nov. [May?] 4, 1868
Ellis Aurelius Bean born Sept. 5, 1850; died [March 20, 1924]
James Washington Bean born April 25, 1853; died [?]
Marquis ["Marcus"] Almonte Bean born Aug. 13, 1854; died [?]
Mary [Nancy?] Elizabeth Bean born Feb. 1, 1856; died Oct. 3, 1893
Thomas Preston Bean born May 11, 1857; died [1935?]
Alkmena Bean born July 30, 1859; died Nov. 10, 1859
William Boone Bean born Dec. 16, 1860; died July 6, 1890

Joseph R[adliff] L[afayette] Bean born July 4, 1863; died [Jan. 6, 1956]
Cornelia Louisa Bean born Feb. 9, 1866; died [1951?]
Alice Bean born Nov. 13, 1869; died [1968?]
Emma Bean born May 17, 1871; died [1941?]

All of this Bible information is fairly consistent in the various court exhibits, except that Isaac's date of birth is mistakenly given as March 14, 1829, in one of them; this was his wife Nancy Boone's birth date. The Bible owned by Emma (the baby) Bean Stephens—which belonged to Candace—had some notes: "Ellis P. Bean come to Texas in 1800; was married in 1818; located in Nacogdoches in 1820." Her father's Bible also recorded that "Isaac T. Bean and Nancy Boon were married at Ruben Boons [house] on Aug. 4, 1847. Cherokee Co. by Revern N. N. Allen." Last of all, Emma certified that "Grandma's [Candace's] Bible was printed by D. Fanshaw in 1831."[7]

This being the case, someone must have copied the information in her Bible from an earlier source. Candace did not, because she could not even sign her name. But a lot of people were illiterate in those days, and they still managed to record entries in family Bibles and leave their mark on Texas history. Those were hard times, so hard that we moderns can scarcely imagine what life was like. And even fewer members of our "wired" generation could go back to those days and be happy and enjoy life as *some* early Texans did.

Isaac and Nancy had twelve kids, as did many other couples of the era, so there are plenty of Beans still squinting at the Texas sun and knocking Texas dust from their heels. Some bear the Bean name, as there were six sons. Issue from the daughters also carry the genes of their notable ancestor. There is no reason to credit William Zuber's opinion to Martin Parmer's grandson that Candace Midkiff was "not respectable" or that Isaac Hix was a "tramp" when she married him (supposedly after Bean's death).[8] Some old-timers of the region remembered her as Candace "Hicks," rather than Candace Bean—small wonder because she used that name and that is what her sons by Colonel Bean called her. Even less credible are the notes that George Crocket assembled in researching his *Two Centuries in East Texas,* wherein it is stated that Bean's "Tennessee wife was an illiterate woman of inferior mental capacity, and her two children are said to have been but little above the grade of morons."[9] Reference must be to her sons Isaac T. and Ellis M. Bean.

These are fighting words, and Crocket was wise not to have published malicious pap such as this in his book. "Said to have been" by whom?[10] Little is known of Ellis, except for the physical abuse charge of his wife and his early death. But Isaac Bean was a respected citizen, just as much as any other Texan of his time. The photographs of him, a handsome man, and his wife Nancy Boone, a strikingly beautiful woman, suggest that their children were fine specimens.[11] On August 4, 1847, Isaac deeded Nancy half of his father's headright league and three slaves. A prenuptial agreement does not necessarily make him a moron, and his bride-to-be certainly had her wits about her in securing a "dowry" of sorts. If the marriage did not work, she at least had some property. But the marriage did last, with gratifying results.

Their earlier children were born in Cherokee County but the later ones in Bell County, where Isaac died at Moody on July 5, 1899; he was seventy-eight, an old man by standards of the day. This was near where Bennett Lay found the ivory portrait of Peter Ellis Bean in the 1950s, owned by a great-granddaughter by the name of Mrs. Leona Hicks. Bob Davis tracked her down at some point in time and made photographs of it and those of Isaac and Nancy as well. Isaac Bean lived longer than his father, even if his life was not so rousingly eventful.[12] Through his children, the past extends into the present. Few Texans have had a forebear more fascinating than Peter Ellis Bean, a man of whom his descendants can justifiably be proud. A bigamist? So it seems, but as Dobie says, "No matter how many wives he had—and he certainly never had a tenth as many as had the wise King Solomon or the psalmist David—he told a bully story."[13] I might add, with his words *and* his life.

APPENDIX A

Certifications of Bean's Military Service during the Mexican Revolution

THE CITIZEN JOSÉ FÉLIX TRESPALACIOS, COLONEL OF CAVALRY OF THE MEXICAN ARMY

I certify on my word of honor that the citizen Pedro Elías Bean, of the Anglo-American nation, was a prisoner before our glorious insurrection in the Province of Texas, because of having fired, in union with others [of] his company members, and in their own defense, on the troops of the King: conducted to the city of Chihuahua, he there remained free on bail four or six years until there arrived the order from Spain that from Bean and his countrymen one out every five should be chosen [to be executed], as thus it was effected, gambling his life with dice on a military strong-box; then they were assigned to Acapulco, from where Bean fended for himself to rejoin Sr. Morelos; by reports that I took in Louisiana and other places, I learned that he was ranked as Colonel for the many services that he had lent in our insurrection and that he had married a decent young woman from Jalapa; and finally, when I was commanding in Béjar, I learned that he did not want to return to this country while its government was monarchical; and so that it may be on record where it is suitable I give the present [certification] at the request of the interested party in Mexico City on Nov. 19 of 1825.

José Félix Trespalacios[1]

• • •

Fourth Seal. One Cuartilla.
For the years of 1824 and [1]825.

Don Antonio de Sesma y Alencastre, Retired Accounting Minister of the Public Treasury, Quartermaster General of the Armies of the South, Alternate Member in the first Supreme Mexican Congress, for the Province of Puebla, and Proprietary [Member] for that of Veracruz; &c, &c.

I certify, in the manner that corresponds to me, that I have known Mister Elías Bean, native of the province of Tenasi, of the States of the North, since the year of 1812, when I joined up with Generalísimo Don José María Morelos; and he impressed upon me the faithfulness, patriotism, and good services that he owed to the aforesaid Elías, telling me that he liked him a lot, for because of his aid and news, he had achieved the complete defeat of [Commandant Francisco] París, which was [the victory] with which he made himself a man, taking from him about 800 arms, more than 500 prisoners, all his artillery, and supplies; [it was] the first force with which he advanced his conquests, and accredited his name, in all the [subsequent] attacks.

From El Veladero, he went on to La Sabana, Aguacatillo, Chichigualco, and the two great actions of Tixtla, a great part of these glories owing itself to the arrangements made by Elías to provide him with powder; which was worked out at all risk and with the greatest activity, by means of his knowledge. Because of these acts [Morelos] gave him the rank of Lieutenant Colonel, having commanded the divisions that were entrusted to him, from which results Elías remained charged with the manufacture of powder and the supplying of niter, and more, while Morelos passed on to Quautla, as in fact, going on to work at Chilapa, the troops of the King withdrew him [caused Bean to withdraw], and he went to Chilpansingo, to manufacture his powder; that which served in the withdrawal from Quautla to again resupply the Army, wherewith he went to protect Trojano besieged in Huajuapa, where the besiegers were defeated completely, losing arms and supplies and even the military strongbox; whence they passed on to set up at the city of Teguacán, having left all that route of the Mixtecs in harmony.

Continuing from Teguacán, we went to Ozumba, to receive the booty that the Sr. Colonel Cano was bringing, taken in Pachuca; at the time that the division that was going to Perote was passing through there, from which we went to the Villa of Orizava, in which withdrawal from this villa for Teguacán, he saw himself with many risks. From Teguacán we passed on to the taking of Oajaca, where, having gone with me to reconnoiter those surroundings, we arranged that powder factories would be set up in one of the high mills; the direction and management of which the

Generalísimo Sr. Morelos turned over to the said Elías. He arranged and elaborated it with prudence, having to burn the said factory when that city was attacked and subjugated by the troops of the King.

Withdrawing to the town of San Pablo Soguitlán, situated in the sierra of Zongualica, from which place the Generalísimo Morelos ordered him to embark promptly for the North of America so as to provide the corresponding advantages in deference to the name of our liberty, and [ordered him] to give notification of those results, and of the state in which Alvarez de Toledo found himself; after which inspections in the Province of Texas, he returned to [New] Orleans, and from there, with sealed documents for Sr. Morelos, to Puruarán, where we found ourselves, from which post there was conferred on him the rank of Colonel, going in company with the commission carried by the Minister Chargé Don José María [Manuel] Herrera, to the States of the North; Elías accompanied them as far as Orleans, from where as soon as he left the Commission, he returned via Boquilla de Piedra and to Guatusco, where he married, and remained until this town was lost; fleeing from here to seek refuge, he was surprised by the Royalists, in a mountain cave, losing all he had; and taken as a prisoner to Veracruz, from where by the aid of Holy Providence he managed to flee, embarking for Orleans. And so that it may be on record I give the present [certification] at the request of the interested party in Mexico City on Nov. 12, 1825.

Ant[oni]o de Sesma[2]

• • •

Fourth Seal. One Cuartilla. For the years of 1824 and [1]825.

I certify, as much as I can, that the North American citizen Pedro Elías Bean, finding himself confined by the Spanish government in the castle of Acapulco, from this fortress joined up in the year '10 with the nascent army of Señor Morelos; and that from then he worked with zeal and faithfulness for the cause of our independence until the year '16 in which he was apprehended by the Royalists, and conducted to the plaza of Veracruz from whence he went to his country. He cooperated in great part, with his valor and sagacity, in the taking of the camp of Commander París, which amounted to no less than eight hundred guns, various artillery pieces, a considerable quantity of munitions, and more than five hundred prisoners, having merited for his gallantry the post of Lieutenant Colonel.

To his knowledge was owed in those beginning [times] the manufacture of the powder, which so usefully and gloriously was employed in the famous actions of El Veladero, Sabana, Aguacatillo, Chichihualco, and Tixtla, and with which the army was provided for the memorable Huajuapan expedition, in which the besieging Royalists of Colonel Trujano were vanquished. In Tehuacan, and Oajaca he continued directing the manufacture of the expressed article, having to burn the workshops constructed in one of the high mills of Oajaca when this province was invaded. Then he withdrew to the town of San Pablo Zoquitlan.

From there he went on to the coast, and succeeded in embarking for the United States of North America where he contributed to the forming of ideas advantageous to our insurrection, and to some Americans' deciding to lend us their assistance. He returned from Orleans with sealed documents from General Albarez de Toledo, which he conducted to Puruarán and put in the hands of the national Government. These sealed documents gave a motive for my being sent to the said United States and earned Bean the commission of Colonel, with which investiture he accompanied me by order of the same government to the cited villa of Orleans, from which he returned at the end of some months; and having remained in the province of Veracruz, he had the misfortune of being surprised by a party of the King['s forces].

And so that all the expressed may give confirmation that the petition [of Bean] may be granted, I give the present [certification] at the request of the interested party. Mexico City, November 14, 1825.

J[ose]ph Man[ue]l Herrera[3]

• • •

FOURTH SEAL. ONE CUARTILLA.
FOR THE YEARS OF 1824 AND [1]825.

Manuel de Mier y Terán, Brigadier General of the Mexican Republic's Army.

I certify: That Don Pedro Elías Bean, native of the United States, was apprehended in the year of 1801 by the Spanish Commander of Internal Provinces Don Nemesio Salcedo in Mexican territory — without more cause, in my judgment, than having introduced himself with other companions within the limits of Mexico — and [was] transferred to the fortress of Acapulco where he was treated inhumanely, maintaining him in shackles until the year 1810, when General Morelos approached the said castle; with which occurrence the Spanish commander, to profit from the services of Bean, set him at liberty, putting him in a militia company; and having set out on a scouting detachment with other company members, two of them North Americans, they were apprehended by the patriots; and with Bean being conducted into the presence of Gen. Morelos, he showed such sentiments in favor of the good cause that this General, trusting in them, permitted him to return to the Royalists to operate among them with greater advantage; that which this official carried out perfectly, for having won over his whole company, which was part of the division of 700 men commanded by París, Bean introduced the patriots by night to the Spanish camp, in which manner that enemy force was surprised and slaughtered.

As a reward Bean received the post of captain of a company; and for the reason that a betrayal had been arranged in which must needs have perished the patriot division, which with the hope of taking control of the Castle had approached the point that the traitors had indicated, Elías Bean took in that incident such prudent measures that the patriots had no loss when those who had contrived that perfidy opened fire. Immediately the attacks on Tixtla were given, in which this official found himself, as in all the subsequent ones up to the taking of Oajaca.

The important services of Bean in that period were those of manufacturing powder on very urgent occasions, in which everything was lacking for making it; difficulties which were conquered only by the activity and intelligence of this individual. After the occupation of Oajaca, in which Bean was present in the employment of Lieutenant Colonel, he constructed in the vicinity of that city a water wheel and a mortar to manufacture powder, in which service he was employed until the year [1]814 when the Royalists again entered Oajaca, [this event] taking Elías in the direction of the sierra after having set fire to his machine and blown it up.

He received orders from General Morelos to go to the United States of the North to solicit aid and put himself in communication with the forces which Alvarez Toledo had gathered in Texas; he returned from this commission, and for his good performance he merited promotion to Colonel and was named again to accompany Don José Manuel Herrera, minister plenipotentiary to the United States; and on his return when the patriots of Veracruz were dispersed, Bean made the greatest efforts to sustain them, and [with these] proving unfruitful, he, at the last moment—and at the time that he was going to be captured, as most of his party were—he presented himself to the Royalists who conducted him to Veracruz to take him to Spain as a prisoner; which he avoided by fleeing, directing himself to the United States where he has remained until last month, when he has presented himself again in this capital. Don Pedro Elías Bean was particularly esteemed by Gen. Morelos for his constant support for Mexican independence; this individual has married a young lady of the land. And so that it may be on record I give the present [certification] in Mexico City on Nov. 15, 1825.

Manuel de Mier y Terán[4]

• • •

Fourth Seal. One Cuartilla. For the years of 1824 and [1]825.

The citizen Vicente Guerrero

I certify that I have known the Anglo-American Don Pedro Elías Bean since the year [1]810 in which, finding himself a prisoner in the castle of Acapulco by the Spanish Government, which held him in suspicion as a revolutionary, he was sent by the Governor of that castle against the troops of the Most Excellent Sr. Gen. Don José María Morelos; and this individual, very far from acting in conformity with his [Royalist] commission, agreed with the said Sr. Morelos that he would serve under his orders but that he should let him return to the castle with the object of enticing [away] the same company in which he had been placed. That thus it was effected, there resulting to our troops the great utility of the arms and munitions of which the said company had made use.

And that since that time Elías Bean began to perform the best and most important services to our liberty and independence, invested with the position of Captain with which Sr. Morelos then gave him the demonstrations of appreciation that his services merited. In that position he was present in the actions of Aguacatillo, Veladero, Sabana, et cetera, et cetera, up to Tehuacan and Oaxaca; being finally sent by the same Most Excellent Sr. Gen. Morelos to his country of North America in a request for aid and to see the state of the Commission of Gen. Alvarez de Toledo, Elías being already at that time Lieutenant Colonel.

And having returned this time, continuing in search of our army as far as Puruarán, he was promoted by the Congress to Colonel, in which position he returned to the United States in the company of Sr. Don José Manuel Herrera; which is as far as I have seen his history, but I learned that he had other commissions and services, maintaining himself in the United States of North America until a month ago, when he returned. And so that it may be on record where it may be suitable to his petition, I give him the present [certification] in Mexico City on the fifteenth of November of 1825.

Vicente Guerrero[5]

• • •

Don Nicolás Brabo [Bravo], Meritorious [Patriot] of the Motherland, Division General, &c., &c.

I certify: That in the year '11 I met Don Pedro Elías Bean lending services to the Motherland in the army of the Most Excellent Sr. Don José María Morelos whom he supplied with powder that he himself manufactured in very straitened circumstances and [those] in which this so-necessary article was lacking. It is on record to me also that in the actions of war he presented himself with his gun in the ranks to defend the rights of the Motherland and at his petition I give him the present [certification] for the mo[tive]s that may be suitable to him, in Chichihualco on Nov. 6, 1825.

Nicolás Brabo[6]

APPENDIX B

Bean to Guadalupe Victoria, November 24, 1825

MOST EXCELLENT SIR.

[*In margin*:] Jan. 9, '27. Pass on to the commissioners. — G. Pedraza

I, the citizen Pedro Elías Bean, humbly, in this capital, to Your Excellency respectfully say: That as they accredit in the six certifications that in 10 legal sheets I duly present, since the year of 1810 I have devoted myself to serve, with [all] possible meticulousness, the Mexican Nation in the terrible struggle that it has sustained for the cause of the independence that it now enjoys, serving principally under the orders of the Most Excellent Sr. Gen. Don José María Morelos y Pavón.

I would have been [one] of the first who presented themselves in this territory for the third time, after the cry of Yguala had been given, if because of my past misfortunes I had not been found at the time in the United States of North America; for besides, I found myself, like them [Mexican exiles?], legitimately married in this Republic; but when I undertook my journey I found out on the way that an Empire had been installed, a form of government that always has disgusted my republican principles, and for which reason I refused to come to increase the number of slaves of the Monarch [Iturbide] who had grasped the scepter, scandalously trampling the sacred rights of these peoples, and making useless their previous sacrifices and efforts to be free.

For a similar reason (to which may very well be added that of distance) I have not appeared at an opportune time before the Board of Compensation to represent my rights so as to receive the demonstration of recompense to which my services have made me entitled; the time has passed, and although this never elapses according to law for the *ignorant, or the disabled,* I understand that Your Excellency is only too well authorized by the constitution and the laws, no less than by the extraordinary powers that have been conceded to you, to reward the worthy.

I have the satisfaction of appealing at this time to the presence of Your Excellency, less as to the first magistrate of the Mexican Nation than as to an eyewitness and . . . let it be permitted me to say it, with a certain noble pride, as to a companion in arms who served under the orders and the voice of the same leader whom I obeyed and loved as the most firm support of our hopes and [the] illustrious adornment of the Mexican Nation and liberty. Therefore, and with Your Excellency being convinced of the truth of my services that I have demonstrated, in conformity with the history of the revolution —

I pray Your Excellency to be pleased to grant me the distinction to which for these [services] you may judge me as entitled. Mexico City, November 24, 1825.

Pedro Ellis Bean

Most Excellent Señor President D. Guadalupe Victoria.[7]

APPENDIX C

Bean to Compensation Board [?], June 7, 1826

Most Excellent Sir:

The Citizen Pedro Elías Bean, Lieut. Colonel of permanent Cavalry with the rank of Colonel, before Your Excellency with the due respect expresses: That since the beginning of November of the year [1]810 he began to serve for the liberty of the Motherland; that on the 20th of December of the same year, in consideration of having distinguished himself in the actions of La Sabana carried out by the Most Excellent Sr. Gen. Don José María Morelos, he was made Captain of Cavalry; that he obtained various commissions and among them that of Commander of Engineers; that because of the victories that the Army to which he belonged had then, he was made Lieutenant Colonel of Cavalry on December 28 by the same Señor General.

In whose employ he was commissioned to [go to] the United States, from where, on his return, he was granted the employment of Colonel of the same branch on May 2, 1815; that having represented his services before Your Excellency with certificates from the Señores Generals, he was granted the employment and rank that he has obtained, but not having received the patent [of] the seniority that belongs to him, he prays Your Excellency that you order it credited to him and that the General Staff, with the presence of the documents that he attached to his first petition, form [and issue] for him the service record that corresponds because of the expressed [services].[8]

APPENDIX D

Certification of Bean's Military Service to Mexico, by Vicente Filisola and Francisco García Conde, January 1, 1828

By certifications of the Citizen Division Generals Nicolás Bravo, Vicente Guerrero, and Ygnacio Rayón [Antonio Sesma?], Citizen General of Brigades Manuel de Mier y Terán, Colonel José Félix Tres Palacios and Sr. José Manuel de Herrera, it is credited to this leader that finding himself confined by the Spanish Government in the Castle of Acapulco, he joined in the year [1]810 the Army of Señor Morelos, gathering an armed Company from the said fortress, and from then on he worked with zeal and faithfulness for the just cause of our Independence until the year [1]816 in which he was apprehended by the Royalists and conducted to the Plaza of Veracruz from which he transferred himself to his [native] country.

He cooperated in great part with his valor and gallantry in the taking of the camp of Commander París, which amounted to no fewer than 800 guns, several pieces of artillery, a considerable quantity of munitions, and more than 500 prisoners, having merited by his heroic valor the post of Lieutenant Colonel. To his knowledge was due in those [years] the manufacture of the powder that so usefully and gloriously was used in the famous actions of El Veladero, Savana, Aguacatillo, Chichihualco and Tixtla, with which he provided the army for the memorable Huajuapan expedition in which the besieged Royalists of Colonel Trujano were vanquished. In Tehuacan and Oajaca he continued directing the manufacture of the expressed article, and had to burn the offices constructed in one of the high mills of Oajaca when this city was invaded by the troops of the oppressing Government.

Then he withdrew to the town of San Pablo Zoquitlan; from there he passed on to the coast and succeeded in embarking for the destination of the United States of North America, where he contributed to there being formed advantageous ideas of our emancipation and to some Americans' deciding to lend aid for our glorious Independence. He returned from [New] Orleans with sealed documents from General Alvarez y Toledo which he conducted as far as Puruarán and put in the hands of the American [Mexican] government. These sealed documents gave occasion for them to send Señor Don José Manuel de Herrera as Plenipotentiary to the United States of America, the Government rewarding the services of this leader [Bean] with the post of Colonel, with which investiture he accompanied Sr. Herrera to the cited Villa of [New] Orleans, from which he returned at the end of some months; and having remained in the state of Veracruz, he had the misfortune of being surprised by the enemy troops. The sufferings of this leader to uphold the present system are notorious, according to the credentials that demonstrate his extreme patriotism and valor. —

Francisco García Conde, 2nd Aide of the G[eneral] S[taff] and agent of the Divisional Section of this State by the Law of May 10 of last year.

I certify that the service record which precedes is in everything formed from the expediente that is returned to the G[eneral] S[taff] according to the time that the Compensation Advisory Board assessed it, there remaining an equal copy of this record filed in this office under my charge. Mexico, January 1, 1828.

Vicente Filisola *Fr[ancis]co G. Conde*[9]

APPENDIX E

Bean to Lewis Cass, February 24, 1833

Sir: My duty as Military Commander of the Northeast portion of the U.S. of Mexico imposes on me a heavy task. I must therefore acquaint you with certain facts that are not consonant with the treaties and friendly relations existing between the Republic of the U.S. of the North and that of the U.S. of Mexico. You will probably deem it advisable to lay these facts before the President to enable him to interpose his authority through his agents or officers and relieve this Government from a calamity which, besides being an usurpation of its territory, may also expose the lives and property of its inhabitants to imminent danger.

It was stipulated in Article 33 of the treaty of 1831 ratified in the city of Mexico, that the outrages or attacks of any description whatever by Indians residing in the territory of either Republic shall be reciprocally repressed. You will acknowledge that both contracting parties bind themselves by the said treaty and article to repress any hostilities and incursions by the Indian tribes living within their respective territory, and that the principal object of said article is to prevent not only the evils and injuries that may result to the inhabitants of both Republics but also the incursions and introduction of tribes living in the territory of the one of the contracting parties, into territories claimed by, and the property of, the other party. A strict and faithful adherence to the above stipulation would undoubtedly bring to an end the evils therein contemplated.

A very short time since, several hundred Choctaw Indians emigrated from Natchitoches, territory of the U.S. of the North, and established themselves in the middle of the settlement of this Municipality, at 24 miles from this post, and they declare that an equal number of Indians of the same tribe have also an intention to settle here. I am satisfied that no less than 700 Indians have introduced themselves in this territory in the course of this month. This, however, is not the principal source of serious apprehension entertained by the citizens of the U.S. of Mexico, but some time since several Seminole Chiefs from Eastern Florida, in company with two white men, passed through this post, on their return from an exploration of the territory South West of the Brazos, and declared it to be the intention of said chiefs to emigrate into this Province, next Spring, with several tribes of the Creek Nation, now living in Florida, a part of the territory of the U.S. of North America.

The mutual good faith and harmony of both Republics demand a reciprocal understanding in regard to this subject, which is evidently of paramount importance, and would awake the just resentment of my Government, if a suspicion could be entertained that the President, or officers, of the U.S. of the North have sanctioned or permitted this trespass on the territory of the Republic of Mexico.

It is a fact that those Indians passed in the vicinity of a Military post of the U.S. of the North (Fort Jesup) on their way to the Sabine river, to introduce themselves into the Province of Texas. It is also a fact that the Choctaws followed the same direction on their way from Natchitoches, which was quite deviating from the course they should have taken, to reach the territory East of the Colorado [Red River?] ascribed to them within the limits of this [your?] Government. By this representation to the U.S. of the North, such measures are requested as may be taken in good faith to prevent any such introduction for the future, and cause the withdrawal of the Indians who have already introduced themselves into this Province back to the territory ascribed them by the Government of the U.S. of the North. This course is demanded by the existing treaty and the friendly relations existing between both Governments and their respective citizens.

I trust that the enlightened policy, as well as the character for morality of the President of the U.S. of the North, will suggest to him the propriety of preventing any attempts on the part of the Creek Indians to trespass on the territory of Mexico and more particularly that of this Province.

You will feel at once the peculiarity of my situation, and acknowledge that it is my imperious duty to inform immediately my Government of these facts, in order to cover my responsibility. I am &c. Pedro Elias Bean[10]

APPENDIX F

Bean to Andrew Jackson, September 11, 1835

Sir: In addressing your excellency, I would feel myself under ordinary circumstances trespassing on the rules of established etiquette; but I trust that the subject on which I have the honor to approach you will, at least, excuse a deviation from the routine of office communications.

As early as the 24th of February, 1833, I addressed a letter to Lewis Cass, secretary of war of the United States, on the subject of the incursions of Indians from the United States into this country, and referred him to the treaty concluded at the city of Mexico, on the 6th day of April, 1831, the 33rd article of which provides and declares that, "Both parties bind themselves expressly, to restrain by force, all hostilities and incursions on the part of the Indians living within their respective boundries," &c. &c. At the date of the letter, small bands of Choctaws were daily making incursions from the United States, and locating themselves in the middle of the settlement[s] of Texas, and I hope you will allow me to call your excellency's attention to one circumstance of a striking character. The Indians were compelled, in pursing their route to this country, to pass by a fortress of the United States (Fort Jessup). The annoyance to the community as well as the danger which has resulted from the fact of their incursion, was clearly anticipated at the time of my letter to the secretary of war. If any measures have been adopted by your excellency, agreeable to the treaty, either to restrain others by force from similar incursions, I have not had the honor to be apprised of the fact.

Within the last winter and spring a project was set on foot by Benjamin Hawkins and another individual to introduce into Texas no less than 24,000 Creeks from the United States for which they were to receive $100,000. The plan was for a while delayed, but from appearances on which I place the most undoubted rehance [reliance?], he has left this section and departed to the United States, with the avowed intention of introducing Apotheyahola, with 5,000 of his tribe, immediately to Texas, and the remainder are to remove as soon as practicable, and all the Indian tribes already here are to be united to those of the Creek nation, as soon as they shall arrive. Previous to the departure of Hawkins and his friend to meet the chief at New Orleans, he applied to me, as superintendent of the Indians in Texas, and informed me that a grand speculation could be made out of the Creeks in the old nation by permitting them to move to lands in this country; that a large sum of money could be obtained from them. I promptly assured him that no such thing could take place—nor be permitted by me, as it was contrary to the laws of the republic, and the existing treaties with the United States. Disregarding my instructions, he persisted in violating the solemn laws of both countries. Your excellency will at once perceive that the avarice and cupidity of [these] individuals, is to make a barter of human life, without [unless] your excellency will most strictly enforce the stipulations of the treaty, and prevent the emigration and incursions of those Indians to any part of Texas.

Your excellency will perceive from the duties devolving on me, as superintendent of all the Indian tribes in this department, and military commander, that I could not acquit my duty to myself and my country, had I remained silent or deaf to the appeals of humanity.

Your excellency will anticipate the propriety of my transmitting, forthwith, a report and copy of this communication to my government. God and liberty. I have the honor to be your excellency's ob't servant. Peter E. Bean, col. of cavalry, commanding the eastern department [of Texas].[11]

ABBREVIATIONS

AHSDN	Archivo Histórico, Secretaría de la Defensa Nacional, Mexico City
AOCCN	Archives from the Office of the County Clerk, Nacogdoches
BA	Béxar Archives, Center for American History, University of Texas at Austin
Bean MSR	Military service record (Pedro Elías Bean), Archivo Histórico, Secretaría de la Defensa Nacional, Mexico City
Blake Transcripts (R) and (G)	Robert Bruce Blake Research Collection (Red) and (Green)
BNAH	Biblioteca Nacional de Antropología e Historia, Mexico City
CAH	Center for American History, University of Texas at Austin
ETRC	East Texas Research Center, Steen Library, Stephen F. Austin State University, Nacogdoches
IED (Coahuila)	Instituto Estatal de Documentación (State Archives of Coahuila), Ramos Arizpe
NA	Nacogdoches Archives, Texas State Library, Austin
NA Transcripts	Nacogdoches Archives typescript collection, Texas State Library, Austin
NCCO	Nacogdoches County Clerk's Office
NHOT	*The New Handbook of Texas*
QTSHA	*Quarterly of the Texas State Historical Association*

SHQ	*Southwestern Historical Quarterly*
SRE	Secretaría de Relaciones Exteriores, Mexico City
TGLO	Texas General Land Office, Austin
TSL	Texas State Library, Austin

NOTES

Acknowledgments

1. The three books mentioned are Maurine T. Wilson and Jack Jackson, *Philip Nolan and Texas: Expeditions to the Unknown Land, 1791–1801;* Jack Jackson, ed., and John Wheat, trans., *Texas by Terán: The Diary Kept by General Manuel de Mier y Terán on His 1828 Inspection of Texas;* Jack Jackson, ed., and John Wheat, trans., *Almonte's Texas: Juan N. Almonte's 1834 Inspection, Secret Report & Role in the 1836 Campaign.*

2. Bennett Lay, *The Lives of Ellis P. Bean.* It is hereafter cited as Lay, *Lives,* in an effort to dispense with the given name that Bean used in his early years as opposed to "Peter Ellis," which he adopted in the mid-1820s and used while he was an Indian agent in Texas.

3. Bean's military service record is in the Cancelados section of the Archivo Histórico, Secretaría de la Defensa Nacional (AHSDN), Mexico City, with the number C46. XI/111/4-701, under the name Pedro Elías Bean, Colonel of Cavalry. Starting in chapter 3 it is given as "Bean MSR" by folio number of the document cited therein. These records are in bound books.

4. I should here note the recently published two volume reference work that Galen D. Greaser has compiled and written for the Texas General Land Office (TGLO): *Catalogue of the Spanish Collection of the Texas General Land Office.* Part 1 is subtitled *Titles, Unfinished Titles, Character Certificates, Applications for Admission, Registers & Field Notes;* Part 2: *Correspondence, Empresario Contracts, Decrees, Appointments, Reports, Notices & Proceedings.* This monumental work will serve researchers at the TGLO greatly for generations to come.

5. See Ron Tyler et al., eds., *The New Handbook of Texas* (hereafter *NHOT*), 4:924, for a brief entry on the Nacogdoches Archives collection (hereafter NA Transcripts). I used the set at the Center for American History, University of Texas at Austin (hereafter CAH), but the Archives Division of the Texas State Library (hereafter TSL) has a set, as well as the original documents. For microfilm of the originals, one must walk down the hall and use the machines in Genealogy. Of the Buquor/Debray Translations at TSL, I mostly used the "2d series" translated in 1856 by X. B. Debray; he called them "Historical Documents found in the Archives of Bexar County." They consist of forty-four packets, written on legal-sized, ruled paper in a very legible hand, filed in box 2004/046. A chronological guide to the collection is available.

6. Tyler et al., *NHOT,* 1:579–80, has an entry on Robert Bruce Blake and how he assembled the ninety-three volumes of this "research collection," seventy-five volumes of

which are bound in red and eighteen as a "supplement" series in green. They are hereafter cited as Blake Transcripts (R) and (G). At the beginning of each volume is a description of Blake's tremendous contribution to students of Texas history written by Jesse J. Lee of Houston. See also the Blake (Robert Bruce) Papers at CAH.

7. James L. Haley, *Sam Houston;* Thomas Ricks Lindley, *Alamo Traces: New Evidence and New Conclusions.* Lindley also shared with me numerous documents about Bean found during the course of his own research, and a few concerning Houston. How the relationship between Bean and Houston changed after 1835 is important to my book and is traced as fully as the documentation permits.

Chapter 1

1. Bean family Bible entries, Blake Transcripts (R), 52:225, 262.

2. Internet post: http://www.larkcom.com/ancestry/bean (see p. 4 of 12). Also at www.larkcom.net/org/ancestry/bean/history.htm (copyright 1999 by LaRK Communications). The watercolor of him that I reproduced in my Nolan book is seen on www.larkcom.net without credit to the source for it.

3. Lay, *Lives,* 4–7, gives a bit of family history as it was available to him in 1960. For a better and more recent treatment see Martha L. Crabb, *Over the Mountain: A Narrative History of the Bean, Selman, and Germany Families,* chapter 3, "The Bean Clan." See also Jamie Ault Grady, *William Bean, Pioneer of Tennessee and His Descendants,* 30–31, 35, 38–41. This is a Bean genealogy by generation; my thanks to Carolyn Reeves Ericson for providing a copy of Grady's information entered on standard family group sheets. There is also a William Bean Internet post that seems to follow Grady's work: www.pearland.com. Yet another Bean "Family Group Sheet" appears on www.varleyphoto.com. The information on these posts does not always agree.

4. For brief mention of Bean's Station see Lay, *Lives,* 7; Crabb, *Over the Mountain,* 118 (giving the text of the historical marker on the site).

5. Internet post as cited in n2 above, p. 4. Crabb, *Over the Mountain,* 101, 118–23, notes the difficulty in sorting out the children of Captain Bean and Lydia Russell. In his 1782 will he named sons William, George, Robert, and Russell, but Jesse, Edmund, and John are usually accepted, along with daughters Jane and Sarah. These given names were usually repeated in subsequent generations, making the Bean family tree hard to sort out.

6. Edmund Been to Peter Ellis Been, 28 Jan. 1827, Eugene C. Barker, ed., *The Austin Papers,* vol. 1, pt. 2, 1595 (vol. 1 is in two parts). Edmund asks about "Aunt Midcalf," suggesting that he was a nephew and that Bean's Tennessee relatives considered Candace Midkiff as his wife. Or Edmund may have been Peter Ellis's brother, and the "Aunt" a tactful reference because he knew about the Mexican wife, as Lay suggests in *Lives,* 132–33. According to Crabb, *Over the Mountain,* 122–23, Russell was stabbed in the back and died on 9 Jan. 1826 in Washington County, Tennessee, at age fifty-seven. He was married to Rosamond Robertson, and his five sons were "skilled and well-known gunsmiths."

7. Robert V. Remini, *Andrew Jackson and the Course of American Empire, 1767–1821,* 115, citing James Parton's *Life of Andrew Jackson,* 2 vols. (Boston: Ticknor and Fields, 1866). The "cats and dogs" fight (without naming Bean) is given in *The Life of Andrew Jackson, President of the United States, by Major Jack Dowling,* 16–18. An illustration of the standoff (dating the event 1802) is in Paul O'Neil, *The Frontiersmen,* 192–93. Crabb, *Over the Mountain,* 122–23, gives the date as 1801. Russell was tried, convicted, branded on the hand, put in stocks, and whipped for his offense. See Grady, *William Bean,* 94–98, for more on Russell and Rosamond Bean.

8. All citations of Bean's memoir are from the original edition found in H[enderson King] Yoakum, *History of Texas from Its First Settlement in 1685 to Its Annexation to the United States in 1846,* 1:403–52, called his appendix no. 2, and hereafter cited as Bean, "Memoir." Quote about Andrew Jackson is on p. 449.

9. Much of this Tennessee background is derived from Lay, *Lives,* 3–12, and Crabb, *Over the Mountain,* 85–126. See also the n2 Internet post (p. 2) for the 1769 birth of Peter Ellis's "Uncle Russell," final child of Capt. William and Lydia Russell Bean.

10. On the Beans during the American Revolution, see Crabb, *Over the Mountain,* 110–17. For a parallel study of another such frontier clan, see Jack Jackson, "The Trammells: Being a History of a Pioneering Family, with Emphasis on the Descendants of Nicholas Trammell Who Blazed 'Trammell's Trace' When Texas Was a Province of Spain" (unpublished, but a copy recently placed at the CAH with my papers).

11. For Terán's letters about how the Anglos did not need to use roads to infiltrate Texas, see Jackson and Wheat, *Texas by Terán,* 31–33, 97–100, 104–105, 178.

12. Josiah H. Shinn, *Pioneers and Makers of Arkansas,* 273. On this migration westward the Trammells and Beans engaged in producing salt. Mark Bean's salt works in old Hempstead County are well documented in official records. In 1825 Gov. George Izard of Arkansas Territory gave him permission to work the salines because he and his brother had "long manufactured good salt at a low cost," and it was a commodity much needed by the settlers and Indians of the region. Grant Foreman, *Indians & Pioneers: The Story of the American Southwest before 1830,* 59–60, 133–34, 152, 156, 167; also Jackson, "The Trammells," 15, 25. Mark Bean, like his cousin Peter Ellis Bean in Texas at the same time, had to deal with the prior claims of Indians to his salt works.

13. Lay, *Lives,* 9–10.

14. Here begins Bean's own memoir account, used by all later writers to summarize his adventures. See especially the treatments in Lay, *Lives,* and John Edward Weems, *Men without Countries: Three Adventurers of the Early Southwest.* Note that Bean says his father did not want him to go at age seventeen (i.e., in 1800), even though Grady (*William Bean,* 30) states definitely that William died in 1798 and the captain's estate was administered by his wife Elizabeth, assisted by Robert Blair. The "larkcom" Internet post, however, has Capt. William Bean Jr. living to about 1825 and dying in Hawkins County, Tennessee. Grady states the following about Peter Ellis's mother: "We feel sure Elizabeth died the year of 1818 when the children were disposing of the [estate's] property and leaving Grainger County." She also believes that Peter Ellis and the next three children were born in Hawkins County instead of Grainger.

15. For a detailed study of Nolan's expeditions, and Bean's role in the final one, see Wilson and Jackson, *Philip Nolan and Texas.*

16. Bean, "Memoir," 404–408.

17. Wilson and Jackson, *Philip Nolan and Texas,* follows the prisoners into Chihuahua, supplementing Bean's memoir by use of Spanish accounts of their captivity and escape attempts.

Chapter 2

1. Quoted in Lay, *Lives,* 42.

2. Wilson and Jackson, *Philip Nolan and Texas,* 98; account taken from seized letters between the conspirators leading up to their attempted escape.

3. Bean, "Memoir," 413.

4. See, for example, Flora Lowrey, "Peter Ellis Bean: A Typical Filibuster of Early

Texas History," 40, where it is stated that "It may be that [Bean's] remarks regarding Jefferson indicate his motive for remaining at least not disloyal to Mexico later."

5. Bean, "Memoir," 415–16.

6. Ibid., 416–19, for all quotes concerning the episode with María Baldonada.

7. Ibid., 418.

8. On this castle, or fortification, called San Diego, see Vito Alessio Robles, *Acapulco, Saltillo y Monterrey en la Historia y la Leyenda,* 1–102; Enrique Cárdenas de la Peña, *Historia Maritima de México: Guerra de Independencia, 1810–1821.* The latter writer used Bean's military service record to supplement his memoir for the action at Acapulco (and on the Gulf Coast as well). This was how I learned that such a file existed and its number, but at that time access to the archives of the Mexican War Department was very difficult for foreigners; it has since improved.

9. Bean, "Memoir," 419–33, for all quotes found in the text.

10. Ibid., 427, 433. Lay, *Lives,* 60, 186, identifies the "old Spaniard" who joined Nolan's venture in Natchez as Luciano García. On the 1801 list of prisoners he gave his age as thirty-nine, native of Real de Charcas and resident of Nacogdoches (Wilson and Jackson, *Philip Nolan and Texas,* 41). For the most assuredly different man of the same name who was briefly governor of Texas in 1823, see Tyler et al., *NHOT,* 3:85.

11. Bean, "Memoir," 433–38, covers his initial services to Morelos in the vicinity of Acapulco; quote on p. 434.

12. Ibid., 439; an account substantiated by depositions in Bean's service record as given in appendix A.

13. Useful in following the activities of Morelos and Bean's part is Wilbert H. Timmons, *Morelos of Mexico: Priest, Soldier, Statesman.*

14. Bean, "Memoir," 441.

15. Ibid., 443.

16. Lay, *Lives,* 81, 83.

17. Bean, "Memoir," 444.

18. Timmons, *Morelos of Mexico,* 127–28, 132.

19. Bean, "Memoir," 445–46. There is much inconsistency in the spelling of placenames in these records by all participants—especially with Indian names.

20. Ibid., 446. See also Timmons, *Morelos of Mexico,* 145–46, for events following.

21. Bean, "Memoir," 446–49. For the situation at New Orleans and in the Neutral Ground at this time, see Harris G. Warren, *The Sword Was Their Passport: A History of American Filibustering in the Mexican Revolution;* Bean's arrival is mentioned on pp. 110–14. He wrote a letter about the Mexican Revolution at New Orleans on 21 Oct. 1814, which was published in the Winchester *Kentucky Advertiser,* 14 Jan. 1815. A copy of this narrative has unfortunately not come to hand. Another useful work is Frank Lawrence Owsley Jr. and Gene A. Smith, *Filibusters and Expansionists: Jeffersonian Manifest Destiny, 1800–1821.*

22. Bean, "Memoir," 449. The voyage back to Mexico is more fully treated in Warren, *The Sword Was Their Passport,* 120–24. Despite this family tradition linking the Bean portrait to Jean Laffite at the time of the Battle of New Orleans, Joseph Musso—an authority on early nineteenth-century American portraiture—believes it to be the work of Jacob Marling (1774–1833). Marling resided in Raleigh, North Carolina, so Bean may have sat for this portrait several years later when he visited his relatives in eastern Tennessee and married the young woman he brought to Texas, Candace Midkiff.

23. Bean, "Memoir," 450. For the arrival of Ambassador José Manuel de Herrera at New Orleans, see Warren, *The Sword Was Their Passport,* 127–34; Carlos E. Castañeda, *Our Catholic Heritage in Texas, 1519–1936,* 6:138–40.

24. Bean, "Memoir," 450. Here Yoakum adds a lengthy note on Almonte and his years at New Orleans.

25. Ibid. How Bean returned to Mexico is uncertain, but Lay, *Lives,* 100–101, suggests it was on the *Petit Milan,* which left New Orleans with a cargo of arms on 15 Jan. 1816. Filibuster ships were coming and going frequently after Herrera's arrival, among them the *Surprise* and the *Firebrand.*

26. Bean, "Memoir," 451 (Yoakum note).

27. On Isaac's trip to meet the Mexican widow, and several different versions of it, see chapter 21, n36.

28. Bean, "Memoir," 451.

29. Ibid., 451–52.

30. According to the depositions in his service record, the story of Bean's escape on his wife's horse given in Lay, *Lives,* 104, cannot be true; see appendix A. Mrs. W. D. Peevey (an old resident of Nacogdoches who claimed to be intimate with Bean's family and a descendant of his half brother William Shaw) had this getaway episode occurring in Texas, Bean using his wife's fresh horse to outrun Spanish pursuers across the Sabine! Ridiculous.

31. Yoakum, *History of Texas,* 1:236; information based on the manuscript "Memoirs" of Bean's half brother in Tennessee, Capt. William Shaw. Interestingly, he later showed up in east Texas; see chapter 18, n45. In two letters written to Mattie Austin Hatcher in Feb. 1937, Bennett Lay asked if she knew what had happened to this Shaw memoir. He also revealed the "intense interest" that later led him to do a biography of Bean: Lay's great-grandmother was Mary Bean Shaw, thought to be Capt. William Shaw's daughter. Hatcher replied in March, not very helpfully, that she had put "all I could find out about him" in her "reprint of Bean's story" for the Book Club of Texas in 1930. Bean Genealogy File, CAH.

32. See the deposition of Trespalacios, appendix A. The 17 July 1822 document, which Bean signed twice, was offered for sale in 1986 and is listed in the catalog titled *Philpott Texana Collection Auction* (Dallas: Altermann Art Gallery, 1986), item 174, with thanks to Dorothy Sloan. I wonder if the year should not be 1824? No other evidence has come to light that Bean was a magistrate at Nacogdoches as early as 1822.

33. Clarke to Austin, 3 Feb. 1824, Barker, *Austin Papers,* vol. 1, pt. 1, 738–39.

34. Clarke to Austin, 12 June 1824, ibid., 828–29.

35. James Gaines is another of those interesting-but-neglected border characters; see the short entry on him in Tyler et al., *NHOT,* 3:42–43, and the longer sketch in Louis Wiltz Kemp, *The Signers of the Texas Declaration of Independence,* 127–34.

36. This incident is covered in Jack Jackson, "Nicholas Trammell's Difficulties in Mexican Texas," *East Texas Historical Journal* 38, no. 2 (2000): 22–23. It is a spin-off of my longer, unpublished history of the Trammell family cited in chapter 1, n10.

37. Ibid., 16–18.

38. Jackson, "The Trammells," 4–14, traces the history of the family following the death of Nicholas Sr. in 1784; copy at CAH.

39. The eviction is treated in Jackson, "Nicholas Trammell's Difficulties in Mexican Texas," 26–36.

40. Ibid., 23.

41. Bean election certification, 5 Mar. 1825, NA Transcripts, 195:160, 172 (CAH, box 2Q298); see also Blake Transcripts (R), 11:18. For Bean to Torres, 6 Sept. 1824, re horse thieves, see NA Transcripts, 26:5.

42. Bean Internet post, 1, 4, 7, as cited in chapter 1, n2. The brother's name is given in this source as William M. Bean, 1785–1867, who married Mary Polly Mauck in Frederick County, Virginia, on 5 Aug. 1804. The family sheets derived from Jamie Ault Grady

give no middle initial for William Bean but say that he married Polly McIlhaney on 23 July 1808.

43. Bean, in the petition for land quoted on p. [34], stated that he built this house in January 1823. It had "cost me a lot of work," said Bean, and William was not mentioned.

44. Jackson, "Nicholas Trammell's Difficulties in Mexican Texas," 23.

45. Ibid., 23–24.

46. NA Transcripts, 196:57–59 (CAH, box 2Q298). I will give the box number for these volumes (and those in other collections at CAH) because finding the documents without this information is a time-consuming chore.

Chapter 3

1. The federal colonization law of 18 Aug. 1824 is given in Carolyn Reeves Ericson, *Nacogdoches—Gateway to Texas: A Biographical Directory, 1773–1849,* 207–8; also in Malcolm D. McLean, ed., *Papers concerning Robertson's Colony in Texas,* 2:214–17.

2. On Iturbide's banishment and execution see Stanley C. Green, *The Mexican Republic: The First Decade, 1823–1832,* 14, 43; Ohland Morton, *Terán and Texas: A Chapter in Texas-Mexican Relations,* 33–34. On Gutiérrez's part in the execution see David E. Narrett, "José Bernardo Gutiérrez de Lara: Caudillo of the Mexican Republic in Texas," *Southwestern Historical Quarterly* (hereafter cited as *SHQ*) 106 (Oct. 2002): 227.

3. The state colonization law of 24 Mar. 1825 is in Ericson, *Nacogdoches—Gateway to Texas,* 209–13; also in McLean, *Papers concerning Robertson's Colony,* 2:269–88.

4. Luis Prosela character certificate for Bean, 6 Apr. 1825, Béxar Archives (hereafter cited as BA); translated in Blake Transcripts (G), 9:27.

5. For Candace's deposition see chapter 4. Her Bible information is given in the epilogue. On the 1822 mortgage that Bean signed at Nacogdoches as a "justice of the peace," see chapter 2, n32; I have not examined this document, to confirm the year, or learned its present whereabouts (it did not sell at the auction).

6. Bean land petition, 5 Apr. 1825, BA (CAH, box 2S161). The box number is given when I have examined the original letter in BA.

7. Robert Collier deposition, 22 Aug. 1826, NA; Blake Transcripts (R), 11:191.

8. Saucedo to González, 26 June 1825, BA; translated in Blake Transcripts (G), 9:39–40. Saucedo's original is in the State Archives of Coahuila (now called Instituto Estatal de Documentación and hereafter cited as IED [Coahuila]), filed as AGEC, FJPB, C11, E65, 2F, ficha 1076. Negative photostats of some of these records concerning Bean are at CAH, which I will cite as Saltillo Archives. The collection is now in the nearby village of Ramos Arizpe and is a state-of-the-art facility with all the documents digitized.

9. See Edward A. Lukes, *The DeWitt Colony in Texas,* 55–56, where it is stated that Bean's interest in the affairs of DeWitt remains unknown. I cannot explain the situation further, unless Bean was repeating gossip at Nacogdoches on DeWitt's checkered past and trying to boost his self-importance to the political chief at Béxar. Virtually all of the Anglo empresarios had strikes against them before coming to Texas, whether for escaping indebtedness or more serious charges.

10. Bastrop to Austin, 16 July 1825, Barker, *Austin Papers,* vol. 1, pt. 2, 1147. Bastrop's political activities on behalf of Texas are fully covered in Charles A. Bacarisse's study, "The Baron de Bastrop," CAH, box 2Q417; see p. 214.

11. Austin to González, 17 Oct. 1825, BA. The proceedings that Austin conducted at San Felipe to clear DeWitt are not available.

12. Yoakum, *History of Texas,* 1:173n (Bean quote about Gutiérrez).

13. Yoakum's source for this 1825–26 notebook, or diary, is unknown. Bean probably left it (along with his manuscript memoir) with family or friends when he moved to Mexico in 1843.

14. Bean, "Memoir," 451. For information on Bean's Mexican wife being called "Deloretta Morelas, the beautiful niece of General Morelos," see the undated, uncredited, transcribed newspaper clipping (eight typed pages) that was sent by Lois Foster Blount to Mattie Austin Hatcher in Jan. 1929, "Romance and Tragedy in the Life of Peter Ellis Bean," in his Genealogy File, CAH.

15. Yoakum, *History of Texas,* 1:236. This date was likely based on Bean's notebook that Yoakum used.

16. Lay, *Lives,* 112, suggests such a motive for Bean's detour to see Gutiérrez.

17. "Memoire Adressé a la Republique Mexicaine," Materials from Various Sources, CAH, box 2Q236, vol. 758 (thirty-six legal-sized handwritten pages) with date of 20 8bre [Oct.] 1825. The "Plan" starts on p. 26, but I shall cite the entire document as "Memoire."

18. On the general's last years in Mexico City, see James Ripley Jacobs, *Tarnished Warrior: Major-General James Wilkinson,* 334–40. Wilkinson's "Reflections on the Province of Texas," prepared for Emperor Iturbide, was harsh in its condemnation of Gen. James Long—who was married to Wilkinson's niece! Wilkinson remained a scoundrel to the end and would say anything to advance his own interests.

19. All quotes as cited in n17 above, "Memoire," 33–34, 22, 26. Reference is to the colonization grant of the Englishman in Mexican service, Gen. Arthur G. Wavell. On him see Robert Amsler, "General Arthur G. Wavell: A Soldier of Fortune in Texas," *SHQ* 69 (July and Oct. 1965): 1–21, 186–209.

20. The letters mentioned are found in the collection of translations of documents "from the Archives of Bexar County" made in 1856 by X. B. Debray, TSL. P. L. Buquor made similar translations at the order of Gov. P. H. Bell in the early 1850s. Some of these originals are no longer in what is now known as the Béxar Archives at CAH; hence the importance of the Buquor/Debray Translations. Most of their translations have also been lost for over a century. Thanks to Jean Carefoot and Dorothy Sloan for calling my attention to this valuable collection.

21. "Memoire," 24, 30. Gaines's second (or possibly third) wife was Susanah Norris, sister to Samuel and Nathaniel. On this clan see Lois Foster Blount, "The Norris Family in Early Nacogdoches," Blake Transcripts (R), 59:290–314, 316–62 (two different drafts of same study).

22. "Memoire," 35–36. This Gaines partial letter to Saucedo, 5 Sept. 1826, is not in BA, nor could I find mention of him in the political chief's subsequent correspondence with the governor. He wrote the governor a similar letter in August 1823, complaining that good-for-nothing foreigners were intruding into the Sabine District without permission or taking an oath of loyalty to Mexico. Gaines said that he, at the beginning of the year, had been elected by the respectable citizens to organize a government and was obliged to try, whip, and expel "six roguish families and ten straggling vagrants." Gaines thought that twenty more families deserved the same treatment if property was to be made secure in the region. He said that the governor would remember him as "Capitán Colorado" (Red Captain) from 1813, when he helped obtain his release; Mrs. "Saliedo" (Salcedo?) would certainly recall the particulars. Buquor Translations, Book A, 21–22, box 2004/046, TSL.

Gaines was not the only "informer" who spoke badly of the Anglo squatters flooding across the Sabine as far as Ayish Bayou "without any kind of leave or permission whatever." See James Dill to Governor of Texas, 21 Jan. 1822, Debray Translations, box 2004/046, TSL. Dill also noted Francisco Garrare's complaint that James Gaines and

Edmond Quirk "have been runing surveys of land & have run through and taken in a considerable part of his land & I wish to know if [the] Government allows them that privilege." Dill was an early alcalde and militia captain at Nacogdoches.

23. "Memoire," 34–35. Reference to Joseph Durst as "Joe" suggests that the writer was intimately acquainted with him and familiar with the political situation at Nacogdoches. Betje Black Klier thinks that the author was Arsene Lacarriere Latour, an associate of Pierre Laffite and Charles Lallemand, who (as a secret agent for Spain) wrote bombastic reports to Spanish officials in Cuba and later to those in independent Mexico. He fought with General Jackson at the Battle of New Orleans, published a book about the War of 1812 with England, and was strongly opinionated about the Trans-Sabine borderlands. The Memorial and Plan of 1825–26 reflect such sentiments, to say the least.

24. Pedro Elías Bean military service record (hereafter cited as Bean MSR), Cancelados, C46. XI/111/4-701, AHSDN. As noted, the only scholar to have used this file on Bean is Cárdenas de la Peña; see his *Historia Maritima,* 1:95n5.

25. Bean MSR, fol. 1.

26. Ibid.

27. Sesma, Herrera, and Terán all mention Bean's capture and imprisonment at Veracruz, so it was no isolated memory lapse or slip of the pen by one person. Bean, of course, may have written about these events in a portion of his memoir either lost or perhaps not included by Editor Yoakum.

28. Bean to Victoria, 24 Nov. 1825, Bean MSR, fols. 14–15. For full text see appendix B. Bean here expresses his disgust for the empire of Iturbide and echoes the republican sentiments found throughout his memoir. His references to Morelos as the "illustrious adornment of the Mexican Nation and liberty," and to Victoria as an "eyewitness" and "companion in arms" who served under the leadership of Morelos, were bound to strike a sympathetic cord with the president.

29. Bean MSR, fol. 16, with board's opinion of 28 Feb. 1826, which is marked "Agreed."

30. Bean to Compensation Board, 4 Feb. 1826, Bean MSR, fol. 26.

31. Board to [Secretary of War] Gómez Pedraza, 4 Feb. 1826, Bean MSR, fol. 21.

32. Victoria to Pedraza, 18 Feb. 1826, Bean MSR, fols. 18–20 (two copies).

33. Ibid., fols. 23–24.

34. Ceballos to Bastrop, 15 Feb. 1826, and Bastrop's undated reply, both in NA Transcripts, 195:85–90 (CAH, box 2Q298).

35. Bean to Secretary of War [Pedraza], 3 Mar. 1826, Bean MSR, fols. 27–30; the remark about Bean joining Terán is on fol. 16v.

36. Yoakum, *History of Texas,* 1:237, citing "Bean's Notes, MS [manuscript]."

37. John Henry Brown, *History of Texas from 1685 to 1892,* 1:135. On the first trip to Mexico City, see Mary Whatley Clarke, *Chief Bowles and the Texas Cherokees,* 20–25. Duwali is variously called Bowles or The Bowl, but I will use Bowl.

38. Bean to Secretary of Foreign Relations [Camacho], 3 May 1826, Fomento [BNAH] Transcripts, 309:81–82 (CAH, box 2Q167). The original documents from the old Fomento archive are now at the Biblioteca Nacional de Antropología e Historia, Mexico City; hence, BNAH. Another copy, made at Saltillo by Juan Antonio Padilla on 18 Sept. 1826, is in the Saltillo Archives, 24:99–100 (CAH, box 2Q320).

39. For Haden Edwards's colonization difficulties in Mexico City, see Jordan Holt, "The Edwards Empresarial Grant and the Fredonian Rebellion," 12–22. This is a very useful and well-documented study based on primary sources.

40. Théodore Pavie did not think too highly of the boundary reserve settlers, especially those at Ayish Bayou; see his 1830 description in Jackson and Wheat, *Texas by Terán,* 190–93.

41. Bean to Compensation Board [?], 7 June 1826, Bean MSR, fols. 31–32. See appendix C for full text.

42. Bean to Nacogdoches Alcalde, 28 June 1826, NA.

43. For a translation of the Edwards contract of 15 Apr. 1825 with Governor González, see Holt, "The Edwards Empresarial Grant," 30–32; also found in Yoakum, *History of Texas,* 1:462–64, as his appendix no. 5. Edwards was authorized to introduce eight hundred families, more than the usual number. Austin's first contract was for only three hundred families. As the crow flies, the twenty-league boundary reserve extended almost to the eastern city limits of Nacogdoches, a measurement not recognized by the old inhabitants with ranches in the area.

44. B. W. Edwards to Austin, 21 July 1826, Barker, *Austin Papers,* vol. 1, pt. 2, 1383.

45. Ibid.

46. Bean to Austin, 5 July 1826, Barker, *Austin Papers,* vol. 1, pt. 2, 1368–69.

47. Eugene C. Barker, *The Life of Stephen F. Austin: Founder of Texas, 1793–1836,* 204–5, 211 (hereafter cited as *Life of SFA*).

48. Bean to Blanco, 14 Sept. 1826, Fomento [BNAH] Transcripts, 309:83–84 (CAH, box 2Q167). Another copy is in Saltillo Archives, 24:101–2 (CAH, box 2Q320).

49. Blanco to Secretary of Foreign Relations, 18 Sept. 1826, Fomento [BNAH] Transcripts, 309:85–86.

50. J. E. B. Austin to S. F. Austin, 23 Sept. 1826, Barker, *Austin Papers,* vol. 1, pt. 2, 1461–62. As seen, this was the time when Governor Blanco gave Bean a copy of James Gaines's self-incriminating letter and Bean passed it on to the settlers of Ayish Bayou. The writer of the Memorial/Plan predicted that Gaines would meet his rightful end because of it: "Gaines, seeing his life in danger, has taken flight, leaving his wife and children. The new attack against him has been occasioned by his letter to the government [Saucedo] . . . Gaines will be assassinated, it is sure." Plan, 30–31, as cited in n17 above. Small wonder that Gaines kept a troop of armed "Regulators" at his service!

Chapter 4

1. Blanco to Saucedo, 10 July 1826, Saltillo Archives, 22:84 (CAH, box 2Q319); another copy at the Spanish Collection, TGLO, box 127, folder 10.

2. Martin Allen deposition, 3 Aug. 1826, Barker, *Austin Papers,* vol. 1, pt. 2, 1397–98. This testimony is also found in Saltillo Archives, vol. 22 (CAH, box 2Q319), and translated as an appendix in Lowrey, "Peter Ellis Bean"; see also Lay, *Lives,* 116–17. Notice that Allen says that Bean has three children (not two), of interest when we discuss Samuel Bean later on. Other witnesses, however, agree that Bean had only a son and a daughter at this time.

3. Sterling Robertson deposition, 24 Aug. 1826, Saltillo Archives, vol. 22 (CAH, box 2Q319). Also in Lowrey, "Peter Ellis Bean," and McLean, *Papers concerning Robertson's Colony,* 2:629–30.

4. Austin to Saucedo, 28 Aug. 1826, BA. The Spanish is in Barker, *Austin Papers,* vol. 1, pt. 2, 1443, and a translation in McLean, *Papers concerning Robertson's Colony,* 2:637.

5. The depositions at Nacogdoches are all in Saltillo Archives, vol. 22, as cited in n1 of this chapter, with translations in Lowrey, "Peter Ellis Bean." Copies of these translations are in the Bean (Peter Ellis) Papers, CAH, box 2B45, along with other miscellaneous Bean documents (mostly photostats).

6. See n5 above.

7. Barker, *Life of SFA,* 106–7, quoting Gaines's letter of 10 Nov. 1824. Gaines was irri-

tated because on 15 Feb. 1824, John A. Williams had asked the political chief if the land warrants or certificates that Gutiérrez had awarded his men on 16 Apr. 1813 were valid; James Dill was the bearer of samples of these items. Saucedo replied on 3 Apr. that they were "worthless," but holders might apply for land according to the laws in force. Debray Translations, TSL. For the 1825 claims on behalf of foreign veterans of Gutiérrez's campaign, see the file in BNAH (Mexico City), 51-4-26. Doc. 16 (eight items). The paperwork was forwarded to the governor of Coahuila y Texas in December 1825.

8. John Sprowl deposition, [Sept. 1826?], NA, translation given in Blake Transcripts (R), 11:88; also in NA Transcripts, 251:59 (CAH, box 2Q310). It is misdated "1825" but clearly pertains to the 1826 testimony-taking process. Sprowl did not think too highly of Captain Gaines. He wrote Austin that "even an aged and defenceless female could not escape the poison of his malice." Sprowl to Austin, 5 Nov. 1826, Barker, *Austin Papers,* vol. 1, pt. 2, 1490.

9. M. B. Lamar, "Information Derived from Col. Heyden Edwards," C. A. Gulick et al., eds., *The Papers of Mirabeau Buonaparte Lamar,* 3:260 (hereafter cited as *Lamar Papers*).

10. Edmund Morris Parsons, "The Fredonian Rebellion," *Texana* 5 (Spring 1967): 25. Many documents concerning the rebellion are in Saltillo Archives, vol. 22 (CAH, box 2Q319); see also the translations in Blake Transcripts (R), vol. 11 and (G), vol. 9. Some of the documents Blake cited as from the BA no longer exist except in these translations, probably taken from the work of Buquor/Debray in the 1850s before the originals disappeared at San Antonio.

11. Robert Collier deposition, 22 Aug. 1826, Blake Transcripts (R), 11:191.

12. Candace Midkiff deposition, 22 Aug. 1826, Saltillo Archives, vol. 22. For translations see n5 above and Lay, *Lives,* 117.

13. Norris to Saucedo, 5 Sept. 1826, BA; also in Blake Transcripts (G), 9:70; Saucedo to Blanco, 1 Oct. 1826, ibid., 74.

14. Blanco to Saucedo, 20 Oct. 1826, NA, translated in Blake Transcripts (R), 11:266; copy also in Saltillo Archives, vol. 22 (CAH, box 2Q319), and translated in Lowrey, "Peter Ellis Bean."

15. Jesús María del Ibarra certification, 14 Oct. 1826, BA, translated in Blake Transcripts (G), 9:79.

16. Lucas Porlamo to *comisario* of Béxar [Erasmo Seguín], 23 Oct. 1826, BA, translated in Blake Transcripts (G), 9:80.

17. Blanco to Saucedo, 24 Oct. 1826, BA (CAH, box 2S192).

Chapter 5

1. Blanco to Saucedo, 23 Aug. 1826, TGLO, "Translations of Empresario Contracts," 105, given in Holt, "The Edwards Empresarial Grant," 111–12.

2. Blanco to Benjamin Edwards, 20 Oct. 1826, TGLO, "Translations of Empresario Contracts."

3. As cited in chapter 4, n9. J. P. Bryan has recently acquired some important papers that came down through the Edwards family. Included in this collection are various "essays" that Haden wrote to defend his conduct after he had lost his grant. They add considerably to the account he gave to Lamar and cast new light on the Fredonian Rebellion from his perspective.

4. Events leading up to the rebellion are developed nicely by Holt and Parsons. The

Fredonian Rebellion, being the first Anglo-inspired uprising against Mexican rule in Texas, has probably received more attention than it really deserves—considering how easily it was contained, lack of actual fighting, etc. It was mostly a war of words with only one small battle. In Mexico, however, the rebellion was regarded as an omen of things to come and made the government very suspicious of its foreign settlers in Texas. See also James G. Partin, "A History of Nacogdoches and Nacogdoches County, to 1877," 125–42.

5. Jackson, "Nicholas Trammell's Difficulties in Mexican Texas," for details.

6. Holt, "The Edwards Empresarial Grant," 90–94, where the Bassett affair is called the "spark" that began the Fredonian Rebellion. Holt covers the Trammell eviction (pp. 51–54, 89) with the assumption that Zertuche had prior rights to the Trinity crossing; Jackson offers contrary evidence as cited in n5 above.

7. See the entry on Parmer in Tyler et al., *NHOT,* 5:67; Kemp, *Signers,* 243–52. He gets much attention in Holt, "The Edwards Empresarial Grant," and in Parsons, "The Fredonian Rebellion." William P. Zuber wrote a lengthy biographical sketch of him, based on information from Parmer's children; CAH, box 2R313.

8. The "Impeachment Proceedings" are in Barker, *Austin Papers,* vol. 1, pt. 2, 1511–23. See the summary in Parsons, "The Fredonian Rebellion," 16–20.

9. Saucedo to Blanco, 12 Nov. 1826, Saltillo Archives, vol. 22 (CAH, box 2Q319), translated in Lowrey, "Peter Ellis Bean."

10. All found in BA (CAH, box 2S194).

11. Ahumada to Bean, 28 Nov. 1826, not located but mentioned in Bean's reply of 25 Feb. 1827; see chapter 6, n16.

12. There is some confusion about when Hunter returned to east Texas. Richard Drinnon, *White Savage: The Case of John Dunn Hunter,* 195–99, postulates that it happened around mid-1826. Ernest W. Winkler, "The Cherokee Indians in Texas," *Quarterly of the Texas State Historical Association* (hereafter *QTSHA*) 7 (Oct. 1903): 123, says it was in the "autumn" of 1826; Bean reached Saltillo early in September. Regardless of the exact time, concern about Hunter's activities among the Indians did not develop with Texas authorities until late in the year.

13. As given in Bean to Austin, 31 Dec. 1826, Barker, *Austin Papers,* vol. 1, pt. 2, 1554; also in Lay, *Lives,* 125.

14. Parsons, "The Fredonian Rebellion," 23–26. The 21 Dec. 1826 treaty of alliance is given in Holt, "The Edwards Empresarial Grant," 116–18; also in Henry Stuart Foote, *Texas and the Texans: Or Advance of the Anglo-Americans to the South-West,* 1:254–56, and in Clarke, *Chief Bowles,* 41–43.

15. B. W. Edwards to Buckner, 26 Dec. 1826, Barker, *Austin Papers,* vol. 1, pt. 2, 1546–47. See the summary in Barker, *Life of SFA,* 167–73, where various letters are quoted.

16. [Ahumada] to Commandant at La Bahía, 30 Nov. 1826, relaying Bustamante's instructions of 16 Nov., BA.

17. See orders dated 11 Jan. 1827, BA.

18. Bean to Saucedo, 6 Dec. 1826, translated in Blake Transcripts (G), 9:81, and cited as BA. I have not located the original.

19. Yoakum, *History of Texas,* 1:246n; see Lay, *Lives,* 118.

20. Austin to Williams and Thompson, 14 Dec. 1826, Barker, *Austin Papers,* vol. 1, pt. 2, 1532–34. See also Barker, *Life of SFA,* 167, and Lay, *Lives,* 119. Austin's letters to Hunter and the Cherokee chiefs are given in Clarke, *Chief Bowles,* 45–47; Clarke reproduces Thrall's portrait of Bean opposite p. 47. Published variants of Bean's likeness are discussed in chapter 21.

21. Austin to Saucedo, 16 Dec. 1826, Barker, *Austin Papers,* vol. 1, pt. 2, 1535.

22. Bean to Austin, 23 Dec. 1826, Saltillo Archives, 22:105–6 (CAH, box 2Q319). This is Bean's earliest letter on the rebel situation, not given elsewhere.

23. Bean to "Roberds," 22 Dec. 1825 [1826], J. P. Bryan Collection. Elisha Roberts, on the day before, wrote Benjamin Edwards about the "great Confusion" at Ayish Bayou between contending factions. One company of men wanted to take down the Fredonian flag and reinstate Alcalde Norris. Roberts called James Gaines a "Devil" who was keeping the citizens stirred up and urged Edwards to "Detect" him. Ibid. His reply to Bean, given in the text, suggests that Roberts (like many other settlers) was trying to play it both ways.

24. Bean to Austin, 28 Dec. 1826, Barker, *Austin Papers,* vol. 1, pt. 2, 1551.

25. Candace Midkiff deposition, 28 Dec. 1826, ibid., 1551–52.

26. See the 1902 William P. Zuber account given in Lay, *Lives,* 121–23, where it is stated that Candace heard from "some man from Mexico" that Bean was dead before she took up with Parmer. This may have been intended to excuse Parmer's behavior more than Candace's, as Zuber was writing to Parmer's grandson A. W. Morris. This Zuber account dealing with Martin Parmer is now at the East Texas Research Center, Steen Library, Stephen F. Austin State University, Nacogdoches (hereafter cited as ETRC), filed as item A-103; another copy in the Crocket Papers, A-12; see chapter 17, n48. I have used "The Bean Affair" letter to Morris in Zuber Papers, CAH, box 2R313.

27. Thomas Parmer, "Last of the Ringtail Family," to Moses Austin Bryan, 15 July 1874, Texas Veterans Papers, CAH, box 2H120; Lay, *Lives,* 123, and "The Bean Affair," 46–49. Zuber claims the "marriage" lasted only "forty-eight hours after its commencement" and says that Parmer "departed for his own residence and never returned." He wondered why Bean did not later kill Parmer; someone else bushwhacked the "Ring-Tailed Panther" near Jasper in 1850. Evidence that Zuber's dates are wrong, and that Parmer was in Nacogdoches on Christmas Day instead of honeymooning with Bean's wife on the Neches, comes with a proclamation he issued to the "Gentlemen of the Committee from Head Quarters, Nacogdoches," 25 Dec. 1826: "As I think it necessary that we all know there are but two sides to proclaim[, and] that all those who are for us should come here & take the oath of allegiance that we may know our enemies from our friends[,] I lay this before you for your consideration and shall expect a communication from you on this subject. Martin Parmer, Col. Commanding." J. P. Bryan Collection.

28. Parsons, "The Fredonian Rebellion," 39. The three negotiators were Richard Ellis, James Cummins, and James Kerr. They were sent to deliver Saucedo's offer of pardon to the rebels at Nacogdoches. See McLean, *Papers concerning Robertson's Colony,* 3:209, for their report to Austin; also in Barker, *Austin Papers,* vol. 1, pt. 2, 1586–87. Haile's interesting letter to Benjamin Edwards of 23 Jan. 1827 names the seven men under his command at, or near, Bean's house and gives other news from the vicinity—all indicating that this was a pocket of resistance that Bean may have bypassed and did not clean out until later. Speaking of the prisoners being transmitted to Nacogdoches, Haile says: "I expect McLain [Daniel McLean?] is a good witness in this case as Bean made his house his home for some time." The flatboat at the crossing was underwater, but Haile had plans to raise it for scouts west of the river. J. P. Bryan Collection. McLean lived at the crossing of San Pedro Creek, a stream just to the west; see Jackson and Wheat, *Texas by Terán,* 73–74, 227–28. He was killed by Indians in 1837.

29. Otto Askins deposition, 15 Oct. 1826; Alcalde Norris order for Parmer's arrest, same day, NA Transcripts, 197A:235–36 (CAH, box 2Q298). Mentioned in Holt, "The Edwards Empresarial Grant," 89–90, 95–96, and Jackson, "Nicholas Trammell's Difficulties in Mexican Texas," 36. Mote's sons were still living with Trammell when he came back to Texas and settled in Gonzales County in the 1850s, their names given as Askey.

30. Bean to Austin, 31 Dec. 1826, Barker, *Austin Papers,* vol. 1, pt. 2, 1553–55. An "ed-

ited" version is in Blake Transcripts (R), 11:310–12. Both "Gressom" and "D. Hays" are mentioned as at Haile's post in his letter cited in n28 above.

31. Yoakum, *History of Texas,* 1:248n (letter to Fields of 26 Dec. 1826, not located); 250n (Bean's spies). The picture often reproduced by historians of a bearded Chief Richard Fields is most certainly not him, as Fields was dead before photography was invented!

32. As cited in n30 above; also in Lay, *Lives,* 124.

33. See n32 above.

34. Parsons, "The Fredonian Rebellion," 34–37, 41.

35. Bean to Edwards, 6 Jan. 1827, Debray Translations, TSL, and NA Transcripts, 198: 143–44, 208–9 (citing BA); also given in Blake Transcripts (R), 11:319, and in Lowrey, "Peter Ellis Bean," as appendix 1. A copy of this Bean item is no longer extant in the BA at CAH. It is a very similar letter to the one Saucedo wrote Edwards on the same day, which is in BA; see Barker's comments in *Life of SFA,* 173–74.

36. Bean to Fields, 4 Jan. 1827, NA, and Debray Translations, TSL. Another "proper English" version is in Blake Transcripts (R), 11:314–15. Both it and the letter above are signed "P. E. Bean." I have not seen the original, but the use of plural "agents" may refer to the backing that Hunter received from General Wavell and other powerful Englishmen in the Mexican capital; on this see Drinnon, *White Savage,* 183–96. After the rebellion was over, an investigation was ordered to see if Wavell had fomented an uprising of the Indians; his assistance to Hunter was common knowledge in Mexico City.

37. Bean to Austin, 4 Jan. 1827, Barker, *Austin Papers,* vol. 1, pt. 2, 1561.

38. Foote, *Texas and the Texans,* 1:251–52.

39. Parsons, "The Fredonian Rebellion," 42–44.

40. Bean to Ahumada, 7 Feb. 1827, NA, and Debray Translations, TSL. There are two versions, one dated Feb. 9. See the translations in NA Transcripts, 198:236–37 (CAH, box 2Q299), and in Blake Transcripts (R), 11:339, and (G), 9:95; also in Lowrey, "Peter Ellis Bean," as appendix 1.

41. Concerning Bean's 118 pesos for putting down the rebels, see Ahumada to Bustamante, 27 Feb. 1827, BA; it was endorsed as "just." Clarke, *Chief Bowles,* 51, speculates that Bean "might have conceived the plan to murder Hunter and Chief Fields, finding a willing accomplice in Bowles." The sources Clarke cites—mostly men who disliked Bean—make this speculation questionable.

42. See the explanation given in Dianna Everett, *The Texas Cherokees: A People between Two Fires, 1819–1840,* 44–47. Yoakum, *History of Texas,* 1:250n, says that Bean was able to detach the Indians "through the instrumentality of John Williams, [William?] Elliott, and others." For this service these "agents" each received a league of land. I have not tried to confirm Yoakum's assertions about the land; the listings in Greaser, *Catalogue of TGLO,* vol. 1, do not so indicate (see chapter 6, n18). Williams, however, was charged by the rebels (Haile?) as "[s]aying that he was a friend to the goverment and did not care who knew it." Another charge was that he had given a "public Dinner to Col. Bean and his party on Christmas day," likely when Bean was scouting the vicinity of his house on the Neches. J. P. Bryan Collection. Judging from a letter that Burrell Thompson wrote Austin on 3 Feb. 1827, the men who were at/near Bean's house on the Neches all fled to Natchitoches Parish, including Haile, Hayes, Capt. John W. Frith, William Jones, and others. They wanted to return to Texas if their safety could be assured, as did Thompson. Barker, *Austin Papers,* vol. 1, pt. 2, 1600. On John Williams see chapter 7, n17.

43. Letter as cited in n40 above. In the third of his three-part series on the early revolutions in Texas (San Augustine *Red-Lander,* 18 Dec. 1845), James Gaines had this to say about Bean's role in the Fredonian Rebellion: "Col. Bean had just returned from Mexico to the Neches, and finding that himself among many others had been plundered, and

being commissioned by the Mexican government Indian agent, he sent young [William?] Bean and [John] Williams to the Cherokee villages of Bolls and Bigmush for them to meet him at Trinity, with which they immediately complied. Bean agreed to secure them their lands if they would kill Fields and Hunter, which they agreed to do, and shortly after punctually performed. Bean then went down the Trinity among the settlers to raise men." Gaines says that he tried to keep several "deluded youngsters" from being arrested at Nacogdoches, "but Col. Bean arriving with a large company, in his Mexican style, acted roughly [against rebels] for a short time, though it was not of long duration."

Chapter 6

1. On these newspaper articles, see Nettie Lee Benson, "Texas as Viewed from Mexico, 1820–1834," *SHQ* 90 (Jan. 1987): 255. The 20 Apr. 1827 issue of *El Sol* is also mentioned in Eduardo Enrique Ríos, "El Insurgente Don Pedro Elías Bean, 1783–1846," *Anales del Museo Nacional de Arqueología, Historia y Etnografía* 5a, tomo 1, no. 3 (July–Dec. 1934): 522n2. Mostly derived from Yoakum, this is nonetheless one of the earliest Mexican studies in praise of Bean's efforts to secure the nation's independence from Spain.

2. As cited in chapter 5, n40.

3. Ahumada to Bustamante and Bean to Bustamante, 9 Feb. 1827, IED (Coahuila), AGEC, FJPB, E62, 4F; copies made at Laredo on 6 Mar.

4. Bean to Bustamante, 9 Feb. 1827, as cited in n3 above.

5. Williams to Ahumada, 12 Feb. 1827, NA, given in Blake Transcripts (R), 11:343–45.

6. There are conflicting accounts of which leader was killed first. Drinnon, *White Savage*, 220–22, says it was Fields, but Haden Edwards told Mirabeau Lamar that Hunter was the first victim: "Fields hearing of the murder fled and was persued across the Sabine where he was overtaken." Gulick et al., *Lamar Papers*, 3:263. Edwards, fleeing across the Sabine himself, should have known. He was counting on both men to rally their Indian warriors to his cause and would have made close inquiries about their fate.

7. Brown, *History of Texas*, 1:135.

8. Mayo's account is in Parsons, "The Fredonian Rebellion," 48–49, citing Foote, *Texas and the Texans*, 1:279–80.

9. As related in Lay, *Lives*, 127–28; William P. Zuber, "Biographical Sketches of Martin Parmer," 39–41, Zuber Papers, CAH, box 2R313.

10. According to George Louis Crocket, *Two Centuries in East Texas: A History of San Augustine County and Surrounding Territory, from 1685 to the Present Time*, 147, the Edwards brothers and Adolphus Sterne were the others. But a number of rebels moved to Louisiana rather than stay and learn how they would fare under the general amnesty—especially those who had signed the Declaration of Independence or taken a military role well known to loyal citizens of the town.

11. He and his family were living in the Tenaha District (near the Sabine, later Shelby County) on the 1835 Nacogdoches census. See NA Transcripts, 252:301 (CAH, box 2Q310). Parmer gave his age as fifty, his wife "Sevina" (Lornt, a widow) as forty-three; they had seven children at home and three slaves. He reentered central Texas from time to time, as indicated by the order for his arrest given by Political Chief Ramón Músquiz on 26 Apr. 1831. Parmer was reported by the authorities of San Felipe as on the way to Gonzales to meet his son Isom. Because of Parmer's past activities, it was suspected they might try to "disturb order and peace." Debray Translations, TSL. On this trip Parmer was traveling with James Bowie, who was about to get married at Béxar. Bowie had to make apologies for keeping such bad company.

12. Saucedo to Vice-Governor, 12 Feb. 1827, Saltillo Archives, vol. 22 (CAH, box 2Q139); Blake Transcripts (G), 9:96, gives a translation from BA. The original is at IED (Coahuila), AGEC, FJPB, C3, E28, 2F.

13. Saucedo to Governor Arizpe, 19 Mar. 1827, forwarding two depositions, Saltillo Archives, vol. 22. Both are translated in Lowrey, "Peter Ellis Bean."

14. Ibid.; see also Lay, *Lives,* 129.

15. Bean bill of sale to Mary Ronald, 14 Feb. 1827, NA, given in Blake Transcripts (R), 11:346.

16. Bean to Ahumada, 25 Feb. 1827, BA (CAH, box 2S198).

17. Signed "Victoria." It is a copy dated 1 Mar. 1827 at Nacogdoches, also signed by Bean with his distinctive rubric. "Bexar Land Papers," TGLO, box 127, folders 5, 18.

18. Concerning Bean's land affairs, here it is again proper to note the usefulness of the recent two-volume *Catalogue of the Spanish Collection of the Texas General Land Office* (prepared by Galen D. Greaser and hereafter cited as *Catalogue of TGLO*), especially its calendar and index. Part 1 contains titles (approved and unfinished) and Part 2 deals with correspondence. For this grant see Part 1, 18 (box 114, folder 4, also 38: 554, and GSC, box 6, folder 8). There is a copy of Gaines's 13 Aug. 1828 field notes for the survey in the Raguet (Henry) Papers, CAH, box 2F380—along with the survey for Martin Lacy's adjoining league on the north side of the road, dated 23 Dec. 1834.

19. See map in text. The vicinity was called "Mound Prairie" because of the three small mounds built by the Southern Caddoans, or Hasinai, on the east bank of the Neches in prehistoric times. (It is presently known as the George C. Davis Site or Caddoan Mounds State Park on SH 21.) The mounds are shown on the Juan Pedro Walker map, along with the Arroyo de los Cerritos, which ran through Bean's later grant. The Walker map, drawn sometime between 1806 and 1816, is reproduced in A. Joachim McGraw, John W. Clark Jr., and Elizabeth A. Robbins, *A Texas Legacy: The Old San Antonio Road and the Caminos Reales,* 189; also in Jack Jackson, *Shooting the Sun: Cartographic Results of Military Activities in Texas, 1689–1829,* 2:330.

20. All the William Bean documentation is found in Greaser, *Catalogue of TGLO,* 2:11 (entry nos. 54–59); for his petition see ibid., 1:18. The grant and sale to Peter Ellis are also found in Deed Book C, 98–99, Nacogdoches County Clerk's Office (records hereafter given as NCCO).

21. Tyler et al., *NHOT,* 4:967, entry on "Neches Saline, Texas."

22. William was in Texas at least until Apr. 1829, when he explained to the Nacogdoches ayuntamiento his reasons for transferring the land to Colonel Bean. The ayuntamiento (town council) confirmed that the hat shop he was about to establish would be a very useful enterprise to the town. See entry no. 59 in Greaser, *Catalogue of TGLO,* 2:11. William Bean does not show on Nacogdoches censuses of the 1830s. Ericson, *Nacogdoches—Gateway to Texas,* 11, says that there is a deed recorded in his name on 16 Nov. 1837, but the correct year is 1827—same documents as at NCCO and TGLO.

23. Ahumada to Bustamante, 27 Feb. 1827, BA (CAH, box 2S198), forwarding "Bian's" petition.

24. Winkler, "The Cherokee Indians in Texas," 150, from BA.

25. Ibid., 150–51. See also the translation of this 7 Apr. 1827 letter from NA given in Blake Transcripts (R), 11:370–71.

26. Bustamante to Ahumada, 9 Mar. 1827, from Laredo, NA, translated in Blake Transcripts (R), 11:355.

27. Bustamante to Austin, 7 Apr. 1827, from La Bahía, Barker, *Austin Papers,* vol. 1, pt. 2, 1626–27.

28. The mop-up operations are described in Parsons, "The Fredonian Rebellion," 49–50; see also Barker, *Life of SFA*, 174–79.

29. Ahumada to Bustamante, 16 Apr. 1827, BA (CAH, box 2S193).

Chapter 7

1. Bustamante signed treaties under Iturbide with the Apaches and Comanches, Ruiz being the envoy who brought the latter to the Mexican capital. Jean-Louis Berlandier, *The Indians of Texas in 1830*, 133–34; Morris E. Opler, *The Lipan and Mescalero Apache in Texas*, 29.

2. The literature on the various Indian tribes of Texas has been steadily increasing since W. W. Newcomb Jr. published his now-classic *The Indians of Texas: From Prehistoric to Modern Times* (1961). Separate books have seen print on almost every tribe, far outstripping the sources listed in Michael L. Tate, *The Indians of Texas: An Annotated Research Bibliography* (1986). For the latest overview see David La Vere, *The Texas Indians.* The following text is a summary of Indian tribal information as seen on maps and presented in Jackson, *Shooting the Sun*, vols. 1 and 2.

3. See Gregg Cantrell, *Stephen F. Austin: Empresario of Texas*, 96–97, 136–42, where it is stated that "Austin might be willing to coexist with Indians if they would agree to be 'subdued' on the white man's terms . . . but like most other Anglo-Americans of his time and place, he never questioned the right of the white man to settle and control Indian-occupied lands." For a harsher view of Austin's anti-Indian bias, see Drinnon, *White Savage*, 212–16, 225–26. Austin admirers, on the other hand, can argue that he was not a racist by the standards of his day and that the reason he was permitted to colonize Texas in the first place was to solve an Indian problem that the Spanish/Mexican government could not.

4. Everett, *The Texas Cherokees*, 16–26, 38–44, gives a good summary of these events.

5. Bustamante to Ahumada, 7 Apr. 1827, NA, translated in Blake Transcripts (R), 11: 368–69.

6. As cited in chapter 6, 29.

7. On José Francisco Ruiz see Tyler et al., *NHOT*, 5:711–12. He and his nephew, José Antonio Navarro, were the only Tejano signers of the 1836 Declaration of Independence from Mexico. Colonel Ruiz had a son named Francisco Antonio, sometimes confused with the father. For the treaties being signed in Mexico City at this time, see also Joseph Carl McElhannon, "Imperial Mexico and Texas, 1821–1823," *SHQ* 53 (July 1949): 128–31, and Thomas W. Kavanagh, *The Comanches: A History, 1706–1875*, 196–98. David McDonald is currently working on a biography of Navarro that will shed new light on Ruiz's exile period in Louisiana and his return to Texas as an agent for the Comanches.

8. Documentation on both Milam's and Wavell's contracts is cited in Greaser, *Catalogue of TGLO*, 2:96–97 (entry nos. 942–57).

9. Milam to Ahumada, 1 Mar. 1827, TGLO, box 127, folder 5, 16–17v (entry no. 951 in Greaser, *Catalogue of TGLO*, 2:96–97).

10. "Mapa del pais de los Comanches formado por el C. Estevan Austin pa[ra] explicar el plan de campana contra dhos. Indios," Béxar, 28 Aug. 1827. Map SA38 1827 at CAH; item 79A(c) in Jackson, *Shooting the Sun*, 2:330. McLean discusses Austin's war plan, refers to the map, and translates the notes on it in *Papers concerning Robertson's Colony*, 3:46–47, 266–67.

11. Ruiz to Ahumada, 14 Apr. 1827, BA, translated in Blake Transcripts (G), 9:100;

Ruiz to Austin, 2 June 1827, Barker, *Austin Papers,* vol. 1, pt. 2, 1653–54, translated in McLean, *Papers concerning Robertson's Colony,* 3:253–54.

12. Ruiz et al. to Ahumada, 3 June 1827, BA, translated in Blake Transcripts (G), 9: 103–4. Bean was one of the eight signatories of this Indian council report at Nacogdoches. A good summary of Wichita relations/depredations in the Mexican period is found in chapter 7 of F. Todd Smith, *The Wichita Indians: Traders of Texas and the Southern Plains, 1540–1845.*

13. Bean to Austin, 3 June 1827, Barker, *Austin Papers,* vol. 1, pt. 2, 1656. Also in McLean, *Papers concerning Robertson's Colony,* 3:255, and Lay, *Lives,* 132.

14. See McLean's remarks, *Papers concerning Robertson's Colony,* 3:45.

15. On this treaty see Barker, *Life of SFA,* 146, and Craig H. Roell, *Remember Goliad! A History of La Bahía,* 30. Austin did not attend the treaty-making ceremony, but Kelly F. Himmel, *The Conquest of the Karankawas and the Tonkawas, 1821–1859,* 51, claims that he signed an agreement dated 13 May—citing Barker, *Austin Papers,* vol. 1, pt. 2, 1639–41. Later correspondence between Austin and Bustamante (ibid., 1641–42, 1657–58) indicates that Jacob Betts signed the treaty as Austin's representative.

16. Bean, "Memoir," 405–7. One daring recovery of horses stolen by the Comanches is given, as well as visits to their villages near a salt lake "so covered with salt, that they can break up any quantity they want." Bean was making mental notes on rich salt deposits at an early age.

17. Ruiz to Ahumada, 14 May 1827, NA, translated in Blake Transcripts (R), 11:378–80. This John Williams was Bean's neighbor who operated a ferry on the Neches crossing of the Old San Antonio Road. See Terán's remarks on him in Jackson and Wheat, *Texas by Terán,* 73–74, 227n109.

18. Blake Transcripts (R), 11:378–80.

19. Ahumada to Bustamante, 16 Apr. 1827, Bean MSR, fol. 38. Also found in BA, a poor translation given in Blake Transcripts (G), 9:102.

20. Bustamante to Secretary of War, 19 Apr. 1827, Bean MSR, fols. 39–39v.

21. Bustamante to Ahumada, 19 June 1827, BA, translated in Blake Transcripts (G), 9: 106. For President Victoria's and Secretary of War Pedraza's instructions, the latter dated 19 May, see Bean MSR, fols. 39v–40.

22. Greaser, *Catalogue of TGLO,* 2:13 (entry no. 71 for Burnet's contract and entry no. 70 for Vehlein's contract).

23. Arizpe to Saucedo, 20 Apr. 1827, Saltillo Archives, vol. 22 (CAH, box 2Q319).

24. Bean to Secretary of War, 31 Aug. 1827, and Bustamante's marginal endorsement of 6 Sept., Bean MSR, fols. 43–45. The president, when informed of Bean's request, considered it "surprising that he should not have been paid for the months in question" and ordered *comisario* Seguín to explain the delay. Ibid., fol. 48.

25. Bean MSR, fols. 31–33.

26. Compensation Board to Head of General Staff, 11 Aug. 1826, Bean MSR, fols. 16v–17; another variant copy dated 7 Aug. is on fols. 21v and 25 (the latter page bound out of order).

27. Bean to Secretary of War, 16 Aug. 1827, with Bustamante's marginal endorsement of same date, Bean MSR, fols. 33–33v.

28. Barker, *Life of SFA,* 146n68, says the treaties are "not available," but Kavanagh, *The Comanches,* 526, cites it as BA under date of 28 July 1827; discussed on his p. 200.

29. As cited in n10 above.

30. Barker, *Life of SFA,* 144–45. See also chapter 6 in Allen G. Hatley, *The Indian Wars in Stephen F. Austin's Texas Colony.* A great deal of documentation for Austin's planned

1826 campaign is found in the Debray Translations, TSL; see especially 2d series, nos. 24 and 25.

31. Milam to Austin, 30 Mar. 1827, Barker, *Austin Papers,* vol. 1, pt. 2, 1621–22.

32. Burnet to Bustamante, 2 July 1827, ibid., 1667–71. Barker notes that when this document was published in the *Telegraph and Texas Register* on 6 Oct. 1838, it also had the signatures of Milam and Austin (both dead by that time). Austin's other writings on Indians strongly suggest that he was the principal author and, for some reason, allowed Burnet to have authorship credit in Commandant General Bustamante's mind.

33. Juan José Urteaga to Erasmo Seguín, 8 July 1827, forwarding from Rio Grande two burlapped boxes and a sword for Bean, BA, translated in Blake Transcripts (G), 9:108; Bean acknowledges receipt of same from Seguín, 4 Aug., ibid., 109.

34. Seguín certification, 30 Aug. 1827, Bean MSR, fol. 3; Seguín to Bustamante, 31 Oct. 1827, ibid., fol. 49 (fol. 54 has another copy made by Seguín on 27 Dec.).

35. Bustamante to Secretary of War, 8 Nov. 1827, Bean MSR, fol. 50; War Department's reply, 1 Dec. 1827, asking Bustamante for the "forgotten document," ibid., fol. 51; Bustamante to Seguín, 3 Apr. 1827, forwarding the president's ruling on pay for Bean, Ruiz, et al., ibid., fol. 52; Bustamante to Secretary of War, 27 Dec. 1827, ibid., fol. 53.

36. Bean MSR, fols. IV–2, printed form under the heading of "Campaigns and Actions of War in Which He Has Found Himself." Appendix D gives the full text. See Bean MSR, fols. 55–56, for the transmission of Bean's service record to the War Department from the head of the General Staff.

37. Pedraza to Cañedo, 2 Feb. 1828, Fomento [BNAH] Transcripts, 309:96 (CAH, box 2Q167).

38. Cañedo to Governor of Coahuila y Texas [Viesca], 22 Apr. 1828, transmitting the president's approval of Bean's project, ibid., 86.

39. Viesca to Cañedo, 5 May 1828, ibid., 87–88. Another copy is in Saltillo Archives, 24:127–29 (CAH, box 2Q320).

40. José María Viesca and Juan Antonio Padilla to Secretary of War [Pedraza], 28 May 1827, Fomento [BNAH] Transcripts, 309:89 (CAH, box 2Q167). This is a copy made at Saltillo on 5 May 1828 by Padilla.

41. Ibid., 90, under date of 20 May 1828.

42. Pedraza to Cañedo, 2 June 1828, ibid., 91.

43. Mora to Músquiz, 1 Mar. 1828, acknowledging the political chief's orders re Bean of 17 Jan. 1828, BA, translated in Blake Transcripts (G), 9:119.

44. Bean to Bustamante, 1 Mar. 1828, Historical Archive of Secretaría de Relaciones Exteriores, Mexico City (hereafter cited as SRE), L-E-1076, fols. 39–39v.

45. Bean to Izard, 4 Mar. 1828, cited in Foreman, *Indians & Pioneers,* 218. See also Skipper Steely, *Six Months from Tennessee: The Story of Old Miller County, Now N. E. Texas and S. E. Oklahoma, from 1816–1830,* 131–34.

46. Bean to Austin, 5 Mar. 1828, Barker, *Austin Papers,* 2:23–24; also given in Lay, *Lives,* 133–34. On the Dayton incident, see Cantrell, *Stephen F. Austin,* 196–98.

47. For the Shawnee land claim see Greaser, *Catalogue of TGLO,* 2:11–12 (entry no. 61), 110–11 (entry nos. 1078–82).

48. Pierson to Izard, 22 Mar. 1828, McLean, *Papers concerning Robertson's Colony,* 3: 176–77. Other letters on the Indian situation along the Red River at this time are also given by McLean.

49. Seguín [?] to Bean, 1 May 1828, translated in Blake Transcripts (G) 9:126. Blake cites the letter as BA, from the political chief, but *comisario* Seguín likely wrote it; original not located. President Victoria and Secretary of War Pedraza became annoyed at the

delay, writing on 27 and 28 Sept. 1827 that Bustamante should have taken care of Bean's payment "without need of appealing to the [Superior] Govt." Bean MSR, fols. 35, 48.

50. For the Zuber account see Lowrey, "Peter Ellis Bean," 54; also given in Lay, *Lives,* 129–30.

51. Lowrey, "Peter Ellis Bean," 52, citing the Belt account in *Lamar Papers,* 1:546, and several communications she had received from Robert Blake and Samuel Asbury expressing the opinion that Belt/Lamar had no legitimate basis for such a statement. They thought it amounted to character assassination.

52. Lafitte power of attorney to Bean, 21 Sept. 1828, Blake Transcripts (R), 1:25.

Chapter 8

1. For Terán's time at Nacogdoches and in the boundary reserve, consult Jackson and Wheat, *Texas by Terán,* 75-140.

2. Galli's 1826 map is reproduced in ibid., 55, and (because of its Bean connection) in this chapter. The original is at CAH.

3. Terán to Secretary of Foreign Relations [Cañedo], 9 June 1828, ibid., 94. Here I should note that this official in 1828 was Juan de Dios Cañedo, not José María Bocanegra as mistakenly attributed throughout the Terán book; see 234n1 therein, which should have alerted me to the correct minister's name. Terán's letters were directed to the head of the agency, not to an individual.

4. Terán to Governor of Coahuila y Texas [Viesca], 29 June 1828, in Jackson and Wheat, *Texas by Terán,* 95.

5. As admitted by Margaret Swett Henson, *Lorenzo de Zavala: The Pragmatic Idealist,* 34, 41–43, 45–53, wherein Zavala's efforts to sell his contract in the United States are discussed and followed through completion.

6. See Juan Suárez y Navarro, *Historia de México y del General Antonio López de Santa Anna,* 395; mentioned in Ríos, "El Insurgente Don Pedro Elías Bean," 524.

7. Piedras to Elozúa, 25 Sept. 1828, BA, acknowledging his orders of 2 Sept.

8. Terán to Secretary of Foreign Relations [Cañedo], 5 July 1828, SRE, L-E-1076, fols. 53–54.

9. Bean to Terán, 11 July 1828, given in Jackson and Wheat, *Texas by Terán,* 106–109, the source for quotes below in the main text. Lay, *Lives,* 138–40, mistakenly says that Terán and diarist José María Sánchez attended the council (as have most other writers). Sánchez's diary gives this false impression.

10. Bean to Terán, 11 July 1828, given in Jackson and Wheat, *Texas by Terán,* 106–109.

11. William Goyens might be added to this list. No doubt there were others who acted as interpreters at these Indian councils, but (according to Susanne Starling) Martin Lacy was not one of them: "Lacy did not speak or write Cherokee; in fact, he was illiterate except for the ability to sign his name." Susanne Starling, *Land Is the Cry!: Warren Angus Ferris, Pioneer Texas Surveyor and Founder of Dallas County,* 60. See the Austin letter about John "Cherokee" Williams's suspected illicit trade with the Indians in McLean, *Papers concerning Robertson's Colony,* 3:428. Some of the interpreters were local Mexicans who rarely got mentioned. Luis Sánchez, a veteran of San Jacinto on the Texan side who spoke twelve Indian languages, was certainly among these neglected men. He is on the 1834 census as a laborer, aged thirty.

12. An original of the two letters in Terán's hand and signed by him is in the Eberstadt Collection (CAH, box 3N189), with thanks to Thomas Ricks Lindley for bringing it to

my attention. John Wheat and I were unaware of it when working on *Texas by Terán;* see 230n124 therein for published versions used.

13. Berlandier, *The Indians of Texas in 1830;* population figures are given for each tribe discussed.

14. As cited in n1 above.

15. Roberts to Austin, 18 July 1828, BA, given in Blake Transcripts (G), 9:138.

16. Mora to Political Chief, 22 July 1828, BA, ibid., 140.

17. Thorn to Austin, 22 July 1828, Barker, *Austin Papers,* 2:74–75. Thorn also mentioned the recent state law that permitted "indented" servitude for slaves and how Amos Edwards—recently arrived from Kentucky with his slaves—had been placed "at ease on that subject" by language of the law. His house above San Felipe may have been the one mentioned by Lundy in 1834, rather than that of his brother Haden, the ex-empresario; see Jackson and Wheat, *Almonte's Texas,* 169n21, for this possible mix-up. According to letters in the J. P. Bryan Collection, there were several other Edwards brothers in Texas during the 1820s, including Asa B. and Gustavus. Thorn's defense to Saucedo for his conduct during the Fredonian Rebellion is in NA Transcripts, 198:244–45 (CAH, box 2Q299). He said he only took his family to New Orleans because of fear for their safety at Nacogdoches.

18. For the paperwork on Filisola's contract see Greaser, *Catalogue of TGLO,* 2:110 (entry no. 1074); on Thorn, ibid., 12 (entry no. 63), 110 (entry no. 1077). Filisola was also unsuccessful as a colonizer of these lands, despite trying to form a "Filisola Association" with Samuel Swartwout and other speculators in the United States. At one point James Treat, who had good contacts in Mexico City, was an agent for this projected enterprise.

19. Bean to Governor of Coahuila y Texas, 30 July 1828, IED (Coahuila), AGEC, FJPB, C8, E99, 2F (Bean's original petition); translation given in Blake Transcripts (G), 9:143–44, cited as a copy in BA.

20. Nacogdoches Ayuntamiento to Interim Political Chief, 14 Oct. 1828, BA (CAH, box 2S227).

21. TGLO, box 114, folder 14 (38:554). Gaines's survey not only shows the Old San Antonio Road cutting diagonally through Bean's grant but another connecting road going north alongside "Serrito" Creek to the Indian villages. This survey is proof that the roads shown from the house of BEAN on Galli's 1826 printed map were in use and could be taken directly from the Neches crossing to reach the Red River settlements. See also GSC, box 6, folder 8, at TGLO.

22. As earlier noted, the documents pertaining to the William Bean league are cited in Greaser, *Catalogue of TGLO,* 2:11 (entry nos. 54–59). There are six items in box 114, folder 5, plus parts of the file in BA and IED (Coahuila). Blake Transcripts (G), vol. 9, has translations of some of the BA items. Bean paid Gaines his surveying fees for the "Salinas League" on 24 Sept. 1828. Deed Book C, 149, NCCO.

23. Cañedo to Pedraza, 2 Aug. 1828, and Cañedo to Governor of Coahuila y Texas [Viesca], same date, Fomento [BNAH] Transcripts, 309:92–93 (CAH, box 2Q167).

24. Viesca to Cañedo, 18 Aug. 1828, ibid., 94.

25. Cañedo to Viesca, 27 Sept. 1828, Saltillo Archives, 24:86–87 (CAH, box 2Q320). Suárez y Navarro, *Historia de México,* 396–97; mentioned in Ríos, "El Insurgente Don Pedro Elías Bean," 524.

26. Document collection as cited in n23 above, p. 98.

27. Ibid., 99–101, under date of 25 Nov. 1828.

28. Suárez y Navarro, *Historia de México,* as cited in n25 above; Ríos, "El Insurgente Don Pedro Elías Bean," 524.

29. Bean to Governor of Coahuila y Texas [Viesca], 6 Jan. 1829, Saltillo Archives, 24:

135–36 (CAH, box 2Q320). Bean's 22 July 1828 "memorial" to the governor has not been found. Terán may have encouraged him to write it, in hopes that Bean could bring order to the boundary reserve.

30. On this revolt—the first of many to plague independent Mexico's leadership—see Green, *The Mexican Republic,* 154–63.

31. This Bocanegra decision of 10 Feb. 1829 is *the* critical document for Bean's empresarial ambitions. Among the copies located are Saltillo Archives, 24:91–93, 137–38; TGLO, box 127, folder 10, 64–65; BNAH, 51-6-54, documents 5/13 and 6/13. It is also given in Ríos, "El Insurgente Don Pedro Elías Bean," 524–25, from José María Bocanegra's *Memorias para la Historia de México Independiente, 1822–1846,* 1:544–45.

32. Vicente Filisola, *Memoirs for the History of the War in Texas,* 2:283–84. Filisola praised the wisdom of Bocanegra for giving the contract to a Mexican instead of a foreigner, even though events had since proved that Lorenzo de Zavala—who took the side of the insurrectionists in Texas—was the wrong man to be so honored.

33. Ríos, "El Insurgente Don Pedro Elías Bean," 525. The writer, however, was not aware that the case pending against Bean involved bigamy. How this would have affected his verdict is unknown.

34. Viesca to SRE, 23 Feb. 1829, and Viesca to Bean, 27 Feb. 1829, Saltillo Archives, 24:94, 139 (CAH, box 2Q230).

35. Winkler, "The Cherokee Indians in Texas," 153, citing Piedras to Elozúa, 8 Jan. 1828, BA. An alternative spelling is Elosúa, used by many historians.

36. The documentation for the Houston County league is cited in Greaser, *Catalogue of TGLO,* 1:18 (116:13).

37. Nacogdoches Ayuntamiento to Political Chief, 19 Jan. 1829, BA, translated in Blake Transcripts (G), 9:188.

38. Bean to Nacogdoches Ayuntamiento, 10 Mar. 1829, BA, translated in ibid., 192. Bean's protest was forwarded to Músquiz on the 17 Mar.; ibid., 196.

39. Ibarvo to Músquiz, 28 Sept. 1829, ibid., 216. Often spelled Ibarbo or Ybarbo.

40. NA Transcripts, 213:149, 157; 211:169–70 (CAH, box 2Q 302). Thomas wrote Dubois of his problems at the salt works on 28 June 1829.

41. Bean to Austin, 18 Mar. 1829, Barker, *Austin Papers,* 2:192–93; also in Lay, *Lives,* 142–43. For the Tampico invasion see Morton, *Terán and Texas,* 83–92.

42. Elozúa to Piedras, 28 May 1829, BA, translated in Blake Transcripts (G), 9:208.

43. Bustamante to Austin, 23 Mar. 1829, conveying his letter to Elozúa of the same day, Barker, *Austin Papers,* 2:194–95, translated in McLean, *Papers concerning Robertson's Colony,* 3:389–90. Here it is proper to give credit to Dr. Malcolm D. McLean for translating many of the Bean-related letters in the BA that other scholars have overlooked. My reliance on his work will become evident as this study progresses.

44. Músquiz to Austin, 28 May 1829; McLean, *Papers concerning Robertson's Colony,* 3:394–95.

45. Mentioned (but inadequately treated) in Hatley, *The Indian Wars,* 59–60. See also Músquiz to Austin, 11 June 1829, Barker, *Austin Papers,* 2:223–24; McLean, *Papers concerning Robertson's Colony,* 3:401–2, where the shift is proposed.

46. Martin Allen to Austin, 5 July 1829, Barker, *Austin Papers,* 2:225–26; also in McLean, *Papers concerning Robertson's Colony,* 3:412–13, and Hatley, *The Indian Wars,* 118–20, as his document 18.

47. Austin to Elozúa, 29 July 1829, and Ruiz to Austin, 23 July 1829, both in McLean, *Papers concerning Robertson's Colony,* 3:422–24.

48. The notes for this 1829 map are in Barker, *Austin Papers,* 2:236–40, and translated more fully in Jackson and Wheat, *Texas by Terán,* 220n71. Austin's map is reproduced in

Jackson, *Shooting the Sun,* 2:441 (an 1836 copy as the frontispiece); see also my Map List entry nos. 79C and D for large, easy-to-read copies in Texas depositories.

49. Bean to Lindsey, 25 Aug. 1829, NA, given in Blake Transcripts (R), 12:171.

50. Lindsey to Nacogdoches Alcalde, 27 Aug. 1829, NA, ibid., 172.

51. Hatley, *The Indian Wars,* 59; DeWitt to Músquiz, 8 May 1829, complaining how the Wacos and Tawakonis were trying to enlist the Comanches in their war with the whites. McLean, *Papers concerning Robertson's Colony,* 3:393.

52. As cited in McLean, *Papers concerning Robertson's Colony,* 3:414, 415n2; see also the Kuykendall account of a Sept. 1829 outing from Austin's colony, ibid., 430–37, and Smith, *The Wichita Indians,* 123–24.

53. Bean land sale to "Liboy Bosgte," 29 Sept. 1829; Bean land sale to Bradshaw, 23 Nov. 1829, both in Blake Transcripts (R), 1:32–33, 33. Blake gives separate pagination for each record book, naming them as "Archives from the Office of the County Clerk, Nacogdoches, Texas," Books A and B (hereafter cited as AOCCN); they are not to be confused with the deed books cited as NCCO. I have not been able to determine when and to whom Bean sold the remainder of this league. Bostick sale to Bean of slave "Qusdet," 30 Sept. 1829, NA Transcripts, 212:68 (CAH, box 2Q302).

54. Estate of Robert Collier, deceased, 20 Sept. 1826, NA Transcripts, 197A:186–88, 194 (CAH, box 2Q298).

55. Susana "Callier" deposition, 9 Sept. 1829, NA Transcripts, 211:136 (CAH, box 2Q302). In this case, Bean's guardianship is doubtful. According to Holt, "The Edwards Empresarial Grant," 97, Robert Collier and Matthew Yocum were involved in a boundary reserve feud called by contemporaries "a falling out of thieves." Collier was killed, and a deputy sheriff from Natchitoches Parish named John S. Roberts fell in love with Collier's widow Harriet while trying to protect her from her late husband's enemies. He was still courting her when he joined Parmer's men in the Nov. 1826 housecleaning at Nacogdoches, was active in the Fredonian Rebellion, and went on to become a signer of the Texas Declaration of Independence, prosperous citizen, etc. See the entry on him in Tyler et al., *NHOT,* 5:610.

56. Mata Medina land sale to Bean, 27 July 1829, Deed Book B, 42, and Flores land sale to Bean, 9 Sept. 1829, Deed Book C, 292, NCCO; on the latter see Lay, *Lives,* 196n6. "Site of Home of Peter Ellis Bean" given in Blake Transcripts (R), 52:152; see chapter 17, n43, for more on this house.

57. Piedras to Músquiz, 4 Aug. 1829 (also other letters on this subject going into Sept.), SRE, L-E-1076, fols. 144–52. Erasmo Seguín wrote on 14 Sept. 1829, enumerating the ills afflicting Texas, fols. 159–159v.

58. For more information on the foregoing chain of events, see Green, *The Mexican Republic,* 170–74, 189–98; Morton, *Terán and Texas,* 92–94, 105–8.

59. McKinney to Austin, 9 Sept. 1829, Barker, *Austin Papers,* 2:254–57, quoted at length in Lay, *Lives,* 143–46.

60. McKinney to Austin, 9 Sept. 1829, Barker, *Austin Papers,* 2:254–57.

61. Ibid.

62. These letters are at the TGLO, box 114, folder 5, along with the 30 Mar. 1829 letter that William Bean wrote to the Nacogdoches ayuntamiento (which seemingly indicates that he was still in Texas at the time). Greaser, *Catalogue of TGLO,* 2:11, lists the documents.

63. Greaser, *Catalogue of TGLO,* 2:11 (entry no. 58). Viesca's verdict of 18 Feb. 1829 is entry no. 54.

64. Bean to Elozúa, 22 Dec. 1829, BA, translated in Blake Transcripts (G), 9:218.

65. Barker, *Life of SFA,* 217.

66. For how Austin was obliged to deed property to Butler on this Texas trip (and later in 1833) because of old indebtedness, see Margaret Howard et al., *Testing at the San Felipe de Austin Townsite (41AU2),* 30–31. Butler made frequent trips to Texas, and he was accused by Mexican officials in Texas of inciting the colonists to attack Anáhuac in 1832—this because the cabinet in Washington was taking an "active, but secret, part" in the revolutionary movements directed toward independence. See Political Chief [Músquiz] to Vice-Governor [Veramendi], 11 Mar. 1833, Debray Translations, TSL. In a letter that Butler wrote to Benjamin Edwards on 14 Dec. 1826 (from the Sabine ferry), he asked for land in the colony and mentioned the date of mid-November "last, when I first visited Nacogdoches." This, of course, was when Parmer's men rode into town and started what became the Fredonian Rebellion! J. P. Bryan Collection.

67. Músquiz, in the letter just cited, recalls that when Butler passed through Béxar at the end of 1829, he was bragging to him—in a confidential manner, of course—about how he was bearing instructions for the purchase of Texas from Mexico by the United States government. It is small wonder that the news preceded Butler to the Mexican capital and jeopardized his mission.

Chapter 9

1. Morton, *Terán and Texas,* 115; Green, *The Mexican Republic,* 190–91.

2. The basic study is still Alleine Howren, "Causes and Origin of the Decree of April 6, 1830," *SHQ* 16 (Apr. 1913): 378–422. Barker devoted an entire chapter to this law in his *Life of SFA,* 256–83.

3. Cantrell, *Stephen F. Austin,* 236.

4. Terán to Alamán, 15 Mar. 1830, AHSDN, Operaciones, XI/481.3/1190, fols. 67–69. The map is labeled "limites de la frontera que se proponen." It has no place-names and may be understood only by reference to the letter. See Morton, *Terán and Texas,* 140.

5. Making the entire department (that is, state) of Texas a territory was still being considered by the government at the time Almonte inspected Texas, and one of his chores was to discourage moves for separate statehood. The subject is treated in detail in Jackson and Wheat, *Almonte's Texas.*

6. Bean petition, 27 Feb. 1830, and Viesca's reply, 29 Jan. 1831, IED (Coahuila), AGEC, FJPB, C14, E81, 2F. See the signature page of this petition reproduced in this chapter.

7. Some new information on the founding of these forts is presented in my yet-unpublished 2002 study for Texas Parks and Wildlife Department, "Fort Lipantitlán: Mexico's Lone Sentinel on the Coastal Corridor to Texas" (a historical background of events at this fort on the Nueces near San Patricio). Copy on file at TPWD, Austin, and at CAH with my collection of papers.

8. BA, under date of 13 Apr. 1830.

9. *Texas Gazette,* 12 June 1830, as given in McLean, *Papers concerning Robertson's Colony,* 4:192.

10. Bean to Elozúa, 22 June 1830, BA, translated in ibid., 4:210.

11. Elozúa to Terán, 6 July 1830, BA, translated in ibid., 4:241–42.

12. Elozúa to Bean, 6 July 1830, and Elozúa to Ruiz, same date, BA, translated in ibid., 4:243–44, 245–46.

13. Ruiz to Elozúa, 22 June 1830, BA, translated in ibid., 4:334–35.

14. Bean to Elozúa, 22 June 1830, and Elozúa to Terán, 6 July 1830, conveying Bean's report, BA, translated in ibid., 4:208–9, 240.

15. Terán to Elozúa, 18 Aug. 1830, conveying his letter to Bean of 19 July, BA, translated in ibid., 4:399–400. See McLean's remarks on these orders and related Indian-fighting activities in ibid., 4:51–52.

16. Brooks to Bean, 7 July 1830, cited in F. Todd Smith, *The Caddo Indians: Tribes at the Convergence of Empires, 1542–1854,* 115–16. The quote is Smith's.

17. Elozúa to Piedras, 2 Aug. 1830, replying to Piedras's notification on the 19th "last," BA (CAH, box 2S256).

18. Piedras to Terán, 14 Sept. 1830, as forwarded by Secretary of War Facio to the Secretary of Relationes Exteriores (SRE) on 8 Nov., Fomento [BNAH] Transcripts, 314: 105–6 (CAH, box 2Q168).

19. Piedras to Terán, 27 Sept. 1830, as forwarded by Terán to SRE on 7 Nov., ibid., 107–8.

20. Bean to Terán, 22 [Nov.] 1830, as forwarded by Terán to SRE on 30 Dec., ibid., 242–43. Morton, *Terán and Texas,* 127–28, gives a brief account of this expedition, citing Terán's orders for it dated 26 May 1830.

21. Piedras to Elozúa, 28 Sept. 1830, BA, translated in McLean, *Papers concerning Robertson's Colony,* 4:552–54; Elozúa to Piedras, 13 Oct. 1830, ibid., 5:76.

22. Elozúa to Terán, 22 Oct. 1830, and Elozúa to Piedras, 23 Oct. 1830, BA, translated in ibid., 5:97–99, 107–9.

23. Bean to Elozúa, 22 Oct. 1830; Elozúa to Terán, same date; and Elozúa to Bean, 23 Oct. 1830, saying he was transmitting Bean's information to Commandant General Terán, BA, translated in ibid., 5:75, 100, 110.

24. Bean to Elozúa, 22 Oct. 1830, BA, translated in ibid., 5:104.

25. Elozúa to Bean, 23 Oct. 1830, and Elozúa to Ortega, same date, BA, translated in ibid., 5:106, 105.

26. Ortega to Elozúa, 22 Nov. 1830, BA, translated in Blake Transcripts (G), 9:239.

27. Bean Internet post, as cited in chapter 1, n2. Interestingly, Robert B. Blake told Flora Lowrey that "Bean was tried for bigamy, in the Alcalde's court in Nacogdoches, and was cleared of that charge." Blake to Lowrey, 13 Dec. 1944, Blake Papers, CAH, box 3G294. I have not found Blake's source for this information, but he said it came "soon after" Candace's 1826 contradictory testimony about their marriage. He—wrongly as it turns out—stated that "the evidence seems to be rather conclusive that he and Candace were never married." Blake did not know about Bean's petition for divorce in 1839.

28. Family Bible "Exhibits" in Blake Transcripts (R), 52:225–26, 262–63, 264; see the epilogue, where the information is given.

29. For the land grant of Isaac Midkiff, see Greaser, *Catalogue of TGLO,* 1:110. It adjoined that of his sister Candace in Leon County. A brief biographical sketch of him is given in Blake Transcripts (R), 59:95–96.

30. Cherel Henderson, East Tennessee Historical Society, to Jack Jackson, e-mail communication, 28 June 2003. Grady, *William Bean,* 30, also notes how the destruction of records for Hawkins County, Tennessee, makes it impossible to say when Peter Ellis Bean's parents married and if his mother Elizabeth's maiden name was Blair for certain; Grady makes a strong case that it was.

31. Elozúa to Ruiz, 24 Oct. 1830, and Ruiz to Elozúa, 12 Nov. 1830, BA, translated in McLean, *Papers concerning Robertson's Colony,* 5:113, 178. Bean, from his arrival in 1826, was routinely entrusted with delivery of military cash on his trips between Béxar and Nacogdoches.

32. Piedras to Austin, 12 Nov. 1830, ibid., 5:183–85.

33. Piedras to Elozúa, 22 Nov. 1830, and Terán to Elozúa, 18 Nov. 1830, BA, ibid., 5: 229, 220.

34. Terán to SRE, 30 Oct. and 7 Nov. 1830, BNAH, 51-6-50, documents 2/9 and 4/9.

35. For the correspondence on Milam/Wavell, see Greaser, *Catalogue of TGLO,* 2:97 (entry nos. 950–57).

36. Henson, *Lorenzo de Zavala,* as cited in chapter 8, n5.

37. See, for example, BNAH, 51-7-58, eight documents dealing with John T. Mason's efforts with Alamán to overcome Terán's opposition to the sale by the three grantees. Larger files on the same subject are ibid., 51-6-35, 51-6-36, 51-6-37, and 51-6-39. The file involving Bean's contest with Zavala is 51-6-54, thirteen documents covering 1828–29; document 9 is a pencil-and-ink sketch map showing the lands awarded to Zavala, Burnet, and Vehlein. The documentation on these three empresarios at the TGLO is also voluminous; see entry nos. 958–95 in Greaser, *Catalogue of TGLO,* vol. 2.

38. On Terán's steadfast opposition see documents cited in the previous note and the summary in Morton, *Terán and Texas,* 125–26, 129–30.

39. Morton, *Terán and Texas,* 128–29, gives the full letter.

40. Santos to Piedras, 12 Jan. 1831 (re slaves), NA; Santos to Political Chief, 15 Feb. 1831, and Bean to Santos, 23 Feb. 1831, translated in Blake Transcripts (R), 52:38–41.

41. Bean to Political Chief [Músquiz], 1 Mar. 1831, and his reply of 29 Mar., TGLO, box 116, folder 13; Músquiz to Governor of Coahuila y Texas, 13 Mar. 1831, IED (Coahuila), AGEC, FJPB, C19, E81, 2F.

42. Letona to Political Chief [Músquiz], 28 Apr. 1831, IED (Coahuila), AGEC, FJPB, C19, E81, 2F. This letter is also in BA, translated in Blake Transcripts (G), 9:245.

43. Músquiz to Nacogdoches Ayuntamiento, 12 May 1831, BA, translated in Blake Transcripts (G), 9:247.

44. Viesca to Bean, 29 Jan. 1831, conceding sale of eight leagues of vacant land, IED (Coahuila), AGEC, FJPB, C14, E81, 2F. This was in response to Bean's petition of 27 Feb. 1830; the governor's reply is attached to Bean's original.

45. See Greaser, *Catalogue of TGLO,* 1:10 (Aranjo/Araujo), 69 (Garza). Bean is noted as the "attorney" for both grantees, later discussed in more detail.

46. Circular to promote the building of a church and school at Nacogdoches, dated 10 Mar. 1831, Debray Translations, TSL. Alcalde Chirino reported a year later that twenty-four children were receiving instruction at the school. Bean's son Isaac (aged ten) may have attended; he was literate, but his mother Candace was not. Partin, "A History of Nacogdoches," 143.

47. Galindo town lot sale to Bean, 29 Nov. 1830, Deed Book D, 70; Pineda town lot sale to Bean, 31 Dec. 1830, Deed Book D, 71; Amador land sale on "la Loma" to Bean, 15 May 1831, Deed Book B, 201—all in NCCO. Lazarin land sale to Bean, 11 May 1831, Blake Transcripts (R), 1:49–50; also in ibid., 4:75.

48. Gary Clayton Anderson, *The Indian Southwest, 1580–1830: Ethnogenesis and Reinvention,* 262.

49. Both letters are given in Jackson and Wheat, *Texas by Terán,* 92–95, 109–10.

50. Quoted in Winkler, "The Cherokee Indians in Texas," 153–54.

51. Ibid.

52. Músquiz to Letona, 25 Sept. 1831, ibid., 154–55.

53. Letona to Músquiz, 22 Mar. 1832, ibid., 155.

54. Ibid., 156. In addition to the TGLO volume Winkler cited in 1903, "Translations of Empresario Contracts," see Greaser, *Catalogue of TGLO,* 2:51–52 (entry nos. 451–63) for the original documents in Spanish.

Chapter 10

1. Piedras to Elozúa, 25 Sept. 1831, and Elozúa's acknowledgment, 10 Oct., BA.

2. See the small on-the-ground study by Don C. Marler, *Fort Terán on the Neches River.* A map of surveys for the Trinity Land Company, probably done by agent George M. Patrick in 1834, shows "Terran" on the west bank of the Neches with roads connecting it to other points; see map in the text. This map served as the basis for the eastern portion of the map in the immigrant's book published by David Woodman in 1835, the intention being to drum up land sales in the region by speculators who owned stock in the Galveston Bay & Texas Land Company and its spin-off groups, such as the Trinity Land Company. National Archives, RG 76, E24, box 27, claim 205, with thanks to Galen Greaser.

3. Actually, the Tyler County grant comprised $4^{22}/_{25}$ (call it five) leagues; see TGLO, box 110, folder 16. Marler, *Fort Terán,* 55–56, notes an early resident of the tract, Peter Cauble. Crocket, *Two Centuries in East Texas,* 153, states that Aranjo was with the "small garrison" at Fort Terán.

4. Lay, *Lives,* 148.

5. Piedras to Elozúa, 9 Apr. 1832, BA; see Marler, *Fort Terán,* 28–29.

6. Béxar Commissariat report, 23 Oct. 1831, BA, translated in McLean, *Papers concerning Robertson's Colony,* 6:491. Bean later claimed that stop-payment notices had cut off his salary in July 1831.

7. Marler, *Fort Terán,* 43–54, discusses Sam Belt's store and ferry, suggesting the possibility of Bean's tolerance of smuggling or taking a cut for himself. This is only speculation, based upon what other Mexican officials (like Piedras) and merchants (like Belt?) were doing. Frost Thorn and John Allen Veatch later planned to form a town at Fort Terán, purchasing Belt's "entire interest." See the agreement of 7 Nov. 1837, Raguet Papers, CAH, box 2F381.

8. Marler, *Fort Terán,* 56–59, gives information on this and other points of interest around remote Fort Terán. See also the two articles by John L. Tompkins in the *Tyler County Booster,* 21 Apr. 1983, written at the time it was feared that "Lake Rockland" would submerge the Fort Terán park site. Lake Rockland was not built, perhaps because Sam Rayburn Reservoir on the Angelina's lower tributaries already served these water needs.

9. Discussed in Jackson, "Fort Lipantitlán," 27, citing letters of 30 Aug. and 1 Sept. 1831, BA.

10. H. Allen Anderson, "The Delaware and Shawnee Indians and the Republic of Texas, 1820–1845," *SHQ* 94 (Oct. 1990): 237–38. The author notes that Bean "often bore the brunt of the Indians' complaints about the slowness of the Mexican officials to act" on their petitions for land.

11. Bowie to Political Chief of Béxar [Músquiz], 10 Dec. 1831, NA, given in Blake Transcripts (R), 12:276–82. For more information on this San Sabá venture, see William C. Davis, *Three Roads to the Alamo: The Lives and Fortunes of David Crockett, James Bowie, and William Barret Travis,* 298–307, 339.

12. Bowie to Political Chief of Béxar [Músquiz], 23 Apr. 1832, given in Blake Transcripts (R), 12:308–10. Davis only devotes one page (341) to this second "campaign," perhaps because Bowie had no spectacular fight with Indians. Both of Bowie's reports are in the Debray Translations, TSL. For why Bowie could not find these tribes see Smith, *The Wichita Indians,* 124–27.

13. Davis, *Three Roads to the Alamo,* 228, where Bowie's "complex set of relationships" with Prather and McKinney are mentioned—but not spelled out clearly. See also Lowrey, "Peter Ellis Bean," 57, for Robert B. Blake's thoughts on when the Bean-Bowie contact

began; he suggests the early 1820s. A carbon copy of Blake's 13 Dec. 1944 letter to Lowrey is at CAH, box 3G294.

Chapter 11

1. The subject is adequately covered in Margaret Swett Henson, *Juan Davis Bradburn: A Reappraisal of the Mexican Commander of Anahuac,* though her focus is on Anáhuac instead of events at Nacogdoches.

2. Piedras to Elozúa, 19 June 1832, NA, translated in Blake Transcripts (R), 12:336; see Henson, *Juan Davis Bradburn,* 106–107.

3. Blake Transcripts (R), 12:336; see also Lay, *Lives,* 148.

4. Gulick et al., *Lamar Papers,* 1:545–47; account of "Judge Harden [William Hardin] of Liberty," ibid., 544–45.

5. Ibid., 546. Lamar's informant said that Bean's wife did not join him in Texas until he commanded Fort Terán, and that Bean refused to acknowledge her because local people knew about his wife in Mexico—along with other malicious and false assertions. Lowrey, "Peter Ellis Bean," 52, repeats this slander but cites letters to her from Samuel Asbury and Robert Blake that place the blame on Lamar, because he wanted to "make Bean as mean as they are made" (this due to Lamar's pro-Fredonian and pro-1832 revolt attitude, he believing that Bean was on the wrong side of both confrontations).

6. Gulick et al., *Lamar Papers,* 1:547; also in Lowrey, "Peter Ellis Bean," 32, and Lay, *Lives,* 149.

7. Henson, *Juan Davis Bradburn,* 109–12.

8. Piedras to Elozúa, 24 July 1832, BA, translated in Blake Transcripts (G), 9:279–80.

9. Piedras to Commandant of Coahuila y Texas, 12 July 1832; Ayish Bayou committee resolutions, 5 July 1832, both in Debray Translations, TSL.

10. Ayuntamiento of Nacogdoches to Inhabitants of Ayz Bayou, 28 July 1832, Debray Translations, TSL. Mary Austin Holley, *Texas,* 324.

11. David B. Edward, *The History of Texas: Or the Emigrant's, Farmer's & Politician's Guide . . . ,* 207–208.

12. Gulick et al., *Lamar Papers,* 1:547.

13. Tyler et al., *NHOT,* 4:923, entry on "Nacogdoches, Battle of." More detail is given in Partin, "A History of Nacogdoches," 158–69.

14. Davis, *Three Roads to the Alamo,* 346–48. See also the account of Piedras's defeat given to the political chief at Béxar by the Nacogdoches ayuntamiento on 14 Aug. 1832, Debray Translations, TSL. Correspondence with Piedras and capitulation documents are attached.

15. Davis, *Three Roads to the Alamo,* 348–49. Medina power of attorney to Bowie, 14 Mar. 1833, executed before Alcalde Miguel Arciniega at Béxar, in Blake Transcripts (R), 1:72–73. His source was given as Book A, 72–73, AOCCN. There is some question about this, as Medina wrote Bean in July 1835 that Edward Gritten was the consignee for his grant—plus the fact that Captain Medina had taken the 12th Battalion to Matamoros long before the month of March 1833. Another forged Bowie land document?

16. Filisola, *Memoirs,* 1:112. Lamar wrote an account titled "Expulsion of Pedres from Nacogdoches, 1832" (*Lamar Papers,* 3:268–72, evidently on the authority of John H. Thompson), which names the prominent merchants at Nacogdoches who wanted a Mexican garrison to remain there "with old Col. Bean in command; their feelings being on the mexican side [with the hope of deriving] great pecuniary advantages from the soldiers."

Thompson said he threatened to burn the town if any Mexican troops were allowed to return.

17. Almonte to Commandant General Pedro Lemus, 4 June 1834, Jackson and Wheat, *Almonte's Texas,* 108.

18. Everett, *The Texas Cherokees,* 64–65, saying that with the ouster of Piedras and the deaths of Terán and Letona, "the paperwork [for the Cherokee land title] was never to be completed."

19. Austin to Political Chief at Béxar, 15 Aug. 1832, Debray Translations, TSL; Thorn to Austin, 28 Aug. 1832, Barker, *Austin Papers,* 2:851.

20. As cited in n17 above.

21. Bean to Nacogdoches Alcalde, 14 and 24 Nov. 1832; 5 Feb. 1833, NA.

Chapter 12

1. Green, *The Mexican Republic,* 227–29; William A. DePalo Jr., *The Mexican National Army, 1822–1852,* 40–42.

2. Vice-Governor [Veramendi] to Political Chief [Músquiz], 14 Feb. 1833, copying a letter that Santa Anna had written to the secretary of treasury on 18 Jan. 1833 that had progressed to him through the secretary of state. Debray Translations, TSL. Veramendi's original is no longer in the BA, but Debray assuredly did not create the document out of thin air. Barker was not aware of this translation in his *Life of SFA,* 362–73, where he discusses the preliminaries for Austin's trip to Mexico. For the many reasons why Filisola could not carry out the planned military occupation of Texas in 1833, see his *Memoirs,* 1:124–40.

3. Vice-Governor [Veramendi] to Political Chief [Músquiz], 14 Feb. 1833, Debray Translations, TSL. As noted in chapter 8, n66, Músquiz wrote a detailed report to Vice-Governor Veramendi on 11 March, describing what he considered to be blatant moves toward independence by Austin's colonists in the convention that was to meet in April (Debray Translations, TSL). For warnings to cease these activities—after Austin showed up in San Antonio, bearing the results of the convention and seeking support for them from Erasmo Seguín and the Tejano political establishment—see Barker, *Austin Papers,* 2:963-68.

4. Haley, *Sam Houston,* 88, 90–94.

5. Ibid., 95; also in Lay, *Lives,* 151–52 (a "proper English" version).

6. Bean to Cass, 24 Feb. 1833, NA, given in Blake Transcripts (R), 13:165–67; for the full text see appendix E. The copy now lost from the BA and given in Debray Translations, TSL, is undated but in sequential order.

7. Houston to Jackson, 13 Feb. 1833, partially quoted in Haley, *Sam Houston,* 95. The entire letter is in Amelia W. Williams and Eugene C. Barker, eds., *The Writings of Sam Houston, 1813–1863,* 1:274–76.

8. The 1833 "Texas Memorial" is given as appendix no. 7 in Yoakum, *History of Texas,* 1:469–82. It had appeared in the 26 June 1839 issue of the *Telegraph and Texas Register* (Houston). Burnet had said that under its own government, Texas could "check the alarming accumulation of ferocious Indians, whom the domestic policy of the United States of the North is rapidly translating to our borders."

9. Bean power of attorney to Thorn, 24 Jan. 1833, in Blake Transcripts (R), 3:44–45. On his extensive land dealings at Nacogdoches, see Lucy May, "The Life and Activities of Frost Thorn," chapter 4.

10. "Notice of the lands that the government has conceded to various citizens in the

vacant lands of the state as purchasers and in the class of settlers," 2 Jan. 1832, NA, translated in Blake Transcripts (R), 12:287.

11. Parsons, "The Fredonian Rebellion," 45. For a fuller description of Prather's activities, see Crocket, *Two Centuries in East Texas,* 145–49. He had a trading post on the Angelina, not far from Bean's environs at the time.

12. A photostat of the original agreement, dated 19 Mar. 1833, is in the Bean Papers, CAH, box 2B45, as is the 14 June agreement with Stephen's son Freeman Prather. See also Blake Transcripts (R), 52:32–33; Lowrey, "Peter Ellis Bean," appendix 3 and p. 39; Lay, *Lives,* 152–53, for a portion. Some writers have mistakenly given the year as 1835—not surprising, as the original in the Peter Ellis Bean Collection, A-139, Folder 1, ETRC, is so listed. The final digit is badly formed, probably accounting for the confusion.

13. Bean Papers, CAH, box 2B45. The text makes it certain that the correct date of Bean's original agreement with Prather was 19 Mar. 1833, not 1835.

14. Morin land sale to Bean and Thorn, 20 Sept. 1833, Deed Book B, 147, in Blake Transcripts (R), 1:69–71; also in volume titled Blake, "Notebook," 344, and in Blake Transcripts (R), 52:46–47. Blake mistakenly thought that Bean moved his Carrizo sawmill to this location, giving the date "about 1836." That was the year that Bean sold his interest in the La Nana property, its sawmill included. See Blake to P. L. Sanders, 18 Dec. 1945, Blake Papers, CAH, box 3G294, and chapter 17 for this sale.

15. The documentation to explain this incident is in NA Transcripts, vol. 234 (CAH, box 2Q307). Oddly, Bean himself posted bond as tutor for John Berry, a minor, on 16 Oct. 1834; Blake Transcripts (R), 11:167. A year later, on 28 Sept. 1835, Bean and George Pollitt posted bond of fifteen hundred dollars for Daniel Wilburn as administrator of the Berry estate and tutor of Berry's heirs; ibid., 1:144–46.

16. Bean to Alcalde Ibarvo, 11 Mar. and 1 Apr. 1833, NA Transcripts, 234:3, 49–50 (CAH, box 2Q307). The outcome is unknown, but Bean did own the slave Solomon. He bought him for a term of seven years from John Berry on 22 Dec. 1831. Bean promised to pay Berry one hundred pesos a year for seven years and at the end of the term Solomon was to be liberated, along with his wife. Samuel Asbury Papers, box 5, folder 71, item 91, Cushing Memorial Library, Texas A&M University, College Station, with thanks to Gregg Dimmick and Rebecca Hankins. There was an Apr. 1834 arbitration in which "attorney" Bean represented Mrs. Berry and Antonio Menchaca represented "two men of color, Solomon and Alfred"; see mention of it in a letter dated 12 Jan. 1835 by Morris May to the alcalde. Texas Veterans Papers, CAH, box 2H120.

17. *A List of Titles Issued by Different Commissioners and Alcaldes, at Nacogdoches, from 1791 to 1835,* 86–87; TGLO, box 115, folder 8.

18. TGLO, box 115, folder 9. The documentation on Bean's eight leagues is also in Deed Book C, 20–27, NCCO, under date of 14 Dec. 1834.

19. TGLO, box 115, folder 9; compare with documents in William Bean's file, box 114, folder 5. My thanks to Archivist Galen Greaser for his assistance with these records.

20. Tyler et al., *NHOT,* 4:929, 965, 967. The first-cited entry on the "Nacogdoches-Neches Saline Road," by Bernard Mayfield, gives some good information on the significance of the saline as tied to the Cherokees and their expulsion.

21. See ibid., 6:478; Lay, *Lives,* 153. For more information on Thorn and his various business activities, see the 1939 thesis by Lucy May cited in n9 above.

22. Bean's petition, 31 July 1833, and other documents under date of 13 Aug., 7 and 26 Sept., and 28 Oct. 1833, all in BA.

23. Bean to Alcalde Ibarvo, 5 Dec. 1833, NA Transcripts, 235:201 (CAH, box 2Q307).

24. Durst to Political Chief, 4 Nov. 1833, BA (CAH, box 2S304); Bean to Alcalde Mora, 24 Nov. 1833, NA Transcripts, 235:183 (CAH, box 2Q307).

25. On Goyens, see Tyler el al., *NHOT,* 3:269. Despite what this entry says about an 1832 marriage, Goyens is on the Nacogdoches censuses of the late 1820s and early 1830s as a single man living with "María Petra" (either called a widow or single), her son Henry, a slave named Sallie, and her four young children. It is not until 1835 that William (aged forty) is shown married to "Marie Pate Goyen" (aged thirty-nine). Besides Henry Goyen (aged sixteen), there are Robert Calare (aged five), a Negro boy James (aged ten), and Sallie, plus her four kids, for a total of ten in the blacksmith's household. If Mary Pate Sibley was "white" and William Goyens "black," it is amazing that they could have lived under the same roof at Nacogdoches for so long without arousing a lynch mob to action. One suspects that both he and she were of mixed blood and their "marriage" was recognized as common-law in the early going. Consult "Nacogdoches Archives," vols. 1 and 2 (reading room at CAH), and NA Transcripts, vol. 252 (CAH, box 2Q310) for these census records.

26. For these transactions see NA Transcripts, 235:61–64, as cited in n23 above. They are in English, probably written by Bean, but Goyens was not illiterate, as proved by his signed letters to Sam Houston in the Andrew Jackson Houston Collection at TSL. Briefly mentioned in Lay, *Lives,* 154.

27. Bean to Elozúa, 17 June 1833, BA, translated in Blake Transcripts (G), 9:319.

28. Bean to Nacogdoches Alcalde, 10 July 1833, NA Transcripts, 234:242–44 (CAH, box 2Q307). Noted as a copy of Elozúa's 8 June letter, forwarding one from the commandant general dated 3 May. On the persecution of Bustamante's ministers, see Green, *The Mexican Republic,* 230–33.

29. Bean to Elozúa, 16 July 1833, translated in Blake Transcripts (G), 9:324–25. Augustus Hotchkiss came to Texas in 1829. On the 1832 Nacogdoches census he gave himself as a merchant, aged thirty-two, with a wife and three children. In 1834 he moved to San Augustine, where he was selected as the primary judge because he was a man of family, honest, and sober. This village had 176 inhabitants by 1835, Hotchkiss being shown as "Judge"; census material as cited in n25 above. Some writers, on uncertain authority, have called him Archibald's brother. This does not appear to be the case.

30. Filisola gave a lengthy and very self-serving account of this centralist revolt in his *Memoirs,* 1:155–94. He claimed that he was on his deathbed as power was wrested from him. When faced with a crisis, Filisola became "ill" and incapacitated on more than one occasion during his military career.

31. As quoted from Winkler, "The Cherokee Indians in Texas," 157–58. For the original documents in this 1833 attempt by the Cherokees to secure title to their lands, see Greaser, *Catalogue of TGLO,* 2:112–13 (entry nos. 1095–1103).

32. Winkler, "The Cherokee Indians in Texas," 158.

33. Ibid., 158–59.

34. Ibid., 159–60.

35. Ibid., 162–63. Veramendi's ruling is dated 21 Aug. 1833. A copy was not obtained and forwarded to interim political chief Juan Seguín by Alcalde Ibarvo until 21 Feb. 1834; see entry nos. 1102 and 1103 in Greaser, *Catalogue of TGLO,* vol. 2. On the death of Veramendi (BA says early Sept.) and Bowie's activities at the time, see Davis, *Three Roads to the Alamo,* 354–63.

36. Greaser, *Catalogue of TGLO,* 2:113 (entry nos. 1097–1101). These letters date from late Oct. to early Nov. 1833.

37. Bean to Elozúa, 7 Oct. 1833, ibid., entry no. 1096 ("Bexar Land Papers," TGLO, box 127, folder 38). This is Bean's original. The other items cited above that bear on this question are in the same box—no doubt once part of the BA before being pulled out because they related to the republic's land affairs. For a different translation see Winkler,

"The Cherokee Indians in Texas," 161; he cites it as "Appendix to Empresario Contracts," 3:288–90 (TGLO).

38. TGLO, box 115, folder 27. Garza power of attorney to Bean, 8 Apr. 1832, in Blake Transcripts (R), 52:42–45. It was not put on record until 1838, a year after Bean had sold the tract for a great deal of money.

39. TGLO, box 115, folder 9. See map of Bean's Saline League in text. By Novermber 1835 the Consultation had ordered all land offices to close, making it unusual that Bean's title—or rather that of the purchaser Archibald Hotchkiss—was allowed to stand.

40. Barker, *Life of SFA,* 358–67. Despite his "Fidelity to Mexico" professions, Austin was talking about independence at the end of 1831. See his letter to Mary Austin Holley of 29 Dec. 1831 in Barker, *Austin Papers,* 3:727–30, brought to my attention by Thomas Ricks Lindley. One suspects that this letter was a simmering reaction to the hated law of 6 Apr. 1830, even though Austin was able to have his colony exempted from most of its provisions: "Do the people of my colony, or of Texas, or *do I* merit this? No; we have been to this Government *true as steel.* . . . I will exhaust all honorable means of obtaining redress of our grievances. *Should these fail the last resort will be taken.* One word from me *now* would annihilate every Mexican soldier in Texas." If the Mexican government, said Austin, would not "treat us as we merit . . . we shall go for *Independence,* and put out trust in our selves, our rifles, and—in God." Briefly mentioned in Barker, *Life of SFA,* 365.

Judging from this letter, General Terán was not entirely amiss when he wrote Minister of State Alamán on 21 Dec. 1831 about how Austin gave proof each day that he was a "solemn scoundrel, occupying himself in nothing more than conspiracies against Mexico." Quoted from Green, *The Mexican Republic,* 223, 282. The empresario's commentators have usually cast the Austin-Terán relationship as warm and mutually trusting, but Cantrell, *Stephen F. Austin,* 211–14, correctly notes that there was a "fundamental incompatibility" in their views about Texas.

41. Barker, *Life of SFA,* 362, 367–87. Cantrell, *Stephen F. Austin,* 267–82, brings a needed reevaluation to Austin's thinking at the time of his arrest. The fact that Erasmo Seguín begged off on going to Mexico with Austin in May 1833 might indicate that Seguín had received warning from Veramendi (or Músquiz) of Santa Anna's January letter even if Austin had not. Considering the close relationship between Austin and Seguín, one is reluctant to believe that Don Erasmo would have kept such a secret from the empresario during the deliberations at Béxar in which the appropriateness/legality of the April Convention's measures were hotly debated. Only Seguín voted in favor of separate statehood, though declining to accompany Austin on his trip. Austin, of course, knew that his mission had its risks. See his letters to Luke Lesassier, 6 May 1833 (reporting results of three-day discussions at Béxar) and Wyly Martin, 30 May 1833 (reporting talks with Filisola at Matamoros and learning that Santa Anna was "very much enraged at the colonists" because of the revolt at Anáhuac), Barker, *Austin Papers,* 2:961–63, 977–81.

Chapter 13

1. For a detailed account of this 1834 inspection (including Almonte's unknown "Secret Report" on measures necessary to safeguard Texas), see Jackson and Wheat, *Almonte's Texas.* In view of the "new" Santa Anna letter cited in chapter 12, n2, the statement I make therein (p. 385n86) might require adjustment—meaning that Butler's "O.P.Q." warnings to the Texans early in 1834 were not lies meant to stir them to insurrection without cause. Santa Anna, it would seem, did wish to direct a campaign against the ungrateful colonists

prior to Almonte's inspection, just as Butler claimed. Internal problems and logistics kept it from happening until 1836.

2. Bean petition to Aldrete, 16 Feb. 1834; Aldrete to Carvajal, 1 [Mar.?] 1834, appointing him surveyor; Carvajal survey notes for five of the eleven leagues, 4 Apr. 1834, IED (Coahuila), AGEC, FJPB, C19, E8, 15F. Vicente Aldrete's kinship to José Miguel Aldrete of Goliad—son-in-law of Martín de León, who was also appointed a land commissioner in 1834—is unknown.

3. For the Aranjo/Araujo six leagues on the Red River, see TGLO, box 110, folder 16.

4. Bean and Thorn land sale to A. C. and J. K. Allen, 22 May 1834, in Blake Transcripts (R), 3:70–72. It was stated that Aranjo had purchased these eleven leagues from the state of Coahuila y Texas on 17 Mar. 1831.

5. See the entry on John Kirby Allen (in which his brother Augustus is mentioned) in Tyler et al., *NHOT,* 1:111. Both appear on the 1835 Nacogdoches census, and they bought more land on the Red River from Bean that year. Deed books at NCCO show the magnitude of their speculations.

6. The *List of Titles,* 86–87, gives this location as "East side [of the Neches], 4 leagues above the San Antonio Road." Bean changed his mind, as indicated by the file in TGLO, box 115, folder 27 (Angelina County). Vicente Aldrete was also land commissioner for this title.

7. Almonte to Secretary of Foreign Relations Lombardo, 4 May 1834, Jackson and Wheat, *Almonte's Texas,* 102.

8. Almonte's "Confidential Instructions," Article 8, ibid., 40–41.

9. On Terán's repulsion at the physical contact and bear hugs that the Indians considered a polite and necessary prelude to formal talks, see Jackson and Wheat, *Texas by Terán,* 51–52, 76.

10. Bean to Músquiz, 16 June 1834, BA, as given in Jackson and Wheat, *Almonte's Texas,* 142.

11. Almonte to Lombardo, 16 June 1834, ibid., 139–41. For the ceremony in which these honors and presents were extended to the chief, see Crocket, *Two Centuries in East Texas,* 151; Clarke, *Chief Bowles,* 53.

12. Almonte to Lombardo, 16 June 1834, as given in Jackson and Wheat, *Almonte's Texas,* 139–41.

13. Almonte's Secret Report, document no. 13, ibid., 274–75.

14. Almonte to Lombardo, 16 June 1834, ibid., 139–41.

15. Almonte to Lombardo, 10 Dec. 1834, ibid., 285–86.

16. Bean to Lemus, 30 June 1834, Bean MSR, AHSDN, Cancelados, C46. XI/111/4-701, fols. 62–63.

17. Lemus marginal endorsement, 25 Sept. 1834, ibid.

18. Lemus to Secretary of War, 25 Sept. 1834, conveying Bean's letter of 4 July, ibid., fols. 59–59v. On these Indian gifts see Bean to Nacogdoches Alcalde, 13 July 1834, NA.

19. Extract dated 29 Dec. 1834 in Ministry of War and Marine; president's order that Bean be paid and the Ministry of Treasury be so notified, 26 Jan. 1835, Bean MSR, fols. 57, 58. See also fol. 61 where Bean's appeal for payment of his salary since July 1831 (saying that Bean had not even received a "half-real" of money during this time) was approved by the president, same date. Almonte's note of 3 Feb. 1835 is on fol. 63, and the order to the Treasury, on fol. 64—last item in Bean's file.

20. Bean land sale to "Enyer," 9 Oct. 1834, in Blake Transcripts (R), 4:111–13. This sale was probably to M. Cryer; he gave two promissory notes, each for $562.50, "for value received" to Thorn and Bean dated 10 Oct.; the first was due on 1 May 1836, the other a year later. Raguet Papers, CAH, box 2F380.

21. Bean land sale to Hotchkiss, 16 Oct. 1834, Blake Transcripts (R), 4:114–16. Lay, *Lives,* 154, 198n8 (citing Deed Book C, 101, same date), mistakenly says that this sale of the Saline League was *from* Hotchkiss *to* Bean. Lay is not always reliable with his land information. Trusting him misled me to state (in *Almonte's Texas,* 302) that Bean obtained an option to buy eight leagues from Zavala's agent on 7 Oct. 1834. But a check of Lay's source (Deed Book J, 260) at the Nacogdoches County Clerk's Office reveals that Bean was petitioning "A. Hotchkiss, agent of Lorenzo de Zavala" to locate five and three-quarters of his eight-league purchase from the state of Coahuila y Texas on Galveston Bay. Hotchkiss granted permission the next day. So this was not an "option" to buy anything; Bean owned the eight leagues and was merely seeking confirmation of his right to have part of it located on the coast in Zavala's grant. As discussed in chapter 12, Bean had already attended to the matter; Carvajal completed the survey in Sept. 1833. It is shown on the Trinity Land Company manuscript map cited in chapter 10, n2.

In his oath taken on 18 Sept. 1834, Archibald Hotchkiss said he was from New York, aged thirty-nine, and had arrived in the present year. He came and went, turning his business affairs over to agents in his absence. "A. Hotchkiss" swore in 1849 that he had seen Bean sign the 1834 petition and signed it himself (Deed Book J, 261); see chapter 18, n63 for Archibald's testimony on Bean's title given around 1843 or 1844. Both Archibald and Augustus signed with the initial "A." so all of this is hard to determine unless their given name is spelled out. Ericson, *Nacogdoches — Gateway to Texas,* 72, has Archibald Hotchkiss returning to Texas and residing in Nacogdoches County. During the Texas Revolution he was styled "Captain," and known for his land deals with Bowie. See also the entry on him in Tyler et al., *NHOT,* 3:708. He is frequently mentioned in Kate Mason Rowland, "General John Thomson Mason: An Early Friend of Texas," *QTSHA* 11 (Jan. 1908): 163–98, along with Nixon, Henrie, and other agents of the Galveston Bay & Texas Company. See especially the letter Archibald wrote on 13 Sept. 1834 describing his hostile reception in east Texas (p. 186). He says that only a "Mr. Hotchkiss" spoke up in his defense at San Augustine (no doubt Augustus) but does not mention their relationship.

22. Williams and Barker, *Writings of Sam Houston,* 1:296–98. According to the Vertical File, Sam Houston Papers, folders 1 and 2 at ETRC, Houston only got a quarter league, surveyed on 5 May 1835. Folders 3 and 4 contain his "married man" application for a league of land in Austin's colony, dated 24 Dec. 1832. Houston wanted to raise cotton on land near Carancahua Bay, or so he said. On 12 May 1835 Houston sold his mulatto slave "Louis" to Frost Thorn for $950; Raguet Papers, CAH, box 2F380.

23. For Candace's league see TGLO, box 44, folder 56, title granted 22 Apr. 1835. Her brother Isaac J. Midkiff's league (ibid., folder 51) was granted a day earlier and the tracts adjoined. The Spanish text of her grant (from TGLO) is given in Blake Transcripts (R), 59:97–99. Henrie's field notes for the survey, dated 21 Apr., are also in the Raguet Papers, CAH, box 2F380. Blake Transcripts (R), 52:49 (also in his "Notebook," 84), says that Candace sold her league to Nathaniel Robbins on 3 July 1836. The entry trails off, but Leon County Deed Book 48, 528, is cited. Robbins acquired the Trinity crossing of the Old San Antonio Road after Nick Trammell was run out of Texas in 1826; like Trammell he operated a ferry at the crossing, which soon took *his* name on Texas maps.

24. The 1835 Nacogdoches census, NA Transcripts, 251:45 (CAH, box 2Q310); also in "Nacogdoches Archives," vol. 2, CAH. This is a very detailed census of the entire jurisdiction, eastward to the Sabine. Also in the Angelina District are Joseph Durst (aged forty-five), wife Delilah Dill (aged thirty-five), and son James (aged fifteen, later to figure into our story with the Bean children). The Dursts have four slaves, and an eight-year-old orphan, "Nancy" Rutherford, lives with them; she—going by the name Carmelita—would marry Samuel M. Bean in 1843.

Interestingly, a George Midkiff was one of Gen. James Long's men taken prisoner at La Bahía on 9 Oct. 1821. He is listed with the rank of lieutenant, a native of Scotland (Debray Translations, TSL). Midkiff asked for a league of land in May 1829. He said he was English, had served in the Mexican navy since 1827, and had been a resident of Goliad three years. A letter in the BA (Ahumada to the La Bahía Commandant, 1 Dec. 1826) seems to confirm this service, sending instructions for George Midkiff who was captain of the boats examining Matagorda Bay. Governor Viesca granted him the land on 5 Feb. 1830 (Eberstadt Collection, CAH, box 3N180). He did not complete the title to his *sitio,* and his relationship to Bean's wife and brother-in-law (if any) is unknown.

Chapter 14

1. Bean to Ugartechea, 7 Apr. 1835, BA, translated in Blake Transcripts (G), 9:364.

2. Bean to Ugartechea, 7 Apr. 1835, BA, ibid., 365; Ugartechea to Bean, 4 June 1835, BA.

3. For this testimony taken in mid-Feb. 1835, see NA Transcripts, 243:189–208 (CAH, box 2Q309). *Coyote,* then as now, was a disparaging term. In this case it means that Hawkins was of mixed blood.

4. Petition dated 28 Feb. 1835, ibid., 258. This was the month that Thomas Jefferson Rusk arrived at Nacogdoches. For his entrance certificate of 11 Feb. (witnessed by Sam Houston and Nathaniel Robbins) see ibid., 208a; also in ibid., 252:204 (CAH, box 2Q310), under "Foreigners who became citizens, 1835–1836."

5. Bean testimony, 24 Apr. 1835, NA Transcripts, 245:89 (CAH, box 2Q309).

6. Thorn land sale to Ware and Perez, 11 Apr. 1835; for the transaction see Kathryn Hooper Davis and Linda Ericson Devereaux, eds., *This I Convey: Deed Book A, Nacogdoches County, Texas, 1837,* 319–23. Bean's power of attorney to Thorn, the basis of this sale, is in Blake Transcripts (R), 3:44–45.

7. Hotchkiss land sale to Thorn, 15 Apr. 1835, with verification of 8 July 1837, Davis and Devereaux, *This I Convey,* 275–77. Another copy of the deed, same date of 15 Apr., is in the Raguet Papers, CAH, box 2F380. May, "Life and Activities of Frost Thorn," 59–61, cites the later lease of the saline by Thorn and Hotchkiss and 1850 lawsuit against them by Gardner.

8. Political Chief Rueg to Nacogdoches Alcalde [Radford Berry], 14 Apr. 1835, NA Transcripts, 246:26 (CAH, box 2Q309).

9. Blake, "Notebook," 344, from Deed Book B, 211, NCCO. This tract is not to be confused with the Bean/Thorn sawmill property on the lower La Nana.

10. Bean land sale to A. C. and J. K. Allen, 6 May 1835 (said to be based on Aranjo's power of attorney to Bean of 27 Oct. 1831), Blake Transcripts (R), 4:135–37. See also Blake Transcripts (R), vol. 1, for this transaction, taken from Deed Book B, 97–99, AOCCN.

11. Bean land sale to H. H. Edwards, 30 May 1835, Blake Transcripts (R), 4:146–48, found in Deed Book B, 213–14, AOCCN. As noted, he was the empresario's son. Lay, *Lives,* 154, says this Haden was Thorn's father-in-law, not realizing that Haden H. Edwards was a different person and Thorn's brother-in-law, by virtue of Thorn having married Edwards's sister Susan. Haden H. took his oath on 9 Dec. 1829, saying he was a single man, aged sixteen, in Texas for four years. He lived with Frost Thorn's family at Nacogdoches, going into business with him as he came of age. The picture reproduced in Tyler et al., *NHOT,* 2:798, and seen in various other books, is probably Haden H. (born 1812). The empresario Haden (1771–1849) was much too old to be this vigorous looking by the time photography reached Texas. Haden H. Edwards married Sarah Forbes (the daugh-

ter of Houston's close friend John Forbes) in 1843, and the papers of both families were recently acquired by J. P. Bryan.

12. Bean town lot sale to Thorn and Edwards, 26 May 1835, Blake Transcripts (R), 4:141–43; Deed Book B, 211–12, NCCO. The Amador sale of 15 May is ibid., 1:111, but I am uncertain how she got the property on Irion Hill back from Bean. Her sale of it (for one hundred pesos) is in Book A, 111–13, AOCCN.

13. Jackson and Wheat, *Almonte's Texas,* 287–90. On the treaties being made with the plains Indians at Fort Gibson, see David La Vere, *Contrary Neighbors: Southern Plains and Removed Indians in Indian Territory,* 77; Brad Agnew, *Fort Gibson: Terminal on the Trail of Tears,* 132–36. More treaties followed in 1835.

14. Bean to Almonte, 12 Jan. 1835, Jackson and Wheat, *Almonte's Texas,* 310.

15. Ibid., 312–17.

16. Forsyth to Castillo Lanzas, 22 Oct. 1835, Carlos Bosch García, ed., *Documentos de la Relación de México con los Estados Unidos,* 2:456–57; also in U.S. Senate, *Executive Document 14,* 32d Cong., 2d sess., 1852–53, vol. 3, p. 10.

17. Almonte to Lombardo, 10 Dec. 1834, Jackson and Wheat, *Almonte's Texas,* 388–89. Even Nixon complained to Mason that Hotchkiss treated people as if they were his "servants" and called him "an overbearing man, and a rough kind of man." If Hotchkiss was kept on as the New York company's agent, Nixon asked to be removed as its commissioner. Rowland, "General John Thomson Mason," 187–88.

18. Rueg to Padilla, 12 Apr. 1835, Greaser, *Catalogue of TGLO,* 2:160 (entry no. 1576).

19. Almonte to Elguezábal, 23 Sept. 1834, and Almonte, "Plan of Attack against the Savage Indians of Texas," (n.d.), given as Secret Report Document, nos. 8 and 9, Jackson and Wheat, *Almonte's Texas,* 183–91.

20. Ugartechea to Bean, 26 Mar. 1835, BA.

21. Bean to Ugartechea, 18 May 1835, and Ugartechea's reply of 4 June, BA.

22. Given in Winkler, "The Cherokee Indians in Texas," 164; Dorman H. Winfrey and James M. Day, eds., *The Indian Papers of Texas and the Southwest, 1825–1916* (hereafter cited as *Indian Papers*), 1:6; Clarke, *Chief Bowles,* 56; and mentioned in Everett, *The Texas Cherokees,* 69. Interesting in light of this land law for the friendly tribes is a letter that Béxar deputy José María Carvajal, from Monclova, wrote his "Dear Cousin" Antonio Menchaca at Nacogdoches on 29 Apr. Carvajal said the government was rapidly going to ruin and Santa Anna was marching on Zacatecas to "*abolish the federal system!!*" He assured Menchaca that "Texas and Coahuila shall never be governed by any other form of Government" and told him that the Cherokees will get "land enough to make them live happy." Buquor Translations, Book B, 100, TSL. Coming events ruled out the possibility, even if the Cherokees had wished to take advantage of the law and obtain lands facing the hostile plains tribes.

23. Ruiz to Nacogdoches Alcalde, 20 Feb. 1835, Winfrey and Day, *Indian Papers,* 1:6; pp. 7–8 deal with the 11 and 29 July 1835 complaints against surveyor "Stroud." See also NA Transcripts, 247:214, 218–19 (CAH, box 2Q309). Jeremiah Strode became a citizen of Texas the same year, so he was new to the Cherokee land situation; see NA Transcripts, 252:208. Another 14 Apr. complaint of intrusion, involving Bean, is cited in n8 of this chapter.

24. Bean to Ugartechea, 21 Apr. 1835, Blake Transcripts (G), 9:366. It is cited as BA, but entry no. 138 in John H. Jenkins, ed., *The Papers of the Texas Revolution, 1835–1837,* 1:80, says it is NA. Other Blake and Jenkins citations display similar confusion, possibly because some of the Buquor/Debray Translations from BA were added to the existing NA collection early in the twentieth century. The bulk of them, however, were lost

in the 1880s and not recovered by the TSL until recently. They are currently filed in box 2004/046, separate from the NA translations.

25. Cos to Ugartechea, 8 June 1835, BA, translated in McLean, *Papers concerning Robertson's Colony,* 10:379; Secretary of War to Secretary of Foreign Relations, 16 June 1835, BNAH, 51-9-70-16.

26. Ugartechea to Bean, 4 June 1835, conveying Cos's instructions of 12 May, BA. It appears that Cos backed off on the idea of a campaign against the Comanches. He told Ugartechea on 8 May (BA) to reestablish the policy of giving gifts to them because their "quietude" depended on it.

27. Barker, *Life of SFA,* 400–9, offers a summary of these speculations, as he does in greater detail for east Texas with "Land Speculation as a Cause of the Texas Revolution," *QTSHA* 10 (July 1906): 83–95. See also Margaret Swett Henson, *Samuel May Williams: Early Texas Entrepreneur,* 62–76.

28. Bean to Ugartechea, 15 June 1835, BA, translated in McLean, *Papers concerning Robertson's Colony,* 10:409.

29. Bean to Ugartechea, 15 June 1835, BA, ibid., 10:410. La Vere, *Texas Indians,* 168–69, makes the outrageous statement that Bean was trying to organize this campaign so the Comanches "would in turn attack Texas settlements." This was not Mexico's policy and certainly not that of local government officials.

30. Secret Report, Jackson and Wheat, *Almonte's Texas,* 225–26.

31. Bowie to Miller, 22 June 1835, BA, Blake Transcripts (G), 9:379; the copy here was made at Béxar on 7 July. This letter was circulated by Miller to Anglo settlements throughout Texas—and to Mexican officials as well.

32. Bean to Ugartechea, 28 July 1835, NA, translated in Blake Transcripts (R), 14:213; also in Jenkins, *Papers of Texas Revolution,* 1:280 (entry no. 435). I will give both volume/page and entry numbers for Jenkins because various writers sometimes inconveniently cite only the latter designation.

33. Davis, *Three Roads to the Alamo,* 447–56.

34. Ibid., 455; on Bowie's doings in Mexico, 420–26.

35. Bean to Rueg, 30 July 1835, NA Transcripts, 82:68 (CAH, box 2Q310). It is tempting to identify Bean's "James Grante" as the deputy from Parras (Dr. James "Diego" Grant) who may have fled the land scandals at the capital of Coahuila y Texas, either with Bowie or on his own; Blake's entry in *NHOT,* 3:282, makes this mistaken link. Stuart Reid's work has established them as different men of the same name. The Apr. 1835 Nacogdoches census has James Grant as a single man, aged twenty-eight, and a merchant. Dr. Grant at this time was in Monclova, forty-two years old, and a married man with seven children (two more in Scotland). Rather than fleeing to Texas, he was arrested with Governor Viesca and detained at Monterrey until the entire party escaped to Goliad with the help of Col. José María González, a federalist, late in the year. Ben Milam made his getaway ahead of the others, also reaching Goliad.

On 15 Apr. 1835 Empresario Green DeWitt wrote a letter "To the People of Gonzales" from Monclova, speaking highly of Dr. James Grant and saying that "Dr. Grant will in all likelihood visit our colony in the fall of the year and will be able to give you satisfactory information [about receiving land titles in the colony] on all points in which you and myself are equally interested." OS box 8, folder 7, TSL, with thanks to Thomas Ricks Lindley. By this time DeWitt's colony had been awarded to the De León family of Victoria, due to DeWitt's failure to introduce enough families. See Ana Carolina Castillo Crimm, *De León: A Tejano Family History,* 113. DeWitt died at Monclova on 18 May, possibly of cholera or a fever, and was buried in an unmarked grave.

36. Entry no. 1615 in Greaser, *Catalogue of TGLO,* 2:164. Rueg's 31 July letter is quoted in the following Bean item as cited in n37 below.

37. Bean to Ugartechea, 11 Aug. 1835, NA Transcripts, 82:45–46; also in Blake Transcripts (R), 14:236–37. The Spanish is given in Jenkins, *Papers of Texas Revolution,* 1:434 (entry no. 610).

38. Davis, *Three Roads to the Alamo,* 426–27.

39. Bean to Ugartechea, 11 Aug. 1835, BA, translated in McLean, *Papers concerning Robertson's Colony,* 11:280–81. Reference was probably to Major Richard Mason, who by 1838 was a lieutenant colonel of the 1st Dragoons and commandant at Fort Leavenworth.

40. Agnew, *Fort Gibson,* 144–48; La Vere, *Contrary Neighbors,* 77–80. The 1834 and 1835 treaties are also discussed in Kavanagh, *The Comanches,* 237–42, and Smith, *The Wichita Indians,* 128–34.

41. Davis, *Three Roads to the Alamo,* 428.

42. Ibid., 428–29.

43. Bean to Ugartechea, 18 Aug. 1835, BA, translated in Blake Transcripts (R), 14:246–47; Jenkins, *Papers of Texas Revolution,* 1:352–53 (entry no. 527). See also the Bean letter in Spanish dated 22 Aug. (name of addressee hard to read) in Bean Papers, CAH, box 2B45. He complained that he had no soldiers nor any aid from the federal government in maintaining his position at Nacogdoches.

44. "Public Meeting at Nacogdoches," 15 Aug. 1835, Jenkins, *Papers of Texas Revolution,* 1:343–45 (entry no. 513).

45. Llerna B. Friend, *Sam Houston: The Great Designer,* 61–62.

46. Medina to Bean, 11 July 1835, Bean Papers, CAH, box 2B45 (a photostat of the original); also in Blake Transcripts (R), 52:50–51.

47. Order to summons Bean, 30 Aug. 1835, Blake Transcripts (R), 14:258.

48. Bean certification, 9 Sept. 1835, NA, ibid., 264. No less than fourteen such 1835 Bean testimonials are in the NA, three of them for Mexicans.

49. Alcalde Berry order of 31 Oct. 1835, NA Transcripts, 250:60 (CAH, box 2Q310); also in Blake Transcripts (R), 14:307.

50. Rusk as quoted in Paul D. Lack, *The Texas Revolutionary Experience: A Political and Social History, 1835–1836,* 199. This statement came in May 1837 when Cortinez was seeking reimbursement for a horse and four rifles, valued at $210, earlier given to the Texan forces. Miguel "Cortinas" is on the 1834 Nacogdoches census, listed as single, aged twenty-nine, and a "journeyman." Oddly, he is shown the following year as a laborer, aged thirty, and married to Jacinta Esparza with a daughter aged six ("Nacogdoches Archives," vol. 2, CAH). It does not seem that Cortinez/Cortinas was a prosperous citizen, but he did witness land transactions and sign other public documents in the 1830s. Everett, *The Texas Cherokees,* 84–85, says that Miguel's brother Eusebio, along with a small group of Cherokees, was killed by Comanches in July 1837 near Matamoros.

51. *Bean v. Thomas,* 13 Nov. 1835, NA Transcripts, 245:136–37 (CAH, box 2Q309); also in Blake Transcripts (R), 14:310. The location of the farm was not indicated.

52. Rueg to Berry, 6 Sept. 1835, Greaser, *Catalogue of TGLO,* 2:175 (entry no. 1752); Berry to Rueg, 8 Sept. 1835, passing the request to Bean, NA Transcripts, 82:246 (CAH, box 2Q310); Bean's reply, ibid., 255:209 (CAH, box 2Q311).

53. Rusk to Berry, 11 Sept. 1835, Jenkins, *Papers of Texas Revolution,* 1:438 (entry no. 612).

54. This cane will be discussed later. For Robert B. Blake's comments on the Bowie-Bean relationship, see Lowrey, "Peter Ellis Bean," 57. As noted, his letter to her of 13 Dec. 1944 is in Blake's papers at CAH, box 3G294.

55. Bean to Jackson, 11 Sept. 1835, Jenkins, *Papers of Texas Revolution,* 1:433–35 (entry no. 609, cited as from the *Niles Register* [Baltimore], 7 Nov. 1835); see appendix F for the full text. Also mentioned in Lay, *Lives,* 157–58, calling it a letter that Bean "obviously did not draft."

56. Forbes et al. to Jackson, 11 Sept. 1835, Jenkins, *Papers of Texas Revolution,* 1:436–38 (entry no. 611, cited as from the *Niles Register* [Baltimore], 7 Nov. 1835). Jack Gregory and Rennard Strickland, *Sam Houston with the Cherokees, 1829–1833,* 148–51, somehow construe this letter as part of Houston's plan to bring these Creeks to Texas to help fight the Mexicans so he could be the "Cherokee Emperor of Texas." They ignore the appeal for Jackson to enforce Article 33 of the treaty and keep the Creeks *out* of Texas, while at the same time saying that Thorn and Rusk on 15 Sept. ordered Houston to "arrest the progress" of Hawkins in his attempt to bring a large "body of Indians from the United States into Texas" (149n46). Their construction makes no sense, as the authors should have realized.

57. Ideas expressed on numerous occasions in 1834; see Jackson and Wheat, *Almonte's Texas,* 98, 102, 124–28, 143, 425.

58. Sawyer to Houston, 3 Oct. 1835, Jenkins, *Papers of Texas Revolution,* 2:27 (entry no. 737); see also Jackson and Wheat, *Almonte's Texas,* 426–27. Houston may have been priming Jackson for the idea of placing more troops on the Texas border to control the grave Indian "menace," an angle that was exploited fully when the revolution came about. It is not likely, however, that the motive for Bean's complaint envisioned trying to involve these U.S. troops in a Texan struggle with Mexico for independence.

59. As cited in n4 above. This was when Rusk wrote his wife about how Houston had made so much money in the legal profession at Nacogdoches, obviously hoping to do the same himself. Friend, *Sam Houston,* 61; Haley, *Sam Houston,* 104–6.

60. Rusk and Houston to Mush, Bowl, et al., 24 Sept. 1835, Jenkins, *Papers of Texas Revolution,* 1:486–87 (entry no. 664).

61. See the speech of Bowl and Mush to the Cherokees, 19 Sept. 1835, as reported by Goyens, ibid., 466–67 (entry no. 646).

62. Ugartechea to Cos, 8 Sept. 1835, Buquor Translations, Book B, 155–56, TSL. Bean's three letters were not copied in this cover letter.

63. Cos to Ugartechea, 3 Oct. 1835, BA, translated in Blake Transcripts (G), 9:414. According to Adán Benavides Jr., ed., *The Béxar Archives (1717–1836): A Name Guide,* 96–98, this is the last item concerning Bean in the BA. Entries for Bean in this guide are extensive, showing his significant role in the affairs of Texas during the Mexican period.

Chapter 15

1. Yoakum, *History of Texas,* 1:272; 2:130; Lay, *Lives,* 159–60.

2. John H. Reagan, "Queries and Answers," *QTSHA* 6 (Oct. 1902): 166–67; also given in Lowrey, "Peter Ellis Bean," 34–35.

3. On the 21 July 1835 formation of this committee (Rusk, Pollitt, Thorn, and Logan, chaired by Forbes), see Jenkins, *Papers of Texas Revolution,* 1:269 (entry no. 412). Its deliberations are scattered throughout subsequent volumes, with some changes of membership; see the Raguet Papers, CAH, for his participation—which extended well beyond the revolution.

4. Nixon to Austin, 10 Oct. 1835, Barker, *Austin Papers,* 3:171–72. Yoakum, *History of Texas,* 1:358; 2:130, states that Bean "was probably at heart in favor of the Texas cause" and that "there is little doubt but Bean's real feelings were in favor of the Texans." This seems

in line with Nixon's report, given at the time that hostilities commenced. Nixon had a half interest in Mason's three-hundred–league purchase at Monclova in 1834, which caused a dispute between them; Rowland, "General John Thomson Mason," 192–95.

5. Lack, *Texas Revolutionary Experience,* 168–69, 173, 199–200; list of people making war donations, 12 Oct. 1835, Raguet Papers, CAH, box 2F380.

6. TGLO, box 116, folder 13, title granted on 20 Oct. 1835. For the subsequent sale see Blake Transcripts (R), 8:180–82. Williams could not sign his name, showing how loosely the term "attorney" was used; in land affairs like this, it really meant "consignee."

7. Royall to Austin, 18 Oct. 1835, Jenkins, *Papers of Texas Revolution,* 2:155–56 (entry no. 905).

8. Ibid., 2:160–61 (entry no. 906).

9. Baker and Johnson to Chairman of the General Council, 23 Oct. 1835, ibid., 2:199–201 (entry no. 952).

10. Lack, *Texas Revolutionary Experience,* 43; Winkler, "The Cherokee Indians in Texas," 164; William Ransom Hogan, *The Texas Republic: A Social and Economic History,* 83.

11. Everett, *The Texas Cherokees,* 70. For the "Solemn Declaration" of 13 Nov. 1835, see Clarke, *Chief Bowles,* 60–61; also in Jenkins, *Papers of Texas Revolution,* 9:284. Houston actively pressed for it, and he signed the document after Branch T. Archer and John A. Wharton.

12. Forbes to Council, 8 Nov. 1835, Jenkins, *Papers of Texas Revolution,* 2:357 (entry no. 1126).

13. Garrett to Houston, 9 Nov. 1835, ibid., 2:366 (entry no. 1137).

14. Smith to Council, 16 Nov. 1835, ibid., 2:438–42 (entry no. 1213, quotation on p. 440).

15. P. Menard to Council, 26 Nov. 1835, ibid., 2:513–15 (entry no. 1302).

16. Ibid., 514 (re meddlers).

17. Houston to Bowl, 22 Nov. 1835, Williams and Barker, *Writings of Sam Houston,* 3:7; see also Clarke, *Chief Bowles,* 62; Everett, *The Texas Cherokees,* 71.

18. Lack, *Texas Revolutionary Experience,* 64–67. John Forbes wrote Lt. Gov. James W. Robinson on 19 Dec. 1835 that Political Chief Rueg and Alcalde Berry had refused to recognize the authority of either the "Convention" or the Council. Forbes was going to demand the archives of "Judge Roag" the next day. He thought that alcalde-elect David Hoffman was a supporter but found that he, no sooner than in office, refused to take an oath to the provisional government or recognize its authority: "Hoffman has grieved me." Gulick et al., *Lamar Papers,* vol. 1 (entry nos. 273 and 294).

19. Appointment of Houston, Forbes, and Cameron, 22 Dec. 1835 (by Robinson) and 28 Dec. 1835 (by Smith); Instructions from Smith, 30 Dec. 1835, all in Winfrey and Day, *Indian Papers,* 1:10–13. On 17 Jan. 1836 Robinson commissioned Byrd Lockhart to treat with the Comanches "now at San Antonio." His fellow commissioners were Edward Burleson, J. C. Neill, John W. Smith, and Francisco Ruiz. Thus Tejano Ruiz—also an officer in the Mexican army (retired)—made the transition as an Indian representative of the insurgent government of Texas, even if Bean did not.

20. Houston to Bowl, 5 Feb. 1836, Williams and Barker, *Writings of Sam Houston,* 1:355–56.

21. Rueg to Rusk, 9 Nov. 1835, Jenkins, *Papers of Texas Revolution,* 2:371–72 (entry no. 1143). Rueg says, "as far as the Mexicans of this place, we have not been able to induce them to start, notwithstanding I had a meeting of them called, in which I red them an adress inviting them to join in the common cause, the most wealthy of them have however furnished horses and money for the equipmt. of the N. Orleans company, and in or-

der to have some benefit of them I have ordered a permanent guard of 25 men of them, for the protection of the families and properties of those who are absent, and keep up the order at home." This arrangement was sorely tested in 1836.

22. The 23 Feb. 1836 treaty is given in Williams and Barker, *Writings of Sam Houston,* 1:358–60; Winfrey and Day, *Indian Papers,* 1:14–17.

23. The 23 Feb. 1836 treaty is given in Williams and Barker, *Writings of Sam Houston,* 1:358–60, and also in Winfrey and Day, *Indian Papers,* 1:14–17. Article 2 is also in Clarke, *Chief Bowles,* 63. For a discussion of why the Cherokees were willing to sign the agreement, see Everett, *The Texas Cherokees,* 71–73; see p. 142n96 for her analysis of the last two tribes named.

24. Houston and Forbes to Smith, 29 Feb. 1836, Williams and Barker, *Writings of Sam Houston,* 1:356–58. If Houston and Forbes visited Fort Jesup in the early part of February, seeking some kind of U.S. military assistance in the coming struggle, proof has not yet been found. Their movements for several weeks after leaving San Felipe are a mystery.

25. Santa Anna to Filisola, 31 Jan. 1836, in Richard G. Santos, ed., *Santa Anna's Campaign against Texas, 1835–1836,* 43. Santos says that the letter seems to confirm the allegation that Bean was in correspondence with the enemy. Lack, *Texas Revolutionary Experience,* 175, follows this reasoning, calling it a "fact." More on this question later.

26. Historians have disagreed about the importance of Houston's Indian treaty. Some have regarded it as taking a holiday when he should have been organizing and training an army. Others consider it as a crucial event, a step that guaranteed that the disorganized Texan rebels would not have to fight a war on two fronts. Houston, of course, argued for the latter interpretation.

27. See Section 10 under "General Provisions" of the Texas Constitution in Holley, *Texas,* 405–6, for the type of land claims declared "null and void." Also, Lack, *Texas Revolutionary Experience,* 91–93; Andreas V. Reichstein, *Rise of the Lone Star: The Making of Texas,* 139–41, 188–91, 255n52.

28. Friend, *Sam Houston,* 66; Marshall De Bruhl, *Sword of San Jacinto: A Life of Sam Houston,* 180; John Hoyt Williams, *Sam Houston: The Life and Times of the Liberator of Texas, an Authentic American Hero,* 134, where he states that Houston was "mortified" at the results of the Nacogdoches election.

29. Everett, *The Texas Cherokees,* 76–77.

30. Santa Anna to Tornel, 16 Feb. 1836, given in Jackson and Wheat, *Almonte's Texas,* 353–59, a letter likely written by Almonte for Santa Anna's signature. The journal kept by Almonte during the campaign does not mention Bean, but James Gordon Bennett, editor of the *New York Herald*—when preparing the journal for publication in the summer of 1836—discreetly deleted the names of all people to whom Almonte wrote letters.

31. Houston to Bowl, 13 Apr. 1836, Williams and Barker, *Writings of Sam Houston,* 1:409; also in Jenkins, *Papers of Texas Revolution,* 5:452–53 (entry no. 2738). See Everett, *The Texas Cherokees,* 77–78.

Chapter 16

1. Big Mush to Committee, 13 Apr. 1836, mentioned in Everett, *The Texas Cherokees,* 78.

2. Judge John A. Quitman from Natchez, as cited in n35 below.

3. J. Gaines to Burnet, 5 May 1836, William C. Binkley, ed., *Official Correspondence of the Texas Revolution, 1835–1836,* 2:656; also in Jenkins, *Papers of Texas Revolution,* 6:173–74 (entry no. 2979); Lay, *Lives,* 159. James Gaines appears on the 1835 census of the San Augustine jurisdiction as aged fifty-three with his wife "Susannah" (Norris, aged thirty-

six) and their four children, ages ranging from seventeen years to five months. "Nacogdoches Archives," vol. 2, CAH.

4. Burnet to M. Menard, 19 Mar. 1836, Winfrey and Day, *Indian Papers,* 1:17–18.

5. On Michel Menard see Tyler et al., *NHOT,* 4:613.

6. Long hinted at by historians, this spin is given with agenda-driven delight by Jeff Long, *Duel of Eagles: The Mexican and U.S. Fight for the Alamo,* 213–16, 296–301, 321–23, 329–30. The "Question of Conspiracy" is also explored in a more objective, convincing manner by Bill Walraven and Marjorie K. Walraven, *The Magnificent Barbarians: Little-Told Tales of the Texas Revolution,* 122–32.

7. Mason to Major Nelson, 20 Mar. 1836, Jenkins, *Papers of Texas Revolution,* 5:149 (entry no. 2380). News of the constitution's nullification of his three-hundred-league purchase (mentioning him by name) had probably not reached Mason yet. On this see Feris A. Bass Jr. and B. R. Brunson, eds., *Fragile Empires: The Texas Correspondence of Samuel Swartwout and James Morgan,* xxi–xxiv, 1–16, 38–39, 41. Mason had sold his three-hundred-league acquisition to Swartwout and associates, but of course was still interested in sustaining its legality under the Republic of Texas—as were the men who had bought this bundle of eleven-league grants from him. Mason paid Houston a fee of two thousand dollars in mid-1836 to get these grants recognized by Congress without waiting for the Land Office to open (xxiv). On the complexity of his land dealings through the years, see Rowland, "General John Thomson Mason," which quotes many documents at length. According to Barker, Mason's papers were burned in 1922; *Life of SFA,* 280.

8. San Augustine Committee Report, 21 Mar. 1836, Jenkins, *Papers of Texas Revolution,* 5:153–54 (entry no. 2388). As noted, Augustus usually signed with an "A." (as he did here), which makes it difficult to distinguish between his writings and those of Archibald Hotchkiss. On them see the entries in Ericson, *Nacogdoches—Gateway to Texas,* 72. She tells me that Archibald had a brother born in 1800 named Charles, not Augustus, and suspects that they were cousins. The eldest son of Augustus was named Charles, shown on the 1835 San Augustine census as nine years old. Harry P. Noble Jr. researched and wrote an excellent series of articles on Augustus Hotchkiss, published in the *San Augustine Tribune,* 12 Sept.–17 Oct. 2002.

9. General E. Gaines to Secretary of War Cass, and E. Gaines to Governors, both of 8 Apr. 1836, Jenkins, *Papers of Texas Revolution,* 5:373–76 (entry nos. 2638 and 2639).

10. Ibid.

11. Chesher and Sims depositions to Nacogdoches Committee, 11 Apr. 1836, ibid., 5:429–30 (entry no. 2703).

12. M. Menard deposition to Nacogdoches Committee, 11 Apr. 1836, ibid., 5:430.

13. Hoffman et al. to Mason, 11 Apr. 1836; Mason to Nacogdoches Committee, same date, accepting the assignment, ibid. 5:432–33, 439 (entry nos. 2706 and 2716).

14. Nacogdoches Committee Resolutions, 11 Apr. 1836; R. A. Irion to Lt. James Carter, 11 Apr. 1836, ibid., 5:438, 437 (entry nos. 2715 and 2713).

15. Houston to Thomas, 11 Apr. 1836, ibid., 5:436 (entry no. 2712).

16. Houston to Hoffman, 13 Apr., ibid., 5:436 (entry no. 2740), giving only the heading, not the letter itself.

17. Yoakum, *History of Texas,* 2:130.

18. Lay, *Lives,* 160.

19. Lowrey, "Peter Ellis Bean," 33, 48. Her citation is Blake, *Nacogdoches,* 18, a little chamber of commerce–type booklet that was first published in 1936 to celebrate the Texas Centennial, but I could not find the quotation therein.

20. Weems, *Men without Countries,* 237, 240. This oath, which Bean took on 3 Apr. 1839, is in Blake Transcripts (R), 52:63.

21. Yoakum, *History of Texas,* 1:358–59; 2:130.

22. Lack, *Texas Revolutionary Experience,* 175, 298n51.

23. Houston to Hoffman, 13 Apr. 1836, Andrew Jackson Houston Collection, TSL, no. 367. Like many other items in this collection, it is a copy—not Houston's original. Perhaps this accounts for Editor Jenkins's statement that the original was "not located," but he should have noted his source as AJHC. Jenkins, I am informed, was instrumental in getting this large collection placed at the Archives Division of the TSL in Austin.

24. Lack, *Texas Revolutionary Experience,* 174; also letter cited in n15 above.

25. Houston to H. Raguet, 7 Apr. 1836, Williams and Barker, *Writings of Sam Houston,* 1:400.

26. Jonathan C. Poole file, RV 839, TGLO, with thanks to Thomas Ricks Lindley—who says he has also found evidence that Houston had express riders going back and forth between his camps and Fort Jesup prior to San Jacinto. I have not located or examined any documents to this effect.

27. Lay, *Lives,* 160. By letter of 6 July 2004 Neal Murphy of the San Augustine County Research Center informs me: "There is absolutely no record found of him [Bean] being arrested as an 'enemy of the Republic' in our files."

28. Unsigned description of affairs at Nacogdoches in mid-Apr. 1836, dated "City of Houston, August 1837" in Raguet Papers, CAH, box 2F381. Robert A. Irion likely wrote this account of the Mexican/Indian hysteria in east Texas during the Runaway Scrape, in which Bean is not mentioned. See Irion to Carter, 11 Apr. 1836 (ordering him to act as a spy in "the neighborhood of our enemy") and Irion to Mason, 12 Apr. 1836, Jenkins, *Papers of Texas Revolution,* 5:437 (entry no. 2713), 448 (entry no. 2729); Córdova to Irion, 14 Apr. 1836 (explaining he had disarmed an American because it was thought he intended to set fire to the town once the troops evacuated) and Raguet to Houston, 17 Apr. 1836 (saying his committee had believed a few days ago that the "enemy in large force was within a few miles of this place" and local Mexicans were ready to join them; this rumor was now proved false), Andrew Jackson Houston Collection, TSL, nos. 378 and 387; see also nos. 345, 379, 381, 383, and 388. Raguet wrote a long letter to his wife in Philadelphia on 17 Apr., describing the panic over the loyalty of local Mexicans; Raguet Papers, CAH, box 2F437. Lack, *Texas Revolutionary Experience,* 170–72, gives the context of Tejano-Anglo suspicions at the time involving Vicente Córdova's militiamen.

29. Cortinez deposition, 12 Apr. 1836, to General Gaines through Nathaniel Amory Jr. as interpreter at Natchitoches, Jenkins, *Papers of Texas Revolution,* 5:446 (entry no. 2726). "Cortinas" gave a similar statement on 10 July 1836 before Alcalde Adolphus Sterne at Nacogdoches, no doubt for Sam Houston's benefit; see next chapter. Blake Papers, CAH, box 3G296.

30. Quitman to Officers at Nacogdoches, 12 Apr. 1836, Jenkins, *Papers of Texas Revolution,* 5:450 (entry no. 2734).

31. Houston to Bowl, 13 Apr. 1836, ibid., 5:452–53 (entry no. 2738).

32. Mason to General E. Gaines, 13 Apr. 1836, ibid., 5:459–60 (entry no. 2747). See also his letter to Gaines of the day before from Thompson's Tavern, ibid., 5:449–50 (entry no. 2732).

33. Carson to Burnet, 14 Apr. 1836, ibid., 5:468–69 (entry no. 2755).

34. Carson to Houston, 14 Apr. 1836, ibid., 5:470 (entry no. 2756).

35. Quitman to F. Huston, 15 Apr. 1836, ibid., 5:484–85 (entry no. 2775).

36. Ibid. Quitman did much to keep the peace with local Tejanos after his arrival at Nacogdoches—as opposed to Alcalde Hoffman, who told them on 9 Apr. to either join the Texas army or pack up and leave the country.

37. Mason to ——, 16 Apr. 1836, ibid., 5:489 (entry no. 2782).

38. Lt. Bonnell to Gen. Gaines, 20 Apr. 1836, ibid., 5:506–8 (entry no. 2804).

39. For an analysis of the U.S. deserters who fought for the Texas side, see Bill Walraven and Marjorie K. Walraven, *The "Sabine Chute": U.S. Involvement in the Texas Revolution,* copy provided to me by the authors at the 2002 San Jacinto Symposium in Houston. Another version of this study appears in *SHQ* 107 (Apr. 2004): 573–601.

40. E. Gaines to Cass, 20 Apr. 1836, Jenkins, *Papers of Texas Revolution,* 5:510–12 (entry no. 2807).

41. Cass to E. Gaines, 25 Apr. 1836, ibid., 6:53–54 (entry no. 2862). Adjutant General Jones told Gaines on 11 Apr. that the president wanted him to arrest any Mexican agent found stirring up the Indians along the Red River; see ibid., entry no. 2714.

42. E. Gaines to Houston, 25 Apr. 1836, from "camp, east of the Sabine waters," ibid., 6:64–66 (entry no. 2868).

Chapter 17

1. E. Gaines to Cass, 2 May 1836, from "Camp Sabine," Jenkins, *Papers of Texas Revolution,* 6:150–51 (entry no. 2952).

2. J. Gaines to Burnet, 5 May 1836, from "Gaines Ferry," ibid., 6:173–74 (entry no. 2979). Is the reference to Martin Parmer and Samuel Benton, residents of San Augustine? Parmer had signed the Declaration of Independence as a delegate from the district on 2 Mar.

3. H. H. Edwards to Rusk, 11 May 1836, ibid., 6:222 (entry no. 3025). Captain "Braddy" was likely John M. Bradley; see the short sketch of him in Blake Transcripts (R), 52:338–39. He was at the top of a list of citizens of Tenehaw who petitioned that they be granted their own ayuntamiento (undated), "Nacogdoches Archives," vol. 2, CAH.

4. Robertson to Rusk, 27 May 1836, Jenkins, *Papers of Texas Revolution,* 6:392–93 (entry no. 3177).

5. Gerald S. Pierce, *Texas under Arms: The Camps, Posts, Forts, & Military Towns of the Republic of Texas, 1836–1846,* 107–8.

6. J. D. Cannon to Family, 14 Aug. 1836, Duncan Cannon file, Court of Claims Collection, TGLO, with thanks to Thomas Ricks Lindley.

7. Ibid. Meaning, one supposes, that General Gaines would not "carry" (tolerate) their desertions. Evidence that he *did* tolerate desertions prior to San Jacinto is presented in the study cited in chapter 16, n39.

8. Peter Ellis Bean file, Republic Claims, TSL.

9. See NA Transcripts, 252:108, 216, 221 (CAH, box 2Q311).

10. Bean land sale to H. H. Edwards and James Carter, 28 June 1836, Blake Transcripts (R), 7:381–83; also in Blake, "Notebook," 296. It is recorded in Deed Book B, 210, NCCO.

11. Bean land sale to Houston, 24 Aug. 1836, Williams and Barker, *Writings of Sam Houston,* 4:38. The metes and bounds of this league are given in a scribbled handwritten copy of the full contract in Peter Ellis Bean, Genealogy File, CAH. Neighboring surveys of Encarnación Chirino to the north, Vicente Córdova to the east, Ignacio Ibarvo to the south, and vacant land to the west are mentioned—the same surveys mentioned when Bean bought Vital Flores's "Carrizo ranch" seven years earlier for four hundred pesos, for which see Deed Book C, 292, NCCO. Clearly, this was Bean's "Plantation" sold to Houston for five thousand dollars. Bean also witnessed a large land sale that Houston and Philip A. Sublett made to W. B. P. Gaines in mid-September. It involved part of a "nine or eleven" league tract east of the Attoyac granted to one Guerrero under Spanish title.

Deed Book D, 203–5, San Augustine County Research Center, with thanks to Neal Murphy. This further suggests that Houston and Bean had a friendly working relationship on land matters in the summer of 1836. "Traitors" are not usually regarded as suitable witnesses to important business transactions.

12. Houston to the Citizens of Nacogdoches, 29 Aug. 1836, Williams and Barker, *Writings of Sam Houston,* 1:445–46. Another version, misdated 1835, is on pp. 298–99. Friend, *Sam Houston,* 75–76, places the proclamation in its proper Aug. 1836 context.

13. Houston to E. Gaines, 29 Aug. 1836, Andrew Jackson Houston Collection, TSL, no. 520.

14. Houston to Lacy, 17 Sept. 1836, Williams and Barker, *Writings of Sam Houston,* 1:447–48, with a short biographical sketch of Martin Lacy containing some errors. Better information on Lacy is found in Starling, *Land Is the Cry!,* 60, 89–90. According to an Ancestry.com post sent to me by Carolyn Reeves Ericson, Martin Lacy (ca. 1789–1842) was a native of South Carolina who married Dorothy Young in Caldwell County, Kentucky, on 22 Apr. 1813. A lawsuit that eldest son William Young Lacy filed in Houston County after his father's death names all six siblings. See 4 Nov. 1843 *Red-Lander* (San Augustine); also the 5 Jan. issue where Martin's widow and administratrix, Dorothy, was offering to rent the "well known and valuable farm, generally known as Fort Lacey." Hattie Joplin (Mrs. V. R.) Roach, *History of Cherokee County (Texas),* 26, gives the location of Lacy's Fort as "on a commanding elevation on the Old San Antonio road two miles west of the present Alto." Thus it was not at the saline but on Lacy's grant (title conferred 3 Jan. 1835) adjoining Bean's original league on the northeast; see also Pierce, *Texas under Arms,* 86–88. Bean's Smith County claim was upheld by the Republic of Texas, meaning that his sale to Hotchkiss was as well. Hotchkiss had also located seven leagues above Bean's Saline League as "attorney" for a Mexican grantee named Tomás Quevedo, title confirmed and dated 23 Sept. 1835.

15. As cited in n13 above.

16. Everett, *The Texas Cherokees,* 80–81.

17. Ibid.

18. Ibid., 82–83. Everett presents a cogent discussion of Houston's Indian activities in the summer of 1836. The "Bascos" that Houston mentioned to General Gaines is revealed as Juan Basquez (or Vásquez). On these events see also Stephen L. Moore, *Savage Frontier, Volume I, 1835–1837: Rangers, Riflemen, and Indian Wars in Texas,* 164–65.

19. Friend, *Sam Houston,* 87–89; Everett, *The Texas Cherokees,* 85; Haley, *Sam Houston,* 186–93. For the speech that Houston made in Dec. 1836, urging that the Senate ratify his treaty, see Clarke, *Chief Bowles,* 69–70. For some of Houston's 1833 land acquisitions from Mexican grantees at Nacogdoches, see Book A, 90–100, and Book B, 67–78, AOCCN, found in Blake Transcripts (R), vol. 1. I was not able to locate the original record books that Blake used.

20. Quoted from Richard Rollin Stenberg, "American Imperialism in the Southwest, 1800–1837," 347–48. See also Everett, *The Texas Cherokees,* 84, 144n31, where a similar report that Butler gave to Gen. Felix Huston at the end of 1838 is cited.

21. Houston to Goyens, 3 July 1837, Gulick et al., *Lamar Papers,* 1:559.

22. Lowrey, "Peter Ellis Bean," 28, says that—judging by the letter—Houston "may have depended on [Bean] to keep the Indians calm." Lay, *Lives,* 163, also gives the letter, saying that it indicates that Bean had "apparently retained his influence with the Indians." Neither writer seems to have made the connection that Houston's debt to Bean on the plantation league of land was about to come due, although Lowrey knew about Houston's "Beware" notice that evolved out of the dispute; see n25 below.

23. Houston "Reply" to Bean, 15 Nov. 1837, Williams and Barker, *Writings of Sam Houston,* 2:150; also in 4:37.

24. Houston to H. Raguet, 16 Nov. 1837, ibid., 2:150–51. It is uncertain if "Egeri" referred to a house that Houston was planning to build in town or to remodeling work on Bean's house that stood on the Carrizo league.

25. Houston "Beware" of Bean Notice, 10 Nov. 1837, published in *Texas Chronicle* at Nacogdoches on 28 Feb. 1838. It is given in Lowrey, "Peter Ellis Bean," 45–46, citing Blake, "Notebook," 183.

26. Bean "Notice" to Public, 2 and 19 May 1838, *Telegraph and Texas Register.* It is a full copy of the Houston-Bean contract of 24 Aug. 1836, including metes and bounds of the tract, as witnessed by Allen, Irion, and Amory and certified as a true copy at Nacogdoches on 7 Apr. 1838. Williams and Barker, *Writings of Sam Houston,* 4:38. Dr. Irion married Houston's former matrimonial prospect, Miss Anna Raguet, two years later.

27. Haley, *Sam Houston,* 201. His payment was $5,907.27; the quote is Haley's, and he suggests that Houston pulled some strings to receive the money. Indicating that Houston did not hold a grudge is the letter he wrote Henry Raguet on 1 July [1838], "If you see Colonel Bean be pleased to say to him that I will be happy to see him, when I go to the east!!" Raguet Papers, CAH, box 2F437. There is always the possibility that Houston was being sarcastic.

28. Clarke, *Chief Bowles,* 71; Everett, *The Texas Cherokees,* 84–85; Bean to Houston, 6 May 1837, Andrew Jackson Houston Collection, TSL, no. 1047. While this is a very detailed report on Chief Bowl's mission to the prairie tribes written from "Bean's farm," there is no reference to Houston's land purchase and the note soon to come due. Bean ends with "I hope you will Drop me aline if you can take time and let me [k]now how things is in the west Mr. Reed is ateaching school for a few of Us hear that have empoyd him." Signed "P. E. Bean" with a more simplified rubric than earlier used.

29. Bowl to Houston, 14 Jan. 1837 (getting ready to go make peace with "our prairie Brothers"); Houston to Goyens, 23 Jan. 1837 (Bowl's commission as a "General of all friendly tribes"); Houston to Rusk, 27 June 1837 (guide got lost; tell chiefs we will meet near Nacogdoches on 2 July), Andrew Jackson Houston Collection, TSL, nos. 777, 800, and 1214. Clarke, *Chief Bowles,* 70–71; Everett, *The Texas Cherokees,* 85–86.

30. William A. Force to Dear Brother & Sister, 10 July 1837, William Force Papers, CAH, box 2D153, brought to my attention by Thomas Ricks Lindley. It is partially quoted without attribution in Williams, *Sam Houston,* 177.

31. Rusk to Wife Mary, 15 Feb. 1835, Jenkins, *Papers of Texas Revolution,* 1:21 (entry no. 44). See also Friend, *Sam Houston,* 67, for William Fairfax Gray's similar description of Houston at the Mar. 1836 Convention. On the Apr. 1835 Nacogdoches census Rusk gives his age as twenty-eight and his wife Mary as twenty-three; they have three children and five slaves.

32. Bean town lot sale to Peck, 10 Aug. 1836, Blake Transcripts (R), 52:52–53; it is recorded in Deed Book D, 72, NCCO.

33. Williams and Whitely sale of Bean's league to Bondies, 24 Dec. 1836, Blake Transcripts (R), 8:180–82. Bean was also involved in some court cases during 1836. On 29 June George Pollitt ordered Dept. Sheriff John A. Veatch to bring Bean in to answer W. R. Wilson's charge of a debt owed. Bean gave testimony in the *Joseph Durst v. José Falcón* case, 3 Oct. 1836, which had to do with one cow and its "increase" over the past three years. See NA Transcripts, 253:231, 255:4–6, both in CAH, box 2Q311. The Skinner case of Feb. 1836 has already been cited.

34. Thomas Goss land sale to Joseph S. Abels, 29 Dec. 1836, given in Davis and Dev-

ereaux, *This I Convey,* 315–16. On Goss's league see Greaser, *Catalogue of TGLO,* 1:74, noted as on the west side of the Neches in present Anderson County. He—along with Martin Lacy and son Young Lacy—is on a "List of Officers and Privates, Company of Militia at Saline West of Nacogdoches," 24 Apr. 1835, "Nacogdoches Archives," vol. 2, CAH.

35. Bean land sale of four leagues to Thorn and "Pinkney," 20 Mar. 1837, Deed Book C, 363. In the Raguet Papers, CAH, box 2F381, there are two deeds of the same date in which Bean—as attorney for Aranjo and Garza—sold Thorn and John T. Pinckney both tracts, each for ten thousand dollars. Bean's son Isaac sold the Garza four leagues in 1856 through his attorney William Young Lacy, so it must not have worked out, even though Bean stated in the deeds that he had received money "in hand," presumably twenty thousand dollars. Bean land sale to George Payne, Richard Parmalee, and Rudolph Roeder, 12 July 1837, Deed Book B, 90, NCCO. This instrument is given in Blake, "Notebook," 286; also in Lowrey, "Peter Ellis Bean," as appendix 3. The buyers sold the tract to John Thorn in October, at which time Mata Medina was called a *padre.* Blake Papers, CAH, box 3G296, from Deed Book B, 195.

36. Lowrey, "Peter Ellis Bean," 47–48.

37. Menchaca bond to "Wiess" on town lot, 9 Aug. 1837, Blake, "Notebook," 281. Menchaca was a major figure in the Córdova Rebellion a year later. He is not to be confused with the Tejano patriot who was a native of Béxar.

38. For the documentation on this Bean suit against Piedras, which began on 12 Sept. 1836 (claiming $595 for "lumber"), see Blake Transcripts (R), 52:1–24. It includes the subsequent sales by Bean mentioned in text.

39. Ibid.

40. *Sterne and Taylor v. Piedras,* 18 June 1836, NA Transcripts, 253:197–200 (CAH, box 2Q311). Other actions against Piedras have not been traced, but there were probably more; he amassed considerable property during his rule as military commandant at Nacogdoches and owed debts when driven out.

41. *Bean v. Medina,* 15 May 1837, Blake Transcripts (R), 52:54–60. Lay, *Lives,* 200, cites both the Medina and Piedras suits as 15 May; see also his p. 163.

42. John Durst land sale to I[ra] R. Lewis, 20 July 1837, given in Davis and Devereaux, *This I Convey,* 312–13, cited in Deed Book A, 363–65. These one thousand acres were the subject of much later litigation with Bean's heirs.

43. Lay, *Lives,* opposite p. 130. Different photos of the Bean house are given in the articles by Lucille Fain, "The Ingenious Colonel," 9 Feb. 1947, *Houston Chronicle;* Robert M. Hayes, "Old Peter Ellis Bean House Still Stands at Nacogdoches," 10 Sept. 1954, *Dallas Morning News,* Peter Ellis Bean, Biographical File, CAH. Its passing was lamented by Johnnie May Sparks Wyres in "Peter Ellis Bean," 13 Sept. 1957, *The Daily Sentinel* (Nacogdoches). Through the courtesy of Francis E. Abernethy, I have received the text on the historical marker at the site where the house once stood: "Home of Peter Ellis Bean, 1783–1846. A Member of Nolan's Expedition in 1800. Captured and Imprisoned in Mexico. Soldier in the Mexican Struggle for Independence. Commandant at Fort Teran, 1831; at Nacogdoches, 1832–1835. Erected in 1829 in the Vicinity of a Sawmill Owned by Bean."

44. Blake Transcripts (R), 52:142, a sketch titled "Candace Midkiff Bean," its authorship uncertain but presumed to be Robert B. Blake. See also Blake's letter to Flora Lowrey, 13 Dec. 1944, Blake Papers, CAH, box 3G294, where he says, "There is nothing in the records to show that Bean and Candace ever lived together after her brief marriage with Martin Parmer, notwithstanding the memoirs of Mrs. Sophia Peavy, which I hope you are not relying upon for any information concerning this interesting couple." More on "Peavy" later.

45. Blake Papers, CAH, box 3G294, as cited in n44 above.

46. Lay, *Lives,* 162. Recorded as entry 22 in Nacogdoches County Marriage Book, A, 11, NCCO. The license is dated 3 Nov. 1837 and the couple were wed four days later. Hix sold his claim for one-third league of land as a single man to Candace's brother Isaac Midkiff on 15 May 1838, seven months after the marriage. Blake Transcripts (R), 59:95.

47. See quotation cited in n44 above.

48. As given in Lowrey, "Peter Ellis Bean," 58, quoted from Zuber's "Manuscript of Martin Parmer." This item is presently in the George L. Crocket Collection, ETRC (A-12, box 23, folder 81), and only one of many documents that Crocket gathered for possible use in his 1932 book, *Two Centuries in East Texas.* Zuber's 1902 manuscript letter to a grandson of Parmer's, mentioning Colonel Bean and his wife Candace Midkiff, is in this file and also listed as a separate item at the ETRC (A-103). Yet another copy of "The Bean Affair" is at CAH. Zuber (1820–1913) told some great tales, but his memory and/or embellishments were not always in line with the facts.

49. Peter E. Bean's Petition to Congress for a Divorce, no. 29, Memorials and Petitions, TSL. I became aware of this petition from an undated, uncredited newspaper clipping titled "Romance and Tragedy in the Life of Peter Ellis Bean," Bean Genealogy File, CAH. On p. 8 of this typescript the writer correctly mentions that Bean petitioned Congress for divorce, but mistakenly says that his wife had married Hicks while Bean was in Mexico "on business," thereby deserting him and giving him just cause to seek divorce upon his return. It appears that Bean was living on the Durst one-thousand-acre Angelina tract at the time Isaac and Candace married, instead of absent on a trip to Mexico.

50. Attachments to Bean's Divorce Petition, Memorials and Petitions, TSL.

51. See next chapter for the fate of Bean's divorce petition.

52. "Report of Standing [Senate] Committee on Indian Affairs," 12 Oct. 1837, Winfrey and Day, *Indian Papers,* 1:22–28. Burton chaired the Committee.

53. Ibid., 26 (quote), 27 (resolution). It was said that "the Treaty was based on premeses that did not exist and that the operation of it would not only be detrimental to the interests of the Republick but would also be a violation of the vested rights of many Citizens." Isaac Watts Burton married Martin Lacy's sixteen-year-old "Blue Eyed" daughter Martha shortly after following the Lacy family to Texas from Louisiana in 1832. He left a detailed account of the 1832 uprising against Colonel Piedras (not mentioning Bean but calling Lacy his "future father-in-law"); Blake Transcripts (R), 53:48–65, and Gulick et al, *Lamar Papers,* 3:287–95. A veteran of San Jacinto and captain of the "Horse Marines," he was elected to represent Nacogdoches as a senator in three congresses of the republic. It was mainly due to his and Lamar's influence that Houston's Cherokee treaty was rejected by the Senate. Burton was a surveyor, lawyer, and pro-Lamar newspaperman (*Texas Chronicle* at Nacogdoches) who spoke often against Indian land rights, regardless of the tribe. Starling, *Land Is the Cry!,* 60–61, 69, 75, 83, with thanks to John Crain for sharing his Burton research.

54. Ernest W. Winkler, ed., *Secret Journals of the Senate of the Republic of Texas, 1836–1845,* 101; Everett, *The Texas Cherokees,* 86–88. Oddly, in later speeches on the Cherokee Land Bill, Sam Houston denied that his treaty had ever been rejected and argued that it was still in force, implying (one supposes) that the Senate had no power to void authorized agreements made before the Republic of Texas was established.

55. See especially the discussion in Clarke, *Chief Bowles,* 71–73; also De Bruhl, *Sword of San Jacinto,* 237, and Haley, *Sam Houston,* 201.

Chapter 18

1. I am among them; see my illustrated book, *Indian Lover: Sam Houston & the Cherokees,* in which Houston's motives for being a "Magnificent Barbarian" are not questioned. This was because I was relying on secondary sources—what other people had written about Houston's Indian relations—without full knowledge of his or Bean's activities as revealed by primary sources. Even so, compared to other white men of the era, Sam Houston and Robert S. Neighbors must rank near the top as champions of Indian rights in nineteenth-century Texas.

2. Houston to Senate, 21 May 1838, Williams and Barker, *Writings of Sam Houston,* 4:6; also in Everett, *The Texas Cherokees,* 88.

3. Everett, *The Texas Cherokees,* 88–89. See her remarks on this so-called marriage to Bowl's daughter, 145–46n52. An indication that the Cherokee dissatisfaction was genuine is the report that Agent Jeff Wright (also a painter of some note) gave Houston on 17 June. Big Mush told him that the Cherokee leadership was being made to look like fools for trusting the treaty promises of the whites and that war would certainly result unless they received their land. Andrew Jackson Houston Collection, TSL, no. 1683.

4. Everett, *The Texas Cherokees,* 89.

5. Ibid., 93, 147n75 (citing NA and described as "Bean letter captured with Miracle documents [1838?]"). The Nacogdoches Archives at TSL do not extend into the Republic of Texas period. In e-mail communications of 8 July and 27 Sept. 2003, Everett recalls that she saw this item with other Córdova documents in an "oversize box" at TSL but could not give me specifics or provide a copy. From the citation sent to me on 27 Sept., it appears that her reference was not to NA but to the translations of captured documents in the Andrew Jackson Houston Collection, no. 4602.19. All these items pertain to the 1839 Flores incident, however, not to the episode with Miracle in 1838; there is no Bean letter among them, nor could I find it elsewhere at TSL.

6. Paul D. Lack, "The Córdova Revolt," in *Tejano Journey, 1770–1850,* ed. Gerald E. Poyo, 92–94.

7. Houston said that he did not get it until the end of August, after the rebellion had commenced—thus shifting the blame for a military solution (as opposed to what he could have done toward a peaceful mediation) to Rusk. Ibid., 96–97.

8. Ibid., 98–99; also discussed in Everett, *The Texas Cherokees,* 90–91. For Córdova to Flores, 19 July 1838, see Winfrey and Day, *Indian Papers,* 1:8. The documents captured from Miracle (including his diary) are translated in U.S. Senate, *Executive Document 14,* 11–17. See Joseph Milton Nance, *After San Jacinto: The Texas-Mexican Frontier, 1836–1841,* 113–20, for a well-documented account of Miracle's mission and his Tejano collaborators. The treatment in Smith, *The Wichita Indians,* 140–45, relegates Miracle to a mere diarist for the expedition instead of its principal spokesman. From the diary it is not even certain whether Córdova rode north with Miracle or met him in Texas.

9. Miracle diary, U.S. Senate, *Executive Document 14,* 15–16. According to Lack, "The Córdova Revolt," 154n31, this diary is "no longer extant." A translation of it, along with other papers taken from Miracle's body, is at the Bancroft Library, filed as BANC MSS [P-O, 110], from the collection of A. L. Pinart. He did not give his source, but it is a handwritten, word-for-word copy of what was published in the U.S. Senate document. As noted, there is no letter to, from, or about Bean among these papers.

10. Anson Jones to Secretary of State John Forsyth, 31 Dec. 1838, U.S. Senate, *Executive Document 14,* 11–12. This letter explains how Miracle was killed and his diary recovered. The event is further described in an article titled "Threatened Indian Hostilities on the South Western Frontier" in the 27 Oct. 1838 *Telegraph and Texas Register,* which was

taken from the Little Rock *Gazette.* After receiving Miracle's diary from the commandant at Fort Towson, General Arbuckle at Fort Gibson sent a copy to the Arkansas governor. Arbuckle sent another copy to the Houston paper, which at some point received a letter dated 21 Aug. from Dr. James G. Wright with his translation in the diary. For the name of the "prisoner" or interpreter/guide (Alexander Pineda) who killed Miracle, I am obliged to Stephen L. Moore, who gave me chapters from his forthcoming vol. 2 of *Savage Frontier.*

11. See Lack, "The Córdova Revolt," 97; for variant copies and a list of the signatories, ibid., 154n28. An outstanding study that traces white Texan fear of an Indian/Mexican combination from the time of the revolution onward is James Ernest Crisp, "Anglo-Texan Attitudes toward the Mexican, 1821–1845," 116–30, 361–63.

12. Clarke, *Chief Bowles,* 73–75; Everett, *The Texas Cherokees,* 91–95. Houston wrote Bowl on 11 Aug. that Mr. Vansickle, despite the trouble, would run the boundary lines. Lamar Papers, TSL, box 1909/1-10, no. 782. Vansickle was captured early in October.

13. Houston to Rusk, 12 Aug. 1838, Williams and Barker, *Writings of Sam Houston,* 2:275–76. Most of the other Houston letters discussed below are also in this volume. He arrived at Nacogdoches on 22 July.

14. Rusk to Houston, 14 Aug. 1838, Andrew Jackson Houston Collection, TSL, no. 1766. See mention in Everett, *The Texas Cherokees,* 93 (along with her erroneous statement that Bean was "in league" with Córdova), and Clarke, *Chief Bowles,* 81 (which says that the meeting between the chief and Rusk's representatives was to take place at Bean's house). An article titled "The Late Mexican Insurrection" (*Telegraphy and Texas Register,* 29 Sept. 1838) states that when Rusk's force reached "Bean's prairie," Big Mush and ten unarmed Cherokees "came into camp and professed friendship."

15. Houston to Big Mush, 10 Aug. 1838; Houston to Bowl, 11 Aug. 1838; Houston to May, 12 Aug. 1838; Houston to Bowl, 12 Aug. 1838; and Houston to Rusk, 13 Aug. 1838, Williams and Barker, *Writings of Sam Houston,* 2:270–75.

16. Houston to Bowl, 14 Aug. 1838, ibid., 277; see also his letter of the following day, ibid. One is reminded of Austin's stream of letters in trying to stop the Fredonian Rebellion without taking the field.

17. Clarke, *Chief Bowles,* 81–85, gives a very detailed account and says that hard feelings resulted between Rusk and Houston because of how the president's orders from Nacogdoches had "cramped" Rusk's operations facing the enemy. The Córdova Rebellion documents in Lamar Papers, TSL, box 1909/1-10, offer more evidence to support this view.

18. "Trials of Mexicans for Treason," 27 Mar. 1839, *Telegraph and Texas Register* (from the San Augustine *Red-Lander,* with thanks to Dianna Everett). The trial results are summarized in Lack, "The Córdova Revolt," 106–8. See also Blake Transcripts (R), 53:271–339. Bean and Durst were called as witnesses on 10 Oct. 1838; their testimony is not recorded in Blake's court proceedings (p. 299) but was given by the newspaper account.

19. Houston to Sims, 15 Aug. 1838 (re the Shawnees); Houston to Rusk, 26 Aug. 1838 (urging Rusk to run the treaty line, as it would unite all the immigrant tribes with the government); Houston "Talk" to the Alabama-Coushattas, 12 Nov. 1838 (sent via Rusk), Williams and Barker, *Writings of Sam Houston,* 2:278–79, 293–94.

20. For treaties made with other tribes in 1838, see Winfrey and Day, *Indian Papers,* 1:30–32 (Lipan Apache, by James Power); 42–45 (Comanche, by Col. Henry Wax Karnes); 46–48 (Tonkawa, by Barnard Bee and George Hockley); 50–52 (Comanche, by Robert Irion and Ashbel Smith); 53–54 (Keechi, Tawakoni, Waco, and Taovaya, by trader Holland Coffee).

21. Albert Woldert, "The Last of the Cherokees in Texas, and the Life and Death of Chief Bowles," *Chronicles of Oklahoma* 1 (June 1923): 201–6; Clarke, *Chief Bowles,* 85–87.

22. See U.S. Senate, *Executive Document 14;* Irion to Jones, 29 Nov. 1838, quoted in Cecile Elkins Carter, *Caddo Indians: Where We Come From,* 290–92. Irion's reference may have been to president-elect Lamar instead of lame-duck Houston.

23. Houston to Rusk, 10 Oct. 1838, Williams and Barker, *Writings of Sam Houston,* 2:288–89, quoted in Clarke, *Chief Bowles,* 73–74.

24. Clarke, *Chief Bowles,* 74–76; Everett, *The Texas Cherokees,* 97–98.

25. Haley, *Sam Houston,* 205.

26. Houston to Texas Congress, 19 Nov. 1838, Williams and Barker, *Writings of Sam Houston,* 2:299–305.

27. De Bruhl, *Sword of San Jacinto,* 255.

28. Lay, *Lives,* 164; Emma Barrett Reeves, ed., *Minutes of the District Court of Nacogdoches County, Book A,* 63.

29. Lay, *Lives,* 164, cited as Bowl to Rusk via Thorn, 28 May 1839, Rusk Papers, TSL. He was John Stephen Thorn, Frost Thorn's son.

30. Probably the most detailed treatment of the 1839 Flores incident, and Córdova's involvement, is Nance, *After San Jacinto,* 123–40.

31. Ibid., 136 (giving William Wallace—not to be confused with William A. A. "Bigfoot" Wallace—credit for killing Flores), 140. Edward Burleson's report of the battle to Albert S. Johnston, 22 May 1839, said that Flores and two others were killed, with the remainder of the twenty or thirty Mexicans and Indians put to flight. Andrew Jackson Houston Collection, TSL, no. 4602.19. The death of Flores is refuted in the *Colorado Gazette* (Matagorda), 28 Mar. 1840, copy at TSL, and by reports of Flores's activities on the northern frontier among the Indians being given by ranger captain Jack Hays as late as Jan. 1844. Everett, *The Texas Cherokees,* 149n11, also questions his death in 1839.

32. As cited in n8 above.

33. See the Woldert, Clarke, and Everett studies aforecited. Also, John H. Reagan, "The Expulsion of the Cherokees from East Texas," *QTSHA* 1 (July 1897): 38–46. Primary documents for the 1839 Cherokee War are in Winfrey and Day, *Indian Papers,* vol. 1.

34. Reagan, "Expulsion of the Cherokees," 39–40.

35. The battle is given in Woldert, "Last of the Cherokees," 214–23 (with maps showing locations); Clarke, *Chief Bowles,* 106–11; Everett, *The Texas Cherokees,* 108–9. Bean's son Isaac and future son-in-law William Young Lacy fought as Texan soldiers in the 1838–39 Indian campaigns.

36. Clarke, *Chief Bowles,* 94–106, chronicles the negotiations before the battle; the wording of the treaty is included. See Lamar's instructions to the commissioners, dated 27 June 1839, in Winfrey and Day, *Indian Papers,* 1:67–70.

37. Lamar to Bowl, 26 May 1839, Winfrey and Day, *Indian Papers,* 1:61–66; also in Gulick et al., *Lamar Papers,* 2:590–94.

38. Martin Lacy Appointment as Indian Agent by Secretary of War Albert S. Johnston, 14 Feb. 1839, Winfrey and Day, *Indian Papers,* 1:55–56. See also Williams and Barker, *Writings of Sam Houston,* 1:448n.

39. Woldert, "Last of the Cherokees," 197, 210, pinpoints Lacy's residence and shows that he still lived on his grant adjoining Bean's original league. Lacy's paperwork for this league (a copy of his 21 Sept. 1834 petition and steps leading to his 1835 title) somehow wound up in the Blake Papers, CAH, box 3G295. Several copies of the survey field notes for Lacy's *sitio* no. 9, dated 23 Dec. 1834, are also in Raguet Papers, CAH, box 2F380. In 1936 a marker was placed on SH 21 near (actually just east of) the site of Lacy's Fort. The note in Williams and Barker, *Writings of Sam Houston,* 1:447–48, has him living "between Nacogdoches and San Augustine," which seems mistaken for these years—as does their Lacy/Lacey family information; see n40 below.

40. Marriage Book A, 34, NCCO. The license (entry 69) was issued on 29 Dec. 1840 and the couple got married on 11 Jan. 1841. See Lay, *Lives*, 167, where William Young Lacy is incorrectly identified as "son of the county clerk at Nacogdoches." The clerk was Daniel Lacey, of unknown relationship (if any) to Martin Lacy and his son William Young Lacy, Bean's son-in-law. On these two families see Ericson, *Nacogdoches—Gateway to Texas*, 82. "Captain" William Y. Lacy wrote a detailed sketch of his life, which was published in William S. Speer and John Henry Brown, eds., *The Encyclopedia of the New West*, 442–43. Born in 1814, he was a surveyor and said that he had spent eight months (starting in Mar. 1834) "examining lands on the Trinity up to the Cross-timbers" (now Tarrant County) under James Bowie, whom he admired as a man of action. See also his historical account in the Mary Kate Hunter Notebooks at the Palestine Public Library, with thanks to Stephen L. Moore.

41. As cited in n33 above; Reagan, "Queries and Answers," given in Lay, *Lives*, 166–67.

42. Reagan, "Queries and Answers," given in Lay, *Lives*, 166–67.

43. [J. H. Brown], "Col. Ellis P. Bean, or Fifty Years Ago in Texas," *DeBow's Review*, 48, copy at CAH. I did not see Brown's name on the article, but it is attributed to him by the University of Texas catalog listing for this item.

44. Brown, *History of Texas*, 1:45.

45. Yoakum, *History of Texas*, 1:236. Actually, Yoakum may not have had to go to Tennessee to "track down" Shaw. He moved to Texas and, in 1849, purchased part of the Lacy league, including the fort site on the Old San Antonio Road; Roach, *History of Cherokee County*, 26. Mary Scott (aged seventy-eight) testified in 1909 that P. E. Bean's half brother "Bill" Shaw told her that her mother, Sarah Selman, was a second cousin to the colonel, she being a Bean before her marriage to Benjamin Selman; Blake Transcripts (R), 52: 267. This Bean-Selman connection is well documented; see chapter 7 in Crabb, *Over the Mountain*. Thus it is likely that Yoakum obtained Captain Shaw's "Memoirs" and some Bean material from him right next door to the original Bean home place in Cherokee County, Texas, and not in White County, Tennessee.

46. "Note," in *History of Texas*, ed. Yoakum, 1:403.

47. Lowrey, "Peter Ellis Bean," 37.

48. See the "unexpurgated" original, with extensive annotation by William H. Goetzmann, in Samuel Chamberlain, *My Confession: Recollections of a Rogue* (Austin: Texas State Historical Association, 1996), as opposed to the tame edition assembled by Roger Butterfield for Harper & Brothers in 1956. For an example of Bean's legendary sexual appeal, see Tom Bean, "Ellis P. Bean: The Señoritas Wouldn't Leave Him Alone," *True West* 30, no. 3 (Feb. 1983), copy in Bean Biographical File, CAH.

49. Isaac T. Bean to Henderson Yoakum, 27 July 1856, Yoakum Papers, TSL, box 2-23/971, a copy in Bean Papers, CAH, box 2B45. Yoakum died suddenly and unexpectedly in November of that year at age forty-six; see the entry in Tyler et al., *NHOT*, 6:1121–22. I have been unable to confirm the story that many of his papers burned after being placed in a Masonic collection.

50. The gory details are given in Clarke, *Chief Bowles*, 108–11; Woldert, "Last of the Cherokees," 223–26. See also Dorman H. Winfrey, "Chief Bowles of the Texas Cherokee," *Chronicles of Oklahoma* 32 (Spring 1954): 38–41. On the death of Watkins, a memoir by his son Jesse J. Watkins was published in the 27 Jan. 1955 issue of *The Daily Sentinel* (Nacogdoches). Watkins was commissioned on 14 Sept. 1837 to make peace with the Keechi, Caddo, Ioni, and Tawakoni tribes, assisted by interpreter Luis Sánchez. After the death of Watkins, trader Holland Coffee made a treaty with these prairie tribes on 2 Sept. 1838. Winfrey and Day, *Indian Papers*, 1:21–22, 53–54. Despite what Sánchez said, it is doubtful that Bowl or his Cherokees were responsible for murdering Watkins. The prairie tribes

are more likely suspects. James H. Starr confirms it, stating that the "venerable" Jesse Watkins was killed by the Indians "to whom he had read the president's 'talk' of peace and friendship." Speer and Brown, *The Encyclopedia of the New West,* 603–5.

51. Most historians have emphasized two aspects of this business/pleasure jaunt: Houston meeting his future wife Margaret Lea in Alabama and the visit with his mentor Andrew Jackson at the Hermitage in Tennessee. See Marquis James, *The Raven: A Biography of Sam Houston,* 307–9; Friend, *Sam Houston,* 93–95; Williams, *Sam Houston,* 194–97; De Bruhl, *Sword of San Jacinto,* 258–68; Haley, *Sam Houston,* 209–15. Only the last two biographers comment on Houston's absence from Texas in relation to the Cherokee War.

52. "On the Removal of the Capital from Austin," 2 and 3 Dec. 1839, Williams and Barker, *Writings of Sam Houston,* 2:315–21.

53. "In Behalf of the Cherokee Land Bill," 22 Dec. 1839, ibid., 2:323–48. See Haley, *Sam Houston,* 216; De Bruhl, *Sword of San Jacinto,* 270. Houston called him "A. Hotchkiss," but his remarks about the Creeks clearly indicate that his reference was to Archibald, not Augustus. Archibald gave Lamar an account, dated 5 Dec. 1838, of the Cherokee settlement in Texas and his connection with Burnet's colony as an agent, which he said began in 1833; the Creeks are not mentioned. Lamar Papers, TSL, box 1909/1-11, no. 905.

54. "Speech [given to the House of Representatives] concerning the Cherokee Bill," 4 Dec. 1840, Williams and Barker, *Writings of Sam Houston,* 2:354–62. In this speech Houston read portions from Edward's *History,* but not so lengthy as he had in his Dec. 1839 speech on the Cherokees cited in n53 above. To dramatize the significance of the 1832 Convention's promise to award land to the Cherokees, a document found in Edward, Houston put on a pair of silk gloves (instead of "mittens") before handling the book.

55. On the harsh political campaign see Friend, *Sam Houston,* 100–101; De Bruhl, *Sword of San Jacinto,* 280–83; Haley, *Sam Houston,* 224–27.

56. Haley, *Sam Houston,* 159 (calling Henderson Yoakum "Houston's own chronicler"), 310 (calling his chosen biographer, C. Edwards Lester, Houston's "Boswell"). See chapter 21, n18.

57. Nacogdoches County Tax Rolls, 1839, 1840, 1841, microfilm at Genealogy Section, TSL. Because some entries were hard to read, the original lists at ETRC (ref no. 126, box 1) have been consulted. The clerk spelled Bean's name Peter E. "Bran," suggesting that he was a newcomer to the region. As described in chapter 4 of Hogan, *The Texas Republic,* these were lean years with virtually no money available and people hard-pressed to pay their taxes.

58. Bean agreement with Flores and Chirino's widow, 6 Apr. 1838, Deed Book D, 358, NCCO. Chirino was a casualty in the 1832 battle with Colonel Piedras.

59. Two land sales to Muckleroy, both dated 5 Dec. 1838, Deed Book, F, 21 and 362; Bean land sale to Long, 1 Apr. 1840, Deed Book G, 27; Long land resale to Bean and Lacy, 18 Nov. 1842, and Bean and Lacy land sale to Graham, 15 Dec. 1842, both in Deed Book G, 235 and 312; Bean land sale to Berry, 15 Nov. 1840, Deed Book G, 140; Bean bond to Arnold and Wood, 30 Mar. 1841, Deed Book E, 548—all from NCCO. According to an uncredited sketch called "Site of Home of Peter Ellis Bean" in Blake Transcripts (R), vol. 52, John F. Graham refurbished Bean's former house near the Carrizo in 1848.

60. Kaufman County, folder 1-221, TGLO. The patent for Bean's league and labor is in the basement, vol. 2, no. 253; see the typescript in Bean Papers, CAH, box 2B45.

61. As cited in chapter 17, n8. Kaufman's proxy was no doubt Kindred H. Muse, formerly a Land Office employee then representing Nacogdoches in the Texas Congress. Muse also presented Bean's divorce petition.

62. Harriet Smither, ed., *Journals of the Fourth Congress of the Republic of Texas, 1839–1840: Volume II, The House Journal,* 122. Robert B. Blake considered Candace's two mar-

riages (to Parmer and Hix) while Bean was alive as bigamous and noted that "no charges were filed against her" for either offense. Blake to Lowrey, 13 Dec. 1944, Blake Papers, CAH, box 3G294.

63. Archie P. McDonald, ed., *Hurrah for Texas! The Diary of Adolphus Sterne, 1838–1851,* 44, 54, 60, 181, 195. See the testimony of Archibald Hotchkiss, John S. Roberts, and Adolphus Sterne concerning Bean's five-and-three-quarter-league grant on Galveston Bay in Raguet Papers, CAH, box 2F437. It is undated and mistakenly filed in the 1836 folder, but was given around 1843 or 1844 and clearly intended as a defense of Bean's title. Hotchkiss said he, as Zavala's agent, had given his consent for Colonel Bean to locate there; he had known Bean since 1826, in Mexico. Sterne claimed to have known Bean since Feb. 1827, calling him "one of the oldest citizens of the country," meaning the Nacogdoches region. There are documents in Raguet Papers (CAH, box 2F437) indicating that Thorn and Pinckney had acquired the tract from Bean by 1839, if not earlier, and were trying to sell it in New Orleans.

64. For a discussion of post–Mexican War claims and how the scam worked to benefit absentee speculators, see Reichstein, *Rise of the Lone Star,* 97-112. Chapter 2 in Elgin Williams, *The Animating Pursuits of Speculation: Land Traffic in the Annexation of Texas,* gives the pre-Revolution background of these dubious claims.

65. Bean's heirs later sold lands besides these—as well as lands that Colonel Bean had once sold himself! See next chapter.

66. Henson, *Lorenzo de Zavala,* 34, 46–49, 51. She gives the middle initial as "R." but it is probably the same individual. See Rusk Papers, TSL, box 2-23/970, for documents about Col. Tomás H. Luckett being with the Texan army of Kemper and Ross at Béxar in May 1813 on General Adair's behalf.

67. Bean, Durst, and Lewis bond for Matilda D. Luckett's security as administrator of estate of her husband Thomas H. Luckett, deceased, 22 July 1842, Blake Transcripts (R), 52:64. Mrs. Luckett had a ferry on the Angelina on what was called the "middle" San Antonio Road. It intersected the upper, or main, road near Lacy's Fort. Roach, *History of Cherokee County,* 36. Thus the Lucketts and Beans (or Colonel Bean at least) were neighbors. See the 3 Apr. 1837 document concerning Ira Lewis's purchase of John Durst's nine leagues on the Angelina in Blake Papers, CAH, box 3G295. Lewis, a resident of Matagorda, owed Durst $13,575 for the land; one of the drafts he gave to secure the purchase was from Thomas H. Luckett of Virginia. Perhaps this is how the widow came to own a ferry on the Angelina.

68. Blake Transcripts (R), 52:65; Lay, *Lives,* 168–69.

Chapter 19

1. George Wilkins Kendall, *Narrative of the Texan Santa Fe Expedition,* 2:391–93; see Lay, *Lives,* 170–71.

2. It ran in the *Picayune* from the beginning of June until the end of Aug. 1842 in fifty-eight articles—making it at least possible that Bean could have read Kendall's remarks about his Mexican wife while still in Texas.

3. "Last Will and Testiment" of P. E. Bean, 6 Feb. 1843, Nacogdoches County Deed Book G, 296, item no. 352; location of the original unknown, if there was one. On this document see Roach, *History of Cherokee County,* 22–23 (calling Samuel Bean his eldest son); Lowrey, "Peter Ellis Bean," 55–56 (saying likewise); Blake Transcripts (R), 52:94–95; Lay, *Lives,* 172–73.

4. There is a typescript copy in Bean Papers, CAH, box 2B45. Land Commissioner

William Walsh certified it on 17 Dec. 1878, and it was filed on 7 Nov. 1879 by A. J. Houston. Sam's son Andrew Jackson Houston? Possibly; he was admitted to the bar at Tyler in 1876 and served as a U.S. District Court clerk from 1879 to 1889.

5. Bean land sale to Helena Nelson, 16 July 1842, Blake Transcripts (R), 52:99. She sued him in 1844 for the same amount; see n10 below. On 1 Apr. 1843, shortly after making his will, Bean sold James Haynes two hundred acres of land for four hundred dollars. The tract was noted as five miles east of Nacogdoches beginning at Long's bridge where the middle road crossed the Carrizo. Deed Book G, 376, NCCO. From this sale, and others made later, it is obvious that Bean did not list or bequeath all of his landholdings in his will.

6. See the 1909 testimony in Blake Transcripts (R), 52:153–70. Other Bean descendants through the colonel's son Isaac denied it vigorously, saying they had never heard of Samuel Bean prior to this litigation. Despite all the conflicting testimony, it seems clear that *if* he was fathered by Peter E. Bean, it must have been by another woman besides Candace Midkiff. All the people who would have known for certain were dead by 1909.

7. The proceedings of this *Vansickle and Debard v. Bean* suit are in ibid., 52:66–77. Bean's lawyers were Rusk and Jennings; see mention in Lay, *Lives,* 169. The Debard grant still shows on Smith County survey maps at the TGLO, about where Bean's litigation said it was; Debard's title was conferred in 1835, like those of Bean and Hotchkiss in the Neches Saline area (see map of Saline League in chapter 12). The Raguet Papers, CAH, box 2F380, has survey notes to Debard's *sitio* no. 12.

8. Blake Transcripts (R), 52:77; partially quoted in Lay, *Lives,* 174–75.

9. *Blair v. Bean,* Feb. 1844 proceedings, Blake Transcripts (R), 52:81–84, 86–88. Notice of this suit appeared in 23 Mar. 1844 *Red-Lander.*

10. Seizure of Bean's property by Sheriff David Rusk, 5 Feb. 1844, Blake Transcripts (R), 52:85. By 20 Apr. Helena Nelson was suing Bean for twenty-two hundred dollars and trying to attach the same slaves.

11. Delilah Allen statement in 1909 lawsuit, ibid., 52:203. Other sources call him Colonel Bean's cousin.

12. Bean to Roark, 9 Apr. 1844, as given and cited in Lay, *Lives,* 175, 201n6. Did "Rogue and a lyar" mean that Sam was claiming the colonel was his father? And, consequently, that part of Bean's property belonged to him and—as executor—he was free to sell what he wished? So it would seem.

13. P. E. Bean sale of slaves to Jesse E. Bean, 3 May 1844, Blake Transcripts (R), 52:98. Frost Thorn attested to Bean's signature on the document in Jan. 1846. He certainly was qualified to say if it was genuine or forged.

14. Ibid., 89. Attorney/agent Jesse Bean sold David Muckleroy two more tracts out of the Vital Flores grant after Colonel Bean left for Mexico. The first came on 20 Nov. 1844 (1,350 acres for five hundred dollars) and the second on 24 Nov. 1845 (769 acres for fifteen hundred dollars). Deed Books H, 278, and I, 102, NCCO.

15. Bean MSR, fol. 60.

16. Jackson and Wheat, *Almonte's Texas,* 450–61.

17. See the summary in Richard Bruce Winders, *Crisis in the Southwest: The United States, Mexico, and the Struggle over Texas,* 81–88.

18. These events are detailed in Pedro Santoni, *Mexicans at Arms: Puro Federalists and the Politics of War, 1845–1848,* 21–23, 33–92.

19. See Charles D. Spurlin, *Texas Volunteers in the Mexican War,* for a masterful treatment; also, Frederick Wilkins, *The Highly Irregular Irregulars: Texas Rangers in the Mexican War.*

20. This date of Bean's death was first given by Yoakum, *History of Texas,* 1:452, and has been followed by other writers since.

21. Given on p. 318 and cited in epilogue, n6. It is strange that Bennett Lay, who had access to two Bean family Bibles, repeated Yoakum's date rather than giving the year correctly as 1847. Weems, *Men without Countries,* 242, did the same: "On an autumn day in 1846 he died . . . " Until evidence is found in Mexico to the contrary, I go with the family Bibles: 3 Oct. 1847.

22. Winders, *Crisis in the Southwest,* 118–30.

23. Stephen B. Oates, ed., *Rip Ford's Texas, by John Salmon Ford,* 66 (quote); 70 (drawing "six-shooters" at Vergara); 77, 102 (camp near Jalapa). For Walker's death see K. Jack Bauer, *The Mexican War, 1846–1848,* 331. Church of the Latter Day Saints (LDS) microfilm for burials at Jalapa recorded at the cathedral do not show Bean in either year, possibly because he was laid to rest on his wife's hacienda rather than in a city cemetery.

Chapter 20

1. As cited in chapter 8, n54.

2. Bracken petition, 20 Sept. 1844, Blake Transcripts (R), 52:90–91. See also Bracken's public notice re Dory in the 11 Jan. 1845 *Red-Lander.*

3. *Bracken v. Bean,* amended petition, 16 Nov. 1849, Blake Transcripts (R), 52:79–80.

4. Ibid.

5. Candace Hicks, Isaac and Ellis Bean land sale to James H. Durst, 21 Dec. 1846, ibid., 102. On him see Ericson, *Nacogdoches—Gateway to Texas,* 45–46; a photo of James (or possibly his uncle John Durst) is opposite p. 2.

6. Sketch of "Candace Midkiff Bean," Blake Transcripts (R), 52:143–44. More of Mrs. Peevey's disparaging remarks about Candace are in the Peter Ellis Bean, Genealogy File, CAH, typed on index cards with the heading "Story by Mrs. Peavey." She said Candace was "little and black and ugly, ambitious. Good to her Negroes. But he [Bean] did not get along with her. He lived on a ranch at Rusk. Viney and her husband [Dory] cooked for him." Although there are grains of truth in Mrs. Peevey's stories, she was responsible for a lot of romantic rubbish about Bean—most of it swallowed by people of the area who were eager to learn more about the famous colonel and his exploits. These include Gladys Hardeman, who wrote a paper called "Peter Ellis Bean, Man with a Story" (on file at ETRC) saying that one of the three reasons Bean *should be remembered* was because he was "closely related to the late Mrs. W. D. Peevey (1839–1934)." Hardeman expounded on this connection at a DRT luncheon reported by Lucille Fain in *The Daily Sentinel,* 14 Feb. 1958, and her entry on Bean made its way into a book called *Nacogdoches County Families,* sponsored by the Nacogdoches County Genealogical Society. A Peevey family heirloom was the platter supposedly used at the "infare dinner" when Bean married Candace Midkiff in Tennessee. This relic—so it would seem—convinced local people that everything Mrs. Peevey said about the Bean family was true.

7. Ellis M. Bean land sale to James H. Durst, 23 Oct. 1849, Blake Transcripts (R), 52:99.

8. John Durst deed to James H. Durst, 15 Mar, 1847, ibid., 105. John Durst died four years later, still a very wealthy man but no longer a resident of the Nacogdoches area. At one point he owned thirty-nine slaves. On him see Tyler et al., *NHOT,* 2:737–38, and Ericson, *Nacogdoches—Gateway to Texas,* 45–46.

9. James H. Durst land sale to William A. Hagood, 8 June 1847, Blake Transcripts (R), 52:110–11.

10. Jesse E. Bean petition re slaves, 11 Feb. 1847, ibid., 103–4. Jesse had been author-

ized by the Commissioners Court in Nov. 1846 to build another Angelina bridge; Roach, *History of Cherokee County,* 36–37. Perhaps he wanted the slaves Dory and Stephen to work on the bridge for him.

11. *William Y. Lacy v. Ellis M. and Isaac T. Bean,* 14 Aug. 1848, Blake Transcripts (R), 52:114–17. Isaac lived in Nacogdoches County, and Ellis resided in Cherokee County, as did the petitioner. "Friendly" suits between extended family members over slaves were fairly common in the late 1840s and throughout the 1850s. Some of these cases reached the Texas Supreme Court and lasted until *after* emancipation, as I learned while researching my unpublished study on the Trammells.

12. Marriage agreement between Isaac T. Bean and Nancy A. Boone, 4 Aug. 1847, Nacogdoches County Deed Book 9, 60, as cited in Blake Transcripts (R), 52:98; also in Blake, "Notebook," 346.

13. Ellis M. Bean petition to administer estate of "Candis Hicks," 25 June 1849; surety agreement and his oath to perform duties of administrator, 2 July 1849, Blake Transcripts (R), 52:118–19.

14. This case no. 5100, which took place in the District Court of Houston County, Mar. 1909, is styled *Chas. Martin et als. v. H. H. Bennett et als.* It is given in Blake Transcripts (R), 52:153–289. The Selman testimony is on pp. 170–91; the Bible information, on pp. 225–26, 262–64. Blake Transcripts (R), 59:95, says that Candace was living at the home of her brother Isaac J. Midkiff when she died and confirms that she was buried in the Selman-Roark Cemetery at Linwood. It lies just east of Alto near the junction of SH 21 and FM 241; see the photo of her grave and historical marker in the epilogue.

15. William Martin petition, 2 Apr. 1850, Cherokee County Probate Book B, 56, Blake Transcripts (R), 52:121. William Martin and Mrs. Carmelita (Rutherford) Bean married on 27 Aug. 1846; they were the second bride and groom in the newly formed county. Roach, *History of Cherokee County,* 38.

16. Hicks appointment as administrator of Peter Ellis Bean's estate, Cherokee County Probate Book B, 38–39, Blake Transcripts (R), 52:122. Roach, *History of Cherokee County,* 27, says that William Hicks settled four miles east of later Rusk in the 1830s, so he was in the general area when Candace married Isaac Hix/Hicks in 1837.

17. Introduction of Bean's will by Wm. Martin, 13 May 1850, Cherokee County Probate Book B, 57, Blake Transcripts (R), 52:123; revocation of Martin's administratorship, ibid., 124. As noted, Bean's will is on pp. 94–95, from Deed Book G, 296, NCCO; it was duly recorded at the time he made it in 1843. Martin did not say where he found the will, at the courthouse or elsewhere.

18. Statement of "Carmelette" Bean, 9 May 1846, Blake Transcripts (R), 52:100; also in Blake, "Notebook," 349. She was conveying Samuel's half of the "Angelina Bridge at Jas. H. Durst's Crossing" to Rebecca Denson as per an agreement between her deceased husband and Denson, dated 2 Sept. 1845. Samuel also sold 640 acres out of his headright to Durst on 8 Mar. 1844; Deed Book I, 182, NCCO. Elizabeth Selman testified in 1909 that Carmelita Rutherford had married Sam Bean at the old Joe Durst place on the hill "this side of Angelina River." They had one child named Joe. A year after Samuel died, she married William Martin (see n15 above). This took place at Denson's, on the bank of the Angelina River, where he had a toll bridge. Their four children were Charlie, Andrew, George, and Helena; Blake Transcripts (R), 52:179–80. Mrs. Selman also stated (several times) that Sam was a son of Peter Ellis Bean's; ibid., 177–78, 185.

19. Petition of Henry and Helena Berryman for title from Bean's estate, 26 Mar. 1856, and associated paperwork, Blake Transcripts (R), 52:125–30. On the notable Berryman family see Roach, *History of Cherokee County,* 18–19 (with pictures of the couple and their

home, Forest Hill). As noted, Helena Nelson was earlier suing Bean for twenty-two hundred dollars; *Red-Lander,* 27 Apr. 1844.

20. Isaac Bean land sale to David Snively, by attorney Wm. Y. Lacy, 3 Apr. 1856, Blake Transcripts (R), 52:96–97. Isaac, "sole heir of P. E. Bean," appointed Lacy as his attorney on 17 June 1853; Deed Book M, 324, NCCO. William Young Lacy's second wife was Elizabeth Lindsay/Lindsey; see Ericson, *Nacogdoches—Gateway to Texas,* 82–83. They married on 30 July 1845 and had nine children, only two of them alive by 1881. There is a copy of José Pineda's eleven-league grant in the Raguet Papers, CAH, box 2F380. Frost Thorn was the "attorney" for it in 1834; how Bean later acquired the grant is unknown.

21. Testimony of Mary Scott, Blake Transcripts (R), 52:271–72.

22. Testimony of various deponents, ibid., 155, 174, 195, 207, 247.

23. This was particularly the line of questioning directed to Bean's known grandchildren Ellis A. Bean (ibid., 217–18, 221–22) and Emma Bean Stephens (ibid., 256, 258–59). Although aware of Bean's memoir that Yoakum had published, they said that their information on their grandfather Colonel Ellis P./Peter Ellis/Pedro Elías Bean came from talks with their parents (Isaac and Nancy) and from the family Bibles in their possession. For a biographical sketch of Ellis A. Bean, see *A Memorial and Biographical History of McLennan, Falls, Bell, and Coryell Counties, Texas,* 472–73; an entry for his father, Isaac T. Bean, is ibid., 985–86, along with names of children and their whereabouts at the time.

24. *Bracken v. Bean,* 5 June 1850, Blake Transcripts (R), 52:131. It is unknown if Dory was surrendered to Bracken or if this judgment was paid—all rather doubtful, as cases like this had a way of going on and on for years.

25. Testimony of Ben McNeill, W. H. Pearson, Henry Hendrix, and W. A. Muckleroy, all of Cherokee County, in 1909, Blake, ibid., 227–50. The quotes are from McNeill (p. 235).

26. Appointment of appraisers John Findley, John F. Williams, and James Cook, 8 Aug. 1850, Cherokee County Probate Book B, 177, Blake, ibid., 132. Blake did not include their evaluation of what was left of Bean's property.

27. *Mary Ann Bean v. Ellis M. Bean,* Divorce Petition, 23 Sept. 1850; writ for Ellis M. Bean to appear, 24 Sept. 1850, Blake, ibid., 133–34. She was represented by lawyers Jasper and Henry.

28. Ibid. W. A. Muckleroy later recalled that "Dick [Ellis M.] was sorter of a rough kind of fellow" (ibid., 249), but it is unknown if he died a natural or violent death in 1851.

29. Family Bible of Ellis A. Bean (son of Isaac), entered as "Exhibit A" in 1909 lawsuit, Blake Transcripts (R), 52:226. I have another transcription of this Bible information made in 1973 by Mrs. Ellis A. Bean of Lueders, Texas, with thanks to Carolyn Reeves Ericson for sharing it.

Chapter 21

1. Edward, *The History of Texas,* 206–9, has the 1832 Convention's "Address to the Sovereign General Congress of the Republic of Mexico." Sam Houston, in his 1839 speech on the Cherokee Land Bill, "imputed" the Memorial to David G. Burnet. Williams and Barker, *Writings of Sam Houston,* 2:336. In his 1840 speech on the same subject, Houston correctly identified Charles S. Taylor as the author; ibid., 361 (see also p. 299 where Taylor is named).

2. On the 1832 Convention and its proceedings, see Barker, *Life of SFA,* 348–53.

3. The 1833 Memorial by Burnet is in Yoakum, *History of Texas,* 1:469–82. After

reading a lengthy portion from Edward's book, Houston said, "This, eminating from an empresario, he thought had some *squinting* at the rights of the Indians." Williams and Barker, *Writings of Sam Houston,* 2:338. The reference could also be to Burnet as an empresario, and not to Haden Edwards.

4. William Kennedy, *Texas: The Rise, Progress, and Prospects of the Republic of Texas,* 1:237–38 (spelling it "Noland"); 363 (quote). "Captain" James Gaines told Mirabeau Lamar more correctly in 1835 that "Bean and some others from their youth were spared, but were imprisoned for years at Chewawa." Gulick et al., *Lamar Papers,* 1:280. Being pardoned is quite different from being "spared" by a youthful roll of dice.

5. See p. 304–305 and n12 below.

6. Wilson and Jackson, *Philip Nolan and Texas,* chapter 8, reviews the literature on "Nolan's Legacy."

7. See chapter 7 for a photo of the original watercolor, still in family hands in Texas; also in Wilson and Jackson, *Philip Nolan and Texas,* 107. The engraving is in Yoakum, *History of Texas,* vol. 1, opposite p. 404, and a photo appears in chapter 7 herein. For what appears to be a later painting of Bean (facing left, the same way as Yoakum's engraving and closely resembling it), see Ericson, *Nacogdoches—Gateway to Texas,* opposite p. 2. Through her courtesy, it is here reproduced in chapter 9. This picture also graced Lois Foster Blount's article "Sidelights on Story of Peter Ellis Bean," 27 Oct. 1974, *The Sunday Sentinel* (Nacogdoches), copy provided by Carolyn Reeves Ericson, and more recently appears in James G. Partin et al., *Nacogdoches,* 54. Another black-and-white photograph of the same image is at the ETRC; it is posted on their Web site entry for the "Peter Ellis Bean Collection" of fifteen items. On the back is a note saying that the painting was done by Haskell Bean, a great-grandson of the colonel's. Records show that the photograph came to the ETRC from the Old Stone House in 1983. Location of this original oil painting is presently unknown. Biographer Bennett Lay corresponded with Haskell Bean in 1958, at which time he lived in California, and provided Lay with genealogical information.

8. See source cited in n6 above for more on Hale and Nolan.

9. Brown, *History of Texas,* 1:46.

10. John H. Jenkins, *Basic Texas Books: An Annotated Bibliography of Selected Works for a Research Library,* 590–93.

11. Jean Delalande, *Les Aventures au Mexique et au Texas du Colonel Ellis Peter Bean,* translated into Spanish by José Ballester Gonzalvo and published as *Aventuras en México y Texas del Coronel E. P. Bean: Sus Memorias.* Use of Bean's memoir by Ríos and Cárdenas de la Peña has already been cited.

12. M. B. Lamar, "Information Derived from Col. Heyden Edwards," Gulick et al., *Lamar Papers,* 3:263.

13. Foote, *Texas and the Texans,* 1:251–52, 278–79. Showing his bias, Foote says that Chief Bowl "met a deserved death at the hands of the Texans eighteen months since" (278). Concerning use of the Indians in the Fredonian Rebellion, this is what Theodore Dorsett wrote Samuel Norris in mid-December 1826: "16 went out in number command[ed] by [Martin] Parmer & B[enjamin] Edward[s] yesterday [and] 20 men went out [today?] under the command of B[urrell] Thompson all making threats what they will do [to those] that don't join them thretning to send all the Cherokee Indians to plunder the settlement & old [Haden] Edwards says scalp men wimen & children & Ef his contract with the Government aint confirm[ed] he will not leave a Spaniard [alive] to the reo grand." Dorsett to Norris, n.d., J. P. Bryan Collection. So much for the mistaken idea that Edwards had noble intentions for his Red-White Alliance. Foote falsely blamed Bean for using these tactics, when actually it was the Fredonians who hoped to employ them.

14. Jenkins, *Basic Texas Books,* 313–14, says that Lamar "came to Texas in 1835 determined from the outset to write a history of Texas." Perhaps this is why Austin's family—concerned that his contribution to the development of Texas would be lost amid all the blood and thunder—asked Lamar to do a book extolling the empresario. Cantrell, *Stephen F. Austin,* 368–70.

15. Yoakum, *History of Texas,* 1:272, 327. On how Houston helped aspiring historian Yoakum, and how Houston later denied that he had had "any connection" with the book, see Jenkins, *Basic Texas Books,* 592.

16. See the Piedras letter of 24 July 1832 given in chapter 11. Who better than the Nacogdoches commandant knew which side Bean was taking?

17. Yoakum, *History of Texas,* 1:358–59; 2:130.

18. The remarks in Jenkins, *Basic Texas Books,* 80–83, make it clear that Houston was resented for claiming the glory at San Jacinto by quite a few of his former comrades. In the instance of Sidney Sherman, whom Houston accused of disobeying orders and cowardice in one of his "spin doctor" speeches, see Sherman's reply: *Defense of Gen. Sidney Sherman against the Charges Made by Gen. Sam Houston in His Speech Delivered in the United States Senate, February 28th, 1859.* Haley, *Sam Houston,* 358, 477n56, mentions and cites the speech but does not comment on Sherman's outraged reaction. See also Friend, *Sam Houston,* 267, for more background on Houston's motives in making this "valedictory" speech of his Senate career, attacking Sherman in the process.

19. Winkler, "The Cherokee Indians in Texas," 164; on p. 161, however, Winkler does say that Bean "did not approve of the course pursued by the Cherokees after Bowles's return from Monclova." Clarke, *Chief Bowles,* 55–56, goes further, claiming that the government "decided to carry out the suggestion of Indian Agent Bean." She, in other words, blames him for the law's removal provision to lands where the Cherokees had no desire to go.

20. Drinnon, *White Savage,* 217 (quote), 218–19.

21. Ibid., 217, 221–22.

22. Ibid., 212–17 (where it is stated, "Upon establishing his colony, Austin had grimly set about clearing out the 'natives of the forest' with the determination of a farmer clearing his field of stones"); 226–27 (quote, where it is also erroneously said that Bean was appointed Indian agent as a reward for "putting out the fire at Nacogdoches"). Older historians all agree, correctly, that Bean returned from Mexico with this commission in hand.

23. Gregory and Strickland, *Sam Houston with the Cherokees,* 59, 70–81 (drinking problem—"Nothing could be farther from the truth"); 32–54, 82–87 (fondness for Indian women); 55–60 (*Gazette* articles); 68 ("Houston was the greatest 'peacemaker' in American Indian history"); 155 ("basic attitudes" quote). The evaluation on p. 68 says much about this study's pro-Houston bias in terms of his relations with the Indians. In fact, Houston believed from early on that the Indians must yield their lands to the march of civilization.

24. Interview with Houston, 7 Apr. 1844. Holley (Mary Austin) Papers, CAH, box 2R40. In a sense, if Bean cannot be blamed for failing to deliver on his promises of land on behalf of Mexico, neither can Houston on behalf of the Republic of Texas. My point is that Bean deserves recognition for his peacemaking efforts with the Indians as much as Houston does—if not more.

25. D. W. C. [DeWitt Clinton] Baker, *A Texas Scrap-Book, Made Up of the History, Biography, and Miscellany of Texas and Its People,* 322–24; full-page portrait of Bean opposite p. 322. On how this portrait evolved, see Robert A. Calvert's remarks in the 1991 facsimile edition by the Texas State Historical Association, pp. xiv–xviii. Homer S. Thrall, *A Pictorial History of Texas, from the Earliest Visits of European Adventurers, to A.D. 1879,*

499–500; portrait of Bean on p. 383, one of the engravings made for Baker's book and obtained by Thrall's publisher. It is superior to Yoakum's 1855 small portrait, and the reproduction in Thrall's 1885 edition has better detail; see reproduction in chapter 8 herein.

26. Colonel Frank Triplett, *Conquering the Wilderness; or New Pictorial History of the Life and Times of the Pioneer Heroes and Heroines of America . . .*, 701–10 (portrait of Bean on p. 704; quote on p. 706).

27. Ibid., 709. *The Texas Almanac* also mentioned Bean favorably through the years; see James M. Day, ed., *The Texas Almanac, 1857–1873: A Compendium of Texas History.* These historical sketches in the *Almanac* no doubt had an influence on other writers.

28. Hubert Howe Bancroft, *History of Mexico, Vol. IV, 1804–1824,* and *History of the North Mexican States and Texas, Vol. II, 1801–1889,* published as vols. 12 and 16 in *The Works of Hubert Howe Bancroft.* Citation is from second book, p. 8. In a lengthy n16, Bancroft criticizes Kennedy's book and says, "Thrall's statements [about Bean] are equally contradictory."

29. Brown, *History of Texas,* 1:45–49, 135.

30. Ibid.

31. Dudley G. Wooten, ed., *A Comprehensive History of Texas, 1685 to 1897,* 1:76 (quote, with small portrait of Bean facing left), 93, 115, 274. A mistake-riddled entry on Bean also appeared in the 1895 *Memorial and Genealogical Record of Texas (East),* 91–93.

32. George P. Garrison, *Texas: A Contest of Civilizations,* 116.

33. Eugene C. Barker, ed., *A History of Texas and Texans by Frank W. Johnson, a Leader in the Texas Revolution,* 1:5, 27; Louis J. Wortham, *A History of Texas from Wilderness to Commonwealth,* 1:224 (portrait of Bean on opposite page), 277 (quote); Drinnon, *White Savage,* 215–16.

34. T. R. Fehrenbach, *Lone Star: A History of Texas and Texans,* 117, 164.

35. Tyler et al., *NHOT,* 1:437. In this entry Weems mistakenly gives Bean's mother as "Lydia" (Russell), who was his grandmother. He repeats Yoakum by saying "neither Texans nor Mexicans trusted him" and gives Yoakum's date of death for Bean. In addition to the "larkcom" Bean family Internet post earlier cited, there is one about Col. Peter Ellis Bean by Wallace L. McKeehan on the "Sons of DeWitt Colony, Texas" Web site at http://www.tamu.edu/ccbn/dewitt/beanellis.htm. McKeehan also presents a selection of Bean documents and letters. This is all very commendable, but Colonel Bean had virtually no connection with DeWitt's colony—except to denounce the empresario as an embezzler in 1825.

36. See the different versions in Blake Transcripts (R), 52:136–38 (quoted from Virdian Alice Barham's 1926 thesis and credited to Mrs. Sophia Peevy), and in Roach, *History of Cherokee County,* 21. For an excerpt from Barham's "History of Nacogdoches," 47–50, with the Peevy information, see Peter Ellis Bean, Genealogy File, CAH. The unreliability of Mrs. Peevy's "memoir" is discussed in the sketch of "Candace Midkiff Bean" (probably by Robert B. Blake) in Blake Transcripts (R), 52:143–44. She claimed that her father was Thomas Jefferson Shaw, the son of Capt. William Shaw. Her name is given as Peevy, Peevey, or Peavey in various references I have seen; chapter 20, n6. In the Bean, Genealogy File, CAH, is an interview with Mrs. "Peavey" that Lois Foster Blount sent to Mattie Austin Hatcher on 31 Jan. 1929, possibly for use in the postscript that Hatcher wrote when the Book Club of Texas—in its first publication— reissued Bean's memoir in 1930. See also the 1974 Blount newspaper article on Bean cited in n7 above; it is a factual disaster, owing to her total reliance on the 1926 information of Mrs. W. D. "Peevey." When Flora Lowrey asked Blake's help with her Peter Ellis Bean thesis at SMU, he warned her not to rely on "any information" concerning the family in the "memoirs of Mrs. Sophia Peavy." Blake to Lowrey, 13 Dec. 1944, Blake Papers, CAH, box 3G294.

37. Unfortunately, the source for this Bowie presentation cane story seems to be the unreliable Mrs. Peevey. It was accepted by J. Frank Dobie in his book cited in epilogue, n2; by Flora Lowrey, "Peter Ellis Bean," 57; and by Roach, *History of Cherokee County,* 21. Bennett Lay makes no mention of such a cane—or even of Bowie—in his 1960 biography of Bean. Peevey also says, "The Spanish wife took quite a fancy to Isaac and insisted that he make his home on her estate, promising to make him her heir. Isaac's loyalty to his mother prevented his accepting the offer." Instead, he hastened back to Texas with some of his father's belongings so Candace would know that he was at rest and decently buried, not scalped by Indians and his body left to rot on some unknown prairie. Blake Transcripts (R), 52:138.

38. See the reproductions in Wilson and Jackson, *Philip Nolan and Texas,* 107, 108. The photographs of Isaac Bean and his wife Nancy Boone are reproduced in chapter 20 herein. The watercolor of Colonel Bean (see chapter 7 herein) lacks the ornate frame seen in the Nolan book that allows focus more on his facial features. Based on its similarity to other known examples of his work, the artist may have been Jacob Marling. My thanks to Joseph Musso on this subject.

39. Lay, *Lives,* 4, 179n2. She was the daughter of Joseph R. L. Bean, who died in 1956. I had failed to notice this "lead" when involved with the Nolan project. At that time I was more interested in locating a picture of Philip Nolan. One has since surfaced; see the color reproduction in Terry Stark, "The Face of Philip Nolan," *Texas Studies Annual* 1 (1994): 54–61, reproduced in chapter 1 herein through his courtesy and that of the owner, Margaret M. Shaffer. It is a small oil painting on ivory, showing that Nolan had shoulder-length hair and wore it loose.

40. An update was done in 1998, titled "The Solomon B. Jackson Family in Texas." By July 1999 I had made a third printing of photocopied, spiral-bound copies and circulated them at cost to relatives who came forth with documents and pictures (all of which were reproduced), urging them to photocopy and circulate it further. My Trammell history was done in similar fashion. Are they published or unpublished books? In this day and age of the "information network" and "desktop publication," I am not sure how they qualify and will leave the question to librarians of the future.

Epilogue

1. Ellis P. [Peter Ellis] Bean, *Memoir of Col. Ellis P. Bean, Written by Himself about the Year 1816, Edited by W. P. [H. K.] Yoakum, with a postscript by Mattie Austin Hatcher,* 109–10.

2. J. Frank Dobie, *The Flavor of Texas,* 21–27. Earlier in the year Dobie wrote several similar articles on Bean for his syndicated newspaper column, "The Flavour of Texas." Copies from different papers are in the Bean Biographical File, CAH.

3. A photograph of the marker is given between pp. 58 and 59 in Lowrey, "Peter Ellis Bean." It still stands at the Selman-Roark Cemetery, placed inside the original red sandstone block wall around her grave; see photo in the text.

4. As cited in chapter 20, n14. There was also an earlier suit over land, mentioned in *M. A. Bean et al. v. H. H. Bennett et al.,* case no. 4679. Blake did not transcribe it.

5. Dobie, *Flavor of Texas,* 22. Roach, *History of Cherokee County,* 22–23, says that Bean "disowned one of his children [Sam]" in his will, but in 1910 a lawsuit "recovered part of the Peter Ellis Bean land for Samuel Bean's heirs," and "proved that Samuel Bean was his oldest son." Lowrey, "Peter Ellis Bean," 56, says, "Bean [in his will] does not acknowledge his eldest son, Samuel M. Bean, but names him as an executor." Lay, *Lives,* 161–62, calls

Samuel "a relative of unknown degree" and says—without giving the result—that the 1909 lawsuit for land was by an heir of Samuel's "who stood to profit by it." Lay implies that the jury's findings were flawed and did not really "prove" that Samuel was Bean's son. No DNA tests in those days.

6. Exhibits of Bean Bible entries in Blake Transcripts (R), 52:225–26, 262–64. As might be expected, some names/dates differ on the Bean Internet posts now circulating. Family Bibles display miscopied information on occasion, nor do birth/death dates on tombstones always agree with Bible entries, but they must be considered more trustworthy than Internet posts with no source given for their information.

7. Ibid., 263–64. The Bible of Ellis A. Bean also had the notation "Joseph Bean died 8 April 1864 at Battle of Mansfield, Louisiana." He was the son of Samuel Bean (executor of the colonel's will and his disputed son) and Carmelita Rutherford; see transcription source cited in chapter 20, n29. This is the only reference to Samuel Bean or his issue in any of the family Bibles. In an article in the *Dallas Morning News,* 28 Mar. 1930, a great-granddaughter of Bean's (Mrs. H. J. Zeranski) is shown holding this Bible, said to have been printed in 1832. Bean Biographical File, CAH. In an undated, uncredited obituary (typescript) for Emma Bean Stevens Staufer, however, the date is given as 1831 with this remark: "She is shown with a 110-year-old Bible, which once belonged to her grandmother, Mrs. Peter Ellis Bean." Blake Transcripts (R), 52:151. There is no photograph of her with the typescript.

8. As quoted in Lowrey, "Peter Ellis Bean," 58, citing Zuber's "Manuscript of Martin Parmer" in Crocket Collection. It is a typescript of fifty-four pages now in A-12, box 23, folder 81, ETRC (title given as "Biographical Sketches of Martin Parmer"); see chapter 17, n48. As noted, there is another copy at CAH, box 2R313, Zuber Papers.

9. Lowrey, "Peter Ellis Bean," 53, citing Crocket's "Notes," from same collection. For some reason she consistently misspells his name as Crockett. The George Louis Crocket materials fill forty-four boxes at ETRC; a guide is available online. Several short typescripts about Bean and his family by Crocket are also in the Peter Ellis Bean, Genealogy File, CAH—including one with the "morons" remark.

10. Issued in 1932 by Southwest Press in Dallas, and an authoritative study of great value. References to Bean are on pp. 142, 144, 152; his wife Candace goes unmentioned, despite the "Notes" that Crocket compiled. Zuber may have been Crocket's source. In his 30 Aug. 1902 letter to A. W. Morris, Zuber said, "I was told that both her sons were almost mental imbeciles, not capable of managing their own business." "The Bean Affair," 44, CAH, box 2R313.

11. The photographs of Isaac and Nancy are presently at the Central Texas Area Museum in Salado, loaned to them by Mrs. Leona Hicks with other Bean family items. I understand from L. H. Hicks (Leona's husband who died while this book was in final editing) that Bennett Lay managed to obtain Colonel Bean's own Bible, a large one "bound in spotted cowhide." In his 1960 biography Lay mentions examining Ellis P. Bean's Bible in the hands of descendants (p. x) but—oddly—does not give any information from it. How (and if) Lay came by this Bible and its present whereabouts are unknown.

12. The entry on Isaac in *A Memorial and Biographical History of McLennan, Falls, Bell, and Coryell Counties,* 985–86, calls him a "prominent farmer of Bell county" and notes his participation in various Indian fights and his service during the Confederacy as a member of the 32nd Cavalry stationed near Galveston. The date of his move to Bell County is given as 1853. This is probably correct, as he, his wife Nancy, and infant daughter "Candis A." appear on the 1850 census for Cherokee County, household no. 393. His uncle William Shaw (aged sixty-six, Colonel Bean's half brother), wife Susannah (aged sixty-four), and cousin John C. Shaw (aged twenty-nine, born in Arkansas) are in household

no. 490. Henderson Yoakum likely obtained the Bean documents he used in his *History of Texas* from "Captain" Shaw and Isaac Bean around this time.

13. Dobie, *The Flavor of Texas,* 27.

Appendices A–F

1. Trespalacios certification, 19 Nov. 1825, Bean MSR, fol. 4. He says that the dice were cast on a strongbox (*caja*), not on a drum as generally thought; see Wilson and Jackson, *Philip Nolan and Texas,* 101.

2. Sesma certification, 12 Nov. 1825, Bean MSR, fols. 5–6. The town where Bean married is given as "Guatusco." Is this modern Huatusco, due west of Veracruz and south of Jalapa? So it would seem, making an investigation of church records there worthwhile.

3. Herrera certification, 14 Nov. 1825, Bean MSR, fols. 7–8.

4. Terán certification, 15 Nov. 1825, Bean MSR, fols. 9–10. This is a particularly valuable account, considering Terán's military training and expertise. He confirms Bean's memoir version of Morelos's betrayal at Acapulco by Royalist forces within the castle, and Bean's critical role in the manufacture of powder. He also says that Bean surrendered to the Royalists, perhaps why our hero did not wish to include this humiliating episode in his memoir. Did Bean make his "escape" from imprisonment at Veracruz in some compromising manner? Or did he effect it by bribing his guards as he almost successfully did years before on the docks at Acapulco? In short, there are unanswered questions about how and exactly when Bean reached the United States in 1816. Bean was always careful to point out that his conduct during the revolution was honorable and without blemish.

5. Guerrero certification, 15 Nov. 1825, Bean MSR, fols. 11–12.

6. Bravo certification, 6 Nov. 1825, Bean MSR, fol. 13. This is the earliest of Bean's six testimonials. Chichihualco is north of Acapulco, off the road to Mexico City near the insurgent congressional site of Chilpancingo.

7. Bean to Victoria, 24 Nov. 1825, Bean MSR, fol. 14–15.

8. Bean to Compensation Board [?], 7 June 1826, Bean MSR, fols. 31–32.

9. Filisola and García Conde certification, 1 Jan. 1828, Bean MSR, fols. 1v–2.

10. Bean to Cass, 24 Feb. 1833, NA, given in Blake Transcripts (R), 13:165–67; also in Lowrey, "Peter Ellis Bean," appendix 2.

11. Bean to Jackson, 11 Sept. 1835, Jenkins, *Papers of Texas Revolution,* 1:433–35 (entry no. 609, cited as from the *Niles Register* [Baltimore], 7 Nov. 1835).

BIBLIOGRAPHY

Archival and Unpublished Material

Archives from the Office of the County Clerk, Nacogdoches, Texas (AOCCN). Books A and B, given in Blake (R), vol. 1; originals not located.

Archivo Histórico, Secretaría de la Defensa Nacional, Mexico City (AHSDN). Manuscript collection, including Bean's military service record (Cancelados, C46. XI/111/4.701) and other Texas-related materials.

Archivo Histórico, Secretaría de Relaciones Exteriores, Mexico City (SRE). Manuscript collection kept by the Secretariat of Foreign Affairs; contains many Texas-related documents and newspaper clippings.

Bacarisse, Charles A. "The Baron de Bastrop." Center for American History, University of Texas at Austin (CAH).

Bean, Peter Ellis. Biographical File, CAH.

———. Genealogy File, CAH.

———, Papers. Miscellaneous items, CAH.

Béxar Archives (BA). Manuscript collection, CAH.

Blake, Robert Bruce, Papers. Correspondence, typescripts, original documents, etc., CAH.

———, Research Collection (cited as Blake Transcripts). Ninety-three volumes—seventy-five of which are bound in red (R) and eighteen in green (G), CAH.

Blount, Lois Foster. "The Norris Family in Early Nacogdoches." Unpublished study found in Blake Transcripts (R), 59:290–362.

Bryan, J. P., Collection, Houston. Edwards-Forbes Family Papers.

Buquor Translations. Handwritten translations of Spanish documents in the Archives of Bexar County, made in 1852, TSL.

Crisp, James Ernest. "Anglo-Texan Attitudes toward the Mexican, 1821–1845." Ph.D. diss., Yale University, 1976.

Debray Translations. Handwritten translations of Spanish documents in the Archives of Bexar County, made in 1856, TSL.

East Texas Research Center, Steen Library, Stephen F. Austin State University, Nacogdoches (ETRC). Manuscript collection with a few Bean papers.

Eberstadt Collection. Manuscript collection, CAH.

Fomento [BNAH] Transcripts. Typescripts gathered from the manuscript collection now at the Biblioteca Nacional de Antropología e Historia, Mexico City, in seventeen volumes, CAH.

Guerra y Marina [AHSDN] Transcripts. Typescripts in twenty volumes, CAH. Originals at Defensa Nacional, Mexico City, as noted above.

Hardeman, Gladys. "Peter Ellis Bean, Man with a Story." Unpublished paper on file at ETRC, n.d.

Holley, Mary Austin, Papers. Manuscript notes, typescripts, CAH.

Holt, Jordan. "The Edwards Empresarial Grant and the Fredonian Rebellion." Master's thesis, Stephen F. Austin State University, Nacogdoches, 1977.

Houston, Andrew Jackson, Collection. Manuscript collection, Archives Division, Texas State Library, Austin (TSL).

Instituto Estatal de Documentación (IED). Manuscript collection at Ramos Arizpe, Coahuila; State Archives formerly kept at nearby Saltillo.

Jackson, Jack. "Fort Lipantitlán: Mexico's Lone Sentinel on the Coastal Corridor to Texas." Unpublished, copy in author's collection at CAH.

———. "The Solomon B. Jackson Family in Texas." Unpublished, copy in author's collection at CAH.

———. "The Trammells: Being a History of a Pioneering Family, with Emphasis on the Descendants of Nicholas Trammell Who Blazed 'Trammell's Trace' When Texas Was a Province of Spain." Unpublished, copy in author's collection at CAH.

Lamar, Mirabeau B., Papers. Manuscript collection, TSL.

Lowrey, Flora. "Peter Ellis Bean: A Typical Filibuster of Early Texas History." Master's thesis, Southern Methodist University, Dallas, 1945.

May, Lucy. "The Life and Activities of Frost Thorn." Master's thesis, University of Texas at Austin, 1939.

Memorials and Petitions. Archives Division, TSL.

Nacogdoches Archives (NA). Manuscript collection, Archives Division, TSL.

Nacogdoches Archives Transcripts (cited as NA Transcripts). Typescript collection bound in eighty-nine volumes, CAH. Also several volumes of census records for the jurisdiction called "Nacogdoches Archives."

Nacogdoches County Deed Books. County Clerk's Office, Courthouse, Nacogdoches, Texas (NCCO).

Nacogdoches County Tax Rolls. Microfilm, Genealogy, TSL. The original lists are at ETRC.

Partin, James G. "A History of Nacogdoches and Nacogdoches County, to 1877." Master's thesis, University of Texas at Austin, 1968.

Raguet, Henry, Papers. Manuscript collection, CAH.

Relaciones Exteriores Transcripts. Typescripts in twenty-one volumes, CAH. Originals noted as SRE above.

Rusk, Thomas J., Papers. Photostats of letters, TSL.

Saltillo Archives. Manuscript collection (photostats) bound in fifty volumes, CAH. See Instituto Estatal de Documentación for the originals.

Spanish Collection, Texas General Land Office (TGLO). Manuscripts related to land affairs, Spanish/Mexican period, Austin.

Stenberg, Richard Rollin. "American Imperialism in the Southwest, 1800–1837." Ph.D. Dissertation, University of Texas at Austin, 1932.

Zuber, William P., Papers. Typescript letters to A. W. Morris, 1902, CAH.

Books and Articles

Agnew, Brad. *Fort Gibson: Terminal on the Trail of Tears.* Norman: University of Oklahoma Press, 1980.

Amsler, Robert. "General Arthur G. Wavell: A Soldier of Fortune in Texas." *Southwestern Historical Quarterly* 69 (July 1965): 1–21; (Oct. 1965): 196–209.

Anderson, Gary Clayton. *The Indian Southwest, 1580–1830: Ethnogenesis and Reinvention.* Norman: University of Oklahoma Press, 1999.

Anderson, H. Allen. "The Delaware and Shawnee Indians and the Republic of Texas, 1820–1845." *Southwestern Historical Quarterly* 94 (Oct. 1990): 231–60.

Baker, D. W. C. *A Texas Scrap-Book, Made Up of the History, Biography, and Miscellany of Texas and Its People.* New York: A. C. Barnes, 1875.

Bancroft, Hubert Howe. *History of Mexico, Vol. IV, 1804–1824.* San Francisco: The History Company, 1886.

———. *History of the North Mexican States and Texas, Vol. II, 1801–1889.* San Francisco: The History Company, 1889.

Barker, Eugene C. "Land Speculation as a Cause of the Texas Revolution." *Quarterly of the Texas State Historical Association* 10 (July 1906): 76–95.

———. *The Life of Stephen F. Austin: Founder of Texas, 1793–1836.* 1925. Reprint, Austin: University of Texas Press, 1980.

———, ed. *The Austin Papers.* 2 vols. Washington: U.S. Government Printing Office, 1924, 1928; vol. 3, Austin: University of Texas Press, 1927.

———, ed. *A History of Texas and Texans by Frank W. Johnson, a Leader in the Texas Revolution.* 5 vols. Chicago and New York: The American Historical Society, 1914.

Bass, Feris A., Jr., and B. R. Brunson, eds. *Fragile Empires: The Texas Correspondence of Samuel Swartwout and James Morgan.* Austin: Shoal Creek Publishers, 1978.

Bauer, K. Jack. *The Mexican War, 1846–1848.* Lincoln: University of Nebraska Press, 1992.

Bean, Ellis P. [Peter Ellis]. *Memoir of Col. Ellis P. Bean, Written by Himself about the Year 1816, Edited by W. P. [H. K.] Yoakum, with a postscript by Mattie Austin Hatcher.* Houston: Book Club of Texas, 1930.

Bean, Peter Ellis. "Memoir." In Yoakum, *History of Texas,* vol. 1, 403–52.

Bean, Tom. "Ellis P. Bean: The Señoritas Wouldn't Leave Him Alone." *True West* 30, no. 2 (Feb. 1983).

Benavides, Adán, Jr., ed. *The Béxar Archives (1717–1836): A Name Guide.* Austin: University of Texas Press, 1989.

Benson, Nettie Lee. "Texas As Viewed from Mexico, 1820–1834." *Southwestern Historical Quarterly* 90 (Jan. 1987): 219–91.

Berlandier, Jean-Louis. *The Indians of Texas in 1830.* Edited by John C. Ewers. Translated by Patricia Reading Leclercq. Washington, D.C.: Smithsonian Institution Press, 1969.

Binkley, William C., ed. *Official Correspondence of the Texas Revolution, 1835–1836.* 2 vols. New York: D. Appleton-Century Co., 1936.

Bocanegra, José María. *Memorias para la Historia de México Independiente, 1822–1846.* 2 vols. 1892, 1895. Reprint, Mexico City: Instituto Nacional de Estudios Históricos de la Revolución Mexicana, 1985.

Bosch García, Carlos, ed. *Documentos de la Relación de México con los Estados Unidos.* 4 vols. Mexico City: Universidad Nacional Autónoma de México, 1983–85.

[Brown, J. H.]. "Col. Ellis P. Bean, or Fifty Years Ago in Texas." *DeBow's Review* (New Orleans), 1853.

Brown, John Henry. *History of Texas from 1685 to 1892.* 2 vols. 1892. Reprint, Austin: Jenkins Publishing Co., 1970.

Cantrell, Gregg. *Stephen F. Austin: Empresario of Texas.* New Haven, Conn.: Yale University Press, 1999.

Cárdenas de la Peña, Enrique. *Historia Maritima de México: Guerra de Independencia, 1810–1821.* 2 vols. Mexico City: Ediciones Olimpia, 1973.

Carter, Cecile Elkins. *Caddo Indians: Where We Come From.* Norman: University of Oklahoma Press, 1995.

Castañeda, Carlos E. *Our Catholic Heritage in Texas, 1519–1936.* 7 vols. Austin: Von Boeckmann-Jones, 1936–58.

Castillo Crimm, Ana Carolina. *De León: A Tejano Family History.* Austin: University of Texas Press, 2003.

Clarke, Mary Whatley. *Chief Bowles and the Texas Cherokees.* Norman: University of Oklahoma Press, 1971.

Crabb, Martha L. *Over the Mountain: A Narrative History of the Bean, Selman, and Germany Families.* Baltimore, Md.: Gateway Press, 1990.

Crocket, George Louis. *Two Centuries in East Texas: A History of San Augustine County and Surrounding Territory, from 1685 to the Present Time.* Dallas: Southwest Press, 1932.

Davis, Kathryn Hooper, and Linda Ericson Devereaux, eds. *This I Convey: Deed Book A, Nacogdoches County, Texas, 1837.* Nacogdoches: Ericson Books, 1995.

Davis, William C. *Three Roads to the Alamo: The Lives and Fortunes of David Crockett, James Bowie, and William Barret Travis.* New York: HarperCollins, 1998.

Day, James M., ed. *The Texas Almanac, 1857–1873: A Compendium of Texas History.* Waco: Texian Press, 1967.

De Bruhl, Marshall. *Sword of San Jacinto: A Life of Sam Houston.* New York: Random House, 1993.

Delalande, Jean. *Aventuras en México y Texas del Coronel E. P. Bean: Sus Memorias.* Translated by José Ballester Gonzalvo. Mexico City: Editorial Patria, 1959.

Delalande, Jean. *Les Aventures au Mexique et au Texas du Colonel Ellis Peter Bean.* Caen, France: Ozanne & Co., n.d.

DePalo, William A., Jr. *The Mexican National Army, 1822–1852.* College Station: Texas A&M University Press, 1997.

Dobie, J. Frank. *The Flavor of Texas.* Dallas: Dealey and Lowe, 1936.

Drinnon, Richard. *White Savage: The Case of John Dunn Hunter.* New York: Shocken Books, 1972.

Edward, David B. *The History of Texas: Or the Emigrant's, Farmer's & Politician's Guide. . . .* 1836. Reprint, Austin: Texas State Historical Association, 1990.

Ericson, Carolyn Reeves. *Nacogdoches—Gateway to Texas: A Biographical Dictionary, 1773–1849.* Fort Worth: Arrow/Curtis, 1974.

Everett, Dianna. *The Texas Cherokees: A People between Two Fires, 1819–1840.* Norman: University of Oklahoma Press, 1990.

Fehrenbach, T. R. *Lone Star: A History of Texas and Texans.* New York: Macmillan, 1968.

Filisola, Vicente. *Memoirs for the History of the War in Texas.* Translated by Wallace Woolsey. 2 vols. Austin: Eakin Press, 1985, 1987.

Foote, Henry Stuart. *Texas and the Texans: Or Advance of the Anglo-Americans to the South-West.* 2 vols. 1841. Reprint, Austin: Steck Co., 1935.

Foreman, Grant. *Indians & Pioneers: The Story of the American Southwest before 1830.* Norman: University of Oklahoma Press, 1936.

Friend, Llerna B. *Sam Houston: The Great Designer.* Austin: University of Texas Press, 1969.

Garrison, George P. *Texas: A Contest of Civilizations.* Boston and New York: Houghton Mifflin Co., 1903.

Grady, Jamie Ault. *William Bean, Pioneer of Tennessee and His Descendants.* Knoxville: Southern Bean Association, 1985. First self-published in 1973.

Greaser, Galen D., ed. *Catalogue of the Spanish Collection of the Texas General Land Office.* 2 vols. Austin: Texas General Land Office, 2003.

Green, Stanley C. *The Mexican Republic: The First Decade, 1823–1832.* Pittsburgh: University of Pittsburgh Press, 1987.

Gregory, Jack, and Rennard Strickland. *Sam Houston with the Cherokees, 1829–1833.* Austin: University of Texas Press, 1967.

Gulick, C. A., Jr., Winnie Allen, Katherine Elliott, and Harriet Smither, eds. *The Papers of Mirabeau Buonaparte Lamar.* 6 vols. Austin: Von Boeckmann-Jones, 1921–27.

Haley, James L. *Sam Houston.* Norman: University of Oklahoma Press, 2002.

Hatley, Allen G. *The Indian Wars in Stephen F. Austin's Texas Colony.* Austin: Eakin Press, 2001.

Henson, Margaret Swett. *Juan Davis Bradburn: A Reappraisal of the Mexican Commander of Anahuac.* College Station: Texas A&M University Press, 1982.

———. *Lorenzo de Zavala: The Pragmatic Idealist.* Fort Worth: Texas Christian University Press, 1996.

———. *Samuel May Williams: Early Texas Entrepreneur.* College Station: Texas A&M University Press, 1976.

Himmel, Kelly F. *The Conquest of the Karankawas and the Tonkawas, 1821–1859.* College Station: Texas A&M University Press, 1999.

Hogan, William Ransom. *The Texas Republic: A Social and Political History.* 1946. Reprint, Austin: University of Texas Press, 1980.

Holley, Mary Austin. *Texas.* 1836. Reprint, Austin: Texas State Historical Association, 1990.

Howard, Margaret, et al. *Testing at the San Felipe de Austin Townsite (41AU2).* Austin: Texas Parks and Wildlife Department, 1999.

Howren, Alleine. "Causes and Origin of the Decree of April 6, 1830." *Southwestern Historical Quarterly* 16 (April 1913): 378–422.

Jackson, Jack. *Indian Lover: Sam Houston & the Cherokees.* Dripping Springs, Tex.: Mojo Press, 1999.

———. "Nicholas Trammell's Difficulties in Mexican Texas." *East Texas Historical Journal* 38, no. 2 (2000): 15–39.

———. *Shooting the Sun: Cartographic Results of Military Activities in Texas, 1689–1829.* 2 vols. Austin: Book Club of Texas, 1998.

Jackson, Jack, ed., and John Wheat, trans. *Almonte's Texas: Juan N. Almonte's 1834 Inspection, Secret Report & Role in the 1836 Campaign.* Austin: Texas State Historical Association, 2003.

———, ed. and trans. *Texas by Terán: The Diary Kept by General Manuel de Mier y Terán on His 1828 Inspection of Texas.* Austin: University of Texas Press, 2000.

Jacobs, James Ripley. *Tarnished Warrior: Major-General James Wilkinson.* New York: Macmillan Co., 1938.

James, Marquis. *The Raven: A Biography of Sam Houston.* 1929. Reprint, Austin: University of Texas Press, 1988.

Jenkins, John H. *Basic Texas Books: An Annotated Bibliography of Selected Works for a Research Library.* Rev. ed. Austin: Texas State Historical Association, 1988.

———, ed. *The Papers of the Texas Revolution, 1835–1837.* 10 vols. Austin: Presidial Press, 1973.

Kavanagh, Thomas W. *The Comanches: A History, 1706–1875.* Lincoln: University of Nebraska Press, 1996.

Kemp, Louis Wiltz. *The Signers of the Texas Declaration of Independence.* Houston: Anson Jones Press, 1944.

Kendall, George Wilkins. *Narrative of the Texan Santa Fe Expedition.* 2 vols. New York: Harper & Brothers, 1844.

Kennedy, William. *Texas: The Rise, Progress, and Prospects of the Republic of Texas.* London, 1841. Reprint, Fort Worth: Molyneaux Craftsman, 1925.

Lack, Paul D. "The Córdova Revolt." In *Tejano Journey, 1770–1850,* edited by Gerald E. Poyo, 89–109. Austin: University of Texas Press, 1996.

———. *The Texas Revolutionary Experience: A Political and Social History, 1835–1836.* College Station: Texas A&M University Press, 1992.

La Vere, David. *Contrary Neighbors: Southern Plains and Removed Indians in Indian Territory.* Norman: University of Oklahoma Press, 2000.

———. *The Texas Indians.* College Station: Texas A&M University Press, 2004.

Lay, Bennett. *The Lives of Ellis P. Bean.* Austin: University of Texas Press, 1960.

The Life of Andrew Jackson, President of the United States, by Major Jack Dowling. Philadelphia: T. K. Greenbank, 1834.

Lindley, Thomas Ricks. *Alamo Traces: New Evidence and New Conclusions.* Lanham, Md.: Republic of Texas Press, 2003.

A List of Titles Issued by Different Commissioners and Alcaldes, at Nacogdoches, from 1791 to 1835. Reprint of the 1838 edition, a larger compilation titled *An Abstract of the Original Titles of Record in the General Land Office.* Austin: Pemberton Press, 1964.

Long, Jeff. *Duel of Eagles: The Mexican and U.S. Fight for the Alamo.* New York: Quill-William Morrow, 1990.

Lukes, Edward A. *The DeWitt Colony in Texas.* Austin: Jenkins Publishing Co., 1976.

Marler, Don C. *Fort Terán on the Neches River.* Hemphill, Tex.: Dogwood Press, 2000.

McDonald, Archie P., ed. *Hurrah for Texas! The Diary of Adolphus Sterne, 1838–1851.* Austin: Eakin Press, 1986.

McElhannon, Joseph Carl. "Imperial Mexico and Texas, 1821–1823." *Southwestern Historical Quarterly* 53 (July 1949): 117–50.

McGraw, A. Joachim, John W. Clark, Jr., and Elizabeth A. Robbins. *A Texas Legacy: The Old San Antonio Road and the Caminos Reales.* Austin: Texas State Department of Highways and Public Transportation, 1991.

McLean, Malcolm D., ed. *Papers concerning Robertson's Colony in Texas.* 19 vols. Fort Worth: Texas Christian University Press, 1974–76; Arlington: University of Texas at Arlington Press, 1977–93.

A Memorial and Biographical History of McLennan, Falls, Bell, and Coryell Counties, Texas. Chicago: Lewis Publishing Co., 1893.

Memorial and Genealogical Record of Texas (East). Chicago: Goodspeed Brothers Publishers, 1895.

Moore, Stephen L. *Savage Frontier, Volume I, 1835–1837: Rangers, Riflemen, and Indian Wars in Texas.* Plano: Republic of Texas Press, 2002.

Morton, Ohland. *Terán and Texas: A Chapter in Texas-Mexican Relations.* Austin: Texas State Historical Association, 1948.

Nacogdoches County Genealogical Society. *Nacogdoches County Families.* Dallas: Curtis Media Corp., 1985.

Nance, Joseph Milton. *After San Jacinto: The Texas-Mexican Frontier, 1836–1841.* Austin: University of Texas Press, 1963.

Narrett, David E. "José Bernardo Gutiérrez de Lara: Caudillo of the Mexican Republic in Texas." *Southwestern Historical Quarterly* 106 (Oct. 2002): 195–228

Newcomb, W. W., Jr. *The Indians of Texas: From Prehistoric to Modern Times.* Austin: University of Texas Press, 1961.

Oates, Stephen B., ed. *Rip Ford's Texas, by John Salmon Ford.* Austin: University of Texas Press, 1987.

O'Neil, Paul. *The Frontiersmen.* Alexandria, Va.: Time-Life Books, 1977.

Opler, Morris E. *The Lipan and Mescalero Apache in Texas.* New York: Garland Publishing, 1974.

Owsley, Frank Lawrence, Jr., and Gene A. Smith. *Filibusters and Expansionists: Jeffersonian Manifest Destiny, 1800–1821.* Tuscaloosa: University of Alabama Press, 1997.

Parsons, Edmund Morris. "The Fredonian Rebellion." *Texana* 5 (Spring 1967): 11–52.

Partin, James G., Carolyn Reeves Ericson, Joe E. Ericson, and Archie P. McDonald. *Nacogdoches.* Lufkin: Best of East Texas Publishers, 1995.

Pierce, Gerald S. *Texas under Arms: The Camps, Posts, Forts, & Military Towns of the Republic of Texas, 1836–1846.* Austin: Encino Press, 1969.

Reagan, John H. "The Expulsion of the Cherokees from East Texas." *Quarterly of the Texas State Historical Association* 1 (July 1897): 38–46.

———. "Queries and Answers." *Quarterly of the Texas State Historical Association* 6 (Oct. 1902): 166–67.

Reeves, Emma Barrett, ed. *Minutes of the District Court of Nacogdoches County, Book A.* St. Louis: Mrs. Frances Terry Ingmire, 1981.

Reichstein, Andreas V. *Rise of the Lone Star: The Making of Texas.* College Station: Texas A&M University Press, 1989.

Remini, Robert V. *Andrew Jackson and the Course of American Empire, 1767–1821.* New York: Harper & Row, 1977.

Ríos, Eduardo Enrique. "El Insurgente Don Pedro Elías Bean, 1783–1846." *Anales del Museo Nacional de Arqueología, Historia y Etnografía* 5a, tomo 1, no. 3 (July–Dec. 1934): 489–526.

Roach, Hattie Joplin (Mrs. V. R.). *History of Cherokee County (Texas).* Dallas: Southwest Press, 1934.

Robles, Vito Alessio. *Acapulco, Saltillo y Monterrey en la Historia y la Leyenda.* Mexico City: Editorial Porrúa, 1978.

Roell, Craig H. *Remember Goliad! A History of La Bahía.* Austin: Texas State Historical Association, 1994.

Rowland, Kate Mason. "General John Thomson Mason: An Early Friend of Texas." *Quarterly of the Texas State Historical Association* 11 (January 1908): 163–98.

Santoni, Pedro. *Mexicans at Arms: Puro Federalists and the Politics of War, 1845–1848.* Fort Worth: Texas Christian University Press, 1996.

Santos, Richard G., ed. *Santa Anna's Campaign against Texas, 1835–1836.* Waco: Texian Press, 1968.

Sherman, Sidney. *Defense of Gen. Sidney Sherman against the Charges Made by Gen. Sam Houston in His Speech Delivered in the United States Senate, February 28th, 1859.* Galveston, Tex.: "News" Book and Job Office, 1859.

Shinn, Josiah H. *Pioneers and Makers of Arkansas.* 1908. Reprint, Baltimore, Md.: Genealogical Publishing Co., 1967.

Smith, F. Todd. *The Caddo Indians: Tribes at the Convergence of Empires, 1542–1854.* College Station: Texas A&M University Press, 1995.

———. *The Wichita Indians: Traders of Texas and the Southern Plains, 1540–1845.* College Station: Texas A&M University Press, 2000.

Smither, Harriet, ed. *Journals of the Fourth Congress of the Republic of Texas, 1839–1840: Volume II, The House Journal.* 3 vols. Austin: Von Boeckmann-Jones, 1931.

Speer, William S., and John Henry Brown, eds. *The Encyclopedia of the New West.* Marshall: United States Biographical Publishing Co., 1881.

Spurlin, Charles D. *Texas Volunteers in the Mexican War.* Austin: Eakin Press, 1998.

Stark, Terry. "The Face of Philip Nolan." *Texas Studies Annual* 1 (1994): 54–61.

Starling, Susanne. *Land Is the Cry!: Warren Angus Ferris, Pioneer Texas Surveyor and Founder of Dallas County.* Austin: Texas State Historical Association, 1998.

Steely, Skipper. *Six Months from Tennessee: The Story of Old Miller County, Now N. E. Texas and S. E. Oklahoma, from 1816–1830.* Wolfe City, Tex.: Henington Publishing Co., 1983.

Suárez y Navarro, Juan. *Historia de México y del General Antonio López de Santa Anna.* 1850–51. Reprint, Mexico City: Instituto Nacional de Estudios Históricos de la Revolución Mexicana, 1987.

Tate, Michael L. *The Indians of Texas: An Annotated Research Bibliography.* Metuchen, N.J.: Scarecrow Press, 1986.

Thrall, Homer S. *A Pictorial History of Texas, from the Earliest Visits of European Adventurers, to A.D. 1879.* St. Louis: N. D. Thompson & Co., 1879.

Timmons, Wilbert H. *Morelos of Mexico: Priest, Soldier, Statesman.* El Paso: Texas Western Press, 1963.

Triplett, Colonel Frank. *Conquering the Wilderness; or New Pictorial History of the Life and Times of the Pioneer Heroes and Heroines of America. . . .* New York: N. D. Thompson & Co., 1883.

Tyler, Ron, et al., eds. *The New Handbook of Texas.* 6 vols. Austin: Texas State Historical Association, 1990.

U.S. Senate. *Executive Document 14.* 32d Cong., 2d sess., 1852–53. Vol. 3.

Walraven, Bill, and Marjorie K. Walraven. *The Magnificent Barbarians: Little-Told Tales of the Texas Revolution.* Austin: Eakin Press, 1993.

———. "The 'Sabine Chute': The U.S. Army and the Texas Revolution." *Southwestern Historical Quarterly* 107 (Apr. 2004): 573–601.

———. *The "Sabine Chute": U.S. Involvement in the Texas Revolution.* Corpus Christi: Self-published, n.d.

Warren, Harris G. *The Sword Was Their Passport: A History of American*

Filibustering in the Mexican Revolution. Baton Rouge: Louisiana State University Press, 1943.

Weems, John Edward. *Men without Countries: Three Adventurers of the Early Southwest.* Boston: Houghton Mifflin Co., 1962.

Wilkins, Frederick. *The Highly Irregular Irregulars: Texas Rangers in the Mexican War.* Austin: Eakin Press, 1990.

Williams, Amelia W., and Eugene C. Barker, eds. *The Writings of Sam Houston, 1813–1863.* 8 vols. Austin: University of Texas Press, 1938–43.

Williams, Elgin. *The Animating Pursuits of Speculation: Land Traffic in the Annexation of Texas.* New York: Columbia University Press, 1949.

Williams, John Hoyt. *Sam Houston: The Life and Times of the Liberator of Texas, an Authentic American Hero.* New York: Simon & Schuster, 1993.

Wilson, Maurine T., and Jack Jackson. *Philip Nolan and Texas: Expeditions to the Unknown Land, 1791–1801.* Waco: Texian Press, 1987.

Winders, Richard Bruce. *Crisis in the Southwest: The United States, Mexico, and the Struggle over Texas.* Wilmington, Del.: Scholarly Resources Books, 2002.

Winfrey, Dorman H. "Chief Bowles of the Texas Cherokee." *Chronicles of Oklahoma* 32 (Spring 1954): 29–41.

Winfrey, Dorman H., and James M. Day, eds. *The Indian Papers of Texas and the Southwest, 1825–1916.* 5 vols. Austin: Texas State Historical Association, 1995.

Winkler, Ernest W. "The Cherokee Indians in Texas." *Quarterly of the Texas State Historical Association* 7 (Oct. 1903): 95–165.

———, ed. *Secret Journals of the Senate of the Republic of Texas, 1836–1845.* Austin: Austin Printing Co., 1911.

Woldert, Albert. "The Last of the Cherokees in Texas, and the Life and Death of Chief Bowles." *Chronicles of Oklahoma* 1 (June 1923): 179–226.

Wooten, Dudley G., ed. *A Comprehensive History of Texas, 1685 to 1897.* 2 vols. Dallas: William G. Scarff, 1898.

Wortham, Louis J. *A History of Texas from Wilderness to Commonwealth.* 5 vols. Fort Worth: Wortham-Molyneaux Co., 1924.

Yoakum, H[enderson King]. *History of Texas from Its First Settlement in 1685 to Its Annexation to the United States in 1846.* 2 vols. New York: Redfield, 1855.

INDEX